Penguin Education

Introducing Psychology

Ann Taylor, Wladyslaw Sluckin
D. R. Davies, J. T. Reason, R. Thomson
and A. M. Colman

Introducing Psychology

Ann Taylor, Wladyslaw Sluckin,
D. R. Davies, J. T. Reason, R. Thomson
and A. M. Colman

Second Edition

Penguin Books

Penguin Books Ltd, Harmondsworth, Middlesex, England
Penguin Books, 40 West 23rd Street, New York, New York 10010, U.S.A.
Penguin Books Australia Ltd, Ringwood, Victoria, Australia
Penguin Books Canada Ltd, 2801 John Street, Markham, Ontario, Canada L3R 1B4
Penguin Books (N.Z.) Ltd, 182–190 Wairau Road, Auckland 10, New Zealand

First published 1970
Reprinted 1971, 1972, 1974, 1975, 1977, 1978, 1980
Second edition 1982
Reprinted 1984

Made and printed in Great Britain by
Richard Clay (The Chaucer Press) Ltd, Bungay, Suffolk
Filmset in Monophoto Times by
Northumberland Press Ltd, Gateshead, Tyne and Wear

Contents

6 Contents

10 Contents

12 Contents

Preface to Second Edition

More than ten years have elapsed since the publication of the first edition of *Introducing Psychology*. Many sections of this second edition are entirely new, while others have been substantially rewritten and updated. The authorship, too, has undergone some changes. Professor S. G. M. Lee died in 1973. Professor D. S. Wright – as he now is – is no longer an author; he has had to withdraw from the venture owing to pressure of other work. Two new names appear among the authors: Robert Thomson and Andrew M. Colman. Whereas all the original contributors in 1970 were in the Department of Psychology at the University of Leicester, now two are elsewhere: Roy Davies is Reader in Experimental Psychology at the University of Aston in Birmingham, and James Reason is Professor of Psychology at the University of Manchester. The joint editors of the present edition are Ann Taylor and Professor W. Sluckin. The primary responsibilities, chapter by chapter, are as follows: Chapters 1, 2 and 3, W. Sluckin, although a great deal of Chapter 3 is based on previous material due to D. S. Wright; Chapters 4 and 5, D. R. Davies; Chapter 6, D. R. Davies, Ann Taylor and W. Sluckin; Chapter 7, D. R. Davies; Chapter 8, J. T. Reason; Chapter 9, D. R. Davies; Chapters 10 and 11, Ann Taylor; Chapters 12 and 13, W. Sluckin; Chapters 14 and 15, J. T. Reason; Chapters 16, 17 and 18, Ann Taylor; Chapter 19, Ann Taylor and W. Sluckin, based on previous material by D. R. Davies; Chapter 20, R. Thomson, partly based on previous material by D. S. Wright; Chapter 21, R. Thomson; Chapter 22, Ann Taylor and D. R. Davies; Chapter 23, A. M. Colman; Chapter 24, Ann Taylor and W. Sluckin. A generation of students have found the first edition of the book useful; we trust that this thoroughly revised edition will continue to be of value to students of psychology and related disciplines.

14 Preface

We are indebted to colleagues and friends who have read and commented upon parts of the manuscript in draft form – among them Graham Beaumont, David Hargreaves, Jim Horne, Mick Hunter, Dylan Jones, Raja Parasuraman and David and Jenny West.

A. T.
W. S.

January 1981

Chapter 1
Modern Psychology: Historical Roots and Current Problems

The main aims and tasks of psychology, and its proper subject-matter, are more a matter of opinion than of fact. There is broad consensus that psychology sets out to explain why we feel and think and act as we do; but there is less than full agreement as to how the explaining is to be done. Initially psychology was to be the science of mind, and so it was to complement the physical and biological sciences. Some said later that psychology must delve into unconscious mental happenings underneath the conscious mind. Others argued that mental events, let alone the unconscious, could not be observed objectively; so psychology was to study overt behaviour – not every kind, of course, for in other ways history, sociology, physiology and other disciplines also study behaviour. The various views as to what psychology is about, or should be, often appear antithetical to one another; but modern psychology tends to absorb them all and generally manages so to conduct its work as to avoid fruitless disagreements about initial assumptions. Such definitions of psychology as have been offered are not only contentious but are also too general and cryptic to be enlightening. To learn what living psychology is, it is best to see what it does. With this in view, we shall now survey, albeit very briefly in the first place, the many different interests and preoccupations of psychology.

Fields of psychology

We all act differently, and psychology has always striven to understand the nature of *individual differences*. Differences in conduct and in attitudes, in abilities and personality, are investigated in a variety of ways; and various explanations of these differences have been put forward. Contrasts among individuals are already apparent soon after birth. Individuality is incipient at conception, and it develops throughout life. The tracing and under-standing of psychological development in childhood and adolescence, at maturity and in the course of ageing, is the subject-matter of *developmental psychology*. In the broadest sense this embraces the study of hereditary influences, or psychogenetics, the environmental influences and the inter-action of the two.

The impact of the environment upon the individual is mainly through *learning*. The study of learning, together with *memory*, is indeed one of the very central interests of psychology. Because all learning processes in human beings and animals appear to have certain features in common, at least at the fundamental level, the psychology of learning is often comparative in its approach. It is also largely experimental, in that knowledge of learning processes is often achieved most readily by manipulating and observing behaviour under varying experimental conditions. Much the same may be said about the study of *perception*. It, too, tends to be *comparative* and *experimental*. In animals we infer perception from responses to sensory stimulation. In human beings we rely to a great extent on the reports of our experimental subjects. They tell us what they are aware of, what they experience. Thus, in the study of perception, experimental and experiential approaches are often complementary.

This is so also in the study of *motivation*. That field of study is concerned with the 'springs of action'; they include at the biological level such 'drives' as hunger and thirst, avoidance of pain, and sexuality. Human beings are, of course, also motivated by love and hate, altruism, pride, compassion, etc. Since motivation enters into everything we do – learning, perception, social activity – some writers do not regard it as a separate area of study. At any rate there is little doubt that, in the layman's view at least, motivation is central to psychology. To understand the biological roots of motivation, or of perception, or of learning, we study *physiological psychology*. This can reveal how our experiences and conduct are controlled by our nervous system, the hormones in our bloodstream, and our senses, such as vision or hearing. This may raise the thorny problem of interaction between body and mind; we shall make some remarks on this in a later section of this chapter.

While physiological psychology constitutes the biological wing of psychology, *social psychology* is the other wing of our subject and links it to sociology. If we say that social psychology is concerned with the influence of the social environment upon the individual, then this is almost tantamount to saying that whenever psychology is not physiological it is social. This may be true in a broad sense, but traditionally social psychology focuses much more on some topics than on others, and in particular it concerns itself with the study of the individual in a group, with his perception of other persons, with beliefs, attitudes and prejudices, and the like.

An area of psychology related to this, and one that is also close to learning and perception, is *cognitive psychology*. As the term implies, cognitive psychology concerns itself with cognizing, that is experiencing and thinking. Thinking also involves problem solving and the use of language. Cognition is not a very sharply delineated field of study; and it is one that is probably closer than any other to the original conception of the 'science of mind'. To what extent some areas of cognitive psychology are scientific is a somewhat controversial matter. We shall return in the last section of this chapter to the question of what is meant by scientific and unscientific.

There are other areas of psychology and approaches to psychology that deserve to be mentioned. One is *mathematical psychology* which is in part concerned with psychological measurement, or *psychometrics*, and in part with mathematical models of behaviour. Most psychology is, of course, empirical in that it involves collecting and interpreting observational and experimental data. Some psychology, however, deals with such matters as private feelings – passions, sorrows, etc. – which are of great interest to the individual but which can scarcely be studied with precision and rigour; this is sometimes called *humanistic psychology*. We should also mention *parapsychology* which attempts to investigate telepathy, precognition and related matters, and which many psychologists regard as being rather outside the confines of psychology.

The areas and approaches so far mentioned are for the most part concerned with features of experience and behaviour which are, as it were, universal and, in that sense, normal. On the other hand, *psychopathology*, known also as abnormal psychology, pays special attention to mental malfunctioning. The question arises immediately as to how we can tell, if at all, the psychologically normal from the abnormal. And this links psychopathology to the study of *personality* and individual differences, or differential psychology. The study of psychopathology is also close to that of clinical psychology, which is one of the applied fields to which we now turn.

Clinical psychology is concerned with the assessment of personality and abilities of the client or patient, with treatments, such as psychotherapy and behaviour modification, and with research into the assessment and treatment procedures. Such a statement may not be acceptable to all clinical psychologists because there is much debate as to what the proper tasks and functions of clinical psychology are. This is partly because psychiatry, which is a branch of medicine, is at the centre of diagnosis and treatment of mental patients, and the division of labour between it and clinical psychology is somewhat uncertain. Assessing children and dealing with their psychological problems in the school setting is the domain of *educational psychology*. More generally, educational psychology sets out to study teaching and learning problems; and it is particularly concerned with the alleviation of mental handicaps of every kind. The sphere of *occupational psychology* extends to vocational guidance and occupational selection and training, as well as to the psychological considerations bearing upon the design of working equipment, and the planning of working arrangements and of social conditions of work.

In rapidly running over the various psychological specialisms, we have tried to indicate, and even to emphasize, how each was related to the one mentioned earlier and/or later. In fact, each field is often so specialized that it may be studied in relative isolation from any other. A subject such as social psychology has not, in practice, much of a common language with, for instance, differential psychology, let alone physiological psychology. And mathematical psychology is very distant from, for example, psychopathology. The great diversity of psychology – the variety of traditions, schools of thought, attitudes and approaches within it – has prompted one writer at least to prefer the term psychological sciences to the term psychology which implies a unity within the discipline which is perhaps not there (Beloff, 1973). Such a term would follow the model set by the physical sciences, the life (biological) sciences, the social sciences and even the behavioural sciences. Of course, psychology may be said to be a behavioural science; and it is no doubt partly a biological and partly a social science. Nevertheless, in emphasizing the inherent plurality of psychology, the term psychological sciences may not be inappropriate; but the reader will be in a position to form his or her private judgement about this later on.

Philosophical origins

In a sense, the beginnings of all the sciences lie in philosophy. The philosophical roots of psychology are particularly interesting, and not purely for historical reasons. Some of the background concerns of psychologists are philosophical in nature, both metaphysical and semantic; that is, some of these issues have to do with beliefs concerning the ultimate nature of reality as well as with the meaning of psychological ideas. Such are the problems of free will, of purpose, and of the relationship between mind and body. Many psychologists believe that these are interesting puzzles rather than serious worries for modern psychology. Nevertheless, they continue to nag, and we shall have some observations to make about them in a later section of this chapter. First, however, it will be instructive to look at some aspects of the history of the emergence of psychology. In addition to philosophy, modern psychology owes its origin to developments in biological studies. These include the Darwinian view of evolution, and progress in physiology and psychiatry. There have also been influences of other disciplines, and psychology has some distinctly indigenous roots as well. However, the philosophical origins of psychology deserve pride of place.

In order not to go too far back into history we may begin with the so-called British empiricist philosophy of the late seventeenth, the eighteenth and the early nineteenth centuries. To begin with, it may be worth making two observations about the words 'British empiricist'. It is not, of course, claimed that there is anything peculiarly British about psychology; it is only that philosophers in a particular tradition – John Locke, David Hume, James Mill and others – were especially influential in shaping the outlook of early psychology. And further, the adjective empiricist does not imply anything empirical about the methods of those writers, but only indicates that in their view all human knowledge came from experience rather than from 'innate ideas', as was believed by Descartes, Leibnitz and not a few other philosophers of that era.

The various philosophers of the empiricist tradition certainly did not speak with one voice, but they did share a certain conception of the human mind which was later adopted by psychology and which persisted in several variants until the turn of the present century. One characteristic of this psychology was that it was *sensationist*, that is it assumed that all experience was ultimately sensory in character. The function of mental philosophy, and later, psychology, was to analyse what was in our minds into the constituent sensations: visual, auditory, and so on. Thus, the turn-of-the-century psychology was also *atomistic*, believing that the whole of mental life is built up from such 'atoms' of sensory experience. The principle governing this building up of experiences, or learning, was one of association of ideas by contiguity. In other words, this early psychology was *associationist* in outlook; this view seemed to make good sense, but was not based on systematic empirical studies of perception and cognitive processes. To all this may be added that the mainstream of psychological thought was also *introspectionist* and *intellectualist*, in that it was assumed that what goes on inside our minds was open to an intellectual analysis by introspection (see Thomson, 1968, for fuller treatment of the philosophical origins of psychology).

In the tradition of the British empiricist philosophy mind was passive; that is, it starts as *tabula rasa*, a clean slate, and it develops as a result of the impact of sensory experience. By the second half of the nineteenth century most psychologists considered, however, that mind was active and possessed a range of faculties. According to this 'faculty psychology' our experiences are weighed by the faculty of judgement, arranged by the faculty of reasoning, stored by the faculty of memory, and so on. It was believed that these faculties, and others, such as observation and will, could be improved by rigorous exercise. The American philosopher and psychologist, William James (brother of the novelist, Henry James), argued against this view and adduced experimental evidence that memory, for instance, could not be successfully trained in that way.

Even though by the turn of the twentieth century psychology had established itself as a separate discipline, relying on systematic observation and experiment as a means of gathering and extending knowledge, it was still to a considerable extent dominated by the assumptions of mental philosophy. New thinking was much in evidence (see, for instance, James, 1890) but the old conceptions of 'armchair psychology', as philosophical psychology was later nicknamed, were much in evidence too. The late Professor C. A. Mace argued that the new schools of psychology which arose and flourished during the first three decades or so of the twentieth century could be regarded as revolts against one or another of the assumptions deriving directly from the tradition of the empiricist philosophy.

The intellectualist conception of mental processes was, of course, brushed aside by Freud on the ground that intellect had no access to the unconscious, as conceived of by *psychoanalysis*, where instinctual urges ruled supreme. *Behaviourism*, as espoused by J. B. Watson, challenged introspectionist psychology, contending that scientific findings must be based on objective observation and not on subjective introspection. Atomism was blown sky-high by *Gestalt* psychology which produced evidence to show that percepts are whole 'Gestalten', or configurations, from the start, and are not normally built up from distinct and separate sensations. This as well as other schools of psychology held the sensationist assumption as untenable. Simple associationism, too, gradually came to be questioned, or at least subjected to qualifications, specifications and reformulations.

The model of mind due to Locke and Hume, that of a passive receptacle of sensations and ideas, the 'bucket theory of mind' as it was later dubbed, was the first to go. It was abandoned by early philosophical psychologists such as Thomas Brown, John Stuart Mill and Alexander Bain, as well as by William James who represents a transition to experimental psychology (Boring, 1957). The view that mind was active, expecting, believing and dependent on bodily conditions was more in keeping with the biological outlook. Late nineteenth century was the time when philosophical and biological streams of psychological thought were coming together. Thus we must now turn our attention to the biological origins of psychology.

Biological origins

The notion that the evolution of organisms is due to natural selection – Darwinism, as it used to be called – has led to viewing human behaviour in the new light of its biological context. One result of this was the emergence of comparative psychology of animals and man. The general climate was also conducive to progress in physiological psychology. One of the many developments in medicine was the rise of psychiatry. This culminated in the work of Freud in Austria which early this century made a striking impact on psychological theories of motivation and personality. At the same time, physiological studies had led directly to the researches of Pavlov in Russia. Pavlov's work influenced profoundly the psychological studies of animal and human learning; it also influenced markedly, if less directly, the study of perception and developmental psychology.

Aside from his general impact on the biological and social sciences, Darwin had a special interest in comparative psychology. In fact he published in his later years a treatise on emotions in animals and man. However, many consider Lloyd Morgan to have contributed more than any other to the founding in Britain at the turn of the century of modern comparative psychology (Hearnshaw, 1964). It was he, perhaps more than anybody else, who put an end to the anecdotal approach to the study of animal behaviour, insisting that reliable knowledge could only be gained by means of experimental observations carried out under controlled conditions. Lloyd Morgan was also critical of anthropomorphic explanations of animal behaviour, that is, of explanations imputing to animals human-like mental faculties. Instead, he favoured the most parsimonious explanations possible, often in terms of relatively simple adaptive and learning mechanisms; this precept came to be known as 'Lloyd Morgan's canon'. Thereafter comparative psychology flourished, and more in America than elsewhere.

Freud has made such an impact on psychiatry as well as on the arts, on social work and, generally, on the educated public that many people suppose that Freud's psychoanalysis must be absolutely central to psychology. In fact, the place of psychoanalysis in psychology is, and has been for many years, very much a matter of controversy. Certainly, Freudian thinking has considerably influenced psychopathology and the psychology of motivation and personality, and also such areas as social psychology and even comparative psychology. However, psychoanalytic tenets have never been universally accepted. This is largely because they depend on uncertain clinical evidence – evidence which is nearly always open to a variety of interpretations. That may well be one reason why there have been so many incompatible derivatives of psychoanalysis (Hall, 1954; Brown, 1961).

It could be said that Freud's influence on psychology is not so much biological as speculative. Without agreeing or disagreeing with this view, it may be remembered that Freud was a medical man, interested in biology and dissatisfied with the psychiatry of his day. The influence of psychiatry on psychology clearly predated Freud; French writers, such as Charcot at the end of the last century, and later Janet, had made some impact; and Freud's own thinking had some roots in French psychiatry, and particularly in its interest in hypnotism. Now it is difficult to single out any particular contribution of psychoanalysis as the most important one; but among the significant ones are: the emphasis on unconscious mental processes and the role of sex motivation, the conception of psychosexual development of the child, and the idea of psycho-dynamic mechanisms, such as repression, sublimation, projection, introjection, etc. Modern psychology attempts to examine the many imaginative thoughts contained in Freud and the post-Freudians with a view to integrating whatever can be integrated into the body of established psychological knowledge (Kline, 1972).

Pavlov was a physiologist and had always regarded his studies of conditioned reflexes as being within the ambit of physiology. His researches, however, essentially involved laboratory investigations of animal learning, and more generally animal behaviour, rather than animal physiology in the narrower sense. The groundwork was originally done early this century; and it has since had an enormous impact on developments in psychology. Modern studies of learning in animals, as well as in human beings, are almost inconceivable without the foundations laid by Pavlov's work (see Pavlov, 1927) and that of his collaborators and followers. All learning theories are also in one way or another indebted to Pavlov's pioneering studies. The different strands of biological influence in psychology, those originating from Darwin, and later from Freud and Pavlov, certainly do not all come neatly together. Still, psychology, as it is today, probably owes more to its diverse biological roots than to any others.

Psychological mainstream

The first exclusively psychological laboratory was set up in Leipzig, Germany, in 1879 by Wilhelm Wundt. In approaching psychology in an experimental manner Wundt followed in the footsteps of physiologists and others who for some time had been conducting psychological studies in the field of psychophysics (psychophysics to this day continues to investigate relationships between physical stimuli and the sensations to which the stimuli give rise). Research in the newly set up laboratory was concerned with vision, hearing and other sensory modalities, with attention, with judgement of time, with reaction times and other such matters. Wundt's own special interest lay in the human reaction time (now often called response latency), that is, the time it takes a person to respond to a stimulus. Many psychologists – German, French, British and American – were trained in the Leipzig Institute of Psychology, as the laboratory was called. These laboratory studies of human subjects were thus the beginnings of what came to be called experimental psychology. The epithet 'experimental' in this context was meant to contrast with 'philosophical'. And the conviction of the experimentalists was that the most important contributions to knowledge come from systematic experimental observations rather than from the 'armchair' contemplation of psychological phenomena.

It is sometimes said that psychology is a very young science. This supposedly justifies what some regard as the meagreness of achievement in the totality of psychological knowledge. The reader may later be able to judge for himself what and how much psychology has or has not achieved. However, to say that psychology is young is not entirely true. Not only do the philosophical origins of psychology go back several centuries, and the biological origins over a century, but even experimental psychology itself predates considerably the first psychological laboratory. We have already mentioned psychophysics; E. H. Weber and G. Fechner in Germany were studying stimulus-sensation problems experimentally in the first half of the nineteenth century; and to this day the so-called Weber–Fechner Law is regarded as valid under certain conditions. Reaction times, too, were already studied before Wundt, and – to mention further examples – so were colour vision and inter-sensory facilitation. It is interesting to note that all these areas are still being investigated today, albeit more deeply and with the aid of more efficient laboratory equipment. Anyway, the last two decades of the nineteenth century witnessed a rapid development of experimentation in the mainstream of psychology.

Experimental psychologists were now investigating not only mainly sensory processes but also memory, learning, problem solving and even aesthetics. Experimental psychology aimed at being empirical and quantitative and at avoiding imprecision and undue speculation. Thus the word, experimental, indicates *an approach* to psychology and *not a branch* of psychology. The hope was that all the branches of psychology would be experimental; in practice, experimentation is more appropriate to some than to others. Physiological psychology is highly experimental; the study of learning and memory is largely experimental; some areas of personality and social psychology are experimental but some are not; much cognitive psychology and, of course, philosophical psychology are non-experimental. It is sometimes hotly debated whether the experimental approach in psychology is, or is not, the best approach. Some regard it as barren because it appears to be inapplicable to vital aspects of human personality and mental life (Joynson, 1974; Gauld and Shotter, 1977). However this may be, it should be noted that the adjective experimental is used as much as ever in the titles of psychology books and journals. Insofar as it appears to some to be out of date, this is mainly because it expresses more of a desideratum or expectation than a reality about *all* the territory of psychology. Nevertheless, many experimental psychology textbooks (e.g. Underwood, 1966; Kling and Riggs, 1972) show clearly the wide applicability of experimental methods to psychology.

Interdisciplinary influences

Not all the roots of modern psychology fit into the three main categories mentioned so far, even though each is broad and heterogeneous, especially the biological one. One further important early influence is associated with the name of Francis Galton who pioneered in the second half of the last century the quantitative approach to the study of individual differences and the use of statistical methods in psychology. Galton could not be described as primarily a psychologist; he was that, but also a biologist and philosopher. Among other things, he was interested in geographical exploration, in meteorology, in anthropology and in criminology; in fact, he was a true polymath. One of the topics of which he made a special study was what he called the hereditary genius (Galton, 1869). This involved him in attempts at assessing human abilities and in investigations of the distribution of abilities within the population as a whole. As we now see it, Galton was handicapped by the absence in his time of the science of genetics; nor did he appear willing to recognize the importance of the environmental influences upon the characteristics of the individual. In spite of all this he was able to initiate anthropometry and mental testing and he developed modern correlational methods. In fact, because of his emphasis on quantitative procedures, Galton greatly helped at about the turn of the century to push the rapidly developing discipline of psychology in the direction of science.

Early this century psychometrics was established as an integral and essential feature of psychology; the core of the discipline was by then undoubtedly experimental; at the same time disparate ideologies, such as psychoanalysis, behaviourism and Gestalt psychology were much in evidence. In the inter-war period new influences began to be felt; one of the main ones was that of social anthropology. Its impact was primarily on social psychology, psychopathology and the study of individual differences. It was initially due in the main to the writings of Malinowski who carried out field studies of societies in the Western Pacific which had remained largely undisturbed by Western civilization (e.g. Malinowski, 1922). He and other investigators, such as Margaret Mead (1928), helped to focus attention on the lasting effects of modes of rearing infants, and of early cultural experiences, in moulding the human personality. They also argued that our ideas as to what is normal behaviour, or what is socially desirable, are shaped by the particular culture within which we are functioning.

Psychology has always been torn by the conflict between two extreme outlooks, that of *environmentalism*, stressing the ready susceptibility of the individual to socio-cultural influences, and that of *nativism*, emphasizing the importance of the innate features of the human personality. Those who regarded the mind of the neonate as essentially *tabula rasa*, such as the British empiricist philosophers or Jean Jacques Rousseau, represent the former tradition. So do, in a large measure, the behaviourists, the Freudians and the Pavlovians, strange bedfellows though they may seem. And the influence of social anthropology upon psychology was in the same direction. Nativism is represented by such philosophers as René Descartes and, more recently, by some psychologists of the first quarter of the present century who stressed the importance of instinct in human behaviour, e.g. William McDougall (1908). Students of perception in the Gestalt-psychology tradition are also essentially nativist; and so are ethologists who initially came to study behaviour from the zoological point of view.

Ethology is an approach to the study of animal behaviour that developed among Continental zoologists, and it is vividly presented in the writings of Lorenz (1952). The more traditional approach of comparative psychology had relied on laboratory studies, mostly of learning in animals, often using small mammals, such as mice, rats and cats. Ethological studies not only covered, as a matter of principle, many more species but they also involved field observations under natural conditions. Initially the main concern of ethology lay in the characteristics of instinctive behaviour (Tinbergen, 1951). While comparative psychologists tended to be interested in general laws of behaviour, irrespective of species, ethologists stressed interspecific differences. This, as well as the ethological researches into genetically determined behaviour patterns, made psychologists more aware of the biological constraints on learning. At the same time the value of laboratory experimentation in advancing our understanding of animal behaviour continues to be as fully recognized as ever. In fact, it looks as if much present-day research in animal behaviour is based on a combination of comparative-psychological and ethological methods (Hinde, 1970). Furthermore, some contemporary research procedures in human developmental and social psychology have also been devised under the influence of ethology (see Chapter 2).

There is a further interdisciplinary influence on psychology deserving a mention, viz. that of cybernetics. Cybernetics has been described as the study of control and communication in man and machine. It is perhaps an interdisciplinary study *par excellence*. As far as psychology goes, cybernetics is mainly concerned with machine models of functioning of living things, including their mentality. Such models have a long history, but only from the mid 1940s on did they begin to be of real interest to psychological theorists. The leading early cybernetician was Norbert Wiener, a professor of mathematics at the Massachusetts Institute of Technology. Others active in cybernetics were engineers, physiologists, psychiatrists and philosophers. Quite a few psychologists, too, were drawn early on towards this ambitious new movement, promising a fresh approach to the study of man.

It is not easy to assess the total impact of cybernetics upon psychology. Without doubt it generated in the first place some new thinking about behaviour by drawing attention to the simple, basic and ubiquitous operation of *negative feedback*. The principle involved underlies the working of most standard electronic apparatus; it also governs the functioning of many simple mechanical devices, such as the thermostat; and it is inherent in the physiology of all organisms. In point of fact, negative feedback, as a principle of functioning of organisms, is to a large extent merely a fresh formulation of what is called *homeostasis*. This regards bodily functioning, and mental functioning too, as a continuous process, whereby departures from the various states of equilibrium actuate mechanisms directed towards the restoration of conditions of balance (Cannon, 1932). Cybernetics has also had side effects; the most important of them has been the application of what is known as information theory to psychology. The contribution of *information theory* has been twofold; it gave some of its language to psychology – such concepts as input, output and transmitted information, 'noise', redundancy, etc.; it also provided psychology with a new way of quantifying certain of its variables in perception, in memory, in verbal communication and other areas. Cybernetic influences in psychology reverberate quite strongly to the present day. The interested reader may refer to such books as those by Ashby (1952), Sluckin (1960) and Apter (1970) which cover progressive developments in this field.

Traditional puzzles

Strange as it may seem, in the early days of psychology there existed a lively debate as to whether psychology was at all possible. The problem was seen at that time to be somewhat as follows. Human beings have free will, that is, they can decide within limits to do whatever they wish; since their actions are not determined in a way that, say, the movements of celestial bodies are determined, how possibly can they be studied? We now know that psychological knowledge can predict behaviour to some degree, that is, our predictions are in terms of probability and not certainty. Human decisions are not wholly capricious; while human beings feel free to decide on one course of action rather than another, we can also establish by psychological study which actions are more likely, and which are less likely, to occur. Free will is what we experience, but we can assume that our decisions have causes, and these causes are investigable. But – some would say – if behaviour is determined, why blame criminals, why express moral judgements? We do this partly because punishment and moral strictures may influence a person away from anti-social behaviour, that is, may cause him/her to desist from certain courses of action. However, approving or disapproving of others and thereby possibly influencing their behaviour is a separate issue from studying behaviour with a view to understanding its underlying causes.

Around the same time another query was being raised. Physical events have causes, but the behaviour of human beings, and even of animals, has also a purpose. We normally study causes, and we can study the causes of behaviour of organisms; but can we study purposes? Views have often been offered on this, but those of the early cyberneticians were perhaps the most unequivocal. Some machines – they pointed out – are so constructed as to behave purposefully, or teleologically; for instance, the thermostat 'aims' at keeping the room's temperature at a certain level, or the ground-to-air missile so adjusts its own flight as to follow and hit the aircraft that it is after. Thus, teleology, or the doctrine of 'final' causes, was now seen to be entirely compatible with mechanical functioning. Organisms exhibit purposive behaviour, and purpose is inherent in mentality. This in itself is no obstacle to a systematic study of mental functioning along scientific lines (Petrinovich and McGaugh, 1976).

Perhaps the most intriguing philosophical problem at the foundations of psychology is the so-called mind–body problem. Briefly, the nature of this puzzle may be said to be as follows. Mind is generally conceived of as being characterized by awareness and thinking. Body, on the other hand, including the brain, is material or physical; like all matter, it occupies space, has weight and so on. Being essentially different 'stuffs', how can mind and body interact? And yet seemingly they do. Therefore some philosophers see the solution in some such word as 'seemingly'; that is, they favour what they call psychophysical parallelism as an explanation of the *apparent* interaction between body and mind. There are also those who regard matter as wholly conceived by the human mind; this is philosophical idealism. And there are others who regard mind as something that emanates from body, which is a form of philosophical materialism, known as epiphenomenalism. One way of thinking about body and mind is to regard them as the structure and function respectively of the human organism. Anyway, the body–mind interaction presents an awkward metaphysical problem for philosophy. It is also a problem in psychology, but a much more down-to-earth one (see Chapter 4).

In more concrete terms, we know that we are sometimes angry when we are hungry; here the state of the body affects the mind. At other times we blush; here our mental state affects the body. In yet other cases, such as 'nervous' indigestion or headache, bodily and mental states mutually influence each other. Psychology is much concerned with the mechanisms of all such happenings. Some branches of psychology, such as physiological psychology, psychopathology and developmental psychology, are especially interested in the interaction between bodily and mental processes. The problems in this sphere are susceptible of empirical study and are, in principle, capable of being resolved. What solution, if any, any of us may personally find for the old metaphysical mind–body problem is scientifically (although not personally) unimportant. This is so because the advancement of psychological knowledge is not really dependent on any particular view of the philosophical mind–body dilemma (Sluckin, 1960).

Methods of psychology

As psychology was becoming emancipated from philosophy into a study in its own right, the question was sometimes raised as to whether this new discipline could be scientific. Indeed, it is nowadays also often asked whether psychology is truly a science. The answer hinges on what is under-stood by science; and the characteristics of scientific inquiry are the proper concern of the philosophy of science (Popper, 1963; Kuhn, 1970). Leaving the complexities of the question aside, it is generally agreed that in science whatever is asserted must stand or fall in the light of empirical evidence. On the other hand, we all have beliefs of one kind or another that are not based on empirical evidence, often because such evidence is just not available; and we do not normally claim that these beliefs are a part of science. In between the two situations there is the no-man's-land where it is debatable as to whether, or to what extent, any particular tenets are scientifically grounded. Quite a lot of psychology is in that category, and notably whole areas of, for example, motivation, personality and social psychology. Now, it can be cogently argued that imaginative speculation is no less valuable than scientifically established facts. While this may be so, it is important to recognize clearly the difference in the logical status between scientific theory and personal belief. To aim at strictly scientific psychology would be to abandon quite large sections of the subject that simply do not lend themselves to fully scientific treatment. To ignore the canons of scientific methodology altogether would be to condemn psychology to perpetual un-certainty or the realm of fancy. And yet, it would be undesirable to expend too much time and energy on debating whether this or that psychological investigation is wholly or only partly scientifically sound. For the true aim of research is to ask interesting and important questions and attempt to answer them as fully and objectively as circumstances permit. This is nicely illustrated by Reed (1972) in his studies of anomalous experiences which shed much light on normal cognitive processes; see also the discussion of explanation in psychology in Bolles (1975).

Ideally, scientific inquiry is objective rather than evaluative; it sets out to establish what the facts are and seeks to understand them; it does not judge them as good or bad. However, values are often implicit, if not explicit, in the biological sciences. Adaptation, for instance, is seen as something valuable. Skill, learning and related psychological concepts have an aura of desirability. Adjustment is good and maladjustment is bad. Prejudice is bad, but tolerance is good. We want mental functions – perception, memory, etc. – to be effective rather than ineffective. Does this mean that we cannot study them objectively? Not necessarily; but we must be watchful that our emotional biases do not distort our observations – that we see facts as they are and not as we should like them to be. From time to time students of psychology become disillusioned with this 'cult of the fact' (Hudson, 1972). We should accept, they say, that psychology is shot through with value-judgements, and no value-free psychology is possible. Without questioning this, it is still the case that in seeking the truth about human nature we are aided in our quest and progress by being as detached as we can and by consciously trying to be as objective as possible in all our observations in the laboratory and in the field.

Is this, however, the only way of making progress? Is systematic observation and experiment the key to the advancement of knowledge? This belief has at times been challenged (e.g. Maslow, 1973; Severin, 1973). It is countered that the way to advance knowledge of oneself (and possibly psychological knowledge in general) is to broaden and deepen one's personal experience. The way to achieve it may be through meditation, or participation in 'encounter groups', or by stimulating one's own imagination and experiential powers by drugs, or by actively seeking religious experience, and so on. Undoubtedly the enrichment of personal experience can be very worthwhile, but it is not an alternative to scientific endeavour. Intuition as a means of understanding is not opposed to reason where pure reason has limited scope. As an aid to intellect, intuition can be a spur and a guiding light but it is not a substitute for intellect.

Intellectual scientific pursuits, born out of curiosity, involve observing, understanding, predicting and sometimes controlling events. Observation provides empirical evidence for such understanding of natural phenomena as we may gain. Understanding gives rise to prediction. Incomplete understanding of all factors involved in a situation permits only actuarial and statistical prediction, whereby we forecast future occurrences in the light of what has happened in the past. Fuller understanding can lead to more precise predictions; this typically occurs in, for example, astronomy, but hardly ever in psychology. When we can manipulate events to achieve certain outcomes, then prediction is tantamount to situational control. Psychologists engaged in research aim at understanding and prediction. Many practising applied psychologists make 'clinical predictions'; these turn out, on analysis, to be imprecise statistical ones, expressed in non-numerical terms. Psychologists working with individuals aim not only at predicting events but also at controlling situations, generally to benefit their subjects or clients.

We have seen that, as a 'pure' discipline, psychology sets out to understand the phenomena of perception, learning and thinking, social behaviour, individual differences and so on. Psychology also seeks, as an applied discipline, to promote the efficient use of manpower, good teaching, mental health and similar objectives. Academic psychology, in seeking the truth, is primarily concerned with the extension of knowledge through empirical research; applied psychology, in attempting to do good, is also concerned with research so as to discover the best ways of achieving its aims (see, for example, Broadbent, 1973). Both kinds of research form a continuum; at one end of it the emphasis is on 'pure' research, primarily aiming at satisfying our curiosity about human (and animal) nature and not designed to be immediately applicable; at the other end is 'operational' research, expressly setting out to solve practical problems of a psychological character which are being faced by industry, or commerce, or government departments. But, just as 'applied' research may add to fundamental knowledge, so even the purest research has the potential of becoming useful. In fact, research findings from traditional areas of laboratory-type psychology – such as visual and auditory perception, psychophysics, problem solving, learning, memory and the like – have, sometimes after many years, found good uses in down-to-earth situations in industry, government, schools and hospitals. A wide knowledge of 'general' psychology, as well as the ability to conduct laboratory experiments and field research, are valuable assets to all intending to become professional psychologists – clinical, educational or occupational. Chapters 2–23, which follow, deal with most aspects of 'general' psychology. The final chapter, 24, serves as an introduction to the main applications of psychology.

Chapter 2
Comparative and Ethological Perspectives

The structure and physiology of species are the result of evolution; behaviour, too, must be considered as having evolved through natural selection. The study of fossils helps to reconstruct the morphological evolution of species; historical clues to the evolution of behaviour are more difficult to come by. However, just as evolutionary inferences can be made from existing anatomical and physiological differences among species, so also the origins and functions of behaviour can often be surmised from behavioural comparisons among animals and man.

This chapter is mainly concerned with problems arising in the study of inter-species differences and similarities in behaviour. Differences are studied not only for the sake of detailed knowledge but also in order to help avoid misleading cross-species generalizations and extrapolations. Noting similarities is helpful in focusing on general laws or principles of behaviour. We shall presently see why comparative animal and human studies in fields such as motivation and learning are regarded by many as an essential aspect of psychological inquiry.

The evolution of behaviour

Comparative studies of physical characteristics have made possible systematic classifications of living things. Closely related species have been grouped into genera, genera into families, families into orders, and so on. Such taxonomic studies of inter-relatedness of organisms help our understanding of the evolutionary development of species, the progressive branching of the 'tree of evolution'. Although the spade work has been done, the task of taxonomy has not yet been completed. In the light of fresh evidence, many of the finer details of the taxonomy of animals have to be revised time and again. Some of this new evidence comes from observations of stable inter-group differences in behaviour. Hinde (1970) quotes many examples of the use of behavioural characters both in taxonomy and in furthering our understanding of the course of evolution. One must, however, be on one's guard against drawing false conclusions from the similarities in behaviour of different species. First, many similarities are determined environmentally rather than genetically. Second, similarities that are due to genetic factors may not necessarily indicate phyletic affinity, for they could be the result of independent development of similar forms of behaviour, the so-called convergent evolution.

To understand behaviour, we study its causes; and to understand the evolution of behaviour we must also study its consequences. Some but not all of the consequences will have a bearing on the animal's survival or reproduction. Thus, some types of behaviour are better adapted than others to the survival of the given species. However, it is sometimes not at all obvious what the survival value of some behaviour pattern might be; one can make an inspired guess, but it is not easy to establish observationally or experimentally whether one's guess is correct. Thus, it is known that animals quite commonly display repeatedly certain sequences of movements which are independent of environmental stimuli. For example, such *fixed action patterns* (FAPs), as they are called, may be observed in the behaviour of certain birds building their nests. The survival value of such nest-building behaviour would seem clear enough. It is more difficult, however, to know what may be the value to the animal of certain FAPs characteristic of courtship displays of various species. Here there is much scope for guessing and speculation. The study of fixed action patterns has been shown to be very useful for taxonomic purposes; we shall return to FAPs later in this chapter in the section on ethology.

Traditional comparative psychology

Many of the early British books on general psychology were especially concerned with comparisons between animals and man, and between one animal species and another. The term, comparative psychology, was introduced in the 1880s and 1890s by writers such as G. J. Romanes, C. Lloyd Morgan and others (Hearnshaw, 1964). Although the phrase might be thought to refer equally to similarities and differences in culture or social class, traditionally it is confined to inter-species comparisons and not to intra-species ones. At least, this was the original aim of comparative psychology. Later, in Britain, America and elsewhere the expression 'comparative psychology' was quite often simply used to refer to studies of animal psychology or animal behaviour. The history of this development is interesting and instructive.

In the first place, in looking for general psychological laws, research workers turned to animals because they were considered simpler and more convenient to study rigorously. Since the laws sought were thought to be universal, it did not greatly matter which species was investigated. And so psychologists concentrated on the study of a few selected species; the most popular was the laboratory white rat, and later, the domestic pigeon. Experimentalists studied the learning of such animals when finding their way to some goal, when acquiring the ability to discriminate between different patterns, and so on. Such animal behaviour studies still went under the name of comparative psychology, possibly because they were regarded as implicitly comparative, and also perhaps because they were usually conducted by psychologists rather than zoologists.

Comparative psychology became indistinguishable from the study of animal behaviour when inter-species comparisons were explicitly investigated without any reference to the human species. The interest in these studies tended to lie in the search for a hierarchy of abilities. Of course, higher up the evolutionary scale animals have greater ability to solve problems than lower down the scale. At the same time, some animals are good at solving some problems but not others; for example, rats are good at solving mazes because that is, in effect, what they are adapted to in their natural environment. Other animals, differently constructed, may be poor at maze running, but good at coping with other types of problem, such as learning manipulations, or learning to respond to auditory signals. Bitterman (1960) argued strongly against rash quantifications of the learning ability of different species, and insisted on the necessity for qualitative comparisons. It gradually became clear that a species hierarchy of general ability was well-nigh impossible to establish; so one could not tell with confidence whether, say, the dog, the cat, or the horse was the most or the least intelligent of the three.

Still, certain quantitative inter-species comparisons may well be valid; these would be comparisons concerning some very specific learning situations, such as, for instance, simple habituation to innocuous stimuli. More sophisticated comparisons of the ability 'to learn how to learn' have also been found worthwhile. Sheldon (1968) has provided a valuable review of the methods suitable for comparative studies of learning abilities. Generally, it is not the speed of simple learning that is indicative of the animal's potential, but rather the intrinsic difficulty of the problems the given animal can overcome, as well as the range of the tasks that it is able to learn.

At one time, those who were critical of the preoccupation of the traditional comparative psychology with specialized studies of a limited number of animal species, but mainly the laboratory-bred rat, dubbed it disparagingly 'rat psychology'. The aim of such laboratory studies of rat behaviour was, as we have seen, to seek general principles of behaviour; and rats, mice, pigeons and the like were merely convenient animals for this type of research (Lockard, 1968, 1971).

From the early days on, investigations of animal discrimination learning have been conducted with a view to elucidating such problems as the use of cues in successful discrimination, the ability of animals to generalize from given learning discriminations to new ones, the matter of delayed responding, and so forth. Figure 2.1 shows in a diagrammatic form an early discrimination box. One of the stimuli leads to a food reward while the other does not. The black and white circles can be interchanged so that the animal must not merely respond by turning right or left, but has to learn whether to go past the white or the black circle. Other patterns have been used to establish which of them are discriminable and which are not.

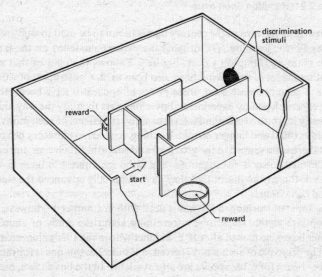

Figure 2.1   Early discrimination box

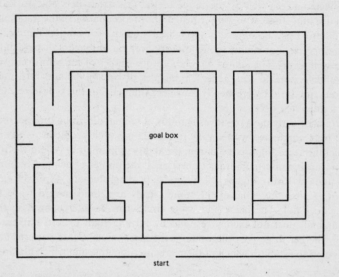

Figure 2.2   Hampton Court maze

As early as the turn of the century mazes began to be used to study animal trial-and-error learning. The original mazes were modelled on the famous hedge maze at Hampton Court. Figure 2.2 shows the plan of that maze, but other mazes of every kind have also been used. Constructed of wood or metal to accommodate a rat, these pieces of apparatus have been very extensively employed by experimental psychologists to study the way animals gradually learn to avoid blind alleys, to study the effects of such motivating factors as thirst and hunger on maze running, to study exploratory behaviour when there is no reward in the goal box, and so forth. Much time and energy was devoted to such investigations, and although interest in them has now declined, there is no doubt that they have materially advanced the study of animal behaviour.

The topic of learning in general is dealt with in Chapter 13; however, it is appropriate at this stage to say something about the study of animals in Skinner boxes, so named after B. F. Skinner who in the 1930s pioneered their use. The principle of such a box is given in Figure 2.3; this one is for rats, but Skinner boxes for other species are also available. In the box shown, pressing a lever produces a pellet of food. The animal soon learns to press the lever

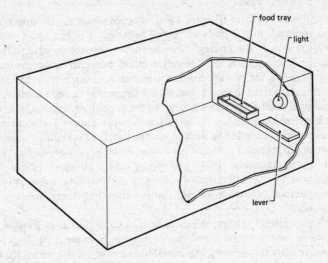

Figure 2.3 Prototype of Skinner box

again and again. The apparatus can also be arranged so that the reward is obtained by pressing the lever only when a light in the box is on but not when it is off; and this the animal can learn fairly readily. Skinner boxes for pigeons have been particularly extensively used; in such a box the bird pecks a key to obtain some grain; this reward reinforces the animal's pecking behaviour. Psychologists have been greatly interested in the behaviour of animals as a function of the way they are rewarded; whether reinforcement is given for each desired action (continuous reinforcement) or only sometimes (intermittent reinforcement). There are various possible ways of providing intermittent reinforcement. These different *schedules of reinforcement*, as they are called, can exert precise control over what the animal does. Schedules of reinforcement of some kind are thought to control also much, if not all, of ordinary day to day human behaviour. The work of Skinner and his many followers illustrates well the view that certain general principles of behaviour may apply equally to all species. Of course, such views are somewhat controversial; we shall have occasion to return to this question later.

Traditional ethology

We mentioned briefly in Chapter 1 the influence which the European zoological approach to the study of animal behaviour has had upon modern psychology. While the interest of comparative psychology originally lay mainly in learning, that of ethology focused primarily upon instinctive behaviour. Thus, the two approaches to animal behaviour might have been complementary from the start; and yet they appeared to be in conflict. For comparative psychology traditionally tended to be environmentalist in outlook, asserting the influence of nurture rather than nature. Early ethology, on the contrary, tended to be nativist, that is, it insisted upon the paramount importance of inherited modes of behaviour. However, writers such as Hinde (1970, 1974), Manning (1976) and many others all agree that despite appearances and a difference of emphasis the two established ways of studying animal behaviour are not contradictory but complementary (see next section).

Although animal behaviour was of interest to zoologists in Europe and America in the last century, and the forerunners of modern ethology were very active early this century, the actual founders of the discipline, Konrad Lorenz, Niko Tinbergen and their associates on the continent of Europe, began their studies only in the 1930s. While many of the original ethological ideas came from Lorenz, the most systematic and complete exposition of the ethological viewpoint and researches with regard to instinctive behaviour was given by Tinbergen (1951). Several major books embodying ethological work appeared in the 1960s (e.g. Thorpe, 1963). However, perhaps the most comprehensive presentation of the traditional ethological approach, exhibiting its strengths as well as weaknesses, is that of Eibl-Eibesfeldt (1970).

Unlike comparative psychology, ethology has greatly concerned itself from the start with the description and categorization of the behaviour of animals under natural conditions. A catalogue, as it were, of the full range of behaviour patterns of any given species is known as the *ethogram*. This was regarded at one time as the *sine qua non* of any further study. The first thing that ethograms would reveal was fixed action patterns characteristic of each species. As mentioned earlier, these are modes of behaviour which are relatively invariable and which possess the features of skills except that, unlike most human skills, they are not acquired through learning. On the contrary, a truly fixed action pattern may be shown to require no training whatever, although this does not mean that it necessarily makes its appearance suddenly in its mature form. Many types of behaviour contain FAP elements. Some skills, such as retrieving eggs by birds, or retrieving their young by mammals, require a minimum of learning, if any. Other skills, such as hunting, certainly contain elements of fixed action, but do involve learning – sometimes a great deal of it.

Ethologists have never regarded behaviour as consisting primarily of responses to stimuli. On the contrary, animals and human beings are active as a result of internal motivating factors; they display *appetitive behaviour*. Searching for food, or water, or warmth, or a mate, are all examples of it. All these culminate in *consummatory acts*. While appetitive behaviour generally exhibits variability and flexibility, consummatory acts are typically fixed action patterns or stereotyped modes of behaviour. More recent studies have, however, cast doubt on the sharpness of this distinction.

Complex sequences of behaviour, requiring practically no learning, are known as instinctive behaviour – a phrase which comparative psychologists have often been reluctant to use because of doubts as to its explanatory value. An animal has to be internally ready for instinctive action, such as courtship and mating, or looking after its offspring. However, instinctive behaviour has to be set in motion by a suitable external stimulus, for example, the sight or smell of a potential mate. Such a stimulus is known as a *releasing stimulus*, or releaser; it allows the potential for instinctive behaviour to be, as it were, released for action. Ethologists have often been particularly interested in discovering what precisely releases the different kinds of stereotyped complex behaviour patterns which may be observed in animals.

Some ethologists went further than that and searched for releasers of various forms of human behaviour. They have not often been successful. In the first place human behaviour is immensely varied and variable; secondly, stimuli that initiate human activities cannot be so readily pin-pointed. Generally, extrapolations from animal to human behaviour can be dangerously misleading. Nevertheless, the skills of ethologists in observing, describing and classifying animal behaviour have been successfully applied to the study of child development (Blurton Jones, 1972). In other spheres, too, the thinking and findings of ethologists have had an impact on animal behaviour studies outside ethology as well as on human psychology.

The merging of approaches

It had been clear for some years how unsatisfactory it was for animal behaviour to be studied in separate camps, working in isolation from each other, when R. A. Hinde published in 1966 the first edition of his book,

Animal Behaviour. The book had then, and the second edition still has, the telling sub-title: 'A synthesis of ethology and comparative psychology'. Animal behaviour is a field of study where the interests of zoology and psychology, as well as physiology, genetics, ecology and even sociology, all overlap. In particular, the central interests of ethology, with its zoological roots, and comparative psychology, which developed in association with experimental psychology, are much the same. Happily, the coming together of the two traditions has now progressed very considerably.

The resulting new horizons in the study of animal behaviour owe much to both traditions. Because of the ethological influence, attention is nowadays given to the full range of the animal's behavioural repertoire and to the environment to which the given species has become adapted in the course of evolution. At the same time, students of animal behaviour now appreciate the importance of the experimental control of conditions, and of the need to quantify observations, so that valid conclusions may be drawn from observational data. Furthermore, it is now generally accepted that both the causes of behaviour, in the sense of behavioural and physiological antecedents, and the ontogeny of behaviour, that is, its development in the individual, need to be investigated if a fuller understanding of the roots of the behaviour of animals is to be achieved.

Many modern books dealing with animal behaviour do not attempt to be comprehensive, but concern themselves with some particular aspect of the subject. Some, for example, focus on the evolution and ontogeny of behaviour (Aronson *et al.*, 1970; Moltz, 1971). Others pay special attention to the social behaviour of animals (Tinbergen, 1953; Dimond, 1970). Scientific papers and books are still written from either the ethological or the comparative psychological angle, but many synthesize the two approaches. Often, edited volumes contain contributions from both stables (e.g. Etkin, 1964; Aronson *et al.*, 1970; Bateson and Hinde, 1976). It may be said with some confidence that the early isolation of each of the two approaches, and the subsequent disagreements and friction between them, now belong more to the history of the study of animal behaviour than to the present.

In recent times a third stream of thought, that of sociobiology, has joined the other two. Sociobiology, which has sprung into existence in North America, focuses on the influence of evolution on the behaviour of animals and man, and seeks simple rules – mathematical, if possible – governing social behaviour. Like ethology, its roots are in zoology rather than psychology, but its preoccupations appear to be rather different from those of traditional ethology. A leading sociobiologist, Edward Wilson, seems to believe that the new discipline, in addition to looking afresh at animal behaviour, can also shed new light on human social functioning. Certainly, topics such as parental behaviour, aggression, altruism and the like have been tackled by sociobiologists (Wilson, 1975; Barash, 1979; Ruse, 1979). There has been some debate as to what is the essential difference, if any, between the sociobiological and ethological positions. What is clear is that both these perspectives, as well as that of comparative psychology, are having a marked influence on modern psychological thought.

Animal behaviour and the human species

What relevance, if any, has the study of animal behaviour for human psychology? Some would say that it has little or none. We shall presently consider the view that comparative studies of behaviour may be of value even to those whose interests are purely human; but first it may be worth stating, in passing, that animal behaviour is studied essentially for its own sake and not because of its implications for psychology. Animal behaviour is a subject that arouses extraordinary curiosity – and understandably so. Some of the actions of animals, even relatively lowly ones like ants and bees, are remarkably efficient in their complexity. Birds and especially mammals are often capable of very effective learning and show good memory. Both laymen and specialists are interested in knowing what precisely animals can and cannot achieve. And discovery in recent years has not been slow to come, perhaps especially so in the field of infra-human primate behaviour (Hinde, 1974).

The biological continuity between animals and man needs no special emphasis; *Homo sapiens* is a mammal within the order of *Primates*. For this reason it used to be thought that, to gain an understanding of human behaviour, one should study the simpler behaviour of lower animals in the first place. However, it soon became clear that the supposedly simple behaviour could in fact be very complex indeed. There is another reason, however, why animal studies may be of relevance to human psychology. The reason is that certain general principles of behaviour may be exhibited both by animals and human beings; and, from a practical point of view, these laws, if there are such, may be much more readily investigated with animal rather than human subjects. The general principles in question often concern modes of learning. For instance, it is not often reasonable to study systematically the effects of punishment in children, but there are fewer objections to such studies when rats or mice are subjects. Again, retention of what has been learned, or memory, may be studied in both humans and animals; but it is more acceptable to study experimentally in animal rather than human subjects the various features of amnesia resulting from shock.

In other spheres, too, animal studies can make a contribution to psychology. Heredity and environment, nature and nurture, are responsible for what we are. Chapter 3 deals with genetic influences; suffice it to say here that there are distinct advantages in using relatively fast-maturing animals, such as rats, as experimental subjects in programmes of selective breeding for psychological characteristics, such as problem-solving abilities or fearfulness. Environmental effects of early experience can also be studied much more readily in animals than in human beings. There have certainly been many follow-up studies of infants reared in institutions rather than by parents; but humane considerations prevent the psychologist from manipulating rearing conditions freely in order to learn as much as is theoretically possible. Young animals, on the other hand, can be raised with or without mothers, in social isolation, under conditions of perceptual deprivation or with a maximum of stimulation, and so on, although here, too, ethical considerations set limits to what may be done. Generally speaking, a wide range of early experiences and their short-term and long-term effects upon the abilities and 'personality' of animals can be studied. As far as human implications are concerned, such animal studies can only be suggestive rather than conclusive. Nevertheless, interesting ideas as to how the environment might influence human behaviour may be gained (especially when such ideas are derived from studies of infra-human primates).

Animal studies are probably most directly useful to human psychology in the areas of physiological psychology and psychopathology. In order to find out how different parts of the brain affect mental functioning, it is necessary to study persons with known brain damage resulting from accidents or disease. What, of course, must not be done for obvious reasons is to use surgical techniques for scientific, as distinct from therapeutic, purposes. These methods, however, may be sometimes justifiable in animal research. Surgical studies of animals have, in fact, often taught the surgeon how to treat human illness. They have also yielded a great deal of knowledge about the physiological bases of instinctive behaviour, perceptual and motor skills, memory and the like.

The effects of drugs on behaviour have, of course, been extensively studied in human beings. They have to be if therapeutic drugs, such as sedatives, stimulants and others are to be prescribed with safety. However, new drugs must always be tested on animals first. To investigate their full effects, general and specific activities of animals have to be observed and measured;

changes in different learning abilities have to be assessed; the sexual behaviour of animals must be studied; in short, every aspect of animal behaviour is of interest to psychopharmacology and psychopathology. Not only are the effects of drugs – all drugs, including alcohol, coffee, etc. – studied in the individual animal, but also the effects of drugs administered to the mother upon her offspring are of great interest. Such experiments cannot be done with human beings and that is where animal behaviour studies can be of great help.

Lastly, we may stress once again that the neuro-physiological and psychological gap between man and even the advanced anthropoid apes is very wide indeed. Hence, extrapolations from animals to human beings can be dangerous. All generalizations across species are risky, and those from animals to man have often been very dubious. And yet, animal behaviour studies, apart from their own great intrinsic interest, have a contribution to make to the study of man. In psychology, whether it is physiological or developmental, or even social, we are never very far from the biological and evolutionary roots of conduct and mentality.

Chapter 3
Psychogenetics and Maturation

Nature and nurture

Well over a century ago Francis Galton began to ask questions about the effectiveness of nature (i.e. inheritance) and of nurture (i.e. environment) in making us what we are. Judging by his book, *Hereditary Genius*, Galton (1869) was himself more interested in the influence of nature than nurture. In this regard he was at variance with the tradition of the British empiricist philosophy. For the dominant interest had been for a long time in the contribution of nurture. The problem, however, is in what way and how far inheritance and environment contribute and interact in producing the mature individual.

We shall, of course, give very much attention in subsequent chapters to the role of nurture under such headings as early experience, learning, skilled performance, and so on. The present chapter, however, deals with influences of heredity upon the behaviour of both animals and human beings. This field of study is known as behaviour(al) genetics, or psychogenetics.

Genetics of structure, function and behaviour

It is well known that the physical structure of an organism is to a large extent determined by its genes. To put it more technically, phenotype is a function of genotype, where by *phenotype* we mean all the observable characteristics of an individual, and by *genotype* we mean the genetic potential that the individual has (and can in part transmit to his offspring). Individual differences in morphology, or form, both between species and within species, can be attributed primarily to differences in genotype. This is not to deny that environmental variation may also be associated with structural differences; a grossly uncongenial environment, prolonged inadequate nutrition, or disease can have permanent structural consequences. But it does mean that, when the environment is 'normal' in the sense of providing the conditions necessary for healthy growth, structural differences between and within species are more closely connected with genotypic differences than with such variation in environment as can occur within the 'normal' range for the organism.

The concern of the behavioural geneticist is to examine the relationship between genotypic variation and differences in *behavioural phenotype*, that is, in the functional properties exhibited by organisms. An organism functions in a context and as a result of stimulation from this context, and therefore to some extent this functioning is shaped by the context; behaviour represents the more or less adaptive transaction between an organism and its environment. We may therefore expect that behavioural difference will be somewhat less closely associated with genotypic difference than is structural variation. But the fact that behaviour is always the functioning of a structure which remains relatively constant from one situation to another, and which is under genetic determination, makes it probable that the influence of genotype upon behaviour will be discernible.

It might be thought that comparisons between species would give us the strongest evidence of genetic influence upon behaviour. Though in general this may be true, there are two complications. First, behavioural differences between species cannot be dissociated from environmental differences; two species may co-exist in the same physical environment, but the behavioural significance of that environment will be quite different for them. Second, one of the respects in which species differ, as a result of their differing genotypes, is in the plasticity or flexibility of their behaviour. Because of his genetic endowment, man is the most malleable of animals; his behaviour is most modifiable through learning. It is because of this genetically determined modifiability that some psychologists have held that genotypic differences between people are not important determinants of behavioural differences between them. The argument that because structure is under genetic determination therefore behaviour will in some measure also be, has less force in the case of human beings, for whom the distinguishing feature of their structure is the capacity for highly variable functioning under the stimulus of environmental change.

Two consequences have followed from these complications. In the first place, behaviour geneticists have concentrated upon the effects of genotypic difference within a species rather than between species. If the focus is upon one species, it is easier to exercise experimental control over environmental factors and thus isolate, in some degree, the effects of genotype. In the second place, students of genetic influence upon human behaviour, and that of other species to a lesser extent, have had to deal with *general* characteristics of behaviour, or broad *behavioural traits*, rather than with specific responses. The concept of behavioural trait is discussed in detail in Chapters 19 and 20. Briefly, it is based upon the fact that individual differences in certain forms of behaviour remain stable from one situation to another. We call a person intelligent, not because on one occasion and in one situation he exhibits behaviour which meets our criterion, but because he does this habitually and in varying circumstances. It is the influence of genotype upon behavioural trait that the behaviour geneticist investigates. More precisely he asks the following questions:

1. Is there an association between individual differences in a behavioural trait and the genotypic differences of the same individuals? Do genotype and phenotypic behavioural trait *co-vary*? This is the initial question and the answer establishes whether, in explaining the variability of a particular form of behaviour in a population, we need to take account of hereditary differences.

2. *To what extent* are genotypic differences related to behavioural differences? What are the relative contributions of heredity and environment to the observed behavioural differences? Plainly, the answer to these questions must always be relative to the range of environmental and genotypic differences sampled in a particular investigation. But it may be possible to show that some behavioural traits are less susceptible to the influence of environmental variation than others.

3. What is the genetic mechanism involved in the production of a given behavioural difference? Is the difference due to forms of a single gene, or is it due to a number of genes acting in a cumulative fashion? Is there evidence of a dominant–recessive relationship between different forms of the same genes?

4. What is the nature of the physiological structure and process which intervene between the primary, local action of the gene and the behavioural trait manifested by the whole organism?

5. In what ways do genotype and environment interact in the production of behavioural differences? For example, the effect of a given environment might be to increase the intellectual functioning of all people. But it might also have a differential effect, making the innately more intelligent better still, and at the same time, perhaps because it is overstimulating, actually depressing the level of performance of the innately less intelligent. Conversely, an environment which stimulates the innately dull may be insufficiently

interesting to promote effectively the intellectual development of the innately bright.

This last question raises an issue which needs further elaboration. Phenotype, whether structural or behavioural, is always a function of the interaction of both genotype and environment. The effects of genotype and environment are not additive but multiplicative, in the sense that, without an appropriate environment, there can be no phenotype. To emphasize the point, it is worth listing some of the complex interactions which occur in the 'gap' between genotype and behaviour. Though genetic material does not all have the same function, the primary effect of those genes which control structural development is the production of enzymes. Thereafter, the following interactions occur: (a) between the effects of similar or different forms of the same genes at corresponding loci on a pair of chromosomes, (b) between the effects of different genes, (c) between the cell and its environment and (d) between the total multicellular organism and its environment. Just as it is the environment which determines whether potential genetic effects are actualized, so it is the genotype which determines which aspects of the physical environment are behaviourally significant.

These considerations make plain the absurdity of saying of a particular person's intelligence, for instance, that more of it is due to heredity than to environment. How is it, then, that we can even raise question 2 above, and what is the significance of the estimates made by many investigators of the relative importance of heredity and environment? To understand the justification for the question and the context which makes answers to it meaningful, it is necessary to be clear on two points. First of all, as we have said, the behaviour geneticist is not studying the single organism, but is trying to find out whether, and how much, in a specified population of organisms, *differences* in genotype *co-vary* with, or are associated with, *differences* in behavioural trait. Second, in analysing the results of an experiment he has to make use of various statistical procedures. He uses, as models to facilitate his analysis, those parts of statistical theory which suit his purpose. Central among these is the statistic called the *variance* or σ^2.

The variance is a single value which represents the degree of variability, scatter or dispersion of a set of scores; it is the average of the squared deviations of each score from the average score. For an adequate account of this statistic, the reader must consult one of the standard textbooks (e.g. Edwards, 1967c). For the present, the importance of this statistic resides in the following fact: if individual differences in a variable A can be attributed to two other independent variables X and Y, then the variance of the scores measuring A can be analysed into three components, one which represents the amount of the variance of A which is due to X, and the other the amount due to Y, together with a third, interaction component, which represents that amount of the variance of A which is due to the interaction of X and Y. These three components are additive and together make up the total variance of A. Now the behavioural geneticist knows that the behavioural variability in the population which he has measured is a function of both the variability of genotype and the variability of environment. It is therefore possible for him, using the variance statistic as his model, to write the following theoretical equation:

$$\sigma_B^2 = \sigma_H^2 + \sigma_E^2 + \sigma_{EXH}^2$$

where:

σ_B^2 is the total variance of a given behavioural trait
σ_H^2 is the amount of σ_B^2 which co-varies with genotypic differences
σ_E^2 is the amount of $_B^2$ which co-varies with environmental differences
σ_{EXH}^2 is the amount of σ_B^2 which can be attributed to the interaction of heredity and environment.

It must be reiterated that this is a purely theoretical equation. In practice, the problem of giving numerical values to the components of the equation is considerable. It would be necessary to have adequate measures of both genotypic and environmental differences, and we should need to modify the equation to take account of error in measurement. But the point remains that, so long as we are talking about the variability of a trait in a population, it is in principle quite possible to say that more of it is due to genotypic than to environmental differences.

It has been argued (Loevinger, 1943) that since we know that the effects of genotype and environment are not additive, it is inappropriate to apply a mathematical model which assumes that they are. The short answer is that, since the model is the best available, we have no choice. But it is possible to go further. Insofar as this criticism has force, it is relevant only to the misapplication of the statistical model. The function of statistical analysis is to summarize in a convenient way the relations between sets of scores; to make inferences about the mode of operation of the factors involved is to go beyond the mathematical analysis, and cannot be justified by it. The assertion that differences in a trait are more closely associated with genotypic differences than with environmental does not conflict with a recognition of the fact that the two determinants interact continuously; for the former is a statement about the variance of a trait in a population, the latter a statement about the processes operating in each individual case.

In the next two sections we shall consider some of the work which has been done in this field. No attempt will be made to give an exhaustive account. Instead the emphasis will be upon the problems that arise and the methods adopted to meet them, with particular reference to the questions listed above. Furthermore, we shall be primarily concerned with the direct experimental approach to the genetic determination of individual differences within a species. Other sources of evidence which bear upon the general question of hereditary influence, such as interspecies comparisons, studies of maturation and the correlating of physiological structure and function with behaviour, will be dealt with in other chapters.

Broadly speaking, the experimentalist is faced with three problems: (a) he must select a behavioural trait which can be reliably measured and which is not trivial; (b) he must be able to manipulate systematically the variable of genotypic difference; and (c) he must be able to control environment. Genes, of course, cannot be manipulated directly. In animal studies, control of genotypic difference is inferred from the nature of the breeding programmes adopted; in human beings it is inferred from the nature of familial relationships, or, as in the case of identical twins, from crucial phenotypic similarities. Since the study of animals and of human beings must necessarily involve somewhat different approaches, they will be considered separately.

Animal psychogenetic studies

Psychogenetic research involves selective breeding, that is mating animals which show a specified behaviour trait in a high degree or in a low degree. Their offspring are again bred selectively, and so on, until after several generations a strain evolves which is characterized by a high or a low degree of the particular behaviour trait; but this will happen only if the trait in question is a heritable trait. A great deal of research has been done on the fruit fly, *Drosophila melanogaster*. This organism has been successfully bred for a number of behaviour tendencies, such as activity, mating speed, positive phototaxis (attraction to light) and geotaxis (movement towards and away from gravity) – see McClearn and DeFries, 1973.

Selective breeding has been successful in producing aggressive strains of domestic fowl, alcohol-liking mice, rats good at running mazes, etc. Genetic studies of rats have quite a long history; Tryon began his psychogenetic investigations of rats in mazes at the University of California in the 1920s. He reported success (Tryon, 1940) in breeding both 'bright' maze learners and 'dull' maze learners. This initially suggested that rats, and possibly higher animals, could be bred for 'intelligence'. However, Searle (1949) showed that maze-bright and maze-dull rats could not be described as generally bright and dull respectively; they just showed different patterns of abilities. The two strains differed not only on cognitive tests but also on motivational ones; maze-bright rats showed stronger food motivation and lower spontaneous activity, so that they were less distracted by alternatives in the maze.

On the physiological side, Tryon's maze-bright and maze-dull rats were used in experiments by Krech, Rosenzweig and Bennett (1956) which provide evidence of a relationship between cholinesterase activity in certain parts of the brain and performance in a learning situation. Subsequent experiments have demonstrated the following: that it is possible to breed strains of rat which differ systematically in cholinesterase activity (Roderick, 1960); that an enriched environment leads to an increased level of cholinesterase activity; and that there is an interaction effect between genotypic difference and environment in the determination of cholinesterase activity (Bennett *et al.*, 1964). For a criticism of these experiments, see Hirsch (1964). The interaction between genotypic and environmental differences in the production of learning ability in rats has been examined in several studies. Hughes and Zubek (1956, 1957) supplemented the diet of bright and dull strains of rat in certain ways from weaning for forty days. The result was a significant improvement in learning by the dull rats, an improvement which lasted at least three months after the cessation of the dietary supplement; there was no improvement in the performance of the bright rats. Cooper and Zubek (1958) raised bright and dull rats in enriched and restricted environments, and compared their performance on learning tasks with a control group reared in 'normal' laboratory conditions. The results showed that bright animals were not improved by the enriched environment, and were retarded by the restricted environment; dull animals, on the other hand, were not affected by the restricted environment, but were considerably improved by the enriched environment.

The work of Broadhurst, initially carried out at the Maudsley Hospital in London, focuses on a different aspect of rat behaviour. Broadhurst began by replicating the earlier work of C. S. Hall (1951) under more rigorously controlled conditions (Broadhurst, 1960). The behavioural trait investigated

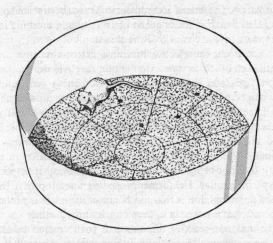

Figure 3.1 The open-field test of emotionality. The animal (here, a rat) is taken from its home cage, placed in the open area shown and subjected to mildly frightening noise and light stimulation. Measures of the animal's response include the number of faecal pellets eliminated and the amount of exploration or move-ment about the area; the floor is marked off in sections to allow a measure of movement. (Adapted from Broadhurst, 1963, Plate 1a)

was that of 'emotionality' in rats, as measured by the 'open-field test' (see Figure 3.1). This test consists essentially of a fear-inducing situation which yields two measures of intensity of response: rate of defecation, and latency and extent of ambulation, or readiness to explore. Because it might be questioned whether these measures are valid indices of what is usually meant by the term 'emotional', Broadhurst substituted the labels 'reactive' for 'emotional' and 'non-reactive' for 'unemotional'. It may be noted that, later, Archer (1973) more thoroughly questioned the value of the concept of emotionality (especially in relation to the open-field test) as a consistent unitary trait.

The experimental manipulation of genotypic difference in animals can be achieved in two related ways: by the *method of selective breeding*, in which the experimenter breeds out of a population of animals two strains that differ consistently on the behavioural trait; and by the *comparative method*, in which strains which have already been selectively bred for some other characteristic such as coat colour are tested for significant differences on the behavioural trait. The second is complementary to the first, and bears witness to the fact that breeding for one trait often results in breeding for others as well. Both methods were used by Broadhurst.

In the experiment on selective breeding, extreme reactive animals were mated with each other, as were extreme non-reactives drawn from the same population. This was then repeated for subsequent generations. Mating schedules can be such as to maximize or to minimize inbreeding. Schedules that maximize inbreeding increase the overall genotypic similarity within each strain and overall difference between strains, and therefore increase the likelihood of breeding for other traits; schedules that minimize inbreeding make it more likely that the two strains will only differ on those genes relevant to the trait being investigated, and that in other respects they will be genotypically similar. The former procedure was adopted in Broadhurst's study, though his opinion is that, on balance, the latter is probably preferable. In practice, it is not easy to keep consistently to either.

Reactive and non-reactive animals had to be reared under as nearly identical environmental conditions as possible to ensure that differences between them could only be attributed to the breeding procedure. In Broadhurst's experiment, feeding, handling and physical environment were rigorously controlled. Important among environmental influences is the influence of the mother. To control for this, the offspring were cross-fostered, which means that half the offspring of reactive mothers were exchanged at birth with half the offspring of non-reactive, thus keeping the influence of the reactivity of the mother the same for both strains. The only way to control for the intra-uterine environment is to transplant some of the foetuses and this is not practicable. However, Broadhurst was able to test for the influence of this factor retrospectively. As soon as two relatively pure strains had been bred, it was possible to mate reactive fathers with non-reactive mothers and non-reactive fathers with reactive mothers. The offspring could then be assumed to be genetically similar and to differ only in their intra-uterine environments. When it was found that the two sets of offspring did not differ significantly on the behavioural trait, it could be concluded that intra-uterine environment was not a significant factor in this experiment.

The results of the main experiment are given in Figure 3.2. It is clear that, within a few generations, Broadhurst had bred two strains of rat which differed significantly and consistently on the behavioural trait. This fact is powerful evidence of the genetic influence upon the trait.

Breeding experiments of this kind do not permit any general assessment of the relative importance of heredity and environment for the obvious

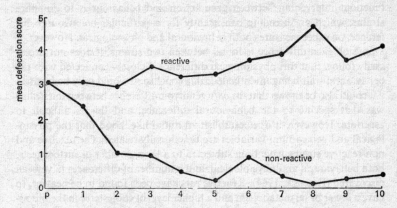

Figure 3.2   Results of selective breeding for high and low defecation scores. The graph shows the mean scores of the reactive and non-reactive groups from the parent generation through successive generations. (From Broadhurst, 1960, p. 51)

reason that environmental variation has been to a very large extent excluded. It is, however, possible to compare two traits for degree of genetic influence, when experimental conditions are comparable, by calculating the heritability quotient or h^2. This value is the ratio between the variance due to breeding procedures and the total variance. If this ratio is high for a given trait, it means that it is relatively easy to breed strains which differ systematically on it and that therefore the genetic influence is strong. In Broadhurst's selective breeding experiment, heritability was found to be high for one measure, defecation rate, and somewhat lower for the other, ambulation scores. It should be noted that in his experiment using the comparative method, the heritability quotients were somewhat different.

An examination of the logic and experimental method involved in analysing genetic mechanisms is beyond the scope of this chapter and the reader is referred to Fuller and Thompson (1960) for a clear account. Essentially, however, it consists of deriving predictions from a genetic hypothesis and testing them by mating schedules involving more than one strain of animal. From his own experiments, Broadhurst was able to conclude that an additive, polygenic system – that is, a large number of genes acting cumulatively – underlies emotionality in rats, and that the trait is not sex linked in any significant way.

A preliminary move in the investigation of the physiological structures and functions intervening between gene action and behaviour is to compare strains, which are breeding consistently for a particular behavioural difference, on other measures both behavioural and physiological. However, if a physiological difference is found between two strains, it does not necessarily follow that this physiological difference is closely connected with the behavioural trait being investigated; this conclusion would only be justified if it could also be shown that the *only* genotypic difference between the strains was that specific to the behavioural difference, and this is difficult to ascertain. However, it does establish an initial likelihood that the physiological and behavioural variables are functionally related. The reactive and non-reactive strains have been subjected to a large number of further tests, both behavioural and physiological, and a number of differences have been discovered (Eysenck, 1964). Reactive rats have been found to be heavier, to have a lower basal metabolism and a higher level of cholesterol in the bloodstream, and so on.

A further problem concerns the interaction between genotype and environment. Experimentally, this means rearing different strains of animal under varied conditions to see if the conditions differentially affect the strains. In Broadhurst's main experiment, such an interaction was ruled out by maintaining a uniform environment for both strains. But in a later study (Levine and Broadhurst, 1963), reactive and non-reactive rats were compared for the effects of handling in infancy. Though for various reasons the outcome was not too clear, the evidence suggested that handling had a greater effect in reducing emotionality in reactive rats than in non-reactive ones.

Extensive experimental psychogenetic studies have been made of the behaviour, and especially social behaviour, of dogs (Scott and Fuller, 1965). Data were gathered on the heritability in various breeds of the animals' abilities to solve problems, of their trainability, their emotional reactivity, etc. Knowledge thus gained is of considerable practical use in breeding dogs best suited to what may be required of them, for instance as watch dogs, as guide dogs for the blind, and so on. Such studies have also proved to be of additional theoretical interest in that they help us to understand behaviour as a factor in phylogenetic evolution (McClearn and DeFries, 1973; Manning, 1976).

Human psychogenetic studies

Investigation into the influence of heredity upon human behaviour faces difficulties not encountered in animal studies. The direct manipulation of genotypic difference through breeding and the direct control of environment are not possible. Genotypic difference cannot be measured directly, nor are there any precise measures of environmental difference; indeed, it would be necessary first to know what aspects of environment are relevant before such measures could be constructed. However, the experimenter is not helpless. On the one hand, the principles of genetics enable him to infer degrees of genotypic similarity between people on the basis of their familial relationships. For example, the genotypic similarity between pairs of siblings is on average greater than the genotypic similarity between first cousins, or unrelated people. On the other hand, though environment cannot be precisely measured, it is possible to infer that some environments are more similar than others. For example, there is some plausibility in saying that siblings reared together experience more similar environments than siblings reared apart. The task before the psychologist, then, is to seek ways of showing that similarities on a behavioural trait are associated with similarities in genotype under conditions in which it is reasonable to claim that they are not also associated with similarities in environment. Since to do this he has to make a number of more or less plausible, but unproven, assumptions, it is hardly surprising that conclusions drawn from human studies are less firm and more vulnerable to criticism than the conclusions drawn from animal studies.

One of the earliest approaches to the problem was to report evidence on the way certain characteristics, such as high ability or mental defect, tend to run in families. Thus, Galton (1869) examined the frequency with which the relatives of eminent men themselves achieved eminence, and he showed that the remoter the relationship, the lower the frequency. As evidence for a genetic effect, such studies are inconclusive, since close relatives are likely to experience a similar environment. If we are to make justifiable inferences from a comparison of close and distant relatives, it must be under conditions in which we can be fairly sure that environmental variability is not affecting the results.

This has been attempted in a variety of ways. Since the most popular method has been to make use of twins, this method will be examined in detail here.

Identical twins, since they derive from the same fertilized ovum, have identical genotypes. Fraternal twins derive from two separate fertilized ova, and therefore are no more alike genotypically than ordinary siblings. Yet both types share the experience of being twins. The argument then goes as follows: similarities on a trait between both identical and fraternal twins are due to both similarities of genotype and environment; but if identical twins are *more* similar to each other than are fraternal twins, this must be because of their greater genotypic similarity, and this difference in degree of similarity on the trait can be taken as evidence of the influence of genotype upon it. The argument can be summarized as follows, when I_a and I_b refer to members of a pair of identical twins, and F_a and F_b members of a pair of fraternal twins:

$I_a - I_b$ is due to environment
$F_a - F_b$ is due to environment and heredity.

Therefore, if $|F_a - F_b| > |I_a - I_b|$, then the difference must be due to the greater genotypic similarity of the identical twins.

A variant of this method is to compare identical twins who have been reared apart with both identical and fraternal twins reared together. Since it is implausible to claim that twins reared apart experience more similar environments than twins reared together, we can argue that, if identical twins reared apart are more similar than fraternal twins reared together, and if they are not much less similar than identical twins reared together, we have strong evidence of the influence of genotype upon behaviour. In practice, of course, it is difficult to find identical twins who have been separated early, and have grown up apart.

In making their comparisons, most investigators have used the correlation coefficient as their index of similarity between twins. A test measuring the relevant behavioural trait is given to both members of every pair of twins in the sample. The scores of one member of each pair are then correlated with the scores obtained by the other member of each pair. A high positive correlation means that the differences between members of pairs of twins tend to be small in relation to the variability between pairs. If the correlation coefficient for identical twins is higher than the coefficient for fraternal twins, it means that the differences within pairs of identical twins tend to be smaller than the differences within pairs of fraternal twins, provided of course that the variability between pairs is the same for both sets.

Using the method of twin comparison, numerous studies have sought to demonstrate a genotypic influence upon intelligence. It is impossible to list them all here. Fortunately, Erlenmeyer-Kimling and Jarvik (1963) have reviewed some fifty-two studies involving subjects from many different countries, and of different generations, ages, ethnic grouping and socio-economic level. They found that the median correlation coefficients were as follows:

for identical twins reared together   0·87
for identical twins reared apart   0·75
for fraternal twins reared together   0·53.

In general, the average difference between fraternal twins reared together was one and a half to two times as great as the average difference between identical twins reared together.

So far, few studies have used twin comparisons to examine the relationship between genotypic difference and personality difference. Two papers (Eysenck, 1956; Eysenck and Prell, 1951) report results for the personality dimensions of neuroticism and extraversion–introversion (for a discussion of these dimensions, see Chapter 19). Identical twins reared together correlated 0·85 on neuroticism and 0·50 on extraversion; the corresponding coefficients for fraternal twins were 0·22 and −0·33. In a later study of the same personality dimensions, Shields (1962) obtained the following results:

	Identical apart	Identical together	Fraternal together
Extraversion–introversion	0·61	0·42	−0·17
Neuroticism	0·53	0·38	0·11

The coefficients are lower than for intelligence but fraternal twins are consistently less similar than identical twins. Gottesman (1963) found that identical twins reared together were more similar than fraternal twins on fifteen out of the seventeen scales of the Minnesota Multiphasic Personality Inventory. The twin method has also been extensively used in the study of psychopathology (see Shields and Slater, 1961).

Results of this kind are often accepted as powerful evidence of the influence of genotype upon intelligence and personality. However, in assessing just how strong this evidence is, there are important qualifications to be made. Consider first the comparison between identical and fraternal twins reared together. The conclusion that the greater behavioural similarity between identical twins is due to their greater genotypic similarity is based upon the assumption that this greater similarity is *not* due to the fact that they experience an environment that makes them more similar. It is doubtful whether this assumption is justified. Earlier investigators found evidence of

environmental pressures towards both greater similarity and greater difference among identical twins. For example, identical twins were more often
mistaken for each other, were in each other's company more, and more often
shared the same friends than was the case with fraternal twins; but on the
other hand they were also more often observed to adopt different roles (one
twin becoming the 'ambassador' for the pair), and the frequency of
differential handedness was greater among them. It has sometimes been
hopefully concluded that these factors cancel each other out. But when we
do not know what aspects of environment are decisive for the trait in
question, and when the evidence is so scanty, this conclusion is hardly
warranted. Moreover, in a study (Husen, 1959) in which a very large sample
of the population was involved, it was found that identical twins were much
more anxious to stress their similarity and much less likely to be competitive.
Furthermore, Husen found no difference in handedness between the types of
twin, and in answer to the question, 'Who usually decides what you are going
to do when you are together?', identical twins were much more likely than
fraternal twins to reply, 'Both of us.' The problem is complex and difficult;
but on balance the safest assumption seems to be that identical twins do
experience more similar environments than fraternal twins and that a
consequence of this could be greater similarity on intelligence and personality
tests. The question we must then ask is whether this greater similarity in
environment is a sufficient explanation of the consistent and markedly
greater behavioural similarity. In the absence of definitive evidence, our
judgement is bound to be influenced by the expectations we form on the basis
of other findings involving different assumptions.

The most striking of these other findings is that identical twins reared
apart are more similar on measures of intelligence and personality than
fraternal twins reared together. In Shields's study (1962) they were even
found to be slightly more similar on personality measures than identical
twins reared together. It does seem very unlikely that identical twins reared
apart share more similar environments than fraternal twins reared together.
But even this assumption is not entirely beyond question. Identical twins
reared apart are not in competition with each other as fraternal twins reared
together often appear to be, and they may not experience environments
which differ much on trait-relevant variables. It is plain that environment can
affect performance on intelligence tests, for identical twins reared apart are
less similar than identical twins reared together; and when identical twins
reared apart are considered alone, there is a high correlation between degree
of difference in educational advantage and degree of difference in intelligence

(Anastasi, 1958). Finally, because identical twins who have been separated early in life are so rare, the use of them in research is especially vulnerable to criticism of a different kind. In order to draw general conclusions from comparing different types of twin, not only must the twins be representative of the population, but the different sorts of twin must be *equally representative*. It should be added that, in recent studies, steps have been taken to meet this criticism. Again we have to judge whether considerations such as these are sufficient and plausible enough to provide an alternative account of the results.

It should now be clear that, in the absence of precise measures of relevant environmental factors, comparisons between twins, and indeed between other groups such as siblings reared together and apart, cannot provide conclusive evidence of genotypic influence. With sufficient ingenuity, it is usually possible to produce some hypothetical explanation in terms of environment. But, at least as far as intelligence is concerned, the cumulative effect of studies involving different comparisons, so that no single environmental explanation can suffice for all of them, makes it at least highly probable that individual differences on the trait are partly a function of genotypic difference.

This cautious and seemingly non-controversial statement would be strongly contested by some psychologists who have thoroughly scrutinized the evidence. At first the strongest support for the genetic component of intelligence, as assessed by mental tests, came from the work of Burt (1955, 1966). There are, however, so many serious doubts about Burt's procedures (Kamin, 1974) that we must look for evidence elsewhere. A close examination of the rest of the evidence from studies of identical twins reared apart shows that that evidence, too, is of rather doubtful validity. However, to conclude that environmental influences alone are responsible for differences in ability is to brush aside findings concerning individual differences which are convincingly explained only in terms of interactions between environmental *and* genetic factors (Mackintosh, 1975; McGuire and Hirsch, 1977).

As far as personality studies are concerned, the assessment of the contribution of inheritance to personality differences is even more difficult. Early eugenicists hoped that criminality, psychopathy and other forms of anti-social behaviour could be investigated from the genetic perspective. This presents insuperable problems, partly because such modes of behaviour are defined legally rather than psychometrically (McClearn and DeFries, 1973). Nevertheless the possibility of a genetic component in personality, both normal and deviant, cannot be ruled out. Large-scale statistical studies of personality serve an essential function, but their interpretation is a matter of debate and controversy. We may hope that they will eventually shed more light on the possible role of genetic factors in personality development.

Maturation, development and growth

In earlier sections we examined some of the evidence which points to the existence of a functional relationship between genotypic difference and behavioural difference, *when behaviour is measured at a particular stage of development*. In the present section we shall be focusing upon the influence of genotype upon behavioural development. More precisely: are differences in genotype related to differences in the way behaviour changes over time in the same individuals?

The behavioural transactions between an organism and its environment are constantly being modified under the control of changing environmental stimulation on the one hand and biological processes of growth and ageing on the other. It is usual to label the changes due to environment as *learning* and the changes due to growth and ageing as *maturation*. It is of the greatest importance to be clear, however, that this conceptual distinction does not imply that there are two independent processes, one of maturing and one of learning, that somehow occur in parallel. The development of behaviour must be regarded as a single, continuous process. The notions of maturation and learning are convenient abstractions from this developmental process and serve to draw attention to the two main classes of influence that bear upon it.

In what follows, we shall inquire into how psychologists use the term *maturation* and into the kind of empirical evidence that justifies this usage; learning will be discussed in later chapters. In defining the concept of maturation, it is useful to contrast it with two other, overlapping terms – namely *development* and *growth*. There is a good deal of confusion and ambiguity in their usage. Some writers use them virtually interchangeably, and those who do differentiate their meanings are by no means in agreement. For the psychologist, the justification for maintaining distinctions between them must lie in the fact that each can be given a distinctive empirical reference. Since the terms can be given such distinctive references, there seems to be good reason for trying to separate them. (For other general discussions, see Ausubel, 1958; Hebb, 1966; Kessen, 1960.)

Development is the most inclusive of the three words in question. This concept refers to the fact that changes in the nature and organization of an organism's structure and behaviour are systematically related to age; 'a characteristic is said to be developmental if it can be related to age in an orderly and lawful way' (Kessen, 1960, p. 36). Such a definition naturally raises the question whether there can be non-developmental changes in behaviour. To say that behavioural change is age-related is to say that in some sense it is cumulative and irreversible. Having once attained puberty, or learned to walk or to read, there is no going back to the condition which existed before these events. And each of these events is the necessary condition of further developments in behaviour. What kind of behavioural change would then be classified as non-developmental? Clearly it would be any learning which is reversible in the sense that it could be 'unlearned', and which could occur equally well over the whole age range. It could be argued that no learning meets these criteria: later learning always builds upon and is affected by early learning; and it could be said that there is never complete 'unlearning' since a learned response which appears to have been forgotten has presumably left some permanent and irreversible trace in the organism. But this is to be too academically precise. Much learning, especially in human beings, can occur equally well over a wide age range and does not appear to be an important condition for later learning. For practical purposes we can designate learned responses of this kind as non-developmental.

We call behavioural change developmental, then, when it follows an invariant sequence over age. To take an obvious example – in the development of motor skills in children, sitting precedes crawling which in turn precedes walking, and so on. Each stage prepares the way for the next and the order of the stage is always the same. Such development is the fruit of the intimate and subtle interaction between spontaneous structural changes on the one hand, and the different experiences and learning made possible by systematic environmental change on the other.

Growth refers, of course, to *incremental increases in amount* of a characteristic. But some psychologists have included in the term other features of the developmental process, such as changes in organization and the emergence of 'new' forms of behaviour. This, however, is to make the term effectively synonymous with development. Growth is best exemplified in such physical characteristics as height, heart size and gland weight. Growth curves have been plotted for a great many physical characteristics and, although there is considerable variation among individuals, the curves do, on average, follow predictable patterns (see Shock, 1951). The concept of growth has also been applied to behavioural traits in the hope that similar stable patterns would be found. However, the application of the term to behaviour is less safe. It is only justifiable to talk of the incremental growth of intelligence when what we mean by this is that, with increased age, individuals solve more difficult versions *of the same kind of problem* that they were solving earlier. But to talk of the growth of intelligence in a more global sense may be misleading, for there is reason to think that the nature of intelligence, in this wider sense, changes with age. To extend the term to age changes in personality traits is even more problematic, for it is highly questionable whether, for example, aggression is the same kind of trait in childhood as it is in adulthood. The essential requirement for evidence of growth is that the same measure be applied at different ages and yield an increase with increased age. It follows that growth in a characteristic ceases when the maximum level is reached.

Maturation is the least easy to define. Gesell (1929) defined it in terms of those phases and products of development which are wholly or chiefly due to innate and endogenous factors. But, of course, no developmental change is wholly due to genetic influence. Both genotype and environment are necessary conditions of all development, but neither is sufficient; and, as was said at the beginning, development is a single process, not two parallel ones. Some writers (e.g. Hebb, 1966) have loosened the term to include, besides innate factors, the influence of those environmental conditions which are the essential prerequisites of the realization of genetic potentiality. Others adopt an operational approach and, like Ausubel (1958), define maturation as 'development that takes place in the demonstrable absence of specific practice experience' (p. 80). But rarely, if ever, can we 'demonstrate' the absence of specific practice. It seems wisest to recognize that precise circumscription of the term is impossible. Its central function is to refer to genetic control of the patterning and sequential ordering of development; maturation is genotype in action. Despite arguments to the contrary, there is still some value in contrasting maturation and learning so long as we remember that this is simply a convenient way of classifying different antecedent conditions of the single process of development.

Some writers would limit the term to progress towards maturity or adulthood. The implication is that maturation ceases when the optimal development level of a trait is reached. This is inconsistent with the term as understood here. There is evidence that genetic influences affect development throughout the life cycle. Kallman and Sander (1949) conclude from their study of twins over the age of sixty years that genotype plays a basic role in determining the ability to maintain physical and mental health into senescence.

Finally, we can usefully distinguish behavioural from physiological maturation. Since behaviour occurs 'between' an organism and its environment, and since the genetic influence upon behaviour is mediated by physiological structure and functioning, behavioural maturation can be defined as behavioural development insofar as it is determined by physiological maturation. The development of physiological structure is, of course, dependent upon an adequate physical environment. Moreover, variations in environment can affect the timing of the process and the ultimate level reached in growth (Tanner, 1962). But the *sequence* in which physiological structures develop seem to be very much under the control of genotype. The order in which the structures develop is highly constant within a species and resistant to wide variations in environment. Studies have shown that the timing of the onset of menstruation is much more similar for identical than for fraternal twins (Tanner, 1962). Patterns of growth in at least some features, such as height, show a 'target-seeking' quality. Tanner (1963) observed that when growth in height is slowed down by illness, there tends to follow a period of accelerated growth until the individual 'catches up' with his growth curve. There is good reason, therefore, for assuming that, given an adequately supportive environment, the differences between individuals in their physiological development are very much a function of their genotypic differences. It follows that one of the ways of investigating behavioural maturation is to study the way in which behaviour change is correlated with physiological development.

A striking feature of physical growth is that in general it follows a negatively accelerated curve. With the exception of the adolescent spurt, growth is fastest in the very beginning and gradually slows up. It is not surprising, therefore, that students of behavioural maturation have tended to concentrate upon the earliest stages of development, for it is then that the effects of physiological maturation are most visible.

So far we have only been concerned with the definition of certain terms. The psychologist is interested in the concept of maturation only insofar as the results of empirical studies require it for their adequate evaluation. Comparatively few studies have been explicitly designed to demonstrate the existence of behavioural maturation, and these stem mostly from the period, now part of history, when investigators tended to adopt somewhat extreme points of view – either that maturation is unimportant, or that development is more or less wholly due to it. In recent years, developmental psychologists have assumed the operation of both maturation and learning and have sought to understand the nature of their interaction rather than to demonstrate the presence of either.

We shall now consider some examples of the different kinds of study which seem to demand the concept of maturation for their adequate description and explanation. Irrefutable evidence of behavioural maturation is hard to obtain. This is because it cannot be separated from the effects of environmental change. Environment does change systematically with age. This is especially true for children. The caretaking procedures of adults are deliberately varied as the child grows older and this could not only provoke changes in the child but also be the effect of those changes in the child which are due to maturation. Nevertheless, there are grounds which support the use of the concept. Six kinds of evidence have been selected for discussion here. They do not all offer equally strong justification for assuming the presence of behavioural maturation, and one or two provide only tenuous support. A brief description of them will be given first and then each will be discussed more fully with illustrations.

The first source of evidence is studies which correlate changes in physiological structure with the appearance of new forms of behaviour. The importance of maturation is manifest if the emergence of certain forms of behaviour is contingent upon specifiable structural developments. Second, the fact that the sequential ordering of behavioural development is constant within a species points to the influence of maturation provided we have no reason to think that the phases of this development are environmentally initiated. Third, there are studies in which subjects with known genetic similarities and differences are tested at regular intervals over a period of development. If similarities and differences in the timing and patterning of behavioural change parallel genetic similarities and differences, we have the most direct evidence of 'genotype in action'. Fourth, attempts have been made to exclude the possibility of learning and to show that behavioural development nevertheless occurs. Fifth, there are the studies which show that the same learning procedures have different effects at different ages. Last, there is the evidence that individual differences in a behavioural trait remain relatively constant through development.

1. All organisms have a life cycle, the pattern and timing of which is genetically controlled through the mediation of physiological maturation. There are two ways in which this process influences behaviour. Certain levels of physiological development are a necessary condition of the appearance of certain classes of behaviour; when these behaviours appear for the first time, they may already be structured and patterned in a species-specific manner. This is most evident in the early stages. The first appearance of reflex

responses is contingent upon neural maturation, as is the pattern of these reflexes (see Carmichael, 1954, and Coghill, 1929, for a detailed account). The maturation of the sexual function is a necessary condition of sexual reproduction. In lower species, whose behaviour is relatively stereotyped, maturation also determines the *form* this sexual behaviour will take when it emerges; the higher the species, the less the form of the behaviour is maturationally determined. In monkeys, for example, gross social deprivation in early life can radically affect the form of behaviour to the extent of making reproduction highly unlikely; though even in these animals, it may be assumed that, with the 'normal' limits of environmental variation, physiological maturation plays an important role in determining the structure of sexual behaviour when it occurs. Among human beings, however, though puberty is a necessary condition of sexual reproduction, the patterning of sexual behaviour is, within the limits set by anatomical structure, much more determined by social factors than by maturation. Even the common assumption that at puberty a maturationally determined increase in heterosexual interest occurs has not been demonstrated. It is true that a change of interest does occur. In an early study, Stone and Barker (1939) compared pre-menarcheal and post-menarcheal girls of the same age, educational and social status, and found that post-menarcheal girls had significantly stronger heterosexual interests. But, as the authors point out, this could be a function of the social expectation that they should have greater heterosexual interests with the onset of menstruation. There is evidence that interests, values and social behaviour vary systematically throughout the life cycle (see Pressey and Kuhlen, 1957); but though common sense suggests that maturation plays a part in this, it cannot be offered as clear evidence of maturation until cross-cultural studies have shown this to be stable across societies which differ in the relevant social expectations.

2. The influence of maturation is also discernible in the way in which the sequential ordering of behavioural development remains constant, at least within the normal range of environmental difference. In human beings, the best evidence of this has come from the work of Gesell and his associates, who studied the motor development of children over the first years of post-natal life. Babies were examined at frequent intervals and under standard conditions, and their behaviour very precisely recorded. The sequential patterning of motor development was found to be remarkably constant; indeed, it was sufficiently constant for Gesell to formulate a number of 'principles of developmental morphology' to describe the sequence (Gesell,

1954). An example is the principle of cephalocaudal progression, previously observed by Coghill and others, which refers to the tendency for the more developed forms of motor behaviour to occur first in the region of the head and only later in lower regions of the body. It is true that Gesell did not examine the effects of gross environmental abnormality upon this sequence; but his observations were so refined and detailed that it is hard to believe that environment played an important part in determining the sequence. Moreover, there is evidence that gross restriction of movement in the early stages may not affect the outcome, though it may interfere with the patterning and timing of the intermediate stages. Dennis and Dennis (1940) compared babies who, in accordance with cultural practice, had been strapped tightly to a cradle board for the first three to six months of life with babies allowed freedom, and found no difference in the age of onset of walking.

Another example is speech development. Research into the development of language strongly suggests that maturation plays a crucial part. Lenneberg (1967) has summarized this research and his argument is briefly as follows: though exposure to language is an essential condition of speech attainment, children are not normally taught to speak by formal instruction; yet by the age of about three years they have usually acquired a considerable skill in it and the sequence of steps in the achievement of this skill remains invariant even though children may differ widely in the amount of speech stimulation they receive; moreover, if for some reason speech development is delayed, children still go through the same stages in its acquisition. The content and structure of the speech to which the child is exposed will, of course, influence the content and structure of his own speech; but provided he is exposed to speech of some kind, the timing of his speech development follows its own course. In short, what occurs over the first three years is not so much a change in the environment as a change in the child's capacity to learn from the environment.

3. The most direct experimental approach to the study of behavioural maturation involves the control of genotypic difference. Scott and Fuller (1965) reared five breeds of dog under controlled conditions and found that the timing of certain critical phases of early development was related to genotypic difference. With human beings, the obvious method is the use of twins. Gesell and Thompson (1941) have reported the results of an intensive developmental study of one pair of identical twins from early infancy through to puberty. The twins were frequently given tests of motor, mental, linguistic and social behaviour, during which the authors made extensive use of film.

Though it is impossible to draw general conclusions from one pair of twins, particularly without fraternal twin controls, the developmental profiles were strikingly similar. This was especially true of motor development, where the similarities were so close that the differences that did occur were small enough in the authors' judgement to pass for similarities in a comparison of unrelated children, or even siblings. A more recent, better-controlled study has been done by Freedman and Keller (1963). Making use of observations and film, they found that, over the first ten months of post-natal life, identical twins were significantly more similar in the timing and patterning of behavioural development than fraternal twins. The method adopted by these investigators deserves to be used a great deal more.

4. Some experiments have sought to exclude all significant environmental influence for a period of time to see whether changes in an organism's behavioural repertoire have occurred without the effects of environment. The classical experiments of this kind were done by Carmichael (1926). He anaesthetized *Amblystoma* (a kind of newt) shortly before the swimming responses would normally appear. Control *Amblystoma* were allowed to develop in the usual way. When the control *Amblystoma* had been swimming freely for five days, the experimental group was released from the anaesthetic. Within thirty minutes, they were swimming as well as the controls. Later experiments (Carmichael, 1927) suggested that the thirty minutes could largely be accounted for by the time taken for the effects of the anaesthetic to wear off. These experiments have sometimes been taken as evidence that structural maturation can occur without practice of the relevant function. However, Fromme (1941), in a similar series of experiments, showed that practice is necessary for the optimal functioning of a structure. That this is so does not alter the fact that the experiments demonstrate the importance of maturation.

5. A further type of study which at least points to the effect of maturation is that in which the same learning procedure can be shown to have different outcomes at different stages of development. The demonstration that such a difference exists noes not necessarily entail an explanation in terms of maturation; but the relevant studies do carry the implication, in various degrees, that maturation may be involved. One method is that of 'co-twin control'. In the well-known study by Gesell and Thompson (1929), one of a pair of identical twins was given practice in climbing stairs while the other was kept away from stairs. Shortly after the trained twin had reached a high

level of proficiency, the other was allowed to climb the stairs. She was found to reach an equal level of skill in a much shorter period of time. The improved learning capacity in the delayed twin cannot be attributed wholly to maturation, since, though unable to climb stairs, she had plenty of opportunity, as had the trained twin, to practise the component elements of the stair-climbing pattern at other times. However, the fact that she was able to recombine these elements into a new pattern more quickly suggests that maturation was at work. In a similar study, using two pairs of twins, McGraw (1940) showed that twins who were given training in bladder control from an early age were no better than their co-twins whose training was delayed until well after the age of twelve months.

There is a very great deal of evidence to show that certain experiences and forms of learning have their optimal effect when the developing organism has reached a stage of readiness for them. We know, for instance, that the formation of the first social attachments in children, and learning to walk, to speak and to read are all contingent upon the attainment of certain levels of development. There is also evidence that in some instances, if the learning is delayed much beyond this optimal period, it may be less easily acquired, or not acquired at all. Investigators commonly assume that this readiness to learn, or special susceptibility to experience, is at least partly a function of maturation. However plausible this assumption is at a common-sense level, its demonstration is extremely difficult. To illustrate, we can consider the development of learning in monkeys. Zimmermann and Torrey (1965) have reviewed the experimental evidence which shows that for some tasks adolescent and adult monkeys learn more rapidly and effectively than young animals under conditions in which experience of the task is held constant. This superiority of the older animals could be due to the fact that efficient performance of the task is dependent upon specific forms of prior learning which the young animal has not had the opportunity to acquire; or it could be due to the facilitating effect of greater physiological maturation; or both factors could be equally important. To be sure that maturation is an important factor, it would be necessary to demonstrate either that specific antecedent learning is not necessary, or, if it is, that it has already adequately occurred in the young animals, or that in the intervening period of development, certain relevant physiological changes have taken place which are not themselves dependent upon particular forms of learning.

6. There is one final type of study which is relevant to the concept of

maturation and that is the study which seeks to show that behavioural differences at a later period of development are predictable from differences at an earlier stage. In this type of study, a group of subjects is tested at regular intervals from early childhood through to adulthood. Performance at the earlier stages is correlated with performance later. (An excellent review of these studies will be found in Bloom, 1964.) A number of such longitudinal studies of intelligence have been made, all of which are in agreement that differences in intelligence, as measured by tests, have a quite high degree of stability over a long period of childhood and adolescence.

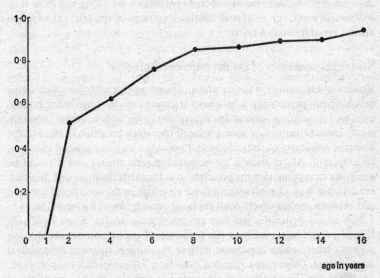

Figure 3.3   Correlations between I.Q.s measured at different ages with I.Q.s at age eighteen years. (Data from Bayley, 1949)

The results for one study are plotted graphically in Figure 3.3. A detailed discussion of these results and the findings of other studies will be found in Bloom (1964). The fact that correlations for the first year are zero or very low is due to the difficulty of creating measures which can be realistically applied to both early infancy and later childhood. This in turn stems from the fact that the nature and organization of intellectual functioning are probably not the same at the two stages.

Though studies of this kind offer firm evidence that differences in intelligence between children remain fairly stable over a long period of development, they provide no clue why such stability should occur. There are two possible explanations. On the one hand it might be a maturational effect in that genotypic differences between children presumably remain absolutely stable throughout life. On the other hand it might be due to the fact that differences in environmental stimulation remain constant throughout development. In order to demonstrate that the stability in intelligence is a function of maturation it would be necessary to show that such stability still obtains under conditions in which it is known that differences in the relevant environmental factors are not stable. At present we are a long way from such a demonstration, for valid and reliable measures of the relevant environmental variables do not exist.

Some characteristics of the developmental process

Besides investigating the innate and environmental conditions which shape development, psychologists have also attempted to characterize the process itself by formulating various descriptive principles of behavioural development. These principles are useful because they draw attention to some of the observable features of the process and point the way to a general theory of development. As yet there is no accepted general theory and it would be a mistake to suppose that the principles put forward constitute one. But they are a useful way of representing those developmental consistencies within and between species which await explanation in terms of a general theory.

Not all the principles put forward are equally useful. Some have very limited applicability, such as the principle of cephalocaudal progression quoted earlier, which is relevant only to the earliest stages of behavioural development. Others are so general as to have little empirical content at all. Examples are the principle of increasing complexity and the principle of diminishing plasticity (i.e. the tendency for individuals to become less flexible and adaptable with age). Others more or less succeed in being empirically informative while having some general application. Three of these will now be briefly discussed.

Differentiation

The concept of differentiation finds its least ambiguous illustration in embryology. Immediately after conception, the fertilized ovum starts to divide and multiply. At first, the cells are structurally and functionally indistinguishable. As the total aggregate of cells begins to take a significant shape, so individual cells begin to differ from each other. Cells progressively differentiate in the sense of becoming increasingly specialized in structure and function. This differentiation is one condition of the aggregate of cells becoming a single organism, within which cells may differ as widely as, for example, blood cells and nerve cells.

At the level of cellular development, differentiation can be defined with some precision. In extending the term to behavioural development, some of this precision is lost, but there is much evidence that the extension is justified. Coghill (1929) was one of the first to document this principle in the field of behaviour. He observed that in the behavioural development of *Amblystoma*, the first responses tended to be total and diffuse, involving the whole organism, and that only later was the organism capable of more precise, local responses. As Coghill puts it: 'The limb arises in complete subjugation to the trunk. It can do nothing except as the trunk acts. From this subjugation, it struggles as it were for freedom.' And again: 'Behaviour develops from the beginning through the progressive expansion of a perfectly integrated total pattern and the individuation within it of particular patterns which acquire various degrees of discreteness.' Gesell (1954) reports evidence of a similar differentiation of local responses from original total responses in the behaviour of babies during the first year of life. When a young baby reaches for an object, he is likely to do so with arms, legs and even head; later he will reach for it with one arm only. Bridges (1932), also in a study of babies, has reported evidence that the emotional responses of joy, fear and anger are progressively differentiated out of an initial response of general excitement.

The concept of differentiation has also been applied to more long-term aspects of development. Werner (1948) has attempted to conceive all mental development in this way. Witkin and his associates (1962) have traced the way children's experience of themselves and their environment becomes progressively articulated with age. The child's conception of the human body appears initially to take the form of a general, schematic impression which subsequently becomes differentiated as the component elements are increasingly articulated. There is also evidence that the development of intelligence can be conceived in terms of the differentiation of special abilities out of a more unitary general ability. The relevant studies have mostly used factor analysis, and have been designed to show that more factors are needed to account for individual differences in adolescence than in childhood. However, the studies are not all in agreement and the issue is still unresolved.

Integration

As cells differentiate in structure and function, so the survival of each cell, and of the whole structure, depends upon the co-operative integration of these different functions. The activity of different organs must be co-ordinated in the service of the organism as a whole and the need for such co-ordination is directly related to the degree of autonomy achieved by the particular organs. That is, the complexity of integration is a function of the complexity of differentiation. In higher organisms, one type of cell, the nerve cell, has been differentiated largely to serve this co-ordinating, integrating function.

Psychologists have applied the concept of integration to behavioural development in order to bring out the observable fact that local reflex units become combined, through learning, into more complex patterns and sequences. In the past, some psychologists adopted a somewhat doctrinaire attitude and claimed that this was indeed *the* way in which behaviour developed. They were in turn opposed by advocates of the principle of differentiation. Though the controversy generated much research, its unreality soon became apparent. Both principles are needed, for each presupposes the other. Moreover, there is an inherent imprecision in both, for it would be difficult to establish that a particular response was really a total response, or that it was entirely local (Kuo, 1939).

It is not difficult to find evidence to support the use of the concept of integration. All learning can be conceived in these terms. Developmentally, it can be evident in the way component skills are organized into more complex patterns, as in learning to walk or play a game; it can be seen in the combination of speech sounds into words and sentences, and in the way abstract concepts are formed through the process of classification. At a more general level, personality theorists make much use of the term to describe the way attitudes, values, motives and opinions tend, with more or less success, to be consistent and coherent (Allport, 1961). The whole process of psychological development in children and adolescents could be said to be in the direction of greater autonomy and self-regulation, and greater independence of social support and influence.

Successive stages

A number of psychologists have described development as proceeding in stages; others have criticized the use of the concept as arbitrary and misleading. This dispute is in some respects a new form of an older controversy, namely, whether behavioural development is continuous or saltatory (i.e. occurring in sudden jumps). This earlier controversy has largely died down through the recognition that development can validly be described as both continuous and discrete, depending upon the perspective of the observer. For example, at the appropriate stages of readiness, the young child will learn to walk with apparent suddenness. From only being able to crawl, he will, in a matter of weeks, be walking quite well. However, when the process is examined in detail, a long period of preparation will be evident. The development of walking can be described as both gradual and sudden. We could put the point another way by saying that growth in a particular characteristic is always continuous and gradual, but that changes in the patterning and organization of growing elements may be relatively sudden.

A necessary condition of the use of the concept of stage is that the limits of a stage can be more or less precisely delineated in a non-arbitrary way. It follows that the term cannot be applied to the process of quantitative, incremental growth, for its use would be arbitrary. But it can be usefully applied to the more qualitative aspects of development, such as changes in behavioural organization, the emergence of new forms of behaviour and the disappearance of old.

A further condition which must obtain if the concept of stage is to be *developmentally* relevant is that the sequential ordering of those qualitative changes which empirically index particular stages must be constant. The age at which individuals enter a given stage may vary; what matters is that all individuals normally go through the same stages in the same order.

The developmental theorists who have made most extensive use of the concept are probably Freud, Gesell and Piaget. Freud (1905, trans. 1949) conceived of the development of the 'sexual instincts' in children in terms of an invariant sequence of stages. Each stage is defined by that area of the body which, at the time, is the salient focus of erotic sensation. The first centre of pleasure is the mouth. By the end of the second year, though the mouth is still an important source of pleasure, the anus is now a more salient centre of erotic concern. Then, by the age of about four or five years, the focus has shifted to the genitals. The primacy of the genitals is at this time precarious and temporary, for, according to the theory, from about this time until puberty, the child is presumed to enter a stage of latency, during which sexual interests recede in importance as a consequence of socially induced repression. Finally, at puberty or shortly afterwards, with increased sexual drive, the primacy of the genitals is firmly established and lasts until old age. These stages of sexual development are presumed to underlie the pattern and quality of the growing child's social relationships. Future adult character is held to be partly explicable in terms of the relative importance which the stages have for the child, and failure to develop properly through these stages is thought to be the basis of later sexual perversions and neurotic disorders.

Though Freud's developmental theory has proved fertile in such fields as the study of family relations and psychopathology and has led to much research which might not otherwise have been done, considered from the point of view of the concept of stage, it has a major weakness. Freud's use of the term meets the second of the criteria mentioned above, in that the stages are presumed to be invariant and universal; but it fails to meet adequately the first. It is extremely difficult to deduce from the theory what sorts of behaviour would be unequivocal evidence that the child had moved from one stage to another. The theory is too loosely related to observable behaviour for an adequate testing of it to be easy or even possible. This probably follows from the fact that its original formulation was not based on systematic observation of children but upon the memories of adults. For the examination of empirical work associated with Freudian theories see Kline (1972).

Gesell's approach was of a quite different kind. With a minimum of theoretical presuppositions, he closely observed the behaviour of children and, so to speak, allowed this behaviour to reveal its own stages. For the resulting account of development see, for example, Gesell and Ilg (1949). Gesell's use of the concept does meet the two criteria we have described. But because his stages are so numerous and remain essentially a convenient way of organizing observations, they are not integrated into a general theory in the way that Freud's psychosexual stages are. On the other hand, Gesell's work, because of its great precision, has facilitated the construction of measures of 'intelligence', or mental maturity, in infancy.

The psychologist who has made the most elaborate and systematic use of the concept of stage is undoubtedly Piaget. Piaget investigated in great detail the qualitative aspects of the development of thinking. He has been concerned with defining and classifying the structures which thought takes at different periods of development. The earliest form of thinking is during the so-called *sensory-motor stage* when, side by side with a gradual integration of reflexes, the child acquires the notion of a stable object. This ends at approximately two years of age, when the long-lasting stage of *'concrete operations'* begins. The child now starts to talk and at the same time gradually acquires the capacity for symbolic thought. Make-believe play makes its appearance. The child's view of the world is during this intermediate stage highly egocentric. Around the age of seven the child can grasp the principle of conservation, that is, it can understand that a given property of a thing does not change despite appearances, for example, the amount of water is the same whether a given quantity is in a wide, shallow dish or a narrow, deep one. This stage finally comes to an end at about eleven years of age. The final stage, one of *'formal operations'*, then sets in. It is during that final stage that real abstract thinking becomes possible; and the cognitive development is completed at about fifteen years of age. According to Piaget and his followers the stages are hierarchical in that each incorporates the mental organization of the preceding one (Piaget, 1952a, b; Flavell, 1963). They are invariant in sequence; indeed one of the criteria Piaget used for defining a stage is its constant position in a sequence of stages. Furthermore, Piaget integrates the structures characteristic of each stage into a general overall theory which appears to be modelled on logic and epistemology.

There are other descriptive principles to be found in the literature. But enough has been said to show that, as the characteristics of the developmental process become defined with some precision, so it is possible to compare individuals in terms of the developmental level they have reached – their developmental age. Individuals of the same chronological age may differ widely in developmental age. It may be said that the total pattern of development is unique to the individual. As research continues, it becomes increasingly possible to specify an individual's developmental age, in relation to others, and this is much more informative than his chronological age. The implications for a society where such things as education and law are based upon the notion of chronological age are considerable.

Chapter 4
The Nervous System and Behaviour

Introduction

The terms 'psycho-biology', 'physiological psychology' or 'neuro-psychology' have been applied to the scientific study of the relation between biological processes and behaviour; psychologists have become concerned with the biological processes which occur within an organism, and especially within the brain, because they believe that the study of such processes considerably extends their understanding of behaviour. Since the range, quality and flexibility of an organism's behaviour seem to be largely determined by the way in which the organism is built, increasing our knowledge of structure leads to a more complete understanding of function. In this chapter, therefore, we attempt to provide an outline of the methods employed in the study of the functional significance of the nervous system, a description of its structure and an account of some of the methodological difficulties and theoretical issues which may be encountered in specifying the interrelationships between the nervous system and behaviour.

Although the nervous system is a functional unity it is convenient to subdivide it (see Table 4.1). The major division is between the *central* nervous system (CNS) and the *peripheral* nervous system (PNS), the former consisting of the brain and spinal cord and the latter of thirty-one pairs of spinal nerves and twelve pairs of cranial nerves. These nerves connect the brain and spinal cord with the sensory receptors, muscles, glands and internal organs of the body. As Table 4.1 shows, the CNS can be divided into the brain and spinal cord, and the PNS into the *somatic* and the *visceral* or *autonomic* nervous systems. The somatic nervous system links the CNS to the external world, relaying information from the sense organs to the brain and spinal cord via a system of *afferent* nerve fibres and conveying information from the CNS to the skeletal or striate (striped) muscles via a system of *efferent* nerve fibres. The autonomic nervous system (ANS) links the CNS to the internal environment, relaying information to and from

Table 4.1

Principal divisions of the nervous system

Nervous system	Central nervous system	Brain
		Spinal cord
	Peripheral nervous system	Somatic nervous system
		Autonomic nervous system

the viscera, a group of internal organs including the heart, the stomach, the lungs, the intestines, various glands and the blood vessels, again via systems of afferent and efferent nerve fibres. As we shall see later, the ANS can be subdivided into the sympathetic and parasympathetic divisions, which have somewhat different functions.

Several methods and techniques are employed in the study of the relationship between the nervous system and the behaviour of animals and human beings and these will be discussed at various points in the sections that follow. Sometimes the ongoing activity of the central and peripheral nervous systems is monitored, as for example when recordings are taken of the electrical activity of the brain as a whole, or groups of nerve cells within it, or of the activity of the heart or the skin, and attempts are made to relate the activity thus recorded to behavioural changes. Sometimes the operation of the nervous system is experimentally interfered with, as when a part of the brain is *ablated* or removed, or when a region of the brain is stimulated electrically or chemically. Experimental ablation is not, of course, carried out with human beings, but occasionally situations arise, either as a result of accidental brain injury or as a result of brain operations to relieve functional disorders, which permit essentially the same type of observation to be made. The behavioural consequences of damage to relatively circumscribed areas of the brain can thus be systematically assessed in human beings as well as in animals. Electrical stimulation techniques have also been used, although infrequently, with volunteer patients.

All organisms are made up of cells and different types of cells have become specialized to perform different functions. Thus sense organs, such as the eyes and ears, contain *receptor cells*, cells which are sensitive to environmental stimulation in the form of energy change; *effector cells* in the muscles are specialized for contraction, while effector cells in the glands are specialized for secretion. As a consequence of having become specialized to perform different functions, cells also differ in structure. For example, receptor cells in the retina of the eye, which are responsive to changes in photic stimulation (that is, changes in the intensity or the wavelength of light; see Chapter 8) differ both structurally and functionally from the receptor cells for audition in the cochlea of the ear.

The basic type of cell within the nervous system is the *nerve cell* or *neuron*, which is specialized both to receive information from, and to transmit information to, other cells as well as, occasionally, to receive information directly from the external environment (as in the olfactory system, where neurons act to all intents and purposes as receptor cells). It has been estimated that there are between fifteen and twenty thousand million neurons in the entire nervous system and between ten and twelve thousand million in the brain. Since most neurons connect with several hundred other neurons the neuronal network provides a communication system which enables information from the receptors to reach the brain, where it can be processed and stored, and makes it possible for decisions to be conveyed from the brain to the effectors. The transmission of information among neurons thus furnishes the basis for all forms of behaviour, and before proceeding to a description of the structure of the nervous system, the process of nervous transmission is briefly outlined.

Nervous transmission

Although they vary in size, neurons are very small, the cell body (see below) being on average no more than about 0·1 mm in diameter. Information concerning the structure of neurons can thus only be gained by examining neural tissue microscopically. Various fixation techniques are used to preserve neural tissue, in order to prevent its decomposition; then the tissue is hardened, for instance by freezing, so that it can be easily sectioned. Sectioning produces thin strips of neural tissue which can be examined by the light, or the much more powerful electron, microscope. Staining techniques selectively highlight various components of neural tissue. Much of the information concerning neuronal structure, for example, has been gained from the use of the *Golgi technique*, in which neural tissue is impregnated with silver, and a highly selective stain is produced, affecting only about 2 per cent of the available neurons. This technique enables the structure of individual neurons to be observed microscopically.

The structure of neurons

There are several varieties of neuron in the nervous system but they all possess a similar basic structure, consisting of a *cell body* or *soma*, which is enclosed by a semi-permeable *cell membrane* and contains a semi-liquid substance known as *intra-cellular fluid* or *cytoplasm*, a branching system of dendrites, and a single *axon* or *nerve fibre* which may have off-shoots known as *collaterals* (see Figure 4.1). The cell body and the dendrites receive information from other neurons, while the axon transmits information in the form of *nerve impulses*. Although there are a number of ways in which cells can communicate with one another (see Bullock, 1977; Schmitt, 1979), the most common are *axo-dendritic* and *axo-somatic* transmission, whereby nerve impulses are transmitted by an axon to the dendrites or to the cell body of other neurons, the point of transfer being known as a *synapse*. Several structures are found in the cell body, among them the *cell nucleus*, which contains the *chromosomes* (long strands of deoxyribonucleic acid or DNA that carry genetic information), the *nucleolus*, which is involved in the formulation of proteins, and the enzyme-producing *mitochondria*, which provide the energy required for nervous transmission to take place. Axons may have two types of covering, a thin membrane on the outside known as *neurilemma*, which is found almost exclusively around axons in the PNS and is involved in the regeneration of damaged fibres, and a white fatty substance called the *myelin sheath*, which surrounds about 50 per cent of all axons, these being generally larger diameter nerve fibres. In myelinated fibres the myelin sheath is interrupted at regular intervals of about 1 mm and the cell membrane laid bare. These points are known as *nodes of Ranvier*, after their discoverer, and the nerve impulse does not proceed continuously along the myelinated nerve fibre but effectively jumps from node to node (a process known as *saltatory conduction*), thus travelling at a faster rate than con-

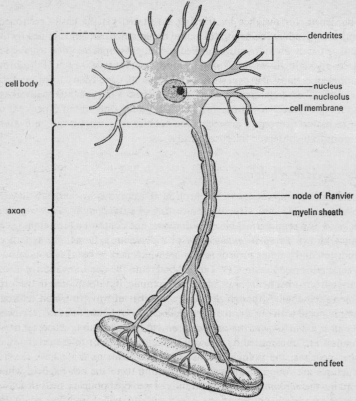

cell body

dendrites

nucleus
nucleolus
cell membrane

axon

node of Ranvier
myelin sheath

end feet

Figure 4.1   Diagram of a nerve cell or neuron with its fibre processes (dendrites and axon)

tinuous progression would permit. In unmyelinated fibres, the nerve impulse spreads more slowly down the axon. The larger the diameter of a nerve fibre the faster the nerve impulse travels, the fastest speeds being around 120 m per second and the slowest around 0·5 m per second. At the end of the axon are small enlargements known as *end feet* or *terminal boutons*, which make connections with other cells.

The nerve impulse and the frequency code

The nerve impulse consists of an electrochemical disturbance transmitted along the axon's cell membrane, lasting for about a millisecond at any one point. When the neuron is *polarized*, or at rest, there is a potential difference of about 70 millivolts (mv) across the cell membrane; that is, the inside of the cell membrane is negative by about 70 mv, with reference to the outside. If a sufficient number of axons transmit nerve impulses to the dendrites at the same time, the permeability of the cell membrane alters and an exchange of electrically charged particles, known as ions, takes place across the cell membrane. The resting potential difference is reversed, the inside of the membrane becoming momentarily positive with respect to the outside by about 40 mv, and the membrane is said to be *depolarized*. The brief potential shift, from negative to positive, known as the *action potential*, spreads rapidly from the dendrites and cell body to the axon, eventually reaching the terminal boutons.

Once an action potential is triggered in an axon, it is propagated without loss or decrement until it reaches the terminal boutons; moreover the potential is *ungraded*, so that its size and duration are in no way dependent upon the intensity of stimulation received by the dendritic systems. The axon thus operates on the *all-or-none principle*: either it fires, producing a potential of fixed size and duration, or it does not fire at all. The output of an axon therefore varies not in terms of size or amplitude, but in terms of frequency, the number of nerve impulses transmitted per unit of time, and neurons convey information by way of a *frequency code*. For a brief interval following the transmission of a nerve impulse, known as the refractory period, the axon is unable to fire again, and there is thus an upper limit to the rate at which nerve impulses can be transmitted. But larger diameter axons have shorter refractory periods and hence can transmit information more quickly, and more intense stimuli can fire the axon at an earlier point in the refractory period and can, therefore, produce a greater number of impulses in a given time.

Neurotransmitters and the synapse

The synapse has already been referred to as the point of transmission between the end feet or terminal boutons of an axon of one cell and the cell body or dendrites of the cell with which it connects (see Figure 4.2). As Figure 4.2 shows, there is a small gap, about 0·02 microns across (a micron being $\frac{1}{1000}$ of a millimetre), called the *synaptic cleft*, which separates the axon of the transmitting cell from the dendrites or cell body of the receiving or post-synaptic cell. Chemical transmitter substances, known as *neurotransmitters*, stored in the synaptic vesicles, convey the nerve impulse from the transmitting to the receiving cell, the energy required for the transmission process being supplied, as noted above, by the mitochondria.

Several different kinds of neurotransmitter have been found in the nervous system (see Table 4.2), some of which are *excitatory* (raising the probability of firing of the post-synaptic cell) while others are *inhibitory* (lowering the probability of firing of the post-synaptic cell) in their effects. Although it is uncertain why so many different transmitter substances should exist, it is possible that a multiplicity of neurotransmitters enables the information crossing a synapse to be varied, since different transmitter substances not

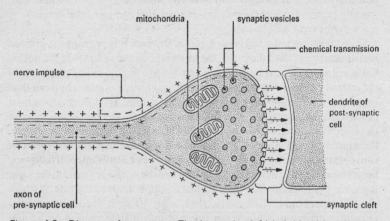

Figure 4.2   Diagram of a synapse. The 'synaptic cleft' is bridged by chemical transmitter molecules released by the synaptic vesicles. The mitochondria provide the energy for the whole process of transmission. (After A. Besterman in *The Science of Man*, vol. 2, B.B.C., 1963, p. 16)

only produce excitatory or inhibitory effects but can also influence the threshold of the post-synaptic cell to varying degrees and for different lengths of time. Furthermore, as Table 4.2 indicates, different neurotransmitters operate in different regions of the CNS and PNS with the result that different 'chemical pathways' within the CNS and PNS are beginning to be defined.

Each of the very large number of axons converging on a post-synaptic cell membrane can thus produce either excitatory or inhibitory effects and these effects can *summate*, either spatially or temporally. Each post-synaptic cell has a threshold of excitation, which must be reached if the axon is to

Table 4.2
The principal neurotransmitter substances, their locations in the nervous system and their probable effects. Adapted from Table 5.1, p. 64 in N. R. Carlson (1977), *Physiology of Behaviour*, Allyn and Bacon, and from Table 2–3, p. 81, in S. D. Iversen and L. L. Iversen (1975), *Behavioural Pharmacology*, Oxford University Press

Transmitter substance	Synonym	Abbreviation	Location	Probable effect
Acetylcholine		ACh	Brain, spinal cord, ANS ganglia	Excitation
			Organs innervated by parasympathetic division of ANS	Inhibition
Dopamine		DA	Brain	Inhibition
Gamma aminobutyric acid		GABA	Brain (especially cerebral and cerebellar cortex)	Inhibition
Glutamic acid		Glu	Brain, spinal cord	Excitation
Glycine		Gly	Spinal cord	Inhibition
Norepinephrine	Noradrenalin	NE	Brain	Inhibition
			Organs innervated by sympathetic division of ANS	Inhibition Excitation
Serotonin	5-Hydroxytryptamine	5-HT	Brain	Inhibition

fire; this threshold corresponds to the potential difference across the cell membrane, which, as noted above, is in the region of −70 mv when the neuron is at rest. The depolarization transmitted by a single pre-synaptic axon will almost certainly be below the threshold of the post-synaptic cell.

Spatial summation can occur when the sub-threshold depolarizations from several axons arrive at the same area of the post-synaptic cell membrane, while temporal summation can occur when sub-threshold depolarizations arrive at the post-synaptic cell membrane in rapid succession; in both cases the depolarizations can be integrated, or added together, thus increasing the probability that the excitation threshold will be attained. The post-synaptic cell can therefore be subjected to both excitatory and inhibitory influences at different places on the membrane surface and at different times, the balance of these effects determining whether its rate of firing is increased, held in check or reduced. But a single pre-synaptic axon produces either an excitatory or an inhibitory effect on the post-synaptic cell membrane, depending upon the type of neurotransmitter stored in the synaptic vesicles.

As noted above, the electrochemical pulses transmitted along nerve fibres provide the principal means whereby information is communicated within the nervous system. Nerve fibres frequently travel together in groups of several million from one part of the nervous system to another, and these collections of nerve fibres are generally known as *pathways*, *tracts*, or *bundles* within the CNS and as *nerves* outside it. Cell bodies also collect together in distinguishable groups having a similar appearance and similar connections. Such groups of cells in the CNS are known as *nuclei*, and in the PNS as *ganglia*. It should be mentioned, however, that there are other types of cell in the nervous system besides receptor, effector and nerve cells, most notably *glial cells*, or neuroglia, which provide mechanical support for neurons and tend to be wrapped around them. Glial cells outnumber the neurons they support by a ratio of about 10 : 1 and perform various protective and 'housekeeping' functions on their behalf. They assist in neuronal metabolism, remove waste products, regulate the chemical composition of the extracellular fluid, in which neurons are immersed, act as insulators, thereby preserving the integrity of neural messages and rid the nerve systems of neurons which have died as a result of injury or from 'natural' causes. It has also been suspected that glial cells may play some part in memory functions (see, for example, Altman and Das, 1964).

The electrical recording of neuronal activity

The electrical activity of the neurons of the brain has been recorded using a variety of techniques. At one extreme, *microelectrodes* (very thin metal or glass tubes insulated except for the tip) can be inserted into the brain and the activity of single cells, known as *single unit activity*, recorded. Slightly larger electrodes, known as *macroelectrodes*, can also be used to record the activity of small groups of cells. Single unit activity can be displayed visually, on an oscilloscope, as a series of spikes, each spike representing a nerve impulse, or can be relayed through an amplifier and loudspeaker, as a series of clicks, and the responses of various populations of single units to different kinds of stimulation can be compared. In this way a great deal of information has been collected concerning how sensory systems operate, particularly from cells in the visual system (see Chapter 8; also Frisby, 1979).

At the other extreme, the *electroencephalogram*, or EEG, provides a measure of changes in the activity of millions of neurons in different regions of the brain in the form of an EEG record. In order to obtain an EEG record, small discs or electrodes are attached to the scalp at various locations, usually in accordance with an internationally agreed arrangement known as the 'Ten-Twenty system' (Jasper, 1958). The electrical activity of the brain, recorded indirectly from the scalp, is picked up by these electrodes and transmitted to an amplifier and thence to a pen write-out, which traces the record on a moving sheet of paper. The EEG provides a continuous record of the voltage functions taking place at the surface of the brain, even though these changes are recorded from the scalp. Provided that certain artifacts of measurement can be excluded (see, for example, Cooper, Osselton and Shaw, 1974), the EEG tracing can be taken to represent a recording of the summed electrical activity of millions of neurons in the brain.

Two measurements are commonly used to analyse an EEG record: first, the amplitude or size of the waves and, second, the number of waves per second. Broadly speaking, the more relaxed a person is the greater the amplitude and the lower the frequency of the waves; this is known as high-voltage slow activity. The lower the amplitude and the higher the frequency (low-voltage fast activity) the more likely the subject is to be in an aroused or excited state. The EEG is commonly divided into a series of 'rhythms', largely on the basis of frequency. These are: delta (0–4 Hz), theta (4–8 Hz), alpha (8–13 Hz) and beta (13–30 + Hz). The frequency and amplitude of the EEG activity from different regions of the scalp is likely to vary, and analytic techniques have been developed which permit the EEG amplitude, or power, at different points in the frequency spectrum to be compared across scalp recording sites (see Shagass, 1972, for a survey). Although EEG recording has proved a useful diagnostic technique in certain clinical areas (see Scott, 1976), one of its main areas of application has been in the study of sleep (see Chapter 5).

The EEG represents the continuous spontaneous electrical activity of the brain and usually little response to external stimulation can be reliably detected in the EEG record since the amplitudes of such *evoked responses* are smaller than that of the spontaneous activity in which they are embedded. It is only comparatively recently that computer averaging techniques have been developed which enable the evoked EEG response, or *event-related potential* (*ERP*) (since such responses may be elicited by stimulus or response events) to be measured (see, for example, Donchin, 1975). The ERP is the result of averaging EEG responses to the repeated presentation of a single event, for example a light flash, a tone or a mild electric shock. It takes the form of a series of positive and negative deflections from a baseline level of activity. Of the various types of ERP two of the more important are the *contingent negative variation*, sometimes known as the 'expectancy wave', and P300. The latter is a positive going brain potential which reaches a maximum amplitude about 300 msec after the eliciting event has occurred. It has been found to be closely related to information processing and other cognitive activities (see Donchin, Ritter and McCallum, 1978, and Hillyard and Woods, 1979, for reviews) and brief reference will be made to ERP studies of attention in Chapter 9.

The structure of the CNS

Before embarking upon a description of the structure of the CNS, some terms commonly used to identify locations within the CNS should be defined. Directions within the nervous system are specified with reference to the *neuraxis*, an imaginary line drawn through the centre of the spinal cord to the front of the brain. In animals whose bodies are horizontal, locations can then be identified in terms of the rostral (anterior)–caudal (posterior) axis, running from head to tail, and the dorsal (superior)–ventral (inferior) axis, running from top to bottom (see Figure 4.3a). However, in animals whose bodies are vertical, the neuraxis takes a 90° turn at the top of the spinal cord, so that the rostral–caudal axis runs from the front to the back of the head and the dorsal–ventral axis from the bottom of the head to the top (see Figure 4.3b). Otherwise, the axes have the same reference as in animals whose bodies are horizontal (see Figure 4.3c). In vertebrates, the CNS is divided at the midline into two halves in a bilaterally symmetrical fashion, with the structures of one half being duplicates of the structures of the other half. The location of a particular structure can

Figure 4.3   Terms used to specify locations within the CNS (see text)

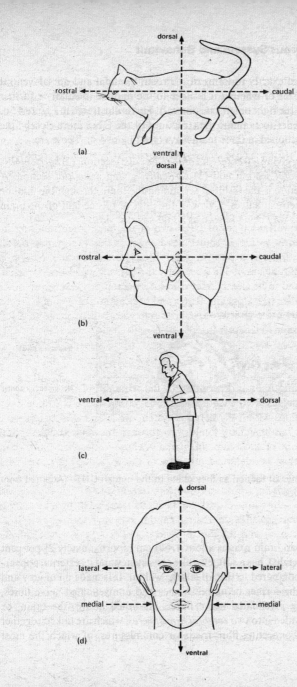

dorsal

rostral ← → caudal

ventral

(a)

dorsal

rostral ← → caudal

ventral

(b)

ventral ← → dorsal

(c)

dorsal

lateral ← → lateral

medial → ← medial

ventral

(d)

thus be specified exactly in terms of the rostral–caudal and dorsal–ventral axes, and in terms of whether it is close to the midline (medial) or further away from it to the right or left side (lateral). This is illustrated in Figure 4.3d.

Finally, in order to examine the structures of the CNS more closely, the CNS can be sectioned in three main ways (see Figure 4.4). These are:

(1) *transversely*, giving a *frontal* (or *coronal*, or *cross*) section; (2) *horizontally*, giving a *horizontal* section and (3) *vertically*, giving a *sagittal* section. A *mid-sagittal* section is the result of sectioning the brain through the midline into two symmetrical halves, a view of the interior of one half of the brain sectioned in this way being known as a mid-sagittal view.

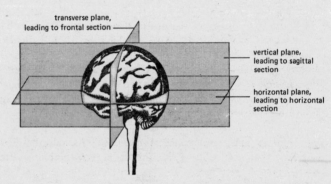

transverse plane, leading to frontal section

vertical plane, leading to sagittal section

horizontal plane, leading to horizontal section

Figure 4.4   Planes of section as they relate to the human CNS. (Adapted from Carlson, 1977, p. 87)

The brain

The adult human brain weighs about 1,440 gm (approximately $2\frac{1}{2}$ per cent of total body weight), has a soft jelly-like consistency and its external appearance has been compared to that of a large walnut. It is made up of grey and white matter, the former being cell bodies and unmyelinated nerve fibres, the latter being myelinated nerve fibres. As noted above, the brain, or *cerebrum*, is divided into two *cerebral hemispheres*, which are linked together by a series of connecting fibre tracts or commissures, of which the most important are the *corpus callosum*, consisting of about 200 million myelinated nerve fibres, and the *anterior* and *posterior* commissures.

The brain consumes between 20 and 25 per cent of the oxygen used by the whole body and nerve cells begin to die after less than a minute without oxygen. In addition, the brain receives a very rich blood supply, between 16 and 20 per cent of the total cardiac output, and the great majority of the brain's energy requirements is obtained from blood glucose. A protective system, the *blood–brain barrier*, prevents many potentially harmful substances from invading brain tissue via the bloodstream. The brain and spinal cord also possess a further fluid supply, the *cerebrospinal fluid* (CSF), which surrounds the brain and fills various cavities within it, known as *ventricles*, as well as the hollow core of the spinal cord, the *spinal canal*. CSF is contained between the inner two of three membranes, the *meninges*, which cover the entire CNS; insofar as it is known, the function of CSF appears to be mainly nutritive, and it also acts as a protective cushion and shock-absorbing medium for the CNS.

We begin our survey of the principal regions of the brain by focusing on the second column of Table 4.3 in which the brain is divided into the *forebrain*, the *midbrain* and the *hindbrain*. The forebrain and the hindbrain can each be subdivided into two major areas. For the former these are the *telencephalon* and the *diencephalon*, and for the latter the *metencephalon* and the *myelencephalon* (see column 3 of Table 4.3). The major constituents of the areas listed in column 3 are shown in columns 4 and 5.

The forebrain (telencephalon and diencephalon). As indicated in Table 4.3, the telencephalon consists of the cerebral cortex, the limbic lobe and the basal ganglia. Cortex means 'rind' or 'bark' and the cerebral cortex forms the outer covering of the brain. It consists of a sheet of nerve cells, arranged in layers, which in man has a surface area of approximately 2 m^2 and varies in thickness from 1·5 to 4·5 mm. The cortex is folded backwards and forwards over the subcortical structures which lie beneath it. Since considerable changes have taken place in the structure of the cerebral cortex in the process of evolution, a distinction is often made between the more primitive *palaeocortex* (old cortex) and the more recently developed *neocortex* (new cortex). The evolution of neocortex resulted in a gradual displacement of palaeocortical structures to positions within the cerebral hemispheres and because of their association with olfaction, these structures are sometimes collectively referred to as the *rhinencephalon* or olfactory brain (see below).

Table 4.3

The subdivisions of the brain

Brain stem Reticular formation	Forebrain	Telencephalon	Cerebral cortex	
			Basal ganglia	Caudate nucleus Globus pallidus Putamen
			Limbic lobe	Amygdala Cingulate gyrus Hippocampus Septal area
		Diencephalon	Thalamus Hypothalamus	
	Midbrain	Mesencephalon	Tectum	Corpora quadrigemina (superior and inferior colliculi)
			Tegmentum	
	Hindbrain	Metencephalon	Cerebellum Pons	
		Myelencephalon	Medulla	

The neocortex possesses numerous convolutions which take the form of ridges (*gyri*) or fissures (*sulci*) and provide useful landmarks for dividing the brain into *lobes*. Figure 4.5 shows a lateral view of the external surface of the left cerebral hemisphere divided in this way. The two sulci which are marked, the *central sulcus* or fissure of Rolando and the *lateral sulcus* or fissure of Sylvius, serve to divide the cortex into the frontal, temporal and parietal lobes, the remaining area being the occipital lobe. Functionally the neocortex can be divided into sensory, motor and association areas (see Figure 4.6). The sensory projection areas of the cortex receive information from the various sensory systems. It can be seen from Figure 4.6 that the projection area for vision is located in the occipital lobe, for audition in the temporal

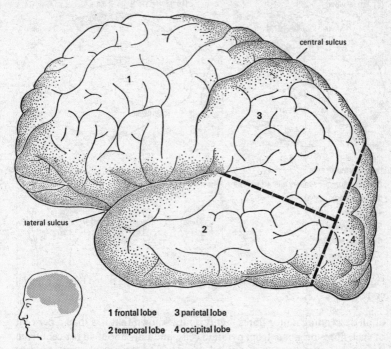

Figure 4.5   External surface of left cerebral hemisphere viewed from the side – human brain, showing the lobes

1 frontal lobe   3 parietal lobe
2 temporal lobe   4 occipital lobe

lobe and for the somatosensory or bodily senses, comprising touch, temperature, pain and kinaesthesis (a sensory system which provides information about bodily position in space), in the post-central gyrus in the parietal lobe. Some kinds of somatosensory information are conveyed to the contralateral hemisphere, that is, to the hemisphere on the opposite side of the body to the point of stimulation. Except in the case of olfaction, information from the various sense organs is conveyed by the thalamus (see below) to the appropriate cortical projection area. The motor cortex, as its name implies, is the cortical division of the motor systems involved in the initiation and control of voluntary movements, known as the *pyramidal* and *extra-pyramidal* motor systems. The pyramidal motor system derives its name from the collection of large cells, shaped like pyramids, which forms part of the motor cortex. It was once thought that these cells were the point of origin

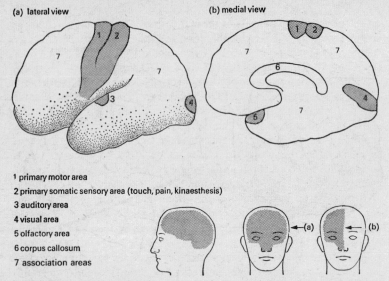

(a) lateral view   (b) medial view

1 primary motor area
2 primary somatic sensory area (touch, pain, kinaesthesis)
3 auditory area
4 visual area
5 olfactory area
6 corpus callosum
7 association areas

Figure 4.6   Primary sensory, motor and association areas of the human cerebral cortex

of all descending motor fibres, but it is now known that less than 5 per cent of such fibres originate from pyramid cells, and only about 40 per cent from the motor cortex as a whole. Approximately a further 20 per cent of motor fibres come from the somatosensory cortex and the remaining 40 per cent from other cortical areas in the frontal, temporal and occipital lobes (Evarts, 1974; Kornhuber, 1974). The fibres of the pyramidal motor system descend via the pons and medulla (see below) to the spinal cord. In man most of these fibres cross over or decussate at the level of the medulla, with the result that limb movements are controlled cross-laterally. That is, movements on the left side of the body are for the most part controlled by the cortex of the right hemisphere and *vice versa*. The motor area of the cortex, like the somato-sensory projection area in the post-central gyrus, is organized somato-topically in each hemisphere, that is, in such a way that different regions are concerned with specific parts of the body, with the amount of cortex devoted to a particular area influencing the degree of precise motor control that can be exercised. Thus in man the fingers, lips, tongue and vocal apparatus have disproportionately large amounts of motor cortex given over to them.

The principal components of the extra-pyramidal motor system are the motor cortex and related cortical areas, and the cerebellum, basal ganglia and reticular formation (see below), these and other structures being inter-linked by a complex series of pathways. While the pyramidal and extra-pyramidal motor systems are probably involved in somewhat different motor functions (Brooks and Stoney, 1971; Kornhuber, 1974) at the cortical level it appears virtually impossible to separate these systems anatomically.

The cortical regions lying outside the sensory projection areas and the motor cortex (see Figure 4.6) constitute the largest part of the neocortex in man and are known as *association cortex*. Association cortex can be divided into two association areas, frontal association cortex and parietal–temporal–occipital, (PTO) association cortex. These areas are thought to be involved in the mediation of cognitive and interpretive functions, includ-ing language, and will be further discussed later in the chapter. Reviews of the functions of the various cortical lobes can be found in Gazzaniga (1979).

The rhinencephalon, or olfactory brain, is one of the most primitive parts of the brain and the structures comprising it can be divided into two groups. The first group contains the olfactory bulbs (the receptors for the sense of smell from which the olfactory nerves arise) and the olfactory nuclei, to which these nerves project. The second group of structures in the rhinen-cephalon make up the *limbic lobe* (see Table 4.3), which has evolved in close association with the olfactory areas, although, in higher mammals, the structures in the limbic lobe have lost their direct connection with the receptors for the sense of smell. The structures in the limbic lobe (see Figure 4.7) are the *septal area*, the *cingulate gyrus*, the *hippocampus* and the *amygdala*. The term limbic lobe is applied to these structures because, taken together, they form a ring on the inner surface of each cerebral hemisphere, around its junction with the diencephalon (*limbus* meaning 'edge' or 'perimeter'). The limbic system is a functional rather than a structural unit, since it includes some brain regions which lie outside the rhinencephalon (see Figures 4.7 and 4.8), and will be briefly referred to in Chapter 7 in connection with emotional behaviour. An overview of the limbic system can be found in Isaacson (1974).

The basal ganglia (see Table 4.3) consist of the *caudate nucleus*, the *globus pallidus* and the *putamen*, although in some classifications the *claustrum* and the amygdala are also included, and the functionally related areas of the *subthalamic nucleus* or *subthalamus*, the *substantia nigra* (black substance) and the *red nucleus*. The basal ganglia occupy a position which is rostral

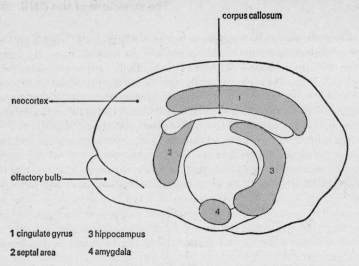

corpus callosum

neocortex

olfactory bulb

1

2

3

4

1 cingulate gyrus   **3** hippocampus

2 septal area   **4** amygdala

Figure 4.7   Schematic diagram of the inner surface of the right hemisphere of the cat's brain showing the limbic lobe (shaded areas). Structures within the limbic lobe, together with the olfactory bulb, make up the rhinencephalon. (From Morgan, 1965, p. 53)

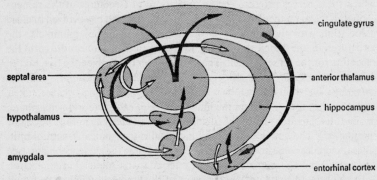

cingulate gyrus

septal area

anterior thalamus

hippocampus

hypothalamus

amygdala

entorhinal cortex

Figure 4.8   Schematic diagram of the limbic system showing the neural areas included in the limbic system together with their interconnecting neural pathways. The arrows show the direction of control exerted by the connecting pathways; double-ended arrows indicate that connecting fibres exert effects in both directions. The closed circuit represented by the black arrows is the Papez circuit (see Chapter 7). The outflow from the hippocampus is the fornix bundle. (From McCleary and Moore, 1965, p. 32)

and lateral to the thalamus and, as indicated above, form a major part of the extra-pyramidal motor system.

Moving from the telencephalon, or 'end brain', to the diencephalon or 'between brain', it can be seen from Table 4.3 that two structures assume importance. The *thalamus* forms the upper region of the diencephalon and the *hypothalamus* (hypo meaning 'below') the lower (see Figure 4.9). Between the two is the *subthalamus*, referred to earlier in relation to the basal ganglia, and the third ventricle, part of the ventricular system mentioned above, is also included in the diencephalon. The thalamus consists of several nuclei which receive inputs from various areas of the brain and send projections to the cortex or connections to other thalamic nuclei (see Figure 4.10). As

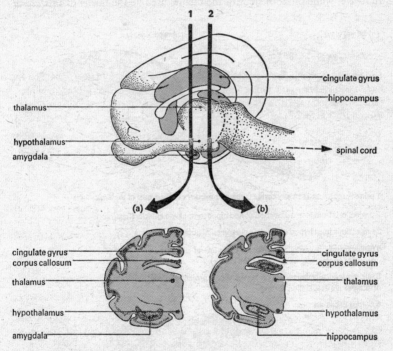

Figure 4.9 Diagram of cat's brain – right hemisphere, medial view. (a) and (b) represent section at points 1 and 2 as they would be seen looking head on. The relative positions of the thalamus and the hypothalamus are shown by dots. (From McCleary and Moore, 1965, p. 25)

well as relaying projections to the sensory projection areas, thalamic nuclei also send projections to other regions of the cortex, as Figure 4.10 shows; virtually all the input the cortex receives comes from the thalamus. Like the thalamus, the hypothalamus consists of several nuclei (see Figure 4.11). The forward (anterior) end of the hypothalamus is bounded by the *optic chiasma*, a junction point in the visual system at which some of the fibres from each retina are sent, via the thalamus, to the primary visual projection area of the contralateral hemisphere. The posterior limit of the hypothalamus is marked by the *mammillary bodies*. The hypothalamus can be divided into two fairly distinct zones; the nuclei of the *medial hypothalamic zone*, including the mammillary bodies, surround the cavity of the third ventricle, while on both sides of the medial area lie the nuclei of the *lateral*

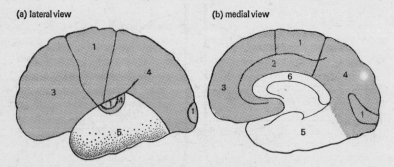

(a) lateral view   (b) medial view

1 primary motor and sensory cortex (projections from ventral group of thalamic nuclei)

2 projections from mammillary bodies and hippocampus via anterior thalamic nuclei

3 projections from hypothalamus via dorsomedial nuclei of thalamus

4 projections from ventral thalamic nuclei via lateral-pulvinar group of nuclei (cognitive association cortex)

5 non-thalamically dependent cortex with some projections from pulvinar (interpretive association cortex)

6 corpus callosum

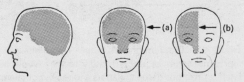

Figure 4.10   Projection zones of the thalamic nuclei on the cerebral cortex

hypothalamic zone. The hypothalamus has many connections with other regions of the brain and is innervated by collateral fibres from the various sensory pathways. It receives a very rich blood supply, is located in close proximity to the third ventricle and is attached to the *pituitary gland*, the major gland of the endocrine system, by the *pituitary stalk*. The hypothalamus is thus well situated to be an integrating centre for many different functions; for example, it is involved in the regulation of water balance, body

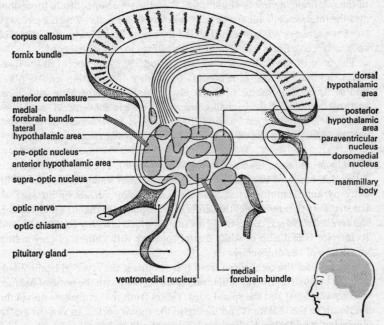

Figure 4.11   Schematic diagram (lateral view) of the hypothalamus

temperature and the metabolism of fats and carbohydrates and influences the activity of the ANS and the endocrine system. The involvement of the hypothalamus, and particularly of the medial and lateral hypothalamic areas, in feeding behaviour will be discussed in Chapter 6 and brief reference to the role of the hypothalamus in emotional behaviour will be made in Chapter 7. An overview of the hypothalamus can be found in Martini, Motta and Fraschini (1970).

The midbrain (mesencephalon). The mesencephalon or midbrain (see Table 4.3) is a relatively small area which forms a bridge between the forebrain and the hindbrain. The fourth ventricle, which, in the midbrain, narrows to a passage known as the *cerebral aqueduct,* divides the midbrain into a roof (tectum) and a floor (tegmentum). The roof contains four groups of nuclei (the *corpora quadrigemina*), comprising the *superior* and *inferior colliculi.* The two superior colliculi are situated in the anterior end of the midbrain, nearer the forebrain, and the two inferior colliculi are situated in the posterior end of the midbrain, nearer the hindbrain. Both the superior colliculi, for vision, and the inferior colliculi, for hearing, are junction points along the pathway from the sense organ concerned to the thalamus. In addition, both pairs of colliculi receive fibres from, and transmit fibres to, the spinal cord.

The floor of the midbrain is an interconnecting system between the forebrain and the hindbrain, and it contains bundles of ascending sensory fibres and of descending motor fibres. It also contains nuclei which send fibres to those muscles of the eyeball concerned with eye movements, as well as other nuclei, the *red nucleus* and the *substantia nigra* which, as indicated earlier, form part of the extra-pyramidal motor system.

The hindbrain (metencephalon and myelencephalon). The *metencephalon* (see Table 4.3) contains two main areas, the *cerebellum* which forms part of the extra-pyramidal motor system, and the *pons.* The *cerebellum,* or 'little brain', is a structure that resembles the cerebral hemispheres in that its outer surface, the *cerebellar cortex,* consists of grey matter which is highly convoluted, and its interior is made up of white matter together with clumps of grey matter consisting of various nuclei.

Fibres enter the cerebellum from three sources, the cerebral hemispheres and the brainstem, the vestibular nuclei (concerned with the sense of balance and equilibrium) and the spinal cord. Fibres from the cerebellum go via the midbrain to the thalamus and thence to the motor cortex, to various motor nuclei in the midbrain, to the reticular formation (see below) and to the spinal cord.

The pons ('bridge') is characterized by very thick bundles of fibres which run across it from one side or hemisphere of the cerebellum to the other. Within the pons are various nuclei which are involved in sensory and motor functions, including some of the cranial nerve nuclei serving the head and face, and various ascending and descending fibre tracts, including part of the reticular formation (see below).

In the myelencephalon is the medulla (see Table 4.3) which joins the spinal cord to the higher centres of the brain. At the level of the medulla the majority of the dozen sets of cranial nerves enter and leave the brainstem and the medulla contains several nuclei associated with these nerves. The medulla also contains nuclei, associated with the ANS, which are involved in the processes of breathing and heart action.

The reticular formation. The reticular formation is a core of nervous tissue, about 5 cm in length, which is located in the centre of the brainstem at the levels of the pons and midbrain, and is clustered around the central canal. Anatomically, the reticular formation is sometimes divided into the midbrain and the pontine reticular formations. The term 'reticulum' means 'network' and the reticular system consists of a collection of over ninety nuclei and short, small-diameter nerve fibres, criss-crossing in all directions.

   The reticular formation appears to possess two distinct functional subsystems. Some groups of reticular cells have axons which project down into the spinal cord, and these are known as reticulospinal neurons. Others have axons which project to higher levels of the brainstem, eventually connecting with the hypothalamus and the thalamus in the diencephalon. The reticular cells which send projections into the spinal cord make up the *descending reticular system*, which is part of the extra-pyramidal motor system, while those which have upward projections form the *ascending reticular activating system*, or ARAS. The ARAS is a polysynaptic pathway which connects to a group of nuclei in the thalamus and thence, by diverse routes, to the whole cortex, particularly the frontal lobes. This projection is diffuse and is not point-to-point, as is the case with the projections of thalamic nuclei concerned with the specific sensory systems. The thalamic extension of the ARAS is known as the *diffuse thalamic projection system* or DTPS. The ARAS, which receives inputs from all the sensory systems, as well as from the cortex and rhinencephalon, acts as an arousal system for the brain and is involved in the maintenance of wakefulness and alertness and, possibly, in the processes of selective attention. The role of the ARAS in wakefulness is discussed in Chapter 5. An overview of the reticular formation can be found in Hobson and Brazier (1980).

The spinal cord

Like the brain, the spinal cord is divided into two symmetrical halves, each half sending fibres to, and receiving fibres from, one side of the body. The spinal cord is housed in the vertebral column made up of the twenty-four individual vertebrae of, in descending order, the cervical, thoracic and lumbar regions and the fused vertebrae of the sacral and coccygeal region of the column. However the spinal cord only extends for about two thirds of the length of the vertebral column, the remaining third being filled by a collection of nerve fibre bundles known as the *cauda equina* or mare's tail. There are thirty-one pairs of spinal nerves, composed of afferent and efferent branches which run through the gaps between the vertebrae (known as the *intravertebral foramina*), dividing just before making contact with the cord itself, input entering the *dorsal roots* and output leaving by the *ventral roots* of the cord.

The spinal cord has two main functions: conduction and control. First, it acts as a conduction path between the brain and the periphery. Nerve impulses travelling from sensory receptors enter the spinal cord at various levels, depending on what part of the body they come from, and then proceed up to the brain. Motor fibres coming down from the brain to the effectors (the muscles and glands of the body) leave the spinal cord for the periphery, again at the level appropriate for their final destination. Spinal cord pathways are of different lengths. Long tracts connect the spinal cord with centres of the brain and are situated primarily in the periphery of the cord. Shorter tracts, known as *intersegmental tracts* or *ground bundles*, connect different levels or segments of the spinal cord. The name of each tract, with some exceptions, is made up first of the place where the tract arises and second of the place where the tract ends. For example, the reticulospinal tract, referred to above, originates in the reticular system and terminates in the spinal cord.

As well as acting as a conduction path between the brain and the periphery, the spinal cord also mediates simple reflexes. There are many different kinds of reflex, some handled by the spinal cord alone, known as *spinal* reflexes, and others involving the brain, known as *suprasegmental* reflexes. In some spinal reflexes, only one segment of the spinal cord is involved, while in others several segments take part. Since spinal reflexes do not involve the brain, they can still be elicited when the connections between the brain and spinal cord are severed.

This outline of the spinal cord completes our survey of the CNS and we now turn to the PNS. Referring back to Table 4.1 it can be seen that the PNS can be subdivided into the somatic nervous system, consisting of the cranial and spinal nerves referred to above, and the ANS. In the next section we outline the structure and functions of the ANS, methods of measuring its activity and also the glandular system known as the endocrine system, to which the ANS is functionally related.

The ANS and the endocrine system

The ANS

The ANS consists of a network of motor fibres which originate in various regions of the brain, particularly the hypothalamus, and are conveyed to their destinations in the PNS by way of the spinal cord. These fibres are connected to the smooth muscles of the visceral organs, to the heart muscles and to various glands (see Figure 4.12). The ANS has two divisions, the *sympathetic* and the *parasympathetic*, fibres of the former division coming from the middle section of the spinal cord and of the latter from the two ends. The majority of the structures connected to the ANS are innervated by both sympathetic and parasympathetic fibres. This reciprocal innervation, as it is called, provides a mechanism for maintaining the activity of a given structure within fairly narrow limits, since the two divisions of the ANS exert somewhat opposing effects. In general, the sympathetic division exerts effects which increase energy expenditure whereas the parasympathetic division exerts effects which promote energy conservation. The effects of sympathetic dominance appear in situations requiring rapid action, for instance, a situation perceived as involving danger; such situations have been described as demanding 'fight or flight' on the part of the organism. Indicators of sympathetic activity include increases in heart rate, respiration or sweat gland activity. Parasympathetic dominance occurs when the organism is at rest, principally in sleep, where heart rate slows and respiration becomes deeper and more regular. However, when one division of the ANS is dominant, the other is not inactive. For example, sympathetic division activity, as well as parasympathetic activity, occurs during sleep. Since both divisions are always active in varying degrees, it is not always possible, by observing changes in one measure of autonomic activity, such as heart rate, to draw a firm conclusion as to which division is primarily responsible for the effects. Some changes in autonomic activity thus reflect the apparent dominance of the sympathetic division, while others reflect apparent parasympathetic dominance. Sympathetic division activity is more global in its effects than is parasympathetic division activity, for three reasons. First, there is much more overlap between sympathetic division interconnections; second, increased sympathetic division activity results in the secretion into

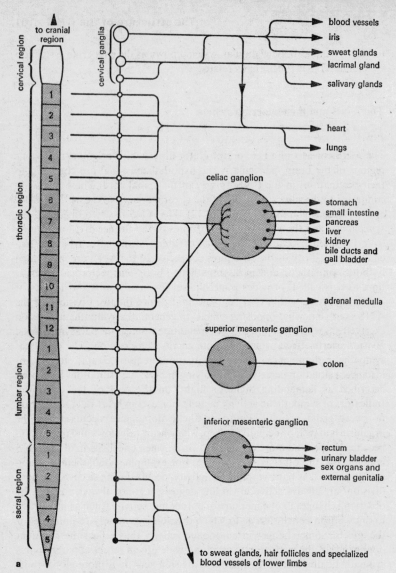

Figure 4.12 Highly simplified diagram of the autonomic nervous system and the parts of the body that it serves; (a) shows the sympathetic division and (b) the parasympathetic division

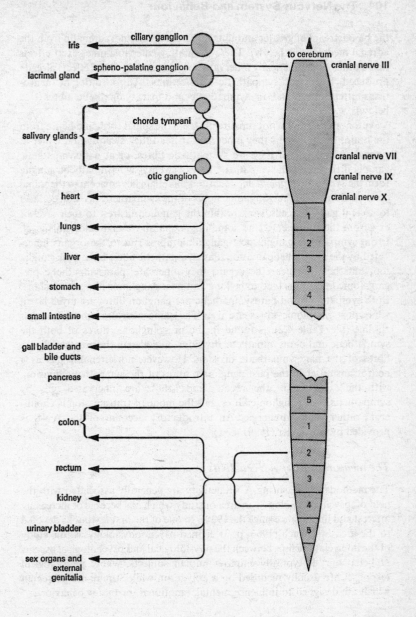

iris

ciliary ganglion

to cerebrum

cranial nerve III

lacrimal gland

spheno-palatine ganglion

salivary glands

chorda tympani

otic ganglion

cranial nerve VII

cranial nerve IX

heart

cranial nerve X

lungs

1

liver

2

stomach

3

small intestine

4

gall bladder and
bile ducts

pancreas

colon

5

1

rectum

2

kidney

3

urinary bladder

4

sex organs and
external
genitalia

5

the bloodstream of greater amounts of adrenalin and noradrenalin from the adrenal medulla (see below). These circulating catecholamines exert effects on all other sympathetically innervated organs, adding to the effects already produced by direct sympathetic connections. Third, different neuro-transmitters are found in sympathetic and parasympathetic fibres (see below).

Autonomic fibres do not run directly from the spinal cord, and hence from the brain, to the organs they innervate. Instead they synapse first either at sympathetic ganglia if they are sympathetic fibres, or at parasympathetic ganglia if they are parasympathetic fibres. Twenty-two sympathetic ganglia form the *sympathetic ganglionic chain* and this chain lies adjacent to the spinal cord on either side. Pre-ganglionic fibres of the sympathetic division connect to several ganglion cells, some within the ganglion nearest to their level of exit from the spinal cord and some in ganglia above and below this level. From sympathetic ganglia post-ganglionic fibres run to the organs inner-vated by the sympathetic division. Parasympathetic fibres have their ganglia too, but these are near the organs they innervate; parasympathetic pre-ganglionic fibres thus tend to be long and post-ganglionic fibres to be short. Both sympathetic and parasympathetic pre-ganglion fibres are myelinated, while post-ganglionic fibres are not. The same neurotransmitter, acetyl-choline (see Table 4.2), is found in the pre-ganglionic fibres of both the sympathetic and parasympathetic divisions, and also in the post-ganglionic fibres of the parasympathetic division. However, noradrenalin acts as a neurotransmitter in the post-ganglionic fibres of the sympathetic division, with the exception of the sweat glands; these are innervated only by sympathetic post-ganglionic fibres, but the mode of transmission is cholin-ergic rather than adrenergic. An introductory account of the ANS is provided by van Toller (1979).

The measurement of ANS activity

The methods of measuring ANS activity are generally associated with the field of 'psychophysiology', an area of study which has become of increasing interest and importance since the 1930s. In one of the first textbooks devoted to the area Sternbach (1966, p. 3) defined psychophysiology as 'the study of the interrelationships between the physiological and psychological aspects of behaviour. It typically employs human subjects, whose physiological responses are usually recorded on a polygraph while stimuli are presented which are designed to influence mental, emotional, or motor behavior ...'

Psychophysiological studies thus attempt to relate behaviour, experience and physiology. Although many such studies have recorded measures of the electrical activity of the brain, such as the EEG or the evoked potential, described on pp. 84–6, they have tended to focus upon the activity of the ANS and this use of autonomic measures is reflected in many of the important concepts and theoretical ideas of psychophysiology, such as *autonomic balance* (Darrow, 1943; Wenger, 1966; Wenger and Cullen, 1972), *autonomic response specificity* (Engel, 1972; Lacey, Bateman and van Lehn, 1953), *autonomic* (Lacey and Lacey, 1958) or *electrodermal* (Crider and Lunn, 1971; Hastrup and Katkin, 1976) *lability*, and *autonomic arousal* (as distinct from electrocortical activation: see reviews by Duffy, 1962, 1972, and Malmo, 1959). Detailed accounts of the theoretical and empirical approaches employed in psychophysiology can be found in the encyclopedic *Handbook of Psychophysiology* (Greenfield and Sternbach, 1972), and an introduction to the area is provided by Hassett (1978).

Many different measures of ANS activity have been adopted. These include measures of *cardiovascular* variables: that is, blood pressure (Lywood, 1967; Brown, 1972); changes in the diameter of arteries and veins – *vasodilation* and *vasoconstriction* – and hence in the volume of blood present in different parts of the body (Lader, 1967; Weinman, 1967) and also in skin temperature (Plutchik, 1956); and changes in heart rate as measured for example by an electrocardiograph (Brener, 1967; Gunn *et al.*, 1972). Since heart rate is affected by respiratory variations, it is customary when recording heart rate to take measures of respiration rate as well; similarly, body movements must also be controlled.

Other measures of ANS activity are electrodermal, that is, concerned with changes in the electrical properties of the skin. The two most common are *skin resistance* and its reciprocal, *skin conductance*; a more recent addition is *skin potential* (Venables and Sayer, 1963). The first two measures are obtained by passing an electrical current between two points on the skin surface and by measuring the resistance of the skin to the passage of the current. The resistance varies with the activity of the sweat glands: the greater the amount of sweating, the lower the resistance and *vice versa*. Thus, in general, an increase in resistance is expected when an individual is relaxed and a decrease when he is aroused or excited.

Two measurements of skin resistance can be taken. The first is the baseline resistance, or the skin-resistance level, which undergoes gradual shifts over a relatively long period of time. The second is the skin resistance response, also known as the galvanic skin response (GSR) or the psychogalvanic reflex (PGR). This can be defined as a change in the waveform of the skin response, in which a negative deflection is followed by a positive deflection. Although skin-resistance responses occur as a result of stimulation, they may also occur in its absence. The measurement of skin potential does not depend upon an externally applied current. As with skin resistance, two measures can be derived, the number of skin potential responses and a measure of basal level. The many problems involved in the measurement of skin resistance are discussed by Montagu and Coles (1966), Brown (1967), Venables and Martin (1967) and Edelberg (1972).

The level of certain hormones (see below) and neurotransmitter substances – the so-called *catecholamines*, particularly adrenalin and noradrenalin – in the bloodstream and in the urine has been measured, and related to various psychological variables, in normal and psychiatric populations (see Mason, 1972, for a general review), with particular emphasis on the response to stress and perceived threat (Lazarus, 1966; Levi, 1966); some of the principal findings relating to emotion will be discussed in Chapter 7. There has also been considerable interest in pupillary activity and its possible relation to information processing and 'mental effort': see Chapter 9, and also Janisse (1977).

The endocrine system

The endocrine system (see Figure 4.13) modulates ongoing processes occurring in the internal environment by the emission of chemical stimulators, known as *hormones*, directly into the bloodstream. This distinguishes *endocrine* or ductless glands from exocrine or duct glands – for example, the salivary glands, which secrete the hormone *ptyalin* through salivary ducts. Hormones circulating in the blood affect cellular activity, modulating the rate at which cellular processes take place, rather than initiating new processes. The number and amount of hormones present in the bloodstream vary with environmental demands. The most important gland in the endocrine system is the *pituitary gland*, which controls the activity of the endocrine system as a whole, stimulating other endocrine glands into action by the release of hormones (although some endocrine glands, for example the *adrenal medulla*, may also be stimulated by other means). The pituitary gland lies beneath the hypothalamus and is joined to it by the pituitary stalk or *infundibulum*. It is divided into three lobes, the *anterior*, *intermediate* and *posterior lobes*. The anterior and intermediate lobes constitute the *adenohypophysis*, which secretes several hormones, among them *somatotrophic*

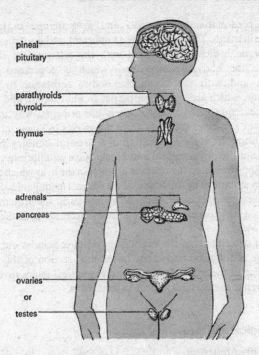

pineal
pituitary

parathyroids
thyroid

thymus

adrenals

pancreas

ovaries

or

testes

Figure 4.13   The endocrine system. (From Hoskins, 1933, p. 19)

hormone, which stimulates the pancreas, *thyrotrophic hormone*, which stimulates the thyroid gland, *adrenocorticotrophic hormone*, which stimulates the adrenal cortex, three *gonadotrophic hormones*, which act on the sex glands, and other hormones which stimulate the secretion of milk or promote the formation of pigment in the skin. The posterior lobe of the pituitary gland, known as the *neurohypophysis*, is an outgrowth of the hypothalamus and secretes two principal hormones, *antidiuretic hormone*, which stimulates the kidneys to retain water in the body, and *oxytocic hormone* which produces contraction of the smooth tissues of the uterus.

The *thyroid gland*, together with the *parathyroid glands* (which regulate calcium metabolism), is mainly concerned, through the agency of its hormone *thyroxin*, with the regulation of the processes of bodily growth. The *pancreas* secretes *insulin* and *glucagon*, both of which are essential to energy metabolism and the *gonads* (the ovaries or the testes) secrete the sex hormones, predominantly *estrogens* and *progesterone* in females and *testosterone* in males. Three of the more important adrenocortical hormones are *aldosterone*, which is concerned with the retention of salt (sodium chloride) in the body, *hydrocortisone* which is concerned with sugar metabolism and with mobilizing the body's resistance to stress, and *corticosterone*, which shares the properties of aldosterone and hydrocortisone. The secretion of hydrocortisone is the principal way in which the adrenal cortex preserves the body from the effects of stress, or repairs the damage resulting from the application of a stressful stimulus. Such stimuli tend to disrupt the physiological and biochemical equilibrium of the body. Hydrocortisone builds up the reserves of sugar in the liver which are depleted in emergency situations by the action of the adrenal medulla. Hydrocortisone maintains these reserves by breaking down into sugar the proteins contained in muscle and by preventing further protein increases until the emergency situation is over.

This brief description of the endocrine system concludes our account of the structure of the nervous system. In the final section of this chapter we examine some of the methodological and theoretical issues involved in the attempt to relate the nervous system to behaviour.

Methodological and theoretical issues

Localization of function

Many of the central questions of modern physiological psychology arise from the anatomical, physiological, neurological and biological investigations of several nineteenth-century scientists and physicians (see Boring, 1957, and Young, 1970 for detailed historical surveys), one of the most important being the problem of the cerebral localization of function. The idea that the mind can be localized in the brain, or in some part of it, has existed for centuries in various forms but it was only in the second half of the eighteenth century that it began to be examined empirically, beginning with the work of Gall and Spurzheim, and the development of the ablation method by Flourens (see below). Ablation has been widely used in the investigation of brain–behaviour relationships and, in conjunction with electrical and chemical stimulation techniques, has provided the bulk of the evidence relating to the localization of function in the brain.

Ablation and stimulation methods. Both ablation and stimulation interfere with the normal operation of the nervous system; ablation by surgically isolating or removing some part of it and stimulation by activating localized areas of the brain, either electrically or chemically.

The term for intentional or accidental damage to neural tissue which results in its temporary or permanent inactivation is a *lesion*, and there are two main methods of producing lesions in the nervous system. First, if the site of the intended lesion is directly accessible, for example, the surface of the brain or spinal cord, neural tissue can be surgically removed. Temporary lesions can also be produced by chemical means in that the application of chemical substances to the cortex can put it temporarily out of commission. The second, and more widely used, method is employed in the production of lesions in less accessible regions of the brain. To make a lesion in a sub-cortical structure, for example, a thin stainless steel or platinum wire, insulated except for the tip, is inserted through the brain into the structure and either a D.C. or a very high-frequency A.C. current is passed through the wire, of sufficient strength to produce a lesion in the tissue in which the uninsulated tip is embedded. A major problem with this procedure is the location of the target structure or region in the first place. To this end, a method known as *stereotaxis* is employed. This method has two components: first an atlas of the brain for a particular species in which the co-ordinates of a particular structure are given, relative to external features of the head, for a series of frontal sections, and second, an apparatus in which the animal's head is clamped while the electrode is inserted in accordance with the co-ordinates provided by the atlas. The location of subcortical lesions is verified by post-mortem examination.

Since one half of the brain is a mirror image of the other, structures of the brain are bilaterally represented. Lesions can thus either be bilateral, when for example a particular hypothalamic nucleus is destroyed on both sides of the midline, or unilateral when it is only destroyed in one hemisphere. In studying the effects of brain lesions on behaviour it is important that bilaterally symmetrical lesions should be made, since the effects of unilateral lesions are often extremely difficult to detect. As it is not particularly easy to locate a particular structure successfully in one hemisphere, it is doubly difficult to locate it accurately twice in the same animal. One way of minimizing this problem is to use *split-brain animals* (see Sperry, 1964, 1974) in which the connections between the two halves of the brain (the corpus callosum and the other cerebral commissures) are cut. The two hemispheres of such split-brain animals have been shown to be independently capable of perceiving, learning and controlling responses (see Dimond, 1972).

In such animals lesions need only be made in one hemisphere, since the intact hemisphere can be used as a matched control for the operated hemisphere.

As indicated above, stimulation methods are of two kinds, electrical and chemical. Neurons can be fired by putting an electrical current near them by means of thin wire probes which are inserted into the brain stereotactically. In this way structures of the brain, usually groups of nuclei, can be activated. As with electrical recording from deeper structures of the brain, the electrodes can be chronically implanted, at least in smaller animals such as rats. However in larger animals, such as primates, various practical problems are associated with this procedure and sometimes miniaturized radio stimulators and transmitters have been employed instead, although this technique also faces certain difficulties. Since the nerve impulse is an electrochemical phenomenon the evidence obtained from electrical stimulation studies has been supplemented and extended through the use of chemical stimulation methods, in which a chemical substance is injected into a chosen brain site using *micropipettes* and *intracranial cannulae*. Using these two stimulation methods it has thus become possible to gain some understanding of the ways in which electrical and chemical information is transmitted to different areas of the brain.

Gall and Flourens. Much of the credit for establishing the brain, or at any rate the cortex, as the 'organ of mind' belongs to the German physician and neuroanatomist Franz-Josef Gall. In partial collaboration with his pupil Spurzheim, Gall published a six-volume treatise on neuroanatomy between 1809 and 1820, but he is best known for his physiognomical doctrine, first put forward in 1808 and later developed and popularized by Spurzheim as phrenology. Drawing on the work on mental faculties of the eighteenth-century Scottish philosophers Reid and Stewart, Gall prepared a list of mental and behavioural functions, or powers and propensities of the mind, and attempted to localize these functions in different regions of the brain. Gall's original list contained twenty-seven such functions, but it was subsequently extended to thirty-seven by Spurzheim. Since Gall believed that 'the difference in the form of heads is occasioned by the difference in the form of brains' he sought to establish a relation between different psychological functions and specific 'cranial prominences'. With hindsight it can be said that this approach to the cerebral localization of function was unlikely to succeed, and although phrenology flourished for a time in the nineteenth century, it soon fell into disrepute. It can nevertheless be regarded as the first scientific expression of an extreme theory of localization of function.

The French physician, Pierre Flourens, born a generation after Gall, is usually regarded as the first to put forward an alternative to the extreme localization of function view expressed by Gall. Flourens used the ablation method in a series of experiments on birds in which six areas or 'units' of the nervous system, the cerebral hemispheres, the cerebellum, the corpora quadragemina, the medulla, the spinal cord and the peripheral nerves, were removed in turn and the resulting changes in behaviour observed. While the results obtained by Flourens clearly showed that these units of the nervous system possessed specific functional properties, each such property being described as the *action propre* of the unit, they also indicated that the nervous system tended to function as a whole, or to exhibit an *action commune*, so that the removal of any one area exerted effects on those remaining. The unitary action of the nervous system in the regulation of function became for Flourens the most important principle of brain organization.

The views of Gall and Spurzheim on the one hand, and of Flourens on the other, were thus in opposition. Gall and Spurzheim held that a particular function could be localized in a specific region of the brain, while Flourens considered that many units of the nervous system made an equal contribution to the mediation of a particular function. Flourens was thus one of the first to put forward the *principle of equipotentiality*, which holds that different areas of the brain may be functionally interchangeable, in the sense that if a particular area is removed the function it subserves can be mediated by another brain area. This principle was evaluated in a famous series of experiments carried out by the American physiological psychologist, Karl Lashley.

Lashley. By the time Lashley began his experimental programme in the 1920s, considerable changes had taken place in the way in which psychological functions were regarded. As noted earlier Gall had identified functions with faculties. These were of two kinds, affective propensities and sentiments such as 'philoprogenitiveness' and 'benevolence' and perceptive and reflective intellectual powers such as those involved in the perception of size or in the appreciation of causality. Although Flourens made a number of cogent criticisms of Gall's faculty psychology, he did not attempt to draw up a more satisfactory list of mental and behavioural functions, preferring to rely upon introspection as the principal source of knowledge about the mind. But gradually, at first as a result of the emergence of Darwinism and later as a consequence of the development of functionalism and the subsequent rise of behaviourism, psychology became less concerned with the study of the mind and more concerned with the study of behaviour. This shift of emphasis enabled the problem of the cerebral localization of function to be approached from a new perspective, although it by no means avoided all the pitfalls of faculty psychology.

Lashley was a student and colleague of John Broadus Watson, the founder of behaviourism, and his experiments on cerebral localization of function were originally intended to provide evidence for certain of Watson's views, although they in fact failed to do so. In his research programme Lashley made lesions in the cortex of the rat and observed the effects upon the learning of mazes of varying difficulty, measured in terms of the number of 'blind alleys'. He found that the number of errors made during learning was positively correlated with the amount of cortex removed, and these correlations increased in size as the maze became more difficult. The location of the lesions did not appear to be important. Lashley also found that the retention of maze habits, once learned, was similarly affected by task difficulty and the amount of cortical loss, with location again playing a minor role. On the basis of these results Lashley considered that the operation of the equipotentiality principle was to some extent constrained by the *principle of mass action* (see Lashley, 1931), whereby the degree of impairment of certain functions is positively and significantly correlated with the amount of cortical tissue ablated in areas equipotential in the mediation of these functions. Areas of the brain which are equipotential in the mediation of a particular function can vary in size; they can be small regions of the brain or they can comprise the whole cortex, as Lashley considered to be the case for maze learning.

Although several alternative explanations of Lashley's results have been advanced (see Zangwill, 1961), Lashley's research programme has been regarded as providing strong evidence against a strict localization of function hypothesis, at least with respect to such higher mental functions as learning and intelligence. Lashley further argued that the effects of brain injury in man did not suggest that the human cortex is more finely differentiated in terms of function than that of the rat, except, perhaps, in the sensory and motor areas. However, the organization of the human brain is both more complex and less symmetrical than that found in animals. It is more likely, therefore, that in human beings the behavioural effect of a lesion in one hemisphere will be different from a similarly placed lesion in the other. Such differences between the effects of a similar lesion in different hemispheres depend to a great extent in man, and to a lesser extent in animals, upon the particular function studied. The way in which the two hemispheres interact to regulate different kinds of behaviour appears to differ for different functions. As was mentioned earlier for some kinds of behaviour, such as motor movements, it appears that the cortex of each hemisphere controls the function cross-laterally, and the demonstration of the relation between the motor cortex and motor behaviour, by Fritsch and Hitzig in the 1870s, provided one of the first pieces of indisputable evidence that specific kinds of behaviour could be controlled by specific and highly localized regions of the brain. But the first 'higher' mental function to be 'localized', by Broca (1861) was language (see Broca, 1865); for language functions one hemisphere appears to be dominant, with the result that damage to well-defined areas in one hemisphere (normally the left) produces language deficits, while damage to the corresponding areas of the other hemisphere does not.

Broca and the localization of language. In a series of presentations before the Paris Anthropological Society, Broca exhibited the brains of two stroke victims each of whom, following the brain injury, had experienced severe speech production difficulties. In each case the brain was found to have a relatively circumscribed lesion in the left hemisphere, specifically in the posterior third of the inferior frontal convolution (see Figure 4.14). Broca believed that articulated speech could thus be localized in this area of the brain, which has since become known as Broca's area. In 1874 Wernicke described an area in the dorsal posterior region of the temporal lobe of the left hemisphere which appeared to be involved in the reception and comprehension of speech. As Figure 4.14 shows, Broca's area and Wernicke's area are connected by the *arcuate fasciculus*; damage to this connection system is associated with *conduction aphasia*, a disorder characterized by an inability to repeat verbal items correctly and by the tendency to make certain kinds of errors and substitutions in spontaneous speech, in the absence of any impairment of verbal comprehension (Benson *et al.*, 1973).

Conduction aphasia is one kind of aphasia, a term which refers to disorders of language functions. There are several varieties of aphasia and these have been classified in a number of ways (see Hécaen, 1979, for a detailed review). The two broad categories into which the aphasias can be divided are the expressive aphasias and the sensory aphasias. The expressive aphasias include conduction aphasia, aphasias resulting from impairments of sound or sentence production, sometimes described respectively as motor and verbal aphasias and the amnesic aphasias, in which the patient experiences great difficulty in correctly assigning names to objects or people. The sensory

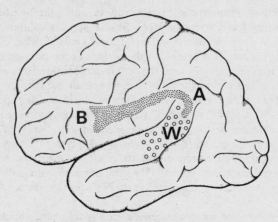

Figure 4.14   Lateral surface of the left hemisphere of the human brain. B, Broca's area, which lies anterior to the lower end of the motor cortex; W (open circles), Wernicke's area; A (dotted area), arcuate fasciculus, which connects Wernicke's to Broca's area. (From Geschwind, 1970, p. 941)

aphasias include 'word deafness', an inability to comprehend speech sounds, and the alexias, in which the deficit takes the form of an inability to read and understand written language. A further category of language disorder comprises the agraphias, in which there is an inability to produce language in written form and it is likely that the agraphias are related to the apraxias, which have in common an apparent loss of memory for a familiar sequence of actions, such as those involved in the use of simple tools, or in dressing (see Geschwind, 1975).

However, the various forms of aphasia do not appear to result from damage to areas of the brain that can be either clearly distinguished histologically or precisely defined anatomically (see Lenneberg, 1967; Marin, Schwartz and Saffran, 1979). The cellular structure, or *cytoarchitecture*, of Broca's area, for example, while different from surrounding areas of the

Figure 4.15   (a) Location of lesions in cases of sensory and amnesic aphasia (word-finding difficulty). (From Conrad, 1954, p. 507), (b) location of lesions producing articulatory disturbances with other language functions remaining intact. (From Conrad, 1954, p. 503), (c) location of left-hemisphere lesions which did not produce language disturbances. The numbered circles indicate cases regarded as anomalous. (From Conrad, 1954, p. 506)

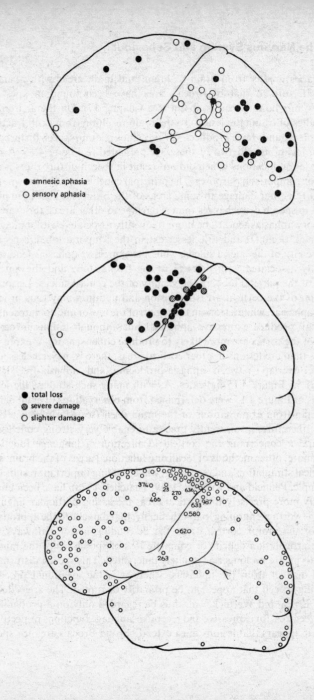

brain, varies greatly from brain to brain, and brain areas with a similar cytoarchitecture to that of Broca's area have been found in apes and monkeys, in whom speech is absent (see Chapter 17). On the anatomical side, studies of traumatic lesions to the brain resulting from skull fractures and missile wounds have produced various maps relating speech disturbance to lesion locations and two of these are presented in Figure 4.15. A map showing lesion locations which did not result in speech disturbances is also shown for comparison purposes. The principal conclusion to be drawn from Figure 4.15 is that damage to some areas of the brain is much more likely to result in speech disturbances than is damage to other areas; for example, the sensory aphasias tend to be more frequently associated with damage to the parietal, occipital and to a lesser extent the temporal lobes, especially in the vicinity of the lateral sulcus, while the expressive aphasias tend to be frequently associated with damage to the frontal lobe and the anterior portion of the parietal lobe, in the vicinity of the central sulcus. Lesions in the region of the cortical areas for vision and audition may thus produce sensory aphasias, while lesions in the region of the motor and somatosensory areas may produce expressive aphasias. But although lesions in certain regions of the cortex are more likely to produce either sensory or expressive aphasias than are lesions in other cortical areas, there is, nevertheless, considerable overlap between aphasia-producing and aphasia-free lesion locations, as Figure 4.15 indicates. As with many such studies, the lesion locations of Figure 4.15 were determined from observations of skull defects rather than from examinations of the brain itself (see Marin *et al.*, 1979) and are, therefore, insufficiently precise to enable very strong conclusions to be drawn concerning the cortical localization of language functions. Furthermore, other methods of localizing functional areas of the brain, such as electrical stimulation and recording, while yielding important results (see, for example, Penfield and Roberts, 1959; Thatcher, 1978), have been unable to specify more precisely the cortical areas mediating particular linguistic skills. It is worth mentioning, parenthetically, that damage to the appropriate region of the motor cortex, or to the descending motor pathways, can produce articulation deficits or complete loss of speech, since the muscles of the larynx are no longer adequately innervated. This speech disturbance is quite distinct from the aphasias, where it is the ideational processes underlying speech that appear to be primarily disrupted. The areas delineated by Broca and Wernicke can thus be regarded only on a probabilistic basis as 'centres' for expressive and receptive language functions respectively. Indeed, it appears that lesions must extend beyond Broca's area for speech production to be more than transiently impaired (Mohr, 1976) and the boundaries of Wernicke's area have proved extremely difficult to determine (see Bogen and Bogen, 1976). It is likely, therefore, that as and when more detailed information becomes available, current models of the way in which the brain might mediate language functions (see, for example, Geschwind, 1970) will require some revision.

Hemisphere differences. As outlined in the preceding section, it appears that aphasia results more frequently from damage to the left hemisphere than from damage to the right, and the left hemisphere thus seems to be specialized for the mediation of speech and language functions. As far as speech and language are concerned, then, the cerebral hemispheres tend to be functionally asymmetrical. But although the right hemisphere, in most people at least, acts as the 'minor' hemisphere for speech and language, it is itself specialized for a variety of functions, in particular the perception of visuo-spatial relationships and the processing of non–verbal information.

The functional asymmetry of the cerebral hemispheres in man has been elucidated by four main lines of inquiry. The first, and perhaps the most productive, has been to observe the performance on various tests of patients with unilateral brain damage, that is with lesions in the left or the right hemisphere (see Benton, 1968). The second has utilized 'split brain' patients in whom, for the purpose of controlling epilepsy, the corpus callosum, the principal communication system between the hemispheres, has been severed. In such patients information can either be presented solely to the left or solely to the right hemisphere and the performances of the two hemispheres on the same task can be directly compared (see Nebes, 1974). Third, techniques have been adapted or developed for assessing the relative performance of the cerebral hemispheres in individuals whose brains are intact (see Cohen, 1977; Moscovitch, 1979); in the dichotic listening task, for example (see also Chapter 9), two different auditory messages can be simultaneously presented, one to each ear, and the subject instructed to recall as many items as possible from both messages. Furthermore, using specially designed apparatus, visual information can be presented to one hemisphere or the other and the performance of the two hemispheres again compared. Finally, EEG or evoked potential activity can be recorded from both hemispheres during the performance of a task considered to involve functions for which the left or the right hemisphere is specialized (see, for example, Galin and Ornstein, 1972; Mayes and Beaumont, 1977; Osborne and Gale, 1975).

Although damage to the left hemisphere is much more frequently associated with language disorders than is damage to the right, the distribution of language, and also of other functions, between the hemispheres depends to some extent upon handedness (see Beaumont, 1974, for a review). Several different self-report and behavioural measures have been employed in the assessment of handedness and although it appears that handedness is a continuous rather than a discrete variable (see, for example, Annett, 1972), a classification is generally made into right-, left- and mixed-handers, the latter two groups sometimes being referred to as non-right-handers. The incidence of left-handedness in the general population is probably in the region of 8–10 per cent (Hardyck and Petrinovich, 1977).

Table 4.4
The percentages of individuals classified as left- or right-handers developing language disorders following left or right hemisphere cortical lesions. Data computed by C. Hardyck and L. F. Petrinovich (1977), 'Left handedness', *Psychol. Bull.*, vol. 84, no. 3, pp. 385–404

Classification	*Site of cortical lesion*	
	Left hemisphere	*Right hemisphere*
Left-handers	22·4%	13·7%
Right-handers	24%	6·7%

The median percentages of left- and right-handers experiencing language disorders following left or right hemisphere cortical lesions, computed by Hardyck and Petrinovich from a survey of large-scale studies reporting the effects of brain damage on a variety of linguistic skills, are shown in Table 4.4. From Table 4.4 it may be seen that following left hemisphere cortical lesions the frequency of occurrence of language disorders is about the same for right- and left-handers, while following right hemisphere cortical lesions the frequency of occurrence in left-handers is twice that in right-handers. The difference between the frequencies of occurrence of linguistic impairment is thus much greater for right- than for left-handers and, as Hardyck and Petrinovich observed, is much more likely to be statistically significant.

A method for determining the lateralization of speech functions, prior to surgery likely to involve areas of the brain in the region of the lateral sulcus, was devised by Wada (1949). The method involves the injection of sodium amytal, a barbiturate, into the left or right carotid artery, thereby deactivating the ipsilateral hemisphere for a brief period and permitting the capacity for speech production of the contralateral hemisphere to be assessed in isolation. The Wada technique has mainly been employed with epileptics about to undergo therapeutic brain surgery; thus virtually all the information concerning the relation between handedness and the lateralization of speech production mechanisms obtained by this method is derived from observations of epileptic patients. Such patients may not be entirely typical of the general population, since epilepsy is associated with a greater incidence of left-handedness, but the results obtained with the Wada method are in good agreement with those found in studies of brain-damaged individuals. The principal findings of a study of epileptic patients conducted by Milner, Branch and Rasmussen (1966) are shown in Table 4.5, and the main con-

Table 4.5
The percentages of epileptic individuals classified as right-handers or non-right-handers with speech represented either in the left or the right hemisphere, or in both hemispheres, as indicated by the Wada method (see text). Data from Milner, B., Branch, C., and Rasmussen, T. (1966), 'Evidence for bilateral speech representation in some non-right-handers', *Trans. Amer. Neurol. Assoc.*, vol. 91, pp. 306–8

Classification	Number in sample	Left hemisphere	Right hemisphere	Both hemispheres
Right-handers	95	92%	7%	1%
Non-right-handers (left-handers and ambilaterals)	74	69%	18%	13%

clusion to be drawn from this table, and from the results obtained with brain-damaged individuals presented in Table 4.4, is that non-right-handers (left-handers and ambilaterals) are more likely than right-handers to have speech functions localized in the right hemisphere or in both the left and the right hemispheres. According to Milner (1974), the left hemisphere is dominant for speech in more than 90 per cent of right-handed individuals but in only 65 per cent of left-handed individuals, and probably about 5 per cent of non-right-handers have speech represented in both hemispheres (see Searleman, 1977). However, left-handedness is not a unitary trait, and the organization of the brain with respect to language may be somewhat different in left-handers with a family history of left-handedness from that in left-handers with no such history, although the evidence is not completely consistent (see Hardyck and Petrinovich, 1977; Searleman, 1977 for discussion). Evidence that the organization of the brain with respect to speech and language may be more diffuse in left-handers and ambilaterals also comes from studies of individuals who have not sustained brain damage. In dichotic listening tasks, for example, right-handers tend to exhibit a right ear advantage (REA), that is, they report the content of auditory messages presented to the right ear more accurately than the content of messages presented to the left (see Kimura, 1967). There appear to be more contralateral than ipsilateral fibres connecting the ear to the auditory cortex and hence material presented to the right ear is likely to enjoy privileged access to the auditory cortex of the left hemisphere. The REA has thus been interpreted as a further demonstration of left hemisphere specialization for language functions, in this case speech perception. However, the REA is less marked in left-handers and ambilaterals (Satz et al., 1965), suggesting that in non-right-handers the left hemisphere is less specialized for the perception of speech.

The functional asymmetry of the cerebral hemispheres has usually been conceptualized along a verbal–non-verbal dimension (Moscovitch, 1979) with the left hemisphere being predominantly specialized for the mediation of speech and language and for the processing of verbal information and the right predominantly for the perception of visuo-spatial relationships and the processing of non-verbal information, although it may also be capable of mediating some linguistic functions (see Searleman, 1977, for a review). It has also been considered that the left hemisphere specialization for language functions may derive from more basic time-related abilities such as those involved in temporal resolution, in the programming of rapid sequences of motor movements and in judgements of temporal order and simultaneity (see, for example, Krashen, 1973), and there is much evidence which supports the view that the left hemisphere is primarily involved in the sequential processing of information, whether linguistic or non-linguistic (see Moscovitch, 1979, for a review). Asymmetries of cerebral function are most apparent in man, and in other animals few instances have been observed, with the exception of the left hemisphere control of vocalization in male songbirds (see Nottebohm, 1979, and Walker, 1980, for reviews).

In man the lateralization of language functions probably proceeds gradually, since regardless of the handedness of the individual, damage to the left hemisphere sustained early in life seldom retards language development, while damage to the right affects speech much more often than it does in adults. The two hemispheres may thus be initially equipotential for the mediation of speech and language (see Basser, 1962; Lenneberg, 1967). However, the age at which lateralization is established has been the subject of some controversy; some investigators have argued that the process is complete by the age of five (Krashen, 1973), while others have contended that it is not completed until puberty (Lenneberg, 1967). But a possible anatomical basis for left hemisphere language specialization seems to be present at the time of birth, since post-mortem examinations of both adult and neonatal brains have revealed differences in the size of corresponding left and right temporal lobe sections, with the left being larger in the great majority of cases (see Galaburda *et al.*, 1978; Witelson and Pallie, 1973).

From this short and selective survey of various attempts to localize mental and behavioural functions in the brain it is clear that such attempts encounter several difficulties. These are in part technical, in that there are differences in the structure of the brain, both across species and within individuals of the same species, and these differences in structure are not easily observable, except by post-mortem examination. Thus, even in two members of the same species, procedures employed in lesion and stimulation studies which may appear to involve the same part of the brain may in fact involve rather different functional areas. The interpretation of data from neuropsychological studies is also beset by logical difficulties (see, for example, Gregory, 1961; Weiskrantz, 1968a). Behavioural changes observed following ablation do not necessarily imply that the behaviour is 'localized' in the part of the brain that has been removed or otherwise put out of action, since the brain area in question may have been part of a larger circuit of nuclei and fibre tracts whose functioning has been disturbed or completely disrupted; it may have controlled the functioning of other brain areas which, following ablation, are now released from control, or the observed behavioural changes may result from malfunctioning of the brain area in question due to the formation of scar tissue, rather than to a complete absence of its influence. But the variety of methods available to the physiological psychologist enables inferences about the functioning of the nervous system to be cross-validated through a series of 'converging operations', with the result that the role of the brain in the mediation of certain kinds of behaviour at least is beginning to be established, and some additional examples are given in later chapters.

Methodological advances have also helped to demonstrate that different regions of the brain subserve qualitatively different functions. One of the principal methodological paradigms employed in the analysis of the behavioural consequences of brain lesions has been 'double dissociation' (Teuber, 1955). For example, a number of experiments have shown that monkeys with lesions of the frontal cortex have difficulty with tasks requiring a delayed response but perform normally on visual discrimination tasks. Monkeys with equally large temporal lobe lesions, on the other hand, exhibit no deficit on delayed-response tasks but perform badly on tests of visual discrimination (Harlow *et al.*, 1952; Pribram, 1954). Teuber (1955) has argued that demonstrations of double dissociation provide the only really incontrovertible evidence that one part of the brain is more important than others in the regulation of a particular kind of behaviour. From this kind of evidence it is impossible to argue either that all lesions of similar size produce comparable behavioural deficits, irrespective of location, or that one type of test is more sensitive to the effects of brain damage than the other. However, even this paradigm is not completely free from difficulties (see Weiskrantz, 1968b), and, ideally, a range of qualitatively different tasks, varying in difficulty, should be employed.

The regulation of different functions by different parts of the brain is not fixed at birth but develops gradually, as has been already noted for language functions. The CNS thus possesses a greater degree of plasticity early in life and several studies have shown that similarly placed brain lesions may produce severe deficits in mature animals but little or no effect in immature animals. Scharlock, Tucker and Strominger (1963), for instance, found that kittens, from whom large areas of cortical tissue, inclusive of auditory cortex, were bilaterally removed, were able to discriminate between different tonal patterns when tested at the age of six months. No difference was found between the lesioned animals and their litter-mate controls in the number of trials required to learn the discrimination. However, adult cats in whom similar lesions were made were completely unable to learn to discriminate between the two tonal patterns. Similarly, the effects of frontal lesions on delayed-reaction performance are age-related (Harlow, Akert and Schiltz, 1964). Rhesus monkeys in whom bilateral frontal lesions were made at age five days, when the ability to solve the delayed-reaction problem is totally absent, or at age 150 days, when this ability is still poorly developed, showed little or no deficit on subsequent learning of the task. In contrast, animals who sustained the same operation at the age of two years showed a marked deficit.

Just as the effects of brain lesions have been shown to vary with age in the same species, so the effects of similar lesions in different species do not necessarily produce comparable behavioural deficits (see, for example, Drewe *et al.*, 1970). There are several reasons for such discrepancies. First, it is extremely difficult to devise tasks which are comparable in terms of the demands they make on different species. Second, the possession of language by human beings implies that the strategies underlying task performance are almost certainly different for human beings than for other primates, and hence different parts of the brain are likely to be involved in superficially similar kinds of behaviour. Third, as a result of evolutionary differentiation the structure of the brain has undergone various changes, which may have produced a different distribution of functions. It is this third possibility that we now consider further.

The evolution of the brain

During the course of evolution, different groups of animate beings have followed different phylogenetic paths of diversification from common ancestral forms, as a consequence of the selection pressures involved in the competition for successful adaptation to a variety of changing environments. On the one hand there has been a trend towards greater specialization of function, permitting adaptation to particular 'ecological niches' to take place, and enabling such mammals as the platypus and the spiny anteater, for example, to survive. On the other there has been a trend towards greater versatility, so that dependence on particular environments for survival has been minimized, as, for example, in the case of man and the other primates.

About 400 million years ago, during the Palaeozoic era, the aquatic vertebrates evolved and were shortly followed by the amphibians and, about 50 million years later, by the reptiles. The reptilian form further diverged into mammals and dinosaurs during the first part of the Mesozoic era, about 200 million years ago, and dinosaurs themselves later diverged into pterosaurs and birds. Of the many different types of mammal which developed during the Mesozoic era, only three have survived: the *monotremes*, examples of which are the duck-billed platypus and the spiny anteater, the *marsupial mammals*, such as the opossum and the kangaroo, and the *placental mammals*, such as the cat, the whale, the hedgehog, the rabbit, the rat, the cow and the horse, as well as monkeys, apes and man. Monotremes produce their young in the form of eggs, while the young of marsupials are at the time of birth very immature embryos which are subsequently raised to maturity in a protective pouch or *marsupium*. The offspring of placental mammals are brought to an advanced stage of embryological development within the mother's body prior to birth, being nourished during this period by the placenta, which monotremes and marsupials do not possess.

Quite clearly a number of changes have taken place in the structure of the central nervous system with evolutionary differentiation, one example being that the corpus callosum is not found in monotremes and marsupial mammals, cross-connections between the two hemispheres being mediated primarily by the anterior commissure and the hippocampus. But the most obvious evolutionary trend in the central nervous system is towards increased brain size. The brain of hominids (primitive and modern man), for instance, has approximately tripled in size during the past five million years (see Tobias, 1971). The evidence for such statements comes principally from the fossil record, and in particular from the examination of *endocasts*, which are essentially moulds of the interior of the skull cavity from which brain volume, as well as external features of the brain, can be estimated with a high degree of accuracy. Comparisons of the brains of different surviving vertebrate species also enable a great deal of information to be gathered about the ways in which the brain has evolved.

The increase in brain size with evolutionary development has taken place as the result of an increase in the size of the cerebral hemispheres and, in mammals, through an increase in the size of the cerebral cortex, especially neocortex, relative to the rest of the brain. Among mammals the size of the frontal cortex also increases relative to the total amount of cortex with greater evolutionary differentiation, being only about 3 per cent of total cortex in the cat but reaching 15 per cent in the chimpanzee and 24 per cent in man (Blinkov and Glaser, 1968).

Speculation as to the significance of these evolutionary changes in the size and structure of the brain has given rise to the view that across, although not within, species, brain size and intelligence are related, and partly in support of this view the principles of *encephalization*, *corticalization* and *frontalization* have been advanced. These principles state in effect that with evolutionary development functions earlier mediated by more caudal structures of the brain are progressively taken over by the later more rostral structures of the cerebral hemispheres and by the cerebral cortex. As an extension of this view the more 'complex' patterns of behaviour exhibited by evolutionarily more developed forms are regarded as being mediated by the neocortex and, particularly, by the frontal association areas.

The simplest way of expressing brain size is in terms of the average weight of the brain for a given species and, for mammals, brain weights range from 6,800 g for the whale to 0·43 g for the mouse, with the average brain weight for adult men being 1,440 g. But since brain size tends to co-vary with body size, some correction for body size needs to be made. Expressing brain weight as a ratio of body weight tends to produce an over-compensation for body size, since as body weight increases, the ratio of brain to body weight decreases. This ratio thus 'favours' smaller animals, the brain to body weight ratio for the mouse being 1:38 while for the man it is 1:44. Several attempts to produce an appropriate correction factor have been made of which the most effective is probably an 'encephalization quotient' which expresses the ratio of actual brain size to expected brain size taking body weight and various other factors into account (see Jerison, 1973). Using this procedure Jerison was able to demonstrate that for fish and reptiles increases in brain size have, on the whole, merely kept pace with increases in body size, while for birds and mammals brain size has increased beyond body size requirements, by an average of some 20 per cent. It is to this additional increase in brain size, which has been greatest for man and the other primates, that 'biological intelligence' may be generally related.

Many of the evolutionary changes in the brain are the result of its faster rate of growth compared to that of the skull cavity in which it is housed. Since in man and the other primates the surface area of the neocortex greatly exceeds the inner surface area of the skull cavity, the neocortical mantle folds backwards and forwards over the subcortical structures of the cerebral hemispheres and brain stem. The result is, as noted earlier, that various wrinkles or convolutions are produced in the neocortical layer. But a number of structural and biochemical features of the brain are extremely highly correlated with its size, including the number of cortical cells, the amount of visual cortex, the size of various subcortical structures such as the hippocampus, the concentration of acetylcholine, the ratio of glial cells to neurons and, probably, the degree of convolutedness. Thus, in making comparisons across species, brain size can be regarded as an index of the degree of corticalization and, to a great extent, as an index of brain complexity. The advantage of possessing large areas of neocortex is not simply that these areas aid subcortical centres in the regulation of behaviour. In addition, the anatomy of the neocortex, in particular the fact that much of it consists of divergent conduction paths (see Hebb, 1958) with short interconnecting nerve fibres, enables it to add flexibility to the list of functions regulated by subcortical centres. The importance of the neocortex is not so much that it provides new functions, although to some extent it does this too, but that it enables old functions to be performed in a new way.

In the first place, the divergent conduction paths of the neocortex make it possible for a response to be delayed, rather than elicited automatically. If the entire CNS consisted of parallel conduction paths, where there is a very high probability of information being transmitted from one synaptic level to the next, there would be little physiological basis for 'higher' forms of behaviour at all, since each above-threshold stimulus would automatically and immediately produce a response. Second, the divergent conduction paths of the neocortex make possible a screening of sensory inputs. Again, if this screening were not possible, as would be the case if there were only conduction in parallel within the CNS, then any intense and varied stimulation would produce an overloading of the nervous system resulting in a breakdown of behaviour. Third, as a consequence of the screening of stimuli, selective responding is possible and the ability to respond selectively is an important feature of 'higher' forms of behaviour. Finally, the great increase in the number of cells in the CNS provided by the neocortex enables a more precise control of function to be exercised by the nervous system; the neocortex can thus be regarded in one sense as the most specialized area of the brain, although this does not preclude a cortical area from involvement in more than one function.

If encephalization or corticalization of function takes place then it would be expected that although the regulation of many functions may be shared between subcortical centres and the neocortex, with evolutionary development the neocortex makes a progressively greater contribution to the control of a particular function. Thus damage to the neocortex should affect the same functions to different degrees in different species; the consequences for vision of damage to the visual cortex, for example, should become progressively more severe. Although there is some evidence for this view, both for sensory and motor functions (see Ades, 1959; Marquis, 1935; Neff, 1960; Ruch, 1935) and also for learning (see Bitterman, 1965, 1968; Noback and Moskowitz, 1962), the interpretation of such evidence in terms of encephalization of function has been strongly criticized (see Jerison, 1973; Oakley, 1979; Weiskrantz, 1961, 1977). Jerison suggested that the evidence for encephalization or corticalization implies 'no more than that several species of mammals have evolved different sets of functions for processing certain information, and damage to cortical or subcortical brain structures has different effects in these species'. As an alternative to functional encephalization he argued that

It is much more likely – and would make good evolutionary sense – that sets of related visual functions were elaborated differently in different species when they entered their varied niches, for example, that form vision is different in the rat, cat and monkey, and hence differently organized, rather than that the same form vision is handled by different neural systems (p. 12).

The evidence for 'frontalization' of function with evolutionary development, which is not in any case particularly strong, can be regarded in much the same fashion, and although frontal lobe damage produces certain behavioural changes in animals, for example in the performance of delayed response tasks, referred to above, in man it appears to be behaviour in general, rather than any specific functions (with the exception of some visual functions; see Teuber, 1964), that is affected, in some fairly subtle ways (see Jouandet and Gazzaniga, 1979, for a review). It does not therefore seem very likely that the increase in the amount of frontal cortex, relative to the rest of the brain, in man and the other primates implies any frontalization of function. Higher mental functions are perhaps best regarded as the product of increases in brain size, of which increases in the amount of neocortex generally, and in the amount of frontal cortex, are consequences.

In the latter part of this chapter we have tended to emphasize the cerebral cortex; in the three following chapters the role of subcortical structures in the regulation of behaviour will receive somewhat greater attention.

Chapter 5
Sleep and Dreaming

The measurement of sleep

Although about one third of the human life span is spent in sleep, the functions of sleep are still poorly understood. Nevertheless, the nature of sleep has been considerably clarified by a massive research effort over the past few decades, and this chapter describes some of the principal findings that have emerged.

We begin by attempting to define sleep, wakefulness and consciousness. Sleep is perhaps most simply regarded as a recurring state of inactivity in which awareness of, and responsiveness to, the external environment is diminished. It can be distinguished from unconsciousness due to anaesthesia, or coma resulting from disease or the ingestion of drugs or alcohol, by the ease with which the sleeper can be aroused. It can also be distinguished from stupor, where there is a reduction in motility but little or no loss of awareness. While hypnotic trances possess some of the features of both sleep and wakefulness, hypnotized individuals, although they may be amnesic for events occurring during the period of trance, behave for the most part as if they are fully in touch with the external world. Sleep can be further distinguished from unconsciousness by the fact that the mental activity which takes place during sleep can be subsequently reported in the form of dreams. There is also evidence that selective responding to internal and external events can occur during sleep (see, for example, Antrobus, Antrobus and Fisher, 1965; Oswald, Taylor and Treisman, 1960; Salamy, 1970).

The terms 'wakefulness' and 'consciousness' are often thought to be synonymous, although it is extremely doubtful whether they can be so considered for all species. The contents of consciousness are generally held to be sensations, perceptions, thoughts, memories and affects (see Izard, 1977) but, more importantly, consciousness is regarded as implying self-awareness, the ability of an individual to appreciate his own relationship to an external world, an ability which, almost certainly, many animal species do not possess. Jerison (1973) has argued that this ability only developed to any significant extent with the evolution of mammals. Consciousness is thus a consequence of increased brain size, while sleep and wakefulness are not, since virtually all species alternate periods of sleep and wakefulness. While it may be possible, therefore, to equate consciousness and wakefulness in mammals, it is more difficult to do so in the case of other species.

Up to the mid 1950s sleep and wakefulness were generally regarded as lying at different points or levels on a continuum of central nervous system (CNS) activation and behavioural arousal (see Figure 5.1). The level of CNS activation is reflected in the electroencephalographic, or EEG, record (see Chapter 4) and the EEG records taken from a sleeping individual differ in frequency and amplitude from those obtained from the same individual in

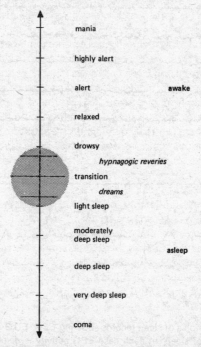

Figure 5.1   A hypothetical view of the continuum of behavioural arousal. (From W. C. Dement, 1973. Commentary in W. B. Webb (ed.), *Sleep: An Active Process* p. 49, Scott, Foresman)

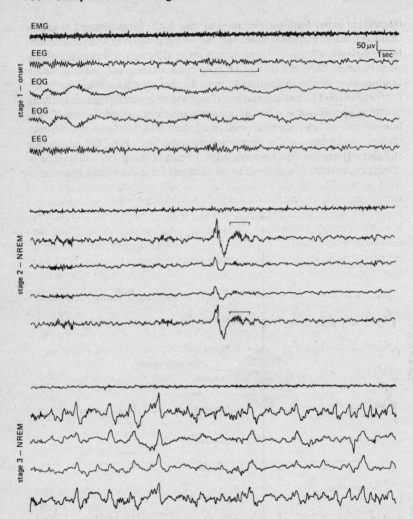

Figure 5.2 Examples of sleep records showing EEG, EOG and EMG activity in different stages of sleep. In each case EEG activity is displayed in the second and fifth channels, EOG in the third and fourth, and EMG in the first. Calibration is 50 μv, 1 second. (Adapted from Figure 1.1, Cohen, 1979, *Sleep and Dreaming: Origins, Nature and Function*, pp. 12–13, Pergamon Press)

the waking state. For much of the time the EEG record during sleep is characterized by high amplitude, low frequency activity. However, the patterns of EEG activity observed during human sleep are not uniform and sleep has been classified into several stages on the basis of EEG criteria. Loomis, Harvey and Hobart (1937) were the first to attempt such a classification and Dement and Kleitman (1957a) later proposed a slightly modified system of sleep stages. Rechtschaffen and Kales (1968), in their standardization of the methodology of sleep stage identification, proposed some revisions and refinements of the system employed by Dement and Kleitman, and this standardized system has gained wide acceptance.

In human adults five sleep stages are generally delineated and to supplement their EEG identification, the electroculogram (EOG) and the submental electromyogram (EMG) are utilized. These stages are shown in Figure 5.2 and consist of stages 1, 2, 3 and 4 and Stage–REM (Rapid Eye Movement sleep). The waking EEG record is shown in Figure 5.3 and the occasional brief periods of wakefulness intervening between periods of sleep are scored as Stage W or Stage 0. For scoring purposes, the all-night EEG record is normally divided up into epochs of thirty or sixty seconds in

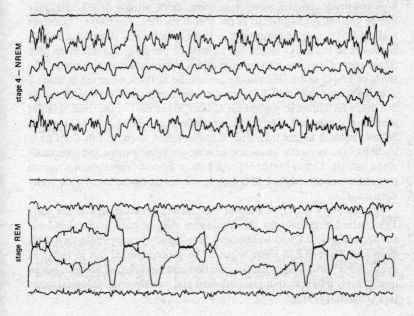

stage 4 – NREM

stage REM

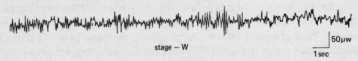

stage — W

$\rceil$50µw

1 sec

Figure 5.3   EEG record accompanying a state of relaxed wakefulness before the onset of sleep. Calibration is 50 µv, 1 second. (From Rechtschaffen and Kales, 1968)

length, and each epoch is categorized as containing one of the six sleep stages (0, 1, 2, 3, 4 and Stage–REM). As can be seen from Figure 5.3 the waking state is mainly characterized by 'alpha' activity (8–12 Hz) with some slightly faster activity. In Stage 1 sleep relatively low amplitude mixed frequency activity occurs, with a predominance of 'theta' activity (4–7 Hz) and very high amplitude sharp waves. The EOG shows slow eye rolling and there is a fairly high tonic EMG, although generally below that of wakefulness. In Stage 2 sleep the EEG shows clear signs of 'sleep spindles' (12–14 Hz) in bursts of 0·5–1 second duration and of 'K complexes', single low frequency high amplitude complex waveforms; some 'delta' activity (0·5–3·5 Hz) may also be present, for as much as 20 per cent of the time. The EOG is quiescent and the EMG may be lower than in Stage 1. In Stage 3 sleep delta activity is present in the EEG record for at least 20 per cent, but not more than 50 per cent of the time, and spindles and K complexes may also occur. The levels of EMG and EOG activity are similar to those observed in Stage 2 sleep. In Stage 4 sleep the EEG record is often completely dominated by delta activity, which must be present for at least 50 per cent of the time. Spindles may also be apparent. The EOG is quiescent and the chin EMG tends to be low, but still higher than that of Stage–REM sleep. In this sleep stage the EEG shows mixed frequency activity, containing theta and sometimes alpha activity, similar to that of Stage 1 sleep. Episodic rapid eye movements (rems) are present and the EMG usually reaches the lowest level found in any sleep stage.

The discovery of REM sleep at the University of Chicago in the early 1950s raised difficulties for the continuum view of sleep and wakefulness shown in Figure 5.1 and wakefulness, non-rapid eye movement (NREM) sleep and Stage–REM sleep began to be conceptualized not in terms of quantitative variations in EEG activation and behavioural arousal, but as qualitatively different, though interlinked and overlapping, biological states (see Dement, 1973).

As will be seen on pp. 138–9, there is good evidence that sleep stages vary in depth, the depth of sleep becoming progressively greater from Stage 1 to Stage 4. As EEG frequency falls, and the amplitude of EEG activity increases, the sleeper also becomes more difficult to awaken. In Stage–REM sleep, however, there is a dissociation between indicators of EEG activation and of behavioural arousal; the EEG record indicates a more aroused state than in sleep stages 2, 3 and 4 yet the depth of sleep, inferred from behavioural measures, is comparable to, and sometimes greater than, that observed in Stage 4. Because of this dissociation between EEG and behavioural measures, Stage–REM sleep became known as 'paradoxical' sleep, and later, in view of the brain mechanisms apparently involved in triggering its onset, as 'hindbrain' or 'rhombencephalic' sleep.

The brain appears to be very active during Stage–REM sleep; for example, the levels of neuronal activity in some parts of the brain are higher during this sleep stage than during wakefulness, and much higher than during NREM sleep. Thus REM sleep has also been described as 'activated' or 'active' sleep (AS) and NREM sleep as 'quiet' sleep (QS), although these terms are generally reserved for the description of sleep in birds and the smaller mammals, and in very young infants, in whom the EEG sleep stages observed in human adults cannot be clearly delineated. However, the EEG records of sleep in primates are fairly similar to those of human sleep, and after about the age of six months or so sleep stages can be differentiated in human infants.

Continuous EEG recording provides the most objective and reliable evidence concerning the activity of the brain during sleep and, as Webb (1973) remarked, the EEG has become 'a primary benchmark or index of sleep' against which other methods of measurement can be evaluated. Information provided by the EEG record is usually supplemented by recordings of EMG and EOG, and frequently also of cardiovascular and electrodermal activity, in order to obtain a more complete picture of the processes occurring during sleep. However, the psychophysiological monitoring of sleep in specially equipped laboratories or clinics is an expensive business, and the collection of reliable data can take a considerable amount of time, around forty hours per subject in many cases. Information concerning the duration and distribution of sleep over relatively long periods under the 'normal' conditions of the home environment has been collected using sleep logs or diaries. The use of sleep diaries is relatively inexpensive and permits data on a large number of people to be gathered, often over a period of weeks or months; hence relatively long term differences in patterns of sleep can be related to age, sex and personality differences using this method, although it depends upon self-reports of sleep behaviour, which may not always be completely reliable. The 'sleep laboratory' and 'sleep diary' methods are essentially complementary, and in the next section studies of sleep as a dependent variable are described, in which one or other of these methods has been employed.

Sleep as a dependent variable

As Johnson (1973) has observed, the ultimate reason for studying sleep is to gain a more comprehensive understanding of waking behaviour and, in pursuit of this goal, the relationship between the structure and patterns of sleep and several temporal, developmental, experiential and behavioural variables has been extensively investigated. We focus here on four aspects of such research: the nocturnal sleep profile, age and sleep, sleep patterns and the quality and duration of sleep and the depth of sleep.

The nocturnal sleep profile

The different stages of human sleep (0, 1, 2, 3, 4 and Stage–REM) are not equally represented in the EEG sleep record. In young adults, Stage 1 occupies about 5 per cent of total sleep time (TST), Stage 2 about 45 per cent, Stage 3 about 7 per cent, Stage 4 about 15 per cent, Stage–REM about 25 per cent and Stage 0 and scoring artifacts together account for about 3

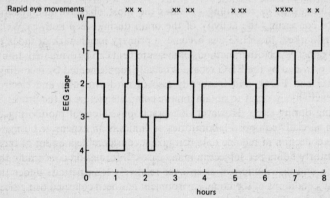

Figure 5.4   Distribution of EEG sleep stages and REMs during a typical night (after Hartmann, 1967, *The Biology of Dreaming*, Thames). REM sleep periods are periods of Stage 1 sleep accompanied by REMs

per cent of the all-night sleep record. Figure 5.4 shows a somewhat simplified sleep stage profile for the young adult. The cycling of these stages, particularly Stage–REM sleep, which appears to have a cycle of about ninety minutes (see Hartmann, 1973), is quite evident and it has been suggested (for example, Kleitman, 1970) that there is a basic rest–activity cycle (BRAC) which is a fundamental rhythm of general bodily activity and is seen both in sleep and wakefulness. However, the existence of the BRAC is still a matter for debate (see Kripke, 1974). It can also be seen from Figure 5.4 that stages 3 and 4 on the one hand, and Stage–REM sleep on the other, are differentially distributed within nocturnal sleep. Stages 3 and 4, known collectively as 'slow-wave sleep' (SWS), occur predominantly during the first half of the sleep period, with successive SWS periods becoming progressively shorter. Although Stage–REM sleep is found throughout the night, successive REM-sleep periods become longer, with the result that the majority of REM sleep occurs in the second half of the night, over 50 per cent in the final third (Agnew, Webb and Williams, 1967). There are differences between individuals both in duration of sleep and in the amount of each sleep stage taken, some of which are described below, but the degree of consistency within any one individual sleep record from one night to the next is quite high (see Clausen, Sersen and Lidsky, 1974; Webb, 1965; Williams, Karacan and Hursch, 1974). The first night of EEG recording is usually discarded since, presumably because subjects are adapting to the unfamiliar laboratory conditions, it tends to yield an atypical sleep profile, with the length of time required to fall asleep being greater than normal, together with an increase in the number of awakenings and a reduction in the amount of Stage–REM sleep, due in part to the delayed appearance of the first Stage–REM period of the night.

Age and sleep

The sleep profile shows very marked changes with age. As is well known, newborn infants sleep for a considerable portion of each twenty-four-hour period. In a study of the duration of sleep in newborn infants, Parmelee, Schulz and Disbrow (1961) found that the mean duration of sleep for seventy-five newborn infants was seventeen hours on the first day of life, and on the second and third days it was 16·5 and 16·2 hours, respectively. The sleep cycle of infants is polycyclic, and the average duration of sleep periods in newborn infants is around four hours. Roffwarg, Dement and Fisher (1964) presented evidence that neonates and infants spend an average of between 50 and 60 per cent of total sleep time in REM sleep. This percentage falls to 29 per cent between the ages of twenty-one and thirty-one months and stabilizes at around 24 per cent between the ages of eight and eleven years (Webb and Agnew, 1969). In premature infants, REM sleep as a percentage of TST increases with the degree of prematurity and REM sleep percentages of 58 per cent at thirty-six to thirty-eight weeks, 67 per cent at thirty-three to thirty-five weeks and 80 per cent (one case only) at thirty weeks of gestational age have been reported (Parmelee *et al.*, 1967). The percentage of Stage–REM sleep tends to decline slightly with increasing age beyond young adulthood, falling to between 15 and 20 per cent after the age of sixty (Feinberg and Carlson, 1968; Kahn and Fisher, 1969; Webb and Agnew, 1969). The percentage of Stage 4 sleep also begins to show a progressive reduction in the late thirties, leading to very low amounts, or even complete absence, in old age, and there is some indication that this tendency is more marked in men than in women (Williams, Karacan and Hursch, 1974). Evidence from sleep diary studies also suggests that the duration and frequency of nocturnal awakenings increase with age and that TST is reduced (see, for example, Tune, 1969). However, the number of daytime naps, in which the percentages of REM sleep and of SWS vary depending upon the time at which the nap is taken, tends to become greater with age. To some extent, therefore, the distribution of sleep with increasing age can be described as a reversion to the polycyclic pattern of infancy. In general, late evening naps tend to contain much more SWS, while naps taken in the morning contain much more REM sleep (Karacan *et al.*, 1970; Maron, Rechtshaffen and Wolpert, 1964).

Sleep patterns and the quality and duration of sleep

The quality of sleep also appears to bear some relation to the nocturnal sleep profile. In a now classic study, Monroe (1967) investigated the sleep of self-reported 'good' and 'poor' sleepers, using a sample of men in their mid twenties, selected from a larger population on the basis of their answers to a questionnaire. Each group ('good' and 'poor' sleepers) was composed of sixteen people. Good sleepers described themselves as usually falling asleep in less than ten minutes and as never taking more than fifteen minutes; they hardly ever woke up during the night and, if they did, almost always experienced no difficulty in falling asleep once more. Poor sleepers, on the other hand, described themselves as normally taking about sixty minutes to fall asleep and as always taking more than thirty minutes; they woke up on average at least once during the night and, when they did so, experienced great difficulty in returning to sleep. Each member of these two groups subsequently slept in a sleep laboratory for seven hours on two nights.

Monroe found that the good sleepers, compared to poor sleepers, spent more time asleep, spent less time in lighter sleep, particularly Stage 2, and more time in REM sleep. They awoke less often and fell asleep more rapidly. However, the proportion of time spent in SWS was about the same for the two groups, although poor sleepers took longer to reach it. This group also took longer to reach the first REM sleep period of the night. The motility of poor sleepers was also higher, particularly in the second half of the night, and rectal temperature was higher throughout the night. In general the level of physiological activity was higher for poor sleepers not only during sleep but also during wakefulness. Monroe observed that differences in the quality of sleep normally obtained by good and poor sleepers may be more marked than is suggested by his study. Most of the good sleepers rated their laboratory sleep as worse than the sleep they typically obtained. The majority of poor sleepers, on the other hand, rated it as considerably better.

This study makes clear that differences between self-reported good and poor sleepers are not merely at the level of verbal report, but that there can be marked differences in their sleep profiles. Nevertheless, some evidence suggests that assessments of sleep quality depend more on the subjective recall of a night's sleep and less on objective measures recorded during sleep (Hauri, 1970).

Differences have also been observed in a number of studies between self-reported 'long' and 'short' sleepers (Hartmann, 1973). The former are defined as individuals who report themselves as normally sleeping for more than nine hours per night and the latter as sleeping for less than six hours, these reports being checked against sleep diaries. Comparisons of the sleep profiles of these two groups with those of 'normal' sleepers have shown that differences between long, short and 'normal' sleepers tend to be principally in the amount of REM sleep taken, long sleepers having more REM sleep than the other two groups. Compared to normals, long sleepers tend to spend more time awake and in REM sleep, while short sleepers spend less time in Stages 1, 2, 3 and REM sleep. The REM sleep periods of long sleepers also appear to be more intense, as inferred from rem density measures, and personality tests indicate that this group is more anxious and introverted, while short sleepers tend to be more extraverted and sociable.

There are thus quite consistent differences among individuals in the amount of sleep that is normally taken and, as Webb (1970) has noted, such individual differences in natural sleep lengths have been observed from birth to old age. However, there is virtually no evidence bearing on the question of the determinants of differences in sleep lengths, although Webb utlined a series of possibilities including stable and transient biophysiological states, early learning, stress, task demands and voluntarily imposed routines. It has frequently been assumed that there is a 'need' to sleep for a particular length of time, although whether such a need should be construed as biological or social remains unclear. On the one hand, there are a few well-documented cases of healthy individuals who seem to be able to manage the demands of their waking lives perfectly well on very small amounts of sleep indeed (Jones and Oswald, 1968; Meddis, Pearson and Langford, 1973), while on the other complaints of insufficient or inadequate amounts of sleep are common. Most people experience insomnia at some time or another but for some individuals it remains a persistent problem. However, the nature and extent of the difficulties encountered in either attaining or maintaining sleep vary considerably from person to person and it is thus difficult to be certain about the prevalence of insomnia in the general population. But in one recent large-scale questionnaire study, cited by Webb and Cartwright (1978), 6 per cent of men and 14 per cent of women reported themselves as experiencing insomnia either 'fairly often' or 'often'. Insomnia can be associated with both organic and functional disorders and may be attributable to any of several causes which may affect the nocturnal sleep profile in different ways. Chronic or acute anxiety, for example, may delay sleep onset, while in depression early morning awakenings are frequent and the time taken to reach the first REM sleep period of the night is reduced (see Stonehill, 1976; Zung, 1970).

The nocturnal sleep profile, which indicates how much of what kind of sleep is being lost, and the assessment of current psychological state, which may reveal potential causes of sleep disturbances, can suggest approaches to the management of insomnia in individual cases (see Kales, 1972). However, the most common way of treating insomnia has been to prescribe hypnotic drugs, of which there are several kinds. Although hypnotics generally reduce the time required to fall asleep, and decrease the number of mid-night awakenings, they may also suppress REM sleep and can lead to various forms of drug dependence (see Clift, 1975; Oswald, 1973).

The depth of sleep

Several measures have been used in attempts to compare the various stages of sleep in terms of their relative depth and, in particular, to determine whether REM sleep is 'lighter' or 'deeper' sleep than that found in other sleep stages. One of the most obvious indicators of the depth of sleep is the intensity of stimulation, usually auditory, required to rouse the sleeper, generally termed the awakening or arousal threshold. However, the results obtained with this measure have been somewhat ambiguous (see Snyder and Scott, 1972), partly because auditory stimuli presented during REM sleep are sometimes incorporated into dream reports obtained from the subsequent awakening. This prolongs the awakening time, resulting in an unduly high threshold value and hence a probable overestimation of the depth of sleep. The threshold values of REM sleep thus tend to be extremely variable (see Price and Kremen, 1980, for a review).

Other studies of sleep depth, therefore, have not defined the criterion response in terms of an awakening, but have required subjects to make a behavioural response (for example, pressing a microswitch taped to the hand) during sleep itself. The response rate to stimuli of varying intensity is taken as an indicator of sleep depth. The results of such studies indicate that both delta sleep and REM sleep are of comparable depth. Williams, Morlock and Morlock (1966) however, argued that the low response rates observed during REM sleep were the result of the sleeper's attention being directed to internal rather than external events, while those observed during delta sleep were the consequence of the depression of physiological activity.

In order to test this hypothesis, they required subjects to discriminate between two tones differing in pitch, one of the tones being designated as 'neutral' and the other as 'critical'. They found that responses decreased from Stage 1 to Stage 4, with REM sleep having a response rate similar to that of Stage 4. However, in the second part of the experiment, subjects were instructed that failure to respond to the 'neutral' tone would entail no unpleasant consequences, whereas failure to respond to the 'critical' tone would be punished. Punishment took the form of a loud siren and a flashing light coupled with electric shock. Williams *et al.* found that the frequency of responding to the 'critical' tone during Stage REM increased markedly under the punishment condition, the response frequency exceeding that of Stage 2, while responding during the remaining stages of sleep was little affected. This finding would appear to provide strong support for the original hypothesis, and some additional support has been furnished, in a similar study, by Langford, Meddis and Pearson (1974).

Sleep deprivation

Many investigators, beginning with Patrick and Gilbert in 1896, have been interested in the effects of loss of sleep, in the expectation that the bio-chemical, physiological and behavioural changes resulting from sleep deprivation might provide some information concerning the functions of sleep. Most sleep deprivation studies have examined the effects of *total sleep deprivation*, that is, of the number of hours of continuous wakefulness, irrespective of the timing of the normal sleep period; several studies of the effects of *partial sleep deprivation*, in which the amount of sleep is restricted to some fraction of that taken normally, and of *selective sleep deprivation*, in which individuals are deprived of a particular kind of sleep, either REM sleep or SWS, have also been conducted.

The length of the deprivation period in the majority of total sleep deprivation studies is generally less than 100 hours, although in some studies it has been in excess of 200 hours and the longest period appears to be 264 hours (Johnson, Slye and Dement, 1965). In this study observations were made on a seventeen-year-old American male high-school student who stayed awake for this length of time in order to beat the previous world record for the number of hours without sleep as part of a research project for the San Diego Science Fair.

The consequences of total sleep deprivation seem to be principally psycho-logical and there are few major biochemical or physiological changes, although body temperature declines progressively and EEG frequency slows considerably, with a corresponding increase in amplitude (see Horne, 1978, for a review). However, sleep deprivation imposes a slight strain on energy production and transfer systems, although it is unclear whether this is attributable solely to lack of sleep or to the increased effort expended in maintaining wakefulness. If, as often happens in sleep deprivation studies, the sleep-deprived individual is required to achieve a reasonable standard of task performance during the deprivation period, compensatory bio-chemical or physiological changes may occur and these will add to the biological cost of continued wakefulness. But although the biological effects of total sleep deprivation can be regarded as mildly stressful and debilitating, they are not long-lasting, and recovery takes place rapidly following a period of sleep taken *ad libitum*, which is always much less than the period of sleep deprivation and only about 50 per cent above the normal duration of sleep. For example, the first recovery sleep of the American student who remained awake for 264 hours lasted for only fourteen hours forty minutes (Gulevich, Dement and Johnson, 1966). In general, studies of the first recovery sleep following total sleep deprivation indicate that the percentage of total sleep time (TST) spent in Stage 4 sleep increases compared to baseline levels, while that spent in REM sleep declines (Berger and Oswald, 1962; Williams *et al.*, 1964). The time taken to reach Stage 4 is reduced and the depth of sleep increases. Sleep gradually returns to normal on subsequent recovery nights, and even after 200 hours of deprivation baseline levels are reached by about the fourth recovery night.

The main psychological effects of total sleep deprivation are on task performance and on mood. The average level of performance at many tasks, particularly those which require continuous information processing with no opportunity for rest pauses, shows a progressive deterioration with the number of hours of wakefulness and the variability of performance also increases (Wilkinson, 1965, 1968). As Broadbent (1963, p. 207) has put it, in summarizing the effects of sleep deprivation on performance, 'a (sleep deprived) man is not like a child's mechanical toy which goes slower as it runs down, nor is he like a car engine which continues until its fuel is exhausted and then stops dead. He is like a motor which after much use misfires, runs normally for a while, then falters again and so on.'

However, the extent of the performance deterioration depends both upon features of the task, such as task duration and task complexity, and on the interest, motivation and probably also the personality of the subject. Furthermore, deterioration can be somewhat reduced or modulated by certain environmental and motivational factors such as loud noise and the provision of knowledge of results and of incentives and also by activating drugs. These findings, and others, suggest that the state of sleep deprivation is one of low arousal, a view supported by the demonstration that lapses of attention associated with 'microsleeps' occur during task performance following sleep deprivation (Williams, Lubin and Goodnow, 1959). These lapses tend to follow a circadian pattern (see Chapter 9) and are negatively correlated with body temperature. The extent of performance deterioration is thus greater at night than during the day. The circadian rhythm is an important mediator of the effects of sleep deprivation on performance and mood; and alterations of normal sleep schedules, while preserving the same total amount of sleep, or even extending the normal duration of sleep (the 'Rip van Winkle effect') also produce adverse effects on performance and changes in mood (Taub and Berger, 1969, 1974).

Some studies have reported psychotic-like signs in some sleep-deprived subjects; these changes are only temporary and generally fairly minor, even if they can be described as 'delusional' or 'hallucinatory'. It would probably be more appropriate to regard them as expressions of irritability and as misperceptions. Certainly the mood changes observed after one night of sleep deprivation indicate that subjects rate themselves as being less good-natured, cheerful, considerate, friendly and relaxed, as well as less lively, alert, efficient and able to concentrate (see Naitoh, 1975) and lack of sleep also impairs visual functions, such as binocular convergence (see Horne, 1975).

The effects of partial sleep deprivation are likely to be of more immediate practical significance than those of total sleep deprivation, since the demands of many occupations probably result in chronic limitations of normal sleep length (see Masterton, 1965), the sleep debt thus incurred being made up on 'rest days' or weekends (see Tune, 1968). Since SWS occurs during the first part of the sleep period and the majority of REM sleep later, the main effect of partial sleep deprivation is to reduce REM sleep time. For effects of partial sleep deprivation to appear in task performance, the limitation of sleep length needs to be quite severe (see Wilkinson, 1972) so that the time spent in SWS is likely to be affected. Moderate restrictions of sleep length thus do not impair performance to any great extent. Webb and Agnew (1974), for example, restricted the sleep of their subjects to five and a half hours per night for sixty days. Although several performance tests and measures of mood were administered each week, only one performance test, vigilance, a test of sustained attention (see Chapter 9), showed any noticeable impairment compared to control levels and the mood scales showed no effects of the régime.

The effects of comparatively short periods of partial sleep deprivation on patterns of sleep take the form of an absolute increase in the amount of time spent in Stage 4 and a reduction in the time devoted to the remaining sleep stages (Dement and Greenberg, 1966; Webb and Agnew, 1965). In Webb and Agnew's (1974) study of prolonged sleep deprivation an increase in the absolute amount of Stage 4 was also obtained, although by the fifth week this had reverted to baseline levels. The initial effect on REM sleep was a sharp reduction compared to baseline values and over the whole study REM sleep was reduced by an average of 25 per cent.

The research on total and partial sleep deprivation suggests both that the physiological and psychological effects of even prolonged deprivation periods are not as dramatic as might be imagined and, perhaps more importantly for theories of sleep function, that SWS is a more critical type of sleep, for human beings at least, than is REM sleep. However, the results of early selective or differential sleep deprivation studies suggested, if anything, the reverse and we now turn to research concerned with the selective deprivation of REM and of Stage 4 sleep.

In 1960, Dement reported the results of the first study of 'dream deprivation'. As soon as REM sleep could be identified from the EEG and eye movement records, subjects were awakened for a brief period and subsequently allowed to go back to sleep. This procedure was used throughout the night on each occasion that an REM period appeared and resulted in a loss of 90 per cent or more of the total REM sleep time, inferred from baseline recordings on uninterrupted nights. Dement deprived his subjects of REM sleep in this way for between two and five consecutive nights. Control subjects were awakened for the same number of times during NREM sleep over a similar period and the effects of both types of deprivation on waking behaviour and subsequent sleep were observed. Further experiments of a similar kind were reported by Dement and Fisher (1963).

The principal results of these experiments were as follows: (1) in all twenty-one subjects who participated the number of awakenings required to suppress REM sleep rose markedly as the number of deprivation nights increased, since REM periods appeared with greater frequency; (2) on recovery nights the percentage of REM sleep increased to up to 150 per cent of the baseline level; (3) the waking behaviour of eleven subjects deprived of REM sleep for five consecutive nights showed a variety of changes. All showed increased anxiety, irritability, lack of concentration and fatigue in varying degrees. Six out of eight men developed an increased desire for food and also put on weight during the deprivation period.

Since other studies (Clemes and Dement, 1967; Dement, 1965; Sampson, 1966) observed similar – and in some cases more dramatic – psychological changes following REM sleep deprivation, it was concluded that REM sleep might be important in the maintenance of mental health. However, such speculations appear to be ill-founded; a number of carefully conducted experiments, while confirming both the progressive increase in the number of awakenings required to maintain REM sleep deprivation and the REM sleep 'rebound' effect (although individual differences in the response to REM sleep deprivation have also been observed: see Cartwright, Monroe and Palmer, 1967), have failed to find any evidence of even minor psychological changes following REM sleep deprivation (see Naitoh, 1975). Many of the earlier studies have also been shown to contain a number of methodological deficiencies (see Vogel, 1975). Although Dement considered that his initial results might be due to the effects of 'dream deprivation' it is now apparent that dreaming occurs in NREM sleep as well (see pp. 155–9, below), and REM sleep deprivation thus cannot be equated with dream elimination. Dement, in fact, has disavowed the idea that impairment of mental health can result from the deprivation of REM sleep (Dement, 1969). Indeed this procedure does not exacerbate schizophrenic symptoms (Vogel and Traub, 1968) and seems to alleviate those of depression (Vogel *et al.*, 1975). However, while the psychological effects of REM sleep deprivation in human beings, including those on task performance (Johnson, 1973), seem to be no greater than those following equivalent amounts of NREM sleep deprivation, except, perhaps, in the case of higher level functions such as those involved in creative thinking (Glaubman *et al.*, 1978; Lewin and Glaubman, 1975), in animals there may be increases in motivated behaviour and in cortical excitability (see Vogel, 1975, for a comprehensive review). Some types of learning may also be impaired. It is possible, therefore, that REM sleep serves different functions in animals and human beings.

As with REM sleep deprivation, the selective deprivation of Stage 4 sleep can only be maintained for any length of time by increasing the number of awakenings, although in general it is an easier procedure to carry out. Stage 4 sleep also shows a 'rebound' effect following deprivation, and although there is little evidence concerning behavioural effects it appears that changes in mood are similar to those observed with total sleep deprivation and that the effects on performance are slight (see, for example, Agnew, Webb and Williams, 1967). However, the effects of prolonged periods of Stage 4 deprivation seem not to have been examined. It can be concluded, therefore, that studies of selective sleep deprivation in human beings have not, as yet, materially assisted the development of theories of sleep function.

Theories of sleep

Theories of sleep can be divided into two broad categories. The first comprises theories bearing on the brain mechanisms and processes involved in the onset and maintenance of NREM sleep, REM sleep and wakefulness. The second category comprises theories bearing on the functions of sleep and can be subdivided into theories of the function of NREM sleep, and in particular of SWS, and of REM sleep respectively. The former tend to be variations on a single theme, that the function of SWS is to promote the restitution of bodily processes of growth and repair, while the latter tend to be much more diverse. This section begins with a description of the physiology of sleep, together with an outline of the biological bases of sleep and wakefulness, and proceeds to a discussion of theories of sleep function.

The physiology of sleep

At sleep onset and during the descent into SWS, parasympathetic activity (see Chapter 4) predominates and there is a gradual slowing down of physiological processes. Breathing becomes deeper and more regular, heart rate and electrodermal activity show a progressive decline, body temperature falls and muscular relaxation occurs (see Snyder and Scott, 1972). The activity of the brain is reduced during sleep stages 1–4, although, as noted on p. 139 above, responsiveness to external stimulation may be greater than in REM sleep, particularly during Stage 2. In general, then, the physiological activity observed during NREM sleep is characterized by relative tranquillity.

Physiological activity during REM sleep. Physiological activity during REM sleep presents a marked contrast to that observed during NREM sleep. As mentioned on p. 132, the term 'REM sleep' derives from the rems, first observed under laboratory conditions by Aserinsky and Kleitman (1953). The eye movements of REM sleep are bilaterally synchronous and conjugate, similar to the saccadic eye movements observable during wakefulness when the individual is fixating points in his visual field. The actual movements have a duration of between 100 and 200 msec, and can be recorded in both the vertical and horizontal planes. They are not continuously present during REM sleep but are only found for between 15 and 40 per cent of the time; rems are thus a *phasic* phenomenon of REM sleep. Another phasic phenomenon of REM sleep, which has been observed in the cat (see Jouvet, 1967), is a series of high voltage spikes, appearing with a frequency of 60 to 70 per minute in the pons, the lateral geniculate nucleus and the occipital cortex. These are known as ponto-geniculo-occipital (PGO) spikes. Muscular 'twitching' also occurs, although there is no change in the number of gross bodily movements, and cardiovascular, respiratory and electrodermal activity all increase and become much more variable (see Snyder and Scott, 1972).

The principal *tonic*, or continuous, physiological changes during REM sleep are the already noted low voltage fast activity of the EEG and a complete lack of tonus (atonia) of the dorsal neck muscles, first observed in the cat by Jouvet, Michel and Mounier (1959). In man there is a loss of tonus in the extralaryngeal muscles, in the region of the jaw (Berger, 1961), and extensor and stretch reflexes cannot be as easily elicited during REM sleep as during other sleep stages (Hodes and Dement, 1964).

Brain activity is markedly elevated during REM sleep; cerebral blood flow surpasses normal waking levels (Townsend, Prinz and Obrist, 1973) and recordings from a number of brain sites, such as the diencephalon and the midbrain reticular system (see Chapter 4), show very high neuronal discharge rates, indicative of massive increases in arousal (see Williams, Holloway and Griffiths, 1973). Hippocampal theta activity, with a frequency of around 6 Hz, which is generally regarded as a further indicator of brain activation, is also present. Evoked potentials to external stimulation tend to be considerably reduced in amplitude. There is thus no doubt that the physiological concomitants of REM sleep are dramatically different from those of any other sleep stage and as will be seen on pp. 151–5, considerable theoretical attention has been devoted to attempts to explain its function.

Hormonal changes during sleep. Hormonal changes also occur during sleep, and it seems that the secretion of human growth hormone is particularly affected. During wakefulness there is little change in growth hormone secretion, although increases may occur following exercise or exposure to stress. But growth hormone begins to rise shortly after sleep onset and reaches maximal levels in SWS (Sassin *et al.*, 1969). The secretion of human growth hormone thus appears to require the presence of SWS. Prolactin, luteinizing hormone and testosterone, all of which, like growth hormone, are concerned with tissue growth and development, are also secreted in large amounts during sleep.

Neural mechanisms of sleep and wakefulness

A parsimonious explanation of the way in which the brain regulates sleep and wakefulness would be to hypothesize that there is a neural system responsible for the maintenance of wakefulness which periodically 'runs down', either in response to a reduction in sensory input, as a consequence of muscular relaxation, through the inhibitory effects of environmental stimulation, or perhaps because the system possesses an inherent rhythmicity, being at times highly active and at others virtually inactive, the result being the onset of sleep. While there is considerable support for the existence of a wakefulness system, as will be seen below, there is little evidence in favour of 'passive theories' of sleep, such as that outlined above, and 'active theories' of sleep, which state that sleep occurs through the intervention of active sleep-inducing mechanisms, have gained widespread acceptance (see Crow, 1975; Williams, Holloway and Griffiths, 1973). We begin by outlining the evidence for the existence of a wakefulness system, and proceed to a discussion of the brain mechanisms thought to be involved in the onset and maintenance of NREM and REM sleep respectively.

The regulation of wakefulness. The ARAS, located in the centre of the brainstem in the vicinity of the central canal (see Chapter 4), appears to be a diffuse tonic energizing system involved in the maintenance of wakefulness (see Lindsley, 1960; Magoun, 1958). The involvement of the brainstem in the regulation of wakefulness began to be appreciated in the 1930s as a result of studies conducted by the Belgian neurophysiologist, Bremer (see Bremer, 1954). Working with cats, Bremer investigated the effects of transections of the brainstem above and below the level of the cerebellum on EEG and behavioural manifestations of sleep and wakefulness (see Figure 5.5). In the former preparation (known as the *cerveau isolé*), in which the transection was made between the superior and inferior colliculi in the midbrain, only EEG and behavioural signs of sleep were observed following recovery from the operation, while in the latter preparation (known as the *encéphale isolé*), in which the transection was made in the lower part of the medulla, alternating periods of sleep and wakefulness were apparent. Bremer interpreted these findings in terms of deafferentation, a reduction in the amount of sensory stimulation reaching the cerebral cortex, and considered that the absence of signs of wakefulness in the *cerveau isolé* preparation was attributable to the reduction of sensory input to the brain from the cranial nerves, the majority of which enter the brainstem between the levels of section producing the *cerveau isolé* and the *encéphale isolé* preparations. Subsequent studies demonstrated this interpretation to be incorrect. Moruzzi and Magoun (1949) showed that electrical stimulation of the midbrain reticular formation in the cat produced or accentuated both EEG and behavioural signs of wakefulness, while lesions of the same area were found to result in a comatose state similar to that observed in the *cerveau isolé* preparation (Lindsley, Bowden and Magoun, 1949). Further, Lindsley *et al.*, (1950), also working with cats, reported that the restriction of input to the brain achieved

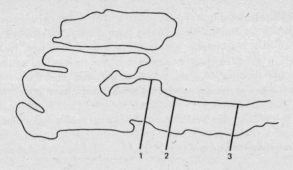

Figure 5.5   Sagittal view of a cat brain showing the level of section producing a *cerveau isolé* (1), a midpontine pretrigeminal (2) and an *encéphale isolé* (3) preparation. See text for explanation

by cutting the ascending somatosensory pathways in the brainstem, while leaving the ARAS intact, did not alter the sleep–wakefulness pattern of the EEG, whereas transection of the ARAS at the same level, sparing the sensory pathways, produced only EEG sleep patterns (see Figure 5.6). Batini *et al.* (1958) transected the brainstem at a point just caudal to the level of the *cerveau isolé* preparation, producing a *midpontine pretrigeminal* preparation (see Figure 5.5). This preparation exhibited greatly increased EEG and behavioural signs of wakefulness, even though the sensory input from the cranial nerves remained the same as for the *cerveau isolé* preparation. Furthermore, when this remaining sensory input was removed, signs of wakefulness were still apparent. EEG and behavioural manifestations of wakefulness and arousal do not, therefore, seem to depend upon the input to the brain from the ascending sensory pathways and the cranial nerves, but upon the integrity of the ARAS. The ARAS can thus be regarded as a mechanism for the promotion of wakefulness. However, for a number of reasons (see Crow, 1975; Williams, Holloway and Griffiths, 1973), notably the observation that over an extended period some recovery of the sleep–wakefulness cycle can take place in the *cerveau isolé* (Batsel, 1960) and midpontine pretrigeminal preparations (Zernicki, 1968), it appears unlikely that the ARAS is the only such mechanism and it is probable that a further 'wakefulness centre', generally assumed to be the posterior hypothalamus, is located above the level of section producing the *cerveau isolé*. The posterior

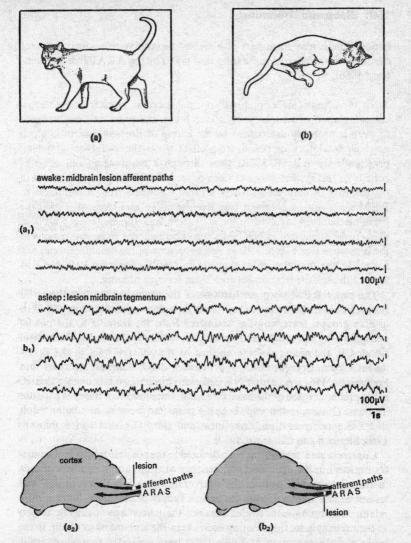

Figure 5.6 Effects of bilateral section of (a) the classical afferent pathways and (b) the ARAS in the midbrain. Cat (a) with bilateral section of the classical afferent pathways in the midbrain sparing the ARAS (a$_2$) stands awake with characteristic waking EEG (a$_1$). Cat (b) with midbrain ARAS interrupted, sparing the classical afferent pathways (b$_2$), lies somnolent with sleeping EEG (b$_1$). (After Lindsley et al., 1950, p. 496)

hypothalamus may form part of a second arousal system which activates the cortex by a different route from that taken by the ARAS (see Routten-berg, 1966).

Sleep mechanisms. Since apparently normal sleep can result from the electri-cal stimulation of various parts of the brain, the onset and maintenance of sleep is probably determined by the action of sleep mechanisms, which exert an inhibitory or deactivating effect upon the wakefulness system, principally the ARAS, rather than through a spontaneous reduction of activity in this system. Since at sleep onset NREM sleep occurs, except in the disorder of narcolepsy, where a rapid transition from wakefulness to REM sleep can be observed (see Rechtschaffen and Dement, 1969), the brain mechanisms involved in the shift from wakefulness to sleep are also likely to be implicated in NREM sleep. There appear to be two regions of the brainstem (see Figure 5.7), as well as an area of the basal forebrain, just rostral to the hypothalamus, that are primarily concerned with NREM sleep, although the relation between them remains obscure.

The two NREM sleep mechanisms of the brainstem are first the *raphé system* (*raphé* meaning 'crease' or 'seam') which comprises a series of nuclei, in nine groups, traversing the brainstem from the medulla to the caudal midbrain (Jouvet, 1967), and, second, an EEG synchronizing mechanism situated in the vicinity of the nucleus of the solitary tract at the pons–medulla boundary (Cordeau and Mancia, 1959; Magnes, Moruzzi and Pompeiano, 1961). A further NREM sleep mechanism is probably located in the preoptic region of the basal forebrain, since lesions of this area produce insomnia (Nauta, 1946), while both electrical and thermal stimulation result in EEG synchronization, drowsiness and sleep (Roberts and Robinson, 1969; Sterman and Clemente, 1962).

Considerable attention has been devoted to the possible function of neuro-transmitters in the onset and maintenance of sleep. Large numbers of cells in the *raphé* system contain the neurotransmitter 5-HT (serotonin), and lesions of this system deplete the brain's supply of serotonin. Since a close relation has been demonstrated between the percentage of cells destroyed in the *raphé* system, the resulting decrease in the amount of serotonin in the brain and the reduction of TST, it has been suggested that serotonin is implicated in the onset and maintenance of sleep (see Jouvet, 1969). But although there is considerable support for this view, some difficulties remain (see King, 1974; Wyatt, 1972).

The onset of REM sleep has been held to result from release of the neurotransmitter noradrenalin from a group of cells known as the *locus coeruleus* (see Jouvet, 1967, 1969), which is situated in the pons (see Figure 5.7). One

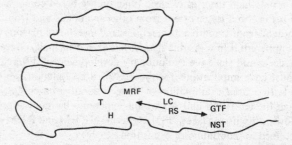

Figure 5.7   Sagittal view of a cat brain showing the location of the principal sleep mechanisms mentioned in the text. T: thalamus. H: hypothalamus. M R F: midbrain reticular formation. L C: *locus coeruleus.* R S: *raphé* system. G T F: gigantocellular tegmental field in the pontine reticular formation. N S T: nucleus of the solitary tract at the pons–medulla boundary

of the effects of activity in the *locus coeruleus* is to activate an inhibitory centre, the *nucleus reticularis pontis caudalis* (NRPC), which is also located in the pons, and destruction of the NRPC abolishes the motor inhibition characteristic of REM sleep. More recent work suggests that cells of the gigantocellular tegmental field (see Figure 5.7), an area of the pons which includes the NRPC, are involved in the initiation and maintenance of REM sleep (Hobson, McCarley and Wyzinski, 1975; McCarley and Hobson, 1975). This area contains cells which trigger both the tonic and phasic components of REM sleep, and alternating periods of increased activity in cells of the *locus coeruleus* and in those of the gigantocellular tegmental field, which are both excited by the neurotransmitter acetylcholine and inhibited by noradrenalin, are probably responsible for the cycling of REM sleep. But although much has been learned about where the neural mechanisms responsible for both NREM and REM sleep are located in the brain, and about their mode of operation, the factors controlling the transition from wakefulness to NREM sleep, and from NREM to REM sleep, are not yet fully understood.

The functions of sleep

The data on which theories of sleep function are based come mainly from human beings, to a lesser extent from other mammals and from birds and scarcely at all from amphibia, fish, reptiles and insects, for reasons which will become apparent below. As this chapter has been principally concerned with human sleep, and since the evolutionary development of different types of sleep must have implications for theories of sleep function, we begin this section with a brief examination of the comparative psychology of sleep. Although the terms QS and AS would sometimes be more appropriate in the following discussion (see p. 133), the terms NREM and REM sleep have been retained for continuity of exposition.

Among warm-blooded animals, with the possible exception of mono-tremes (egg-laying mammals), both NREM and REM sleep are found, and in cats and primates NREM sleep is generally divided into deep (equivalent to SWS) and light sleep on the basis of both EEG and behavioural indi-cators. Greater emphasis tends to be placed on behavioural indicators (such as regular and prolonged periods of immobility accompanied by charac-teristic postural changes and raised response thresholds) in amphibia, fish and especially reptiles, where because of the lack of cortical development compared to mammals, the EEG record is less useful in providing un-ambiguous evidence of the presence of sleep. Mammals vary widely in TST, the amount of time in each twenty-four-hour period spent in sleep (see Meddis, 1975, 1979, for reviews). There are also wide variations in the amounts of time spent by different mammalian species in NREM and REM sleep and in the length of the NREM–REM sleep cycle (the length of time elapsing between the end of one REM-sleep period and the end of the next, which is about ninety minutes in man).

Correlational studies suggest that factors related both to energy conserva-tion requirements and to the demands and pressures imposed by the environment are important determinants of species differences in sleep behaviour. For example, metabolic rate (the rate at which bodily tissues consume oxygen) has been shown to be positively related to TST (Zepelin and Rechtschaffen, 1974) and inversely related to the length of the NREM–REM cycle (Hartmann, 1973); large mammals with low metabolic rates, such as the elephant, spend less time asleep (around four hours, about half of which is NREM sleep) and have comparatively long NREM–REM cycles (about 120 minutes), while small mammals, with high metabolic rates, such as the mouse, sleep for more than thirteen hours (about twelve hours of which consists of NREM sleep) and have very short NREM–REM cycles (about twelve minutes).

Using factor analytic techniques, Allison and Cicchetti (1976) surveyed thirty-nine mammalian species in order to assess the interrelationships between several ecological and constitutional variables and the amounts of time per twenty-four-hour period spent in SWS (which in their sample accounted for, on average, 82 per cent of TST) and in REM sleep. The ecological variables they examined included the degree of protection afforded by the normal sleeping place and the extent to which the species was in danger of being preyed upon, while the constitutional variables consisted of brain and body weight, life span and gestation time. Allison and Cicchetti found that body weight was the best predictor of SWS, smaller mammals taking more SWS, and since brain weight and metabolic rate are strongly related to body weight, these variables are also highly predictive of the duration of SWS. Allison and Cicchetti also found, however, that an overall danger index, in which measures of vulnerability to predation and of the safety of sleeping quarters were combined, was a good predictor of the amount of SWS and proved to be the best predictor of the amount of REM sleep. A further finding was that REM sleep duration was strongly associated with gestation time. Together, body weight and overall danger accounted for 58 per cent of the variability in SWS, and the combination of overall danger and gestation time for 66 per cent of the variability in the duration of REM sleep. In general, the amounts of time spent by different mammalian species in NREM and REM sleep tend to be positively correlated, although REM sleep seldom exceeds 25 per cent of TST or 33 per cent of the time spent in NREM sleep (see Meddis, 1979).

Two hypotheses have been put forward concerning the function of sleep in mammals on the basis of the kind of evidence outlined above. The first hypothesis, the energy conservation hypothesis (see, for example, Zepelin and Rechtschaffen, 1974), suggests that a principal function of sleep, and in particular of SWS, is to provide a means of promoting the conservation of energy through periods of rest and inactivity. Evidence for such an hypothesis comes from the observed relationship between TST and SWS duration and such variables as brain and body weight and metabolic rate. Since both resting metabolic rate and the energy cost of a standard level of activity tend to be higher in smaller mammals, the energy conservation function of sleep would be particularly important in small mammalian species (see Horne, 1977, for a discussion). But, as Allison and Cicchetti pointed out, an alternative explanation of the relation between SWS duration and body size might be that long periods of enforced inactivity spent in sleep would be disadvantageous to large mammals. Many large mammals are herbivores, which are not only especially vulnerable to predation but must also spend considerable amounts of time in the quest for food. Furthermore, the energy conservation hypothesis does not account for the strong association between SWS duration and overall danger.

A second hypothesis, in which sleep is viewed as adaptive behaviour, emphasizes the extent to which the sleep behaviour of different species, including its structure and timing, has been moulded by the necessity of adapting to environmental threats and pressures (see, for example, Meddis, 1975, 1979; Webb, 1972). Evidence for the 'adaptive hypothesis' comes from the observed relationship between the duration of SWS and REM sleep and environmental factors such as the probability of being attacked during sleep.

In line with the energy conservation hypothesis of mammalian sleep function, theories of SWS function in humans have emphasized the role of SWS in the restitution of bodily processes (see, for example, Oswald, 1976). In support of this point of view the apparent dependence of growth hormone secretion on SWS has frequently been cited (see p. 146), and it is generally assumed that the main function of growth hormone secretion is to promote protein synthesis and thereby to set anabolic processes in motion. However, as a critical review of the restitution hypothesis by Horne (1979) makes clear, the action of growth hormone is extremely complex and the evidence supporting the restitution hypothesis is not completely consistent. For instance, several studies have examined the effects of daytime exercise on subsequent amounts of SWS; some studies have found that SWS increases (for example, Baekeland and Lasky, 1966), as might be expected on the basis of the restitution hypothesis, while many others have not (for example, Horne and Porter, 1976). Furthermore, the restitution hypothesis also appears to exclude the brain from any restitutional benefits that SWS may provide.

If, nevertheless, it is accepted that the functions of NREM sleep are primarily conservative and restorative, then what are the functions of REM sleep, and why did this type of sleep, which is only found in birds and mammals, suggesting that it is a comparatively recent evolutionary development, evolve at all? Snyder (1966) proposed a 'sentinel' function for REM sleep, and suggested that a period of REM sleep brings an animal to a state of near-waking readiness, so that it can take rapid evasive action, if necessary, upon awakening. Since REM periods are frequently followed by spontaneous awakenings, the animal is able to sample the environment for potential dangers. Ephron and Carrington (1966) put forward a 'homeostatic' hypothesis of REM sleep function, arguing that the activity of the brain must be kept within certain limits for optimal functioning and that the function of REM sleep was to periodically 'tone up' the cortex, thereby preparing it for wakefulness. Berger (1969) noted that the ability to co-ordinate eye movements binocularly depended upon the extent to which optic nerve fibres coming from each eye cross over to the opposite side of the brain at the optic chiasma (see Chapter 8) and reported that the degree of crossover or decussation appeared to be related to REM sleep as a percentage of TST. In view of this relationship Berger suggested that a possible function of REM sleep is to provide a periodic innervation of the oculomotor system in order to maintain the integrity of the binocularly co-ordinated eye movements which facilitate stereoscopic acuity in mammals. In order to explain the large amounts of REM sleep seen in infant mammals (see pp. 135–6), Roffwarg, Muzio and Dement (1966) have proposed that REM sleep provides endogenous afferent stimulation necessary for the development and differentiation of the CNS in foetal and neonatal life, when the growth of the brain is maximal. Other hypotheses have emphasized the role of REM sleep in the consolidation of new learning (see, for example, Dewan, 1969; Greenberg and Pearlman, 1974), a view for which there seems to be some support, at least for some kinds of learning in some species (see McGrath and Cohen, 1978, for a comprehensive review).

Several hypotheses have thus been advanced to explain the function of REM sleep, although probably no single one of them is capable of accounting for all of the available evidence. An alternative view, in marked contrast to those outlined above, is that expressed by Meddis (1977), in which the evolutionary development of REM sleep is considered to precede that of NREM sleep. Meddis suggested that the evidence for the absence of REM sleep in reptiles is inconclusive since many of the phasic events of REM sleep, such as rems and muscular 'twitching', seen in animals with higher metabolic rates, would not be expected to occur in reptiles. He further pointed out that many of the physiological concomitants of REM sleep are likely to be disadvantageous to homeotherms, but not to reptiles, amphibia and fish. A notable example is the internal regulation of body temperature, which is important to the survival of warm-blooded animals and which functions adequately during NREM sleep but not during REM sleep. Meddis therefore put forward the hypothesis that NREM sleep evolved to prevent long periods of REM sleep which could, ultimately, have fatal consequences for mammals. Thus a possible function of NREM sleep in mammals is to break up the continuity of REM sleep. Whether this hypothesis concerning the phylogenetic primacy of REM sleep is valid or not remains to be seen; yet it does appear to avoid the necessity of postulating a function for REM sleep in adult mammals and provides an explanation of why the discovery of such a function has proved so difficult. Probably the only statement that can be made with confidence about current theories of sleep function is that they will be compelled to change by the continuous emergence of new and often unexpected findings. But many such theories are ingenious and thought-provoking and it is likely that some of them will survive, at least in modified form.

Dreaming

Dreams have been a source of fascination for centuries but it is only comparatively recently that they have become the subject of scientific attention. Freud gave the study of dreaming special impetus by assigning dreams a crucial role in the preservation of sleep and by claiming that the analysis of dream content was a powerful instrument for the exploration of the unconscious (see Chapter 21). His classic monograph, *The Interpretation of Dreams*, first published in 1911 (see Freud, 1954), has thus provided a rich mine of testable hypotheses for dream researchers, although, it should be added, many of his ideas about dreaming have not stood the test of time.

Dream research in the sleep laboratory began with a now famous study conducted by Dement and Kleitman at the University of Chicago in 1957. They awakened each of nine subjects during each sleep period, sometimes during REM sleep and sometimes during NREM sleep Stages 2, 3 and 4. Before retiring subjects were instructed that they would be awakened from sleep by the ringing of a loud doorbell placed near the bed and that upon awakening they should report into a microphone whether or not they had been dreaming and, if they had, narrate the content of the dream. There was no contact between subject and experimenter until the subject had completed his narrative.

Subjects were considered to have been dreaming only if 'they could relate a coherent, fairly detailed description of dream content. Assertions that they had dreamed without recall of content were considered negative' (Dement and Kleitman, 1957b, p. 341). Using this criterion, Dement and Kleitman found that 83 per cent of 191 REM-sleep awakenings produced reports of dreaming as compared to 7 per cent of 160 NREM-sleep awakenings. The great majority of negative reports from REM periods occurred in the first half of the night.

This finding, which was soon followed by many others of a similar kind, did not in itself establish that REM sleep was the type of sleep in which dreaming occurred, since the possibility remained that dreaming takes place in NREM sleep but is most easily recalled following REM sleep. Dement and Kleitman therefore approached the question of whether REM sleep was dreaming sleep or dream recall sleep in a number of different ways and were able to conclude that REM sleep was indeed dreaming sleep. There is thus little doubt that REM sleep is the type of sleep from which dreams are more likely to be reported (see Dement, 1965) and that dream reports obtained from REM-sleep awakenings refer to mental events which have taken place in the preceding few minutes.

But dreams are not invariably reported following awakenings from REM sleep, and a variety of factors appear to influence whether dreamlike content, thoughtlike content or no content at all is obtained. Individuals who describe themselves as seldom or never dreaming (non-dreamers) produce fewer dream reports following REM-sleep awakenings than do individuals who describe themselves as dreaming frequently (dreamers), although the two groups do not differ in the number of REM periods (Goodenough *et al.*, 1959). Such subjects may in fact experience fewer dreams but they may also disguise, suppress or simply forget the content of some of the dreams they do experience (see Foulkes, 1966). Furthermore, in non-dreamers particularly, awakenings from REM periods late in the sleep period are more likely to produce dreamlike content than are REM-sleep awakenings made earlier, and abrupt awakenings are more likely to produce dream reports than are gradual awakenings (Goodenough *et al.*, 1965). The depth of sleep, whether subjectively judged or objectively observed, and the type of physiological activity occurring during the REM period (see Rechtschaffen, 1973) also appear to influence the nature of the content obtained from it.

Cohen (1970, 1974), in reviewing the factors affecting dream recall, considered three possible variables: repression, salience and interference. He concluded that the evidence supporting the repression hypothesis was negligible but that there was quite strong support for the salience hypothesis, while few studies relevant to the potentially important interference hypothesis had been conducted. Cohen also proposed a preliminary model of dream recall which takes into account individual differences, and pre-sleep, sleep and post-sleep factors which render mental events during sleep more or less salient and which could interfere to a greater or lesser extent with their recall.

In general, then, mental activity during sleep is more easily recalled if it is in some way distinctive and if there are few distractions present at the time of reporting. It is possible therefore that the low percentage of dream reports from NREM sleep is attributable either to the low salience of the mental events occurring during this type of sleep or to the high degree of interference present at recall. Yet there is in fact considerable variation in the percentage of dream reports obtained from NREM sleep in different studies and there are a number of reasons for this. Undoubtedly one of the most important is the experimenter's criterion of what constitutes a dream report, and several studies have demonstrated that the percentage of dream reports from NREM sleep increases dramatically if less stringent or broader criteria of dreaming are adopted (see Foulkes, 1966). Different experimenters have also induced different expectations in their subjects as to the type of mental activity they are supposed to report, some specifying that only dreams and nothing else should be reported, while others have indicated that the subject should report anything that is going through his mind. But even when these procedural differences are accounted for, it is clear that a certain amount of dreaming does occur during NREM sleep, and it is extremely improbable that dream reports from NREM sleep represent either awakening experiences or material remembered from previous REM-sleep awakenings or from uninterrupted REM periods (Foulkes, 1962, 1966; Rechtschaffen, Vogel and Shaikun, 1963). However, dream reports from NREM sleep can be clearly distinguished from those of REM sleep (Monroe *et al.*, 1965) and generally contain fewer characters, fewer shifts in scene and less emotional involvement in the activity described, and are less likely to involve bizarre elements or to be rated as dramatic in character. Dream reports from NREM sleep are also more likely to include references to recent events in the dreamer's life. Dream reports have also been obtained during sleep onset, reports of such 'hypnagogic experiences' being quite similar to dream reports from REM sleep (Foulkes and Vogel, 1965; Foulkes, Spear and Simmonds, 1966) and from relaxed wakefulness (Foulkes and Fleisher, 1975). Rechtschaffen, Vogel and Shaikun (1963) suggested that REM-period dreams 'do not arise *sui generis* as psychologically isolated mental productions but emerge as the most vivid and memorable part of a larger fabric of interwoven mental activity during sleep' (p. 546); this statement can probably now be extended to include wakefulness as well. Furthermore, dream reports from REM sleep can be accurately attributed, at better than chance levels, to a particular person and a particular night (Kramer *et al.*, 1976), implying that dreams reflect both permanent and transient individual characteristics. Dreams are thus not random events but form part of the structure of mental activity which is preserved throughout sleep and wakefulness.

Chapter 6
Motivation

The concept of motivation

We customarily speak of behaviour as being 'motivated' when it is clearly directed towards some goal. Reflex responses, such as the knee-jerk or patellar reflex, are not normally regarded as motivated; nor is the behaviour of a man falling under a bus when pushed from behind; and nor, for the most part, are such habitual and more or less automatically performed actions as coughing, or pulling up (in a car) at a red light. On the other hand, motivational explanations are generally seen as appropriate for the behaviour of people cooking a meal, writing a novel or rubbing two sticks together to make a fire. In other cases the appropriateness, or inappropriateness, of regarding behaviour as motivated is less clear, but activity does seem to be more organized and directed at some times than at others. Often, as Ryan (1970) has put it, 'we may speak of the organism as "idling" . . . certain basic activities continue to carry on even though they are not being used to carry activity in any one direction.' The distinction between 'directed' and 'idling' behaviour is not a simple dichotomy but is a matter of degree; behaviour may be more goal-directed at some times than at others. For example, it may be more vigorous in its expression, be more resistant to distraction, seem to involve a greater expenditure of effort, be more persistently maintained, and so on, and the level of motivation characterizing an individual's performance of a particular goal-directed activity may be inferred from such indicators.

Motivation, then, is generally conceived of by psychologists in terms of a process, or a series of processes, which somehow starts, steers, sustains and finally stops a goal-directed sequence of behaviour. But 'goal-directed behaviour' is very diverse: it includes foraging for food, wooing a mate, painting the house, painting a picture, having one's hair cut, seeking a Nobel prize, and so on. The diversity of motivated behaviour, in fact, is very nearly as great as the diversity of behaviour itself. It follows inevitably that motivation is a 'rag-bag' topic, and that many very different approaches, with widely varying generality of application, have characterized its study. The history of psychological concepts of motivation is largely the history of psychology, and consequently the treatment of motivation in this chapter is strongly historical: we shall consider the intellectual origins of motivational concepts, different views which have been taken of the nature of motivation and the ways in which these views have shaped empirical research.

Current concepts of motivation have emerged from numerous speculations about human and animal nature begun by the ancient Greeks and fiercely debated down the centuries by philosophers, theologians and scientists. Man's nature was long considered to be fundamentally different from that of animals since man alone possessed the faculty of reason. This enabled him to subdue the passions, which also formed part of his nature, and to choose, freely, the path of virtue. Plato and Aristotle both argued that animals did not possess rational souls and the Stoic school, founded by Zeno in about 300 B.C., seems to have been the first to put forward the notion of instinct to explain animal behaviour. The views of Thomas Aquinas, in the thirteenth century, were not greatly different from those of Plato and Aristotle some 1,500 years before; animals were regarded as being pushed into action by 'sense impulses' which were directed towards the pleasurable, while man's activity was primarily motivated by 'rational insight'. It was also argued that animals did possess 'sensitive' souls, which were inferior to 'rational' souls, but which were capable of inspiring purposive activity directed at the attainment of goals which would be useful to the animal, principally in terms of species preservation. The behaviour of both human beings and animals could thus be explained *teleologically*: that is, in terms of its purpose, the goal towards which it was seen to be directed.

Despite the fact that the rationalist view of human nature occupied a dominant position in Western thought for some 2,000 years, and is still held in some quarters, at least in modified form, it was never accepted universally, although its opponents were generally a small minority. However, the watershed of the rationalist position came in the seventeenth and eighteenth centuries with the writings of René Descartes and Thomas Hobbes and the emergence of the British empiricist school. Descartes accepted the applicability of teleological explanations to human behaviour but argued that animal behaviour was merely mechanical; input, in the form of sense impressions, both internal and external, determined output (behaviour) completely, without the intervention of reason. Thus explanations of animal behaviour should be *mechanistic*, rather than teleological: in terms of *causes* rather than of goals. Hobbes argued further that the behaviour of human beings did not have to be accounted for in teleological terms and extended the mechanistic explanation of animal behaviour, put forward by Descartes, to encompass human behaviour.

Hobbes was a precursor of associationism, which was established and developed by the eighteenth-century British empiricists, particularly Locke and Hume (see also Chapter 1). The British empiricists argued that the mind at birth is a *tabula rasa* or 'blank slate', that our knowledge of the world is built up from experience, in the form of sense impressions, and that associations are formed between the ideas to which sense impressions give rise. Our knowledge of the world is thus limited by our experience of it, and there is no residual 'human nature' over and above that formed on the basis of human experience.

The empiricists, like Hobbes, espoused a kind of *determinism*: human behaviour was held to be determined by ideas, sensations and desires which originate in experience, and it was therefore appropriate to seek causal explanations of that behaviour. Further, such ideas, sensations and desires were held to be either reducible to physical events or at least dependent upon them, a view known as *materialism*. In general, too, the British empiricists accepted *hedonism* as a fact of life: human activity, like that of animals, was seen as being directed largely towards the attainment of pleasure, either one's own or, in altruism, that of others. Although the basic assumptions of the empiricist school have been challenged, and in some cases invalidated, by philosophical argument and psychological investigation (see Chapter 1 and also Thomson, 1968), its views are still reflected in much thinking about motivation.

In the nineteenth century, Darwin's theory of evolution provided a completely new perspective on the operations of Nature, and one which reinforced an empiricist rather than a rationalist position. As mentioned in Chapter 4, the theory emphasized the continuity of man and animals and argued that the range of living organisms which now exists was the result of initial random variation of species characteristics and the subsequent and continuing operation of the process of natural selection. The behaviour of men and animals alike, in common with their other characteristics, was thus *biologically* determined. Finally, in the early years of the present century, Freud delivered what has often been regarded as the *coup de grâce* to any distinction between human beings and animals based on reason as a determinant of behaviour, by demonstrating that some human behaviour at least appeared to be the result of the operation not of conscious rational forces, but of unconscious and irrational ones.

As a result of these intellectual influences from other disciplines, most psychologists interested in the understanding of motivational phenomena probably share at least an implicit belief in *universal determinism*: all behaviour has a cause, and it is in principle possible to discover systematic laws of causality governing both human and animal behaviour. This belief has not gone unchallenged, although the challenge has perhaps come more often from philosophers than from psychologists. There have been attempts (see, e.g., Peters, 1958) to argue an essentially rationalist view in which human behaviour is seen as generally rule-following and purposive, most appropriately explained in terms of 'reasons' rather than causes. In this view causal explanations of human behaviour are only appropriate if there is some deviation from the normal rule-following purposive model. As Benn and Peters (1965, p. 236, emphasis in original) put it, 'we know why a parson is mounting the pulpit not because we know much about the causes of his behaviour but because we know the conventions governing church services. We would only ask what were the causes of his behaviour if he fainted when he peered out over the congregation or if something similar *happened* to him. Most of our explanations of human behaviour are couched in terms of a purposive rule-following model, not in causal terms.' Causal explanations of human behaviour are thus considered to be appropriate only when an individual's behaviour results from the operation of forces over which he has little or no control. Obsessional behaviour, or a slip of the tongue, might be explained in causal terms but normal rule-following purposive behaviour is to be accounted for in terms of reasons, and the two types of explanation are considered to be very different. However, it has been argued that the logical distinction between 'reasons' and 'causes' is more apparent than real (see Davis, 1979; or, for a more advanced discussion, Bhaskar, 1979); and in any case, for good or ill, revivals of rationalism have not in general received much support from psychologists investigating motivation.

Beyond a generally determinist attitude, there is probably more diversity than agreement among the various views that have been taken of motivation. Many of the concepts utilized have either been borrowed from other sciences or been modelled upon concepts that other sciences use; and although early psychological theories of motivation (such as those of William McDougall and Clark Hull, discussed below) were designed on the grand scale, with intended applicability to all human and animal behaviour, most, if not all, attempts at motivational explanations can be applied only to restricted areas of study. Nevertheless, there is probably some measure of agreement as to what the components of a theory of motivation might be.

For example, it seems likely that both human beings and animals are equipped with a set of 'basic needs', although the size of the set and the degree to which particular needs are innate or acquired remains a matter for debate. Nevertheless, it seems clear that learning and experience enable a system of 'derived motives' to be gradually established, largely through the operation of associative processes, and that in human beings, and perhaps some animals, such motives become strongly linked with the development of attitudes and values, producing dispositions to seek particular satisfactions which may appear to have little connection with basic needs. Furthermore, some needs at least have a physiological basis and much has been learned in the past forty years about the physiology of motivation. Needs, whether innate or acquired, are activated by internal and/or external stimulation and, somehow, although the mechanism is far from clear, the activation of these needs, with the assistance of internal energizing forces, comes to initiate and maintain goal-directed sequences of behaviour. But the activation of needs does not occur in a mental vacuum. Human beings, and probably many animals, can respond to the existence of particular needs, can select goals likely to satisfy those needs, can estimate the chances of those goals being attained, can devise and utilize strategies for attaining them and can, if necessary, fall back on alternatives. Cognitive processes, therefore, play a most important part in organizing and directing sequences of goal-directed behaviour. We shall now consider these components of motivational theory in more detail.

Views of motivation

Instinct theories

The idea that animal behaviour could be explained in terms of instincts originated with the Stoic philosophers of ancient Greece who, according to one historian of the concept of instinct, suggested that 'the natural promptings called instincts are purposive activities implanted in the animal by nature or by the world reason or creator for the guidance of the creature in the attainment of ends useful to it, in its own preservation or the preservation of the species and the avoidance of the contrary' (Wilm, 1925). Up until the eighteenth century instincts were reserved, virtually exclusively, for the explanation of animal behaviour, and the operation of instincts tended to be contrasted with the operation of reason and intelligence, instinct being regarded as a motivating force which produced action in the absence of any idea of what the consequences of the action would be. In the nineteenth century, however, attempts were made to bridge the gap between human and animal behaviour. Lamarck pointed out that much animal behaviour appeared to be characterized by intelligence and Darwin's evolutionary theory provoked a search both for the operation of instincts in human behaviour and for the operation of intelligence in animal behaviour. But although the attempt was made to demonstrate that human beings have instincts and that animals are able to exercise reason, the distinction between 'instincts' and 'reason', as explanations of behaviour, were preserved (Beach, 1955).

The view that some human behaviour might have an instinctive basis was adopted by many early psychologists, notably Herbert Spencer and William James. James, for instance, suggested in his *Principles of Psychology* (1890) that many more different instincts can be found in man than in other animals, although he considered that the influence of these instinctive tendencies on behaviour tended to be obscured by learning. James defined instinct as 'the faculty of acting in such a way as to produce certain ends, without foresight of the ends, and without previous education in the performance' (1890, p. 383), but this definition was not adhered to in his examples of human instinctive behaviour which ranged from sneezing, coughing and walking, to sympathy, cleanliness, jealousy and parental love. However, for James, much human behaviour was not to be regarded as instinctive, since the greater part of it was determined by what he called *ideation* and *habit*. But for the British psychologist, William McDougall, who further developed the application of the concept of instinct to human behaviour in the early twentieth century, all behaviour was to be thought of as ultimately instinctive in character.

McDougall was one of the first psychologists to define psychology as the science of behaviour. In what is probably his best-known book, the *Introduction to Social Psychology*, first published in 1908, he wrote that 'psychologists must cease to be content with the sterile and narrow conception of their science as the science of consciousness and must boldly assert its claim to be the positive science ... of conduct or behaviour' (McDougall, 1908, p. 4). Above all behaviour was purposive; 'the striving to achieve an end is ... the mark of behaviour, and behaviour is the characteristic of living things' (McDougall, 1912, p. 20). The term 'hormic', which is often used to refer to McDougall's conception of psychology, comes from the Greek word meaning 'urge'.

McDougall believed that behaviour was to be explained in teleological terms, that is, by referring to its goals or purposes. Above all, human and animal behaviour was goal-directed, and goal-directed behaviour possessed four principal and observable characteristics: persistence; variability; termination of the activity upon reaching the goal; and the improvement of the behaviour with repetition. But the formulation of goals towards which behaviour was directed depended upon the existence of certain basic needs and preferences, or fundamental motives, from which other motives could be derived as a result of experience. McDougall thus drew up a list of such fundamental motives, which he called initially 'instincts' and later 'propensities'. He did not, however, conceive of instincts as mechanical forces pushing the organism in one direction or another but as 'purposive strivings' towards some goal. Instincts were primitive mental processes which influenced behaviour in three main ways. First, the operation of a particular instinct would, on the receptive side, predispose the organism to pay attention to certain features of the environment; second, on the executive side, it would predispose the organism to perform certain actions, and third, on the emotional side, it would predispose the organism to experience certain feelings.

McDougall's original catalogue of human instincts comprised food seeking, sex, fear, curiosity, parental protectiveness, disgust, anger, self-assertiveness, submissiveness, constructiveness, gregariousness and acquisitiveness; but the instincts, or propensities, of appeal (for assistance), laughter, comfort, rest or sleep and migration were later added, and a group of very simple propensities subserving bodily functions (for example, coughing and sneezing) was also included. McDougall believed that the influence of these 'pure instincts' on behaviour becomes complicated in various ways. One result is the formation of *sentiments* or dispositional tendencies, such as patriotism or love; patriotism, for instance, was regarded as being formed from a combination of the protective, self-assertive, anger and appeal instincts. As children grow older sentiments begin to motivate behaviour directly to an increasing extent, although the emotional substrate of the behaviour remains instinctive.

McDougall's hormic psychology was severely criticized by the behaviourists, many of whom believed that the concept of purpose was unscientific. The behaviourists also insisted that behaviour was principally determined by environmental rather than by innate factors and hence objected to explanations of behaviour couched in terms of instincts. J. B. Watson, the founder and leading proponent of behaviourism, originally accepted the existence of instincts in animals and of a number of human instincts, emphasizing the importance of 'unlearned' behaviour in providing the basis for the formation of habits and for the development of more complex activity (Boden, 1972; Woodworth, 1963). However, for Watson, the range of behaviour which could be explained in terms of instincts became progressively narrower, while the number of instincts postulated by McDougall and his followers continued to proliferate, with the result that Bernard (1924), in a critical review of the concept of instinct, could point to classification schemes containing over a hundred instincts. Since McDougall conducted little or no empirical research designed to demonstrate the operation of instincts, this proliferation was viewed with great scepticism by the behaviourists. Indeed, in a review of McDougall's *Outline of Psychology*, published in 1923, Watson concluded that the book was 'unsafe' and should be kept away from the general public, since 'it breeds a lazy, genial, speculative arm-chair attitude' (see Cohen, 1979, p. 228). McDougall's hostility to behaviourism was no less marked, and, writing of Watson, he stated 'by repudiating one half of the methods of psychology and resolutely shutting his eyes to three-quarters of its problems, he laid down the program of behaviourism and rallied to its standard all those who have a natural distaste for difficult problems and a preference for short, easy and fictitious solutions' (McDougall, 1926, pp. 277–8). Since behaviourism rapidly came to dominate American psychology, however, it is perhaps not surprising that support for McDougall's hormic psychology and, in particular, for the role of instinct in the explanation of human behaviour, gradually declined. But one influential behaviourist, E. C. Tolman, who was also a rigorous experimentalist, agreed with McDougall about the fundamental importance of purpose in behaviour and the controversy between Tolman, who favoured a 'purposive behaviourism', and C. L. Hull, who became the foremost exponent of a mechanistic approach to the explanation of behaviour, later occupied a central position in the psychology of learning.

Yet despite the criticism made of McDougall's hormic psychology, the notion of instinct did not wither away entirely. Freud had put forward a 'dynamic psychology' (see next section) which included a theory of motivation employing the concept of instinct (Freud, 1915). Furthermore, as indicated in Chapter 2, the ethologists developed theories of the motivation of animal behaviour based on the idea of instinct (Tinbergen, 1951), with implications for human motivation, although these theories have subsequently been criticized on several grounds (see Bolles, 1975).

It is of historical interest that the term 'instinct' was used by the early ethologists to refer to an 'inborn movement form' or 'a fixed action pattern', that is, to a specific response or sequence of responses which can be described as 'unlearned', highly stereotyped, internally co-ordinated and species-typical. The form of a fixed action pattern is presumed to be innate and hence genetically determined, examples being the nut-burying behaviour of the squirrel (Eibl-Eibesfeldt, 1970) and the 'following response' observed in young nidifugous birds (Sluckin, 1972). But specific environmental stimuli, known as 'releasers' or 'sign stimuli', are generally necessary for the appearance of fixed action patterns which, in the absence of the appropriate releaser, are inhibited or prevented from appearing, by 'innate releasing mechanisms'. Yet the ethologists did not regard motivated behaviour as being entirely mechanical and, as mentioned in Chapter 2, Tinbergen (1951) distinguished between consummatory activity, which refers to the relatively stereotyped sequences of behaviour that occur when a goal has been reached, and appetitive behaviour which is much more varied and flexible behaviour associated with goal seeking.

The dynamic element of the instinct theory of motivation put forward by the ethologists was provided by the notion of 'action specific energy'. In Lorenz's 'psycho-hydraulic model' of motivation (Lorenz, 1950), each fixed action pattern is held to possess its own reservoir of action specific energy on which it can draw. The ease with which a fixed action pattern can be elicited by its sign stimulus, and perhaps also the vigour of its expression, are related to the amount of action specific energy which has accumulated since the last appearance of the appropriate releaser. The continued absence of the releaser leads to an increasing accumulation of energy which must eventually be dissipated and the principal evidence for the psycho-hydraulic model, and indeed for the existence of action specific energy, comes from the observation of types of behaviour described respectively as 'vacuum' or 'overflow activity' and as 'displacement activity'. Vacuum activity refers to the appearance of a fixed action pattern in the absence of its releaser, and displacement activity, of which the most common example is grooming, is said to occur when, despite the presence of a releaser in the environment, the emergence of the fixed action pattern is frustrated in some way.

Tinbergen (1951) modified and extended Lorenz's model and proposed a hierarchical functional organization for instinctive behaviour. At the top of this hierarchy is an 'instinct centre', an energy source which supplies 'drive specific' or 'instinct specific' energy to lower centres. The second level of the hierarchy contains a number of centres each of which controls a specific type of behaviour; for example, a 'territorial centre' is hypothesized to control the territorial behaviour of the three-spined stickleback, which Tinbergen analysed in detail. The centres at the second level obtain energy from the 'instinct centre' and are also influenced by hormonal and metabolic activity, by internal and external sensory stimuli and by 'intrinsic motivational impulses'. But the downward flow of energy from the 'instinct centre' is prevented from extending beyond the second level of the hierarchy by the operation of a series of innate releasing mechanisms which only permit a further downward flow of energy when the appropriate releasers are encountered in the environment. Drive-specific energy is therefore diverted into appetitive or goal-seeking behaviour, and the innate releasing mechanisms at lower levels of the hierarchy are progressively activated by their appropriate releasers, eventually allowing the relatively stereotyped fixed action patterns involved in consummatory behaviour to take place. A particular kind of behaviour, for instance searching for food, thus begins by the activation of the animal's 'feeding centre', perhaps by changes in hormonal activity or in internal stimuli. Drawing upon energy from the 'instinct centre' the animal engages in appetitive behaviour which, depending upon the opportunity presented by the environment and also upon past experience, may take a variety of different forms. Once food is encountered one of a number of behaviour sequences will be released depending upon the kind of food and how easy it is to obtain. Finally the food is obtained and the fixed action patterns associated with the consummatory behaviour of the ingestion of food occur. Thus in Tinbergen's hierarchical model the term 'instinct' was no longer restricted in its application to a fixed action pattern and its associated action specific energy and innate releasing mechanism, but was applied to a range of appetitive and consummatory behaviours which are functionally equivalent – that is, they have the same goal – and which are set in train by the same determinants – that is, are initiated by the same physiological changes.

The achievements of the ethologists in the observation and analysis of animal, and more recently human, behaviour are notable, but their theoretical speculations have been severely criticized (see Bolles, 1975; Hinde, 1970) and even the existence of, as well as the explanation for, vacuum and displacement activity, has been questioned (see, for example, Zeigler, 1964). Perhaps the most important of several objections which have been directed at their theoretical approach to motivation concerns the presupposition that a large part of animal behaviour is innately determined and also the extension of this view to some human behaviour, most controversially, perhaps, in the case of aggression (Lorenz, 1966). As more evidence has been gathered about the details and determinants of behaviour, especially behaviour in animals, it has become more difficult to label unequivocally specific types of behaviour as being innately determined, or, for that matter, as being solely the result of learning (Lehrman, 1970). This is not to deny that some kinds of behaviour, in both animals and human beings, are innate, the most obvious instance being reflex responses. But the word 'innate' is somewhat imprecise. As Thorpe (1963) has indicated, it may imply any or all of the following: '(1) inherited or genetically fixed and therefore characteristic of the species; (2) internally co-ordinated; (3) internally motivated. Both instinct and reflex may be innate in senses (1) and (2). Only instinct has an internal drive or motivation in sense (3)' (Thorpe, 1963, p. 15). Although there has been disagreement among ethologists as to the value and scope of the term 'innate', it appears nevertheless that instinct theories of motivation of the kind put forward by Lorenz and Tinbergen suggest that the innate component of goal-directed behaviour consists of a 'pre-programmed disposition of the nervous system' which ensures that 'energy (is) channelled in some particular direction under appropriate conditions' (Beloff, 1973, p. 83). However, as greater emphasis has been placed on the analysis of the physiological, neurological, hormonal and sensory determinants of goal-directed behaviour, the question as to whether the determinants of such behaviour are exclusively innate or acquired does not nowadays seem to be either as appropriate or as significant as it did earlier on.

Psycho-dynamic theories

In the spring of 1915 Freud wrote a paper entitled 'Triebe und Trieb-schicksale' (translated as 'Instincts and their Vicissitudes'), which represented an attempt to develop a theory of human motivation. He began by emphasizing that the principal function of the mind was to achieve mastery over stimulation, so that a condition of equilibrium, a pleasurable state of bodily quiescence, could be restored. Stimulation is of two kinds, external, which occurs episodically and can be dealt with or ignored relatively easily, and internal, which is constantly present, although the amount of excitation or tension engendered by internal stimulation can be temporarily diminished by appropriate goal objects. Freud regarded instincts as possessing four characteristics: a source, an aim, an impetus and an object. First, processes of excitation occurring in various bodily organs constitute the source of a particular instinct, and the immediate aim of the instinct is the removal of this organic stimulus, which can be thought of as a need (Jones, 1955). Instincts also possess an impetus, or 'impulsive force' which is related to the strength of the underlying need. The organic stimulus can be removed, and excitation reduced, by an object which will satisfy the particular need and, through learning and experience, a variety of objects may come to fulfil this function.

Freud considered that there were two fundamental categories of instincts, the self-preservative or ego instincts and the sexual instincts, known collectively as the 'primal instincts'. This suggestion was developed on the basis of his experience of treating psychoneurotic patients, in whom the ego and sexual instincts were regarded as being in conflict. The primal instincts are the 'psychical representatives' of basic, innate human needs such as hunger, thirst and sex, but in order to understand the ways in which these instincts are expressed behaviourally, it is necessary to provide a brief outline of Freud's view of the structure of the mind. Freud viewed the mind as being divided into three parts, *the id*, *the ego* and *the superego* (see the discussion of Freud's theory of personality in Chapter 21). The id is said to contain the instincts which provide the source of energy for behaviour, and to operate on the 'pleasure principle', as opposed to the 'reality principle' of the ego. The mental processes of the id are not available to consciousness and are known as primary processes. In infancy and early childhood, the tension aroused by the instincts can often be reduced by primary process thinking – that is, through fantasy and wish fulfilment, rather than by seeking out appropriate goal objects in the real world. The ego has direct contact with the external world and essentially performs an executive function, attempting to determine the consequences of behaviour directed at satisfying instinctual demands and eventually deciding, in accordance with the reality principle, whether such behaviour should be proceeded with or be postponed, or whether another course of action altogether should be adopted. The mental processes of the ego are mainly conscious, although some are preconscious, that is, capable of becoming conscious, while others are, and remain, unconscious. Conscious and preconscious processes are referred to as secondary processes. The superego is the internalized representation of social and cultural expectations, values and standards of conduct acquired through the process of socialization and functions, in effect, as a 'conscience', capable of censoring unacceptable ways of satisfying the instincts.

The task facing the ego, therefore, is to preserve a balance between the unremitting pursuit of pleasure (represented by the instinctual demands of the id) and the strict adherence to a code of behaviour which will secure the approval of society in general (represented by the social and moral prohibitions imposed by the superego) while taking into account the realities of the environment and the opportunities it affords for implementing different courses of action. Frequently the balance between the id and the superego is preserved, the environment offers the possibility of choice, and the ego is able to select a suitable course of action and to direct behaviour towards an appropriate goal object on the basis of conscious and rational decisions. A great deal of human behaviour is thus said to be directed and determined by the secondary processes of the ego. Sometimes, however, the instinctual demands of the id are so strong, or the conflict between the id and the superego so difficult to resolve, that a state of anxiety develops, against which the ego is protected by the operation of one of a number of ego-defence mechanisms, such as repression, sublimation, compensation, projection, introjection, conversion and reaction formation (see Kline, 1972, for a discussion of these). The activation of these defence mechanisms is not consciously initiated by the ego; instead it occurs automatically, and which mechanism is operative on any particular occasion is largely determined by environmental influences and past associations. Gradually, unconsciously determined patterns of behaviour which are effective in resolving conflict between the id and the superego, and hence in allaying anxiety, become habitual. Thus behaviour can also be determined and directed by unconscious processes of which the ego is unaware. These same processes are responsible for the 'parapraxes', deviations from intended courses of action, such as slips of the tongue or pen and certain kinds of forgetfulness, as well as for the latent, or disguised, as contrasted with the manifest, or superficial, content of dreams. Finally, Freud also developed a detailed theory of psychological, or more specifically psychosexual, development, which attempted to explain many features of adult personality structure (see Chapter 21). This theory postulated a sequence of developmental stages, the so-called oral, anal, phallic and genital psychosexual stages, and accounted for certain 'abnormalities' of behaviour, particularly of sexual behaviour, in terms of 'fixation', that is, a failure to pass through a particular psychosexual stage.

In summary, Freud's theory of motivation suggests answers to a number of questions about goal-directed behaviour. The instincts are held to provide the energy which fuels goal-directed behaviour; goals are thought to be selected through the operation of learned expectancies and consciously and unconsciously formulated wishes; slips of action or unintended deviations from a goal-directed sequence of behaviour are considered to be explicable in terms of the operation of unconscious processes and, it is argued, some people persist in directing their sexual behaviour towards goals which receive minimal cultural sanction because their psychological development has not proceeded normally. The model of motivation adopted by Freud is a hedonistic tension-reduction model, which implies that each individual's principal goal is to obtain pleasure by removing or reducing the tension aroused by innate bodily needs. The explanation of goal-directed behaviour adopted by Freud is thus primarily mechanistic. Although it can be argued that there are several conceptual difficulties in Freud's account of motivation (see Peters, 1958), the major problem that this complex, ingenious and wide-ranging theory faces is a lack of empirical support, since most of its major propositions remain untested and, indeed, may be in principle untestable. As a theory of motivation, therefore, Freud's viewpoint, though undeniably influential, is speculative rather than substantiated.

Freud's view of motivation is known as psycho-dynamic because it gives an account of human motives in terms of the supposed underlying active conflicts. Followers of Freud have not all been in agreement about the interpretation of his theorizing. There have also been others who originally went along with Freud, such as Adler and Jung, but who later constructed psycho-dynamic theories of their own. All such theories of motivation are inextricably intertwined with theories of personality. These derivations and deviations from Freudian psychology are considered in Chapter 21. It may be said, however, that Freud's model of human motivation is generally considered to be the most important of the extant psycho-dynamic models, and it has certainly been the most culturally influential of them, perhaps even more outside the domain of psychology than within it. Psycho-dynamic views of motivation are explicitly or implicitly rooted in an instinct-type theory, but they attach much more importance to environmental influences than instinct theories proper. Drive theories of motivation, to be considered next, lay even more stress on the role of experience and learning in the development of motives.

Needs and drives

The starting point for the 'drives' view of motivation is that animals and human beings are active; and this activity is said to be brought about by stimulation which has both a discernible *direction*, in the sense that it appears to be goal-seeking, and a degree of *intensity*, in the sense that the goals can be pursued with more or less vigour and persistence. The instigation of directed behaviour derives both from the internal state of the organism and from external stimulation; it is a function of complex interaction of these two sets of conditions. For some types of directed behaviour the internal state of the organism can be readily identified as the primary instigating condition. When this is the case, it has been convenient to designate the internal condition as one of *need*. The concept of *drive* is used to refer to the purposive activity which is initiated by both the internal and external stimulation. It will be seen later that many drives, if such there are, appear to be initiated more by external stimulation than by any clearly definable state of need. Nevertheless needs are thought to be basic for the understanding of motivation, and they are rooted in the so-called mechanism of *homeostasis*.

The mechanism has to do with the physical and chemical stability of the immediate environment of all the living cells of the body. The environment in question, consisting of blood and lymph, is known as the *internal environment*. Early studies made it clear that (a) certain specifiable character-istics of the internal environment are the normal and optimal conditions of physiological functioning, and that (b) when these conditions are upset physiological and behavioural mechanisms are set into action whereby the equilibrium is restored. Typically, the level of sugar in the bloodstream necessary for efficient functioning is periodically restored by food intake, the requisite amount of fluid in the body is kept constant by the mechanism of thirst, the maintenance of the correct chemical composition of the blood is helped by the operation of the various, so-called specific hungers, and so forth. Cannon used the term 'homeostasis' to refer both to the state of physiological equilibrium of the body and to the tendency, characteristic of so much of the activity of living things, to keep on continually restoring this equilibrium. Many of the restorative processes show themselves as recurring rhythms or cycles of activity. One such process, in diurnal organisms, is waking up in the morning and falling asleep at night, over and over again. Another consists of becoming hungry, feeding to satiation, gradually getting hungry again, and so on. Sex activity, too, tends to go in cycles. All such behavioural cycles are rooted in the physiological functioning of the body, the so-called *endogenous rhythms*.

Disturbances of equilibrium are normal occurrences, as some substances in the bloodstream are used up and others accumulate. Some disturbances also arise from changes in the external environment, to which the organism must continually attune. Thus, disequilibria of one kind or another develop; and these are often subjectively felt as needs – for example, a need for warmth, or hunger or the sexual urge. While the word 'need' refers in one sense to experiences of a particular class, it is also used in an impersonal way. Thus, it is quite customary to refer to the physiological disequilibria themselves as needs; these are often described as homeostatic or *biogenic needs*. And it has been suggested that such needs are the ultimate springs of all action.

One consequence of this suggestion is that features of behaviour, human and animal, which cannot be readily seen as arising from homeostatic needs, have been assumed by many theorists and investigators to derive indirectly from these needs, namely through learning. This has stimulated animal behaviour research concerned with establishing how various acquired behaviour tendencies are built upon initial biogenic needs. At the same time other observational and experimental studies have indicated that some tendencies – for example, investigative behaviour or affectional behaviour – do not always appear to spring from biogenic needs of the type described above, depending perhaps upon their own 'built-in' mechanisms. This situation has been a challenge to anyone interested in theories of motivation.

However, some needs never manifest themselves as drives, and some drives are certainly not based on physiological needs. Thus, oxygen deficiency, the lack of certain vitamins, or exposure to carbon monoxide, do not bring forth drives for corrective action. On the other hand, animals and people will sometimes actively seek saccharin, although the body has no need for it; see, for instance, experiments reported by Sheffield and Roby (1950). Furthermore, animals, and especially human beings, often acquire strong drives that are physiologically harmful: for alcohol, for drugs and for various forms of maladaptive action. It could be argued that such drives are a manifestation of homeostasis in a very broad sense of the word; for the word 'homeostasis' is not an unambiguous one. Some psychologists have extended the concept to cover all motives, such as curiosity and aggression. Such extensions imply that the organism and its environment are being conceived of as forming a single system, which can be in a state of equilibrium or disequilibrium. Though this way of looking at all motives can be illuminating, it is apt to be untestable, and therefore ultimately unfruitful.

Many more-or-less convenient classifications of motives are possible. For example, we can distinguish between those which are cyclic and those which are not. In the latter category are those motives which have to do with the continued adaptation of the organism to changes in the external environment. Animals avoid excessive cold and heat, and withdraw from painful stimulation; human beings go further by putting on or removing clothes, and by taking a variety of steps to relieve pain. The needs that instigate action of this kind are not normally cyclic and are induced by environmental conditions. The typically cyclic activities are internally rather than externally aroused, for instance, by the recurrent needs for sleep, food and elimination. Sexual motivation, however, does not easily fit into either of these categories. It is to some extent cyclic, and depends ultimately on the presence of sex hormones, male and female, in the bloodstream. On the other hand, it is clear that this drive is moulded, and sometimes profoundly so, by a range of environmental factors. Like sex, the parental drive in some of its forms has roots in the physiology of the endocrine system, but can be considerably modified by environmental conditions.

A more frequently used classification is that between *basic* drives and those others which, however strong they may be, are acquired or learned by organisms in the course of their lives; sometimes the labels 'primary' and 'secondary' are used for these two kinds. This classification runs into the problem of providing criteria for distinguishing between the innate and the learned. However, though this is a controversial and difficult matter, there are a number of motives which are sufficiently universal and which appear without any discernible opportunity for them to be learned, for us to be fairly confident that they are 'inbuilt'. These motives include, of course, those called 'self-preservative' and 'species-preservative'. But there are other drives, such as the tendencies to be active and to explore (curiosity), and the tendency to form attachments to living things (proximity seeking), which do not spring from biogenic needs in the narrow sense, but which none the less appear in the light of the evidence to be primarily innate rather than acquired.

Now the term, drive, is generally credited to the American psychologist R. S. Woodworth, who employed it in his *Dynamic Psychology*, published in 1918, to refer to a hypothetical push mechanism which would impel an organism to action. Drive was really a new name for an old idea, but since it lacked the implications of mentalism, teleology and innateness that were generally associated with the term, instinct, it rapidly became popular among comparative psychologists (see Young, 1936) and eventually became a cornerstone of one of the most ambitious theoretical undertakings that psychology had yet produced (Hull, 1943, 1952). Before Hull began to construct his theory during the 1930s, the drive concept, although considered as a valuable addition to psychological theorizing, faced a number of difficulties. It was unclear, for instance, whether drive – like instinct – was supposed to provide both the energy and the direction for behaviour, or only the former. It was uncertain, furthermore, whether there were to be a number of specific drives or just one general drive, whether drive was to be regarded as being centrally or peripherally represented and, finally, whether drive should be defined in behavioural terms or considered to be an unobservable cause of behaviour.

In an autobiographical sketch written for *A History of Psychology in Autobiography*, Hull noted that around 1930 he reached 'the definite conclusion ... that psychology is a true natural science' and 'that its primary laws are expressible quantitatively ...' (1954, p. 155). He therefore took as his model for theory construction the mathematico-deductive system of Newton's seventeenth-century treatise on mechanics, the *Principia*. In attempting to provide a systematic account of adaptive behaviour Hull, following Darwin, viewed such behaviour as being directed at the survival both of the individual and of the species. Survival depended upon the satisfaction or reduction of various biological needs which, for the most part, were the result of tissue deficits. Among these biological needs were included the need for air, for water, for food, for sex, and for the avoidance of pain. The presence of a biological need constitutes a source of stimulation which possesses both general and specific properties. Each need is assumed to give rise to, and contribute to the level of, a general state of drive, whose function is solely to energize behaviour. Most commonly the level of drive is inferred from the time for which the organism has been deprived of something which satisfies a biological need, such as food or water, but it is sometimes also inferred from the level of general activity. A specific pattern of stimulation is also associated with each need (for example, dryness of the throat with thirst) and each pattern of stimulation acts as a drive stimulus, which activates responses in the organism's repertoire and hence directs behaviour. These responses can be either learned (habits) or 'unlearned' reactions, and new responses can become attached to drive stimuli through processes of conditioning and, particularly, reinforcement. The term, reinforcement, has been somewhat differently defined by different investigators (see Wilcoxon, 1969, and our Chapter 13) and is regarded by some as an unnecessary concept (for example, Walker, 1969). Hull defined reinforcement in terms of *drive reduction* (although later, in terms of drive stimulus reduction) and suggested that any reaction which was associated with a reduction in drive had a higher probability of being elicited by the original drive stimulus, since the association bond between stimulus and response was considered to be strengthened by reinforcement. The role of drive in Hull's theory was to energize such stimulus response (S–R) associations, or habits, as well as the innate reactions mentioned earlier, although the latter were thought to be of comparatively little importance in human behaviour.

In Hull's final version of his theory (1952), habit strength, the strength of the associative bond between a stimulus and a response, was regarded as being a function of the number of prior reinforcements. The theory employed two motivational constructs, drive and incentive motivation, and there are a number of differences between them. The antecedent condition for a state of general drive was a state of bodily need, and the satisfaction or reduction of that need was both a necessary and sufficient condition for the occurrence of drive reduction. In contrast, the major variable affecting the level of incentive motivation was the magnitude of the incentive, or the amount of prior reinforcements, and the antecedent condition for incentive motivation is the conditioning of either the goal response itself, or of some fractional part of it, to stimuli present in the experimental situation. The effect of incentive motivation upon behaviour thus depended upon learning, whereas drive could energize behaviour in the absence of any previous learning. External stimuli were said to produce incentive motivation, whereas internal stimuli were thought to produce drive, and there was a biological basis for drive but a psychological basis for incentive motivation.

Hull was of course aware that a great deal of behaviour is not directly attributable to the small number of needs, including hunger, thirst, sex and the avoidance of pain, which were considered to be innate and which acted as primary sources of drive; for example, money and social approval can clearly exert powerful motivating effects. He therefore proposed that hitherto motivationally neutral stimuli could come to acquire, through conditioning, similar energizing properties to those of the primary sources of drive, and in this way secondary sources of drive could be established. Stimuli which were effective in reducing these 'secondary drives' could also, through a process of secondary reinforcement based on conditioning, come to possess reinforcing or rewarding properties similar to those of stimuli which reduced biological needs. Thus new sources of drive could be acquired and, through the operation of secondary reinforcement, new stimuli could come to function as reinforcers.

One of the principal virtues of Hull's theoretical system was that its hypotheses were capable of being tested experimentally, and indeed the system was continually undergoing modification in the light of fresh experimental evidence. By the time of Hull's death in 1952, however, the conception of drive, on which his theory largely rested, was increasingly being called into question and subsequently the considerable amount of research devoted to testing Hull's theory, and Spence's modification and extension of it, has cast further doubt on the utility of the drive concept.

Some of the earliest evidence questioning the Hullian conception of drive was provided by the studies of Sheffield and his associates (Sheffield and Roby, 1950; Sheffield, Wulff and Backer, 1951). As mentioned earlier, in the first of these experiments it was shown that saccharin, which has no nutritive value and thus cannot be satisfying any bodily need, could function as a reinforcer for the acquisition of an instrumental response by hungry rats. This result suggested that reinforcement could occur in the absence of any reduction in bodily need, although it is possible that some reduction in drive can be said to have occurred (Miller, 1957). However, in a second experiment, Sheffield *et al.* (1951) demonstrated that copulation without ejaculation could also act as a reinforcing agent and hence that reinforcement could take place in the absence of drive reduction. Neither need reduction nor drive reduction, therefore, appeared to be necessary conditions for the occurrence of reinforcement, and Sheffield concluded that reinforcement principally depends upon the occurrence of a consummatory response, rather than upon any reduction in drive (Sheffield, Roby and Campbell, 1954).

For a variety of reasons, including the difficulty of maintaining that drive had a biological basis, Hull (1952) finally adopted a definition of drive originally put forward by Miller and Dollard (1941) in which drive was divorced from bodily needs. This definition stated that 'a drive is a strong stimulus which impels action' and that any stimulus, provided that it was sufficiently strong, could function as a source of drive. Drive reduction thus became the reduction of noxious internal stimulation which did not necessarily result from the presence of a bodily need. However, this view of drive also encountered difficulties, since it soon became apparent that increases in internal stimulation could be highly rewarding. For example, animals were shown to learn new responses in order to obtain direct electrical stimulation of certain areas of the brain (Olds and Milner, 1954), to explore a new environment (Montgomery, 1954) or to gain a brief glimpse of their surroundings (Butler, 1954).

As mentioned earlier, Hull maintained both that any source of drive (say, hunger) could energize the appropriate consummatory response (eating), instrumental behaviour culminating in the consummatory response (for example, running by a rat to a goal box containing food) and general activity (as measured, for instance, in an activity wheel), and that different sources of drive, such as hunger and thirst, were motivationally equivalent. The vigour or strength of behaviour should thus co-vary with drive strength, which different sources of drive combine additively to affect. When the energizing effects of drive were subjected to critical scrutiny, however, a number of different studies, using different methods of assessing consummatory and instrumental behaviour and general activity, obtained inconsistent results. While there is clear evidence for a relation between drive strength and the strength of instrumental behaviour, the relation between drive strength and the strength of consummatory behaviour appears to be highly dependent on the measures selected, and that between drive strength and general activity to be virtually non-existent. There is also little evidence for the proposition that different sources of drive can be regarded as motivationally equivalent (see Bolles, 1975, for an extended discussion of these issues).

Although measures of the strength of instrumental behaviour and measures of drive strength tend to co-vary, it still may not be necessary to invoke drive as the explanation of the relationship between these measures. For example, conditions of deprivation, which are assumed to increase the level of drive, could equally well be assumed to increase the level of incentive motivation by affecting the value attached to a particular incentive. In view of the problems faced by the drive concept, it is generally considered to have outlived its usefulness and several alternative theories of motivation based on reinforcement and incentive motivation have been put forward to explain the persistence and direction of behaviour (see Bolles, 1975). The search for a general 'push mechanism' which energizes all behaviour has thus been largely abandoned and although attempts have been made to equate drive with the more recently developed concepts of arousal and activation (see Bartoshuk, 1972), they have not proved particularly successful. Instead interest has tended to be focused upon the specific determinants of a number of relatively simple kinds of motivated behaviour, such as feeding, drinking and mating, and much research has been devoted to gaining an understanding of the physiological processes underlying such behaviour.

The physiological approach

In this section we take feeding as an example of motivated behaviour and describe the physiological mechanisms and, to a lesser extent, the environmental factors, which appear to be important in the initiation, maintenance and cessation of feeding behaviour in animals and human beings. As an illustration of the physiological approach to motivation feeding possesses several advantages: first, such behaviour is clearly motivated and indeed is essential to survival; second, a considerable body of evidence concerned with feeding behaviour exists, and this has resulted in the development of a variety of theoretical approaches; third, it is indisputable that the brain is intimately involved in the control of feeding; and, finally, the analysis of feeding behaviour may have practical applications, for example in increasing our understanding of human obesity.

In order to maintain a constant body weight, food intake and energy expenditure must be kept in balance. If energy expenditure exceeds caloric intake (the calorie being the standard unit of heat energy), then the energy stored in the body, mainly in the form of glycogen (animal starch, which is converted into glucose by the action of the hormone glucagon) and fats, begins to be utilized, and the individual loses weight. If caloric intake exceeds energy expenditure, and the processes of the digestion and absorption of food proceed normally, more energy is stored, and the individual gains weight.

Even when food is freely available, the feeding behaviour exhibited by most mammals is intermittent rather than continuous, the daily supply of food being consumed in a small number of meals. Food intake can thus be regulated either by varying the frequency with which meals are taken or by varying the amount of food consumed at a particular meal. In rats able to feed *ad libitum*, meal size seems to be unrelated to the time that has passed since the previous meal but is strongly related to the time elapsing before the next meal; furthermore, there is little or no correlation between the amounts of food consumed at successive meals (Le Magnen, 1971). If the interval of time for which the animal has not eaten is considered to be related to its need for food, and hence to its state of hunger, it would appear that the timing of food intake, and thus the frequency with which meals are taken, is regulated in accordance with need-associated factors. Meal size, on the other hand, would seem to be determined by other factors, some of which probably have to do with the gustatory, olfactory and visual sensations that accompany the ingestion of food. In man, however, meal frequency is largely determined by social and cultural factors, and meal size becomes the principal way of regulating food intake.

How do we know when to start, and when to stop, eating? Following a period of food deprivation a variety of physiological changes occur which signal a state of hunger to the brain and similarly, following the ingestion of food, physiological changes take place which signal a state of satiety. The hypothalamus (see Chapter 4) has long been considered to be the area of the brain most intimately involved in the integration of information concerning states of hunger and satiety and two hypothalamic regions in particular, the medial hypothalamic zone in the vicinity of the ventromedial (VM) nucleus (see Figure 4.11 in Chapter 4) and an area in the lateral hypothalamic (LH) zone appear to play a crucial role in the control of feeding behaviour. Electrical stimulation of the VM area produces a decrease in food consumption (Olds, 1958), while the effect of bilateral lesions in this area is to double or treble an animal's food intake, a condition known as *hyperphagia* (Hetherington and Ranson, 1942). In contrast, stimulation of an area in the lateral hypothalamic (LH) zone produces an increase in food consumption (Delgado and Anand, 1953), while lesions in this area produce either *hypophagia*, a marked reduction in food intake, or *aphagia*, a failure to eat at all (Anand and Brobeck, 1951). When lesions are made in both the VM and LH areas, the animal behaves as if only the LH area had been ablated, that is, it refuses to eat or eats very little. Changes in feeding behaviour brought about by ablation in the LH area are known as the LH syndrome: those produced by such experimental interference in the VM area alone are known as the VM syndrome. The LH syndrome is briefly described first, and a discussion of the VM syndrome in animals, and of obesity in humans, then follows.

As well as becoming aphagic, LH-lesioned animals also exhibit adipsia (a refusal to drink); even when food and drink are freely available, such animals will die of starvation unless force-fed. But if food is gradually re-introduced in stages, beginning with a highly palatable liquid diet, LH-lesioned animals will eventually, after a period of several weeks, again drink water and eat normal dry food (Teitelbaum and Epstein, 1962). This recovery of normal feeding behaviour may be the result of cortical areas of the brain assuming the functions of the LH area (Teitelbaum, 1971). In addition to aphagia and adipsia, LH-lesioned animals also show some disturbances of sensory and motor functions and appear less able to cope with stressful environments.

Following lesions in the VM area of the hypothalamus, feeding behaviour follows two distinct post-operative phases, the dynamic and the static phases (see Hoebel and Teitelbaum, 1966). During the dynamic phase, which lasts for between four and twelve weeks, lesioned animals consume up to four times their normal amount of food and frequently double their body weight. However, they do less work, and generally appear less motivated, to obtain food (Miller, Bailey and Stevenson, 1950), although lesioned animals whose body weight is maintained at pre-lesion levels will work as hard if not harder than will unlesioned animals to receive food as a reward (see, for example,

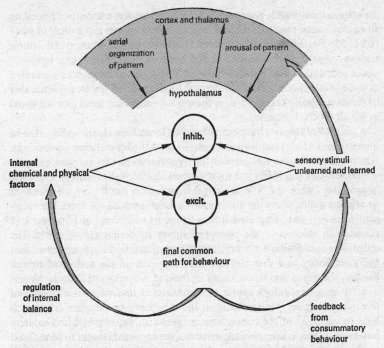

Figure 6.1   Schematic diagram of Stellar's model of the physiological factors contributing to the control of motivated behaviour. (From Stellar, 1954, p. 6)

Wampler, 1973). VM-lesioned animals also appear to be more sensitive to the taste of food, a condition known as 'finickiness'; the intake of palatable foods increases markedly, whereas unpalatable foods are rejected. For example, lesioned animals detect the presence of quinine, a bitter tasting substance, in food at lower concentrations than do unlesioned animals. Thus the hyperphagia shown by VM-lesioned animals is under sensory control (Teitelbaum, 1955), and takes the form of an increase in meal size, rather than an increase in meal frequency. During the static phase of the VM syndrome, body weight no longer increases, having reached a level higher than before the operation, and food intake is regulated so as to maintain the new weight level.

Several similarities between the behaviour of VM-lesioned rats and obese human beings have been noted by Schachter (1971). For example, just as animals in the dynamic phase are less likely to perform a variety of responses to obtain a food reward, so obese human beings appear less willing to work for food. Furthermore, like lesioned animals in the static phase, obese persons appear more sensitive to the taste of food. The eating habits of obese individuals also parallel those of VM-lesioned animals in a number of other ways, such as the amount of food eaten *ad libitum*, the number of meals normally taken per day, the amount eaten per meal and the speed at which food is consumed.

A number of theories have been proposed to account for these data. Anand and Brobeck (1951) put forward a *dual-centre* theory of feeding behaviour, which stated that the LH area of the hypothalamus was an 'eating centre' which initiates the feeding response when the animal is hungry and food is available, while the VM area was a 'satiation centre', which shuts off or inhibits eating when the animal has satisfied its need for food. The dual-centre theory was integrated into a more general view of hypothalamic function in relation to the biological drives by Stellar (1954, 1960). The cornerstone of Stellar's conception of hypothalamic functioning was that both inhibitory and excitatory centres for each of the biological drives, hunger, thirst, sex and so on, could be located in the hypothalamus. Neural activity in an excitatory centre was considered to lead to the arousal of the relevant drive, while activity in the inhibitory or satiation centre was held to occur when the consummatory response associated with the drive had taken place. The level of the drive in question was thought to be reduced by the activity of the inhibitory centre depressing that of the excitatory centre or by the inhibitory centre blocking the output of the excitatory centre, thereby terminating the arousal of the drive and the associated consummatory behaviour. The dual control system proposed by Stellar was believed to be affected by blood-borne, sensory and learned influences (see Figure 6.1), which were presumed to be capable of initiating or terminating activity in both excitatory and inhibitory centres.

The VM area can thus be regarded as a satiety centre, and so-called 'energy balance models' consider that its function is to defend a body weight set point, which is shifted upwards when the VM area is destroyed so that in effect the animal does not know when to stop eating. Similarly, the set point for body weight is altered, in the opposite direction, by lesions in the LH area, the feeding centre. Various sources of information have been presumed to be important in enabling the defence of a body weight set point to be made. These include changes taking place in body cells, such as the utilization of glucose (Mayer, 1955), and the level of fat stores (Keesey and

Powley, 1975), both of which are probably monitored by hypothalamic receptors, although the liver has also been held to be critically involved in the monitoring of metabolic changes (Friedman and Stricker, 1976). But perhaps the most obvious cue for the termination of eating is the feeling of a full stomach, although the maintenance of an appropriate energy balance requires a mechanism sensitive to caloric intake, which the stomach does not possess. It has therefore been suggested that satiety is a conditioned reaction and that the relatively long-term after-effects of food ingestion, such as the absorption of nutrients, can come to be associated with gustatory and gastro-intestinal sensations, so that an appropriate energy balance is maintained (see Booth, 1977; Stunkard, 1975).

While the notion that the VM and LH areas function respectively as satiety and feeding centres has been extremely influential, it also faces a number of difficulties. For instance, electrical stimulation of hypothalamic nuclei, and particularly of the LH area, has been shown to produce many different kinds of behaviour (see, for example, Valenstein, Cox and Kakolewski, 1970). Such findings cast doubt on the view that there are distinct hypothalamic 'centres', each controlling a specific kind of behaviour. Furthermore, both Gold (1973) and Grossman and Grossman (1973) have demonstrated, for the VM and LH areas respectively, that it is not the hypothalamic regions themselves but rather some of the bundles of nerve fibres that traverse them, which appear to be primarily responsible for the VM and LH syndromes (see Grossman, 1975, for a review). The hyper-phagia exhibited by VM-lesioned animals has been shown to be eliminated by cutting the vagus nerve, a cranial nerve which relays information between the brain and the organs in the thoracic and abdominal cavities (Powley and Opsahl, 1974). These and other findings have led to the 'cephalic phase hypothesis' of the VM syndrome (see Powley, 1977), which suggests that VM lesions heighten the cephalic reflexes of digestion, and emphasizes the role of the autonomic and endocrine systems in the regulation of feeding behaviour.

On the basis of his studies of the feeding behaviour of obese individuals, Schachter (1971) proposed a *stimulus control* theory of feeding behaviour in which it was suggested that normal-weighted individuals regulate food intake with respect to internal cues associated with feelings of hunger and satiation, such as the level of gastric contractions, whereas obese individuals regulate food intake with respect to external cues, such as the sight, smell and taste of food. Thus whether the stomach is full or empty should make little difference to the consumption of freely available tasty food by the obese, but should make a considerable difference to the subsequent intake of normal-weighted persons, a prediction confirmed by Schachter, Goldman and Gordon (1968). However, more recent research does not provide consistent support for Schachter's stimulus control theory (see Leon and Roth, 1977, for a review), and evidence from clinical studies of obese persons suggests that there is a strong link between food intake and anxiety and other states of emotional arousal (see, for example, Atkinson and Ringuette, 1967; Silverstone, 1968). In rats, Rowland and Antelman (1976) found that a mildly stressful, but apparently not painful, stimulus (tail pinching), applied twice per day, increased the daily intake of sweet-tasting food by over 120 per cent, compared to that of a non-stressed control group. Mild stress appears to have the effect of releasing dopamine, one of the principal catecholamines (see Chapter 4), which is probably the dominant chemical transmitter substance in some of the nerve fibre systems which traverse the LH area of the hypothalamus. It is possible, therefore, that there is a biochemical basis for the apparent connection between stress and food consumption.

The cognitive approach

The approaches to motivation that were discussed in the four previous sections have, for a variety of reasons, placed little emphasis on the way in which an individual's goal-directed behaviour is influenced by the utilization of his conscious knowledge of the world. Cognitive approaches to motivation emphasize that in many situations human beings have a fairly accurate perception of their own needs, and a reasonably clear appreciation of how these needs can be satisfied. People are also able to estimate the availability of various potential sources of satisfaction and to formulate expectations about the chances of certain courses of action resulting in the attainment of appropriate goals. Contemporary cognitive theories of motivation have their origins in the approaches to behaviour developed by E. C. Tolman, K. Lewin and H. A. Murray in the 1930s. Although Tolman was a behaviourist he was critical of the ambiguity with which the behaviourists, and Watson in particular, approached the definition of behaviour. While Watson generally favoured an atomistic, reductionist approach, whereby behaviour was to be broken down into its underlying constituents, he was also aware that behaviour had, in Tolman's words, 'descriptive and defining properties of its own' and was not merely 'the sum of its physiological parts' (Tolman, 1932). Tolman called these two approaches 'molecular' and 'molar' and, unlike Hull, who followed the molecular tradition, maintained that behaviour could only be understood holistically, that is, in molar terms. Tolman placed great emphasis on the richness, flexibility and variety of goal-directed behaviour, even that of a hungry rat seeking food in a maze; and his observations of such behaviour convinced him that goal-directed behaviour has the appearance of purpose and should therefore be described as 'purposive'. This description does not imply that any conscious purpose or intention must be ascribed to the agent, but merely that the agent behaves 'as if' a purpose were present. Furthermore, a hungry rat with experience of a particular maze behaves 'as if' it expected to find food at the goal box. The animal eventually learns the most direct route to the food, takes a progressively shorter time to reach it and, in general, its behaviour appears to be clearly directed towards the goal. Tolman employed such constructs as 'demand', 'expectancy' and 'value' in order to explain goal-directed behaviour, and thus anticipated modern *expectancy value theories*, which will be discussed shortly.

Lewin was much concerned with the problem of theory-construction in psychology, and contrasted descriptions of the determinants of behaviour couched in terms of an individual's past history and enduring characteristics with those given in terms of current environmental influences (Lewin, 1936, 1938). For Lewin, behaviour was a joint function of both the person and his environment and an individual's motivation was regarded as depending upon his perception of environmental influences, which would be guided by his past experiences. Lewin's approach influenced the development of *cognitive consistency theories* of motivation. Murray stressed that many human needs were psychological in character, and had little or no biological basis. He was primarily interested in the motivational processes stemming from the operation of psychological needs in naturalistic, non-laboratory settings, and with the ways in which the strength of such 'motives' could be measured in individuals. Needs were regarded as hypothetical constructs intervening between a pattern of stimulation and a pattern of behaviour; needs have a directional component, in that different needs exert different effects upon behaviour, and these can be distinguished from each other, and also an arousal component, in that the activation of a need can initiate goal-directed behaviour (Murray, 1937, 1938). Murray sought to measure the presence and strength of particular needs in different individuals by using a projective technique known as the Thematic Apperception Test or T.A.T. (see Murray, 1943, and our Chapter 21), in which the subject is presented with a set of black and white pictures depicting various scenes, and is asked to describe what is happening in the picture, what led up to the events depicted and what the outcome will be. A profile of an individual's psychological needs, such as those for achievement or for affiliation, can then be constructed from an analysis of the responses to the pictures. Much work has subsequently been conducted on how individual differences in the strength of a particular need are related to individual differences in motivated behaviour, particularly by McClelland in relation to the need for achievement (see McClelland, 1961; McClelland *et al.*, 1953).

Cognitive theories of motivation thus emphasize the perception of the strength of psychological needs, the expectancy of goal attainment and the degree to which a particular outcome is valued as determinants of motivated behaviour. The emphasis on cognitive factors as determinants of behaviour has also suggested to some investigators that cognitive consistency is a major psychological need, and the striving for achievement has also been regarded as an important and pervasive human motive, particularly in Western industrialized societies. Much research has been conducted within all these approaches. The main categories into which cognitive theories of motivation can be placed are, therefore, expectancy-value theories, cognitive consistency theories and achievement motivation theories.

Several different versions of expectancy-value theory have been put forward by investigators working in a number of diverse fields, ranging from the motivation for academic achievement of black American children, to the work motivation of industrial managers (see, for example, Atkinson and Feather, 1966; Irwin, 1971; Katz, 1967; Porter and Lawler, 1968; Vroom, 1964). Most of these versions maintain that motivation is a joint function of expectancy, defined as a belief concerning the probability that a particular course of action will be followed by a particular outcome, and valence, a term used by Lewin to refer to the value attached to the various possible outcomes of an action, and which depends upon the structuring of psychological needs in a particular individual. Thus if the most probable outcome of an action is also highly valued then the motivation for that action will be high, while if either the likelihood of goal attainment is low, or the most probable outcomes are not highly valued, then motivation will be reduced. Expectancy-value theories view people as making essentially rational choices between the possible outcomes of their actions. But since human beings are regarded as being inherently active, there is no necessity for a theory of motivation to explain the arousal or energizing of behaviour. The computation of expectancies and the assessment of values do not therefore initiate behaviour; they merely direct the ongoing stream of behaviour along certain lines. External factors, such as financial incentives, do not have a direct effect upon behaviour but are mediated by the expectation of certain outcomes and by the relative values with which these outcomes are invested. For example, Lawler (1971) has summarized, from the point of view of expectancy-value theory, some of the conditions which must obtain for pay to motivate job performance.

The underlying theme of cognitive consistency theories is the maintenance of equilibrium, or homeostasis, in the cognitive sphere. When beliefs about the world are incompatible, a need to resolve the cognitive conflict is aroused which persists until a resolution is achieved. Perhaps the best known example of a cognitive consistency theory of motivation is the theory of cognitive dissonance put forward by Festinger in 1957. Cognitive dissonance is regarded by Festinger as a negative affective state, which has the properties of a drive and leads to behaviour which will reduce the drive-associated tension. As an approach to motivation, however, cognitive consistency theories really only postulate an additional psychological need which remains hypothetical, and cannot be seen as providing anything remotely resembling a complete account of motivated behaviour, though such approaches have generated a considerable amount of research, much of which is relevant to the formation and maintenance of attitudes. For reviews of work in the field of consistency motivation, see Deci (1975) and Korman (1974).

McClelland (1961) has extensively studied differences between individuals in the need for achievement, known as n Ach, and has suggested that the strength of the achievement motive results from child rearing practices and is fairly consistent throughout a person's life. He has also described several differences between people in the strength of the achievement motive and their consequences for behaviour outside the laboratory. McClelland reports, for example, that managers with a high need for achievement obtain more promotions and pay increases, are judged more effective and work for more successful firms than do managers whose achievement motivation is low. Although McClelland's method of measuring achievement motivation has been criticized (see Weiner, 1972), the achievement motivation approach remains a plausible one.

The place of motivation in psychology

On pp. 160–64 of this chapter we claimed that motivation is a rag-bag topic in psychology, and pp. 164–89 have given some examples of the diversity of concepts, methods and areas of application subsumed under its heading. There are, or course, 'motives' which have not been specifically mentioned but which are or have been of great interest to psychologists: curiosity (see, for example, Berlyne, 1960), fear (see Sluckin, 1979), aggression (see Johnson, 1972) and so forth. As with the material reviewed here, it is likely that these examples of motivated behaviour will best be conceptualized by 'miniature' theories of limited application rather than by any attempted integration within some all-inclusive theory.

The place of a concept of motivation in psychology is a matter of controversy. On the one hand, it can be claimed that it is of central importance, since 'motivation' characterizes nearly all behaviour. On the other hand, it has been argued that motivation is not a topic in its own right at all, precisely because its applicability is total. According to this view, there can be no theory of motivation apart from and superordinate to theories of organized behaviour in more limited areas such as perception, learning, memory, personality and social behaviour; and there is no compelling reason to suppose that motivational concepts useful in one context will necessarily be useful in others. Further, it may be more profitable, at least at present, for psychologists interested in motivational phenomena to ask not 'why' such behaviour occurs but rather 'how' it occurs – how sequences of goal-directed behaviour develop, how they are sustained and how they come to be terminated. When this is done, the motivational concepts on which psychologists have traditionally relied may be of comparatively little use in providing satisfactory explanations of goal-directed behaviour.

Although we shall not discuss further the concept of motivation *per se*, motivational issues will be raised in many other chapters: for example, in those concerned with perception (Chapter 10), learning (Chapter 13), skilled performance (Chapter 14), memory (Chapter 16), psychological assessment procedures (Chapter 19) and personality (Chapter 21). Perhaps the closest link of all is that between the topics of motivation and emotion. The two terms have the same etymological root, in the sense of *movement*, and a common philosophical heritage, and the crucial questions in both areas of study overlap: the identity or diversity of various 'motives' and various 'emotions'; the continuity or discontinuity between man and animals, and the question of man's 'rationality'; the relative contributions of physiological and cognitive factors in the definition of motivational and emotional states. To some extent, therefore, issues raised in this chapter are illustrated and extended further in the next.

Chapter 7
Emotion

Introduction

Until comparatively recently the emotions were described as 'passions', a word whose Latin and Greek origins refer to 'suffering'. Emotions were thought of as states of mind in which the responsibility for actions was wrested from rational control, as for example in a *crime passionnel*, and the emotional side of human nature was considered by such influential philosophers as Descartes to be quite separate from, and morally inferior to, the rational element. As Averill (1976) has expressed this distinction, which lingers on in current thinking about emotion (Leeper, 1965), 'emotions are something that happens to us (passions), not something that we deliberately do (actions)'. Descartes viewed reason as a means of subduing the passions and as thus conferring the capacity for choice upon human beings; animals however, lacking this faculty, were at the mercy both of environmental input and of the passions and were therefore little more than automata. This view persisted virtually unchanged until the mid nineteenth century when Darwin put forward his theory of natural selection and followed this with his monograph on the *Expression of the Emotions in Man and Animals*, first published in 1872. Darwin's observations led him to emphasize the essential continuity between man and animals, in emotion as in everything else. The scientific study of emotion was thus placed squarely on a biological footing, and these beginnings have strongly affected its later development. Darwin pointed out that many animals, especially primates, have developed extensive repertoires of expressive behaviour, which in many cases appear to fulfil the functions of communicating emotion and of preserving social cohesion. The ability to communicate emotion through expressive behaviour is almost certainly the result of learning; for example, monkeys reared in isolation seem to lack these communicative skills and are severely impaired in their social relationships (Miller, Caul and Mirsky, 1967).

Facial expression is particularly important in the communication of emotion in human beings and there are some grounds for thinking that certain universal features exist in the facial expression of emotion (see Izard, 1971). A number of studies, for instance, have shown that high degrees of concordance are found among members of different cultures in the judgement of facial expression from posed photographs (Ekman, Friesen and Ellsworth, 1972; Izard, 1977). On the basis of such findings theories of primary affects, or fundamental emotions, have been put forward (Izard, 1971; Tomkins, 1962, 1963) and it has been suggested that there are underlying innate motor programmes and other neural changes associated with particular universal facial expressions, and that feedback from the facial muscles plays an important part in the self-attribution of emotion. But although certain facial expressions appear to have some generality across human cultures, the range of emotions which these patterns of facial muscle activity can reliably convey seems quite limited, and it is doubtful whether a particular facial expression always has the same meaning, irrespective of the situation or context in which it is perceived (see Mandler, 1975, pp. 145–9 for a discussion of these points).

One of the major problems for the study of emotion is the demarcation of emotions from non-emotional states; the closely related concept of mood, for example, has been regarded as being distinguishable from emotion by the greater length of time for which it is sustained and by the lowered intensity of experience with which it is associated (Nowlis, 1963, 1970). As Mayes (1979) has remarked, there is no consensus of opinion either on this point or on the similar question of how one emotion can be distinguished from another. Psychological research on emotion has tended to focus on a few relatively well-defined affective states such as fear and anger (or rage), whose behavioural manifestations can be observed both in human beings and animals and for which there is some evidence of physiological differentiation, both peripherally and centrally, and to consider the analysis of these basic or 'biologically primitive' states as paradigmatic for the analysis of emotions in general. Yet the number of emotion words in everyday usage is very large indeed (see Averill, 1976; Peters, 1969) and it seems clear that the concepts to which they refer cannot all be analysed in the same way. Philosophers have not been slow to chide psychologists for what they regard as naïvety in the conceptual analysis of emotion (see Kenny, 1963; Peters, 1969), pointing out that emotion has often been defined *as* bodily change or *as* behaviour and that neither definition will do; although both bodily change and behaviour can sometimes be taken as evidence for the presence of a particular emotion, neither of them *is* the emotion in question, nor indeed are they *necessary*, separately, as indicators of the emotion (West, 1969). Kenny emphasized that emotion is an 'intensional' concept: that is, an emotion must have an object. As West (1969) has put it, 'talk about emotion necessarily implies talk about the relationship between a man and the object of his emotion'. This relationship frequently requires analysis from a sociocultural or moral perspective in order to determine the nature of the emotion, as for instance, with remorse, shame or indignation. Many emotions can thus be considered primarily as 'social constructions' (Averill, 1976).

Averill argued that there are three categories of emotion: '*biologically determined responses*' (such as the startle reflex or the pain reaction) which are automatically evoked by a variety of appropriate stimuli, '*standard emotional reactions*' (such as anger) in which thinking remains highly structured, although some standard emotional reactions incorporate elements of biologically determined responses while others are almost entirely socioculturally determined; and '*transcendental emotional*' states (such as anxiety) in which thinking becomes disorganized. The first is the smallest category and the second is the largest.

It can thus be concluded that 'emotions are directed towards objects in a way in which physical processes are not; a physical state is not about something, as guilt is about having done something that is, or is believed to be, wrong' (Mischel, 1975). Feelings of anger or fear, or of remorse or indignation, are directed towards a target unlike, say, feelings of sleepiness or nausea, and this is one means of distinguishing between emotions and non-emotional states. Furthermore, emotions, unlike physical states, can be deemed to be appropriate or inappropriate, reasonable or unreasonable, justified or unjustified, depending upon the context and the situation in which they occur. However, both emotional and non-emotional feelings may provide reasons for action, although both in emotional and non-emotional states the agent may perceive the actions which result as being minimally self-determined. Many emotions arise from and are embedded in an intricate network of social and moral relationships, while others possess strong biological overtones. Emotions can thus to some extent be differentiated from each other in terms of the mix of their determinants.

Emotions and 'affective-cognitive orientations' (Izard, 1977) are also an essential part of the stream of consciousness, towards which attention is sometimes directed and sometimes not. Intense emotions, and perhaps particular kinds of emotion, are likely to capture attention, and hence cognitive structures, and thus to take over the direction of behaviour. An emotion is something which is experienced, and the experience of a particular emotion is inferred from a complex set of behaviours including actions, facial expressions, bodily movements and verbal communications, and/or from patterns of physiological activity which may vary in degree as well as in kind. Some of these behavioural and physiological reactions may be innate while others may be acquired. Furthermore, in human beings at least, the experience of an emotion usually entails a set of cognitions, attitudes towards and beliefs about the world, which has been brought to bear on the appraisal of a particular situation, and which thus influences the way in which that situation is perceived.

Psychological theories of emotion

Two theories, appearing at approximately the same time in the late nineteenth century, have exerted important effects on subsequent thinking about emotion. The first of these theories, that of William James (1884, 1890), has been an important influence partly in its own right, as the first psychological theory of emotion, and partly because the criticisms of James's position by Cannon (1927, 1931) have stimulated a great deal of empirical research. The second theory, that of Lange (1885), although less important than that of James, has exerted some influence on the development of activation theories of emotion (see, for example, Lindsley, 1951).

The theories of James and Lange are often considered together as the James–Lange theory of emotion although they are in fact somewhat different. The merging of the two theories has been regarded as unfortunate by some investigators (for example, Izard, 1971, 1977) since it has focused attention on their similarities and disregarded their differences. Unlike Lange, for instance, James emphasized the importance of feedback from the voluntary (striate) muscles in the determination of emotional experience (see Angell, 1916), but this aspect of his theory has been somewhat overlooked in subsequent research, which has tended to concentrate on autonomic activity as the most important kind of bodily change occurring during emotional states. Nevertheless, a substantial literature concerned with the contribution of the somatic system, and in particular that of the facial muscles, to emotional experience and expression has gradually accrued; the origins of this approach can be traced back to Darwin, as noted in the Introduction.

Lange's theory further differs from that of James in that it places little or no emphasis on emotion as a mental event. Instead, the bodily changes, particularly those occurring in the viscera, which accompany emotional states are thought to define an emotion completely. Thus, for Lange, emotion is vasomotor disturbance. A more recent statement of Lange's view can be found in Wenger (1950) and Wenger, Jones and Jones (1956), who define emotion as 'activity and reactivity of the tissues and organs innervated by the autonomic nervous system. It may involve, but does not necessarily involve, skeletal muscular response or mental activity.' Furthermore, 'change in emotional behaviour is altered activity or reactivity in a part of one, or more, tissue or organ innervated by the autonomic nervous system'.

Criticisms of this kind of definition of emotion were presented in the Introduction, and although an amalgamation of the views of James and Lange is presented here, the emphasis is placed firmly on James.

James's theory of emotion

James attempted to explain the relationship between visceral and muscular changes and feelings of emotion and the main point made by his theory is that emotional experience is dependent upon visceral and muscular feedback to the brain. To summarize James's theory very briefly: stimulus information processed by the brain is transmitted to the visceral and somatic systems where it evokes patterns of visceral responses via the ANS (autonomic nervous system: see Chapter 4) and patterns of motor responses via the skeletal muscular system. These two classes of response themselves act as stimuli which in certain circumstances result in a particular kind of emotional experience being 'recognized' by the cerebral cortex. This theory is depicted in Figure 7.1, and its essentials are expressed in James's well-known statement that 'we are afraid because we run, we do not run because we are afraid'. Emotional experience is thus based on the appreciation of changes occurring in the viscera or the motor system, and these changes are initiated directly by the perception of an appropriate stimulus, 'the exciting fact' as James termed it.

Criticisms of James's theory

Because of its emphasis on autonomic and somatic response patterns as determinants of emotional experience, James's theory is known as a *peripheral theory of emotion*. This theory soon came under attack, first from Sherrington and later from Cannon who, as will be seen on pp. 213–17, considered the CNS, and in particular the diencephalon (see Chapter 4),

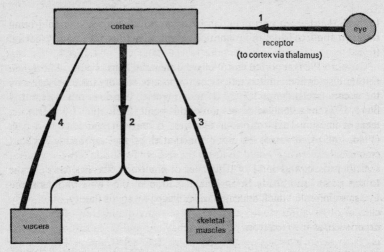

Figure 7.1 Schematic diagram of James's theory of emotional experience (see text)

to play a critical part in the mediation of emotional experience and behaviour, and hence favoured a *central theory of emotion*. Cannon put forward a series of criticisms of James's position which remains controversial (see Fehr and Stern, 1970; Mandler, 1975; S. Schachter, 1964), and both the criticisms and their *sequelae* will be enumerated in some detail.

The abolition of feedback from the visceral and somatic systems neither impairs emotional behaviour nor emotional experience: Sherrington (1906) objected to James's theory on the grounds that he had observed emotional behaviour in dogs deprived of a large part of the sensory feedback from the viscera and skeletal musculature; all the viscera and most of the skeletal musculature were isolated from the brain (paths 3 and 4 in Figure 7.1). Sherrington stated that 'anger, joy, disgust, and, when provocation arose, fear, remained as evident as ever following such operation'. Furthermore, he anticipated a possible criticism of his argument by stating that 'it may be objected to these experiments that although the animals expressed emotion they may yet have felt none. Had their expression been unaccompanied and had they not led on to trains of acts logically consonant with their expressed emotion, that objection would have weight. Where the facies of anger is followed by actions of advance and attack with all appearance of set purpose, I find it difficult to think that the perception initiating the wrathful expression should bring in sequel angry conduct and yet have been impotent to produce angry feeling' (p. 265).

Cannon (1927) reported essentially the same findings in cats, although in neither his nor Sherrington's experiments was the sensory feedback between the viscera, skeletal muscles and cortex completely eliminated (see Fehr and Stern, 1970 for a detailed discussion of this point). Nevertheless, no impairment of emotional expression was observed. It has been pointed out by Hebb (1946, 1949) that James did not claim that emotional *expression* but that emotional *experience* would be lost if the sensory feedback between viscera, skeletal muscles and cortex was reduced or abolished. Sherrington's answer to this point has already been cited. But despite some observations made by James himself, which appeared to lend support to his theory, other early clinical observation studies did not suggest any diminution of emotional experience, as inferred from patients' behaviour and verbalizations, following fairly severe losses of visceral and motor feedback (Cannon, 1927; Dana, 1921). However, Dana's study involved only one patient, in whom afferent feedback from the viscera cannot be ruled out, and a later study by Hohmann (1966), in which twenty-five paraplegics and quadriplegics were interviewed about their capacity for emotional experience before and after injury, yielded results which are consistent with James's theory. Hohmann found that the higher the location of the lesions in the spinal cord and hence the greater the deprivation of peripheral visceral and somatic sensation, the more severe was the reported reduction in emotional experience, at least as far as fear, anger, grief and sexual excitement were concerned. His patients described themselves as exhibiting emotional behaviour but as feeling nothing. In view of Hohmann's findings, and of the failure of either Sherrington or Cannon to abolish completely visceral and somatic feedback to their animal experiments, it has been concluded that Cannon's first criticism of the Jamesian position must be regarded as not proven and probably ill founded (Fehr and Stern, 1970; Mandler, 1975).

Different emotional states, and non-emotional states, are accompanied by similar patterns of visceral activity: a second objection to James's theory made by Cannon (1927) is that (a) different emotional states – for example anger and fear – show the same patterns of automatic discharge and are not therefore distinguishable on this basis, and (b) non-emotional states – for example, those resulting from physical exercise or exposure to high temperatures – are accompanied by similar patterns of autonomic activity to those found in emotional states. Virtually all the studies bearing on this criticism of James's theory have attempted to differentiate emotional states in terms of their concomitant autonomic response patterns. The principal experiments of this kind are those conducted by Ax (1953), Lewinsohn (1956) and J. Schachter (1957), and in spite of the different measures taken, the different ways in which these measures were scored, and the different situations from which the experiences of fear and anger were inferred, there is some agreement among their findings. Broadly speaking, and with certain qualifications, diastolic blood pressure appears to increase from the resting level to a greater extent in anger than in fear, while heart rate, cardiac output, palmar conductance, respiration rate and frontalis muscle tension all appear to increase more in fear than in anger. A difficulty with laboratory experiments in which fear is to be differentiated physiologically from other emotions is that the laboratory situation itself may produce feelings of apprehension resulting in bodily changes which confound the assessment of possible physiological changes due to experimental treatments (see Fehr and Stern, 1970). That is, anger and fear situations, whatever their differences, may share the property of being fear, or anxiety, arousing. But fear and anger have also been differentiated physiologically outside the laboratory. Wolf and Wolff (1943), for instance, were able to study over several months a patient with a chronic stomach fistula, in whom the blood flow to the stomach as well as gastric activity could be observed in different, naturally occurring situations. Whenever this patient was afraid, or sad, a pattern of sympathetic discharge could be seen; the stomach lining became white, being virtually drained of blood, and gastric contractions were considerably reduced. When he became angry or resentful, a pattern of parasympathetic discharge was noted; blood flow to the stomach increased, producing a reddening of the stomach lining and the gastric activity was elevated. However, these two patterns were the only ones that could be observed over the period of study.

In other studies the physiological differentiation of emotions other than anger and fear has been reported. Averill (1969), for example, examined autonomic response patterns during sadness and mirth using two contrasting films (*John Kennedy 1917–63*, which emphasized the assassination, funeral and burial of the American President, and a Mack Sennett silent comedy, *Good Old Corn*) in order to induce the different emotions. Changes in respiratory patterns, to some extent attributable to the laughter evoked by the comedy film, were considered by Averill to be more characteristic of mirth, while changes in cardiovascular activity were more typical of sadness.

Changes in autonomic response patterns occurring in different emotional states are likely to be associated with alterations of hormonal balance in the endocrine system, and it has been suggested that anger is characterized by a greater secretion of noradrenalin as opposed to adrenalin, whereas fear and anxiety are characterized by a greater secretion of adrenalin (Ax, 1953). This suggestion is supported by the results of a number of studies (Elmadjian, Hope and Lamson, 1957; Funkenstein, King and Drolette, 1957; Silverman and Cohen, 1960). Injections of adrenalin and noradrenalin also appear to produce different patterns of autonomic response which broadly correspond to those observed in fear and anger. Martin (1961) concluded from a survey of the physiological reactions accompanying injections of adrenalin and noradrenalin that in general the former leads to increases in palmar conductance, systolic blood pressure and heart rate, and decreases in diastolic blood pressure, hand temperature and salivary output. Fewer measures have been taken in studies of the effects of injected noradrenalin, but such effects include increased diastolic and systolic blood pressure and no change or a slight decrease in heart rate. In a carefully conducted study, Wenger and his colleagues (1960) found that injections of adrenalin produced a marked increase in cardiac output (rate and stroke volume) while noradrenalin produced a decrease; both drugs were found to decrease the flow of blood to the skin, but it was inferred that adrenalin constricts the blood vessels of the skin to a lesser extent than noradrenalin, while constricting to a greater extent the blood vessels supplying the skeletal musculature. However, Wenger reported that no feelings of emotion accompanied injections of either drug. It thus appears that, in spite of some overlap, there are differences between the effects on physiological responses of adrenalin and noradrenalin, at least at the dosage levels used in the above experiments, and that there is some correspondence between the physiological changes seen in fear and anger and those which follow adrenalin and noradrenalin injections. However, an important factor in the analysis of emotional responses, namely the appraisal of stimuli, is missing from the experiments just mentioned. We shall return to the problems involved in the 'artificial' induction of emotional states and their concomitant physiological reactions (pp. 204–13).

But there is some evidence which suggests that the relationship between fear and adrenalin-like reactions, and between anger and noradrenalin-like reactions, is rather a dubious one. Levi (1965) showed his subjects a series of feature films, some of which (such as *The Devil's Mask*) were considered anxiety- or fear-arousing, as assessed by subjects' ratings, while others (such as *Charley's Aunt*) were not; another film, *Paths of Glory*, seemed to contain both anxiety- and aggression-arousing features. The urinary excretion of adrenalin and noradrenalin was measured before and after each film and before and after a control film consisting of landscapes and scenery. *The Devil's Mask*, rated as the most anxiety-arousing film, increased both the adrenalin and the noradrenalin level and, although *Paths of Glory* produced ratings high in anxiety and in aggression, the associated adrenalin level was similar to that produced by *Charley's Aunt*, which was rated neither as anxiety- nor as aggression-arousing. Patkai (1971) obtained broadly similar results, finding that the excretion of adrenalin was greater in either pleasant or unpleasant situations compared to neutral ones.

Levi suggested that there is a positive correlation between the intensity of emotional arousal, whatever the expressed emotion may be, and the urinary excretion of adrenalin and possibly also that of noradrenalin, while Patkai concluded that the release of adrenalin was related to 'the level of general activation', rather than being associated with a particular emotional reaction such as fear or anger. It is also possible that the available repertoire of 'coping' responses and the extent to which they are utilized in an emotionally arousing situation determine the balance between the secretion of adrenalin and noradrenalin. Elmadjian *et al.* (1957), for example, found that the excretion of noradrenalin increased in hockey players actively involved in a game, while those watching from the bench showed elevated adrenalin levels. Thus situations in which active coping with an emotionally arousing situation is possible may be associated with different levels of catecholamine excretion than are situations in which the individual's role is restricted to that of a passive spectator. Research bearing on the relation between the catecholamines and emotion is surveyed by Frankenhaeuser (1975) and Schildkraut and Kety (1967).

Insofar as there appear to be discriminable differences between the autonomic response patterns observed in different emotional states induced by laboratory procedures, Cannon's second criticism of James's theory can be regarded as uncorroborated. But in view of the difficulties of interpreting the results of these experiments – for example the possible contaminating effect of apprehension and anxiety in the studies of anger and fear, and in the light of the very limited number of visceral patterns observed in naturally occurring situations such as that investigated by Wolf and Wolff – it would seem that James's position cannot easily be sustained. Furthermore, the evidence relating to hormonal balance in the endocrine system and the differentiation of emotions does not provide much support for James's theory. The burden of Cannon's second criticism of James's theory would thus appear to be justified.

The viscera are too insensitive to act as a basis for emotional experience: even supposing that an outside observer, using polygraphic recordings and computer analysis, can distinguish reasonably accurately between the physiological changes associated with fear and anger, can the individual experiencing the emotions do so? This is the basis of Cannon's third criticism of James's position. Cannon argued that the visceral organs are poorly supplied with nerve fibres and hence transmit little information. It would therefore be difficult to make fairly subtle discriminations between patterns of visceral activity, or indeed to be aware of them at all. While it seems that the viscera proper may contain few fibres that mediate pain sensations, there is plenty of evidence that visceral organs possess stretch, pressure and temperature receptors, and differential stimulation of these receptors is presumably reflected in such common expressions as 'a sinking stomach' and 'a lump in the throat' – both of which are often linked to different emotional states. Yet as was noted in the discussion of Cannon's second criticism of James's theory, the number of different visceral patterns that have been observed is fairly small, and it seems likely that the range of discriminable cues provided by the ANS, on which, according to James, the perception of emotional experience is based, must be quite restricted. However, given that the range of internal cues may be limited, is it possible nevertheless to make accurate discriminations among them?

Although this question has been answered in different ways (see, for example, Brener, 1977; Mandler, 1975), and despite the fact that in some bio-feedback studies a remarkable degree of control of autonomic responding has been demonstrated (for example, Schwartz, 1975), the majority view would appear to be that the ability to perceive small differences in visceral activity is negligible. Support for this view comes principally from a series of studies by Mandler and his associates. Mandler and Kahn (1960) required a prediction to be made concerning which of two lights would come on next, the response being the depressing of a key. Unknown to the subject, one light went on when his heart rate increased by at least two beats per minute, the other when it decreased by the same amount. After about 5,000 presentations, there was no evidence that subjects had learned to make the discrimination. Although the visceral changes accompanying emotional experiences are usually of considerably greater magnitude than the small changes in heart rate investigated in this experiment, it is still presumably a difficult task for individuals to discriminate differences in their own autonomic patterns.

There are considerable differences between individuals in the degree to which changes in their own physiological states are reported. Subjects given an autonomic perception questionnaire listing common physiological changes and asked how often they observed such changes taking place in themselves were found to differ markedly in their responses. When these self-reports were correlated with the magnitude of physiological changes occurring in response to a laboratory stress situation, the overall correlation was found to be positive but of low magnitude. However, when subjects were divided into extreme groups on the basis of their questionnaire responses and the intermediate group omitted from the analysis, highly significant differences in physiological reactivity emerged. Those subjects who reported observing physiological changes frequently were much more reactive in the stress situation, while those subjects who reported a low incidence of such changes were much less reactive (Mandler and Kremen, 1958; Mandler, Mandler and Uviller, 1958). In a study of the perception of gastric changes, Stunkard and Koch (1964) reported that in people whose weight was in the normal range reports of hunger sensations were related to measures of gastric motility, while in obese subjects no relation between the two indices was observed. But although some subjects may be fairly accurate monitors of their internal physiological states, it is notable that *patterns* of physiological response seem to be more highly correlated with subjects' reports of visceral activity or to self-reports of activation than any single autonomic measure (Mandler, 1960; Thayer, 1970). Mandler (1960) suggested that 'if people react to anything referentially in their visceral upheaval, it is likely to be a rather global, general condition of arousal'. Cannon's third criticism of James's theory thus appears to have some validity, since whether or not the viscera are insensitive structures, and they are almost certainly not as insensitive as Cannon supposed (see Fehr and Stern, 1970), human beings do not seem to be particularly efficient either at detecting or at discriminating among their own physiological reactions.

Visceral changes occur too slowly to act as a basis for emotional experience: Cannon also suggested that the effects of visceral changes are transmitted to the brain too slowly for them to be a direct source of emotional feeling, since there is evidence (Lehmann, 1914) that (a) reports of emotional feeling occur extremely quickly after the presentation of an emotion-provoking stimulus, and that (b) specific autonomic changes almost always follow the verbal report. Although later evidence (Newman, Perkins and Wheeler, 1930) suggests that there are two distinguishable experiences (one fast and one slow) separated by the visceral response consequent upon the presentation of an emotion-provoking stimulus, the later one being dependent upon visceral feedback, it seems unlikely that the verbal report of emotional experience can be determined solely by visceral changes and, indeed, emotional responses to a stimulus situation can sometimes precede stimulus identification (Guthrie and Wiener, 1966). It is probable, therefore, that Cannon's fourth criticism of James's theory is also valid.

The artificial induction of visceral changes known to occur in specific emotional states does not produce the associated emotional experience: The final objection made by Cannon to the Jamesian position was that the 'artificial' induction of those visceral changes known to occur in emotional states does not produce reports of emotional experience or emotional behaviour. Specifically, he argued that the injection of adrenalin, which, as already mentioned, is a sympathetic nervous system activator, should produce emotional feelings. However, adrenalin does not appear to affect the activity of either the parasympathetic or the somatic nervous system which James also considered to be important in producing emotional experience.

In the experiment of Wenger *et al.* (1960), cited above, the injection of adrenalin and noradrenalin did not produce any spontaneous reports of emotional feelings. In earlier studies, for example Marañon (1924), it had been found that some subjects injected with adrenalin and questioned about their emotional states reported 'as if' emotions, while others reported no emotional feelings at all. About a third of Marañon's subjects said that they felt as if they were afraid or as if they were awaiting good news. When Marañon talked to them about emotionally toned events, then the appropriate emotional feelings were reported without qualification. Thus, although Cannon's original criticism appears to be well-founded, it also seems clear that the provision of situational or instructional cues, coupled with visceral arousal, can shape emotional experience and behaviour.

This point is well made by an experiment performed by S. Schachter and Singer (1962) which led to one of the most influential of psychological theories of emotion, Schachter's attribution theory (see S. Schachter, 1964). But before describing Schachter's theory, and the experiments relevant to it, we shall briefly summarize the Jamesian position in the light of Cannon's criticisms. We have seen that James argued that emotional experience was dependent upon the perception of visceral and muscular feedback, although the subsequent debate concerning the role of feedback in emotional experience has focused almost exclusively upon the viscera. Many of Cannon's criticisms of James's theory seem to be valid and it is thus unlikely that emotional experience is determined by the perception of patterns of autonomic activity. It is possible, however, that emotional experience is based, at least in part, upon the perception of a gross, undifferentiated change in autonomic arousal. But why is a change in physiological arousal sometimes given one emotional label and sometimes another? The group of theories to be considered next argue that this question can be clarified by considering how situational cues interact with an individual's cognitions against a background of physiological arousal; they can thus be classified as cognitive theories of emotion.

Cognitive theories of emotion

Under this heading we shall concentrate principally upon Schachter's attribution theory, the criticisms that have been made of it, and the research it has provoked, although other cognitive approaches to emotion, notably those of Valins and Lazarus, will also be discussed.

Schachter's attribution theory of emotion. Ruckmick (1936) had argued that cognitive factors were of great importance in determining emotional experience but it was not until over twenty years later, with the re-emergence of cognition in experimental psychology, that this argument began to be seriously considered. Although, therefore, Ruckmick anticipated the development of cognitive theories of emotion, the first major theory of this kind, the attribution theory of emotion, was not put forward until the 1960s (S. Schachter, 1964, 1970; S. Schachter and Singer, 1962).

The attribution theory of emotion assumes that a state of physiological arousal is a necessary but not a sufficient condition for the occurrence of an emotional experience. It suggests that after a state of physiological arousal has been induced, an awareness of that state ensues, evaluative needs are activated, the environment is searched for an appropriate explanation of the arousal state, and finally the state is labelled with reference to the environmental–cognitive information available at the time; once a label has been applied, appropriate behaviours manifest themselves. Hence emotional experience results from an attribution process which determines the most likely explanation for a state of physiological arousal in the light of the cognitive information available. Schachter and Singer (1962) subjected the attribution theory of emotion to experimental test. They began by reviewing the experiments of Marañon (1924), referred to earlier, and, in commenting upon his procedure and results, made the point that his subjects were aware that they were receiving an injection of adrenalin and that they probably knew something of its effects. That is, they knew why they felt the way they did. However, if an individual was unaware that he had received an injection of adrenalin, although in fact he had, he would have no readily available explanation for his physiological state. The verbal label used to describe his internal state in the absence of an appropriate explanation would, Schachter and Singer hypothesized, be determined by his interpretation of the situation in which he found himself. However, if an individual knows very well why he feels the way he does, then it is improbable that he will label his feelings in terms of new interpretations of the situation. Finally, the label applied to the internal state in the absence of physiological arousal is unlikely to be an emotional one.

Schachter and Singer investigated the emotions of euphoria and anger in an experiment in which the subject's state of physiological arousal, the availability of an appropriate explanation for that state and the situation to which the subject was exposed were manipulated. Volunteer subjects came to the laboratory ostensibly to participate in an experiment concerned with the effects of a drug, 'suproxin', on vision. The drug was in fact adrenalin, which increases the level of physiological arousal. In the euphoria condition subjects, who were male university students attending an introductory course in psychology, were divided into four groups. Those in the first group were correctly informed about the effects of the injected drug, and were told that they would experience mild hand tremor, increased heart rate and a flushed feeling in the face. Subjects in the correctly informed group were thus provided with an appropriate explanation for their state of physiological arousal. Subjects in the second group were misinformed about the effects of the drug; they were told that it would produce numbness in the feet, itching sensations and a slight headache, and were thus provided with an inappropriate explanation for their state of physiological arousal. Subjects in the third group were given no information about any side effects the drug might have and, like subjects in the misinformed group, had no readily available explanation for the bodily feelings they experienced. Subjects in the fourth group, who were also given no information, received an injection of saline solution as a placebo. In the euphoria condition of Schachter and Singer's experiment, therefore, there were four treatment groups: correctly informed, misinformed, ignorant and placebo. In the anger condition, the number of groups was reduced to three, the misinformed group being omitted.

The second and third parts of the experiment were identical for all groups. Each subject was shown to a waiting room where another subject was waiting to participate in the experiment. This subject was actually a confederate of the experimenters. The confederate went through the same standardized behavioural repertoire with each subject and, depending upon the subject's reactions, behaved in much the same way on each occasion. In the euphoria condition he began by doodling and ended by twirling a hula hoop on his arm, while in the anger condition, in which both the subject and the confederate were given an insulting and offensive questionnaire to complete, the confederate began by complaining about the length of the questionnaire and finally tore up the questionnaire and stamped out of the waiting room. During the time that the subject was in the waiting room, his behaviour was observed through a one-way vision screen and evaluated in terms of the degree to which it resembled the behaviour of the confederate or showed other signs of the emotion that the experimenters were attempting to induce. Finally, in the third part of the experiment, the subject was given a scale on which to rate his feelings of euphoria or anger, and to check the bodily symptoms he had experienced, and his pulse rate was also taken.

Schachter and Singer hypothesized that the degree of experimentally produced euphoria or anger, as inferred from the subject's behaviour in the waiting room, and his subsequently reported emotional experience, would be greater for the misinformed and ignorant groups than for the correctly informed and placebo groups. The results they obtained are shown in Table 7.1. From this table it can be seen, firstly, that the adrenalin-injected groups all experienced an increase in pulse rate following the injection, while the pulse rate of the placebo group decreased following the injection of saline solution. The increase in pulse rate for the adrenalin-injected groups was statistically significant in each case, and the pulse rates of all three groups were significantly higher than that of the placebo group at the end of the experiment. If pulse rate is regarded as an index of arousal level, therefore, the adrenalin-injected groups were significantly more aroused than the placebo group. This difference in arousal level was also reflected in the self reports of bodily feelings obtained at the end of the experiment, although these are not shown in Table 7.1.

Secondly, in both the euphoria and anger conditions, the self reports of emotional state indicated that a greater degree of the relevant emotion was reported by the ignorant group, and, in the euphoria condition, by the misinformed group, than by the correctly informed group, as Schachter

Table 7.1

A summary of the principal results obtained in the euphoria and anger conditions of Schachter and Singer's experiment. High self-report scores indicate greater *positive* affect; N indicates the number of subjects contributing to each mean score. (Adapted from Schachter and Singer, 1962)

| | Saline-injected group | Adrenalin-injected groups | | |
| | | Correctly | | |
	Placebo	Informed	Ignorant	Misinformed
1. *Euphoria condition*				
Pulse rate	Pre 80·4	Pre 85·7	Pre 84·6	Pre 82·9
(beats per minute)	Post 77·1	Post 88·6	Post 85·6	Post 86·0
	(N = 26)	(N = 27)	(N = 26)	(N = 26)
Self-reported emotional state (0–4 scale)	1·61 (N = 26)	0·98 (N = 25)	1·78 (N = 25)	1·90 (N = 25)
Euphoric activity rating	16·00 (N = 26)	12·72 (N = 25)	18·28 (N = 25)	22·56 (N = 25)
2. *Anger condition*				
Pulse rate	Pre 84·5	Pre 85·9	Pre 85·0	
(beats per minute)	Post 79·6	Post 92·4	Post 96·8	
	(N = 23)	(N = 23)	(N = 23)	
Self-reported emotional state (0–4 scale)	1·63 (N = 23)	1·91 (N = 22)	1·39 (N = 23)	
Angry behaviour (composite index based on observations of the subject's behaviour)	+0·79 (N = 22)	−0·18 (N = 22)	+2·28 (N = 23)	

and Singer predicted. But in the euphoria condition neither the ignorant nor the misinformed group reported themselves as feeling significantly more euphoric than the placebo group. In the anger condition, furthermore the critical comparison between the correctly informed and the ignorant groups was only marginally significant, and again the difference between the ignorant and the placebo groups failed to reach even a marginal level of significance. With respect to the ratings of emotional behaviour, however, the results were more clear-cut, at least for the anger condition, in which the anger scores of the ignorant group were significantly higher than those of the correctly informed and placebo groups. In the euphoria condition, only the comparison between the scores of the correctly informed and misinformed groups reached a satisfactory level of statistical significance.

Although, therefore, the overall pattern of average scores within each condition conformed to Schachter and Singer's predictions, as Table 7.1 shows, the statistical analysis of their original data only partially confirmed their expectations, since the emotional experience and behaviour scores of the placebo groups were not, as they should have been, significantly different from those of the ignorant and misinformed groups, and those of the ignorant groups did not consistently differ significantly from those of the correctly informed groups. Schachter and Singer advanced two explanations of these deviations from the predicted result, based on a re-analysis of their data. First, despite the fact that they had received an injection of saline solution, some subjects in the placebo groups became physiologically aroused, presumably in response to the confederate's behaviour in the waiting room. When the emotional behaviour scores of subjects in the placebo groups whose pulse rate decreased following the injection were compared with those of subjects whose pulse rate either increased or remained the same, it was found that the latter exhibited significantly more euphoria or anger than did the former. It thus appears that the degree of emotional behaviour displayed increased with arousal level. Second, some subjects in the ignorant and misinformed groups correctly attributed their bodily feelings to the injection they had received. These subjects were described by Schachter and Singer as 'self-informed'. When the emotional behaviour scores of self-informed subjects were compared with those of subjects who were not self informed, it was found that the former manifested significantly less euphoric and angry behaviour than did the latter and the behaviour scores of self-informed subjects closely resembled those of subjects in the correctly informed groups.

The re-analyses of their data by Schachter and Singer provide an explanation, on the one hand, of the comparatively high emotional experience and behaviour scores of the placebo groups and, on the other, of the failure to obtain consistent differences between the scores of the ignorant and correctly informed groups at an acceptable level of statistical significance. But they also raise questions about how individual differences in cognitive appraisal and in emotionality can be accommodated by the attribution theory of emotion; it is unclear, for example, why some subjects, and not others, in the ignorant and misinformed groups attributed their bodily feelings to the injection of the drug or why some subjects in the placebo group became physiologically aroused while others did not. In an attempt to control one of these factors, the level of physiological arousal, Schachter and Wheeler (1962) injected one group of subjects with an ANS blocking agent, chlorpromazine, and compared their reactions to a fourteen-minute excerpt from a comedy film *The Good Humor Man*, with those of an adrenalin-injected group and a saline-injected placebo group. Although the pulse rates of subjects in the chlorpromazine-injected group in fact increased following the injection, it appears that many subjects were unaware of this, since their reported bodily symptoms were similar to those of subjects in the placebo group. As predicted, subjects in the adrenalin-injected group showed most amusement during the comedy film, followed by the placebo and chlorpromazine groups. However, the three groups did not differ significantly in their evaluations of the film as funny or enjoyable. Thus, despite the fact that the perceived level of arousal seemed to affect emotional behaviour during the film, it did not affect cognitive evaluations of the film once it was over. This finding weakens the attribution theory of emotion, which assumes that cognitive evaluations are linked to emotional experience and behaviour.

While the point of view put forward by Schachter and Singer has been extremely influential, several criticisms have been directed against both the design and procedure of their experiment and their interpretation of their results (Erdman and Janke, 1978; Kemper, 1978; Leventhal, 1974; Maslach, 1979; Plutchik and Ax, 1967; Shapiro and Crider, 1969). It has been argued, for example, that pulse rate alone is an inadequate index of physiological arousal and that a combination of psychophysiological measures should have been recorded throughout the experimental session, rather than only at the beginning and the end. The method of compiling the indices of euphoria and anger, and the differential weightings attached to different kinds of behaviour displayed by the subject in response to the confederate, have also been questioned. It has been further pointed out that the euphoria and anger conditions were not truly comparable, since they apparently differed in duration and in the amount of activity that took place. The amount of activity could have influenced the pulse rate measure obtained at the end of the experiment. Alternative interpretations of Schachter and Singer's results have been put forward in terms of information processing

(Leventhal, 1974) and in terms of the experimenter–subject relationships involved (Kemper, 1978).

In view of the criticisms of such an important study, and the alternative interpretations that have been advanced, it is surprising that so few replications have been conducted. Marshall (1976; cited by Maslach, 1979) replicated in modified form the euphoria condition of Schachter and Singer's experiment. He obtained little support for their findings since regardless of the behaviour exhibited in response to the confederate, subjects who were physiologically aroused reported themselves as experiencing a negative affective state rather than euphoria. Maslach (1979), who employed both a euphoria and an angry condition, and increased physiological arousal level by hypnotic induction to a specific verbal cue, obtained similar results to those of Marshall. Subjects who had no explanation for their state of physiological arousal reported negative emotions, in both experimental conditions. Maslach suggested that an unexplained state of physiological arousal is not a neutral variable which exerts no effect on the search for a probable explanation, but rather imposes a bias in the direction of negative affect, perhaps as a result of learning, or perhaps because such a state is anxiety-arousing. Erdman and Janke (1978) investigated states of happiness, anger and anxiety, as well as a neutral control condition. They employed a completely disguised method of drug administration, used both blood pressure and heart rate as indices of physiological arousal and controlled for the amount of activity in the different experimental conditions. The results obtained for happiness and anger confirmed the findings of Schachter and Singer, but those for anxiety did not, since the emotional effects of the anxiety condition were independent of the drug-induced arousal level. Anxiety reactions occurred in a low state of physiological arousal (placebo condition) and did not increase following the administration of ephedrine, the drug employed.

Thus attempts to replicate Schachter and Singer's findings have been only partially successful and the validity of Schachter's attribution theory of emotion must remain in some doubt. Schachter's theory seems to suggest that an individual becomes aware of his state of physiological arousal and that the perception of his bodily feelings, together with the observation of his emotional reactions in a particular situation, lead him to label his emotional experience in a certain way. But neither reports of emotional experience nor cognitive evaluations of a situation appear to be necessarily related to emotional behaviour, and a state of physiological arousal for which there is no immediately available explanation seems to be linked to the experience of negative emotions, rather than being emotionally neutral. Furthermore there is some evidence, reviewed by Leventhal (1974), which indicates that when an individual focuses attention on his own reactions to a situation, the intensity of his emotional experience is diminished, although there appear to be quite marked sex differences in this effect. To what extent, therefore, does the perception of autonomic reactions contribute to emotional behaviour and experience, and must this perception be veridical? These questions were considered in an ingenious series of experiments conducted by Valins and his associates (see Valins, 1970, for a review).

The effects of false autonomic feedback. The studies carried out by Valins demonstrated that non-veridical information concerning an individual's level of physiological arousal, in the form of false heart-rate feedback, could affect a variety of behaviours, ranging from long-term preferences for *Playboy* nudes to the desensitization of snake phobias. In the latter study, for example, Valins and Ray (1967) showed that snake-phobic subjects who had been led to believe that they were hearing their own heartbeats while viewing a series of slides, and that their heart rates were unaffected by slides of snakes but increased to other anxiety-arousing slides, subsequently approached a real snake more closely than did snake-phobic subjects who viewed the same series of slides while listening to the same sounds, but believed them to be meaningless. Such results were interpreted as providing support for the hypothesis that an individual's beliefs concerning the state of his internal environment, irrespective of the actual state, are the primary determinants of emotional responses. However Valins defined emotional responses either in terms of stimulus evaluation, for example, attractiveness ratings of female nudes, or in terms of approach–avoidance behaviour, for example, the degree of proximity to a previously feared object that the subject was willing to tolerate, and no attempt appears to have been made to measure emotional experience. In a later false heart-rate feedback study, Hirschmann (1975) showed that measures of stimulus evaluation and of emotional experience tended to be unrelated.

Some attempts to replicate Valin's findings have proved to be unsuccessful (Kent, Wilson and Nelson, 1972; Sushinsky and Bootzin, 1970) while others have demonstrated that the administration of false heart-rate feedback itself influences the actual level of physiological arousal, which in turn affects emotional responses (Gaupp, Stern and Galbraith, 1972; Goldstein, Fink and Mettee, 1972; Hirschmann, 1975). In a review of false heart-rate feedback studies and their implications for the psychology of emotion Hastrup and

Katkin (1976) proposed that there are two types of emotion, primary and secondary. Primary emotion was considered to be dependent in part upon a state of autonomic excitation and upon the individual's veridical perception of that state, whereas secondary emotion, which was considered to be dependent upon a learned association with a primary emotional experience, was not; it is possible, therefore, that some kinds of emotional behaviour, such as stimulus evaluation, may occur in the absence of visceral arousal. Hastrup and Katkin also suggested that the experiments of Valins were concerned with secondary, rather than with primary, emotion. Visceral arousal may thus be a necessary condition only for the occurrence of certain types of emotional behaviour and experience.

Lazarus's theory of emotion: cognitive appraisal and coping behaviour. An even more thorough-going cognitive approach to emotion than that of Valins has been put forward by Lazarus and his associates (Lazarus, 1966, 1968; Lazarus, Averill, and Opton, 1970). Lazarus views emotion as resulting from the cognitive appraisal of a stimulus situation and physiological changes as following the appraisal. Situational, personality and cultural factors influence the kind of appraisal that is made and hence the physiological changes that occur. Lazarus's work on situational determinants of the process of appraisal has emphasized coping processes, and his experiments have demonstrated that threatening or anxiety-arousing films are associated with different patterns of physiological response depending upon the coping strategies that are made available. Preferences for certain coping strategies are also related to personality and to cultural background (Averill, Opton and Lazarus, 1969). Although Lazarus's theory of cognitive appraisal and coping processes was presented as a theory of emotion, it has sometimes been regarded as a theory of coping with threat (Shapiro and Schwartz, 1970), and it is certainly true that comparatively little attention is devoted by Lazarus to the more positive or 'benign' emotions.

However, one of the beneficial consequences of the work of Lazarus and his associates has been the broader perspective given to the determinants of the attribution of emotion. Averill (1976), for example, argued that 'the attribution of emotion, whether to oneself or to another, is essentially an interpretation of behaviour and ... that such an interpretation is based, in part, on the conformity of the behaviour to certain cultural standards or norms'. In support of his view of the part played by feelings of passivity in the attribution of emotion, mentioned in the Introduction, he presented experimental evidence that if an individual wishes to claim responsibility, or to take credit, for an action he is unlikely to label it as being inspired by emotion, whereas if he wishes to disclaim responsibility or to avoid censure, then the self-attribution of emotion is one way of doing so.

The cognitive theories of emotion discussed above have emphasized the interaction between physiological and cognitive factors in the self-attribution of emotion. Schachter's theory suggests that emotional behaviour and experience are the products of a state of autonomic arousal, the accurate perception of that state and the cognitive interpretation of a social situation based on internal physiological and external environmental cues. The work of Valins implies that cognitive factors are the most important determinants of emotional responses, since it is the individual's beliefs about his physiological state, rather than the actual state itself, that determines emotional behaviour, at least in certain circumstances. The investigations of Lazarus and others indicate that the nature of prior information and the availability of coping strategies, which influence the processes of cognitive appraisal, can also alter the level of physiological responding in a stressful situation. Thus not only can the perception of physiological responses affect the cognitive interpretation of a situation but cognitive interpretations can affect physiological responding.

A major assumption made by cognitive theories of emotion is that whatever the resulting emotion, the underlying physiological responses are the same, and hence that the various emotions cannot be differentiated physiologically. It is unclear whether this assumption is warranted and, as mentioned above (pp. 197–201), there is some evidence from studies of autonomic response patterns in anger and fear that it is not. The extent to which different regions of the brain are involved in emotional behaviour and experience is also uncertain, and in the final section of this chapter some studies concerned with emotion and the brain are briefly described.

Emotion and the brain

Since most of the research concerned with the brain mechanisms mediating emotional experience and behaviour has been conducted with animals, this section is mainly devoted to such 'biologically primitive' emotions as anger and fear, or, more precisely, to the expression of these emotions in 'fight' and 'flight' behaviour. Early work in this field implicated subcortical structures in the mediation of emotional behaviour since decortication (in cats) was found to produce animals in which thresholds of emotional excitation were markedly lowered, emotional behaviour was intense, diffuse and poorly directed and the timing of emotional responses was dislocated (Dusser de Barenne, 1920). Increases in autonomic activity were also apparent. These observations were extended by Cannon and his associates who regarded such phenomena as pseudo-affective behaviour, or the expression of 'sham' emotions, since it was assumed that without the cerebral cortex the animals were incapable of any emotional experience. The cortex was also assumed to exert an inhibitory influence on the subcortical structures primarily involved in the mediation of emotional behaviour.

The hypothalamus

Subsequent research pointed to the hypothalamus as an important integrating centre for 'fight' and 'flight' behaviours. Bard (1928), for example, working in Cannon's laboratory, found that an integrated 'sham rage' response was still possible in animals decerebrated above the level of the hypothalamus, provided that the posterior hypothalamus remained connected to the brainstem; at about the same time Hess (see Hess, 1954) demonstrated that integrated attack behaviours could be elicited by electrical stimulation of the perifornical region of the hypothalamus in the vicinity of the ventromedial nucleus. Bard further showed that destruction of the posterior hypothalamus largely, but not completely, abolished the 'sham rage' response and it is probable that the residual components of the response are organized by the lower brainstem (Woodworth and Sherrington, 1904).

In what is often described as the Cannon–Bard 'thalamic' theory of emotion, Cannon (1927) argued that the hypothalamus integrated the somatic and autonomic aspects of emotional behaviour, subject to the control of the thalamus, and stated that 'the peculiar quality of the emotion is added to simple sensation when the thalamic processes are aroused'. The thalamus, which relays and partially integrates information passing between the cortex and the viscera and skeletal muscles, is thus considered by the 'thalamic' theory to be involved in the experience of emotion. There is, however, little support for this hypothetical function of the thalamus from subsequent experimental or observational studies, although the involvement of the hypothalamus in emotional behaviour has been repeatedly confirmed. But Cannon was certainly correct in not attributing emotional experience to the hypothalamus, since in human patients electrical stimulation of the hypothalamus affects emotional experience very little, if at all (see Sem-Jacobson, 1968), and it seems likely that diseases of the hypothalamus produce few marked changes in subjective emotional reactions (see Bauer, 1954).

Yet it has also become apparent that the hypothalamus is not uniquely involved in emotional behaviour, or even in the organization of 'fight' behaviours. Ellison and Flynn (1968), for example, working with cats, devised an ingenious technique whereby the hypothalamus could be isolated from the rest of the brain and found that some kinds of aggressive behaviour could still be obtained, both as a response to 'natural' stimulation (tail pinching) and as a result of electrical stimulation of the midbrain, although the intensity of stimulation required was higher than before the operation. The hypothalamus cannot therefore be solely responsible for the mediation of aggressive behaviour. Indeed, there are several different kinds of aggressive behaviour (at least seven according to Moyer, 1968), and in some cases little is known about the underlying physiological mechanisms. The importance of the hypothalamus in the regulation of 'fight' and 'flight' behaviours, as with the regulation of eating behaviour (see Chapter 6), presumably derives from the fact that it is a point of convergence for a great many fibre systems, all of which act on lower systems initiating and facilitating 'fight' and 'flight' responses. The involvement of the hypothalamus with the activity of the autonomic and endocrine systems also helps to provide the peripheral physiological changes characteristic of these behaviours.

The limbic system

Early theories of limbic system functioning emphasized its role in olfaction; it was not until the 1930s that much interest was shown in the possible involvement of limbic structures in non-olfactory functions. In 1933 Herrick suggested that the limbic system might serve as a non-specific activator of all cortical activities and in the following year Kleist suggested that limbic system structures might be important in emotional behaviour. Three years later, on the basis of clinical experience with brain-damaged patients and of data from animal studies, Papez (1937) suggested that neural activity within the limbic system and, in particular, in the circuit that bears his name (see Figure 7.2) might underlie the experience of emotion; and in the late 1930s, Klüver and Bucy published the results of a series of experiments in which the behavioural consequences of temporal-lobe damage in monkeys, first investigated by Brown and Schaefer in 1888, were re-examined (Klüver and Bucy, 1937, 1938, 1939). Klüver and Bucy removed both temporal lobes, including the amygdala, the entorhinal cortex (a rhinencephalic structure; see Figure 7.2 and Chapter 4) and most of the hippocampus; the subsequent

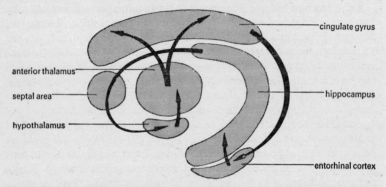

Figure 7.2 The Papez circuit. The pathways of this circuit (black arrows) form a closed loop running from the hippocampus to the hypothalamus, from the hypothalamus to the anterior thalamus and from the thalamus back to the hippocampus by way of the cingulate gyrus and the entorhinal cortex. (Adapted from McCleary and Moore, 1965, p. 32)

behavioural changes they observed have become known as the Klüver–Bucy syndrome. First, the monkeys were no longer particular about what they ate, eating food which was normally rejected and showing a tendency to put anything movable into their mouths. Second, they seemed unable to recognize familiar objects in their cages, a condition described as visual agnosia. Third, they displayed increased sexual activity, much of it towards inappropriate objects, such as pieces of cloth. Fourth, they became tamer and safer to handle and, finally, they showed no fear, in that they would repeatedly put their fingers into the flame of a burning match. In this last example, changes with respect to fear rather than changes in the awareness of or sensitivity to pain have been inferred from the observed behaviour, largely because the electrical stimulation of certain of the brain areas removed in the Klüver–Bucy experiments can produce behavioural signs of intense fear. These structures, then, appear to be involved in the mediation of fear, while pain appears to be mediated by different, although related, parts of the brain. Subsequent research has confirmed these results and examples of the Klüver–Bucy syndrome in full or modified form have also been documented in man (Marlowe, Mancall and Thomas, 1975; Terzian and Ore, 1955).

Both the theoretical speculations of Papez and the empirical studies of Klüver and Bucy engendered much interest in the relationship of the limbic system to emotional experience and behaviour. On the theoretical side, Maclean (1949, 1970) has considerably modified and extended the ideas of Papez, assigning a central role to the hippocampus and amygdala in the mediation of emotional experience but de-emphasizing that of the cingulate gyrus. Unlike Papez, Maclean did not attempt to designate specific neural circuits as representing 'the stream of feeling', regarding the limbic system as a whole as important in the integration of emotional experience both because of its extensive subcortical connections, particularly with the hypothalamus, and because it is the only region of the forebrain in which the viscera are represented. The limbic system is thus considered as the 'visceral brain'. Klüver and Bucy's experimental studies stimulated a rapid growth of research concerned with the functions of the limbic system, especially those of the amygdala and hippocampus. This literature is now very large indeed and reviews can be found in Goddard (1964), Isaacson (1974), Kaada (1972) and Mayes (1979). But although a considerable amount of evidence has been collected on the involvement of limbic system structures in such emotional reactions as fear and aggression, no central theory of emotion has gained general acceptance. While central mechanisms clearly play an important part in the mediation of emotional behaviour and probably also of emotional experience, therefore, an integration between central, peripheral and cognitive theories of emotion remains to be effected.

Chapter 8
Sensory Processes

Introduction

The senses have never been the exclusive preserve of psychologists. It would be presumptuous of us to claim anything but a part share in this field of study, and even that as very junior partners of less than 100 years standing. Long before psychology existed as a separate discipline, artists, philosophers, physicists, physiologists and scientists of many persuasions were engaged in what for centuries had been regarded as one of the most important areas of human inquiry, since it was believed that only through the agency of the senses did we acquire knowledge of the world and of the consequences of our actions. Today it remains more than ever an inter-disciplinary enterprise, and in this chapter we shall attempt to show how the differing techniques and approaches of the neurophysiologist and the experimental psychologist in particular have within the past two decades merged to yield important new insights into the way the senses function.

Before doing that we need to put these developments into some historical context. To this end, the first part of the chapter will be devoted to a comparison of some classical and contemporary views of the senses. The second and third parts deal with receptor function and discuss how the neurophysiologist's microelectrode studies of single units in the rabbit's eye and the cat's brain are beginning to fit together with psychophysical investigations of human illusions (negative after-effects) to create a coherent story of how the senses and their associated nerve pathways extract essential informational features from physical changes in our environment. The final part is concerned with the correlated function of the body's various position and motion senses, and with the consequences of rearranging these inputs in biologically unnatural circumstances.

A word about general emphasis: many textbooks or chapters dealing with the senses tend to present their material in a compartmentalized form, usually devoting a separate section to each sense (see Geldard, 1972). While this approach permits the author to concentrate upon the special attributes of each of the senses, it is often at the expense of those features that are common to all of them. This chapter seeks to emphasize the general rather than the unique aspects of sensory processes, and to stress the high degree of overlapping function that exists between structurally distinct modalities.

Some classical and contemporary views of the senses

Johannes Muller's doctrine of specific nerve energies

By what means do we sense objects in the world around us? The ancient Greeks answered this fundamental question by proposing the *image theory*. Objects, they argued, gave off from their surfaces faint images of themselves which, on being transmitted to the mind via the senses, formed the basis of our awareness. In other words, they believed that sensations derived *directly* from the properties of external objects; the senses served merely as channels through which these images were conducted to the mind or *sensorium*.

Although many philosophers and scientists from the seventeenth century onwards (particularly John Locke, Thomas Young and Charles Bell) had produced cogent arguments against such a view, the image theory was sufficiently intact in the first quarter of the nineteenth century for Johannes Muller to feel it necessary to formulate in 1826 his famous doctrine with the express purpose of laying these ancient but still insistent beliefs to rest. The essence of the doctrine is contained in the following statement:

Sensation consists ... in receiving through the medium of the nerves, and as the result of the action of an external cause, a knowledge of certain qualities or conditions, *not of the external bodies, but of the nerves of sense themselves*; and these qualities of the nerves of sense are in all different, the nerve of each sense having its own peculiar quality or energy (Dennis, 1948, p. 162).

Very simply, Muller was asserting that since the mind is only in direct contact with its nerves, it can only be immediately acquainted with the qualities of these nerves, not with the properties of the external world. He cited many phenomena to support his doctrine, but just one example will suffice to bring the point home:

It is well known that by exerting pressure upon the eye, when the eyelids are closed, we can give rise to the appearance of a luminous circle ... The light thus produced has no existence external to the optic nerve, it is merely a sensation excited in it. However strongly we press upon the eye in the dark, so as to give rise to the appearance of luminous flashes, these flashes, being merely sensations, are incapable of illuminating external objects (Dennis, 1948, p. 159).

Sensations, therefore, derive from the specific energies of the sensory nerves. Muller maintained that there were five such energies, one for each of the classical five senses. Subsequent writers did not dispute the basic doctrine. They had no wish to return to the image theory which, in any case, they had probably abandoned long before the publication of this formal doctrine. Instead, they extended the number of specific nerve energies. Some twenty years earlier, Thomas Young had already suggested the existence of three different optic nerve fibres, each transmitting information relating to a primary colour (red, green or blue). In 1852, Helmholtz built upon this earlier foundation by proposing three specific visual nerve energies to account for colour vision; and, in 1863, when he published his theory of hearing, he assumed a different specific energy for each of the discriminable tones, a total amounting to many thousands.

The influence of the extended doctrine was immense (see Boring, 1942, pp. 73–8), and it still remains central to our present understanding of sensory processes. But the doctrine is not without its contemporary critics, as we shall see when we come to discuss the work of the distinguished American sensory psychologist, J. J. Gibson. Before considering these objections, however, we need to understand how Muller's doctrine became the keystone of the most widely used classification of the senses, that developed by the British physiologist Sir Charles Sherrington in 1906.

Sherrington's classification

In his classic work, *The Integrative Action of the Nervous System* (1906), Sherrington put forward a scheme for classifying the senses which has remained the accepted orthodoxy until recent times. There were two assumptions underlying this classification. First, that there are a certain number of clearly defined senses. Second, each sense has specialized receptors that can excite corresponding sensory nerves. In keeping with Muller's doctrine, it was assumed that the brain deduced the nature of the stimulating event from *which* of these receptors and their corresponding fibres were active.

Sherrington initially divided receptor-organs into two broad groups: those lying within the *surface* sheet of cells covering the organism, and those lying within the *deep* cellular field beneath it. The former were further subdivided into two groups: the *exteroceptors*, senses such as the eyes, ears, nose, mouth and skin that are in free contact with the external world; and the *interoceptors*, lying mainly along the surface of the alimentary canal and visceral organs. Those senses lying within the 'deep field', principally in the inner ear (the vestibular system) and in the muscles, tendons and joints, he termed *proprioceptors*. These receptor groups give rise to three kinds of sensation as summarized in Table 8.1.

Table 8.1
Sherrington's classification

Receptor group	Type of sensation	Basis of
Exteroceptors	Sensations of external origin	Perception
Interoceptors	Vague sensations of internal organs	Feeling and emotion (?)
Proprioceptors	Sensations of position and movement	Kinaesthesis

The problem of proprioception

According to Sherrington's scheme, a person's sensations of his own movements occur as the result of activity within receptors specifically adapted for the purpose, the proprioceptors. Proprioception was therefore regarded as a separate and distinct sense modality that supplemented the classical five: sight, hearing, taste, smell and touch.

In 1968, J. J. Gibson challenged the Muller–Sherrington orthodoxy in his book, *The Senses Considered as Perceptual Systems*. The principal weakness of the Sherrington classification, he argued, was 'the fallacy of ascribing proprioception to the proprioceptors'. We obtain a sense of our own movement not only from specialized receptors in the inner ear, joints, tendons and muscles, but also from what we can see, hear and feel. Clearly, therefore, kinaesthesis does not depend solely upon the proprioceptors alone. Nor does our knowledge of external events depend solely upon the exteroceptors. When we are moved passively by some vehicle or device, we can register these events through the excitation of proprioceptive pathways from the vestibular system and from the joints and tendons. From these observations, Gibson (1968, p. 34) concluded:

Evidently something is wrong with the whole theory of the special senses and with the doctrine of specific nerve energies. More precisely, something is wrong with the theory that all experience is correlated with activation of specific receptors and their nerves.

Gibson's classification

As the basis of his classification, Gibson proposed two distinctions: between *exteroception* and *proprioception*, and between *imposed* and *obtained* stimulation. Exteroception is concerned with the detection of environmental events; proprioception with bodily events. Imposed stimulation falls upon the passive organism; obtained stimulation derives from the organism's own activity. The latter distinction is comparable to that made by von Holst (1954) between exafferent stimulation (stimulation of sense organs produced only by changes in the external world) and reafferent stimulation (sensory feed-back stimulation dependent upon self-produced movements). The resulting Gibsonian classification is shown in Table 8.2.

The purpose of Gibson's classification is thus to distinguish between (a) the senses as passive channels of *sensation*, and (b) the senses as active gatherers of *information*. Muller's doctrine of specific nerve energies, Gibson claims, can only be meaningfully applied to the former. For the latter, he uses the term perceptual systems to emphasize that their overlapping functions cut across the classificatory boundaries imposed by Sherrington. The following example will help to illustrate the nature of this distinction. When the head is tilted, say, towards the left shoulder, the action is accompanied by sensory inputs along a large number of distinct sensory channels that together comprise the position and motion senses (i.e. the eyes, the semicircular canals, the otolith organs, and various specialized mechano-receptors located in the muscles, skin and joints). Despite the multiplicity of channels involved, giving rise to a diversity of sensory qualities, the essential information conveyed to the brain is the same in all cases, namely that the head has tilted so far in a particular direction. Moreover, the message communicated by these various feedback channels is, under natural conditions, exactly that expected on the basis of the original command to move the head. The fact that this correspondence can break down in unusual or biologically atypical circumstances, creating illusory perceptions and other more unpleasant effects, provides direct evidence for the existence of perceptual systems as something distinct from sensory channels, and we shall be considering these phenomena in the last part of the chapter.

Table 8.2
Gibson's classification

| | Type of stimulation | |
	Imposed	Obtained
Exteroception	Arises from classical five senses when they act as passive channels of sensation, detecting events that result from environmental changes alone	Arises from classical five senses when they are actively orientated toward environmental events so as to obtain information. The active senses are termed perceptual systems
Proprioception	Occurs when parts of the body are moved by some external agency, or when the whole body is transported passively	Occurs as the result of self-induced movements or whole-body locomotion. There are at least six feedback channels that could be involved: muscular, articular, vestibular, cutaneous, auditory and visual proprioception

Visual kinaesthesis

The traditional view, derived from Sherrington's classification, is that vision is solely concerned with obtaining information about the outside world. Gibson, as we have seen in Table 8.2, rejects this view and maintains that vision is also kinaesthetic in that it registers movements of the body just as much as do the vestibular receptors and those in the muscles, joints and skin. Vision, he asserts, obtains information about *both* the environment *and* the self. To set against this view, however, we have the everyday observation that being plunged into darkness does not cause us to fall over. We can maintain our balance quite adequately through the traditional proprioceptive channels. So how can we establish the relative importance of vision as a source of position and motion information?

If vision is a primary rather than a secondary or merely supplementary source of kinaesthetic information, it should be possible to demonstrate its importance for the control of our upright posture and in generating false sensations of whole-body movement. A particularly convincing demonstration would be to show that vision is capable of overruling the mechanical proprioceptors, even when only they are conveying accurate information about the body's position in space. This was the task that David Lee and his co-workers at Edinburgh University set themselves, and the results of their

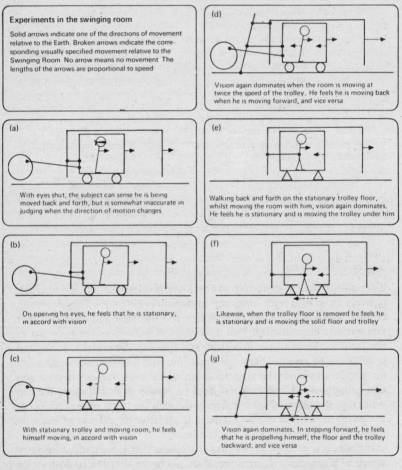

Figure 8.1   Experiments in the swinging room (From Lee and Lishman, 1975, p. 60)

investigations provide compelling evidence for the view advanced by Gibson that vision is a powerful kinaesthetic sense.

They began by analysing the precise nature of the kinaesthetic information that vision furnishes during the course of normal self-propelled locomotion (Lee, 1974). Consider what occurs within the visual field as we walk through a room. Our progress creates a continuous change in seen perspective, and it can be shown mathematically that these purely visual changes specify precisely one's motion relative to the stationary walls of the room. What would happen then if we reversed the normal arrangement? Suppose we kept the observer still and moved the whole room (or something that looked like a room) relative to him? Would the orientation centres of the brain respond only to the veridical information derived from the mechanical propriocep-tors? Or would they be dominated by the visual information so that the observer experiences the illusion of self-motion?

Lee and Lishman (1975) explored these possibilities using a Swinging Room device. This was a large box-like structure, approximately 4 m long by 2 m across, open at the bottom and one end, and suspended just above the floor by four ropes from a high ceiling. The inside of the 'room' was covered by patterned wallpaper, and the whole structure could be swung silently to and fro along its length. The observer stood in a trolley which could be moved passively or actively by his own efforts when a section of its floor was removed. The results of these experiments are summarized in Figure 8.1.

From these studies and other similar investigations (Dichgans and Brandt, 1978), it is evident that vision functions proprioceptively as an integral part of the control system for maintaining posture. Since vision can furnish more sensitive position and motion information than the mechanical pro-prioceptors, it appears to exert a dominant influence in the fine control of posture. Vestibular and other mechanical proprioceptors allow us to main-tain our balance with eyes closed so long as the support surface is adequate; but there is a considerable increase in the amount of body sway under these conditions. The primary role of vision, particularly during the course of infancy and childhood, seems to be in tuning up mechanical proprioception. Congenitally blind children are generally retarded in learning to stand and walk, and in developing other motor skills.

These observations may also help to explain why we sometimes experience dizziness when looking out from high buildings or mountain tops. In these circumstances, the stationary objects within our field of view, in relation to which we detect body sway, are far removed, and thus fail to provide the fine tuning information normally present in our immediate surroundings. It is interesting to note that when experienced climbers are subject to these feelings of vertigo and bodily instability, they overcome them by looking at the rock face near to. In this way they obtain good visual proprioception which is also in close accord with sensations derived from the mechanical senses.

Receptor function

Some general principles

Regardless of which particular sense is involved, our awareness of both external and internal events is the product of a series of information-processing steps within the central nervous system (CNS). In the first place, a *stimulus* constituting some temporal or spatial change in either electro-magnetic, mechanical or chemical energy impinges upon the sense *receptor* that is specifically adapted to detect it. At the receptor, the energy changes are transduced or encoded into *neural impulses* in such a way as to preserve the information concerning the stimulus event. This sensory message embodied in the neural code is transmitted via a series of way stations to the higher levels of the CNS whereupon it is decoded to form a basis of our conscious awareness of the stimulus event.

We know very little about the final stages of this process, but the work of neurophysiologists and psychophysicists over the past fifteen years or so has begun to reveal what happens at the early stages of analysis and at some of the intermediate levels. But before considering this evidence in further detail, let us attempt to state a number of general principles that appear to hold true for all senses at all levels within the animal kingdom.

The brain is essentially a change detector. All sensory systems are biased to accentuate the differences in our surroundings and to attenuate the constant features. In order to detect these changes, the nervous system must make comparisons between the output of the same receptor at different times, or between different units at the same time. When a change is noted, a 'comparator' unit produces a vigorous but relatively short-lived response; if no change is detected, the output remains more or less constant.

The basis of this comparison at all levels of analysis is achieved by adding and subtracting the inputs to individual neurons. This relatively simple pairing of *excitatory* and *inhibitory* processes provides all the necessary computational power to analyse the sensory message into its component features, and thus reduces the total amount of information carried by the message as it passes from one level to the next.

Lateral inhibition

A fairly simple way of discovering how this process operates at a physiological level is to consider what happens within the compound eye of *Limulus*, the horseshoe crab. This animal has taught us a great deal about the basic physiology of visual function since it has a large, readily accessible eye with easily dissected nerve fibres, and in contrast to most other eyes its neural organization is relatively simple.

The coarsely faceted compound eye of *Limulus* has about 1,000 ommatidia or 'little eyes'. Each ommatidium is roughly the size of a pencil lead and contains about a dozen cells arranged like the segments of a tangerine around the dendrite of an associated neuron – a single eccentric cell within each ommatidium. Working at Johns Hopkins University in Baltimore during the 1950s, Hartline and his co-workers found that by inserting microelectrodes in the eccentric cell they could record the nerve impulses (the sensory message) leaving the ommatidium. By this means, they could study the response of single sensory units to a controlled light stimulus; but, more importantly, they were able to investigate the interaction between adjacent units. In particular, they demonstrated that neighbouring ommatidia have a mutually inhibitory effect upon each other, and it is this process of *lateral inhibition* that constitutes the key to understanding how the sensory message is analysed, and its crucial features extracted, at successive stages in the sensory system.

Before moving on to these wider implications, let us first briefly examine what it was that Hartline and his collaborators discovered. When light is directed at a single ommatidium (let us call it A) it generates a volley of impulses whose frequency is directly related to the light intensity. At high intensities, the nerve fires at about thirty times per second. As the intensity is reduced by factors of ten, firing drops off in uniform steps, falling to a low of two to three impulses per second.

When this narrow light beam is directed at an adjacent ommatidium (B), no response is recorded from A, but B yields the same pattern of firing as described above. However, when *two* adjacent ommatidia are illuminated at the same time, each produces a diminished neural response. The amount of inhibition exerted upon each receptor unit in the steady state depends upon the frequency of firing of the other; the more widely separated they are, the smaller the inhibitory effect. When several ommatidia are illuminated at the same time, the inhibition of each is proportional to the sum of the inhibitory effects from all the others.

What, then, is the biological significance of this inhibitory interaction between adjacent receptors? Because the more intensely illuminated receptors exert a stronger suppressive influence on the activity of the less intensely illuminated units than the other way round, the differences between the firing rates of units from differently illuminated regions of the eye will be exaggerated. As a result, the contrasts between darker and lighter regions of the visual field are enhanced to accentuate the boundaries between them in a way that is not present in the pattern of light energy falling upon the eye. A comparison between the pattern of light energy at a dark–light boundary and the rates of firing from corresponding receptor units is shown in Figure 8.2. It will be seen that firing rates are increased on the bright side of the light intensity step and decreased on the dim side. The activity of those ommatidia lying on the bright side away from the step will be suppressed as a result of the mutual inhibitory influence that occurs in a region of uniformly high illumination. But those near the step on the bright side will receive less inhibition from their less active neighbours on the dark side; consequently their firing rates will be greater than those further away on the bright side. The same argument can be reversed to explain the dip in firing rates close to the boundary on the dark side. These less active units will be strongly inhibited by their more active neighbours on the bright side of the intensity step.

Although we have been considering the neural activity of a relatively primitive eye to illustrate the basic mechanism of lateral inhibition, a similar process leading to contrast heightening at contours can account for perceptual phenomena within our own experience. Good examples are the Mach bands, named after the Austrian physicist–philosopher, Ernst Mach. If we inspect a pattern, such as that shown in Figure 8.3, consisting of a series of uniform grey bands graded from white to black, we do not see the constant shade at each step that is actually present in the physical stimulus. Instead, each band appears to be lighter towards the next darker band, and darker towards the lighter band, producing a scalloped effect overall. Artists such as van Gogh and Gauguin were clearly familiar with this heightened border contrast, and even took pains to enhance it in their paintings by bordering objects in black. As is evident from simple line drawings, significant information is conveyed by contours alone. Having this effect 'wired in' at a neurological level provides the first essential step in the complex process of pattern recognition. Although we have illustrated the mechanism of lateral inhibition with exclusively visual examples, the process is likely to be present in all sensory channels. Georg von Bekesy of Harvard University has suggested

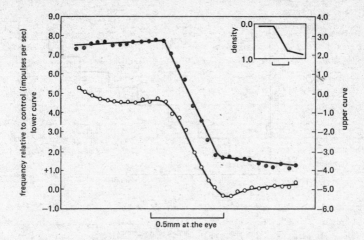

Figure 8.2 Contour enhancement in the *Limulus* eye. This is demonstrated by passing a 'step' pattern of light across the Limulus eye. The
graph shows the rate of a single ommatidium as a function of the
position of a luminance gradient (shown in inset). When the eye is
masked so that the light strikes only one ommatidium, the discharge rate
forms a simple step-shaped curve as the pattern moves across the eye
(upper curve with solid circles). But if the eye is unmasked so that the
neighbouring ommatidia are also illuminated, the discharge frequency
of the single ommatidium is inhibited in varying degrees, as illustrated
by the lower curve with open circles. The net effect of this lateral
inhibition is to accentuate the contrast at the light–dark borders. (From
Ratcliff and Hartline, 1959, p. 1250)

that a similar reciprocal inhibition in the auditory system would lead to a
sharpening of the sense of pitch. For more detailed discussions of this
phenomenon see Held and Richards (1972), Lindsay and Norman (1977),
and Schiffman (1976).

We will now consider how these excitatory and inhibitory processes
operate at different levels of the CNS to extract essential features from the
pattern of stimulation impinging upon the receptors.

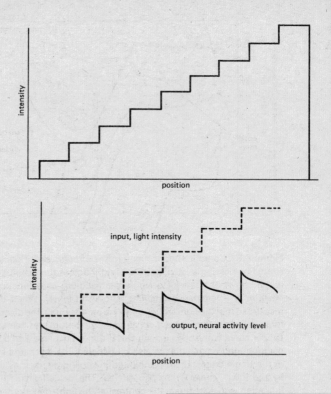

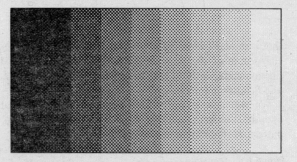

Figure 8.3   Mach bands. (From Lindsay and Norman, 1977)

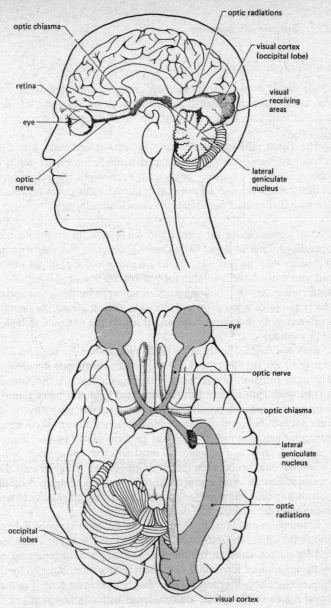

Figure 8.4 Visual pathways from retina to cortex. (From Lindsay and Norman, 1977)

Levels of processing

Once again, we will be drawing on examples from the visual system as this has been the most extensively studied modality. However, it is reasonable to assume that analogous levels of processing operate within other sensory systems.

The visual pathways connecting the retinal receptors with the visual (occipital) cortex are shown diagrammatically in Figure 8.4. For convenience, we can subdivide the visual system into three levels of processing: at the *retina*, in the *lateral geniculate nucleus* (LGN) and in the *visual cortex*. Here we shall restrict our attention to work on mammals.

Retinal processing. In the complex visual systems of mammals, the retinal operations differ in detail from those of the crab, but the basic functions served are essentially similar. In the *Limulus* eye, for example, one receptor cell can only have an inhibitory effect on its neighbour. But in the mammalian eye, neighbouring receptor units can both increase and decrease the response of a ganglion cell (i.e. cells that combine the neural signals from receptors in various ways and transmit the outcome to higher levels of processing).

Rods and cones. The structure of the mammalian eye requires a trade-off between light sensitivity and the power to discriminate detailed patterns. The more receptors connected to a single ganglion cell, the more sensitive it is to weak light signals. But the increased light sensitivity gained by this arrangement exacts a penalty in that it is relatively insensitive to different light patterns falling upon the receptive region of the retina covered by that particular ganglion cell. If details of patterns are to be discriminated, the *receptive fields* should be small; the most sensitive arrangement being a one-to-one relationship between retinal receptors and ganglion cells. Different species achieve different compromise solutions depending upon the demands of their habitats. Humans, for example, need both the ability to see in dim light and to discriminate fine detail in daylight.

In monkeys and humans there are two different types of light-sensitive unit in the retina, the *rods* and the *cones*. There are about 120 million rods and six million cones in the human eye. They are distinguished not only by the anatomical forms that gave them their names, but also by the quite different functions they serve. The cones, present most densely in the central *foveal* region of the retina, are concerned with colour vision and fine discrimination. The fovea is richly supplied with bipolar and ganglion cells, and almost each cone has its own 'private line' to the optic nerve. The cone system is arranged anatomically to have high acuity under daylight conditions, but to be relatively ineffective in dim illumination.

The rod is about 500 times more sensitive to light than the cone, but it is 'colour blind'. Whereas the cones contain a variety of photochemical substances necessary for colour vision, the rods contain a substance called *rhodopsin*, or visual purple, which is bleached in the presence of light and contributes to the rod's light sensitivity in a way that is not fully understood.

On-centre and off-centre receptive fields. Kuffler (1953) carried out the first study of the spatial extent of the retinal area which could be stimulated to produce a response in a mammalian ganglion cell. He used an intraocular microelectrode to record the activity of cells within the cat's retina. Employing a small spot of light which could be projected onto different parts of the retina, Kuffler showed that each ganglion cell was most sensitive to illumination at a point close to the cell body. But the response of a cell to stimulation at this point could be one of two kinds: some cells fired when the light spot was turned on ('on' responses); others were activated when the light was turned off after being on for some time ('off' responses). Nothing Kuffler did changed this characteristic of a cell's behaviour, and he concluded that there were two distinct kinds of ganglion cells: *on-centre cells* and *off-centre cells*.

Although each ganglion cell was most readily stimulated when the light spot was projected onto the retina close to it, it could also be influenced by a spot falling anywhere within a roughly circular region around the optimum position. Stimulation of these surrounding regions produced a response opposite to that of the centre area. Those cells giving 'on-centre' responses produced 'off' responses when the light spot fell in the surround, and *vice versa* (see Figure 8.5). Thus we can distinguish two kinds of receptive fields: on-centre/off-surround and off-centre/on-surround. Simultaneous stimulation of both centre and surround regions of the receptive field had little effect on the cell's discharge rate, whereas two spots of light shone on separate parts of an 'on' area produced a more vigorous 'on' response than either spot alone.

It would appear that each of these ganglion cells was comparing the illumination of the centre of its receptive field with that of the surround. The main concern of these cells seems to be the *contrast* in illumination between one retinal region and surrounding regions. Ganglion cells with this type of receptive field have now been found in the retinae of every vertebrate so far studied (Michael, 1969).

X, Y, and W cells. Subsequent research has shown that Kuffler's classifi-

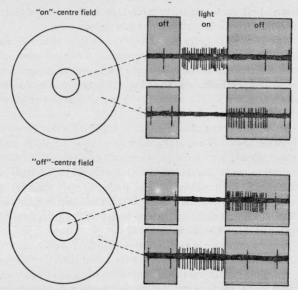

Figure 8.5 'On-centre' and 'off-centre' fields. (From David H. Hobel, 'The visual cortex of the brain'. Copyright © 1963 by Scientific American, Inc. All rights reserved)

cation of the retinal ganglion cells of the cat into on-centre and off-centre types can be extended still further. Cells with concentrically organized receptive fields can be divided into two groups: X and Y cells

Type X cells have small cell bodies and axons. They tend to be located in the central part of the retina, and send relatively slow sustained signals up the optic pathway. Type Y cells are relatively large centre-surround units that tend to be situated in the periphery of the retina and send comparatively fast transient signals up the optic pathway. Type X cells are sensitive to continual stimulation, and to light contrasts; type Y cells tend to be sensitive to movement and respond to changes in stimulation.

A third group of cells, termed W cells, do not appear (like the X and Y cells) to be centre-surround units. They have very small cell bodies and slowly conducting axons that project not to the LGN as do the X and Y cells, but to the *superior colliculus*, a part of the brain concerned with movements and with object position. They include units that respond to specific directions of stimulus movement, but the full extent of their behaviour is not yet understood.

Lateral geniculate nucleus (LGN). Neural signals from the retinal ganglion cells are (for the most part) transmitted upward to the next relay station en route to the visual cortex, the LGN. Since cells of the LGN receive their main excitatory input from only one, or at most a small number of retinal ganglion cells with adjacent receptive fields, it is not surprising that they behave in a similar fashion to the retinal ganglion cells. Although their responses are rather more transient than the corresponding retinal units, they too can be subdivided into X (sustained) and Y (transient) types.

Since the LGN seems to pass on retinal messages more or less unchanged, it is not clear what role it plays in the processing of visual information. Certainly inputs to the LGN do not come solely from the retina; some signals are received from the reticular formation. It has been suggested that the activity in these non-sensory pathways may help to determine whether visual information is relayed to the cortex. There is also a possibility that the LGN acts like an intensity control. But these suggestions are still highly speculative.

Visual cortex. Fibres from the LGN terminate mainly in the fourth and fifth layers of the visual cortex, and fibres from adjacent regions of the retina end up at adjacent parts of the cortical receiving areas. The analysis of the incoming sensory message begins at these layers and continues through successive cortical layers in a progressive region-by-region extraction of significant features. Our understanding of these processes derives in large measure from the pioneering work by David Hubel and Torsten Wiesel at the Harvard Medical School (Hubel, 1963).

Hubel and Wiesel identified three major classes of form-sensitive cortical cells in the visual system of cats and monkeys, each tuned to detecting and signalling the presence of such features as edges, light and dark areas, slits of light, orientation and specific directions of seen motion. These three types were termed *simple*, *complex* and *hypercomplex* cells.

Simple cells. These have receptive fields that can be mapped with stationary stimuli. The fields are subdivided into excitatory and inhibitory regions separated by straight parallel boundaries. The top part of Figure 8.6 shows such a cell giving an 'off' response to a slit stimulus in one region (i), and a small 'on' response to a stimulus in the other region (ii). Simple cells respond selectively to lines, edges, bars and slits in specific retinal regions.

Complex cells. These also respond to bars, slits and edges provided that, as with simple cells, the stimulus shape is suitably orientated for the particular cell under observation. In addition, they respond to moving lines (depending on the direction of motion relative to the cell's preferred tuning). The second part of Figure 8.6 shows a complex cell responding vigorously to movement in one direction (i), and being largely inhibited by movement in the other direction (ii). Complex cells are not so discriminating about the retinal location of the stimulus provided it is correctly orientated. In this sense, therefore, the information extracted by the complex cells is more abstract than that obtained by simple cells, since they are less place-bound

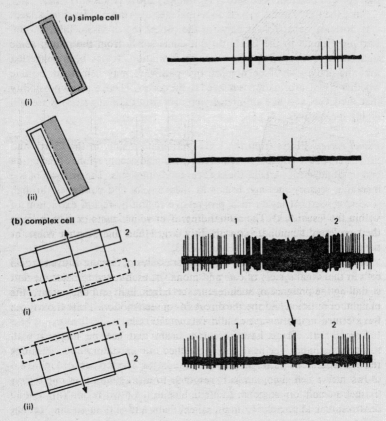

Figure 8.6 (a, b, c)   Simple, complex and hypercomplex cells in the cat's visual cortex (From Charles R. Michael, 'Retinal processing of visual images'. Copyright © 1969 by Scientific American, Inc. All rights reserved)

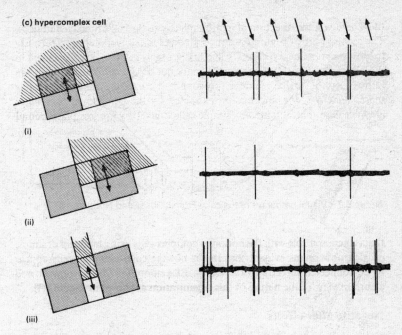

(c) hypercomplex cell

(i)

(ii)

(iii)

within the visual field. The retinal areas over which complex cells react to their preferred stimuli are considerably larger than the receptive fields for simple cells.

Hypercomplex cells. These too respond only to moving stimuli, again usually in a directionally selective fashion. The unique feature of these cells is that the moving edge or line must be terminated properly to give the maximum response. As the third part of Figure 8.6 shows, this type of cell has a central activation region and antagonistic surrounds. It responds best to stimuli that are restricted in length. In this instance, the longer stimuli affect both kinds of region (i and ii), but the most limited one only influences the activation area (iii).

Just a few years ago, it was believed that these various levels of feature extraction were organized in a simple hierarchy of processing with retinal centre-surround units forming simple cells which then formed complex cells which in turn formed hypercomplex cells. But we now know that this view of cascading feature extractions is too simple. It has been found, for example, that certain complex cells respond faster than simple cells, an observation

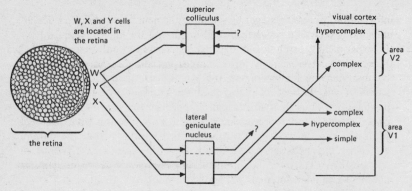

Figure 8.7   Visual pathways of the cat. (From Lindsay and Norman, 1977)

that is incompatible with the notion of complex cells being made up of simple cells. It now seems evident that this is not the case: complex cells appear to be connected directly to the LGN. Blakemore (1975) has summarized a current view of the nature of this organization as shown in Figure 8.7.

Negative after-effects

Gibson's principle

In the previous section we considered some of the major advances that have been made in our understanding of how the CNS extracts essential informational features from the sensory message. The research discussed so far has involved the insertion of microelectrodes into specific receptor units within the sense organs or brains of experimental animals. But these techniques are clearly not applicable in the case of human subjects. So how can we investigate comparable processes in man?

The answer to this question lies in a widespread class of perceptual illusions termed *negative after-effects*, phenomena that have been noted and studied since the time of the ancient Greeks, but whose true significance for elucidating human sensory processes has only come to be properly appreciated within the last two decades. The methods used to investigate these after-effects are predominantly those of the experimental psychologist. They use as their basic data the perceptual judgements of human observers as they vary in response to controlled and systematic manipulations of those stimulus factors that are suspected of influencing some dimension of the illusory experience. Whereas the neurophysiologist seeks to identify critical information-processing stages by sampling the neural activity of particular units along the route between the end-organ and the higher brain centres, the experimental psychologist takes as his starting point the outcome of this sensory analysis, namely, an anomalous perceptual experience, and then by observing how it alters in response to changes in the inducing conditions strives to make testable inferences about the nature of the underlying neural mechanisms. Thus the two disciplines approach the sensory system from opposite ends. The neurophysiologist tends to work forwards from the input, while the experimental psychologist works backwards from the output. Taken together, however, these two complementary approaches have proved remarkably successful of late in identifying common sensory mechanisms in both experimental animals and man.

We can experience a negative after-effect whenever we have been exposed to a steady-state stimulus for a sufficient time to 'fatigue' or diminish the activity of those feature analysers specifically concerned with its detection. When this stimulus is removed, our perceptions are briefly distorted in a number of fairly predictable ways depending upon the nature of the inducing conditions. These consequences have been described by Gibson (1937) as follows: 'If a sensory process which has an opposite is made to persist by a constant application of its appropriate stimulus conditions, the quality will diminish in the direction of becoming neutral, and therewith the quality evoked by any stimulus for the dimension in question will be shifted temporarily towards the opposite or complementary quality.'

This statement is really in three parts. In the first, Gibson states what kind of sensory dimensions are governed by this principle of 'adaptation with negative after-effect'; namely, those which have an opposite, for example, the complementary colours yellow and blue, red and green, or seen motion in one direction and motion in the opposing direction. All of these *oppositional* dimensions have a number of common properties. They run from a maximum of one quality, through a neutral point (which possesses the attributes of neither quality, but which is a point of departure for both of them) to a maximum of the opposite quality. In the case of colour, the dimension runs from, say, the most saturated blue, through grey the neutral point, to the most saturated yellow; and so on for the other oppositional dimensions.

The second part of Gibson's principle defines the process of *sensory adaptation*. He states that if we are exposed to a steady stimulus from some point along the dimension, we become increasingly less aware both of that particular stimulus and of other levels of the same stimulus quality. Thus, continuous exposure to travelling at 70 m.p.h. along a motorway makes it feel a good deal slower than it really is. Indeed, it is to combat this potentially dangerous illusion that yellow lines, designed to enhance the impression of speed, have been painted across the exit roads from some British motorways. Similarly, if we stare at a patch of blue for a long time it appears to become increasingly greyish in hue. As we indicated in the previous section, the central nervous system is essentially a change-detector. It is programmed to take note of the changes in our surroundings and to ignore the constant features. Sensory adaptation is yet another manifestation of this general mode of operation. It is one way in which the nervous system conserves its finite information-handling resources: by assigning different levels of priority to different kinds of stimulation. Those sensory inputs which reflect change receive a high priority, while those inputs that maintain a steady state receive the lowest priority.

Yet, as the final part of Gibson's principle implies, this is a two-edged process. While it blunts our awareness of a steady-state stimulus, at the same time it sensitizes us to the absence of that stimulus, or to any other change in its quality. Prior to exposure to the constant stimulus, our sensory mechanisms are equally sensitive to both ends of an oppositional stimulus dimension; after it we are less sensitive to the stimulated end, but more sensitive to the opposite or unstimulated end. The consequence of the exposure is thus to shift temporarily the balance of sensitivity so that we are biased towards detecting the hitherto absent quality. A corollary to this is that if we are now presented with the neutral point of the sensory dimension, it takes on the characteristics of the opposing end; that is, the end to which we are now sensitized. Thus, after continuous exposure to, say, a seen motion to the right, a stationary object falling upon the previously stimulated area of the retina appears to be imbued with apparent velocity to the left. If we stare into the centre of a waterfall for some time and then direct our gaze to the bank of the river, it seems to be moving (although not actually going anywhere) in a direction opposite to that of the falling water. Likewise, after staring at a blue patch, a grey patch appears yellow, and so on. Hence, we use the term *negative* after-effect.

For all that it neatly encapsulates the basic features of the phenomenon in a single sentence, Gibson's principle does not constitute much of an explanation. In psychology, as in other sciences, there are many different levels of explanation. At a purely behavioural level, Gibson's principle is useful in so far that it clearly indicates we are dealing with a general property of the sensory system as a whole rather than with the peculiarities of particular modalities. It also points to a causal relationship between sensory adaptation and its *sequelae*, the negative after-effects – a relationship, incidentally, that has not gone unchallenged (Over, 1971). There is also evidence to show that after-effects are not restricted to the 'opponents-process' systems described by Gibson, but can occur in one form or another in virtually all receptors in response to most forms of steady-state stimulation (Mollon, 1974). To find a more satisfactory explanation, therefore, we need to penetrate to the level of the feature analysers and determine how the neurophysiological studies can help us to understand the neural origins of negative after-effects. To this end, we will focus upon a particular class of after-effects, the *visual after-effects of motion* (VAMs). VAMs have been extensively studied over many years, and there is reason to believe that their underlying mechanisms have important features in common with those involved in other perceptual after-effects.

Visual after-effects of motion

A clear and interesting account of the early investigations of the VAM can be found in the excellent monograph by Holland (1965). The illusion was known to Aristotle and probably to many before him, but the first modern 'discovery' of the illusion is attributed to the Czech physicist, Purkinje, who observed it accidentally while watching a lengthy cavalry parade pass before his window. On looking across to the houses on the far side of the street, he noticed that they appeared to be drifting in the opposite direction to the horsemen. In 1852, Lotze proposed that when an individual is asked to fixate a limited area on a uniformly moving structured stimulus, his mind becomes accustomed to the movement, so that, eventually, this habitual movement appears normal. That is, it has the same significance as a stationary stimulus. By contrast, therefore, cessation of the stimulus appears to the observer as an equal rate of movement in the opposite direction.

A basically similar explanation was advanced by Sylvanus Thompson (1880) in his notion of 'retinal fatigue plus contrast': 'The retina ceases to perceive, as a motion, a steady succession of images that pass over a particular region for a sufficient time to induce fatigue; and, in a portion of the retina so affected, the image of a body not in motion appears by contrast to be moving in a complementary direction.' These remarkably prescient views were also echoed by Exner (1888) and by Wohlgemuth (1911) whose monograph on the VAM is still a valuable source of information and methodological guidance to contemporary investigators. Anticipating Gibson's principle, Thompson went on to comment on the similarity between the mechanisms underlying the VAM and those implicated in 'kindred ... physicopsychological after-effects'. These included complementary subjective colours, smells, sensations of heat and cold, and the apparent diminution in loudness of a steady sound of constant pitch until one is made aware of it by its cessation.

With the exception of Gibson's (1937) principle, little further theoretical progress was made until the early 1960s when two very significant papers appeared. The first of these was by Sutherland (1961). Two years after the first report by Hubel and Wiesel of directionally-specific motion detectors in the visual cortex of the cat, Sutherland suggested that similar receptors might underlie after-effects of motion and orientation. He argued that motion after-effects arose because of an *imbalance* in the ratio of activities in two sets of directionally-tuned mechanisms, each sensitive to opposite directions of stimulus motion. Immediately following the cessation of the stimulus motion, the resting discharge of the receptors tuned to the opposite direction of motion would be greater than that from the previously stimulated receptors. This sensory message – the ratio between the two levels of activity – would then form the basis of the illusory perception of reversed motion.

Two years later, the main points of this *ratio hypothesis* were largely supported by the work of two Cambridge physiologists, Barlow and Hill (1963). While investigating motion sensitive units in the rabbit's retina, Barlow and Hill made some observations concerning the effects of prolonged exposure to a constant velocity stimulus. Previously it had been found that these motion sensitive units gave a vigorous discharge in response to stimuli moved in certain specific directions. Motion in the 'preferred direction' gave the maximum discharge, while motion in the opposite (null) direction caused no change in the resting activity. The 'preferred direction' was found to differ in different units, and the information as to the direction of stimulation was provided by which of the cells was currently active. With a microelectrode inserted into a movement-sensitive retinal ganglion cell, Barlow and Hill rotated a patterned stimulus disc in front of the eye for a period of approximately one minute. The stimulus motion was in the 'preferred direction' for that particular unit, and they recorded its activity for a period of fifteen seconds prior to the onset of motion and for a period of some fifty-five seconds after its cessation. The same procedure was then repeated with the stimulus motion in the opposite (null) direction. The results are summarized in Figure 8.8.

There are two important points to notice about these data. First, while

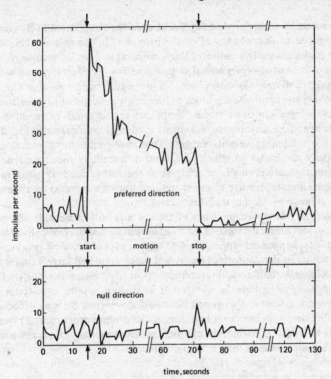

Figure 8.8   The results of Barlow and Hill (1963) (see text). (From Barlow and Hill, 1963)

motion in the preferred direction caused the unit to fire rapidly at first, this activity declined quite quickly during the first fifteen to twenty seconds of motion stimulation; but motion in the null direction elicited no change in the discharge rate. Second, immediately after the stimulus stopped, the firing rate of the preferred direction unit fell to zero – below the resting level preceding the stimulus. During the following thirty seconds, it climbed slowly back to its previous resting level. As predicted by Sutherland, therefore, these results clearly suggest a neural basis for the VAM. But because we have identified a possible mechanism for producing motion after-effects in the rabbit's retina, we must not assume that similar processes occur within the retinae of other mammals, particularly man. The rabbit's retina, along with that of the ground squirrel and even the frog, is relatively complex compared to that of the cat or the primates. In the case of these latter, the evidence strongly indicates that comparable levels of processing occur within the visual cortex rather than the retina. Furthermore, the work of Sekuler and his associates (see Sekuler, 1975) suggests that, in man, mechanisms for detecting motion are sensitive not only to direction, but also to speed. In other words, it appears that a group of receptor units sensitive to one direction of motion are made up of subsets tuned to different (but overlapping) velocity ranges. This implies that both direction and velocity are coded by which of several differentially tuned analysers are maximally active; this is in contrast to the rabbit's retinal ganglion cells where all units sensitive to one direction of motion respond over the entire speed range by varying their firing rates.

We have discussed the work of Barlow and Hill in some detail because it provides a clear example of the complementarity of the neurophysiological and psychophysical approaches to the study of sensory processes. In particular, it demonstrates how hypotheses formulated largely on the basis of behavioural observations receive support from microelectrode studies of single receptor units. In the next section, we shall see how this cross-fertilization can operate the other way as well: how the discovery of increasingly specialized feature detectors by neurophysiologists can prompt experimental psychologists to seek, and to find, the experiential counterparts of these mechanisms in the judgements of their human observers.

Contingent after-effects

The investigations carried out by Hubel and Wiesel on the properties of neurons in the visual cortex of the cat revealed that single units are simultaneously sensitive to more than one specific feature, such as, say, orientation and direction. If the same is true for feature detectors in the human cortex, and if we accept the neural basis of negative after-effects as outlined in the previous section, then it is reasonable to expect that we may also experience after-effects with more than one component. This interesting possibility was first explored by Celeste McCollough of Oberlin College. She argued along the following lines: (1) human beings probably have line detectors similar to those found in the cat's cortex; (2) unlike cats, we also have colour vision; (3) in which case, it is not unreasonable to expect that we possess line detectors that are tuned not only to a specific orientation but also to a particular colour; and (4) if these assumptions are correct, it should be possible to demonstrate orientation-contingent colour after-effects.

She proceeded to test these ideas as follows: subjects inspected grids of horizontal blue and black lines which alternated with grids of vertical orange and black lines. After some ten minutes of these alternating displays, the subjects were shown both horizontal and vertical grids of black and white lines. The horizontal lines appeared to have a faint orange colour while the vertical lines were tinged with blue. When the head was tilted, the colour disappeared at approximately 45°, and the colours were reversed with the head at 90°. It was thus made evident that the colour after-effect was dependent on the orientation of the bars on the retina. The illusory after-effects are therefore 'contingent'. They are only seen in conjunction with lines of appropriate orientation. This phenomenon has been termed the *McCollough effect*.

Since McCollough's initial discovery, a wide range of contingent after-effects has been reported. It has been shown, for example, that colour after-effects can be made contingent upon the direction in which a pattern is seen to move. In the first of these experiments, Norva Hepler (1968) of McGill University required her subjects to view alternately green bars moving up and red bars moving down. After several accumulated hours of exposure, upward moving black and white stripes appeared pinkish, and when moving downwards, they seemed to be tinged with green. A stationary pattern produced no colour after-effects. Stromeyer and Mansfield (1970) found similar effects using a rotating spiral pattern.

A number of investigators (see Favreau and Corballis, 1976) have also shown that it is possible to induce the converse of this contingency. After watching a green clockwise spiral alternating with a red counterclockwise spiral, subjects reported that a stationary spiral seems to move briefly counterclockwise when it is green and clockwise when it is red. This is called a colour-contingent motion after-effect; its converse, described earlier, is a motion-contingent colour after-effect. Both can be made to reappear if an observer is shown the test patterns some twenty-four hours after the original exposure.

The comparatively long periods over which these contingent after-effects can be made to persist was initially taken as evidence that they were a different class of phenomena from the simple after-effects of colour, tilt and motion, discussed earlier. However, Masland (1969) has shown that features of the VAM may be present for as long as a day after the initial stimulation, while Favreau (1976) has found that it may be present for as long as a week. It would therefore appear that all after-effects have both short-term and long-term components; the former lasting for a matter of seconds, the latter for hours and even days. The theoretical significance of these two components is not yet clear, but it has been suggested (Masland, 1969) that the rapidly decaying component is directly due to the adaptation of the specific feature detectors, while the more persistent component may arise from *conditioned adaptation* in which the inducing stimulus becomes associated with fatigue. Thus, when the same stimulus is presented many hours later the appropriate detectors are caused to return to a state resembling fatigue. These suggestions have prompted a good deal of research, but as yet the issue is far from resolved. For all their apparent simplicity, after-effects are proving to be far more complex than was initially imagined, and will continue to be intensively studied for many years to come.

Sensory rearrangement

Visual and inertial distortion

During normal self-propelled activity, the kinaesthetic senses function in harmony to provide a single unified impression of our posture and movements. Seen changes in the visual world correspond exactly to felt changes conveyed by the joint–muscle–skin system, and these are correlated with the more covert inputs from the vestibular receptors concerning the tilting and turning movements of the head. But this concordance of spatial signals is a fragile matter and can be disrupted in a wide variety of ways to produce different forms of *sensory rearrangement*. This term was coined by Held (1961) to describe situations in which one or more of these normally synergistic inputs is at variance with the remainder so that a conflict exists between the signals currently being received from the orientation senses and the pattern expected on the basis of past experience, or what Held called 'exposure-history'.

Two experimental techniques for achieving various types of sensory rearrangement have been widely used: *visual distortion* in which optical devices are used to displace, reverse or invert the retinal image while leaving inputs to the vestibular and non-vestibular proprioceptors unchanged; and *inertial distortion* in which subjects are exposed to atypical force environments that disturb the normal pattern of inputs to the vestibular system and other mechano-receptors while leaving the visual inputs largely unaffected.

The first systematic investigation of sensory rearrangement was performed by Stratton (1897) who wore an optical system that both inverted and reversed the visual field. Following Stratton, many investigators have used a variety of lens, prism and mirror devices to study the consequences of both short- and long-term visual distortion. The work has been reviewed by Epstein (1967) and by Howard and Templeton (1966), while Held (1961), Harris (1965), Rock (1966), and Howard (1970) have considered some of the theoretical implications.

Although the literature is less extensive, manned space flights over the past two decades have focused considerable interest upon the problems associated with exposure to atypical force environments (particularly weightlessness and prolonged rotation), and detailed accounts of this work can be found in Reason (1974, 1977a) and Reason and Brand (1975). An important outcome of this work has been a better appreciation of the stimulus factors that elicit motion sickness. While neither the underlying neural mechanisms nor the biological significance (see Treisman, 1977) of this widespread and exceedingly unpleasant disorder are fully understood, it now seems apparent that some form of sensory rearrangement involving the vestibular system is present in all the many and diverse circumstances that cause motion sickness. Moreover, in almost all susceptible individuals, continued exposure to a provocative motion stimulus leads to the diminution and eventual disappearance of established motion sickness reactions (see Reason and Brand, 1975). This reduction in symptomatology takes place without any change in the nauseogenic stimulus; indeed, it is the absence of such variation that promotes its occurrence. These observations are clearly of importance for elucidating the factors involved in the production of motion sickness, as they demonstrate the existence of processes within the individual that are capable of counteracting the disturbing properties of the sensory rearrangement without recourse to any external agency. It follows, therefore, that a better appreciation of how 'Nature's own cure' operates must bring us closer to understanding how these curious and inappropriate reactions become established in the first place, since adaptation and provocation appear to be two sides of the same coin.

Perceptual adaptation

There are close similarities in the adaptive effects and after-effects produced by both visual and inertial distortion. In all cases, events follow a fairly standard sequence – although their time-course may vary from one form of rearrangement to another.

During the period of *initial exposure* to the sensory rearrangement, the various disturbances associated with the particular form of conflict are experienced most acutely. A person wearing a distorting optical device misses things he reaches for and bumps into objects he is trying to circumnavigate. He is also likely to experience nausea triggered by the unaccustomed relationship between the visual and vestibular inputs whenever he moves his head. Likewise the vehicle passenger or astronaut suffers the worst ravages of motion sickness and disorientation during the early stages of exposure to the unusual force environment. But with *continued exposure*, these adverse effects gradually diminish and can eventually vanish, indicating the establishment of some internal adjustment which renders the abnormal to feel like the normal. Finally, there is an *after-effect* phase in which the individual, having been restored to his previously typical circumstances, suffers the reinstatement of the earlier disturbances. As a consequence of adapting to the unusual conditions, he now has to readjust to what hitherto constituted the natural arrangement of the sensory inputs. It is interesting to note that where these after-effects possess a directional component, as in illusions of apparent motion or in reaching movements of the arm, the direction of the after-effect is opposite to that of the initial exposure effect. Although in its pattern of adaptive effects and after-effects, perceptual adaptation bears some superficial resemblance to the phenomenon of sensory adaptation, discussed earlier in relation to negative after-effects, the two processes are fundamentally different. Whereas sensory adaptation leads to a reduction in the response associated with a steady-state stimulus to *one* sense organ (or, more specifically, to a single set of feature detectors), perceptual adaptation is initiated by a discrepancy between the inputs of *two* or *more* functionally correlated senses, and results eventually in an absence of distortion, ill-effects and illusory perceptions. Thus, sensory adaptation leads to a *neutralization* of the sensory experience, while the outcome of perceptual adaptation is the *normalization* of previously distorted perception. Another important difference is that while sensory adaptation is mediated by a fatigue-like process within specific feature analysers, perceptual adaptation appears to involve something very akin to learning. Some possible mechanisms of perceptual adaptation are considered below.

Theories of perceptual adaptation

The nature of perceptual adaptation is still a matter for considerable debate among contemporary investigators. Several theories have been proposed which fall very roughly into three main groups: those concerned with *where* the adjustments take place, those dealing primarily with *how* they occur, and those theories which seek to specify the *necessary conditions* for perceptual adaptation. It must be stressed, however, that these are distinctions of emphasis rather than substance, since there is a good deal of overlap between these various kinds of theory.

Location theories. Theories concerned with the location of the adaptive changes relate mainly to experiments in which the subjects wear prisms that displace the apparent locations of seen objects to one side. Typically, these subjects are required to make stereotyped pointing movements at a target with the pointing arm concealed from direct view. If the prisms displace to the right, then initially the pointing movements will miss the target to the right by an amount roughly equivalent to the displacing power of the prisms. But after a few more attempts, the aim will be improved sufficiently to allow the pointing to coincide with the direction of the target. On removing the prisms, the initial tendency will be to point too far to the left.

In keeping with the traditional view that vision is only a supplementary spatial sense, and that touch is the primary sense (see Berkeley, 1910; Dewey, 1898), some investigators have argued that adaptation occurs through *altered visual perception.* That is, adaptation involves a perceptual reinterpretation of the retinal image so that a target which at first looked off to one side is now seen to be straight ahead. The immediate consequence of this, on removing the distortion, is to see a target which is actually straight ahead to be displaced some distance in a direction opposite to the original distortion. Explanations along these lines have been offered by Taylor (1962) and Kohler (1964) among others.

At the present time, however, it would seem that the bulk of the recent evidence favours the contrary point of view advanced by Harris (1965), namely the *proprioceptive-change-hypothesis.* This argues that when vision and the proprioceptive position senses provide discrepant information, it is the latter and not the former that is recalibrated. In other words, the felt position of the arm changes to correspond with the seen location of the target. One consequence of this is that the subject's judgement of that arm's position relative to any other part of the body will be incorrect. Only when judging the location of his arm relative to objects seen through the prisms will he be accurate.

Such a view has important implications for understanding the relationship of vision to the other position and motion senses. It suggests, for example, that vision is the prepotent spatial sense which lays down largely inflexible standards regarding the locations of objects in the environment to which the more labile sense of felt position becomes tuned. Harris (1965) summarizes the consequences for perceptual development as follows:

It seems more plausible to assume that proprioceptive perception of parts of the body (and therefore of the locations of touched objects) develops with the help of innate visual perception rather than vice versa ... So when a baby stares raptly at his outstretched hand, he is probably finding out where his hand is, not what his visual sensations mean. He is making use of an adaptive mechanism that keeps his position sense accurate despite extensive and uneven growth of the body. This mechanism enables us to use the precise, detailed information that vision provides, as a means of continually readjusting our vaguer and more variable position sense.

A further demonstration of visual dominance is provided by the phenomenon of *visual capture*. This was originally observed by Gibson (1933) who had his subjects run their hands along a straight edge while wearing an optical device that made straight edges appear curved. When subjects observed their hands moving along this objectively straight edge, they saw it to be curved. Although the sense of touch indicated the true nature of the edge, they experienced no conflict: the edge *felt* curved. Similarly, Rock and Victor (1964) demonstrated that when subjects viewed a square object through a minifying lens, but remained unaware of the precise nature of the visual distortion, judgements of the size of the object depended upon its perceived visual size even when they were able to grasp the object in their hand. In yet another study (Pick, Hay and Pabst, 1963) subjects were asked to point with one hand hidden from view at a finger of the other hand which they viewed through an optical device that displaced the visual field laterally by 11°. Subjects pointed very near to the optical position of their target finger rather than to its felt position. Many subjects were not aware of the discrepancy between the two sensory modalities. Readers interested in pursuing the question of visual dominance further should consult Posner, Nissen and Klein (1976).

'How?' or mismatch theories. In the majority of the visual displacement studies mentioned above, the subjects' heads were fixed by a dental bite or by some other means of restraint. Limiting head movements in this way restricts the sensory conflict to that between the seen and felt senses of object position, and thus it is meaningful to consider within which of these sense modalities the adjustments occurred. But such an exercise becomes increasingly less worthwhile the more sensory channels are party to the sensory

rearrangement, as in the case of freely moving subjects in either visual or inertial distortion in whom head and body movements create complex vestibular and non-vestibular proprioceptive inputs not present in the situations considered above. Not unnaturally, therefore, the more centrally-biased 'how' theories of perceptual adaptation have in the main emerged from studies involving multi-sensory conflicts, where there may also be some risk of motion sickness. These theories can be subsumed under the general heading of *mismatch theories.*

One such theory, designed to account for the effects and after-effects of exposure to nauseogenic force environments, embodies many of the features present in earlier models (Held, 1961; Rock, 1966), and will serve as an exemplar for this type of theory. Two neural components are postulated: a *storage unit* that retains 'traces' of the informational characteristics of previous inputs from the position and motion senses; and a *comparator unit* that compares the most recent contents of the neural store with the prevailing inputs from these senses. In regard to motion sickness, the most important comparisons are between the visual input and the inputs from the vestibular receptors, for it is only when the latter are implicated, either directly or indirectly, that sickness will ensue.

It is suggested that during the initial period of sensory rearrangement, the contents of the store will be markedly different from the signals currently arriving from the spatial senses. This incongruity is detected by the comparator unit, which, as a result, generates a mismatch signal reflecting both the sign and the extent of the discrepancy. The mismatch signal is then directed along reflex pathways to the neuronal and neurohumoral mechanisms responsible for the production of symptoms and associated disturbances. It is also assumed that the severity of these disturbances is in direct proportion to the strength of the mismatch signal.

With continued exposure, the contents of the store are generally updated by incorporating informational traces relevant to the rearranged sensory inputs; so that, eventually, the traces selected by the comparator are compatible with the stimulus characteristics of the provocative environment. When this occurs, the mismatch signal is no longer generated, and the disturbances are no longer experienced. At this point, the individual is said to be adapted to the rearranged environment.

When the individual is restored to the previously typical environment, the recent contents of the store, having adjusted to the atypical conditions, are again at variance with the incoming sensory information. This causes the reinstatement of the mismatch signal and, with it, the reappearance of motion sickness and associated phenomena. After further time in the typical environment the contents of the store are rapidly readjusted to be compatible to the existing sensory inputs. This part of the adaptation cycle is likely to occur much more rapidly than the initial adaptation to the rearranged inputs since the informational characteristics of the typical environment will be 'over-learned'. That is, the appropriate stimulus traces are well consolidated and easily retrievable from the store for matching within the comparator. More detailed versions of this theory, citing experimental support, are given in Reason and Brand (1975) and in Reason (1977a, 1978).

Active movement. Several studies by Held and his colleagues have shown that active movements are superior to passive movements in acquiring adaptation to visual distortion involving the displacement, curvature or tilt of the seen environment (Held and Freeman, 1963; Held, 1965). Although some other investigators (see Howard, 1970) deny the essential role of active movement in adaptation to optical distortion – having shown that adaptation can occur with passive motion under some conditions – the present consensus is that active, self-initiated movements on the part of the subject facilitate the process of adaptation; but they are not, as Held (1961) originally suggested, a necessary condition for its occurrence. A recent study (Reason and Benson, 1978), involving inertial distortion, also supports this conclusion.

Held maintained that it was the command or efferent components of the active movement which promoted the acquisition of perceptual adaptation. Its importance derives from the fact that 'only an organism that can take account of the output signals to its own musculature is in a position to detect and factor out the decorrelating effects of both moving objects and externally imposed body movement' (Held, 1961). Within the terms of the mismatch theory outlined in the previous section it could be argued that when an active movement is initiated, a copy of the command signal is transmitted to the neural store where it retrieves and reactivates the reafferent (feedback) trace combinations 'previously associated with it. In this way, it accelerates the rate of adaptation by accessing appropriate traces more rapidly from the store for matching within the comparator. In other words, the command signal 'addresses' the expected trace combinations and allows them to be found more quickly than in the passive-movement case where such means are not available. The different consequences of active and passive movement are further discussed in Chapter 15.

Chapter 9
Attention

Introduction

The topic of attention was considered to be of prime importance in the early history of experimental psychology. Edward Titchener wrote in 1908 that 'the doctrine of attention is the nerve of the whole psychological system, and that as men judge of it, so shall they be judged before the general tribunal of psychology'. William James observed that 'my experience is what I agree to attend to. Only those items which *I notice* shape my mind – without selective interest, experience is an utter chaos' (1890; italics in original). Yet with the ascendance of *behaviourism* research concerned with attentional phenomena went into a decline, since the concept of attention was thought to be too closely allied to that of consciousness and the study of consciousness was seen as an impediment to the study of behaviour (see Boring, 1957). Since the 1950s, however, with the resurgence of interest in cognitive processes, and against a background of rapid development in the neurosciences, the concept of attention has come to be regarded as lying 'at the very core of cognitive psychology' (Keele and Neill, 1978).

As Posner (1975) has noted, 'attention is not a single concept, but the name of a complex field of study'. Although Moray (1969) listed six categories of attention, including mental concentration, vigilance, selective attention, search, activation and set, Posner suggested that three senses of the term predominate. These are: (1) *selection*, 'of some information from the available signals for special treatment'; (2) *effort*, 'a sense of attention related to the degree of conscious effort which a person invests'; and (3) *alertness*, 'an organismic state which affects general receptivity to input information'.

Attention thus involves a variety of processes: a *selective process*, whereby some information coming from the internal or external environment is analysed and perceived, while other information is ignored; an *intensive process*, whereby the amount of attention devoted to a particular information source can be varied, so that people sometimes feel that they are concentrating so hard on a particular task or activity that they are oblivious of their surroundings, while at others they are easily distracted by whatever is going on around them; and an *alerting and sustaining process*, whereby the receptivity to input information can be heightened over the short-term, as for instance when the arrival of a signal requiring action is imminent, or maintained over the long-term, as when a task requiring vigilance or sustained attention is being performed. Each of these processes, to a greater or lesser extent, is capable of being voluntarily controlled, although even when attention is being focused upon one source of information to the exclusion of others, the environment is under constant surveillance and any significant change, such as the introduction of a novel, intense or incongruous stimulus, is liable to capture attention involuntarily. At any one time, therefore, both voluntary attentional processes, which serve to increase awareness of a particular input, and involuntary monitoring processes, which maintain a residual awareness of other inputs, are in operation.

Selective attention

If it were impossible to attend selectively to environmental inputs or trains of thought, then the flood of stimulation impinging on awareness would be so overwhelming that we should be unable to function adequately. As James (1890) put it, 'selection is the very keel on which our mental ship is built'. The selection of information is necessary not only because there are peripheral limitations on the intake of information from the environment (for instance, we are unable to focus upon the whole of a visual scene at the same time and can only register a small fraction of the total information available at a single fixation) but also because there are central limitations which restrict the amount of information that can be analysed or processed at any one time. In common with all other systems, whether biological, electronic or mechanical, the mind thus has an upper limit placed on its capacity to process information. Were it not for this limitation, it has been suggested, 'the term "attention" would be unnecessary in psychology' (Townsend, 1974). A number of different tasks have been employed in the investigation of selective attention: see, for example, the classificatory scheme of Treisman (1969), shown in Table 9.1. Such tasks can be classified as either focused attention tasks or divided attention tasks and within each of these categories a further classification can be made based on the nature of the selection involved. In focused attention tasks subjects are instructed to focus their attention upon one of two or more sensory inputs (for example, the

Table 9.1
A classification of selective attention tasks. (From Treisman, 1969, p. 287)

Type	Divided attention	
	Object of attention	*Example of task*
1D	Two or more sensory inputs	Listen to messages on both right and left ears
2D	Two or more dimensions to analyse	Analyse both spatial location and loudness
3D	Two or more targets defined by critical features	Listen for the words 'one', 'five', and 'eight'

Type	Focused attention	
	Object of attention	*Example of task*
1F	One sensory input	Listen to message on left ear only; ignore message on right ear
2F	One dimension	Analyse loudness, ignore spatial location
3F	One target or set of critical features	Listen for the word 'eight'; ignore other words

message coming from one loudspeaker), upon one of two or more stimulus attributes (for example, the colour of a circle as opposed to its size) or upon the occurrence of a 'target' (for example, each occurrence of the number 'six' followed by the letter 'E' in a series of numbers and letters). Within the category of divided attention tasks the same subdivision into inputs, attributes and targets may be made but subjects are instructed to divide their attention between two or more sensory inputs, two or more stimulus attributes or two or more targets. More generally, a divided attention paradigm can require the simultaneous performances of two different tasks, for example, reading and copying dictated words (Spelke, Hirst and Neisser, 1976). Experimental tasks may also consist of combinations of focused and divided attention tasks and/or of selection requirements.

Focused attention tasks

One of the most widely used focused attention tasks has been the dichotic listening task, in which one auditory message is presented via headphones to one ear, while a different message is simultaneously presented to the other. The rate of presentation is quite high, usually between 100 and 150 words per minute. The listener is instructed to 'shadow' one of the two messages: that is, to repeat aloud each word in the message as soon as it has been presented. The degree to which attention is focused can be assessed by various measures of shadowing efficiency, for instance, the number of words omitted or mispronounced, the shadowing latency, that is the time intervening between the pronunciation of each word in the shadowed message and the number of intrusions from the unattended or secondary message. The shadowing task has been regarded as the most effective means of focusing the subject's attention on one input, although it has also been criticized as being unrepresentative of focused attention under 'normal' conditions (Underwood, 1976). A visual version of the shadowing task has also been developed (Neisser, 1971) in which alternate lines of prose are printed in different colours, for instance black and red, and the subject is instructed to read aloud the lines printed in one of the colours.

Studies of focused attention tasks have demonstrated that people possess a highly developed ability to focus their attention on one of several competing inputs. For example, it is possible to monitor, with a very high degree of accuracy, target events occurring in one video recorded game when another visually similar game is superimposed upon it and when eye movements are restricted by establishing a fixation point (Neisser, 1976; Neisser and Becklen, 1975). Similarly, in the visual shadowing task referred to above material in one colour can be read with little or no loss of speed, accuracy or comprehension (Willows and McKinnon, 1973) and in auditory shadowing tasks one message can be shadowed more or less perfectly without intrusions from the other (Cherry, 1953; Cherry and Taylor, 1954).

Selection between competing inputs is made much simpler when relevant and irrelevant information can be differentiated in terms of physical characteristics such as spatial location, pitch, loudness, size, colour and shape. It is thus relatively easy to focus attention on one of two simultaneously presented auditory messages which come from different spatial locations (Broadbent, 1954; Moray, Bates and Barnett, 1965) but extremely difficult to select one of several competing auditory messages, spoken in the same voice and at the same intensity, coming from the same location

(Treisman, 1964a). In the latter situation physical cues can no longer be used to differentiate the messages and only semantic cues remain. Semantic characteristics thus appear to be much less effective bases for selecting between competing auditory messages than do physical characteristics.

In general, subjects performing an auditory shadowing task do not appear to be aware of changes in the semantic content of the secondary or unattended message. For instance, although they notice if the speaker's voice changes from a male to a female voice or *vice versa*, they do not notice a change from poetry to prose, from English to French or even, sometimes, that the secondary message consists of reversed speech (Cherry, 1953; Cherry and Taylor, 1954). Furthermore, subjects are able to remember very little if anything of the material presented in the secondary message even when the message contains the same brief list of words repeated over and over again (Moray, 1958), except, possibly, when the interval between message presentation and the retention test is very short indeed (Norman, 1969). But the semantic content of the secondary message, and the semantic relationship between items in the shadowed and secondary messages, can interfere with shadowing efficiency and thus disrupt the focusing of attention. When the unattended message contains instructions prefaced by highly familiar words, such as the subject's own name, these instructions are occasionally followed and the shadowed message neglected (Moray, 1959). Lewis (1970) recorded shadowing latencies for lists of unrelated words during a dichotic listening task and varied the meaning of simultaneously presented words in the unattended message. When the word in the unattended message was a synonym of the word in the shadowed message, shadowing latencies were significantly increased, compared to a condition in which the two words were unrelated in meaning. However, this effect may only be found when attention has not yet been fully focused on the shadowed message (see Treisman, Squire and Green, 1974).

Although it is relatively easy to focus attention on one of two competing inputs, it is often very difficult to focus attention on one of two or more stimulus dimensions or attributes. A striking example of a failure to focus attention on one attribute of a stimulus and to 'filter out' an irrelevant attribute is provided by the Stroop Test (see Dyer, 1973, for a review). In this task subjects are presented with a series of three types of card, one of which (card C) bears a colour patch, another (card W) a colour name printed in black and the third (card CW) a colour name printed in a conflicting colour (for instance, the word 'red' printed in green). In the third case subjects are required to name the ink colour in which the colour word is printed, as quickly as possible, or to sort cards into piles using the ink colour as the relevant dimension. Both of these tasks prove to be extremely difficult, and it seems that subjects are unable to ignore the colour word and focus attention upon the colour in which it is printed. Naming latencies or classification times for CW cards are thus unduly prolonged, due to the interference between relevant and irrelevant dimensions. In both auditory and visual selective attention tasks then, the amount of interference produced by unattended inputs or irrelevant stimulus dimensions provides evidence concerning the extent to which attention can be focused in a particular task situation.

Divided attention tasks

Experiments with divided attention tasks provide evidence concerning the extent to which the simultaneous or parallel processing of different sources or kinds of information is possible and the optimal conditions for its occurrence. Studies of both auditory and visual selective attention have demonstrated that subjects can divide their attention between two competing inputs or among several different targets. Moray and Fitter (1973), for example, showed that two different auditory targets, presented simultaneously in different spatial locations, could often be detected as accurately as when only one target of either type was presented. But although divided attention within the same modality is possible, it is usually easier to divide attention between different modalities (Treisman and Davies, 1973) and a number of studies have found little or no decrement in the accuracy with which simultaneously presented tones and lights are detected, compared to conditions in which either a tone or a light is presented (Eijkman and Vendrik, 1965; Moore and Massaro, 1973). However, in such situations the visual and auditory targets do not seem to be perceived as having occurred simultaneously and the visual target tends to be detected first (Egeth and Sager, 1977), a phenomenon referred to as visual dominance (see Posner, Nissen and Klein, 1976).

In a well-known series of experiments on visual search, Neisser (1963a) required subjects to search for a target letter located somewhere in a fifty-line list (see Figure 9.1), each line containing the same number of letters, usually six, and found that the total search time per line increased linearly with the number of lines searched. One of the most striking results obtained in this series of experiments was that following extensive practice, subjects could search as rapidly for ten targets, drawn from a constant set, as for

```
S L R A                S T F M Q Z
J C E N                R V X S Q M
Z L R D                M Q B J F T
X B O D                M V Z X L Q
P H M U                R T B X Q H
Z H F K                B L Q S Z X
P N J W                Q S V F D J
C Q X T                F L D V Z T
G H N R                B Q H M D X
I X Y D                B M F D Q H
Q S V B                Q H L J Z T
G U C H                T Q S H R L
O W B N                B M Q H Z J
B V Q N                R T B J Z Q
```

The letter *K* is the target in the list at left, and the 'critical item' is the one
that includes it. A more difficult task is a search for an item that does *not* include
a specified letter. In the list at right, for example, there is only one item that
does not include a *Q*.

Figure 9.1   Examples of visual search task materials. (From Neisser, 1964, p. 4)

only one (Neisser, Novick and Lazar, 1964); that is, when they were required
to find the line containing an instance of any one of ten items (in this case
letters and digits), the search time per line was no longer than that taken
when an instance of only one item was sought. With practice, therefore,
a large number of targets can be searched for in parallel and the recognition
of a target appears to become 'automatic' so that well-practised and highly
familiar targets cannot easily be ignored (see Shiffrin and Schneider, 1977).

Theories of selective attention

The revival of research on attention, and especially on the selective processes
involved, during the 1950s was greatly influenced by contemporary developments in communications engineering and computer science. The mathematical theory of communication, or 'information theory' (Shannon and
Weaver, 1949), appeared to provide a measure of human information processing capacity in 'bits' per second, which was independent of the type
of information being processed, and the design features of the digital
computer suggested a conceptual framework for the investigation of human
information processing. The models of information processing that were
developed in the 1950s and 1960s attempted to depict the flow of information
through the organism following the presentation of a stimulus, and por-
trayed sensory data as undergoing various transformations while progress-

ing through a linear sequence of processing stages, the transformed output from one stage becoming the input to the next. As information passed through these various stages of processing, proceeding 'deeper' into the limited capacity information processing system, the degree of cognitive analysis performed upon the original sensory input was assumed to become greater (see, for example, Craik and Lockhart, 1972).

Within an information processing framework, selective attention can be regarded as a mechanism for selecting relevant from irrelevant information at various points in the information processing sequence, thereby reducing the throughput of information so that the performance of the system as a whole is optimized. But how many selection points are there, where are they located and what criteria form the basis for selection? Theories of selective attention put forward in the 1950s and 1960s argued that there was only one locus of selectivity (Broadbent, 1958; Deutsch and Deutsch, 1963) but held different views about whether this one selection point should be located 'early' or 'late' in the information processing sequence. However, both early and late selection theories agreed that because of the limited capacity for processing information of a particular processing stage a 'bottle-neck' in the flow of information is created which necessitates selection among inputs competing for admission to that stage. Early and late selection theories can thus be described as 'bottleneck' theories.

'Filter' theory (Broadbent, 1958) maintained that because of the limited capacity of the processing stage at which pattern recognition and identification took place, selection occurred early in the information processing sequence, before stimulus information reached this stage of processing and hence before any semantic analysis of this information had been conducted. Selection was effected by a 'filter' which, on the basis of the physical characteristics of the relatively unprocessed stimulus representations held in a large capacity but fast-decaying sensory store, admitted some representations for further processing and rejected the remainder. Since stimulus representations could only be maintained in sensory storage for a very brief period, representations not selected by the filter during this time were liable to be lost. In effect, therefore, the filter determined which stimulus information was recognized, identified and, ultimately, consciously perceived. In contrast, late selection theories (Deutsch and Deutsch, 1963; Norman, 1968) maintained that all incoming information was recognized and identified but only some of it was responded to, because of capacity limitations at the processing stage responsible for the selection and generation of responses. Selection was thus considered to take place comparatively late in the information processing sequence, at or just before this stage of processing was reached. In an extension of the point of view adopted by late selection theories, it has been suggested that all highly practised and well-learned stimuli, such as words and numbers, are processed automatically, without drawing on information processing capacity and hence without requiring the direction of attention (see, for example, Posner and Snyder, 1975).

Many experiments have attempted to decide between the accounts of selective attention given by early and late selection theories. The main points of dispute have been whether unattended information is processed to the point of recognition and identification, whether true division of attention can occur, rather than attention being rapidly alternated between competing inputs, and, more recently, whether well-learned and highly familiar stimuli are invariably processed automatically.

A critical experiment in the development of filter theory was performed by Broadbent (1954). Broadbent devised a split-span task in which a series of pairs of digits was presented dichotically at a rate of two pairs per second and subjects were asked to write down the digits they had heard following each trial. Three digit-pairs were presented on each trial, for example, 7–4–5 to the left ear and 9–2–8 to the right, since the recall of six digits presented binaurally (a procedure in which the same digit is presented to both ears) at a presentation rate of two pairs per second is well within the memory span. Broadbent found that binaural presentation of the three digit-pairs resulted in a correct reproduction score of 93 per cent, but this score fell to 65 per cent when dichotic presentation was employed, largely because items from the input channel reported second tended to be forgotten. Correct reproductions were almost always organized by ear, or input channel, of arrival; that is, all the digits presented to one ear were written down first, followed by the digits presented to the other ear. When subjects were asked to write down the digits they had heard in order of presentation, rather than by ear of arrival, the percentage of items correctly reproduced dropped to 20 per cent. This result suggested that subjects found it much easier to group or 'tag' simultaneously presented information by input channel and to deal successively with the information on each channel, rather than to switch rapidly between input channels and to report digit pairs in the order in which they had been presented; that is, in the above example it is easier to report in the order 7–4–5–9–2–8 than in the order 7–9–4–2–5–8.

The results of this experiment were interpreted as indicating that information entering the nervous system was first grouped according to the input channel on which it had arrived, that the information carried by one input channel was then selected for further processing and, finally, the information carried by the second input channel, which had been held in a short-term store while the information from the first channel was being processed, was dealt with. Simultaneously presented information, as in the split-span task, was thus considered to be handed successively, channel by channel. But the concept of an 'input channel', originally defined with respect to physical characteristics such as spatial location, soon had to be broadened, since it became clear that classes of information, or semantic categories, could also act as input channels (see, for example, Gray and Wedderburn, 1960). This finding weakened filter theory and raised some doubts concerning the way in which early selection was supposed to operate.

Late selection theories are supported by evidence that unattended inputs can receive at least some processing (see the experiments by Lewis, 1970, and Moray, 1959, referred to on p. 257.) Furthermore, in investigations of the galvanic skin responses elicited by words presented to the unattended ear in a dichotic listening task, Corteen (see Corteen and Dunn, 1974; Corteen and Wood, 1972) obtained evidence that unattended words were processed to the point at which recognition of their semantic characteristics must have occurred, even though subjects were usually unable to remember the words that had been presented. Although difficulties in replicating Corteen's results have been reported (Wardlaw and Kroll, 1976), other studies of a broadly similar kind provide confirmation of his findings (Forster and Govier, 1978; von Wright, Anderson and Stenman, 1975). Experiments suggesting that divided attention can occur, some of which were referred to on pp. 258–9, have also been interpreted as providing support for late selection theories (see, for example, Duncan, 1980).

Filter theory, as originally conceived by Broadbent, is therefore inadequate, and modifications to the theory have been put forward by Treisman (1960, 1964a) and by Broadbent (1971). Treisman's filter amplitude theory proposed that unattended inputs were not rejected altogether but merely attenuated, or reduced in intensity, and that highly familiar words, notably the subject's own name, or words which were contextually highly probable, could activate their representations in memory even when attenuated. Filter amplitude theory hypothesized not only early selection on the basis of physical characteristics, as in Broadbent's filter theory, but also a selection point later in the information processing sequence at which a selection was made among possible hypotheses concerning the nature of current stimulus inputs, generated by a range of stimulus representations in long-term memory activated to varying degrees by incoming information.

These two modes of selection, or types of selective attention, have been respectively described as *filtering*, or stimulus set, and *pigeonholing*, or response set (Broadbent, 1970, 1971, 1977; see also Keren, 1976). Broadbent (1977) defined filtering as 'the selection of a stimulus for attention because it possesses some one feature that is absent from irrelevant events'. The basis for filtering is thus a simple physical or sensory feature, such as the spatial location of a voice, or its pitch, or the type in which a word is printed (for example, upper and lower case). Broadbent further observed that 'in the case of pigeonholing ... the relevant and irrelevant stimuli do not differ by any single feature. Rather there is a set of responses or pigeon-holes which are distinguished from each other by various combinations of sensory features, and into which any event in the environment will be forced if possible or rejected if it fails to fit any of them' (Broadbent, 1977). A task requiring filtering would be one in which a response had to be made on each occasion that a word printed in red appeared in a list of words printed in black, a response that would usually be made very rapidly. A task requiring pigeonholing, on the other hand, would be one in which a response had to be made on each occasion that a French word appeared in a list of English words, a response that would take rather more time to make. The

Table 9.2
Filtering and pigeonholing (see text)

cat	EIGHT	CHAIR	seven
two	dog	JARDIN	tree
BOOK	egg	time	PAPIER
soon	X	pig	door
nine	livre	FOUR	arbre
five	CLARINET	rideau	LEFT

difference between the two modes of selection is illustrated in Table 9.2, in which filtering would be used to select the capitalized words, or to select the single letter in the array, while pigeonholing would be used to select the digits, or the words in French. These modifications of Broadbent's original filter theory allow for some processing of unattended inputs and for the possibility of divided attention. There are thus three kinds of selection which various theories of selective attention assume to be operating at different points in the information processing sequence: first, an early selection process (filtering), which operates on the representations of stimulus inputs briefly held in a sensory storage system; second, a middle selection process (pigeonholing), which operates on the memory representations of possible stimulus inputs to be considered by the pattern recognition system; and, third, a late selection process, which admits some of the outputs of the pattern recognition system to conscious awareness. Some theories of selective attention accept all three kinds of selection, others two and still others only one. As Francolini and Egeth (1980) have pointed out, the existence of the first kind of selection, filtering, has tended to be rejected on the grounds that some processing of unattended inputs can be shown to occur, a finding that could not be accommodated by unmodified filter theory. In consequence, few attempts have been made to demonstrate that early selection can take place. But the results of studies conducted by Francolini and Egeth (1979, 1980), while not altogether refuting the concept of automatic activation proposed by late selection theories, clearly indicate that 'automatic' processing can be constrained by early selection.

Attempts have also been made to provide psychophysiological evidence for the different kinds of selection proposed by theories of selective attention. Evoked potential studies (see Chapter 4) have shown that the amplitude of certain components of the evoked potential, in particular N100, are reliably enhanced during the presentation of relevant items, possessing easily identifiable physical characteristics such as pitch, or spatial location, to which the subject has been instructed to attend (see Hillyard and Picton, 1978, for a review). The amplitude of N100 is also reduced when irrelevant items are presented. The tentative conclusion has thus been drawn that the amplitude of N100 reflects the operation of early selection or filtering. However, one study in which brainstem evoked responses were measured provided little evidence for the attenuation of all input to the unattended ear in a dichotic listening situation (Woods and Hillyard, 1978). Late components of the evoked potential, in particular P300, have been related to performance indices in a variety of information processing tasks (see Tueting, 1978, for a review) but few studies have attempted to provide correlates of late selective attention processes.

It is reasonable to conclude, therefore, that early, middle and late modes of selection can all be employed, singly or in combination, depending upon the specific requirements of the task being performed, although the employment of different modes of selection may make different demands upon processing resources. This possibility is further discussed below.

Attention and effort

The processing of information by the nervous system depends first upon the quality of the stimulus input, second upon the availability of mental structures to perform the mental operations necessary for processing the input, and third upon a supply of mental resources or capacity which provides the energy required for those operations to be carried out. The 'bottleneck' theories discussed on pp. 259–64 regard certain of the mental structures involved in the processing of stimulus input as having a fixed supply of mental resources available to them. For example, in Broadbent's original filter theory the pattern recognition system is limited in this way, with the result that there is a 'bottleneck' in the flow of information at this processing stage.

However, instead of regarding attention as a device for filtering information, as in 'bottleneck' theories, attention can be equated with processing capacity or non-specific mental effort, as in the 'variable allocation capacity model' of Kahneman (1973). Capacity theories maintain that the processing capacity of a particular mental structure is not fixed, and that there is a general pool of capacity or mental resources on which the mental structures engaged in processing operations can draw. Kahneman suggested that there are no 'bottlenecks' in the information processing system and that processing is restricted only by the limited supply of mental resources available to the system as a whole. The allocation of resources to particular activities is held to be influenced by several factors, including an evaluation of the *processing load* imposed by processing demands and the *level of arousal* (discussed below). Demands on processing resources increase as a task becomes more difficult and/or as the criteria for successful performance are made more stringent.

Processing load and attention

In order to maintain the integrity of information processing operations, and to prevent any decline in the efficiency with which incoming information is dealt with, a balance has to be preserved between the available supply of processing resources and the demands made upon it. Mental resources are thus selectively distributed to the mental structures involved in the processing of information, in accordance with the processing load placed upon them. The distribution of resources or capacity is determined by control processes which form part of or are linked to the memory system and in which attention is either equated with momentary capacity or non-specific mental effort (Kahneman, 1973) or is itself a control process 'which directs translation to an orderly (intended) completion' (Shaffer, 1975). The selective distribution of processing resources or capacity is an operation that absorbs capacity and any increase in the processing load placed on the information processing system adds to the demand for processing resources.

The relation between processing load and the expenditure of mental effort has been investigated in experiments employing the secondary task method and in studies utilizing psychophysiological techniques, notably pupillometry (see below, and Chapter 4). If the capacity for processing information is limited and if the performance of each activity absorbs some processing capacity, with some activities absorbing more than others, then the relative 'mental loads' imposed by different tasks can be assessed from the amount of 'spare' or residual capacity that is left over (see Rolfe, 1971). The greater the capacity devoted to a 'primary' task, Task A, the less will be the residual capacity that can be devoted to a subsidiary or 'secondary' task, Task B, and in consequence the performance of the secondary task is likely to deteriorate, provided that the performance of the primary task is maintained at its normal level. Although the secondary task method suffers from certain limitations (see Brown, 1966), and the underlying assumption that there is just one kind of processing resource has been severely criticized by Allport (1980), the method has been widely employed in studies of human performance, in order to assess the processing demands imposed by different tasks. For example, novice drivers have been shown to exhibit poorer performance than experienced drivers when carrying out a secondary short-term memory task administered while they were driving a prescribed route; the secondary task method can also reveal the inadequate mastery of a skill, which is not apparent from measures of performance on the primary task alone.

If selective attention absorbs capacity, then it should be possible to measure the relative demands imposed by different kinds of selection using the secondary task method. In a series of experiments, Johnston and Heinz (1978), using a dichotic listening task in conjunction with a secondary visual reaction time task, compared the demands imposed by selecting between two different auditory messages presented binaurally, on the basis of various combinations of physical or sensory cues (voice pitch) and semantic cues (similarity of meaning), with those of a control condition in which no selection was required. Their results indicated not only that the process of selection consumes capacity, as indicated by a greater performance decrement on the secondary task, but also that more capacity is expended as the basis of selection is changed from sensory to semantic cues, that is, from 'early' to 'late' modes of selection.

Working in the presence of distractions, such as loud noise, is also more difficult, and although performance at many tasks can be maintained at normal levels when loud noise is present (see Broadbent, 1979, and Davies and Jones, 1982, for reviews) the cost of so doing can sometimes be revealed in the performance of tasks carried out after the noise has ceased, and Glass and Singer (1972) provide several examples of the 'after-effects' of working in loud noise at comparatively high levels. These after-effects, which include impairments of task performance, a reduction in the tolerance for frustration and a diminished ability to resolve cognitive conflict, are particularly marked when the onset of the noise is unpredictable and beyond the individual's control. Such effects have been attributed to a depletion of attentional capacity, or to an accumulation of 'cognitive fatigue', and have also been shown to become more severe both as the mental load imposed by a task, and the length of time for which a task lasts, even in the absence of loud noise or any other extraneous stressor, are increased (Cohen, 1980; Cohen and Spacapan, 1978). High attentional demands, which are increased by the presence of distractions, can thus produce behavioural after-effects, which appear to be related to the effort invested in the task.

Pupil size appears to be a sensitive index of momentary fluctuations in the expenditure of mental effort (Kahneman, 1973). Hess and Polt (1964), for example, examined changes in pupillary activity during the performance of four mental arithmetic tasks of varying levels of difficulty and found that pupillary dilation gradually increased following the presentation of the task, reaching a maximum immediately before the subject reported his solution. Subsequently, pupillary constriction occurred until the initial level of dilation had been achieved. Pupillary dilation was greater when the problem was more difficult. Kahneman and Beatty (Beatty and Kahneman, 1966) obtained similar results in a series of experiments using mental tasks, and further showed that in a dual-task situation, in which a digit transformation task was performed in conjunction with a secondary visual detection task, thus increasing cognitive load, pupil size increased compared to a single-task condition. Beatty and Wagoner (1978) suggested that high-level cognitive processes demand the mobilization of greater amounts of brain activation for their execution than do low-level cognitive processes, and have produced quite strong evidence that pupil size varies with cognitive load, or the level of cognitive functioning that the performance of a particular task requires, and since the expenditure of mental effort is assumed to vary directly with cognitive load, that pupil size varies with the expenditure of mental effort.

Arousal and selectivity

The concept of arousal has its origins in the 1930s, when various investigators attempted to relate variations in behavioural intensity and the quality of task performance to variations in psychophysiological activity (for example, Duffy, 1932; Freeman, 1940). This work suggested that behaviour could be regarded as varying along a continuum of intensity, from deep sleep to extreme excitement, and attempts were made to specify the physiological changes taking place at crucial points on this continuum, which became known as the level of activation or arousal (Duffy, 1962; Lindsley, 1951; Malmo, 1959). The development of the concept of arousal was also influenced by research on the neural systems involved in the maintenance of wakefulness (see Chapter 5), which suggested that the ascending reticular activating system and the diffuse thalamic projection system together formed a system which was highly responsive to environmental stimulation and which in turn contributed strongly to the level of activation manifested by the cerebral cortex (see Lindsley, 1960, and Magoun, 1958, for reviews). Research on the consequences of exposure to sensory deprivation demonstrated that perceptual and cognitive processes were thereby impaired and led Hebb (1955) to emphasize the importance of sensory variation in preserving the efficiency of the brain. Hebb pointed out that environmental stimulation performed two functions, the first a 'cue' or 'steering' function and the second an 'energizing' or 'activating' function.

Research concerned with the effects on task performance of various stressors, such as loud noise, sleep deprivation and heat, and with those of motivational factors such as the provision of incentives and knowledge of results, has lent credibility to the concept of *behavioural* arousal. Out of this work came the 'arousal theory of stress' (Broadbent, 1963, 1971) which assumes that there is a general state of arousal or reactivity which is increased by loud noise or by incentives and reduced by boredom or loss of sleep. The arousal theory of stress makes a further assumption, that the relationship between the level of arousal and the level of performance takes the form of an inverted U. The inverted-U hypothesis holds that performance is low when the level of arousal is much above or much below an optimal point, although the nature of the performance deficit at high and

low levels of arousal may well be different. Easterbrook (1959) proposed
that an increase in arousal level brings about a restriction of the range of cues
that a subject utilizes in performing a task. He further suggested that when
arousel level is low, selectivity in the utilization of cues is also low, and
irrelevant cues may be accepted uncritically. As arousal level increases, so
does selectivity, and attention is diverted away from irrelevant task components. Further increases in arousal diminish still further the range of
usable cues, so that eventually some relevant cues are no longer utilized and
task performance deteriorates. States of high and low arousal are thus
presumed to affect the allocation of attention in different ways.

Hockey (1970a), for example, required subjects to perform a combined
tracking and multi-source monitoring task for forty minutes, the former
being designated as the 'high priority' task and the latter as the 'low priority'
task. He found that tracking performance was unaffected by loud noise
(which is assumed to increase arousal level), compared to a quiet condition,
although signals appearing in peripheral locations were detected less frequently. In a further experiment, Hockey (1970b) found that sleep deprivation (which is assumed to decrease arousal level) produced changes which
could be interpreted as being the opposite of those found with loud noise,
impairment of performance being greater on the high priority task (tracking).
Such results suggest that states of high and low arousal exert opposite
effects on selectivity, and thus provide support for Easterbrook's hypothesis.
Monetary incentives are also frequently assumed to increase arousal level
and Davies and Jones (1975) compared the effects of noise and incentives
on selectivity in a short-term memory task. As in an earlier experiment in
which the same task was employed (Hockey and Hamilton, 1970), noise was
found to have no effect on intentional learning but to reduce incidental
learning, a result which was interpreted as evidence for increased selectivity
in noise. Incentives also increased selectivity, but the pattern of results was
different from that obtained with noise, intentional learning being increased
while incidental learning remained unaffected. In a similar study, Fowler
and Wilding (1979) found that incentive improved incidental learning while
loud noise impaired it. It thus appears that two variables which are both
regarded as increasing arousal level can have somewhat different effects on
selectivity.

In fact, difficulties with the traditional formulation of arousal theory
(see, for example, Gale, 1977) have led to the view that there may be
'qualitatively different activation states', rather than a single arousal continuum, resulting from the combination of specific processing demands

required by task situations and the presence of particular 'stressors' (Hamilton, Hockey and Rejman, 1977; see also Eysenck and Folkard, 1980). As Eysenck and Folkard remark, 'there is a potentially important distinction between arousal in the sense of what is done to the individual (e.g. exposure to white noise or electric shock) and arousal produced as a by-product of active processing effort'. While this hypothesis has scarcely begun to be developed it is likely that any statement of the relation between arousal and selectivity will need to take this distinction into account.

Alertness and sustained attention

Alertness

The term alertness refers to the receptivity of the organism to external stimulation. Receptivity may change either because of the modification of a particular pathway in the chain linking sensory input to response (as, for example, in the case of habituation) or because the organism's general state has been altered, so changing receptivity to all or to a broad class of incoming stimuli. Thus an individual may be sober or intoxicated, deprived of sleep or fully refreshed, be suffering from influenza or in the peak of condition and so on. All these factors may be assumed to affect a general state of receptivity.

This general state of receptivity also appears to change as a function of the time of day at which the tests of receptivity are made. Since the work of Kleitman in the 1920s and 1930s (Kleitman, 1939, 1963), it has been known that oral temperature fluctuates over the twenty-four-hour cycle and that the performance of many simple tasks appears to co-vary with such temperature changes. Measures of autonomic nervous system and endocrine activity, in particular the blood plasma levels of adrenal cortical steroids, also follow a diurnal rhythm (Colquhoun, 1971; Perkoff *et al.*, 1959).

Improvement in performance throughout the day appears to occur only for tasks involving a direct response to external stimulation, such as detection, cancellation or reaction-time tasks (Hockey and Colquhoun, 1972): in reaction time studies, for example, responses are made more quickly and fewer errors occur. Tasks which involve a short-term memory component, on the other hand, do not show the same improvement over the day (Folkard, 1975; and see Chapter 16); if anything, a deterioration in the performance of such tasks occurs (Baddeley *et al.*, 1970; Hockey, Davies and Gray, 1972). Thus it seems to be specifically alertness, rather than general efficiency, which is affected by time of day.

The alertness changes discussed so far are probably not under the individual's voluntary control; they are referred to as *tonic changes in alertness*. We turn now to what are known as *phasic alertness changes*, which take place very rapidly (within the space of a few hundred milliseconds) and probably can be controlled voluntarily. A typical situation for studying such changes is one in which fluctuations in the level of alertness are examined between the presentation of a warning signal and the delivery of a stimulus to which some response has to be made. It is clear from a number of studies of this kind that the presentation of a warning signal shortens the reaction time to the stimulus requiring response, although the degree of facilitation varies with the length of the interval separating the warning signal from the signal to be responded to (Posner, 1975). During this interval several psychophysiological changes occur, some excitatory and others inhibitory in their effects. However, although many changes in autonomic, EEG and motor activity can be observed to accompany the alteration of phasic alertness, no one of them, taken in isolation, is a very accurate predictor of response speed.

The contingent negative variation in the EEG, sometimes referred to as the 'expectancy wave', which is induced by the presentation of a warning signal, has been shown in split brain preparations to spread from one hemisphere to the other, when the warning signal is presented only to the first hemisphere (Gazzaniga and Hillyard, 1973). Such spreading of electrical signs of cortical activity is generally not observed when a specific stimulus, such as a letter or a digit, has to be identified. Since in split brain preparations there is little possibility of direct transmission from one hemisphere to the other, such evidence suggests that the presentation of a warning signal activates a subcortical mechanism, probably in the reticular activating system, and the resulting subcortical activity is transmitted to the cortex as a whole. Thus phasic alertness appears to be a general state, reflected by a large variety of psychophysiological indicators, rather than being confined to a specific pathway in the nervous system.

Sustained attention and vigilance

The British neurologist, Sir Henry Head, used the term 'vigilance' to denote a state of maximum physiological efficiency, not unlike the state of optimal receptivity or alertness referred to above (Head, 1923). Subsequently the term has been employed to refer to a state of the nervous system which is thought to underlie performance at certain kinds of task, known as 'vigilance tasks'. Thus N. H. Mackworth, who pioneered this area of research in the 1940s, defined vigilance as 'a state of readiness to detect and respond to certain specified small changes occurring at random time intervals in the environment' (Mackworth, 1957). Vigilance tasks are tasks in which attention is directed to one information display, although occasionally more than one, over long, unbroken, periods of time, for the purpose of detecting infrequent changes in the state of the display that are extremely difficult to discriminate. Such tasks are also known as 'monitoring' or 'watchkeeping' tasks.

Vigilance research began as an attempt to solve a serious practical problem. N. H. Mackworth (1950) noted that 'towards the end of 1943, the Royal Air Force asked if laboratory experiments could be done to determine the optimum length of watch for radar operators on anti-submarine patrol, as reports had been received of overstrain among these men'. Furthermore, 'there was evidence that a number of potential U-boat contacts were being missed', and after some preliminary experiments had been carried out by Mackworth, Coastal Command began an operational study of the detection of submarines by radar operators, the results of which suggested that after about thirty minutes on watch a marked deterioration in efficiency rapidly occurred.

Mackworth's research programme began with an examination of the working conditions of Coastal Command airborne radar operators. These operators were mainly engaged in flying sorties over the Bay of Biscay and westward, from Cornwall, to the mid-Atlantic. As the result of a report from Middle East Command, Coastal Command had recommended that radar watches should last for no longer than one hour, although in practice the length of watch varied from thirty minutes to two hours (Craik and Mackworth, 1943). The radar operator's task was often a matter of waiting for nothing to happen since the anti-submarine search patrols were frequently unproductive. 'False alarms' were not unusual; for example, Spanish fishing vessels in the Bay of Biscay were registered on the radar screen and were indistinguishable from military vessels until visual contact was established. Mackworth (1950) observed that 'the chance of an aircraft pilot agreeing to investigate a contact reported by his radar observer was only one in eight; there was no more than one chance in thirty that any such contact investigated would prove to be an enemy submarine'. The radar operator worked in isolation, except for occasional telephone calls, and no check on

Alertness and sustained attention 273

his efficiency was made. The target he was searching for was difficult to discriminate, being a small spot of light about one millimetre in diameter appearing on a radar screen covered in 'noise'. The target was present for a few seconds and if action was to be taken, it had to be taken quickly.

Mackworth designed a laboratory task which simulated the essentials of the radar operator's job. This task, known as the Clock Test, consisted of a blank clock face with a white background, around which traversed a black pointer, moving in discrete steps. Occasionally, in fact twelve times during each thirty minutes, the pointer moved through twice its normal distance and these 'double jumps' were the signals the observer had to detect by pressing a response key. The observers in Mackworth's experiments were experienced and inexperienced radar operators and it was found that almost all of them showed a decrement in performance over the two-hour watch period. After the first half-hour of observation the detection rate was around 85 per cent, after one hour around 77 per cent and after two hours around 72 per cent. Similar performance decrements were obtained by Mackworth in two other monitoring tasks, the 'Synthetic Radar Test' and the 'Main Listening Test'. Having established that performance deteriorated with time at work in such situations, Mackworth was also able to show that there were a number of ways of abolishing the 'vigilance decrement'. The most successful were rest pauses, the provision of knowledge of results and the administration of small doses of the drug 'benzedrine' (amphetamine sulphate) before the watch began.

Efficiency during vigilance is usually assessed by recording the number of occasions on which a change in the state of a display, known as a 'signal', is correctly reported, and this measure is called the 'detection rate' or, sometimes, the 'hit rate'. A second measure, which is inversely correlated with detection rate, is the detection latency, the time taken to detect a signal. In some vigilance tasks, known as 'unlimited hold tasks' (Broadbent, 1958), in which non-transient signals are employed, the signal is repeatedly presented until a detection response is made, and the measure of efficiency here becomes the number of repetitions required, either at the same level or at progressively easier levels of discriminability, for the signal to be reported. A final measure of efficiency in vigilance tasks is the number of occasions on which a signal is reported when none has, in fact, been presented. Such errors are variously described as 'commission errors', 'false alarms', 'false positives' or 'type one errors'. Thus the principal measures of performance during vigilance are the detection and false alarm rates and detection latencies. All three measures are necessary for the understanding of the way in which vigilance performance varies with time on task, across different experimental conditions and between different individuals.

Until the late 1960s, most investigators of vigilance restricted themselves either to detection rate or to detection latency as a measure of vigilance performance and false alarm rates were largely ignored, since there appeared to be no satisfactory way of combining these three performance measures into a common metric. But it became increasingly apparent that similar levels of detection rate could be associated with both high and low false alarm rates and, furthermore, that changes over time in detection rate were sometimes accompanied by concomitant changes in the false alarm rate and sometimes not. Consider a situation, for example, where a vigilance task consists of 100 event presentations and twenty of these presentations are of signal events which the observer is required to detect. One observer in the experiment presses his response button twenty times, each time correctly identifying a signal. A second observer presses his response button 100 times also obtaining a perfect correct detection score but at the same time making eighty false alarms. The correct detection scores do not distinguish between the efficiency of these two observers, although their performances would appear to differ in important respects. What is needed therefore is a way of distinguishing between, on the one hand, the observer's perceptual efficiency or sensitivity, which reflects the ability to discriminate between signal and non-signal events, and, on the other, his *response criterion*, which reflects his willingness to report a signal as being present. Some observers may adopt strict response criteria, requiring very strong evidence that a signal has been presented before making a detection response and, in consequence, make comparatively few false alarms while also failing to detect some signals. Other observers may adopt lax response criteria, requiring minimal evidence that a signal has been presented before making a detection response and, in consequence, detect many signals while also making many false alarms.

A method of distinguishing between the effects of sensitivity and of criterion placement has been provided, most notably, by signal detection theory (see McNicol, 1972; Swets, 1977). The application of a signal detection theory analysis to vigilance performance suggests that the frequently observed decline in the number of correct detections as a function of time on task, the vigilance decrement, can arise either from a decrease in the observer's sensitivity, indicating a reduction in the ability to discriminate signals from non-signals, or from an increase in the strictness of his criterion for responding positively. In the former case the hit rate declines with time at work, while the false alarm rate is likely to remain stable or to increase slightly; in the latter case the hit and false alarm rates are likely to exhibit concomitant declines.

Most commonly the vigilance decrement is attributable to response criteria rather than to sensitivity changes. As the task proceeds, the observer makes fewer confident responses and becomes more cautious about reporting that a signal has been presented. The speed with which detection responses are made is also related to criterion placement (see Parasuraman and Davies, 1976). In some vigilance situations, however, a reduction in sensitivity with time at work occurs, but only when the task requires the observer to discriminate between signal and non-signal events presented successively, and when the rate at which events are presented for inspection is high (see Parasuraman, 1979; Parasuraman and Davies, 1977). If the rate of event presentation is low, or if signal and non-signal events are presented simultaneously, rather than successively, the vigilance decrement, if it occurs, tends to be associated with changes in the response criterion.

Theories of vigilance have attempted to provide explanations both of the vigilance decrement and of the overall level of performance achieved in different vigilance situations. Several different theories have been proposed (see Broadbent, 1971; Davies and Parasuraman, 1982; Davies and Tune, 1970; and Warm, 1977, for reviews) but comparatively few of them seem able to account for the two types of vigilance decrement outlined above. The most useful concepts for an explanation of vigilance performance are probably expectancy (Baker, 1963), mental effort (Kahneman, 1973) and arousal. As noted earlier, sensitivity decrements tend to occur only in high event rate successive discrimination tasks, and are not observed when simultaneous discriminations and/or low event rates are employed. It is possible that a combination of memory load, time pressure and mental effort accounts for the occurrence of sensitivity decrements, while failures of expectancy are more important in those situations in which criterion increments are found in the absence of any change in sensitivity. In the latter case it is likely that the observer periodically revises his criterion setting to one of greater strictness, in accordance with his progressively lowered estimate of signal occurrence. Changes in the level of arousal also occur during the performance of a vigilance task, although it appears improbable that arousal theory can provide an adequate explanation of the vigilance decrement. Concomitant changes in electrocortical arousal and detection efficiency have been reported in vigilance situations (for example, Davies and Krkovic, 1965; O'Hanlon and Beatty, 1977) but similar declines in electrocortical arousal are found when there is no vigilance decrement (Hink *et al.*, 1978; Wilkinson and Haines, 1970) or when the vigilance decrement is attributable either to a sensitivity or to a criterion shift (Davies and Parasuraman, 1977). Indeed, the only prerequisite for obtaining concomitant changes in electrocortical arousal and detection efficiency appears to be that the task be prolonged and carried out in monotonous conditions (see Davies, Shackleton and Parasuraman, in press). It seems, therefore, that at best arousal is merely of secondary importance in explaining the performance decrements found in vigilance situations, although it may be useful in explaining variations in the level of performance under different environmental conditions (see, for example, Broadbent, 1971).

Conclusions

Writing in 1890, William James considered that 'everyone knows what attention is'. While people clearly know from experience what it is like to focus attention on an object, an attribute or a train of thought, it is also apparent that the theoretical analysis of attentional phenomena lags far behind this intuitive knowledge.

We began this chapter by outlining three varieties of attention, selective, intensive and sustained attention, and proceeded to describe the principal findings and theories in each area. In the discussion of selective attention the emphasis was placed on auditory selective attention, largely because the major theoretical approaches to selective attention were derived from studies in which auditory focused and divided attention tasks were employed. The construct most frequently used to account for the operation of auditory selective attention has been a selective filter and much research has been devoted to locating the filter, or filters, within the conceptual nervous system. But a number of studies have also been concerned with visual selective attention, and it is far from clear whether the theoretical analysis of auditory selective attention can be extended to encompass visual selective attention. An excellent review of research concerned with visual selective attention is provided by Rabbitt (1978).

Because of problems that have arisen over the location of the selective filter, an alternative view of selective attention, expressed in terms of mental effort, has gained some acceptance, and this concept is sufficiently flexible to be applied to intensive and sustained attention as well. But while the notion of mental effort is appealing, there are difficulties in distinguishing effort from capacity and from arousal. Furthermore, while filter theory made clear predictions which were capable of being falsified, it is more difficult to derive such predictions from capacity theory and subject them to experimental test.

Filter theory has also been used to explain the performance decrement in vigilance tasks, although as with other theories of vigilance which attempt to account for very diverse phenomena in terms of a single construct, it is not completely satisfactory. There seem to be two kinds of vigilance decrement that can occur, one associated with an alteration of criterion placement in the direction of increased caution and the other with a reduction in perceptual sensitivity. Two kinds of explanation of the decrement would thus appear to be necessary, and expectancy, mental effort and, possibly, arousal appear to be useful concepts in the explanation of vigilance performance. In general it is unlikely that any one theory will be capable of explaining all varieties of attention, and even when a single variety is considered, more than one kind of explanation may be required. It can be expected that as research on attention develops further, the tendency to devise 'miniature' theories to account for attentional phenomena will increase.

Chapter 10
Perceptual Organization

Sensation and perception

There are essentially three aspects to man's perception of his environment. In the first place, obviously, objects (including people and events) exist in that environment; these provide what has often been called the *distal stimulus* for perception. Second, there is the stimulus pattern produced by environmental objects at the sensory receptors, such as the retina of the eye; this has been termed the *proximal stimulus*. Third, there is 'what we see' – the appearance of objects to us, the way in which we experience and describe them. The basic aims of the psychologist interested in perception must be to examine the characteristics of perceptual experience – its *phenomenology* – and to observe the relation between that experience and the distal and proximal stimulation which give rise to it. Psychologists have in fact attempted to describe perceptual processes in very varied ways and with varying emphasis upon the physiological and neurological bases of sensation, the analysed qualities of sensory experience, and the role of past experience, expectation and perhaps personality in determining what is perceived. The field of perception, in fact, is broad and its boundaries fluid; it is bordered on the one hand by the field of 'sensation' and on the other by that of 'cognition' – a study of the ways in which the individual schematizes and utilizes the information he receives from the environment, via such functions as learning, memory, thinking. Such cognitive processes will be the concern of later chapters, while in Chapter 8 we have already considered some aspects of sensory processes.

Given this wide variation of approach and of content within the psychological study of perception, the most striking characteristic of everyday perception is that it is *organized*, and that, in particular, it does not appear to be directly and completely determined by proximal stimulation. For example, a car parked 100 yards away 'appears' to be a real, normally sized car although the image projected by it upon the retina is many times smaller than that projected by a car parked beside us (a phenomenon known as 'size constancy'); objects 'appear' to be three-dimensional, or to be moving towards or away from us, although the retinal image is two-dimensional and therefore, at least on the face of it, would seem incapable of representing depth; and in Chapter 9 we have seen that there may be considerable selectivity in our attention to sensory information. For the most part our experience of the world corresponds closely to the physical environment around us, and our responses to that environment are appropriate and successful. Nevertheless, perception is also subject to error, sometimes transitory (as in the case of hallucinations) and sometimes systematic (as in the case of *visual illusions*, to be discussed later). Thus it is impossible to explain why things appear as they do simply in terms of their real nature, because perception is often illusory and because some 'real' characteristics of objects, such as three-dimensionality, cannot be directly represented at receptor areas; and at the same time it is also impossible to explain why things appear as they do simply in terms of the proximal stimulation to which they give rise.

One classic solution to this difficulty of explanation was the distinction between *sensation* and *perception* – a distinction which in fact antedated the science of psychology and was central to British empiricist philosophy, particularly of the eighteenth and nineteenth centuries (see Chapter 1). According to this view, initial sensations are not organized; perception results from the interpretation of sensation. To the empiricists such interpretation was on the basis of knowledge and past experience, and in particular by the *association* of sensations with images and ideas.

However, there was from the start some opposition to this view, and a rival claim that perceptual organization was in some sense inherent in sensory experience rather than acquired by 'outside' association. Alongside the empiricist tradition was a *nativist* tradition, explaining perceptual phenomena in terms of innate ideas, *a priori* intuitions or, as in the case of Müller (discussed in Chapter 8), in terms of specific energies or other properties inherent in proximal stimulation which might give rise immediately to organized and discriminative perception. We have seen in Chapter 8 that there is in fact considerable evidence for some inherent organization, for example in the sense of specific cortical projection areas for different sense modalities and specific receptors for specific sensations within a modality. Objections to the sensation–perception distinction were advanced most notably by the *Gestalt* school of perception (for example, Koffka, 1935), which was particularly concerned with the investigation of perceptual (and other psychological) phenomena principally through the medium of self-report, and their correlation with physical and physiological (and in particular *cortical*) events. The German term 'Gestalt' means in English 'form' or 'pattern'; Gestalt psychology, which may be said to have been founded in the University of Frankfurt in the early decades of the twentieth century by three men, Max Wertheimer, Kurt Koffka and Wolfgang Köhler, started from the basically philosophical assumption that 'the whole is more than the sum of its parts' and that the proper approach to the understanding of behaviour should be the study of experience in all its complexity, rather than the molecular study of sensations and actions then common in the psychological laboratory. The Gestalt psychologists argued that if 'sensation' means anything it must mean an immediate conscious experience which 'perceptual' judgement can then interpret; but introspection shows clearly that our 'immediate' experience is not of elemental sensations which are then intellectually organized into wholes, but of 'real things' – objects, people, events – experienced directly as wholes, not as the sums of parts. Again, infants and animals can be shown to exhibit distance perception and constancy, although they may be inexperienced and are unlikely to be making intellectual judgements about their sensations. Gestalt psychology argued further that most perceptual organization, if not all, was inherent rather than learned, in that it arose directly from (or, strictly speaking, was *isomorphic* with) the cortical events evoked by sensory stimulation patterns and in particular the interaction among such patterns. Thus this school of psychology can be regarded as favouring a kind of nativism.

Because of these difficulties and counter-arguments, and also because of such trends as the demise of introspection and the advent of behaviourism (see Chapter 1), the sensation–perception distinction as a theoretical issue has virtually disappeared from contemporary psychology; as Boring expressed it in 1942, 'in Gestalt psychology, therefore, perception has absorbed sensation, whereas in physiological psychology sensation has absorbed perception'. Nevertheless, the influence of its ideas can still be traced in current thinking; the terms 'sensation' and 'perception' are still used in rather distinct contexts, and the general notion that perception is influenced not only by sense impressions but also by past experience and knowledge is still very widely held. For further discussion of 'sensation and perception', 'nativism' and 'empiricism' see, for example, Boring (1942); Hochberg (1962); Thomson (1968); and Pastore (1971). We shall return briefly to what may be described as the 'innate–learned' controversy, and to the hypotheses of Gestalt psychology and the notion of perceptual learning, in our discussion of perceptual development in Chapter 11; in the rest of this chapter we shall be concerned further with examples of perceptual organization in everyday experience and their closer investigation in the laboratory.

Non-specific stimulation, and 'laws' of organization

It is undeniable that the importance of sensory stimulation is non-specific as well as specific. It appears that an optimal amount of stimulation is needed to maintain efficient behaviour and that disruption may occur if stimulation either greatly exceeds or falls far short of the desirable amount.

A number of experiments have been carried out in the United States and Canada to observe the effects of sensory deprivation – that is, severe reduction of sensory stimulation. The experiments carried out are not uniform in procedure but most of them have in common that subjects (normally college students who are paid for taking part) are required to stay in isolation in sound-proofed cubicles, wearing opaque goggles and with arms and hands bandaged to cut down tactile cues. One alternative method is that employed by Lilly (1956) who kept his subjects suspended in water at body temperature, blindfolded and wearing breathing apparatus, so that not only environmental but also kinaesthetic cues were drastically reduced. After a period of time spent under these conditions, which may be anything from one to four days, subjects typically exhibit certain disturbances in behaviour, varying in severity according to the exact procedure employed and the length of the isolation period. The most general report of subjects is that after a time in isolation it becomes harder to occupy oneself with organized trains of thought; concentration is difficult and instead 'the mind wanders'. Some subjects drift further into a confused state in which they cannot tell whether they are waking or sleeping and in which they become emotionally labile, experiencing considerable swings of mood. Occasionally – and more often in some experimental situations than in others – visual and auditory hallucinations occur, ranging from fluctuations in light intensity to complex and colourful everyday scenes. There is also some distortion of the alpha rhythm of the EEG (see Chapter 4), which becomes slower and irregular in form. In many cases experimenters have reported disturbances in behaviour to persist for perhaps days after the termination of the experiment.

However, there are considerable differences among the results obtained by different investigators and the effects of sensory deprivation upon different subjects. In some cases it appears that *perceptual* deprivation is more disturbing than *sensory* deprivation: for example, more disruption or distress may be experienced by subjects wearing translucent goggles, which allow diffuse but unpatterned light to reach the eye, than by subjects kept in darkness. Further, it has been reported that subjects who are very highly motivated to stay in the experimental situation do not report the typical disturbances in experience; that subjects who are mature, non-neurotic and self-reliant (by varying criteria) can tolerate sensory deprivation better than the less mature and stable; perhaps most important, that the reported experiences of subjects may to some extent be influenced by the expectations of the experimenter. For more discussion of these points, see, for example, Zubek (1969). Nevertheless, it appears generally true to say that subjects under conditions of reduced sensory input are likely to function below their normal level of efficiency. The same can be said of subjects in less extreme situations than these, as we saw in our discussion of vigilance and sustained attention in Chapter 9.

While too little stimulation can disrupt behaviour, too much may also be harmful. Experiments dealing with the effects of excessive stimulation – sensory overload – are few in comparison with the number dealing with the opposite condition. Sensory overload can involve either the stimulation of several sensory modalities at the same time, or intense stimulation of one modality, though some writers (e.g. Lindsley, 1961) would restrict the term to one or other of these situations. Roughly speaking, the first situation described leads to disruption of behaviour because of the extreme 'distraction' involved, while the second does so because it produces extreme discomfort. Intense stimulation is painful and can produce marked effects upon behaviour; human subjects exposed to short periods of intense noise, for example, have reported muscular weakness and excessive fatigue, feelings of dizziness and sometimes burning of the skin, while intense auditory stimulation can be shown to kill some insects and to produce fatal seizures in rats. Again, perhaps analogous though less extreme situations are those in which subjects are asked to perform two different tasks at the same time, or to work in loud noise (see Chapter 9), although findings here are somewhat variable and an interpretation in terms of sensory overload is doubtful. Thus behaviour, and in particular the integration of behaviour, is affected by the intensity of environmental stimulation to some extent independently of its nature. Moreover, when sensory deprivation or overstimulation occurs in early life its effects may be long lasting if not permanent; this will be discussed later in Chapter 12.

Nevertheless, our principal interest here is with the nature of perceptual organization, and thus with the *specific* characteristics and effects of

(a)

(b)

(c)

Figure 10.1   Simple and ambiguous figure–ground stimuli. (a) A simple instance of figure on ground, (b) the 'twins and vase' reversible figure (from Rubin, 1921), (c) the 'wife and mother-in-law' ambiguous figure (from Boring, 1930)

perceptual input. Clearly, as we have seen, organization is a striking and universal characteristic of perceptual experience. Even our simplest perceptions are of integrated objects which in some way 'stand out' or are separate from their context. The characteristics of such *figure–ground* perception were classically described by Rubin (1921). The figure appears to possess form and contours, and to be nearer the observer than the ground, which is relatively formless and appears to extend continuously behind the figure; the figure has an object- or thing-like quality while the ground has no such identity. The fact that the distinction of figure from ground is not completely determined by proximal stimulation is illustrated by the existence of ambiguous or reversible-perspective stimuli, in which either one or another part of the stimulus pattern may be perceived as 'figure': see the simple and complex stimuli in Figure 10.1. Nevertheless, in many percepts there seems to be a 'natural' figure–ground interpretation, which may be reversed with more or less difficulty and whose stability is increased with experience; some of the factors influencing the definition of a figure – 'surroundedness', orientation, colour, size, symmetry – are discussed by, e.g., Rock (1975).

Organization is thus evident even in the perception of single, simple figures; it is even more striking when a number of stimulus elements are combined within a visual array. To demonstrate the complexity of even commonplace perceptual behaviour, so readily lost in the analysis of 'pure' sensation, the Gestalt psychologists, notably Wertheimer (1923, trans. 1938) and Koffka (1935), collected a number of examples of perceptual organization which were said to illustrate the general laws of perception. Some of

---

Figure 10.2   Some principles of perceptual organization. (a) Proximity: the dots in this arrangement are readily seen in groups of two, according to their spatial proximity, (b) similarity: these equally spaced dots are seen as falling into horizontal groups of three, similar units being grouped together, (c) direction: although lines B and C are closer to one another than are A and C, the immediate impression is of one horizontal line, A + C, with an oblique line, B, meeting it – not of a line A and an angle B + C, (d) good curve: a 'special case' of the law of direction. The curve segments are seen as a single continuous curve, not as parts of three independent figures, in spite of the law of closure (see below), (e) closure: where possible, figures are organized into symmetrical and self-enclosed units. Figure (i) is viewed as two overlapping units rather than three. Figure (ii) is usually seen immediately as a circle and a diamond; in fact both forms are incomplete, (f) the 'good Gestalt': the form shown in (i) is present also in (ii), but is recognized only with some difficulty; the difficulty can be explained by recourse to several of the principles above. (From Wertheimer, 1923)

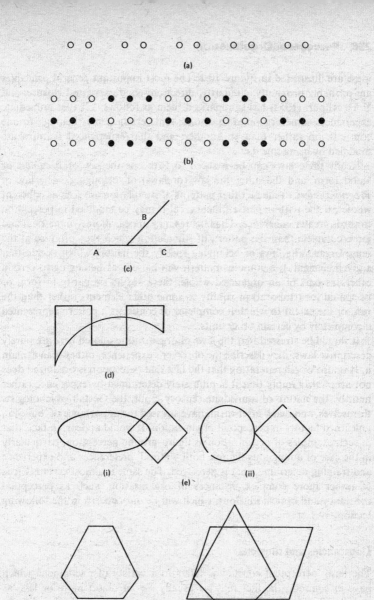

(a)

(b)

(c)

(d)

(i)   (ii)

(e)

(i)   (ii)

(f)

these are illustrated in Figure 10.2. The most important general principles are probably proximity, similarity, direction, good curve and closure, and F. H. Allport (1955) has summarized them as follows: '... that immediate experiences come organized in wholes; that certain items "belong" to one constellation rather than to another; and that experienced features are modified by being together'.

Really these laws can be reduced to two: one the law of *Prägnanz* or 'good form' and the other the law (or laws) of 'belonging'. The law of *Prägnanz* refers to the fact that patterns of stimulation are seen as coherent wholes; if the pattern is itself incoherent it may be modified in perception towards greater coherence. Thus figures may appear more symmetrical and more complete than the pattern of stimulation which they produce at the sense organ. The laws of belonging specify the factors which decide that a given element in a stimulus pattern will be seen as belonging to certain others as part of an organized whole: these are its similarity in form or its spatial (or temporal) proximity to some other elements rather than the rest, or the extent to which it completes or continues a pattern represented incompletely by certain other units.

It should be stressed that the laws of organization quoted here are purely descriptive laws; they describe the observer's experience, rather than explain it. It is also worth reiterating that the fact that perception is organized does not *necessarily* imply that it is ultimately determined by experience rather than by the nature of immediate sensory input; the Gestalt psychologists themselves, and many after them, have stressed the importance of 'built-in', unlearned factors in perceptual organization. It would appear, in fact, that in such examples of organization as figure–ground perception, particularly in the case of ambiguous figures, both 'natural' preferences and experience and training determine what is perceived. The same is almost certainly true of rather more complex instances of organization, such as perceptual constancy and optical illusions, which will be our concern in the following section.

Constancies and illusions

The term 'perceptual constancy' refers to a variety of phenomena which have in common the fact that we usually see an object more or less 'as it really is', even when it is presented under unusual or distorting conditions. A man usually looks more or less man-sized, whether he is near or far away, and a house looks real and not a toy, even when seen on the horizon. Yet the stimulus patterns produced at the retina and at the visual cortex by the same object at different distances are vastly different in size; the fact that our immediate impression of their size corresponds more closely to real than to retinal size is referred to as size constancy. Similar phenomena are apparent in regard to other object characteristics. A plate on the dinner table looks round to the person sitting behind it, although its retinal shape, for that person, is almost certainly elliptical (shape constancy); a sheet of white paper looks white both in sunlight and in shade, although the light reflected from its surface will vary enormously under the two conditions (brightness constancy).

In size constancy and shape constancy the perception of depth or distance is clearly crucial. Many experiments, as well as everyday observation, have shown that accuracy in estimating the size or shape of an unfamiliar object is reduced sharply if cues to its distance from the observer are eliminated - for instance, when only monocular, rather than binocular, viewing is permitted, or when the object is viewed through a small aperture or narrow tunnel which blocks its surroundings from sight. Thus a common statement of the nature of size constancy is in terms of *size–distance invariance*. This *invariance hypothesis* states that any given retinal size determines a unique and invariant relation between perceived size and perceived distance. If we perceive the distance of an object correctly, we will also perceive its size correctly; if we underestimate its distance we will correspondingly under-estimate its size, and so on. Again, if two objects appear to be at the same distance but one has a retinal size double that of the other, it will appear twice as large.

The invariance hypothesis is a useful description of size constancy phenomena, and has been extended also to cover other constancy phenomena - for example, shape constancy, in the form of a shape–slant invariance hypothesis. It does not, however, fit all situations. Size constancy sometimes breaks down, especially over long distances: people seen from aeroplanes, for example, look like ants, and houses like toys on a Monopoly board. Under less extreme conditions perceived size is often less than its real size but greater than the size of the image it projects upon the retina. This tendency for size (and other) estimations to represent some point between retinal and real values has been termed 'phenomenal regression to the real object' (Thouless, 1932), and many reviewers of the evidence have claimed that compromise is a fundamental characteristic of constancy phenomena. It appears, however, that whether or not compromise occurs is to some extent dependent upon the particular experimental techniques adopted.

Under some circumstances observers may show overconstancy – for instance, they may report a particular stimulus object to be not only bigger than its retinal size but also bigger than it really is. Thus a general principle of compromise does not seem tenable. It could be argued, of course, that where less than perfect constancy is attained in the case of perceived size it may be because perceived distance, too, has been underestimated: thus the invariant relationship between the two is preserved. However, experiments which have adopted the procedure of requiring both size and distance judgements from their subjects in the same situation have often found a correspondence between the two which is distinctly less than perfect; thus the invariance hypothesis needs to be viewed with some caution. For a recent discussion of the evidence, see, for example, Dember and Warm (1979).

Perceptual illusions, like perceptual constancies, may be taken as evidence of perceptual organization, but with the difference that they represent inaccurate rather than accurate perception of real objects. Certain illusions have become standardized and are regularly used in the psychological study of such phenomena; some of these are shown in Figure 10.3. An illusion occurring in everyday life is the so-called 'moon illusion': the moon commonly looks smaller when it is at its zenith than when it is at the horizon. This illusion was known in Ptolemy's time and has been of enduring interest to students of perception, not least because it appears at first sight to contravene the 'law' of size constancy. It appears also to be a genuinely 'psychological' phenomenon, since there are no good physical reasons for the difference in appearance (although one or two have been suggested: for example, the relative distances of zenith and horizon moon from the observer, or differences in the degree of refraction of the moon's image through the atmosphere at zenith and horizon). Moreover, the illusion can still be experienced when photographs of the moon in its visual context in different parts of the sky, rather than the moon itself, are viewed.

There is no universally accepted explanation of these phenomena, and indeed the visual illusions are too diverse to make a single, general

Figure 10.3 Some visual illusions. (a) The Müller–Lyer or 'arrowhead' illusion: the longitudinal lines, in fact equal, appear different in length as a function of the 'arrowheads' or 'fins', (b) two forms of the Ponzo or 'railway lines' illusion: of the two equal lines, or circles, the upper appears larger than the lower, (c) the Hering illusion: the horizontal lines, although straight and parallel, appear curved, (d) the Poggendorf illusion: the diagonal line is in fact on a single plane, but appears too high on the right-hand side of the figure for continuity, (e) the horizontal–vertical illusion: the two lines are of equal length, but the vertical appears longer

(a)

(b)

(c)

(d)

(e)

explanatory principle plausible; for an account of different types of illusion, see Robinson (1972). Theories are usually very restricted in their applicability, even within a given type such as that of the so-called 'geometrical optical illusions': that is, illusions relating to the judgement of size, length and other features in line drawings, some of which are represented in Figure 10.3. Offered theories of the geometrical optical illusions have been many and varied, ranging from hypotheses concerning retinal mechanisms and eye-movements to accounts in terms of apparent distance (for a review of theories see, e.g., Robinson, 1972; Rock, 1975). The 'apparent distance' theory is one of the most widely accepted, and one of the most interesting conceptually in that it seeks to account for illusions as 'special cases' of constancy. For example, it has been argued that the Müller–Lyer figure (see Figure 10.3a) gives an impression of depth, because of its similarity to certain stimulus configurations, associated with three-dimensionality, which are encountered in everyday life. The diverging arrowheads suggest the ceiling and floor of a room as they appear at a distant corner. The stimulus pattern of a line between converging arrowheads gives no such impression; if anything it suggests the reverse, that the line is nearer than the 'arrowhead' lines which recede from it. Since the two lines, retinally of the same extent, appear to be at different distances, the principle of size constancy requires that the line which seems further away must be bigger – hence the illusion. Similar arguments can be applied to certain other illusion figures – for example, the Ponzo illusion (Figure 10.3b). The argument in this case is illustrated in Figure 10.4.

A similar explanation was put forward by Kaufman and Rock (1962) for the moon illusion. They argued that the sky at the horizon looks further away than the sky at its zenith (and were able to produce evidence for this assertion); thus the moon, retinally the same size whether at horizon or zenith, appears to be further away when seen at the horizon and so 'must be bigger'. This explanation of the moon illusion is probably the currently dominant one, although there are alternatives, notably the *angle-of-regard* theory of Boring (1943) which has received some more recent support (e.g. van Eyl, 1972), and an interpretation by Restle (1970) in terms of *relative size* of the moon and its visual context.

Such accounts of the nature of visual illusions are not really, of course, explanations in a basic sense. What does it mean, psychologically, to say that 'the principle of size constancy requires' perception of a particular kind, or that an object has a particular appearance because it 'must be' so? What this type of explanation achieves, and this is not a negligible achievement,

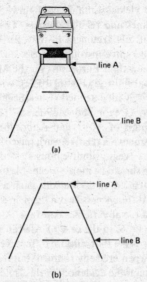

Figure 10.4 Constancy and illusion compared. In both pictures (a) and (b) line A appears longer than line B, although they are in fact equal in length. This phenomenon in picture (a) is termed constancy; in picture (b) it is termed illusion. The difference is that line A can be interpreted as 'really' longer than line B (because the lines are incorporated in a representational context which implies depth) in picture (a), not in picture (b)

is to suggest that at least certain perceptual illusions and perceptual constancies may be two sides of the same coin, illustrating the same underlying principles. In both types of situation the observer views a particular stimulus configuration which conveys the impression of a particular three-dimensional spatial arrangement. If he is looking at the corner of a room this interpretation is veridical – it corresponds to geographical reality. If he is looking at the arrowhead figure of the Müller–Lyer illusion the impression is non-veridical; but as far as explanation is concerned the veridicality or non-veridicality of the impression is strictly irrelevant. The task of the psychologist is to discover why a particular impression is received.

Proponents of the apparent-distance theory have tended to stress the importance of experience; for example, it has been argued that susceptibility to the Müller–Lyer illusion is dependent upon experience of a 'carpentered environment' which yields stimulus configurations consisting largely of rectangles, straight lines and regular corners. There is some cross-cultural evidence in favour of this argument in that, for example, certain African groups, whose members live in round houses on flat plain and scrubland, show much less illusion than Europeans on the Müller–Lyer, but more on the horizontal–vertical illusion (Figure 10.3e), which has been ascribed to their greater familiarity with extended vistas (Segall, Campbell and Herskovits, 1963). However, Gregor and McPherson (1965) compared the performance of two groups of Australian Aborigines, one group living in a 'carpentered' environment – a relatively urbanized settlement – and the other in the open air with only very primitive housing structures; they hypothesized that the former group should be more susceptible to the Müller–Lyer illusion and the latter to 'extended vista' illusions such as the horizontal–vertical, but found no reliable differences between them, in a study which they claimed to be the first to hold racial variables constant. A similar lack of effect was reported by Jahoda (1966) in the case of African groups living in different environments. It is possible that cultural differences arise not from differential experience of a carpentered environment but from differences in training and education (although the evidence for this is not strong; see the negative findings of Jahoda and Stacey, 1970) and perhaps even from physiological differences between races, in particular ocular pigmentation differences (Pollack and Silvar, 1967).

Gregory (1966) has argued that constancy, and the illusions reflecting misapplied constancy, are triggered by two types of 'constancy scaling', one of them essentially automatic and unlearned, the other a higher-level processing more dependent upon experience and awareness. In the first, *primary constancy scaling*, the perspective features of a line-drawing illusion directly trigger a relatively primitive scaling process which enhances the 'apparently' distant parts of the figure. The word 'apparently' is here in parentheses because primary constancy scaling does not involve *awareness* of apparent distance; this argument would explain why illusions are experienced even though the observer appreciates that the figures are drawn on paper, flat and two-dimensional. The second, *secondary constancy scaling*, is triggered by differences in apparent distance of which the observer is at least potentially aware and which he would accept as 'real': it then proceeds to adjustment of apparent size in line with distance information. Gregory has provided further evidence of the involvement of constancy scaling, and to some extent of the independence of primary and secondary constancy scaling, in studies involving the observation of illusion figures drawn in luminous paint and observed in total darkness, so that two-dimensionality is not an inevitable interpretation of the figure. However, while other studies too provide support for Gregory's theory and in general for the apparent-distance interpretation of certain illusion figures, some evidence conflicts with it (see Robinson, 1972).

It is also worth pointing out that the perception of depth or distance, crucial for size and shape constancy and perhaps also for certain illusions, is based upon many and diverse cues (see, e.g., J. J. Gibson, 1950, 1968). Among these are relative accommodation of the lens of the eye, and con-vergence of the two eyes, in viewing a distant or near object. Another is *motion parallax*, which refers to the fact that the relative position of objects at different distances from the observer changes as the observer moves, the change in relative position being greater with greater differences in distance. There is also distance information derived from *binocular disparity*, the difference in the images received by the two eyes, which is again greater with increased differences in the distances of objects in the visual field. Then there are what could be described as *pictorial* visual cues, information about distance which can be seen in two-dimensional representations, such as drawings and photographs, as well as in the three-dimensional visual field. Of these, we have already touched upon *linear perspective* in our discussion of illusions; another important source of information is *texture gradient* or *pattern density*, terms which refer to the fact that in a patterned surface the pattern elements become retinally smaller and denser (that is, there are more elements per unit retinal area) with increased distance from the observer (see Figure 10.5). Other pictorial cues to distance include relative size and height, brightness, shading and shadow, and *interposition*: that is, the partial blocking of a retinal image by another which overlaps it on the retina when the object producing the 'blocking' image is nearer than the object producing the 'blocked' image. Clearly, some of these cues rely upon binocular vision while others do not; some can apply to the perception of apparent depth in two-dimensional figures while others cannot; and it is likely that different sources of distance information are differentially affected by experience and training. It would be naïve, therefore, to seek any very general 'explanation' of, or any universal statement of the role of experience in, the phenomena of constancies and illusions.

Perceptual set and 'motivated perception'

In this final section of Chapter 10 we are concerned with evidence of perceptual organization in a rather different sense from that of earlier

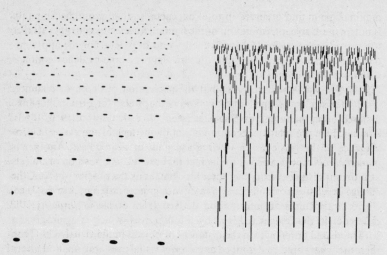

Figure 10.5 Texture gradients, each giving the impression of a receding surface (Gibson, 1950, pp. 84 and 86). The patterns as shown here give the impression of a 'ground scene' on which the observer looks down; a 'ceiling scene' appears, particularly in the case of the 'spot' pattern, if they are viewed upside down

chapters. As Rock (1975) has cogently pointed out, there are several aspects of perceptual experience to be distinguished in the perception of an object. First, we distinguish its shape, size, distance and other physical character- istics; second, we may *recognize* it as familiar; third, we may *identify* it in terms of its function and meaning. As we have already seen, it has been much debated whether, and to what extent, the perception of form and other characteristics is a function of experience; but the recognition and identifica- tion of known stimuli must by definition be the result of experience and learning. The significance of verbal stimuli such as individual words, for example, is arbitrary and must have been previously learned for identifica- tion to be possible. We shall now consider evidence that identification, and in particular the *ease* of identification of words or pictures, may be influenced by *varying* prior experience with different percepts or of different perceivers.

It seems reasonable to argue that where known stimuli are presented un- ambiguously and clearly, relatively minor variations in prior experience are unlikely to result in differences of identification; conversely, the fainter or more ambiguous a stimulus is, the more influential might prior experience be in determining identification. Experiments attempting to show the influence of experience upon perceptual identification have therefore employed techniques which render the stimulus ambiguous: subjects may be asked to identify stimuli presented visually at very dim illumination or for a very brief exposure interval (termed 'tachistoscopic' perception), or auditory stimuli may be presented at very low intensity or accompanied by masking noise. Using techniques such as these it has been found, for example, that common words are more readily identified than words (of the same length) which occur less frequently in the language and therefore have, presumably, occurred less frequently in the subjects' experience; and that subjects recognize words which are related to their own interests (and are therefore more familiar to them) more readily than other words. Other examples of differential ease of identification are given in Chapter 9; and for fuller accounts of experimental work see, for example, Vernon (1970); Haber and Herschenson (1973).

The effect of experience, it is usually argued, is to establish in the perceiver a *set* or readiness for some stimuli rather than others. As a result of differential experience he is set to attend to some stimulus characteristics rather than others when stimuli are ambiguous. If a word, tachistoscopically presented, is only partly perceived, the perceiver will think first of 'probable' words (that is, words which have been frequently encountered in the past and which therefore appear likely to be encountered again) in trying to fit a word to the partial information derived from the stimulus. Only if 'probable' words are found unsatisfactory is he likely to consider 'improbable' words as possible identifications.

A perceptual set can be established rapidly, by instructions or by immediate context, as well as by prolonged experience. If subjects are told that they will be shown tachistoscopically words of a particular kind (for example, names of animals) and are then shown a nonsense word, they will 'identify' it as an animal name; other subjects will interpret the same nonsense word as belonging to a different category if that category has been specified in instructions. Similarly, if subjects are instructed to attend to a specific stimulus characteristic (for example, the number or spatial arrangement of items) and are asked after presentation of the stimulus to report on all its characteristics, they are generally unable or less able to report accurately characteristics other than the one to which they have been set to attend. In an intermediate situation, Postman and Leytham (1951) showed that subjects who, without explicit instructions, were required to identify words which were all trait adjectives developed a set for such words which resulted in delayed identification for other words (although the set was apparently very quickly abolished by presentation of one or two words which were not congruent with it). Leeper (1935) also showed, in a classic study, that a subject's perception of an ambiguous figure (such as the 'wife-and-mother-in-law' picture shown in Figure 10.1) may be affected by prior experimental experience of a stimulus which stresses one asset of the 'test' figure rather than the other. Whether established gradually by pre-experimental experience or, implicitly or explicitly, in the laboratory, a set can thus be shown to determine to a considerable extent the ease and the nature of stimulus identification.

However, some studies suggest that other factors than set – for example, in Leeper's experience, the recency with which a stimulus has been encountered, rather than an expectation of its present occurrence – might be responsible for some of the evidence. Also, it is not always clear whether the effect demonstrated is strictly speaking 'perceptual' or whether it rather represents a variation in response readiness or immediate memory. Lawrence and Coles (1954), for example, reported that 'set' instructions were equally effective whether given, as usual, prior to stimulus presentation or immediately *after* presentation, before the subject's report. They argued from this and other evidence (Lawrence and LaBerge, 1956) that although set influences *perceptual threshold as it is customarily measured*, by verbal report, its effect is upon memory and response processes, not upon perception itself. Evidence on the effectiveness of 'subsequent set' is not, however, conclusive, and in any case such evidence does not necessarily invalidate the notion of perceptual set, since its interpretation depends upon one's definition of the perceptual process. Haber (1966) argued that set can be shown to operate upon *perceptual encoding*, and not only upon response processes (see also Haber and Herschenson, 1973). The difficulty of distinguishing between perceptual and non-perceptual effects upon perceptual threshold is one to which we shall return later in this section.

The hypothesis we have so far considered is simply that we see most readily what is usual and, therefore, what we expect to see; in William James's (1890) classic phrase, 'perception is of definite and probable things'. Some psychologists have claimed further that we see not only what we expect to see but also what we want to see – that perception may be influenced by motivation. This claim has been usefully discussed by F. H. Allport (1955) under the heading of 'directive-state theory', since the assertion is that perception is to some extent directed by the internal states of the organism. Often this has been linked to Freudian theories of wish-fulfilment, 'autism' and repression (see, for example, the argument of Murphy, 1947, and the review of evidence by Kline, 1972). This linking is not inevitable; it can, for example, be argued more simply by analogy with the phenomena of learning and memory that the association of certain percepts with reward or punishment may well influence the readiness with which these percepts are evoked in the perceiver.

A wealth of evidence has been produced in support of the hypothesis that certain aspects of perceptual experience may be influenced by the motivation of the perceiver; for reviews of the evidence, see Vernon (1970); Kline (1972); Dember and Warm (1979). It has been claimed, for example, that pictures of food appear brighter than other pictures of equal objective brightness when subjects are hungry, but not when they are sated; that poker chips are overestimated in size by children who have been able to exchange them for sweets, but not by children for whom the chips have had no value; that coins are overestimated in size as compared with plain discs of the same objective size; that when one aspect of a reversible-perspective figure has been associated with monetary reward it becomes more readily noticeable than the other aspect, which has not been associated with reward. Incidentally, the last finding does not seem to work in reverse; punishing one of two possible percepts (for example, by administration of electric shock) does not make that percept less likely to occur and may have the opposite effect. This finding is of interest in connection with 'perceptual defence', which is discussed later.

Another widely used procedure has been to compare the *ease of recognition* of neutral stimuli (usually words) with that of stimuli which have some relevance to the subject, when each stimulus is presented tachistoscopically or by some other suitable procedure until it can be verbally identified. It has been reported many times that recognition of stimuli is more rapid when they are related to some interest, value or need of the perceiver. For example, *hungry* or *thirsty* subjects recognize words related to their need more readily than other words; subjects with a high *need for achievement* recognize success-related words more rapidly than other words, while the same is not true of subjects who appear to have relatively little need for achievement. Moreover, when stimuli are ambiguous, attempts at identification appear also to be influenced by motivational factors: when subjects guess wrongly at the identity of a word they tend to use as guesses words which are related to their own needs and interests. For instance, hungry subjects asked to 'identify' ambiguous or nonsense pictures tend to use more responses related to food than do non-deprived subjects. Finally, subjects may take longer than 'normal' to recognize words which are of unpleasant connotation or are anxiety-arousing. These words have sometimes been socially 'taboo' words, mainly sexual in connotation; other investigators have used words which are presumed to be unpleasant but not socially taboo, or words which are selected, on the basis of personality tests, as being associated with areas of anxiety for a particular subject or group of subjects.

Thus, it has been claimed, perception may be influenced in various ways by the needs and values of the perceiver. Perception of positively need- or value-related stimuli may be enhanced; that of threatening, anxiety-arousing or unpleasant stimuli may be delayed or 'warded off' – a phenomenon which came to be known as 'perceptual defence'. It has often been pointed out that there are methodological flaws in much of the evidence, and several studies appear, at least at first sight, to be mutually contradictory. This is particularly true of studies of perceptual defence, some of which have actually demonstrated not decreased but *increased* ease of identification for threatening stimuli; thus directive-state theorists must attempt to explain not only a difference in identification thresholds for neutral and critical stimuli but also opposing evidence as to the direction of differences, in what appear often to be essentially similar situations. For a close consideration of these difficulties and of possible resolutions see W. P. Brown (1961). It appears reasonable to conclude – though the statement here must be dogmatic – that enough evidence remains for motivated perception to command serious consideration as to its value; but, again, there are further difficulties in *interpreting* the evidence.

Some writers have argued that the effect of motivation upon perception can be reduced to a simpler one, that of *word frequency*. Words which are related to interests and values of the subject are more familiar to him, because of selected reading and conversation, and may for this reason alone be recognized more readily. On the other hand, words which are associated with anxiety and threat are less likely to be encountered, partly because of social taboos on unpleasant material, partly because subjects will when possible avoid unpleasant situations and their concomitant verbalizations; these words are thus less readily identified because of their relative unfamiliarity, not because of their emotional connotation as such. Others have suggested similarly that the 'motivated perception' effects are really effects of *set*: that, for example, we expect to encounter stimuli related to hunger and thirst when an experimenter has asked us to abstain from food and drink prior to his experiment, and that, other things being equal, we expect to encounter affectively neutral, rather than unpleasant, material and are therefore slower to identify the latter, not because it is threatening but because it is unexpected. These are important criticisms of much of the evidence, although some studies at least have produced evidence in support of the motivated perception hypothesis when word frequency and set have been controlled.

It has also been claimed that the idea of motivated perception is logically absurd, since it implies that the perceiver somehow 'looks' to see if a given object is 'worth seeing': this problem is particularly acute in the case of perceptual defence, since some characteristic of the stimulus must be perceived before it can be recognized as anxiety-arousing and consequently 'not identified'. Bruner and Postman (1949), among others, proposed a way round this paradox. They suggested that reception of a stimulus triggers off not one but a number of responses: one of these is the process of verbal identification, another is an automatic, affective (positively or negatively emotional) reaction which can be measured via the psychogalvanic reflex (PGR). These responses may have different thresholds – that is, they may require different stimulus intensities, or different amounts of stimulus information, for the correct response to be elicited. 'Autonomic identification' of a stimulus may precede verbal identification, and an autonomic response to threatening stimuli may conceivably inhibit completion of the perceptual process and thus delay verbal identification, the indicator generally used to determine whether recognition has occurred. Thus it has been argued that the notion of perceptual defence is not logical nonsense, and moreover, that there is some supporting evidence, from studies of *subliminal perception* or 'perception without awareness', that autonomic discriminations can precede verbal discriminations in a perceptual identification task. However, the evidence for subliminal perception is controversial; moreover, it has been argued (notably by Eriksen, 1960) that the lower threshold of autonomic, as compared with verbal, discrimination may simply reflect the relative difficulty of the two indicators of perception, the verbal discrimination usually being the more difficult of the two. For a more recent defence of the subliminal perception hypothesis, and a review of the various kinds of evidence in its support, see Dixon (1972).

Partly because of the difficulty of equating verbal and non-verbal measures of perception, it has been argued by various writers in various terms that motivated perception may be a verbal, not a truly perceptual, phenomenon. Howes and Solomon (1950) argued that subjects may see anxiety-arousing words as quickly as others but may hesitate to report them; this seems to be a likely criticism of some studies but not of others. Goldiamond (1958) claimed that differential recognition thresholds simply reflect a bias in the subject's readiness to produce various words as guesses when he cannot see what is being shown. A subject may be more likely to produce neutral or pleasantly toned words than to produce anxiety-arousing words; thus his guesses are more likely to be correct when neutral or pleasant words are in fact used as stimuli than when unpleasant words are presented. The effect upon ease of recognition is purely verbal, not perceptual in any real sense, since it is independent of the particular stimulus being shown and dependent simply upon the relatively chronic response bias of the perceiver. There is some evidence to support the response-bias interpretation of perceptual defence, and also support for a similar interpretation of the word-frequency effect and, as already mentioned, of the effects of set. On the other hand, some studies suggest that stimulus information and the expectation of the subject may play a more important role than such interpretations allow (Broadbent and Gregory, 1967; Minard, 1965). A third interpretation has been advanced by Natsoulas (1965), termed by him the stimulus-effect hypothesis; he points out that changes in perceptual threshold might be the result of response processes which are not 'chronic' or pre-existent, as is response bias, but evoked by the presentation of the stimulus. In other words, a *response* disturbance is set up by a 'disturbing' percept. This interpretation is distinct from the perceptual interpretation (as it is from the response bias interpretation) in principle, but it is extremely difficult to distinguish between the two in practice.

'Motivated perception', then, in many cases involves essentially a discrepancy between verbal identification and some other index of perception – for example, the equivalent *objective* stimulus intensity of neutral and critical stimuli, or other behavioural indices such as the PGR. The problem of the accuracy of verbal indicators does not apply only to motivated perception. It is relevant to the effects of set, to virtually all aspects of perceptual organization, to perceptual development and indeed to all areas of psychology in which the subject's 'inner state' – what he has learned, what he can remember, how he is thinking or feeling – is largely inferred from his verbal report. The verbal indicator is not necessarily a 'bad' one, but it is bound to be imperfect, and it is as well to interpret it with caution.

Chapter 11
Perceptual Development

The innate–learned controversy

Much, although by no means all, of our knowledge of perceptual development has been gained in the context of, or at any rate under the shadow
of, the theoretical debate between nativism and empiricism already mentioned in Chapter 10: that is, the aim of research has often been to determine the extent to which perceptual organization is innate and the extent
to which it is learned. There have been many, and very varied, approaches
to this problem. The Gestalt psychologists adduced *introspective* evidence, in
the first instance, to support their contention that organization is immediate
and unlearned; and certainly, if we are asked to report upon our own perceptual experiences, what generally emerges about perception of a particular
stimulus complex is that 'it just appears to be like that', immediately and
without conscious inference. However, this is hardly a crucial test. If an
observer is unaware of any process of inference this does not necessarily
mean that no such process occurs; it may rather be that the observer is
simply unaware of its occurrence – he is not attending to it. The fact that most
of us would find it difficult to give an accurate description of the motor
processes involved in walking upstairs, and that we are not ordinarily aware
of our sequence of actions when performing this rather complex skill, does
not compel belief that the skill is innately organized.

The 'distorted room' designed by Ames (see Ittelson, 1952) illustrates this
point. When we view a room like that shown in Figure 11.1, we assume that
it is a 'normal' room in which the two distant corners are rectangular and
all four walls of equal height; but exactly the same appearance can be given
by a room in which one of the far corners is further away than the other
and in which the ceiling slopes upward (at a calculated angle) to the distant
corner. There are, in fact, many different combinations of angularity and
ceiling slope which would give the same impression to the observer, but the
impression is 'immediately' one of rectangularity, and this impression
persists even if, in a distorted room, two people are viewed at the far corners

Figure 11.1 Normally sized people viewed in a distorted room (see text). (Adapted from Gregory, 1966, p. 178)

so that their different distances from the observer produce differences in retinal size. This immediate and persistent appearance of rectangularity must be a function of learning, derived from experience of 'everyday' carpentered environments. Immediacy of experience, therefore, would be decisive evidence of unlearned organization only in the case of an organism with no opportunity for learning.

More pertinent to the innate–learned controversy have been more or less direct studies of the brain processes involved in sensory reception. Some such studies have been discussed in Chapter 8: for example, the work of Hubel and Wiesel (1962) and of McCollough on the mapping of specific form- or orientation-sensitive cortical cells, and evidence of the dominance, and comparative inflexibility, of visual evidence in sensory rearrangement. Where there is clear evidence that some discrimination of formal characteristics may be 'built in' to the sensory system, the obvious implication is that learning is relatively unimportant for such discriminations, although it may still have a part to play in the perceptual organization of sensory input.

Further studies which might be mentioned in this context include the investigation, notably by Gestalt psychologists such as Wertheimer, of the visual conditions under which illusions may occur, and the interpretation of these illusions in terms of the Gestalt theory of cortical action. Work on the so-called *phi phenomenon* constitutes an example: the successive illumination of two lights in a horizontal or vertical plane may produce the impression of a single light moving between the light sources. This effect is said to be predictable in terms of the overlap of contours of electrical activity produced, at the visual cortex, by the two stimuli, contours which fuse in accordance with the principle of *Prägnanz* to produce the contours of a single moving object; but there have been attempts (moderately but not entirely successful) to explain the results of these and similar studies in other terms (see Hochberg, 1964).

Finally, it is interesting to consider studies of the characteristic perceptions resulting from stabilization of the retinal image. The maintenance of an image on the retina involves constant scanning and stimulation of many different receptors. When retinal stimulation is stabilized in location by, for instance, requiring the subject to wear a contact lens with an attached mirror and projection system (Pritchard, 1961), the image disappears after two or three seconds and may fluctuate in and out of vision thereafter. Pritchard observed that these fluctuations have certain characteristics of interest to the Gestalt thesis. When a projected image is very simple – for instance, a line – it disappears rapidly, and reappears, as a single unit. When the image is more complex it may again fluctuate in vision as a unit, or parts of it may disappear and reappear independently of other parts. These partial units are usually 'meaningful' rather than completely fragmentary. Lines and corners function as units, as do potentially meaningful parts of complex wholes, and figure and ground – in the case of stimuli which can be described as having figure and ground elements – vary independently (see examples in Figure 11.2). It is also noteworthy that some irregular figures undergo successive modifications in appearance which are predictable from Gestalt laws of closure and good form, these modifications sometimes involving not only selective appearance but actual distortion and 'hallucination' of parts of the modified figure. For a discussion of the possible theoretical implications of this work, see Pritchard (1961).

However, most of our evidence concerning the origins of perceptual organization has come from *behavioural* studies. Although these are very varied, they have all derived from one or the other of two basic premises. First, if perceptual organization is innately determined, it should appear in the human or animal which has not had experience, that is, in the neonate.

Figure 11.2 Fluctuations in a stabilized retinal image. The left-hand diagram on each line represents the stimulus shown; others on the line indicate fluctuations in perception. Note the 'hallucination' of part of the figure on line 3. (From Pritchard, 1961, pp. 75–6)

Conversely, if organization is acquired through experience it should not be evident in those observers – again, human or animal – who have had no opportunity to acquire it. Second, if perceptual organization is innately determined it should take essentially the same form for all perceivers, at least to the extent that they share the same sensory apparatus. Conversely, if organization is a function of experience one would expect differences among perceivers, to the extent that different perceivers have had different perceptual experiences. These differences may be appreciable among individuals of the same culture; they are even more likely when, for example, people of different cultures are compared.

From the first premise come studies which compare the perception of neonates with that which is expected of an adult of the same species; also, some studies examine the perceptual performance of subjects who, although not newborn, are without experience in the particular sensory modality of interest to the experimenter (for instance, the congenitally blind man who regains his sight and animals which have been reared in darkness). There are also studies in which the amount, or the type, of experience is different for different subject groups. Representing the second approach, there are some studies comparing the perception of peoples of different cultures, and individual differences within a culture.

Studies of the perceptual abilities of human and non-human neonates and infants will be discussed on pp. 309–14, summarized briefly, they indicate that there may well be considerable 'innate', or at any rate very early, perceptual organization in several species, and particularly visual organization in humans. There is, of course, considerable difficulty in devising situations in which the perceptual experience of a neonate can be accurately inferred; the need is for subjects who are on the one hand perceptually naïve and on the other hand capable of unequivocal responses during testing. In the attempt to meet both requirements some investigators have reared animals in darkness from birth: that is, with no opportunity for visual experience but in otherwise favourable conditions for development of normal responses. Animals of various species have been reared in this way – rats, rabbits, pigeons and other birds, and primates such as the chimpanzee. A summary of studies has been presented by Beach and Jaynes (1955).

It seems clear from these experiments that the visual ability of animals reared in darkness, when they are first exposed to the light, is considerably inferior to that of the normally reared animal. Riesen (1947), for example, reported that a chimpanzee reared in total darkness for the first few months of life showed deficiencies of normal vision and took many times longer to learn simple visual discrimination tasks than animals normally reared. However, there is a complication in that animals reared without exposure to light are frequently found, on post-mortem examination, to have some degree of retinal degeneration and sometimes, after a prolonged deprivation, degeneration of the optic nerve. In other words, physical abnormalities of the optic system may result from visual deprivation and obscure the comparison between naïve and experienced animals. This difficulty can be surmounted by rearing animals in diffuse, unpatterned light; under such conditions of deprivation animals did not show anatomical degeneration, but did exhibit difficulty in avoiding obstacles and in the performance of visual discrimination tasks. Their performance, in fact, appeared to be intermediate between that of the totally deprived and that of the normally reared animal. However, Riesen (1947) also showed that a chimpanzee reared for seven months in darkness but admitted to a normally lighted environment for one and a half hours per day did not show impairment of visual ability, but performed in all observed respects like a normally reared animal. Thus while some visual experience may be necessary for efficient performance the experience needed is not extensive.

It may also be reiterated that the type of experience – for example, whether actively or passively produced – may also be important, as is the opportunity for integration of information derived from different sensory modalities. Held and Hein (1963) demonstrated the importance of active, rather than passive, visual experience by means of the 'kitten carousel' shown in Figure

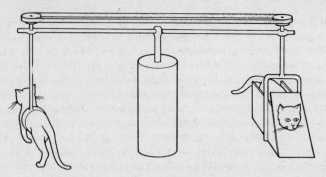

Figure 11.3   The 'kitten carousel' used by Held and Hein (1963)

11.3. Two- to three-month-old kittens were paired in the carousel, one in the restricting carriage and the other in harness, so that it could move about and so that the carriage moved with it. The kittens were put in the carousel for three hours a day and were otherwise reared in darkness. Thus both received the same amount of visual experience; but for only one (the 'active' kitten) was visual experience correlated with movement. When the kittens were tested after about ten days training, the 'passive' kittens showed impairment on various tests of depth perception while the 'active' kitten did not.

Further, it appears that *selective* deprivation may produce selective deficits in later performance: for example, kittens raised in visual environments restricted to either vertical or horizontal stripes may later show insensitivity to objects in a normal environment whose orientation they have not previously experienced. Thus, kittens deprived of exposure to vertical stripes may characteristically bump into chair legs, but not into (horizontally aligned) chair seats or table tops. For a review of such studies, see, for example, Dember and Warm (1979).

No investigator has reared a human subject in darkness from birth, but it sometimes happens that congenitally blind persons gain their sight, for instance, after an operation for removal of cataract. Such persons might be considered to be in an analogous situation to the animal, reared in darkness, which is exposed to light for the first time. A number of case histories (sixty-five in all) dating chiefly from 1700 to 1928 were collected and published by von Senden (1932, trans. 1960). The vision of these patients is reported to have been severely defective; they were for the most part initially capable only of very gross distinctions between figure and ground and took perhaps months to learn to distinguish between even simple shapes, while some were unable ever to proceed beyond this level of ability. This evidence would seem to support the idea that perceptual organization depends upon extensive learning; but as evidence it leaves much to be desired. The case histories are variable in the accuracy and detail of reporting, some providing only anecdotal evidence. The patients concerned also varied widely in age at operation, in the degree of visual experience (if any) prior to operation and in the amount and quality of vision granted after operation. Two factors in particular may have impaired performance. In the first place, when patients had learned, and had practised for many years, to perform various skills with the aid of senses other than vision, they found it extremely difficult to forsake their earlier methods and concentrate on learning to rely on visual cues; thus their old skills may have interfered with the learning of new ones. Second, largely because of inadequate psychological preparation for 'the new world of vision' in which they found themselves after operation, the patients appear often to have been confused, unsettled and intimidated by the new experience; unwillingness and inability to adapt to the new situation may therefore also have impaired performance. A more recent study (Gregory and Wallace, 1963) illustrates rather clearly the severe motivational disturbance which may follow operation and which may well affect visual performance for the worse. Thus in the case of human and animal alike it cannot be said with assurance that the visually deprived subject can be compared directly with the neonate, or that the perceptual development of a visually naïve adult is strictly analogous to that of the normal infant. For further discussion of the effects of early sensory deprivation or additional stimulation, see Chapter 12.

As has already been said, a rather different approach to assessing the importance of learning in perception is to examine whether the differential experiences of perceivers are reflected in differential perceptions. For example, some workers have compared certain perceptual characteristics of individuals of different cultures, notably their differential susceptibility to visual illusions and constancies. Such work, particularly with respect to visual illusions, has been discussed in Chapter 10; it was concluded that the relation between cultural differences in 'experience' and cultural differences in susceptibility to illusion is often, to say the least, obscure. Similar obscurities have been pointed out in the evidence for the effects of various experimentally or extra-experimentally induced 'experiences' – such as 'set', physiological need, reward and punishment.

Finally, there have been attempts to demonstrate individual differences in general 'modes of perceiving' which might be related to personality: for example, perceivers have sometimes been classified as 'synthetic' or 'analytic', as 'levellers' or 'sharpeners', as 'field dependent' or 'field independent'. All three dichotomies are based upon some notion of perceptual integration although in rather different senses. The distinction between synthetic and analytic modes of perceiving refers to the extent to which perception of a stimulus is independent of its context, and would reveal itself, for example, in size constancy, in which the observer's estimate of size depends upon the extent to which contextual factors are taken into account. The distinction between levelling and sharpening is defined largely by the extent to which present stimuli are assimilated in perception to previous percepts – that is, one might say, the importance of the temporal context rather than the spatial. Field dependence or independence refers to the extent to which judgements of orientation can be based upon kinaesthetic cues in the absence of 'external' visual cues to verticality or in the presence of visual cues which are misleading. These schemes, and others, have been summarized by Vernon (1970). One difficulty is that they appear often to be measuring differences in experimental or general cognitive attitude, rather than directly perceptual differences (see, for example, the discussion of field-dependence in Chapter 21); another is that the validity of methods of measurement and in particular the generality of any individual's classification – his consistency of response across different perceptual situations – are often doubtful.

As far as the nativist–empiricist controversy is concerned, the results of such studies suggest both that more of perception is 'learned' than the nativist position would allow and that more of perception may be innately organized than would be accepted by an extreme 'learning' position. For example, some aspects of depth perception and perhaps the perception of movement may be, if not innate, at least very rapidly learned, and there is some evidence for innate discriminability of certain spatial or formal properties. Finer discriminations and certain other aspects of object perception seem fairly clearly dependent upon experience for their emergence and development. To adhere to either the nativist or the empiricist position with any rigour would now be factually inappropriate and an obstacle to progress. It is ultimately as meaningless to talk of perception as being *either* innate or learned as it is to talk of behaviour as being determined either by heredity or by environment; factors of both types interact or summate in shaping our apprehension of the world around us. This is not to deny the interest and importance of attempts to establish the contribution of learning to a given perceptual experience, or to specify the type of learning which may be involved (we shall return to this question in the final section of this chapter). Above all, the value of the nativist–empiricist controversy was in initiating and encouraging, the accumulation of a great deal of empirical evidence concerning the perceptual world of babies and children, its similarities, differences, and developing approximation to that of adults: such evidence will be the concern of the following sections.

The perceptual abilities of infants

In assessing the perceptual abilities of very young children, an obvious first question concerns the efficiency of the sensory apparatus, since any initial limitations of the sensory system must to some extent limit the nature of perceptual experiences. The visual system is clearly immature in certain respects at birth (see, e.g., McGurk, 1974). For example, although the retina is fairly well developed its macular region (the area of greatest acuity) is not very well differentiated; the optic tract is only partially myelinated (see Chapter 4), so that neural transmission is slower than in adults; and accommodation of the lens is virtually non-existent at birth, so that the newborn infant is extremely shortsighted, with an ideal focal distance of about eight inches. Myelinization of the optic tract is completed, and accommodation has achieved an adult level of efficiency, by about four months of age, while differentiation of the macular region of the retina takes perhaps a year or so for completion. There are thus initial visual limitations, but these are fairly rapidly reduced; and some important features of the visual system, such as the pupillary reflex, convergence and conjugate tracking of the two eyes, are well developed very early in life. Although the visual system is immature at birth its immaturities do not constitute any very big obstacle in the way of visual perception.

How are we to measure a young child's perceptual abilities? Clearly we cannot rely upon verbal report, as is usually the case in the measurement of perception in adults. The methods by which perception has been studied in infants are many and ingenious (Gibson, 1969). Some investigators have used gross behavioural measures: for example, arm-reaching towards an object as an index of distance perception, or readiness to crawl across an apparent 'cliff' (see later) as an index of the perception of depth. Others have used rather more subtle measures of attention: for example, head-turning towards a sound as a measure of its localization, or the duration of visual fixation of a pattern as an index of 'preference' for that pattern over others, and hence of its discriminability from others. The reflex following, with the eyes, of a moving pattern (known as optokinetic nystagmus, or OKN) has also been used to study visual acuity, since if a pattern evokes the following response its elements must have been discriminated. Classical discrimination learning has also been used with quite young children: for example, the child may repeatedly be presented with a cube and a triangular block, the cube always having a sweet concealed beneath it. If the child learns to look always under the cube, never under the triangular block, he must be capable of discriminating their shapes. Other techniques have been based upon habituation or operant conditioning, in either case to a standard stimulus; generalization of the learned response, or habituation tendency, to other stimuli can then be taken as an *inverse* measure of their discriminability from the original (see Bower's work, discussed later, for exemplification). Perhaps in some contrast, there are also rather more qualitative observations of behaviour: for example, a young infant may view his mother on the far side of a soundproof screen, while her voice is relayed to him via loudspeakers. If the relative volume of the two speakers is manipulated the mother's voice may be made to come apparently from her visual position, or from a source to the right or to the left of her. The child's capacity for sound localization, and his tendency to integrate visual and auditory information, are inferred from vocal and postural indications of 'disturbance' when visual and auditory information do not match (Aronson and Rosenbloom, 1971).

Such methods have yielded a great deal of information concerning the young infant's perception of space and shape, of which we can give only examples here. For more detailed accounts, see, for example, Gibson (1969); McGurk (1974); Bower (1974, 1977).

The perception of depth has been studied in a series of experiments (for example, by Walk and Gibson, 1961) using young animals of several species – lambs, kids, kittens, chicks, rats, turtles – as well as young humans as subjects. Their apparatus naturally varied in detail according to the species tested, but essentially consisted of the 'visual cliff' shown in Figure 11.4, which presents to a subject the choice between a 'shallow side' (one giving the appearance of a shallow drop) and a 'deep side' (one giving the impression of a steep drop), although in fact the surface of the apparatus is at the same level on both sides of the central platform.

Walk and Gibson (1961) tested young animals as soon as they were able to move about with minimal skill. With most species tested a clear preference emerged for the shallow side of the cliff; the animal would readily step on to the shallow surface and move about freely upon it, but would not move

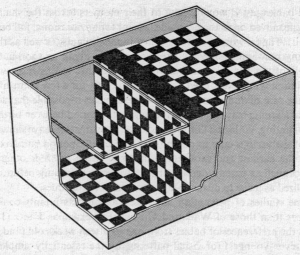

Figure 11.4 The 'visual cliff' used by Walk and Gibson (1961) in the study of depth perception

on to the deep side. The preference was not only definite but also seemingly resistant to learning, since if an animal were placed directly upon the deep side, so that it was supported by the glass surface but to the eye was suspended in space, it typically did not move about but would instead 'freeze', exhibiting apparent fear, and was no more likely to choose the deep side of the cliff when again placed on the central bar. Young rats, who showed no preference for either side when they were able to feel the glass surface with their vibrissae, nevertheless chose the shallow side when this tactual cue was removed by a modification of the apparatus. This finding incidentally underlines the indirect nature of the evidence with which we have to deal; the reason for a lack of discrimination may be either that the animal lacks the ability to discriminate or that it is not exercising it. For this reason the only entirely crucial experiment is one in which no other cues to discrimination exist apart from those in the specific sense modality which the experiment is designed to study.

Human babies of ages ranging from six to fourteen months were also tested on the visual cliff. The technique employed was to place the baby upon the central bar and to observe whether it would approach its mother when she called, either from the deep or from the shallow end of the apparatus. Most of the babies tested would crawl to their mothers across the shallow side, but none moved on to the deep side (except for an occasional fall backwards on to it). Thus it would seem that most human infants, as well as the young of many non-human species, can discriminate depth as soon as they are capable of independent locomotion. The fact that testing must wait until locomotion is achieved, even if that delay is only for a few hours after birth as in the case of domestic chicks, of course makes it possible that some perceptual learning may have occurred during the period between birth and the time of testing. Walk and Gibson, and other investigators, have shown further that of the various cues to depth (see Chapter 10) motion parallax appears to be the earliest and most important cue to be utilized; other characteristics such as pattern density appear to require learning before they can be utilized as a cue to distance in the absence of other cues.

Some studies of perception have used as subjects infants considerably younger than those of Walk and Gibson. For example, Fantz (1961) has tested the preferences of babies from one to fifteen weeks old (and, in some cases, even younger) for visual patterns, by the essentially simple method of presenting the child with two patterns side by side and observing the length of time for which each was fixated. Even the youngest infants showed consistent preferences for some patterns over others, thus revealing themselves capable of discriminating one from another in a situation in which they were unlikely to have had appreciable experience with such patterns. Fantz also compared the attractiveness (in terms of length of fixation) of two diagrams, one a schematic drawing of a face, the other a 'scrambled face' containing the same elements as those of the first figure but differently arranged. The children tested showed a slight but consistent preference for

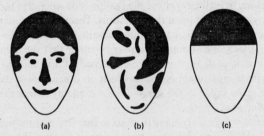

(a)　　　　　　(b)　　　　　　(c)

Figure 11.5　'Face' stimuli used in the study of fixation preferences of babies. (a) A diagrammatic face, (b) a 'scrambled face', (c) a black and white oval. (From Fantz, 1961, p. 69)

the 'real' over the 'scrambled' face, while both were preferred to a third diagram comprising the same proportion of black to white as in the other two figures but with the black in a solid block (see Figure 11.5). Fantz (1961, p. 71) concludes from this finding that there is 'an unlearnt, primitive meaning in the form-perception of infants'. It is of course true that even young infants have almost certainly had the visual experience of a human face bending over the cot; but it is expecting much of the neonate's capacity for learning and categorization to argue that it has learned 'from scratch' to discriminate between a face and a scrambled face in so short a period.

Still further evidence of the far from negligible perceptual ability of very young infants has been provided by Bower and his associates (Bower, 1974). Bower, Broughton and Moore (1970), for example, studying infants of one to two weeks of age, were able to observe defensive behaviour when a large object was moved towards the infant: this behaviour took the form of eye widening, head retraction, and interposition of the hands between face and object. They then found that the same defensive behaviour could be obtained, although with reduced intensity, if the moving object was behind a rear-projection screen, so that only its shadow on the screen was visible, producing the visual expansion pattern associated with decreasing distance (a positively accelerated expansion of the image, often termed 'looming'). This appears to indicate some perception of changes in distance based on visual cues alone. Bower (1966) has further shown that size constancy is also present to some degree in very young children. He first conditioned a head-turning response to the presentation of a 30 cm cube at a distance of 1 metre, then observed the extent to which the response generalized to test stimuli (a) of the same size but at a greater distance, (b) of greater size at the same distance, and (c) of greater size at greater distance. Response to stimuli (a) and (b) was 50–60 per cent of that to a stimulus identical to the original; response to test stimulus (c) was much lower, although its retinal projection size was in fact the same as that of the original. Thus there seems clearly to be some perception of distance and its relation to retinal size; and Bower was able to demonstrate similar evidence for shape constancy.

Precision in distance perception, however, may take some months, at least, to develop. In a classic experiment Cruikshank (1941) found that infants five to six months old would stretch out their arms towards distant objects, well out of reach, which may be taken to indicate that their perception of distance was faulty. However, it is not certain that the error was in visual distance perception rather than in the infants' perception of their own arm length, or indeed that such arm extensions are genuine attempts to reach the object;

other investigators have found that reaching responses can be fairly accurately made at this age (White, Castle and Held, 1964).

The evidence so far reviewed relates to visual perception, and there is in fact very little work on other modalities. What evidence there is does point to the existence of some capacity for auditory localization, in that an infant will make responses (head-turning or arm-reaching) appropriate to the location of a sound source in front of him, to his right or to his left; this has been demonstrated in the case of an infant tested immediately after birth (Wertheimer, 1961), although again *precision* of auditory localization takes time to develop, lagging behind that of visual localization at least over the first few months of life. A fuller review of this area of research, and of the related areas of motor performance and visual-motor co-ordination in infants, is given by Bower (1974).

The perceptual, and in particular visual, abilities of babies appear to be considerable but to leave plenty of room for development to the reasonably accurate perceptual performance of adults. Some characteristics of perceptual development from infant to adult will be the concern of the following section.

Perceptual development beyond babyhood

Most studies of perceptual development beyond infancy are comparative and *cross-sectional*: groups of subjects differing in age are compared with respect to some aspect of perceptual performance. The obvious alternative – the *longitudinal* method, whereby the same subjects would be repeatedly tested over a number of years between infancy and adulthood – has so many problems, both of principle and above all of practice, as to be virtually unused in this area; but the cross-sectional method too has some basic, and fairly obvious, disadvantages. It may be difficult to make the subject groups comparable in respects other than age: for example, in intelligence (since *comparable* estimates of intelligence in young children and in adults are hard to achieve, and since in some testing situations only the more able children may be able to understand instructions), and also in such age-related variables as height and interocular distance, which might be expected to influence size and distance judgements. Further, testing situations cannot always be identical for different age groups, although they should ideally be so, since the experimenter is likely (especially with younger children) to have to modify procedures, or instructions, or both, to ensure that the subjects are capable of understanding instructions and performing the required response.

Again, it is unlikely that motivation, persistence and attention will be equivalent for all age groups tested. Thus, it is not perhaps surprising that with respect to basic discriminations children are typically 'worse' than adults (although this depends upon task difficulty), and improve in accuracy with age. We shall concentrate here upon some findings concerning the perception of space and form; for fuller reviews see, e.g., Gibson (1969), Vurpillot (1976).

Studies of the perception of space include observation of size, distance and depth judgements, and also the measurement of size constancy and distance constancy. Clearly such judgements are interrelated; for example, size estimation is always, of necessity, of an object at some distance from the perceiver, not at the retina; and constancy, which is defined in terms of an invariant relation between apparent size and apparent distance (see Chapter 10), will obviously be affected by any deficiency of size or distance judgement. In fact, a general finding is that in the perception of space children (at least up to the age of, say, ten), are less accurate than adults and become more accurate with age; but the results of studies are somewhat conflicting, which seems to be due often to an interaction between size and distance, and also to the testing methods used. It has often been reported that children may be very inaccurate in their judgement of the size of distant objects, but as accurate as adults in the case of nearer ones. Inaccuracy, then, seems (at least after the first three or four years of life) to be largely a matter of the failure of constancy; and this in turn seems to result largely from inaccuracies of distance perception. The work of Bower, Walk and Gibson and others (see above) has shown that some perception of distance or depth is present even in extremely young children, but that precision may be lacking. A chief problem, for children and indeed to some extent for adults, appears to lie in *distance constancy*, in that distance judgements become more difficult if the extent to be judged is further away from the observer: if we stand at a roadside, looking across two fields which stretch away in front of us towards the horizon, our judgement of the extent of the more distant field may well be less accurate than our judgement of the extent of the nearer field, stretching away from our feet. One method of illustrating this difficulty in controlled laboratory or field experiments is that of *bisection*: the perceiver stands at one end of an extent – say, a corridor – and is asked (in one of several ways) to mark the point halfway down the corridor towards the other end. Typically, the bisection point chosen is inaccurate, and will often be *too near* to the perceiver, indicating that he judges the more distant part of the corridor as being shorter than it actually is. Thus, the typical finding in distance constancy experiments is *underconstancy*: and several observers have found this underconstancy to be more marked in children, diminishing with increased age (e.g. Harway, 1963; Wohlwill, 1965).

However, any such generalization should be made with caution, since findings depend, as we have already mentioned, on the methods and conditions of testing. For example, two studies by Wohlwill (1963, 1965) showed that the difference between children and adults in distance constancy might be *either* that children showed underconstancy while adults were more accurate in judgement, *or* that children were reasonably accurate and adults showed overconstancy, the result depending upon the method of testing. Again, studies of size constancy in children carried out by Piaget, Lambercier, Vurpillot and others (see Vurpillot, 1976) show that fine details of constancy estimation methods – the method of comparison, the nature of the comparison stimuli from which a 'match' must be chosen for the test stimulus, the relative distances from the subject of test and comparison stimuli – may very considerably affect the result obtained. Most important of all, the instructions given to the subject are likely to affect the result, and even when instructions are standardized for all age groups tested the interpretation of those instructions may well be different, and unexpected, in the case of younger children. Vurpillot (1976, p. 70) in fact concludes from her assessment of the development of size constancy: 'the changes in performance with age seem to us to be much more a matter of how the child approaches the task and understands the instructions than of any perceptual change'.

A not dissimilar picture emerges from studies of form perception (which includes the perception of shape and of orientation). It has often been found that shape constancy, conventionally measured, is poor at about three years of age and improves to an adult standard by perhaps fourteen years. On the other hand, the experiments of Bower, already mentioned, indicate that shape constancy is far from negligible in infants as young as fifty–sixty days, and several discrimination learning studies have shown that shape discrimination can be reasonably efficient in six-month-old infants (although discrimination of two-dimensional shapes and pictorial representations lags behind that of three-dimensional objects). Indeed, Meneghini and Leibowitz (1967), for example, reported that under certain testing conditions four-year-old children exhibited more nearly perfect constancy than adults. When poor constancy appears in children, therefore, it may result largely from misunderstanding of instructions or from other failures of rapport between experimenter and subject.

The perception of orientation is an interesting area of study, involving a certain element of paradox. On the one hand, recognition of form must be *transposable*: an object must be identified as the same object even when it is rotated or inverted in space. On the other hand, orientation – say, rotation or inversion – is crucial for certain discriminations. In reading, for example, the child must learn to discriminate among the shapes b, d, p and q – identical or near-identical forms differing only in orientation. Thus 'successful' perceptual development must involve both sensitivity to orientation differences and the capacity to ignore them when irrelevant.

Young children often invert (top-to-bottom) or reverse (left-to-right) letters when they are writing, and look at books and pictures upside down. It has sometimes been suggested that this indicates an ability to tolerate orientation differences; but although some studies have shown that children can happily identify objects when they are inverted or reversed, this generally obtains only when the identification task is relatively easy and the objects used as stimuli are realistic and highly familiar. Ghent (1960), for example, showed that when *tachistoscopic* identification was required (a relatively difficult task) three-year-old children found rotated stimuli much harder to identify than those presented 'the right way up', the effect declining with age up to seven years, the age of the oldest children tested. Probably the most celebrated study of the perception of form in children is that of Gibson *et al.* (1962), which employed 'nonsense' rather than realistic stimuli and an unusually difficult recognition task. Each 'standard' stimulus figure was presented along with a series of thirteen figures, one of them identical with it and the other twelve derived from it but with small variations. Some of these were *orientation* differences of rotation or inversion; in some, *line-to-curve* transformations were carried out; some were *perspective* changes, in which the figure was made to appear slanted or tilted backwards; others were '*close and break*' transformations, in which open lines were joined or joined ones broken. The stimulus figures used, and their transformations, are shown in Figure 11.6. Subjects were required to identify, from the array, the figure which was identical with the test stimulus; the subjects tested were four, five, six, seven or eight years of age.

Gibson *et al.* (1962) found, firstly, that confusion errors showed an overall decline with age; secondly, that some types of confusion error were more frequent than others; and thirdly, that the pattern of age changes was rather different for different types of error. *Orientation* errors were very frequent in the youngest age group, declining swiftly to near zero in the oldest; *line-to-curve* errors were fairly frequent in the youngest group and again very low

Figure 11.6   Stimulus figures, and their transformations, used by Gibson *et al*. (From Gibson *et al*., 1962, p. 898)

in the oldest; *perspective* errors were very frequent and remained so throughout the age range, and *'close and break'* errors were very infrequent throughout, and virtually non-existent at eight years of age. One possible explanation, at any rate, for these findings is that with the advent of formal schooling, including learning to read and write, children learn that rotations and inversions which are unimportant for object identity *are* important for letter identity, while perspective changes are not relevant in either case. Thus, confusions are frequent for those transformations which do not violate identity; less frequent, and declining with age, for those which do: and more frequent, but declining sharply with age, for those which become important. According to this view, the developmental trend is one of increasing sensitivity to perceptual variations, and increasing awareness of their relative importance for object or symbol identity.

How are we to conceptualize perceptual development? Even from the few examples of evidence quoted here, a few suggestions emerge. It is clear that some development does occur, although that development is not 'from scratch' and is not always to be equated with increasing 'accuracy'. The very fact of development has sometimes been taken to support a kind of empiricism: the view that development proceeds by *perceptual enrichment*, whereby an uncoordinated and rather impoverished initial sensory input is supplemented by evidence from other senses, by experience and to some extent by the acquisition of more or less formal knowledge and training. In contrast to this view, however, Gibson and Gibson (1955; Gibson, 1969) have argued that the process underlying development is rather one of *perceptual differentiation*. The evidence of our senses is not impoverished or inadequate; it contains the information needed for the appropriate perception of space, objects and events, but it has to be analysed, and its crucial features isolated, if perception is to be efficient. In the case of size constancy, for example, 'the major developmental change is not the acquisition of constancy, but rather the abstraction of independent dimensions from earlier perception of an unanalysed object' (Gibson, 1969, p. 367).

An account in these terms is also appropriate for the improvement observed in part–whole perception (notably the perception of embedded figures) with age in children, and for some developmental changes in susceptibility to visual illusions (see Wohlwill, 1960). In future research, then, a major need is for more investigation (conceptual as well as empirical) of the features already present in sensory input which become analysed and distinctive, and the mechanisms of perceptual learning which mediate the development of distinctiveness.

Finally, it appears to be appropriate to consider perceptual development not in isolation but in the context of general cognitive development. The notion of differentiation, used by Gibson and Gibson in the context of perceptual learning, has also been used (although not identically) notably by Werner (1948), to apply to a general characteristic of psychological functioning which may vary in degree both developmentally and among individuals; in this sense it has formed the conceptual basis for studies of 'field-dependence' (see pp. 307–8 and also Chapter 21). Again, it is clear, and we have argued the point both implicitly and explicitly in our discussion of perceptual organization, that perception is not simply of stimuli but rather of 'things' and 'events' which have objective reality and which we recognize as belonging to the world as we know it – conceptually as well as sensorily. It is not improbable, then, that perception will develop alongside the formation of conceptual 'maps of the world'.

Many of the most interesting studies in this area are in a very real sense studies of cognitive, as much as perceptual, development. The experiments of Bower and others on size and shape constancy in infants, for example, are concerned essentially with the infants' appreciation of the cognitive reality of objects existing independently of their spatial context. Piaget (1937) has offered a classic treatment of the development of the 'object concept': in particular, the realization that an object still exists when it has moved from, or been occluded within, the field of vision. A young baby will not pursue (by gazing, reaching or crawling) an object which has moved out of vision; somewhat older infants (say, beyond two to four months old) will do this but will not make any move to retrieve a normally desired object which has been covered (in the infant's view) with a cloth. At a later stage infants will readily retrieve the object from under the cloth, but if on a subsequent trial the object is placed under a second cloth in a different location they may look for it under the original cloth instead; if an object is placed under one of two cloths and the position of the two cloths then reversed, infants may look under the cloth occupying the place where the object disappeared, not the cloth under which it was hidden. Children are perhaps eighteen months old before they are 'successful' in tasks of this type (for more detail, see, e.g., Bower 1974, 1977). An extension of this issue is Bower's exploration of what might be termed the 'mother concept'. If an infant of five months or less is presented with a multiple image of his mother (by a simple optical device) he will happily respond to all images in turn; an older child will be disturbed by multiple images of his mother, although not by presentation of his mother-image plus images of strangers.

The line between studies of perceptual development and those of cognitive development can be a fine, and often an uncertain, one; and Rock (1975), for example, has argued that much of the perception of children and of adults can be characterized as a kind of perceptual problem solving which has similarities with, as well as differences from, the problem-solving activities which are involved in thinking. Such activities, and to some extent the characteristics of cognitive development, will be the concern of Chapter 18.

Chapter 12
Early Experience

Introduction

Rudyard Kipling (1937) began his autobiography with the maxim, 'Give me the first six years of a child's life and you can have the rest'. The implication of this is clear: early years are formative years and thereafter personality is set. Such a view of human nature is held by many, ranging from Jesuits to Freudians. A variety of opinions has been expressed concerning the span of the formative period in life and the significance of the different types of early experience. To insist that early experience is all-important is an expression of faith; it is for empirical research to establish how important it is, and what precisely is important early in life in moulding the mature individual. Answers to such questions can only be pieced together as a result of many systematic observational and experimental studies. In this chapter we shall consider what is known about the effects of early experience; and we shall look at animal and human studies side by side. It will be seen that while some findings are clear-cut, others are only tentative; while a great deal of research has been done, far more will be needed before confident statements about the lasting effects of early experience can be made with justification.

Very generally, two aspects of early experience have been studied. Some workers have varied the amount of sensory stimulation received by young subjects and have observed the later effects of such variation upon behaviour. Others have been concerned with variation in rearing which is qualitative rather than quantitative – involving, for example, experience of certain stimuli rather than others, of various types of mothering and so on. Although the two kinds of study are only partly distinct (some variations in the type of early experience also involve variations in the amount of stimulation received) they will be dealt with separately here: the first under the title of *sensory stimulation* and the second under the heading of *social experience*. The latter is a useful title in view of the sorts of experiential manipulation and resultant behavioural change which have been of concern; however, we shall see that it may also be, to some extent, a misleading one.

We shall end the chapter with a brief discussion of the cognitive and affective development of the individual under the title of *early development of individuality*.

Sensory stimulation

Additional stimulation

One way of studying in the laboratory the influence of early experience upon later behaviour of animals is to expose the young experimental subjects to a given type of stimulation, and compare them later with control subjects not so stimulated but otherwise treated in the same manner. This is done with a view to finding out how various kinds of early stimulation affect different modes of the animals' behaviour later in life: their activity, reactivity, learning abilities and so on. It is clear that considerable and continued physical differences between the experimental and control environments, such as differences in food supply, temperature and the like, are likely to have physiological repercussions and could, therefore, produce as a consequence some marked behavioural differences. However, probably more interesting psychologically are changes in behaviour other than those mediated by major physiological events resulting from altered physical conditions – that is, changes in later behaviour due to sensory stimulation of one kind or another occurring intermittently and not lasting very long.

A method adopted by a number of experimentalists has been to apply to animals such as infant mice or rats some such treatment as handling them for a few minutes a day, or 'gentling' (handling and stroking) them, or giving them electric shocks. Handled young animals have been found in adulthood to be more active but less 'emotional' (as indicated by lower defecation scores in the open-field test – see Chapter 3) than animals without this kind of experience (see, for instance, summary of findings in Denenberg, 1963). Furthermore, Levine (1956) and others in the late 1950s found that handling rats in infancy improves their later ability to learn, at any rate in certain types of task; and this has since been reported in other animals also. Somewhat more surprisingly it appears that occasional administration of electric shock to infant mice improves the ease with which they can later be conditioned (Denenberg, 1959; and for a discussion of *conditioning*, see Chapter 13). It looks, then, as if gentle handling, as well as painful shocks, helps animals to develop the capacity to cope with a wide range of stressful situations (see Levine, 1960).

At first sight this might suggest that the more stimulation in infancy the better for the behavioural development of the animal; and further, that stimulation as such, no matter what its nature may be, could be beneficial. It might even be wondered whether human infants would benefit from being talked to more than is customary, from frequent handling and from extra stimulation generally. The value of this, however, may be doubted; too great a range of stimulation could even sometimes be a hindrance to later learning (see Chapter 13 on the role of latent inhibition in conditioning). It would appear that extra stimulation in infancy results later in life in an improvement in the individual's ability to cope with stress and in his greater learning capacity only in certain circumstances – namely, when otherwise the infant, animal or human, would suffer from inadequacy of stimulation or some degree of sensory deprivation (see below).

Laboratory rodents, however, before they are weaned, do not suffer sensory under-stimulation; rather the opposite is the case (Daly, 1973). Ecological studies of rats and mice in their habitats show that breeding burrows effectively shelter the infant animals from external changes in stimulation and, thus, laboratory rearing tends to be over-stimulating (although it is under-stimulating *after* the infants have been weaned). Furthermore, the so-called low emotionality which results from handling in infancy, far from being adaptive, may cause the animal to be vulnerable to predators; immobility associated with fear in the open field has in nature a survival value. Now animal studies providing additional stimulation in infancy had been undertaken partly or largely because of the implications of such work for human developmental psychology (Levine, 1969). We may conclude that as far as animals are concerned the effects of early additional stimulation on later learning are not clear-cut (Daly, 1973). With regard to human implications of such animal studies, the utmost caution is necessary; for example, we are not justified in regarding high reactivity in rats as comparable with neuroticism in people, or in assuming that extra stimulation in babies will inevitably result in higher intelligence later in life.

Early sensory deprivation

Much has been learned about the effects of early experience from studies in which the experimental animal subjects have suffered from some form of deprivation. We shall briefly survey in this section the effects of rearing in a dull, monotonous environment, that is, under conditions of perceptual deprivation; affectional deprivation will be considered in a later section. The problem facing researchers in this field is, in principle, relatively simple; it is to ascertain how important are certain perceptual experiences early in life for the development of various abilities. The experimental methods are essentially straightforward: deprived experimental subjects are compared later in life with control subjects on such traits as activity, curiosity, conditionability and adaptability. Studies of very severe and prolonged sensory deprivation are excluded from consideration; this is because under extreme conditions, for example rearing in complete darkness, some degeneration of sense organs is known to occur. Such studies are of greater interest to physiologists than to psychologists who are primarily concerned with functional relations between behavioural variables.

Many studies were carried out in the 1950s with a view to investigating the effects of different environments during infancy, and particularly the effects of some form of restriction of early experience, upon adult behaviour; the experimental subjects were at first mainly rats. The findings in the main have been that animals with limited initial experience are later less active and markedly poorer at problem solving than control animals. Furthermore, it has been established that the lack of varied sensory input, such as limited visual experience, rather than the lack of motor experience, is the cause of the relative lack of ability in the mature animals; see, for instance, Hymovitch (1952).

A little later, dogs began to be studied. It was found that puppies raised in a restricted and unstimulating environment showed great 'curiosity' in their behaviour, but were apparently unable to profit from the experience afforded by exploration; they would be slow, for example, in withdrawing from painful stimulation, and (as in the case of rats) proved later to be poor learners. The effects of early sensory experience are quite persistent (see the summary of findings in Thompson and Melzack, 1956). In view of the findings concerning subprimate mammals, it may be a little surprising to note that monkeys reared in isolation have been found to be as good at many problem-solving tasks as feral monkeys. On the other hand, monkeys reared in isolation are less active than those reared in freedom; they also prefer later in life stimuli of relatively low complexity, they shun manipulative tasks and they show little curiosity. And such deprived animals are characterized later by grossly abnormal sexual and parental behaviour (Sackett, 1965).

Our knowledge of the lasting effects of an unstimulating environment in childhood upon the abilities of the human adult is somewhat uncertain. This is because no children are ever brought up in conditions of isolation and restriction equivalent to those used in animal studies. Furthermore, in assessing the influence of rearing conditions which are relatively unstimulating perceptually and intellectually, one must compare children brought up under such conditions with control-group children that are otherwise comparable. Thus, the experimental and control groups must be matched for genetic endowment – a well-nigh impossible task. Nevertheless, there is some evidence to indicate what the effects of cognitive deprivation in infancy may be.

Lack of varied experience in early childhood, insufficiency of cuddling, of verbal communication and so on, have all been said to result in a general retardation of physical and mental development (Dennis, 1960). This type of deficit of stimulation occurs inevitably in some otherwise good institutions in which sick or orphaned children have to stay for a long time (but see references to Bowlby's views in the sub-section entitled 'Parental care' later in this chapter). It is, however, very probable that lack of stimulation at one stage can to a considerable degree be rectified by more stimulation and training in later stages. It is uncertain to what extent poverty of initial linguistic experience and of intellectual stimulation in childhood could have lasting adverse effects. Though such deprivation may do damage, human beings are perhaps more adaptable – in so far as such comparisons are at all meaningful – than infra-human species. Evidence has been marshalled by Clarke and Clarke (1976) showing that children can be remarkably resilient and arguing against the view that the environment in the early years necessarily 'exerts a disproportionate and irreversible effect on a rapidly developing organism'.

'Social' experience

We turn now to consider those observational and experimental studies which compare the effects of *qualitatively* different early experiences. Studies of *imprinting* and *socialization in mammals*, may be regarded as an extension of 'additional stimulation' studies: that is, they are concerned with the effect of 'extra' exposure to specific stimuli. Similarly, studies of the importance of *parental care* represent an extension of deprivation studies, in that they consider the effects of deprivation of a specific (affectional) kind.

Imprinting

Certain effects of some infantile experiences are known as imprinting (see Sluckin, 1972). More specifically, imprinting, in the original and narrow sense of the term, refers to attachments which newly hatched birds of various species (primarily ground-nesting but also others – see last paragraph of this section) form quite speedily in relation to living things and inanimate objects simply as a result of being with them. The study of imprinting is bound up with the name of the pioneer ethologist, Konrad Lorenz, who, although not the first to observe such rapid learning, aroused great interest in it and attempted to describe its character relative to other aspects of animal behaviour (see the early paper in English, Lorenz, 1937).

Newly-hatched chicks, ducklings, goslings and the like, tend to follow anything moving which they may encounter. The tendency to behave in this way is innate and probably because of this some writers have in the past referred to imprinting as instinctive. In fact, attachments which *develop out of* following responses, as distinct from the original following responses, are acquired. A fledgling can become imprinted to its own mother, or to any mother substitute such as an animal of another species, a person, a moving box, and even a stationary object. Thus, imprinting is a learning process. Some writers have been quite explicit about this, listing imprinting among simple learning mechanisms or animal training procedures.

Precocial species are those in which the newly-hatched or newborn young have well-developed sense organs and are capable of locomotion. The initial response of such young animals to stimuli of medium-range intensity tends to be approach. Lambs, kids, calves and other such young mammals, as well as chicks, ducklings, etc., approach sources of intermittent visual and other stimulation. Following responses are approach responses to receding objects. Some investigators have believed that following, in particular the effort expended in following, is essential to imprinting (see E. H. Hess, 1959). There is evidence, however, that sensory exposure to an object is the only condition that is necessary for imprinting to take place to that object, even though effort on the part of the animal is often needed to maintain visual contact with the object the characteristics of which the animal is learning (Bateson, 1966; Collins, 1965). This learning of the characteristics of a figure is, of course, necessary if a specific attachment to the figure is to occur.

But what, precisely, enables us to say that imprinting has taken place? One test of imprinting is the 'recognition' test. Young animals are exposed individually to some figure and later the responses of these animals to the figure are compared with the responses of control animals – that is, those without any prior experience of the figure. If the experimental animals are found to approach the figure more readily than the controls, then the initial exposure to the figure must have brought about a degree of imprinting to it.

Another test of imprinting is the 'discrimination' test. In this case some experimental animals are individually confronted with one figure while others are confronted with another figure. Later each subject is tested with both figures together. If it is found that the animals' preferences are influenced by their prior experience in such a way that the familiar figures tend to be approached and the strange ones avoided, then imprinting is considered to have taken place during the initial confrontation.

The discrimination or choice test of imprinting is probably the best single criterion by which to judge whether imprinting has occurred. There are, however, also some other useful indicators of imprinting (Sluckin, 1970). One of them is 'distress' peeping at separation from the figure to which the infant animal is attached. Another indicator of imprinting is that a chick or duckling will run to the substitute mother, i.e. seek close proximity to the 'mother-figure', when frightened by any external disturbance. Yet another sign that a young animal is imprinted to a figure is that the animal will work for reunion with that figure; this will occur in the Skinner box (briefly described in Chapter 2) when the reward for work, such as bar-pressing or pecking, instead of being food is the sight of a familiar figure.

Apart from showing itself as attachment to familiar objects, imprinting can lead later in life to the courtship of familiar but biologically inappropriate figures. Some investigators consider that such *sexual imprinting* is one of the manifestations of the imprinting phenomenon, while others incline to the view that imprinted attachments and sexual imprinting develop separately. However this may be, many workers have reported cases of misdirected sexual approaches by males of various species of birds – approaches which appear to be directly due to early exposure to figures other than the usual mother figure. Unusual attachments do not by any means inevitably result in signs of sexual imprinting at maturity. However, rearing pairs of drakes together was found to lead to homosexual behaviour in these animals in later life; see, for example, Schutz (1965).

The most remarkable experiments in this field have been carried out by Immelmann (1972). He cross-fostered three species of Estrildine finch: one Australian, one African and one Bengalese. The method was to place a single egg of one species with a clutch of another species; the hatchling was then reared by its foster parents. Later such youngsters were separated from their foster parents and isolated. At sexual maturity, birds that had been reared in this way courted only individuals of the foster-parent species and not those of their own kind. Of course only some birds become sexually imprinted in this manner. The most striking examples of birds that always direct courtship towards their own species, no matter who the foster parents may be, are the cuckoo in Europe and the cow-bird in North America. Whether sexual imprinting of any kind can occur in mammals is quite uncertain.

Socialization in mammals

The development of social behaviour in birds has been studied both in relation to imprinting and in other contexts. In mammals the study of the formation of attachments has an entirely separate history from the study of imprinting, although the interests of these fields of research have in recent years tended to converge. Two main lines of investigation concerning mammals stand out: one has to do with the socialization and training of puppies, the other with the affectional development of infant monkeys. We shall deal with them in that order.

After many years of research an eminent student of animal behaviour, J. P. Scott, was able to conclude that certain kinds of early experience are crucial for the shaping of the later behaviour of dogs, and particularly for their sociability (see Scott, 1958a, 1962, 1968). Sociability in one sense may be assessed by the extent of the animal's fear reactions towards people. Experiments indicate that puppies become fully tame only if reared by people during the first three to four weeks of life. If allowed to run wild until about twelve weeks of age, then no matter how trained, such puppies will grow into somewhat timid dogs. Scott suggests that a distinction must be made between primary and secondary socialization. *Primary socialization* in dogs, and in other animals too, takes place in the first stages of active life. This is a process which normally attaches the individual to his species; but attachments may be formed to other species as, for instance, when dogs become tame in relation to human beings. *Secondary socialization* or later social learning is not considered by Scott to be of the same character; and it has repeatedly been reported to be less effective. We shall not here enlarge upon such evidence or upon Scott's definition of secondary socialization, which he views as a form of *instrumental learning* which is susceptible to *extinction*; these terms will be defined and discussed in Chapter 13.

One feature of primary socialization is of great interest, namely, its apparent independence of conventional rewards. While feeding during social training helps, it is not an essential factor in the development of sociability; the only necessary condition is social contact between the young animal and some person or persons. Thus, lasting social bonds which develop between the given individual and other animals or people depend less on reward learning than on familiarization with, or exposure to, others.

It may be added that it is thought that this is also the case with early human social learning. The dominant view in the 1940s and 1950s was that social learning in children depended on primary drive reduction – that is, that a tie to a mother and acceptance of her values were contingent upon the reduction of hunger and alleviation of pain which were attained through her. There is evidence that much social learning depends on such factors, but most probably not all social learning, and especially not the earliest social learning. Social ties in infancy would appear to develop primarily as a result of the infant's sensory experience of its social environment and especially of its mother (see, for instance, Walters and Parke, 1965).

At any rate it has been shown that the love of an infant monkey for its mother – if one may use human terms in this context – is not 'cupboard love'. H. F. Harlow and co-workers established this conclusively in laboratory situations in which the food source was separated from the source of 'contact comfort'. The former was a wire structure provided with a milk supply obtainable through a protruding nipple – the wire mother, as it was called; the latter was a rather similar structure but covered with a towelling fabric – the so-called cloth mother. Infant monkeys were found to prefer the cloth mother, which provided the right 'feel', to the food-giving wire mother (see Harlow, 1959; Harlow and Zimmermann, 1959). We have mentioned earlier the open-field test used to judge animals' fearfulness. Infant monkeys reared with wire and cloth mothers were so tested in a room larger than the familiar cage and containing some strange objects. Without the cloth mother an infant would huddle in a corner, showing the usual signs of fright. The presence of the wire mother had no effect on such behaviour, but an introduction of the cloth mother altered the infant's conduct radically. The baby monkey would first cling to the cloth mother and then begin to explore the strange environment, returning every now and then to the security of contact with her.

There is evidence that the very early experience of a monkey and in particular the attachments it forms to specific stimulus figures tend to have lasting effects. These lie partly in the specific preferences that the monkey has acquired and partly in the general behaviour of the animal later in life in such spheres as social and sexual. It has been argued that the ties, individual and species-specific, which primates develop are much like imprinting in precocial birds (Sackett, Porter and Holmes, 1965). The similarity of these learning processes is particularly clear in relation to the development of fear responses. As far as imprinting is concerned, it was reported in the earlier studies that the onset of fear coincided with the end of the so-called *critical period* for imprinting. It was believed that maturation brought about fear responses and that these inhibited following responses and, therefore, prevented further imprinting. It is now clear that fear is often entailed by imprinting in that the objects that are recognized as familiar are sought, but those that are recognized as strange are avoided or feared; likewise with the growth of affectional responses in infant monkeys: known objects, provided they have the 'right' texture, are sought and strange ones are initially avoided. Thus a teddy-bear and similar toys may be either loved or feared, depending on whether they are familiar or unfamiliar; and the same toy can, therefore, be a love-object to one monkey and a 'monster' to another (for further discussion see Hebb, 1946; for discussion with reference to human infants see Schaffer, 1966, and Schaffer and Parry, 1969). However, the great importance of early experiences, as far as monkeys are concerned, lies in their long-term effects upon the animal's personality, as indicated in the next section.

Parental care

It is one thing to be deprived of a wide range of stimulation and another not to be given specific care and affection that parents, and especially the mother, normally provide. Studies of maternal deprivation in human beings have quite a long history. On the other hand, the effects of maternal deprivation in other primates have become the subject of research only relatively recently. It has been established that infant monkeys readily accept mother substitutes and cling to the so-called cloth mothers as much as to real mothers or other adult animals. But it is clear that cloth mothers do not provide any true mothering; and unmothered infants, even if reared with inanimate mother surrogates, grow up into abnormally behaving adult monkeys. However, it is remarkable that the company of other infant monkeys makes up in many ways for any lack of mothering (Harlow and Harlow, 1962). The socially deprived monkeys have been found to be very disturbed in their later sexual behaviour; and unmothered females become themselves very inadequate mothers. One may wonder what the effects of the lack of maternal care and affection in human infancy may be. Obviously one must not jump to any conclusions from the study of monkeys to human beings. Fortunately one need not be tempted to do so because there is a great deal of information available from studies of deprived children. The findings are not always easy to interpret, and somewhat differing conclusions have on occasions been drawn from the same set of data.

The most extreme forms of parental deprivation occur either when a child is brought up in an institution, or when a child is separated from the parents, most commonly when it has to spend a long time away from home in hospital. An early systematic investigation of the effects of institutionalized upbringing was made in America by Goldfarb (1943). Fifteen boys and girls, ten to fourteen years old, who had been in an institution from the age of a few months until about three years of age, were compared with fifteen children (of comparable heredity so far as could be judged) brought up in foster homes. Detrimental effects of institutional upbringing were said to be apparent in almost every sphere of intellectual and social development. In England, Bowlby (1944) in his account of forty-four juvenile thieves, reported that, as compared with youngsters in a control group, the young delinquents had certain personality traits typical of those deprived in childhood of maternal care and affection; many of the delinquents had indeed suffered maternal separation of more than six months during the first five years of their lives. Spitz (1945, 1946) was much concerned with the effects upon the child of hospitalization and separation from the mother generally. He described the symptoms of what he called *anaclitic depression* in emotionally deprived children: apathy, slow development and so on. He found that recovery was rapid whenever the child was reunited with its mother after a short separation. However, after separations of over three months recovery tended to be slow and incomplete.

These early studies were conducted by psychoanalytically oriented workers and they tended to confirm the view that personality development is adversely affected by early deprivation of affectionate mothering occurring in broken homes, during separation from the mother and so on. Later studies brought out clearly the need for caution in interpreting data and in generalizing. Some earlier conclusions had to be qualified and modified. For instance, Bowlby *et al.* (1956), who studied children who had spent some time away from their mothers in a tuberculosis sanatorium, found them to be more often maladjusted than control-group children; however, the research showed that institutionalization did not commonly lead to the development of an affectionless or psychopathic character, as Bowlby (1951) had earlier suggested. Indeed, many individuals who have suffered maternal deprivation are known – both from everyday observation and from systematic studies – to be very well adjusted by every criterion which can be applied.

More recently attempts have been made at reassessing the effects of the deprivation of maternal care. We may ask in the first place what precisely is meant by maternal or parental deprivation. The term covers many distinct conditions: for example, institutionalization, lack of adequate mothering, lack of ability to interact with mother figures, maternal rejection. And each kind of deprivation may be experienced at various levels of severity. Many questions concerning the effects of deprivation are controversial. For example, different views have been expressed about 'multiple mothering', that is, when the child is given care and affection by more than one person; such a controversy can only be resolved by further empirical studies. The question of the effects of *paternal deprivation* is now more actively investigated. Both maternal and paternal deprivation can have quite varied effects upon later behaviour. Many hereditary and environmental variables are relevant to the problems mentioned in this section; they are considered in some detail by Ainsworth *et al.* (1962) and by Rutter (1972).

Critical periods

We have mentioned the critical period in imprinting; but critical periods are said to occur in other aspects of development of most higher animals, including man. Before psychologists became interested in critical periods, embryologists had found it necessary to think about development in these terms; they had noticed that certain physical abnormalities depended less on the character of the stimuli producing them than on the *time* at which the embryo was stimulated. Later the question arose whether the development of behaviour in the young also depended on the existence of certain sensitive or critical periods. Now the concept of behavioural critical periods is not identical with that of stages of development of behaviour: a developmental stage may be, but need not necessarily be, critical. And a number of claims have been made about the criticality of certain developmental stages.

It has already been noted (in Chapter 3) that Freud held that a child goes through a sequence of psychosexual stages, each of which is in effect a critical period for the development of various personality traits. The first twelve months or so of life are considered by the psychoanalytic school to be the oral stage, that is one when gratification is obtained mainly through the mouth. This is thought to be followed by the anal stage, the phallic stage, the latency period and finally, the genital stage. Each stage is said to be characterized by certain modes of behaviour, which in due course give way to the interests and activities of the next stage. Furthermore, it is said that inadequate or excessive gratification and anxiety at any one stage result in a fixation of the characteristic feelings of the stage and of forms of behaviour deriving from those appropriate to that stage. Thus, greed in an adult would derive from oral fixation, conformity would be described as an anal fixation, and many other features of personality would be related in this manner to various early experiences of the child. Whether such an account of critical periods in personality development is true is entirely uncertain. In order to be confirmed or refuted such suggestions must be tested by rigorous observations. And nothing like enough observational studies in this vein have yet been carried out.

The notion of critical periods in a more readily testable form has been put forward by Konrad Lorenz (1937) in relation to imprinting and by J. P. Scott (1958b) in relation to the early socialization of mammals. Concerning imprinting, all that need be added to what has been said earlier is that Lorenz and others found that it took place within a few hours, or at most during the first day or two, after hatching. Thereafter, it was generally accepted that imprinting could occur only during a strictly critical period some time early in the life of the individual, and that if it did not occur at that time then it never would. However, Guiton (1959) and others after him established that chicks kept in isolation remained capable of being imprinted to moving objects considerably longer than chicks reared in groups. The apparent shortness of the period of imprintability in communally reared chicks is due to the fact that such birds become imprinted to one another, and having become so imprinted, show fear of strange figures instead of approaching them. Thus it is misleading to think of imprinting as occurring solely during some short, genetically determined critical period; environmental factors influence the duration of the sensitive period and, generally, there are simply *more likely* and *less likely* times during which the formation of imprinted attachments is possible.

The acquisition of attachments by mammals has been said to occur mainly during certain sensitive periods in their development. Williams and Scott (1953) reported such critical periods in the development of social behaviour patterns in the mouse. Scott concentrated later on the study of socialization in the dog. He also surveyed findings concerning other animals (Scott, 1962) and concluded that the period of primary socialization, mentioned earlier in this chapter, is a critical one; during a short period early in life, experience determines who will be treated by the animal as its close relatives – members of its own species, or members of another species. Later, Scott (1963) equated the process of primary socialization in puppies, and in human infants, with imprinting. This is debatable. Even the view that primary socialization takes place during a critical period has been challenged (see Fuller and Clarke, 1966, Schneirla and Rosenblatt, 1963). Clearly, much more research is needed in this field of developmental psychology.

Early development of individuality

We may now draw together some of the findings surveyed above in order to consider the cognitive and affective development of the individual in relation to his earliest experiences. We have seen that it is fairly well established that the intellectual development of orphanage children is somewhat impaired. This may be because the institutional environment provides relatively little sensory stimulation and/or because the infant's intellect cannot function optimally unless motherly love is there to provide the necessary emotional stability. McCarthy (1954) has gathered evidence to show that institutionally reared infants are particularly retarded linguistically; and language is, in turn, an important means towards further cognitive development.

The contrast between institutional and home environments may be regarded as a special case of possible 'cultural' differences in child-rearing practices. Both social, subcultural differences and national differences in methods of treating infants have been extensively studied. One particular in which cultures vary is the freedom of movement given to the young infant. While the Western way is to allow the baby to move its arms and legs freely, in parts of Eastern Europe swaddling is or used to be customary. Swaddling entailed a severe restriction of movement and it was sometimes combined with keeping the infant away from strong light and from contact with objects. Some American Indian tribes have also followed similar practices. It is fairly clear that motor development of swaddled children is not effectively retarded, although intellectual development might conceivably be.

However, it is the *personality* of the child which might be supposed most likely to be affected by early experiences typifying different cultures; and such evidence as is available favours the supposition. Strictness or permissiveness in upbringing in general, and in feeding habits and toilet training in particular, are thought to be markedly influential. Whiting and Child (1953) collated information about seventy-five primitive societies in order to test several specific hypotheses concerning personality development as a function of child-rearing practices. Cross-cultural investigations, and there have been several in recent years, have produced much factual and suggestive information; but such findings are too varied and often too controversial to be conclusively summarized.

Now many of the lines of investigation derive from psychoanalytic theory which attaches great importance to early experience, treating it as formative and crucial for personality development (see the useful summary in C. S. Hall, 1954). This chapter is not the place to discuss the speculative aspects of psychoanalytic thought; however, such thinking has given rise to experimentation aiming in part at testing specific aspects of Freudian theory (Kline, 1972). Perhaps somewhat surprisingly a great deal of work has been done with animals, no doubt partly because it is possible in laboratory studies to control closely the animals' early environment. Although such studies have not on the whole made it possible to confirm or refute conclusively many psychoanalytic tenets, they have added substantially to our knowledge of the lasting effects of early experience. Thus, mice have been studied in order to see whether single traumatic experiences, severe defeats for instance, would permanently influence the animals' behaviour. Experiments have also been carried out on mice to find out whether having to compete for food in infancy would influence the animals' behaviour at maturity. In fact, it turns out that severe defeat depresses the level of aggression later in life and that experience of competition raises it. However, perhaps the best-known studies are those which have set out to discover, using rats as subjects, whether frustration of the hunger drive in infancy would produce certain permanent 'personality' characteristics such as a tendency to hoard food. On the whole this proved to be so, even though research findings have tended to be somewhat equivocal (see Hunt *et al.*, 1947).

The mature individual, animal and human, has been moulded into what he is by the impact of his earlier experience upon his genetic make-up. However, as far as human beings are concerned, the indications are that 'the whole development is important, not merely the early years' (Clarke and Clarke, 1976). It is uncertain whether any particular stage is more formative than any other; and in the long term all developmental stages may be influential. Both specific early events and protracted early learning can be important. The task of research is to discover all manner of lawful relationships between happenings in the course of development and later behaviour patterns in animals and in man. Work to this end has started only relatively recently. Our ignorance of the effects of early experience is still immense, but the prospects to all those engaged in this field of research are exciting because of its great intrinsic interest and its potential practical implications for child and educational psychology.

Chapter 13
Learning

Introduction

Generation by generation species adapt to changing conditions by natural selection. This adaptation includes the development of physiological bases for advantageous patterns of behaviour. An individual member of an animal species adapts to its environment mainly by learning how to cope with problems presented by changing conditions. Learning shows itself in modifications of behaviour, but many behavioural changes are the result of maturation or disease. Only adaptive and lasting changes, resulting from past experience and not due to maturation or disease, are ascribed to learning.

In common-sense terms, we learn when we get to know something we did not know before. To think of it this way focuses attention on the conscious aspect of experience. Learning may require following instructions, or it may need practice, or both. We learn when we acquire skills and habits – manipulative, intellectual, social. These are modifications of behaviour, generally, but not necessarily, accompanied by a consciousness of gaining knowledge or skill. We learn, in the broad sense of the word, most of the time when we are awake, whether or not we are actually aware of what is being learned.

Learning a subject at school, learning a motor skill such as riding a bicycle, learning how to behave well, learning to value money or to value friendship – how much in common have all these situations? Does the word 'learning' refer to some essential process or is it a label that points to a region of activities only vaguely delineated? It must be said that there is no real agreement among students of learning about such issues. Many of them, however, have attempted to describe and explain complex learning processes by reducing them to some prototype or prototypes of learning. These prototypes represent various learning situations that have seemed to be relatively simple and fundamental. Furthermore, these learning situations – Pavlovian conditioning, problem solving in animals, and some others, to be considered shortly – have been studied in minute detail. Again it must be said that such attempts at reducing complex learning to prototypical learning have not been crowned with unequivocal success. Nevertheless they have been highly illuminating and have been instrumental in advancing knowledge of learning processes.

To gain an understanding of learning we need not aim at well-rounded knowledge provided by a complete theory of learning. Theories there are in plenty and we shall briefly consider types of learning theory and some theoretical controversies later in this chapter. However, a view of learning may be adopted whereby varieties of learning situations are identified and the conditions that govern learning in these situations are specified (Gagné, 1967). Such an aim, if not very ambitious, is a practicable one. We cannot in this book set out to give a comprehensive survey of varieties and conditions of learning; we can and will, however, give a sample of learning situations that have been extensively studied. We shall begin with relatively simple learning, and then move on to more complex learning, the transfer of training and some theorizing about learning.

Simple learning situations

Classical conditioning

A training procedure, developed early in the century by Pavlov and extensively investigated since the 1920s, has come to be known as classical conditioning. It may be noted that this type of learning was known in outline even before Pavlov's work; without the modern terminology, Jennings (1906) was able to describe such conditioning at some length. However, it was Pavlov who made a detailed study of it and constructed theories around it (see Pavlov, 1927). Classical conditioning is built upon *respondent behaviour*, as it is called by some writers, that is, reflexes which are directly elicited by certain stimuli. Pavlov used as a basis for conditioning the reflexive salivary response in the dog to the smell of food; other workers have used the pupillary reflex (contraction of the pupil in bright light), the knee jerk, sweating, nausea and so on. All such responses, occurring naturally, are called unconditioned (or unconditional) responses, known in technical literature as UCR or UR; stimuli which elicit such responses are described as unconditioned – in abbreviated form, UCS or US.

If some other stimulus, be it visual, auditory, olfactory, tactile, etc., is repeatedly presented at the same time as or shortly before some US, then this other stimulus will tend to acquire the power of evoking the response which initially could only be evoked by the US. In order to achieve this effect it may have to be co-presented with US anything from once to many hundreds of times. The stimulus thus co-presented with the US is called the conditioned stimulus, or CS. In this manner the sound of a bell, for instance, may be made to elicit salivation in a dog, or pupillary contraction in a human subject. The response to the CS is somewhat slower and weaker than that to US, and, so that we may distinguish it from UR, it is labelled CR, or conditioned response (sometimes called anticipatory or preparatory response).

The crucial feature of such training is that the conditioned and unconditioned stimuli are paired; the US reinforces the response to the CS. Without this *reinforcement*, the conditioned response would gradually become extinguished. *Experimental extinction* of CR may be deliberately achieved by providing it with no reinforcement. But such extinction is not necessarily permanent. After a time interval the conditioned response, that is, the response to CS, may make a reappearance, even though it is then weaker than directly after training. Such a reappearance of CR is described as *spontaneous recovery*.

Having been conditioned to respond to a given CS, the subject tends to generalize this response to other, similar stimuli; this is known as *stimulus generalization*. The more these other stimuli are like the CS, the stronger the CR; the relationship between the intensity of responses and the degree of similarity between new stimuli and the original CS is called the gradient of stimulus generalization. If the conditioned responses to the CS are reinforced, but the responses to a given stimulus similar to CS, which at first did evoke some responses, are not reinforced, then the subject will learn to discriminate between the two stimuli, responding to the former and not responding to the latter; this we call *stimulus discrimination*. The various features of conditioning just mentioned: reinforcement, extinction, recovery, generalization, discrimination, as well as several others, have been extensively investigated both in animals and man.

The original experiments in this field were based on the salivary reflex of the dog (see Pavlov, 1927). Later, other subjects as well as other types of response began to be used. Hovland (1937), for example, used human subjects; the US was a light electric shock to the subject's wrist, the UR to which is sweating; the magnitude of this response could be conveniently measured by electrical means because the more sweating the lower the skin resistance and, hence, the higher the galvanic skin response, or GSR (see pp. 105–6). The CS in these experiments was a tone of a particular frequency which was paired a number of times with the electric shock to produce a CR to the sound of the tone, i.e. a GSR score. Using such procedures Hovland was able to demonstrate the necessity for reinforcement in conditioning, the extinction of the CR after the removal of reinforcement, spontaneous recovery of the CR, stimulus generalization to tones other than the one originally used (see Figure 13.1) and other features of conditioning.

Pavlov himself was interested in the physiological processes underlying conditioning. He postulated two complementary processes in the nervous system; *excitation*, as conditioned reflexes are formed, and *inhibition*, as responses to non-reinforced stimuli are prevented from occurring. According to this account, the spontaneous recovery of an unreinforced conditioned reflex would be due to a disinhibition of an inhibition. It is clear that this is

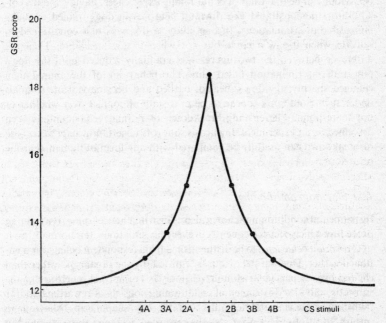

Figure 13.1   Stimulus generalization. Response was conditioned to stimulus 1; responses to other stimuli – tones of frequencies below and above CS – were progressively weaker as the stimuli diverged from CS. (After Hovland, 1937, p. 136)

no more than speculation; we are in a position to know with certainty some particular features of behaviour before, during and after conditioning but not the physiological functioning associated with these features.

To what extent does classical conditioning enter into everyday learning? There is some uncertainty about this, but it appears that many involuntary emotional responses are classically conditioned. Some students of behaviour believe that emotional responses of the autonomic nervous system become commonly associated with many initially neutral stimuli. Thus, fear, for instance, may easily come to be attached to any number of visual or auditory, or even tactile or olfactory, features of the environment (see, for example, Eysenck, 1977). This could be the explanation of various common irrational phobias (see Eysenck and Rachman, 1965).

At any rate, it has certainly been shown that some kinds of abnormal behaviour can be the result of conditioning experiences. Pavlov and his collaborators demonstrated experimental neuroses in dogs trained to make impossible discriminations. In one study, a dog was first conditioned to salivate when it saw a circle but not when it saw an ellipse. Then the difference between the two figures was gradually reduced until the dog's power of discrimination failed him. The behaviour of the animal then changed sharply; the dog squealed, barked and became violent. Animals under such conditions appear to be in a state of conflict over whether or not to respond. The ensuing breakdown of normal behaviour has been described as an experimental neurosis; but it is uncertain whether this type of breakdown can usefully be compared with any form of human neurotic behaviour.

Instrumental conditioning

Instrumental conditioning (known also as instrumental learning) is a training procedure which occurs frequently in everyday situations. It is normally built upon *operant behaviour*, to be distinguished from respondent behaviour mentioned earlier. Operant behaviour is 'emitted' by the organism, rather than elicited by any particular stimuli; it simply is the normal repertoire of the subject's activities. Instrumental conditioning consists of rewarding and/or punishing some acts and not other acts, thereby 'shaping up' behaviour in certain directions. This occurs as the rewarded acts tend to be stamped in and the punished ones stamped out. Roughly speaking, this tendency is what E. L. Thorndike (1911) called the 'law of effect'.

A particular instrumental training procedure developed by B. F. Skinner is known as operant conditioning;* see Skinner (1938). Training of this kind involves the use of the Skinner box, illustrated in Chapter 2; this contains some simple mechanism which may be operated to deliver a limited amount of food or water. Such a box made for small mammals, commonly the rat, has a lever which the animal learns to press in order to obtain a pellet of food or a drop of milk; a box made for birds, usually the pigeon, has a disc which the bird learns to peck to obtain some grain. If the required response is not made, no reward is forthcoming. Thus the reward reinforces the response.

As reinforcement follows a particular feature of operant behaviour, this feature is produced more and more frequently; it is thus acquired or learned. Whereas in classical conditioning the unconditioned stimulus is the reinforcement, in instrumental conditioning the reinforcing stimulus is one that is associated with, and *follows*, some particular response, which initially is only one of the many responses within the organism's repertoire. If, after the operant response has been acquired, the reinforcement is no longer provided, then the response will gradually disappear. Behaviour extinguished in this way will, however, recover spontaneously to some extent after a time interval during which the subject has been away from the conditioning situation.

Whether the removal of reinforcement will result in a rapid or very slow extinction depends on the conditions of initial training. A number of experimental studies have shown that when some, but not all, occurrences of the requisite response are reinforced then, even though learning is slower, it is much more resistant to extinction; see, for instance, the findings of Jenkins and Rigby (1950) concerning the extinction of lever-pressing in rats trained with partial or *intermittent reinforcement* (see also Figure 13.2). Such intermittent rewarding occurs frequently in everyday situations; some of the most strongly established habits arise from learning under inconsistent reinforcement. Operant conditioning procedures have been developed using several different schedules of reinforcement, each having its particular effects; these procedures are discussed in detail by Ferster and Skinner (1957); see also Cohen (1969) and Blackman (1974).

The Skinner box is only one of many possible situations in which instrumental conditioning may be studied. Another one is the T-maze; in this

---

* Paradoxically, while operant conditioning may be regarded as a type of instrumental conditioning, from another viewpoint instrumental conditioning is one form of operant conditioning (Blackman, 1974; Cohen, 1969); a discussion of this matter is, however, beyond the scope of the present chapter.

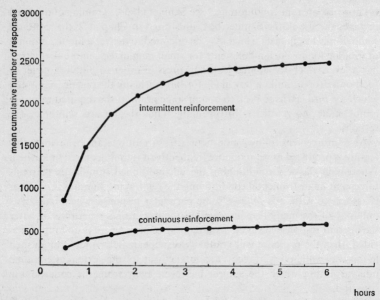

Figure 13.2   Rate of extinction in pigeons after intermittent and continuous reinforcement. Pigeons showed slower response extinction after intermittent than after continuous reinforcement. (After Jenkins, McFann and Clayton, 1950, p. 158)

simple maze the animal coming up to the T-junction faces a choice between turning to the right and turning to the left (see also the discrimination apparatus shown in Chapter 2). The reward is to be found at the end of only one of the two arms. The animal learns by trial and error which way to turn and it may take it a few or a great many trials before it invariably makes the correct turn. In this situation the subject is instrumentally conditioned to make what is termed position discrimination. However, discrimination learning more often involves learning to choose one of two patterns, or one of two colours, entirely irrespective of their position.

Operant learning and discrimination learning described above are forms of reward training. Other instrumental conditioning procedures are avoidance training, omission training and punishment training (see Hilgard and Marquis, 1961). Avoidance training teaches the subject to respond to a signal in some particular way and thereby prevent a noxious stimulus from appearing. Omission training teaches the subject not to respond to certain stimuli by

rewarding it for not so responding. Punishment training involves the punishment of the subject in some manner for certain acts; we shall consider further
the role of punishment in learning later in this chapter.

Some procedures combine two or more of these types of training. For
instance, the Yerkes box for learning position discrimination may provide
a reward for the animal for taking one of the two paths and a punishment
in the form of electric shock for taking the other. In the Lashley discrimination apparatus for training rats to choose between differently patterned cards, the animal is made to jump off a stand on to one of the two
cards in front of it; jumping one way results in hitting an immovable card
and falling into a net – a punishment of sorts – and jumping the other way
shifts a card so that the animal lands on a platform and obtains its reward,
usually a quantity of food.

An animal may readily be trained to make several correct choices in
sequence, that is, to learn to run a maze. Mazes have been used in studies
of animal learning since the beginning of the century. The original maze
which white rats were trained to solve was contained within a 6 × 8 ft
rectangle and was modelled on the hedge maze in Hampton Court (see also
Chapter 2). The goal box of the maze contained food and the animals could
be tested repeatedly for their ability to run the maze. Many different maze
patterns have been used for various animal species.

Serial verbal learning, such as learning the alphabet, has been compared
with maze learning in that in both situations what is learned is a sequence
of responses, each response being contingent on the response that precedes
it. A great deal of learning in children appears to have the features of
instrumental conditioning: learning how to behave and how not to, learning
simple skills and so on. Followers of Skinner tend to believe that academic
study is essentially a type of operant conditioning and that the child's
acquisition of language may also be explained in these terms (see Skinner,
1957; and Chapter 17). Also, some at least of social learning appears to be
instrumental in character. However, that is not to say that complex human
learning can always or often be analysed into simple component acts which
exhibit the typical features of instrumental conditioning.

Indeed, relatively complex learning in animals, such as solving mazes,
cannot readily be analysed into elementary instrumental acts, even though
such learning may be put into the category of instrumental reward training,
very broadly interpreted. It was suggested at one time that, in finding the
way to the goal, an animal learns a chain of specific responses to specific
stimuli at each junction within the maze. It later became clear, however,

that animals do not just blindly learn series of muscular movements; an animal, like a human being, learns the topography of a maze and, having learned the layout, the animal can solve the maze whether it requires running or swimming or wading to the goal box (Macfarlane, 1930; Restle, 1957).

Habituation

Learning what not to do is as important to any animal or human being as learning to respond to signals, or to act in particular ways. A sudden noise can startle us or simply make us look for its source. However, we get habituated to noises such as those of passing traffic and cease to take notice of them. Habituation is learning not to respond to innocuous stimuli. It has been argued that it is a most basic form of learning, necessary for survival of animals. By learning to ignore harmless stimulation the organism's energy is conserved for other functions (Thorpe, 1963). Unlike sensory adaptation which involves changes in the sensitivity of sense organs, habituation is a learning process, viz. not to respond to stimuli which continue to be experienced.

We noted in the section on classical conditioning the phenomenon of extinction. Animals and man all exhibit what is termed the *orientation reflex* in response to stimulus changes. It is of great value to learn to extinguish this reflex whenever it serves no useful purpose, but to retain it when it does. Extinction of the orientation reflex is essentially what we mean by habituation. Although habituation is fundamental to the behaviour of animals, there is no general agreement as to whether it involves more than one learning mechanism, and how precisely it is related to other forms of learning (Groves and Thompson, 1970; Hinde, 1970).

Exposure learning

Classical conditioning and various other types of conditioning, grouped somewhat arbitrarily under the umbrella of instrumental conditioning, differ from each other in many ways. At the same time they are all alike in that they unquestionably require rewards and/or punishments. There are, however, some experimental findings which indicate that learning, as distinct from the performance of what has been learned, does not necessarily depend on conventional reinforcement. Moreover, there is evidence to suggest that the exposure of the organism to sensory stimulation may in itself result in some learning. Whether we take the view that such exposure learning requires no reinforcement, or is self-reinforced, or is reinforced in some special way, depends in part on how we define the term 'reinforcement' which is not beyond controversy; we shall return later to this difficulty of definition.

Consider, to start with, a conditioning process whereby a subject learns to respond to, say, a particular sound – an initially neutral stimulus. Consider, further, a procedure prior to the classical conditioning whereby the sound is repeatedly presented to the subject together with another neutral stimulus, say, a light; such a procedure is known as *sensory pre-conditioning*. Now if, after both some pre-conditioning and the conditioning sessions, the subject is tested with the light only, it may be found that it responds to the light, albeit weakly, even though no specific training to respond to it has been given (see review of such studies in Hilgard and Marquis, 1961). In our hypothetical experiment, the ability to respond to the sound alone is the result of conditioning; but the ability to respond to the light alone is the result of pre-conditioning or exposure of the organism to certain stimuli occurring together with those which are later conditioned. Thus, post-conditioning tests may be said to reveal the occurrence of some exposure contiguity learning prior to conditioning.

The effects of sensory exposure to relevant stimuli before actual training may be readily detected in many learning situations; such effects have been extensively investigated in animals learning to run mazes. In the usual experimental situations animals improve at running mazes if they are motivated to do so; thirsty rats will learn a maze if rewarded with water at the end of each trial run, hungry rats, if rewarded with food, and so on. Unmotivated, unreinforced animals do not show any overt learning. But, if just allowed to explore the maze, they nevertheless do learn it, although such learning is not immediately manifest. That the animals benefit from having been exposed to the environment becomes clear when they are properly trained to run the maze. Animals with prior experience of the maze learn it much more quickly than those without such experience. This was clearly demonstrated in such early experiments as those of Blodgett (1929) and Tolman and Honzik (1930). Such learning without reinforcement – learning which is inferred from subsequent behaviour – is known as *latent learning*, sometimes also called incidental learning (although the latter term is also used in a somewhat different sense to denote learning, in humans, which occurs without the intention to learn).

Learning resulting from sensory experience may show itself in yet other ways, especially in the young of precocial species of birds, and possibly mammals. Such learning, considered in Chapter 12, goes by the name of imprinting. It involves the learning of the characteristics of figures to which the young organism is exposed, i.e. the acquisition of the ability to discriminate between familiar and strange sensory stimulation. Imprinting, or the formation of attachments without conventional rewards, is of course procedurally different from classical conditioning or instrumental learning. We may take the view that behind this actual acquisition process there may be some form of exposure learning, that is, a modification of a disposition or potentiality for overt action.

Specific attachments are one possible result of exposure to fellow-beings. Others are imitation and *observational learning*. Here the subject does nothing to start with other than observe another, the *model*, doing something. Later, as a result of this experience, he may perform a sequence of responses made earlier by the model. For the subject, as distinct from the model, these are new responses which, not having occurred previously, could never have been reinforced. During the first two decades of this century the reality of observational learning in animals was much debated. Some workers claimed to have demonstrated it, but E. L. Thorndike and the early behaviourists denied that animals were capable of true imitation. Warden and Jackson (1935) showed conclusively that under certain conditions monkeys may perform better on selected tasks when given the opportunity to observe the successes and failures of models (demonstrators) on these tasks. More recent animal studies have confirmed the effectiveness of observational learning in animals, although the interpretation of such studies is debatable (see K. R. L. Hall, 1963), as indeed is the interpretation of modelling in children (see, for instance, Bandura, 1962).

Special problems of learning

How is the affection of a child for his mother acquired? It could be through classical conditioning – the sight of mother is a signal for food, and as such is valued. It could be through instrumental conditioning – the child's affection for his mother is well rewarded by her approval and continued love she gives the child. It could be through imprinting – the child gets attached to his mother who is the most familiar figure in the child's environment. It could be all these things at once and more besides. Much that is learned in life cannot be ascribed without uncertainty to one or another of the known training methods. Does this mean that we cannot readily gain any understanding of everyday learning? Not at all; learning can be profitably studied in ways other than reductionist. Learning processes can be investigated to elucidate the various factors that help and hinder acquisition. Problems concerning learning may be stated, conceptually clarified and then tackled experimentally. In this section we shall consider some such problems.

Reinforcement

The term 'reinforcement' is not unambiguous. It is sometimes used to mean a *process* – the (hypothetical) strengthening of a response tendency, which can be measured by an increase in the frequency or probability of occurrence of that response. Thus, a response has been reinforced if it has become more likely to occur. In a somewhat different sense reinforcement may be used to denote a *technique* adopted by the experimenter: reinforcement of a response is the application of a *reinforcer* – some stimulus event which is expected to have the result of increasing the probability of the response which precedes it. For example, food administered to a hungry rat when it presses a lever in the Skinner box is a reinforcer because its administration increases the likelihood of the lever-pressing response. In this sense the US in classical conditioning can be regarded as a reinforcer, even though it precedes the response it reinforces; generally speaking, however, a reinforcer can be defined as 'a member of a class of events which, when they follow a response, strengthen the tendency for that response to occur' (Hill, 1972). Thus, whether reinforcement is defined in terms of a strengthening process or in terms of a training procedure, it is tautologous to say that reinforcement of a response increases its probability of occurrence, since this must be so by definition.

A few investigators have defined reinforcement, rather differently, simply as the presentation of a stimulus which provides the opportunity for learning. For example, in paired-associate learning, where the subject's task is to produce the second item of a pair when the first is presented alone as a stimulus, any presentation of both stimulus and response items together constitutes a 'reinforcement'; presentation of the stimulus item alone constitutes a 'test' (Estes, 1950).

Given that reinforcement is generally defined in terms of its consequences for behaviour, can we say anything more about the nature of reinforcers? Many investigators and theorists of learning have sought other respects in which reinforcers are alike, so that the characteristics of reinforcement can be more clearly understood. It has often been claimed that reinforcers serve to *reduce drive*, and that it is the reduction of drive associated with a response which increases its frequency. Some reinforcers, such as food and water, clearly can be thus described. Others, such as money for human subjects, might be described as having acquired reinforcing value through their association with primary drive reduction: these are sometimes called secondary reinforcers. In yet other cases, however, it is difficult to trace an association between drive reduction and an event which appears to be reinforcing – when, for example, exposure learning occurs or when people take up hobbies demanding the acquisition of knowledge and skills. Again, reinforcers can be described as *rewarding*: a definition which, apart from its appeal to common sense, is almost if not quite circular.

Alternatively, some theorists have claimed that the function of reinforcers is less to reward than to inform the responding subject, to manipulate his attention to various aspects of the learning situation or to alter the learning situation to such an extent that the responses acquired in it are 'preserved' from the interference which might result from further responding in the same situation. Finally, it has been argued that different kinds of learning may involve different kinds of reinforcement and thus of reinforcers (see, for example, Hill, 1972; Mowrer, 1960). It is, consequently, not easy to avoid circularity in the description of reinforcers; ultimately, what such events have in common is their effect upon behaviour.

Certain qualifications should be added here. In the first place, we have discussed reinforcement in terms of an increase in response probability; but some procedures may have the effect of decreasing, rather than increasing, the occurrence of associated responses. Further, certain procedures which on other grounds one might expect to decrease response probability may in fact increase it. These possibilities will be further discussed in the following section concerned with punishment.

Finally, while reinforcers are generally held to be externally applied stimuli whose effect is mediated by sensory reception, there is evidence that *direct electrical stimulation* in some parts of the brain may constitute positive reinforcement, in that animals will make responses which result in such stimulation. In other areas of the brain electrical stimulation may be negatively reinforcing, in that animals will make responses which avoid it.

Olds and Milner (1954) placed electrodes in various parts of the brain such that by pressing a lever, animals (in this case, rats) could deliver a brief burst of current to the part of the brain where the tip of the electrode was located. They compared the number of bar pressings when the current was turned off with the level when the current was turned on. With electrodes in some areas of the brain whether the current was on or off made little difference to the rate of bar pressings. However, with electrodes placed in other brain areas the rats learned to press the bar more and more rapidly.

In the same year, Delgado, Roberts and Miller (1954) found that brain stimulation could serve as punishment in a learning situation, that is, animals (in this case cats) would perform a variety of responses to avoid such stimulation. In the usual avoidance situation animals learn to avoid peripheral stimulation, for example, an electric shock to the feet, but, in general, there appears to be little difference between the rate of acquisition of avoidance responses to peripheral or central stimulation. Those areas which are positively reinforcing are principally areas of the midbrain, most of the hypothalamus, parts of the thalamus and the septal area. From the hypothalamus in particular an extremely high rate of bar pressing (as much as 8,000 per hour) can be obtained and this can continue for periods of twenty-four hours or more, until the animal is exhausted. The placements which are negatively reinforcing appear to be in the reticular system and parts of the thalamus. In addition there are areas in which stimulation appears to be neither positively reinforcing nor negatively reinforcing and areas in which stimulation has both effects. In this section we shall consider only positive reinforcement.

Although the majority of the work on the positively reinforcing effects of electrical self-stimulation has been performed with rats, similar effects have been produced in cats and monkeys, and human beings report feelings of pleasure when stimulated in these areas (Heath, 1955). Animals will also cross an electrically charged grid from which they receive a painful electric shock to obtain electrical stimulation of the brain and they will withstand a stronger shock to obtain electrical stimulation than they will to reach food when hungry (Olds, 1961). In general, stimulation of the brain seems to produce effects which are stronger than those produced by 'natural' reinforcing agents, such as food and water.

There are thus some similarities between the effects of electrical self-stimulation and those of 'natural' reinforcers, and the results of self-stimulation experiments have been taken as support for hedonistic theories of motivation and reward. However, there are also some important differences between the effects of the two kinds of reinforcement, natural and electrical. First, as already mentioned, little or no satiation of the drive for brain stimulation occurs: animals continue bar-pressing to obtain brain stimulation until they are exhausted and the rate of bar-pressing does not appreciably deteriorate. For habits based on food or water rewards, the rate of responding slows down when an animal has received enough food or water.

Second, very rapid extinction of the bar-pressing response takes place when brain stimulation is used as reinforcement. That is, if the current is turned off, bar-pressing ceases almost immediately, whereas when food or water is used as reinforcement the rate of responding slows down gradually before ceasing altogether. Linked to extinction studies are studies of different reinforcement schedules in which, instead of receiving brain stimulation every time the response is made, the animal receives reinforcement intermittently. For example, an animal may be given reinforcement at regular intervals – say, every two minutes – regardless of its rate of response; this procedure is termed *fixed interval reinforcement*. Again, an animal may be reinforced after, say, every seventh occurrence of the response – *fixed ratio reinforcement*. Animals which are reinforced with food will respond at very high fixed ratios, for example, 100 unreinforced responses to one response reinforced; but for animals reinforced with electrical stimulation the ratios have to be much lower unless the animal is very carefully trained. Similarly, the time between successive reinforcements of food and water can be quite long and the animal will still keep responding, whereas in the case of electrical stimulation if the interval extends much over fifteen seconds the animal ceases to respond. It thus appears that the drive for electrical stimulation of the brain decays extremely rapidly when the animal is not receiving stimulation.

The third main difference concerns secondary reinforcement. Secondary reinforcement can be demonstrated in situations where a neutral stimulus, such as a tone, is paired with a primary reinforcer such as food or electric shock; in such cases the neutral stimulus alone comes to produce the same (positive or negative) effects upon behaviour as the primary reinforcer. But in general secondary reinforcement has been difficult to demonstrate using brain stimulation as a primary reinforcer. There is some evidence for it, but the evidence is not entirely free from other interpretations (see Gallistel, 1964).

It is not clear why the effects of electrical self-stimulation should in some respects resemble and in others differ from those of 'natural' reinforcers; for a theoretical account of the possible relation between self-stimulation effects and the neurological bases of drives and reinforcement, see Deutsch (1960) and Gallistel (1964).

Learning and punishment

We have said earlier that punished acts tend to be stamped out. This is perhaps a simple view, but one prompted by everyday observation of the way in which animals and children appear to learn. Are we, then, justified in thinking that punishment generally helps learning? The answer which emerges from empirical investigations is that it 'all depends'; that is, one general answer will not do. Whether punishment is conducive to learning or otherwise has much to do with the type of learning situation in question. Let us, therefore, turn to factual studies of different learning situations.

E. L. Thorndike (1932), well known for his researches into animal learning, subsequently investigated human verbal learning and reported that punishment in the form of criticism did not speed up the acquisition process. He used subjects who knew no Spanish, and presented them repeatedly with a Spanish word together with five English words. The subject's task was to guess which English word was equivalent to the Spanish one; and on giving a response, the subject would be told whether he was right or wrong. It was found, as might be expected, that the correct or rewarded responses tended to be repeated on later occasions whenever the subject was tested on the full list of 200 words; however, there was no tendency for the incorrect, punished response to disappear. Thus, the probability of reappearance of a given response increased when the response was rewarded, but did not decrease when it was punished – a somewhat unexpected asymmetry of reward and punishment effects.

Thorndike's study proved influential. On the one hand, many educationalists began to take the view that punishment was unhelpful in school learning. On the other hand, experimentalists were stimulated to examine more closely the conditions under which punishment was ineffective. Tilton (1939) carried out under strict controls an experiment with nonsense syllables and found that rewarded items tended to be retained while punished ones were eliminated; thus, both reward and punishment were helpful in the learning of lists, and so common sense seemed to prevail again. Having later surveyed the research in this field, Postman (1962) concluded that 'sheer frequency of repetition produces only small amounts of learning', that 'reward reliably strengthens stimulus–response connections and is the single most powerful determinant of learning', and that 'punishment does not weaken connections directly: whatever beneficial effects punishment does have must be attributed to the variability of behaviour produced by annoyers, which in turn leads to the substitution and reinforcement of correct responses' (p. 396).

While verbal reinforcement, such as saying 'right' or 'wrong', tends to have certain effects on the learning of lists of words or syllables, it could have somewhat different effects in the learning of concepts. This indeed was found to be the case by Buss and Buss (1956). In a series of experiments concerned with perceptual learning of concepts, these workers found that saying 'wrong' for the incorrect responses, and doing nothing in the case of correct ones, was an effective method of learning. It was more conducive to learning than saying 'right' for correct responses and saying nothing for the incorrect ones.

Nevertheless, the ineffectiveness of punishment in some human learning situations has often been confirmed; and ineffectiveness has also been shown to prevail in some types of learning in animals. Estes (1944) reported an experiment in which rats were trained in a Skinner box to press a lever to obtain food. The experimental animals were then shocked whenever they pressed the lever; the control animals just received no reward. It was found that the punished group retained the response longer than the control group. Here punishment, far from suppressing responses, actually helped the retention of what had been learned.

Paradoxically, then, punishment can sometimes be rewarding. This can occur, for example, when electric shock has become firmly associated with food. In such circumstances the animal can learn discriminations for the secondary reward of shock. Human beings sometimes appear to seek punishment as if it were rewarding; and perhaps it can be in providing much sought after attention. But apart from such complications punishment is the one instrument of learning in avoidance training, mentioned earlier. And a very effective instrument it is, for avoidance training has been found to be remarkably long lasting after even a few punishing trials (Masserman, 1943; Solomon, Kamin and Wynne, 1953).

The belief that punishment is of doubtful value in learning is surprisingly widespread. Solomon (1964) has questioned 'persisting legends concerning the ineffectiveness of punishment as an agent for behavioural change', and also 'the inevitability of the neurotic outcome' of punishing procedures. Likewise, Church (1963), while surveying the varied effects of punishment, concludes that responses are very effectively suppressed in the presence of noxious (punishing) stimuli whenever these stimuli are directly associated with the responses; in simple words, we learn well from our own mistakes. And further, the closer the time of punishment is to the response, the more marked is the suppression; that is, punishment is best when it is immediate. However, the effects of punishment cannot be predicted without taking into account additional factors in the situation: the restrictiveness/permissiveness of the prior régime, the consistency/inconsistency of previous punishing acts, etc. It may fairly be said that punishment of specific acts is effective in learning, but general punitiveness is not (Marshall, 1965; Sears, Maccoby and Levin, 1957).

Mediating and cognitive processes

A great deal of human learning involves understanding what is being learned and thinking about it. Sometimes animals, too, behave as if they had some *insight* into the situation to which they are adapting. Köhler (1925) observed chimpanzees learning to pile up boxes on top of one another, or join sticks together, in a seemingly intelligent manner, in order to solve specific problems. Tolman (1939) reported *vicarious trial-and-error behaviour* in rats, 'crouching to jump at one door and then crouching before the other door, before finally jumping'; and rapid learning by rats tended to be preceded by such symbolic trial-and-error demeanour.

Human beings are aided in their learning by images, or ideas, or symbolic representations of sensory experiences. Much animal learning appears to be reflexive, or sense-dominated; but some of it looks decidedly as if it involved some symbolic processes – for example, problem-solving behaviour or observational learning. This type of evidence will be briefly discussed in Chapter 18. Although we have no means of knowing anything about such symbolic processes directly, we must presume them to intervene between stimulation and action. They have often been described as *mediating processes*. In human beings, symbolic representations may likewise be regarded as mediating between sensory experiences and behaviour that is not under the sole control of sensory events.

The units, as it were, of mediation are specific mediating responses. We may distinguish between two sorts of such responses: the stimulus-producing and the observing (Hill, 1972).

By *stimulus-producing responses* are meant responses whose role in a behavioural sequence is to provide stimuli for further responses; Hull (1943) called such responses 'pure stimulus acts' and several theoreticians of learning have employed this or similar notions in explaining behaviour. There is, for example, a traditional distinction between *immediate* and *mediate* associations, particularly with reference to verbal associations (for a general discussion, see Jenkins, 1963). If we suppose, from various kinds of prior evidence, that a stimulus item A is associated with another item B;

if we then require subjects to learn an association between another item, C, and item A, and then require them to learn an association between item C and item B, there will almost certainly be *facilitation* in the learning of the association C → B. The association C → A has been learned; the association A → B has been inferred already to exist; thus both prior associations *mediate* the acquisition of the new association C → B. We may suppose that item C, presented as a stimulus, evokes the response A, and that the response A *mediates* the production of response B, by serving as a stimulus for its evocation.

The notion of mediation has also been relevant in describing conditioning. For example, Hull (1943) hypothesized that when a stimulus complex is associated with a response complex, certain portions of the response complex tend to become *anticipatory* (basically via some form of stimulus generalization; we shall not be concerned with possible mechanisms here). If, for example, a rat is trained to run a maze for food, some of the feeding responses which occur in the goal box will become conditioned to maze stimuli which occur earlier in the maze-running sequence. Clearly, not all feeding responses can become anticipatory in this way, since some require the presence of food, while others would interfere with maze running, would therefore not be *reinforced* and would therefore be *extinguished*. Thus, only fractional parts of the 'goal reaction' become anticipatory: responses which do not interfere with the activity needed to reach the goal and which are light-weight in terms of energy expenditure. Nevertheless, such responses are *distinctive* to the goal reactions which they represent. They have *proprioceptive consequences*, and the proprioceptive perception of such responses can serve as a *cue* or stimulus for (and thus *mediate*) specific further responses. To stay with our example, maze stimuli at any point in the maze-running sequence may produce fractional anticipatory responses, specific to the final goal response, which provide a stimulus for the continuation (and appropriate variation) of the 'running' response sequence.

It must be stressed that 'mediating responses', and the 'mediated stimulation' to which they give rise, are hypothetical events. Sometimes an overt response can be seen as mediating further responses by its proprioceptive consequences – for example, in the *internal feedback* involved in much skilled performance (see Chapter 14). More often, what is meant by mediating response is some more or less implicit internal representational response which may be muscular, glandular, subvocal (in the case of humans possessing a language system) or even purely neural; it is impossible within so broad a specification to predict and test the occurrence of a mediating response in a specific situation. The notion of mediation has nevertheless been used quite widely to extend essentially stimulus–response (S–R) explanations of learning, and more generally of behaviour; for example, in explaining the phenomena of set and the acquisition and functioning of secondary drives, and in the analysis of meaning and purpose. For accounts, see Hill (1972) and Osgood (1953); we shall also refer again to the notions of mediation and internal representation in Chapter 18.

Such S–R analyses have helped to visualize what goes on during learning; but they have not been adequate to explain fully even the basic facts of conditioning (Mackintosh, 1978). It is said that conditioning is not reducible to the strengthening of stimulus–response associations; somehow animals and human beings detect relations between events. Thus a cognitive perspective in analysing learning processes is very helpful. It is, of course, traditional even within the context of behaviourism (for example, Tolman, 1932). It is significant that discussions of cognitive processes in animal behaviour (Hulse, Fowler and Honig, 1978) are not thought to imply anthropomorphism, i.e. imputing human modes of experiencing to animals. As for human learning, some form of cognitive approach is necessary in accounting for language learning, modelling and so forth (e.g. Levine, 1975). Generally speaking, however, ambitious global learning theories are regarded as less fruitful than specific theories concerned with particular types of learning (Bolles, 1979; see also later sub-section of this chapter entitled 'Constraints on learning', pp. 358–60).

Before turning to problems of transfer of learning, it may not be out of place to refer again to what might be regarded as mediating responses of a special kind, viz. observing responses. These responses have been said to underlie the *acquisition of distinctiveness of cues*, or learning to which cues in a given type of situation attention should be given. Such acquisition occurs frequently in everyday life, but can also be demonstrated in animal learning in the laboratory when a subject has to learn which aspects of a situation are crucial and which are incidental. Thus, observing responses are presumed to occur when an animal learns – to give examples – that moving a particular object regardless of its position is always rewarded or that touching an object on the right regardless of its nature is punished, and so on. This kind of learning, as well as many other kinds, depends in some way on a process known as transfer. The elementary facts and rules of this process will now be considered.

Transfer of training

Our interest in learning goes beyond the study of either acts of simple learning or the learning of complex tasks in isolation from one another. Indeed, a great deal of study has been devoted to the influence of one act of learning upon another, that is, to the transfer of learning from one task to another task. The general problem is one of assessing the benefit which is derived from past experience – what value has education, for instance, in preparing the child for adulthood. We may ask how useful is industrial or military training which, of necessity, is only up to a point concerned with tasks which will be tackled later. We may wonder whether one set of acquired emotional attitudes carries over to new processes of attitude acquisition. In order to attempt to answer such questions it is necessary to start at the root of the problem of transfer.

Our basic concern is the interaction between different learning tasks. Let us call the earlier task A, and the later task B. *Positive transfer* from A to B is said to occur when learning A facilitates learning B. *Negative transfer* from A to B is said to occur when learning A hinders learning B. To what extent do the two forms of transfer occur in everyday situations? There is evidence that there is some positive transfer of training in such activities as sport and in the acquisition of some manual skills; there is also positive transfer from some intellectual tasks to some other intellectual tasks. Negative transfer, too, occurs quite commonly – in general, when two tasks are superficially similar, though requiring, in fact, quite different responses.

Interaction between different learning tasks may also show itself in the way in which learning one thing affects the *retention* of another. Effects of this kind are known as retroaction and proaction, and are dealt with in Chapter 16. It should be noted that one of the tests of retention is delayed recall. Thus, since the dividing line between immediate and delayed recall is somewhat arbitrary, transfer phenomena cannot always be easily separated from phenomena of memory.

Certain rules of transfer may be given in terms of the stimulus and response elements of the learning tasks between which transfer is possible. Consider a task such as learning the meaning of a number of words in a foreign language; here we have a list of foreign words and their English equivalents such that the former are stimulus words and the latter response words. Or think of the task of assembling, say, an electrical instrument: the sight of each stage of the task is a stimulus, and the next step in the assembly is a response to this stimulus.

Suppose, then, that an individual has to learn two such tasks in turn, first A and then B. If the stimuli of A and B are quite different, and so are the responses in A and B, then there will be no transfer, either positive or negative. There is a proviso here: there will be no transfer of specific learning but there may be some positive transfer of general information. This was shown to be so in some studies of human subjects in early experiments reviewed by Woodworth and Schlosberg (1954); these showed some 'transfer through principles' even where the two tasks had no 'identical components'. Transfer of principles or 'learning how to learn' has also been observed in monkeys coping with simple discrimination problems (Harlow, 1949). Such *learning sets* – as this type of transfer has been called – have been shown to exist in mammals as lowly as the opossum (Friedman and Marshall, 1965).

When a person learns two tasks, A and B, the stimuli of which are different and the responses are alike, then the transfer from A to B will tend to be positive, especially in non-verbal tasks. Furthermore, the less dissimilar the stimuli, the more pronounced will be the transfer. In other words, whenever old responses have to be attached to new stimuli, transfer is positive; and this is especially so when the stimuli are similar, this situation bearing the character of stimulus generalization.

Lastly, when one learns first A and then B such that the stimuli in the two tasks are the same but the responses are different, then the transfer from A to B is negative. The second learning task disturbs an established habit of responding in a particular way, and tends to give the subject a sense of confusion. If, for example, task A consists of learning to ride a motor-cycle and task B is learning to drive a car, then there will be some positive transfer of 'road sense', but also some negative transfer owing to the fact that the same signals call in the two tasks for different manipulative responses, hand-twist acceleration in A, foot-pedal acceleration in B. Likewise, negative transfer may occur if a person has to learn first a list of English–Spanish and then a list of English–French words, where the English words are the stimuli and are the same in both lists.

The situations mentioned above are relatively simple ones. Transfer phenomena are being extensively studied in a number of fields; they are of relevance to the acquisition of skills and also to the phenomena of retroaction and proaction to be considered in Chapter 16.

Constraints on learning

It has been known for a long time that some of the old 'laws' of learning do not hold in all situations. For instance, learning used to be regarded as a gradual, incremental process, but many research workers were finding that sometimes learning would be completed in one trial only. Skinner (1953) noted that a single reinforcement could at times exert full control over behaviour, as when animals (and people) show 'superstitious behaviour' – that is, actions serving no useful purpose and yet performed again and again because on one occasion in the past such an action occurred by chance shortly before a strongly reinforcing stimulus. In human verbal learning, too, it appeared that simple items were learned in an all-or-none fashion (Rock, 1957; Hill, 1972). Thus 'practice makes perfect' in many situations, but some-times it is not needed, as in one-trial learning, or indeed, as in no-trial learning (observational learning, modelling or imitation).

Another traditional belief, cherished by psychologists until comparatively recently, had been that the more promptly a reinforcement follows an action the more effectively reinforcing it is, that is, that delayed reinforcement can only be weak. There is no doubt that this is the case in very many cir-cumstances, but not in all. Sometimes reinforcement is of necessity delayed for many hours, and yet it may bring about after a single experience some very effective learning. This clearly occurs when animals, such as rats and mice, become 'bait-shy'. When an animal gets ill some time after eating a poisonous substance, it tends not to touch it again (Garcia *et al.*, 1968). Conditioning to such 'homeostatic effects' shows somewhat different charac-teristics from conditioning resulting from external punishment (pain) or rewards (quenching thirst or hunger). Distaste for illness-producing foods in animals and man may be developed without any mediation of consciousness; an aversion can be acquired by a subject under anaesthesia at the time of the administration of the agent resulting in subsequent illness (Garcia, Hankins and Rusiniak, 1974).

While bait-shy rats avoid only the taste of food associated with illness and nothing else (not, for example, the place where they fed), quail avoid only the colour of the food connected with later illness (Wilcoxon, Dragoin and Kral, 1971). This phenomenon of selectivity in the acquisition of aversions, the fact that such avoidance responses become attached to some stimuli and not to others, brings us to the heart of the problem of constraints on learning. Now the established view of association learning has been that 'any physical energy change that an organism can respond to in any observable fashion can serve as a conditioned stimulus; there appears to be no evidence contrary to this generalization' (Walker, 1967, p. 20). Seligman and Hager (1972) show at length how this traditional view derives from the writings of Pavlov, Skinner and others. This view, the so-called 'equipotentiality premise' which has latterly been challenged, is in effect that *any* discriminable stimuli and *any* elicitable responses can form the basis of conditioning. Many research workers, but especially Shettleworth (1972), have now shown that this is very far from being the case.

An early discussion of limits to learning such as operant conditioning was contributed by Breland and Breland (1961). They drew attention to the 'misbehaviour of organisms' trained in the operant manner; they found that, no matter how trained, domestic fowl tend to scratch the ground prior to eating, while pigs tend to root before they eat. These authors regarded such persistent behaviour as 'instinctive drift' within the conditioning process. Thus learning is restricted to certain biological boundaries. While members of a given species are unable to learn some tasks, their make-up is such that they show a 'preparedness' to learn certain other tasks (Seligman, 1970; Hinde and Stevenson-Hinde, 1973). Some of the special abilities and disabilities to learn are built in. Other kinds of preparedness to learn, and other constraints on learning, result from early experience.

We saw in Chapter 12 that early sensory deprivation can have adverse effects on later learning. However, a great deal of stimulation does not necessarily facilitate all learning, for certain kinds of experience impose constraints on later learning. This may be advantageous rather than maladaptive. It could be that the animal, or human being, as a result of some early learning will later learn less well generally, but will learn more readily that which is relevant to its wellbeing. This is speculation but there are some empirical grounds for it.

Consider, for instance, the findings of Revuski and Bedarf (1967). They studied the way aversions are acquired by rats to familiar and unfamiliar tastes. The illness from which food aversions developed was brought about, as in many other such investigations, not by anything in the food consumed, but by X-irradiation administered some time after eating. It was found – not unexpectedly – that aversions to novel tastes were much more readily learned than aversions to familiar tastes. The constraint on such learning, resulting from prior experience, ensures that tried and tested types of food continue to be acceptable to the animal. Again, consider the phenomenon known as *latent inhibition* (Lubow, 1973). This refers to the well-attested finding that pre-exposure to a conditioned stimulus hinders subsequent classical conditioning to that stimulus. In other words, exposure to an unreinforced stimulus reduces the power of that stimulus later to associate with reinforcing stimuli. This is useful to the organism in that it prevents commonly occurring stimuli from becoming unreliable signals for specific reactions. Yet another example of early experience imposing constraints on later learning may be cited; in discrimination learning, prior exposure to the discriminanda presented conjointly was found to interfere with the ability of such animals as chicks and monkeys to learn the discriminations in question (Bateson and Chantrey, 1972). This constraint on learning helps animals to maintain their acquired knowledge of environmental configurations.

In summary, much exposure learning early in life limits later learning. Thus, familiar stimuli cannot readily become conditioned stimuli; and familiarity with configurations can hinder learning to discriminate between elements of the configurations. Generally, passive early learning canalizes in various ways subsequent learning. This has, of course, to do with the transfer-of-training effects in the broadest sense. It has implications for our understanding of child development, skill acquisition, behaviour modification, etc. The lesson may be said to be that teaching and training are not imposed upon neutral ground, but build on foundations prepared both to facilitate and to hinder what may later be learned; in practice, to help an individual, it is useful to know as much of his/her learning history as possible.

Some theoretical issues

We started this chapter by wondering how much in common the various learning situations have. This problem – whether there is a central feature which characterizes all learning, whether there is basically a single kind of learning or several kinds – is one that has exercised learning theorists for some time. In particular, there have been advocates of the view that conditioning is essentially one, as well as those who have maintained that there are two different types of conditioning, classical and instrumental. This particular controversy is surveyed and the latter view is cogently argued in terms of the available experimental evidence by Rescorla and Solomon (1967).

However, this is by no means the only or the most important controversy in the field of learning theory. Learning theorists do not speak with one voice about the role of drives, or incentives, or rewards, and, as implied earlier, about the role of punishment in learning. And there is as much disagreement about the importance of practice and of understanding and insight in the learning process. Students of learning have striven to produce theories that are both all-embracing and fully consistent with the factual knowledge of learning phenomena. However, more than one theory appears to meet well these desiderata; and yet, all the theories cannot be equally valid.

The difficulty is that the different theories approach the problems of learning from quite different angles. An example of this is the cleavage between stimulus–response theories and cognitive theories (Hilgard and Bower, 1966). The former tend to assume that learning has to do with the chaining of responses; the latter lay stress on 'central' processes. Again, S–R theories regard learning as essentially an acquisition of habits, whereas cognitive theories are concerned with changes in 'cognitive structures'. Now we cannot choose between these approaches by referring to crucial observations or experiments. The competing theories can 'explain' all factual findings, albeit in different terms.

The classification of learning theories into S–R and cognitive ones is only one possible way of grouping them. Another, to give an example, is according to whether the theory is at all concerned with 'intermediaries', that is, with factors intermediate between stimulus and response variables, and if so, with what kind. Skinner (1950) has argued against intermediary concepts, and indeed, against broadly conceived learning theories. However, other approaches find it necessary to postulate some *intervening variables* or some *hypothetical constructs* (MacCorquodale and Meehl, 1948). Very briefly, intervening variables are constants of measurement, expressed in mathematical symbols, which relate observable phenomena but have no independent existence. Hypothetical constructs, on the other hand, are inferred intermediaries which could prove to be real. Thus, a theory might postulate certain qualities of the nervous system which facilitate learning. Only further research would then show which, if any, of such qualities are actual. It is also worth noting that the same term can sometimes be given either status. *Inhibition*, for example, is in Pavlov's sense a hypothetical construct, since it is used to denote brain processes which might be independently observed; the same term is used by Hull in a purely formal sense, to denote an intervening variable by means of which stimulus and response variables might be mathematically related.

Enough, perhaps, has been said to indicate how recondite the theoretical issues of learning can be. Theories of learning are ingenious and may be intensely interesting. They give hope of a deeper understanding of learning processes, but being largely irreconcilable, they have disillusioned many. The trend in more recent years has been to be somewhat sceptical of theories that claim a measure of completeness (Drever, 1961; Beloff, 1973). On the other hand, theories with a limited scope and concerned with explaining particular learning processes, for example, discrimination learning in animals, vicarious learning in children and so on, are most valuable. They inter-relate items of knowledge and they provide guide posts for further empirical research.

Chapter 14
Skilled Performance

What is skill?

Definitions of skill

One of the first difficulties encountered by anyone seeking to understand the work that psychologists have done in this area is the absence of any universally accepted definition of what is meant by 'skilled performance'. A consequence of this has been that research on skill has, as Adams (1971, p. 112) put it, '... studied anything that looked skilful to the common sense eye'. And this has been taken to embrace the full span of human performance from simple reaction time and eye-movement experiments to studies of highly complex activities like driving a car or piloting an aircraft.

Nevertheless, most definitions are agreed on one thing: that the term 'skill' should be reserved for complex rather than simple activities. Bartlett (1948, p. 31) wrote '... perhaps the beginnings of skill are to be found in the graded response'. A graded response is one in which a person is required to make a controlled movement of definite extent; it is not simply triggered intact by some external stimulus but is guided during its execution by the perceived consequences of the person's own actions. Bartlett was thus emphasizing the importance of *feedback* information in the control of skilled movement. He also argued that we should only begin to apply the term 'skill' when a considerable number of receptor and effector functions are interlinked and related together in a *series* which possesses clear directional characteristics and moves towards an end-point or goal. In a not dissimilar vein, Fitts (1964) stressed the high degree of *organization*, both temporal and spatial, that is evident in skilled activity and which is relatively independent of the specific senses or muscles involved. He concluded: 'spatial–temporal patterning, the interplay of receptor–effector–feedback processes, and such characteristics as timing, anticipation, and the graded response are thus seen as identifying characteristics of skill' (p. 245).

While these statements by Bartlett and Fitts fail to give us any precise

364   Skilled Performance

indication of what the term 'skill' encompasses, they succeed in focusing our attention on what are generally agreed to be the major issues in this area. Perhaps the best way to learn more about what psychologists actually do when they study skill is to look briefly at some of the more important periods in the history of skill research.

The pioneers (1890–1920)

The interesting thing about this early period is that so many of its issues and debates are still very much alive today. In fact, it could be argued that most modern theorizing has merely involved the reinstatement of these early ideas in the form of metaphors and models made possible by technological advances outside psychology, especially in the fairly recent development of complex machines for performing control, communication and computing operations.

One of the most influential of the pioneers was Robert S. Woodworth who, in his investigation of the accuracy of voluntary movements, anticipated by a half-century the implications of more recent studies of motor skill. In a paper written in 1899 he put forward the view (which he later elaborated in his book on the *Dynamics of Behaviour*, published in 1958) that the building blocks out of which complex skills are fashioned are 'two-phase motor units'. These consist of a 'pre-set' or preparatory act, analogous to cocking a gun, and the act itself. Thus, in using a hammer or a golf club there is an up-stroke followed by a down-stroke. The significance of the present or readiness phase is that it selects or 'pre-programmes' the force, amplitude, direction, rate and so on of the subsequent act. In other words, actions can be set up in advance of their initiation, and may be run off as a preformed sequence. This notion clearly anticipates contemporary concern with the preprogramming of responses that will be considered later in the chapter. Woodworth also postulated that these basic two-phase units are usually combined in sequences or 'polyphase motor units' as in, say, continuous hammering or walking. These more complex motor units were believed by Woodworth to be under the control of *feedback loops*; that is, they could be modified by their perceived consequences.

Perhaps the most frequently cited studies of this period are those carried out by two American psychologists, Bryan and Harter (1897, 1899), in which they observed the development of skilled performance in two telegraphists, and described 'plateaus' or lengthy periods in which no obvious improvement occurred. They explained this as follows: 'a plateau ... means that the lower-order habits are approaching their maximum development, but are not yet sufficiently automatic to leave the attention free to attack the higher-order habits (1899, p. 357).' Although the plateau phenomenon itself is now regarded as suspect, Bryan and Harter's explanation of it in terms of a hierarchy of habits is very close to current thinking on the organization of complex skills (Miller, Galanter and Pribram, 1960).

In his book, *Principles of Psychology*, William James (1890, p. 115) made a clear statement of *response chaining* (or 'reflex-chaining' as it was then called): 'In action grown habitual, what instigates each new muscular contraction to take place in its appointed order is not a thought or a perception, but the sensation occasioned by the muscular contraction just finished.' This represents one of the earliest references to the importance of feedback – in this case, *proprioceptive feedback* (see below) – for the control of well-established sequences of actions. As James put it '... the only impulse which the intellectual centres need send down is that which carries the command to *start*'. The rest are then triggered automatically by stimuli generated internally as a consequence of the preceding action.

The idea that each action in a habitual sequence provides the stimulus for the next makes proprioceptive feedback an essential part of movement control, and constitutes what has come to be known as the *peripheralist* viewpoint. Support for these arguments came from a number of animal learning studies carried out during the first decade of the present century. The most influential of these was a series of studies performed by J. B. Watson in 1907. He found that rats which had learned to run a maze in the light could perform the same task with reasonable success in the dark. Similarly, rats whose senses of hearing, sight, smell and touch had been eliminated (singly, not all together) also had little difficulty with the maze. Watson concluded that *proprioception* (sensory signals generated by receptors in the muscles, tendons and joints) was of primary importance in maze learning.

The opposing or *centralist viewpoint* originated with some clinical observations made by Lashley in 1917 of a man whose spinal injury had resulted in almost complete anaesthesia for one leg. Although this patient's movements were not perfectly co-ordinated, they showed normal accuracy in their direction and extent. Lashley argued that since the spinal injury had effectively eliminated proprioceptive feedback, the control of these movements must reside centrally in the brain and be independent of sensory feedback.

This finding gave rise to a number of animal studies in which rats were first taught to run a maze, then they were operated upon to cut the afferent nerves carrying proprioceptive feedback to the brain, after which they were set to relearn the maze post operatively. The outcome was that although the animals' movements were poorly co-ordinated after the surgical intervention, they had little difficulty in running the maze. As the result of these and later experiments, Lashley concluded that the maze habit was centrally organized rather like a gramophone record which once begun could set off the appropriate actions without the need for further modifications from sensory feedback. Although it is now felt that these conclusions were not entirely warranted by Lashley's data (see Adams, 1969), the arguments themselves are echoed by contemporary workers who claim firm experimental support for the existence of what are called *motor programs* (Stelmach, 1976). These will be discussed again at a later point.

In summary, we find that the early skills researchers were concerned with many of the major theoretical issues of the present day: the role of sensory feedback, the hierarchical organization of skilled behaviour, and the centralist–peripheralist debate (now often called the *inflow–outflow* issue). Now let us look briefly at some of the more important developments of the last thirty years.

The post-war period to the present

After the comparative doldrums of the inter-war years, a major impetus for the study of skilled sensory-motor performance came from the military and economic pressures created by the Second World War. People had to acquire new skills and acquire them quickly. Civilians were needed to take on highly skilled military activities and, on the home front, more skilled industrial labour was needed to fill the vacancies created by the rapidly expanding armed forces. Moreover, it soon became apparent that our existing knowledge of sensory-motor performance based, on the one hand, upon simple reaction time studies, maze-learning experiments and investigations into the formation of simple habits, and on the other hand, upon our industrial experiences with such techniques of time-and-motion study, was an inadequate foundation for understanding the complex skills needed in modern warfare. Consequently, research organizations were set up in universities and government departments with the urgent task of investigating the fundamental characteristics of human skill and of devising suitable training and selection methods.

Wartime pressures to understand the behaviour of the skilled human operator in complex weapon systems were also responsible for another, more subtle development. Scientists and technologists were constantly striving to improve existing weapon systems, and the need to assess the results of their efforts by evaluating the *man–machine system* as a whole, rather than by considering the man and the machine separately, brought psychologists into close contact with the thought and methods of other disciplines, notably those of the engineering sciences. Partly because it eased the communication problem, and partly because a rapidly developing technology made the exercise increasingly meaningful, psychologists began to consider the human operator in terms similar to those used by engineers to describe the function of their machines. As the result of this collaboration, a number of machine-oriented concepts found their way into skills theory. Three 'machine models' for the human operator were found to be particularly useful in stimulating research and in providing a conceptual framework for organizing human performance data.

The advent of complex communication systems and the related development of *information theory* (Shannon and Weaver, 1949) provided the means for analysing the human operator as an *information-processing* system: that is, one that receives, stores, collates and emits information in a way that shares many important features with sophisticated telecommunication networks. An important advantage of this approach was that it provided a more meaningful model for skilled performance than the simple stimulus–response or S–R notions that had emerged from animal learning studies.

Although self-regulating machines had been in use long before the Second World War, it was only during this period that sophisticated *servo-mechanisms* or feedback control systems (such as the autopilot, for example) came into widespread use. The idea of using servomechanisms as a model for the human operator was proposed by Craik (1948), and later elaborated by Hick and Bates (1950), and has represented a considerable growing point in our knowledge of skilled performance. In 1948, Norbert Wiener proposed that a separate discipline – *cybernetics* – should concern itself with the study of self-regulation in both physical and biological systems. The most generally used control system concept is that of *negative feedback*. Although this notion has a long history in psychology, it was only within the framework of cybernetics that it achieved any degree of precision or quantification. The role of feedback in skilled activity is to provide information about the extent to which our actions depart from our intentions, or the degree of *error*. In many important respects, the human operator – like the self-regulating machine – is error-actuated. That is, if everything is running to plan there is no modification of action because the system is so organized that information conveying the absence of error tends to be largely disregarded.

The third and most important model for skilled behaviour has been provided by the development of stored-program data-processing systems such as the digital computer. As Newell, Shaw and Simon (1958) pointed out:

The real importance of the digital computer for the theory of higher mental processes lies not merely in allowing us to realize such processes 'in the metal' and outside the brain, but in providing us with a much profounder idea than we have hitherto had of the characteristics a mechanism must possess if it is to carry out the complex information-processing tasks (p. 163).

Digital computers are governed in their operation by *programs* (and here we usually accept the American spelling), or sequences of instructions. Parts of these programs, like the actions of the driver or pilot, may be repeated many times over in one operation, and these relatively invariant sequences of instructions are termed *subroutines*. Subroutines are under the control of higher-level instructions termed *executive programs* which define the overall plan of action and call into play the various subordinate routines at appropriate points within the data-processing operation. Like human skill, therefore, computer programs are organized in a hierarchical fashion, and it is this feature together with their considerable adaptive potential that makes them such attractive analogies for complex performance in man (see Miller, Galanter and Pribram, 1960).

Two research teams in particular dominated the postwar scene. The first was that of Sir Frederic Bartlett and his associates at Cambridge, and the second was under the direction of Paul Fitts at Ohio State University. Although, as we have already seen, both Bartlett and Fitts emphasized the holistic or *Gestalt* nature of human skill and both subscribed to its hierarchical organization and the central roles played by anticipation and timing, their respective research efforts were directed along somewhat different (though ultimately complementary) lines. British workers stressed the limitations of the human operator, arguing that he behaves like a single communication channel of limited capacity. This view led them to concentrate upon the input or sensory end of this limited channel, and to study the gradual development of a perceptual organization which sifts and orders the incoming signals so that only the most important of them is processed by the channel at any one point in time. The American investigators, on the other hand, tended to concentrate on the output or motor end of the channel and sought to elucidate the mechanisms underlying the *automaticity* of highly skilled performance. Both lines of research will be considered in more detail later.

The most recent research on skills has been largely centred in the United States, and can perhaps best be exemplified by the work of Adams (1971) and his associates at the University of Illinois. In common with many other American investigators, they have largely abandoned the earlier concern of Fitts and Bartlett for studying complex skills in real-life settings, and have returned to the laboratory where they are engaged in the detailed study of simple motor learning.

Stages in the acquisition of skill

One of the major problems in the study of skilled behaviour is to determine what changes occur within the operator between his initial fumbling and laborious attempts at a complex sensory-motor task and his subsequent polished and apparently effortless performance. It is evident that this transitional area between skilled and unskilled activity must be filled with training and practice, and a considerable amount of research has been devoted to discovering the best techniques for training various types of skill (see Holding, 1965). Our concern in this section is not with the methods of training themselves, but with the underlying changes in the organization of perceptual-motor behaviour that they seek to bring about. Although they do not necessarily exist in any clearly demarcated or chronological sense, it is convenient for the purposes of explanation to divide the acquisition of skill into stages. These are set out below.

Plan formation

Though it may not feel like it at the time, very few of us have to start from scratch when it comes to learning a skill. Confronted with mastering a new activity, an adult brings to the task a whole range of previously acquired skills. All new skills are built upon the foundation of those already established. But before these existing skills can be redeployed and extended to serve new ends, the learner needs to acquire a *plan*: a set of instructions which serves to guide and organize his actions. This is what Fitts (1965) has termed the 'cognitive phase' of skill learning. In this initial phase, 'the learner must understand what the task or skill calls for; that is the nature of the task and its objective or purpose' (Robb, 1972, p. 52).

Now as Miller, Galanter and Pribram (1960) point out, knowing what to do – that is, having in one's head a clear plan of action – does not by itself lead to the necessary actions being performed adequately; but it is an essential first step in the acquisition of a skill.

Adams (1969; 1971), in particular, has stressed the importance of verbal responses for covertly guiding motor actions during the early stages of skill learning, and has described the initial phase of skill learning as the *verbal-motor stage*. But although motor responses may be under verbal control in the early stages of skill learning, this does not remain true of later stages. As Adams (1971, p. 115) pointed out: 'It would be silly to postulate a theory where *all* motor behaviour is under verbal control because words are crude when compared with the fineness of motor movements. The fingers of a concert violinist are not under verbal control, but they probably were in the beginning when he first started with his teacher.' In other words, verbal control gradually drops out as the learning progresses: or as James (1890, p. 114) put it: 'habit diminishes the conscious attention with which our acts are performed'.

Perceptual organization

A number of British investigators (see Annett and Kay, 1956; Welford, 1968, 1976; Bartlett, 1943) have suggested that the most important of the processes underlying the acquisition of sensory-motor skill, and the one upon which other changes ultimately depend, concerns the input aspect of the task. That is, the gradual development of a perceptual organization which sifts and orders the incoming signals so that the maximum amount of information can be handled by the operator's limited-capacity information-processing system in a given time period. The basis of this organization appears to be an increasing appreciation, on the part of the trainee operator, of the *redundancy* that exists in the information reaching his senses. In other words, as his experience of the task increases much of the information coming in through the senses becomes redundant in that it conveys nothing new or important. Continued experience of a relatively simple sensory-motor task, for example, may allow the operator to identify certain sequences of signals that appear in a relatively fixed order at various points in the operation, i.e., that signal A is always followed by signals B, C, D etc. When these invariant sequences have been identified, the operator learns that all the information contained in a particular series is conveyed by the first signal, the remainder being redundant.

In more complex tasks, such as driving a car or flying an aeroplane, the occurrence of these relatively invariant sequences of signals is rare; in this case, the operator has to learn to appreciate the various *sequential possibilities* of signals present in the inflow of information. Thus, instead of learning that signal A is always followed by signal B, he learns, for example, that the probability of signal A being followed by signal B is greater than the probability of its being followed by itself or by C, D, etc.

As the trainee operator becomes more aware of redundancy in the sensory input, he has more time to concentrate upon the genuinely useful cues which indicate what action is needed, guide its course, give advance warning of changing conditions, or indicate the success or failure of past actions. This greater efficiency in processing the sensory input is reflected on the output side by an *increased economy of motor action.*

Economy of motor action

The unskilled operator has to work a good deal harder than the skilled man to achieve even a pale reflection of the latter's polished ease of execution. The apparent effortlessness and economy of highly skilled performance is not altogether an artifice to impress the uninitiated; to a large extent, it is a reality. And these characteristics have their foundation in the fact that the skilled operator knows *what* cues to respond to, and *when* to act upon them.

It is possible to illustrate the way motor economy emerges out of perceptual structuring by considering a fault commonly observed among student pilots (or among tired ones – see Bartlett, 1943). This is the problem of 'chasing the needle' which occurs most frequently when the trainee pilot is being taught to fly on instruments without reference to the outside world. When the only attitude information available to the student is that represented by his basic flight instruments: artificial horizon, airspeed indicator, altimeter, vertical speed indicator, turn and slip and directional indicators, he often shows a tendency to concentrate his whole attention on each individual instrument in turn and tries to maintain a particular component of the flight path, such as altitude, at the expense of other components. As he follows the fluctuations of the altimeter pointer with his control column, other instruments begin to deviate undetected from their desired readings. When he finally notices these discrepancies he has to make large corrections to restore them. These in turn upset his height maintenance, and so on. But with further training and practice, the student pilot gradually acquires a scanning pattern. He no longer finds it necessary to concentrate on the details of each instrument but abstracts the required information from a global impression of the whole display. As a result, his control movements become both more economical and more efficient in maintaining the required flight path.

Clear signs of a developing skill, therefore, are the changes that occur in the way the learner uses his eyes. In the early stages of learning to drive a car, for example, the novice driver needs to *see* where his hands and feet are in relation to the controls; he is not yet familiar enough with the task to achieve this by 'feel'. This, of course, is very wasteful of his limited attention span. But with practice, the learner driver comes to rely more and more upon proprioceptive feedback information. As a result, he is able to employ his visual sense more efficiently.

Eye-movement studies carried out at Ohio State University (Rockwell, 1972) have shown that skilled drivers adopt quite different scanning techniques to those used by learner drivers. The latter spend a good deal of their time looking just ahead of the vehicle, and within this 'near zone' of viewing they change their point of fixation frequently, looking at irrelevant features like trees and lamp-posts. Skilled drivers, on the other hand, spend most of their time looking far ahead of their vehicles, relying on central vision for directional information and using peripheral vision to tell them where they are in relation to their correct lane position; consequently, they have little need to look just ahead of their vehicles as learners do. It was also found that the experienced driver adjusts the length of his forward focus to the rate at which he is travelling in order to give himself adequate warning time. The faster he goes, the further ahead he tends to look. But novices continued to sample the visual field close in to the fronts of their vehicles, irrespective of speed. Moreover, they also tend to look longer at any one point in the field of view than do skilled drivers.

These findings taken together with laboratory studies (see Pew, 1966) indicate that unskilled operators place more reliance on central or *foveal* vision than do skilled operators. But with experience, the focus of control shifts away to proprioceptive feedback, or to peripheral vision where this is appropriate; and with this shift comes a lessening of the demand placed upon conscious attention. On the output side, this increasing perceptual efficiency is reflected in a gradual reduction of the motor workload. This is what Fitts (1965) has termed the 'fixation phase' in skill acquisition when the learner begins to 'fix' individual actions into an appropriate temporal and spatial organization. It is at this stage that the learner begins to have that most precious commodity of the skilled operator: *time to spare*. He starts to acquire that most distinctive feature of the skilled operator, namely the appearance of 'having all the time in the world'.

Timing

Accurate timing is one of the most important features of skilled behaviour, and also one of the last to be acquired. Bartlett (1958, p. 15) stated that:

... timing has little or nothing to do with the absolute speed at which any component response in the skill sequence is performed. Efficiency depends, more than upon anything else, upon the regulation of the flow from component to component in such a way that nowhere in the whole series is there any appearance of hurry, and nowhere unnecessarily prolonged delay.

Timing permits the skilled operator to manipulate the temporal distribution of responses within the inherent limits of the particular task. Good timing does not simply mean producing the fastest possible response; rather, it means that the operator should organize his activities so that the optimal temporal conditions are provided for each response.

Conrad (1951, 1953) has demonstrated experimentally that bodily skills inevitably have a characteristic temporal structure, and that this can become defined and smoothed through practice, so that initially long intervals between components are shortened and short intervals become lengthened. Bartlett (1958, p. 15) has summarized these experiments as follows:

No single component in skilled behaviour is a function merely of that signal which immediately starts the response going. Within limits that can be experimentally determined and measured, surrounding signals and responses in both directions are contributing their shares. In the actual performance of most, and perhaps all, forms of bodily skill the temporal limits of this kind are rather narrow. It is only the near past and the near future that count. Moreover, it seems as if it is the near future – 'anticipation of what is coming next' – that plays the principal part in producing that objective smoothness of performance which is the hall-mark of a high quality of skill.

Timing, as we have seen, is one of the last characteristics of skilled performance to be acquired by the trainee operator. But it is also perhaps the most fragile and most easily disrupted feature of human skill. Timing is usually the first aspect of skilled behaviour to be lost under stressful conditions. The organization of skilled behaviour, like the trade unions, appears to follow the axiom: 'last in, first out'. For a fuller review, see Schmidt (1968).

Automatic execution

During the final phase of skill learning, the component actions become increasingly more automatic in their execution. Whereas the beginner needs to attend consciously to each step, the experienced operator performs the same movements 'unconsciously' and is thus able to direct his attention and his thoughts elsewhere. Fitts (1965) labelled this the *autonomic phase*; others refer to it as *automatization* (Schmidt, 1968). The largely automatic actions of the skilled operator suggest that one of the essential changes underlying skill acquisition is the gradual transference of control from a high level in the nervous system to lower levels in which the demands made upon consciousness are minimal. Theories as to how this relegation of control comes about, and how we might reconcile automatization with the notion of man as a limited-capacity information-processing system, will be considered in the next section.

Although we talk of 'automatic execution' as the final stage of skill acquisition, it should not be assumed that the process of learning stops here. A number of studies (see Fitts and Posner, 1967) have shown that skill continues to improve almost indefinitely until limited by the basic constraints of the task, or until the trend is reversed by the ageing process. Crossman (1959) took measures of the time taken to make cigars on a hand-operated rolling machine from operators of varying levels of experience up to seven years. It was found that the speed of performance increased as a power function of the number of items previously produced for about four years, at which point further improvement was restricted by the minimum cycle-time of the cigar-making machine.

The ability to maintain this automatic mode of performance requires continued effort on the part of the skilled operator. Complex skills like those involved in driving a car need constant practice to preserve their fragile integrity. Their 'keen edge' can be blunted by even a few days of inactivity. In practical terms, this means that the 'weekend driver' is less skilled than the man who uses his car every day. It is not so much that the former forgets how to change gear, or that he forgets the rules of the road. The degradation of his skill is far more subtle than that, and hence more dangerous. What deteriorates is his ability to process the incoming information effectively. He uses up more of his spare mental capacity than he would if he were in practice, and in consequence is less able to respond effectively when the demands of the task are suddenly increased as in an emergency. The fragility of skill has long been recognized by pilots. To retain his flying rating, a pilot must show that he is in current flying practice.

The control of skilled performance

Everyday experience and a wealth of experimental evidence (see Welford, 1976) indicate that our capacity to process information is limited: we can only handle so many signals in a given time. One view that has remained influential for a long time is the *single channel hypothesis*. This states that the human operator can be meaningfully regarded as a single-channel communication system whose capacity for receiving, storing, processing and acting upon information is limited. It argues that a person performing a skilled task has one central communication channel linking input and output functions through which each signal has to be cleared before others can be dealt with (Broadbent, 1958; Poulton, 1971; Annett *et al.*, 1974).

Although there is now an impressive body of evidence to indicate that the single channel hypothesis holds for many situations, more recent findings have challenged its universal applicability (Moray, 1967; Allport *et al.*, 1972; Shaffer, 1975). What is disputed is not so much that human operators have a limited capacity to process information, but that they should only do so along a *single* channel or transmission line. Of late, there has been a shift away from the notion of man as a communication channel towards a more flexible metaphor that likens human control processes to those involved in a digital computer.

Computer analogies for human performance owe much to the seminal book by Miller, Galanter and Pribram, *Plans and the Structure of Behavior* (1960). These authors proposed an alternative to the S–R reflex as the basic unit of behavioural analysis. They called it the TOTE unit, where TOTE is an acronym for 'Test-Operate-Test-Exit'. This is a cyclical control process involving two phases: a *test* phase that checks for any incongruity between the actual and desired state of affairs; and an *operate* phase which is set into action if the test detects a mismatch. Then a further test is made. If the mismatch still exists, then the 'operate' phase is activated again – and so on until the 'test' phase detects no incongruity, whereupon the cycle is ended. The essential feature of the TOTE unit, and one that makes its application to the understanding of skilled performance particularly appropriate, is that the 'operate' phase can be expanded hierarchically to incorporate any number of subordinate TOTE units (see Miller, Galanter and Pribram, 1960; Annett, 1969).

In addition to its hierarchical organization, the TOTE unit has two further characteristics that make it a powerful conceptual tool in the analysis of skilled performance. First, the *test* phase implies that we have a clear image of the desired outcome against which to assess our progress. This means that behaviour is orientated towards the attainment of some future goal rather than being controlled exclusively by immediate or past stimulus events, as in the case of the S–R analysis. A major weakness of the behaviourist approach was, as Luria (1973, p. 246) put it, that 'it ... closed its eyes to those forms of behaviour which are controlled, not by the past, but by the *future*, which are constructed as the putting into effect of intentions, plans or programmes, and which, as it can easily be seen, constitute the greater part of all specifically human forms of activity'. Second, the provision of feedback loops which shift control from the 'operate' to the 'test' phases and back again means that the behaviour so described is highly flexible and adaptive. Every time we perform a task like hammering a nail into a piece of wood, we are likely to use a different number of hammer blows that vary in force from occasion to occasion; but the outcome, having the nail lie flush with the wood, will not change. To quote Luria (1973, p. 248) again: 'It is a most important fact that the invariant motor task is fulfilled not by a constant, fixed set, but by a varying set of movements which, however, lead to the constant, invariant effect.'

A hierarchical plan of action of the kind just described is essentially the same as a computer program. But it is important to emphasize that the comparison being made here is *not* that between the human brain and the 'hardware' of a digital computer (i.e. comparisons between, say, neural synapses and electrical relays), but rather, as Newell, Shaw and Simon (1958) pointed out, the proper comparison is between the *sequences of operations* executed by a skilled human operator and by a correctly programmed computer.

In other words, we are arguing that the plans and actions of the skilled operator can be understood, in part at least, as being similar to the *executive programs* and *subroutines* employed by the computer programmer. Executive programs are analogous to human plans in that they define the goal to be achieved, specify the tests and control the ordering and timing of the components required to achieve the desired ends. In writing a computer program, it is usual to make all subroutines end by transferring control to the executive program, which then orders what to do next. In complex programs, subroutines will call in subordinate routines, and so on. However, as Neisser (1967, p. 296) explained, '... the regress of control is not infinite: there is a "highest" or executive routine which is not used for anything else'. And he continues (p. 296):

Note that the executive is in no sense a *programmulus*, or miniature of the entire program. It does not carry out the tests or searches of the constructions which are the task of the subroutines, and it does not include the stored information which subroutines use. Indeed the executive may take only a small fraction of the computing time and space allotted to the program as a whole, and it need not contain any very sophisticated processes. Although there is a real sense in which it 'uses' the rest of the program and the stored information, this creates no philosophical difficulties; it is not using itself.

In skilled performance, subroutines are analogous to oft-repeated command signals governing habitual sequences of action, which demand little or no conscious involvement to execute. But subroutines do not arrive ready made. Each can be thought of as a 'has been' executive program. The simple act of tying a shoelace, for example, initially required a conscious plan to control the individual actions. But with increasing practice, it gradually takes on the status of an automatic subroutine within the overall plan of dressing. As a person acquires greater proficiency at a task, each repeated set of actions comes to be relegated to a lower more automatic level of control within the hierarchy. And the more complex the skill, the larger is the number of subroutines contained in the hierarchy.

This gradual down-grading of control with continued practice offers a way of resolving an apparent paradox: namely, the notion of man as a limited capacity information-processing system, on the one hand, and, on the other, the fact that the actions of the skilled operator have a strict routine and make comparatively small demands upon this supposedly limited capacity. The key to this resolution is to make the assumption that only executive programs occupy time in the central processor (loosely identified with consciousness). The corollary to this assumption is that when, at any particular moment in the execution of a sensory-motor task, control resides within an automatic subroutine, the central processor is temporarily free to occupy itself with matters other than the task in hand.

Another way of regarding these changes underlying the acquisition of skill has been to propose that they reflect a transition from a continuous *closed-loop* mode of control to a condition where control is intermittently *open-loop*; that is, one not actuated by feedback. Keele (1973, p. 118), has described this transition as follows:

Early in practice, individual movements may be made, the outcome analysed by the visual system, a correction initiated, feedback analysed again, and so on. Such a skill is said to be under closed-loop control, reflecting the circular relationship between feedback and movement. But gradually, the skill may shift to the open-loop mode, in which movements, at least for some short period, may be autonomous of visual feedback.

If skilled movements are not constantly under closed-loop visual control, as our experience indicates, we are left with two alternatives to consider: either that the movements are under proprioceptive or internal feedback control, as James suggested in his *response chaining* hypothesis (see earlier in this chapter); or that movements are controlled by a *motor program* independently of peripheral feedback, as Lashley (1917, 1951) maintained. Central to this latter concept is the idea that movement patterns must be represented centrally in the brain, or perhaps the spinal cord, and are run off in the absence of modification from any kind of feedback. Thus, a motor program is a sequence of centrally stored commands that is organized prior to the actual execution of the movements. This issue of peripheral feedback control versus centrally stored motor programs is the peripheralist–centralist debate that was touched upon in an earlier part of this chapter.

The experimental evidence (see Glencross, 1977) does not provide convincing support for either an exclusively peripheral control system or for an exclusively central system. Rather it suggests that *both* central and peripheral control processes are combined within an integrated system. How this integration could be achieved has been discussed by a number of authors (see Stelmach, 1976), but the control system suggested by Keele and Summers (1976) is reasonably typical (see Figure 14.1). They postulate two basic components: a template or comparison centre and a movement generator or motor program system. The former is a representation of how the feedback should appear if the skill is correctly performed; and the latter generates a series of movements via efferent outflow to the muscles. These movements create kinaesthetic and other forms of feedback, depending upon the nature of the actions. The feedback is matched to the template, and any resultant discrepancy between what is actually occurring and what should be happening leads to correction of the motor program. This control system contains as its essential feature a central feedback loop between the template and the motor program system that owes much to the reafference principle of von Holst (1954), discussed at some length in the next chapter.

Finally, it must be emphasized that this and other contemporary models of skilled performance do not draw any sharp distinction between

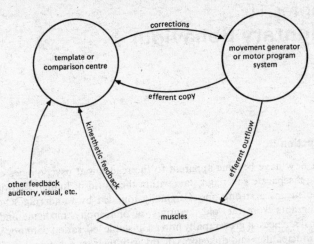

Figure 14.1   A model of skill learning and a mechanism for the detection and correction of errors

perceptual-motor skills and the more exclusively cognitive skills involving language, thinking, remembering and so on. As several writers have pointed out, they share a number of important common properties: they all have directional qualities in that they move towards a goal or solution, they all involve the uptake and processing of information, they are mostly characterized by a hierarchical organization, and they all manifest some degree of automatization. Those readers wishing to pursue the relationship between perceptual-motor and cognitive skills in greater depth should consult Bartlett (1958); Fitts and Posner (1967); Neisser (1967, 1976); Guilford (1972); and Shallice (1972).

Chapter 15
Voluntary Behaviour

Introduction

It must now have become apparent to the reader that psychology's claim to being a separate sovereign state within the world of human knowledge is by no means a strong one. Originally founded by wandering scholars and emigrants from the 'old countries' of philosophy, medicine and the biological sciences, it grew rapidly into an unstable federation of minor kingdoms, principalities and dukedoms, many with their own distinct languages and cultures, and with the whole only loosely held together by the dictates of academic and professional convenience. As is common in new and still unsettled territories, the urge for a coherent identity gave rise to frequent and bitter internal disputes. One of the most apparently decisive of the early psychological 'civil wars' was fought between the then mentalist establishment and a revolutionary group calling themselves behaviourists. Although there were few pitched battles, it was widely held that the behaviourists were the victors, and while strong pockets of mentalist resistance continued to hold out, the behaviourist's word was law for nearly four decades until the end of the 1950s. During this period there were many purges, and one of the first victims was the concept of *volition* or *will*; other proscribed notions included consciousness, mind, intention and purpose, mental imagery and the like.

So effective was the suppression of mentalistic concepts that the term 'volition' largely vanished from the psychological literature between 1920 and 1960. The feeling that prevailed towards the end of the behaviourist era is well captured in the following quotation from an influential textbook of that period. The passage is quoted at some length for two reasons. First, it touches upon many of the issues that will be discussed later in this chapter. Second, it serves to convey the confident finality with which notions such as volition were dismissed, and, at the same time, highlights the explanatory void that was so created.

In an earlier day the nervous system was thought of as a collection of direct S–R connections. As we have seen, this would imply a direct sensory control; so that whenever the control was absent, the behaviour became a mysterious business, to be explained only by a mind or soul which was *not* a part of the brain's activity, but separate. Volition or will was a power of this separate agency, which somehow could be exerted on the brain to make it behave in a way that it would not otherwise. 'Will-power' thus was something that one might have a lot of, or little. 'Free will' for many workers meant that voluntary behaviour was not subject to scientific law, not determined by cause and effect.

But all this was related to a very crude idea of how bodily machinery operates, and especially the machinery of the brain. If the higher animal responds in two different ways to the same total pattern of stimulation, it is because the activity of the central switchboard is not the same on the two occasions but 'set' differently; as a result the sensory input is routed to different muscles. It is evident that we are as yet far from understanding these problems in detail, and must not be dogmatic about their eventual explanation in terms of brain processes; but at the same time there is no fundamental philosophic problem about voluntary behaviour as such.

Consequently, in modern psychology the terms 'volition' and 'will' or 'will-power' have disappeared. 'Voluntary behaviour' still has a certain usefulness, as a rough classification; it is, in short, behaviour that cannot be predicted from a knowledge of the present environmental stimulation alone because a systematic variability is introduced by mediating processes (Hebb, 1958, pp. 63–4).

One of the reasons why this passage is particularly interesting is that Hebb himself, although committed to the identification between mental activity and brain processes, would not regard himself as a spokesman for the behaviourist tradition; indeed, in an earlier book (Hebb, 1949) he was critical of their simplistic views of stimulus control. So it is surprising to find him resorting to very similar arguments here, albeit lightly disguised by the central switchboard metaphor. Let us examine the points he was making in more detail.

1. It is asserted that volitional explanations of behaviour require the postulation of some mysterious 'mind-stuff' that exerts an effect upon the brain but which is not itself a part of it. While this is indeed true of the Cartesian account of human action in which movements are controlled by the flow of 'animal spirits' emanating from the 'soul' (see Dennis, 1948), it is by no means an accurate representation of later *psychological* views of volition, as we shall see when we come to consider William James's (1890) *ideomotor theory* of voluntary action. James made no functional distinction between the original stimulus and the mental image that subsequently comes

382 **Voluntary Behaviour**

to initiate the voluntary act. There was no impalpable 'mind-stuff' at work there.

2. The 'free will' issue is a red herring, at least in this context. The question 'is human behaviour determined or is there freewill?' is a metaphysical one, concerning the way the universe *is*, irrespective of what man may think about it. As Westcott (1976) put it: '... the metaphysical question is not the business of psychologists; as psychologists, it is not a realm to which they bring any expertise, and to which they have brought only confusion.' Freud and William James, for example, each resolved this issue in different ways: Freud in favour of determinism ('what is thus left free from the one side receives its motive from the other side, from the unconscious, and the determinism in the psychic realm is thus carried out uninterruptedly', Freud, 1938, pp. 61–2), and James coming down somewhat reluctantly on the side of freewill. But they made these decisions on personal or ethical grounds, not on the basis of rational, scientific or psychological arguments. James (1890, p. 323) expressed it thus: 'the fact is that the question of free will is insoluble on strictly psychological grounds.'

So what then is the business of psychologists in regard to free will? Westcott (1976) argued that psychologists '... should study free will as an experience which is the consequence of identifiable processes, and as a belief that has further consequences for behaviour'. Regardless of whether it is real or illusory, the fact is that we feel we make free decisions daily, and it should be the concern of psychologists to explain this experience, not to explain it away. Not only that, the lack of a personal conviction that we are, to some extent at least, 'masters of our fate' can have profound implications for our well-being and behaviour (see Lefcourt, 1973).

It is not within the scope of this chapter to pursue any further the age-old debate between the determinists and the libertarians. As Hospers (1973) pointed out, to argue that the notion of volition runs counter to determinism, an assumption basic to science, and hence can have no place in a science of psychology, is to misconstrue determinism. Stated simply, determinism is the view that everything that happens has a cause. It does *not* specify whether that cause should be mental or physical. Those readers who would wish to plunge further into this murky pool are recommended to consult the excellent account given by Hospers (1973).

3. Having rejected volition, what does Hebb offer in its place? The short answer is that he provides nothing except an outdated telephone exchange model of the central nervous system in which control still resides in the sensory input, except that once in a while the system emits different responses

to the same inputs. And this is due to 'unspecified changes' in the 'activity of the central switchboard'. Hardly a satisfactory solution to the basic psychological problem of how actions are initiated, how they are guided to their intended outcomes, and, not least, how they are terminated once this goal is achieved.

Curiously enough, Hebb is willing to retain the term 'voluntary behaviour' – which the dictionary tells us is behaviour that flows from the will – because, presumably, it has suitably mechanistic and physiological overtones, as distinct from the taint of philosophy and metaphysics that he evidently perceives as attaching to 'volition' and 'will'. But what is so special about this behaviour that it cannot be predicted on the basis of environmental facts? Hebb's answer: because it stems from a 'systematic variability' that is introduced 'by mediating processes'. A rose by any other name, indeed! It is this non-explanation which gives the lie to the preceding assertions, and which brings us full circle back to the problem of volition.

In Hebb's account of the status of volition in 1958, we find some of the causes for its fall from psychological grace: the fact that it was regarded as emanating from some 'mind-stuff' belonging neither to the explanatory realm of the body nor that of the environment; and where this was compounded by the metaphysical taint of 'freewill', something that could have no place in a scientific psychology committed to the notion of a deterministic universe. Yet we can also see that the fundamental problems concerning the initiation and control of behaviour have not been solved, nor even properly grappled with. They are either ignored, or else merely obscured in unsuitable mechanistic metaphors.

It is not easy to date when the notion of volition began to find its way apologetically back into psychological discourse since, as we mentioned earlier, there were always groups of mentalistic resistance fighters active during the period of behaviourist domination, but the year 1960 was certainly a significant one in that it marked the publication of *Plans and the Structure of Behavior* by a trio of distinguished American life scientists, George Miller, Eugene Galanter and Karl Pribram. This highly influential book was prompted not so much by the rumblings of the mentalist 'underground' as by post-war technological advances quite outside psychology in the field of self-regulating machines and, in particular, of the digital computer (see Chapter 14). The Test-Operate-Test-Exit (TOTE) unit they propose as an alternative to the behaviourist's S–R unit of behavioural analysis has already been discussed in Chapter 14. It is sufficient for our present purposes simply to observe that this book not only gave expression to a growing mood of discontent with the behaviourist supremacy at that time, but it also offered a viable scientific alternative, and so gave impetus to the development of the 'new mentalism' in the shape of contemporary cognitive psychology. It is inevitable that in the wake of such a counter-revolution, the bones of some of the 'martyred' mentalist concepts should be exhumed and their substance re-evaluated.

Before going on to look at theories of voluntary behaviour, it is worth noting in passing that to the world outside psychology, the notion of volition has continued to play a useful, and in the case of the law, a fundamental role. The following passage from a distinguished writer on jurisprudence, H. L. A. Hart (1968, p. 114) will help to put the matter into a wider perspective:

All civilized penal systems make liability to punishment for at any rate serious crime dependent not merely on the fact that the person to be punished has done the outward act of a crime, but on his having done it in a certain frame of mind or will. Those mental and intellectual elements are many and various and are collected together in the terminology of English jurists under the simple sounding description of *mens rea*, a guilty mind. But the most prominent of these mental elements, and in many ways the most important, is a man's intention ...

Ideomotor theory: past and present

If we choose to disagree with the assertion that 'a scientific analysis of behaviour dispossesses autonomous man and turns the control he has been said to exert over to the environment' (Skinner, 1971, p. 205), then we are thrown back upon the basic question: how are voluntary movements initiated? A suitable point to begin searching for an answer is with the *ideomotor theory* of William James, presented in a lengthy chapter contained in the second volume of *The Principles of Psychology* (1890). Although earlier writers had expressed essentially similar ideas (Buchanan, 1812; Lotze, 1852; Sechenov, 1863), James's theory was by far the most comprehensive and influential, and as such can legitimately be regarded as the classical psychological theory of volition.

Ideomotor theory: the classical version

James's basic idea was that actions are triggered by 'ideas of movement', or by images of what the movement feels and looks like during its execution. Voluntary movements occur as the result of forming a clear mental image of the kinaesthetic and other sensory feedback normally associated with the particular actions. In other words, actions are initiated as an almost automatic result of imagining their sensory consequences, or what von Holst (1954) has termed their *reafference* (see pp. 392–5).

To overcome the logical difficulty of having the *effects* of an action precede the action itself, James argued that all these imagined consequences of voluntary movements are derived originally from the experience of involuntary or reflex behaviour. 'When a particular movement, having once occurred in a random, reflex or involuntary way, has left an image of itself in the memory, then the movement can be desired again and deliberately willed.' According to James, then, we need first to acquire a stock of these 'ideas of movement', stored within the nervous system as a consequence of previous involuntary movements, before we can achieve any degree of voluntary control.

The imagined consequences of a movement eventually come to have the same power to initiate it as did the external stimulus when the movement was entirely under environmental control. James suggested that this is achieved through the establishment of neural connections between sensory and kinaesthetic centres within the central nervous system, both of which feed into the motor centres responsible for activating the movement. Thus, in their ability to evoke action, no distinction is made between the original stimulus and the image of its sensory feedback. So far as the motor centres are concerned, the stimulus and the image are of the same currency.

One of the cardinal features of a voluntary act is that it can be withheld. Within James's theory, this restraint is achieved by '... an antagonistic representation present simultaneously to the mind'. On occasions, these contrary images overrule our best intentions, as when we struggle unsuccessfully to get out of a warm bed on a cold morning. It is under these circumstances that an express fiat, or act of will, is required to neutralize, in this case, the powerful and seductive images of comfortable immobility. However, there is nothing particularly mysterious about this fiat, as James himself points out with characteristic clarity: 'The essential achievement of the will ... is to attend to a difficult object and hold it fast before the mind. The so doing is the fiat; and it is a mere physiological incident that when the object is thus attended to, immediate motor consequences should ensue.' But James was also careful to stress that when the conditions are simple, and no antagonistic images are present, the action will follow in a quasi-reflex fashion from the mental image alone without any accompanying effort of attention.

The nature of the image changes as actions become increasingly more practised. In the first place, the image makes less and less demand upon conscious attention. In the second, a single image may serve to initiate a lengthy sequence of familiar actions through the process of *response chaining*, discussed at length in Chapter 14.

As discussed in the previous chapter, there is still considerable dispute about the way in which highly skilled actions are controlled at a non-conscious level. An early critic of James's explanation of how 'habit diminishes the conscious attention with which our acts are performed' was Woodworth (1906, p. 375) who felt that James placed too much emphasis on imagining the means rather than the ends. He wrote:

If I wish to cut a stick, my intention is not that of making a certain back and forth movement of my arm while simultaneously holding the fingers pressed tightly towards each other; my intention is to cut that stick. When I voluntarily start to walk, my intention is not that of alternately moving my legs in a certain manner; my will is directed towards reaching a certain place. I am unable to describe with any approach to accuracy what movements my arms or legs are to make; but I am able to state exactly what result I design to accomplish ... It is not so much a supply of ideas of the various movements that are possible as a knowledge of the various effects that can be produced, that is the first prerequisite of mental life.

As it happens this criticism is a little unfair, since James himself made a very similar point ('What interests us are the ends which the movement is to attain'); but the quotation is useful because it conveys the flavour of more modern thinking both in psychology (see Miller, Galanter and Pribram, 1960) and in the field of jurisprudence (see Hart, 1968).

Ideomotor theory: subsequent developments

In the early years of this century, ideomotor theory came under attack from many quarters. Experimentalists like Bair (1901) and Woodworth (1906) claimed that their subjects were unable to identify any conscious 'ideas of movement' prior to executing a voluntary act. Burnett (1906), on the other hand, set out to demonstrate that mental images were too slow to provide the trigger for voluntary movements. He asked his subjects to imagine that they were following the course of a swinging pendulum, then he required them to track the arc of the pendulum by pointing with a finger. He found that it took significantly longer to imagine a given number of swings than it did to follow them with a finger.

A more decisive onslaught, however, came from early behaviourists like Thorndike (1913) and Watson (1930) who found mentalistic concepts such as perceptual images unacceptable within a rigorous analysis of behaviour rooted to conditioning. To them, James's ideomotor theory was incompatible with conceptual schemes that relied upon environmental control and upon special reinforcing events to cement together the stimulus–response units of behaviour. Although the ideomotor theory would inevitably have fallen into disrepute during the years of behaviourist domination, it is nonetheless interesting to note the very flimsy grounds upon which James's ideas were dismissed. Thorndike, for example, based his attack in part upon the results of an opinion survey carried out among members of the American Psychological Association! He also resorted to a curious form of argument by analogy along the following lines:

… the idea of throwing a spear or of pinching one's ear, or of saying 'yes' tends to produce the act in question no more than the idea of a ten-dollar bill or of an earthquake tends to produce that object or event. (Thorndike, 1913, p. 94).

As mentioned earlier, there has, over the past twenty years or so, been a considerable revival of mentalistic concepts such as imagery. This renewed interest arose partly from the increasing use of computer programs as models for human cognitive function, models that relied heavily upon internalized representations of the world for the initiation and guidance of action (see Miller, Galanter and Pribram, 1960; Simon and Newell, 1971); and partly as the result of improved experimental techniques for investigating non-verbal mental phenomena (see Sheehan, 1972). In a climate where many psychologists have come to acknowledge once again that their science is centrally concerned with the phenomena of mental life, the ideomotor theory has been restored to a place of major importance. Although the theory is now eighty years old, it would seem that the full impact of James's ideas has only recently been felt. This is to some extent due to the convergence of a number of hitherto unrelated lines of research, as indicated by Konorski's comments (1967, p. 194) upon the ideomotor theory: 'it is most encouraging to know that we have come to exactly the same concept by quite different considerations – namely, through the physiological analysis of (voluntary) movements.' More recently, Greenwald (1970) and Kimble and Perlmuter (1970) have devoted lengthy review articles to a favourable reappraisal of the ideomotor theory. Indeed, Greenwald and his associates (Greenwald, 1970, 1972; Greenwald and Shulman, 1973) have elaborated the theory further in an attempt to explain how external stimulation and internal sensory feedback are involved in the regulation of skilled performance.

Another factor that has directed contemporary theorists to take a renewed interest in ideomotor theory has been the prolific growth in the literature relating to the learned manipulation, using *biofeedback*, of physiological processes previously regarded as being outside the scope of voluntary control. Brener (1974), although specifically concerned with the phenomena of learned cardiovascular change, has developed a general model of voluntary control that is based, like James's theory, upon the assumption that sensory feedback processes are fundamental to the exercise of volition. Also central to Brener's theory is James's proposition that the elicitation of the response image leads inevitably to the activity represented.

Evidence relevant to the ideomotor theory

Experimental studies. On the face of it, it does not appear too difficult to test the basic proposition that a mental image of an action causes the action to occur. In theory, all that is necessary is to present the subject with the feedback stimuli normally contingent upon a particular act, and then observe whether or not the action is produced. In practice, however, such an apparently unequivocal test has not been easy to contrive.

The first attempt to verify the theory along these lines was made by Bair (1901) who set his subjects the ingenious though somewhat bizarre task of learning to waggle their ears at will, with and without the aid of electrical stimulation applied to the appropriate ear-moving muscle. The rationale was as follows: if the theory were correct, the sensations contingent upon the electrically-induced ear twitch should be sufficient to enable the subject to move his ear voluntarily immediately afterwards.

According to this strict interpretation, the results failed to support the theory. Even with the help of electrical stimulation, the subjects required a great deal of practice before they were able to make ear waggles at will. But a closer examination of the results reveals a pattern that is by no means contrary to the predictions of the theory. For example, those subjects who received the electrical stimulation obtained some degree of control over their ear movements much sooner than those who were denied this augmented feedback. These latter individuals found the task exceedingly difficult because they had little idea of what they were trying to achieve. In other words, they did not know what the desired response *felt like*. Evidently sensory feedback contributed in some important way in the process of gaining mastery over this hitherto largely involuntary response.

It is also of interest that the first voluntary ear-movements occurred as part of a wider series of facial contortions. Once the subjects began to appreciate the feelings associated with ear-movements, even though they constituted only a small part of the generalized facial activity, they became increasingly more successful in producing them in relative isolation. In order to achieve the desired movements, however, the subjects stressed how important it was to focus their attention on the ear movements alone, while at the same time making a positive effort to ignore the sensory feedback produced by associated movements. These attentional activities are very much in accord with James's description of the production of a voluntary act.

More recently, Easton and Shor (1975) have sought to investigate aspects of the ideomotor theory using the Chevreul pendulum illusion. This was a device originally employed by nineteenth-century spiritualists, and involves holding between finger and thumb a cord from which a pendulum bob is suspended. The subject is instructed to 'will' or imagine the pendulum to move in a particular direction whilst keeping the hand still. The illusory experience arises because the subject can frequently see the pendulum bob obeying the mental instructions, but he cannot feel the muscles initiate and guide the swinging movements, when in fact they are producing the only forces acting upon the pendulum.

Theoretically, this appears to be a clear demonstration of the ideomotor process, where visual images of the pendulum swinging in a particular way are actualized through the agency of covert hand or arm movements. Also implicated is the phenomenon of *visual capture* (see Chapter 8) in which the monitoring of kinaesthetic information is pre-empted in consciousness by the presence of simultaneous visual impressions.

To eliminate the possibility that the pendulum moves simply because the hand cannot be kept absolutely still, Easton and Shor measured the pendulum swings, using a photographic time-exposure technique, under the following conditions: when subjects imagined the pendulum swinging back and forth; when they imagined it to remain absolutely still; and when they adopted a completely neutral attitude with regard to pendulum movement. The result was that the pendulum actually moved above ten times as much when they imagined it swinging as in the other two conditions. This suggests that the pendulum swings arise as the result of deliberate imaginal processes.

A subsequent study showed that when subjects confined their attention to imagining the pendulum movement, the resultant oscillations of the bob were more extensive than when they were required to carry out simultaneous mental tasks that, presumably, interfered with the imaginal activity. Pendulum swinging was also boosted by visual and auditory prompts, consisting in the former case of the experimenter moving his hand back and forth beneath the pendulum, and in the latter of the experimenter speaking in a to-and-fro cadence. Both prompts were in the harmonic period of the pendulum.

A further experiment (Easton and Shor, 1975) confirmed the facilitatory effects of these imaginal prompts, although visual oscillating stimuli were more effective than their auditory counterparts. It was also found that the extent of the swinging was markedly reduced when the pendulum was not visible to the subject. But the fact that the pendulum *did* move when sight of the actual pendulum was denied, *and* when no imaginal prompts were available, strongly suggests the presence of pure ideomotor control. Taken together, therefore, this series of investigations provides convincing support for James's theory.

Developmental studies. A second category of evidence bearing upon the ideomotor theory comes from investigations of how children acquire voluntary control over their actions. Perhaps the most extensive developmental research bearing on this issue was conducted by Luria (1961) and his colleagues in Moscow. The investigators recorded children's responses to verbal instructions in regard to squeezing an air-filled rubber ball at different ages. On the basis of these observations, the following developmental sequence was described.

(a) *At $1\frac{1}{2}$ years.* The child can obey the instruction 'squeeze the ball' if not engaged in some other activity at the time of the request. However, he could not inhibit ongoing responding when told 'don't squeeze'.

(b) *At $2\frac{1}{2}$ years.* The child can respond to a delayed signal, 'squeeze when the light goes on'. Once started, the movement can be inhibited either by telling the child to do something else (move hand to knee), or by giving him a distinctive signal contingent upon the response ('squeeze to put the light out').

(c) *3 years.* With the help of repeated verbal instructions accompanying each stimulus presentation, the child can squeeze to one signal, a red light, and stop squeezing when he sees a green light.

(d) *$3\frac{1}{2}$ years.* The child can talk *himself* through initiating responses, but not inhibiting them. Thus he can give two successive squeezes to a delayed signal with the help of saying 'go! go!' on presentation of the stimulus. But while he can learn to say 'squeeze' to one signal and 'don't squeeze' to a second, he is still more likely to squeeze the ball on both occasions, rather than on the first only. The task is better performed if he remains silent on the presentation of the second signal.

(e) *5 years.* Now the child becomes able to use his own speech to inhibit responding. In other words, he can successfully carry out the 'squeeze–don't squeeze' experiment mentioned above. He can also regulate his performance on a variety of other complex tasks. At about the same age, the child also begins to be able to accomplish various complex tasks in silence, indicating a transfer of control from externalized to internalized speech.

Although these investigations were not carried out specifically to investigate the ideomotor theory, the slow appearance of successful inhibitory control of performance is in accord with James's assertion that a response image 'awakens in some degree the actual movement which is its object' unless 'kept from so doing by an antagonistic representation simultaneously present to the mind'. More recent investigations of the growth of voluntary control in young children are discussed in Connolly (1971) and Connolly and Bruner (1974).

Neurophysiological studies. As indicated earlier, a particularly strong source of support for the ideomotor theory comes from studies investigating the relationships between thoughts of movements and the electrophysiological recordings taken from the muscle groups involved (i.e. electromyogram or EMG recordings). This technique was employed by Jacobson (1932) and Max (1935, 1937) in an attempt to find evidence to support the motor theory of thinking. Max's results were particularly impressive because of his careful procedures. He used deaf-mute subjects and monitored the EMG activity in their hands during dreaming, using normal subjects as controls. He found a greater frequency of hand muscle potentials during the dreaming of deaf-mutes, a result that is consistent with the expectation that their dreams would include thoughts of hand movements (i.e. language) more than would those of normals. These findings, and other similar ones reported by several Russian investigators, fit closely with James's view that the thought of a movement 'awakens in some degree' the actual corresponding movement.

More recent neurophysiological studies by Kornhuber and his associates (Deeke, Scheid and Kornhuber, 1969; Kornhuber, 1974) have measured the electrical potentials generated in the cerebral cortex immediately prior to the execution of a simple willed action. The movement investigated was a rapid flexion of the right forefinger. The subject was required to initiate this action 'at will' at irregular intervals of many seconds. With the aid of a computer, it was possible to average the very small potentials recorded from the surface of the skull over a period of two seconds *before* the movement actually occurred. The investigators observed a slowly rising negative potential – which they called the *readiness potential* – beginning as long as 800 msec before the onset of the movement. Associated with the growth of this readiness potential, there was a developing specificity in the signals being sent to the motor cortical areas. Although these data do not bear directly upon James's ideomotor connection, they nonetheless demonstrate the existence of activity within the brain during the process of 'willing' a movement to occur. With the availability of such a technique, the possibility now exists to examine the correlation between this 'readiness potential' and concurrent imaginal activity. Far from being a mysterious 'mind-stuff', therefore, it is clear that the notion of volition is something that can not only be subjected to experimental test, but which may also be seen to possess a neurophysiological basis.

The reafference principle

William James set out to tell us in some detail how a movement gets started, but he had relatively little to say about the mechanisms that bring it to a halt. More recent theorists, particularly those employing computer metaphors for human cognitive function (see Miller, Galanter and Pribram, 1960), have stressed the importance of 'stop-rules' that are incorporated into the image or plan that initiates action. Of these theorists, von Holst (1954) is not only one of the most influential, but also one whose ideas, embodied in the *reafference principle*, accord most closely with the ideomotor theory – a rather surprising convergence of thinking considering that von Holst was a zoologist while William James was essentially a philosopher.

The reafference principle is based largely upon neurophysiological ideas and is directed primarily at explaining certain biological control processes. Nevertheless, it has considerable relevance to the understanding of human voluntary behaviour, particularly in accounting for why active, self-induced movements have different consequences from those produced passively by some external agency.

Two notions are central to the *reafference principle: efference* and *afference*. Those neural impulses arising from the motor ganglia and directed towards the effectors, von Holst termed efference; those arising from sensory receptors of whatever kind, he called afference. Whereas the former impulses are present only when the ganglion cells are active, the latter can have two quite different sources. One kind of afference originates from the organism's own activity – *reafference*; the other kind are sensory impulses produced by stimuli from the outside world – *exafference*. Von Holst (1954, p. 161) offered the following examples to distinguish between these two forms of *afference*:

... when I turn my eyes, the image present on the retina moves over the retina. The stimuli so produced in the optic nerve constitute a re-afference, for this is the necessary result of my eye movement. If I shake my head, a re-afference necessarily is produced by the labyrinth. If, on the other hand, I stand on a railway platform looking straight at a train when it starts to move, the moving image on the retina of my unmoving eye produces an ex-afference; likewise when I lie in a tossing ship, the impulses of my labyrinth will constitute an ex-afference. If I shake the branch of a tree, various receptors of my skin and joints produce a re-afference, but if I place my hand on a branch shaken by the wind, the stimuli of the same receptors produce ex-afference. We can see that this distinction has nothing to do with the difference between the so-called proprio- and extero-receptors.

The reafference principle is concerned with specifying the relationship between efference, the command signals, and reafference, the internal feedback information. The essential feature is that a command signal or efference, originating from a higher centre in the brain, leaves an 'image' of itself somewhere in the CNS. This 'image' is termed the *efference copy*, and it is rather like a carbon copy of the original order to the effectors. Specified within this efference copy is the nature of the reafference that would be expected on the basis of the movements being executed as planned. This reafference is then fed back and compared with the efference copy. If the two are compatible, the movement ceases. But if the two are mismatched, either because the reafference is greater or less than expected, then a number of perceptual or behavioural consequences will ensue. We can explain these steps in more detail by reference to a particular example, that of moving the eyes.

If we detect the motion of objects in the outside world by the movement of their images over the retina, how do we maintain the stability of the visual world during eye-movements? When we move our eyes voluntarily, the images of stationary objects will track across the retina in much the same way as the images of moving objects track across the stationary retina. Or to put the question in von Holst's terms: how does the brain distinguish between exafference and reafference when the same sensory receptors are involved in both? Clearly this must happen since the world does not move whenever we change our direction of gaze.

The explanation according to the reafference principle goes as follows: consider the case where the eye is moved voluntarily with a single stationary object in the field of view. The higher brain centre generates a command signal, say, 'turn the eyes a given distance to the left'. This efference is delivered both to the appropriate eye muscles *and* to a lower brain centre where an 'image' or *efference copy* is stored. As a consequence of the eye-movement to the left, the image of the stationary object in the field of view will track across the retinal mosaic producing a reafferent signal that is entirely in accord with the original command signal. In other words, this reafference is the expected result of that particular efferent command. The reafference is fed back to the efference copy and is compared to it 'as the negative of a photograph compares to its print; so that when superimposed the image disappears'. In this case, therefore, the reafference simply cancels out the efference copy; the eye-movement is brought to a halt and the stationary object in the field of view is correctly perceived as such. Conversely, when the object in the field of view moves independently of the eye, the absence of an efference copy indicates that this is an exafferent signal. And again veridical perception is maintained.

But what happens when the reafference fails to match the efference copy? Instead of moving the eyes in the normal manner, suppose we were to move one of them passively by pressing the eyeball with a finger. The eye will move relative to the stationary object in the field of view causing its image to track across the retinal receptors. But this reafferent signal has been produced in the absence of a normal efference. Consequently it is not cancelled by the efference copy, and we experience an illusory perception – in this case of the stationary object moving in a direction opposite to the passively induced eye-movement. You can try the experiment for yourself by closing one eye and gently pulling the skin at the edge of the open eye.

It is also possible to produce the opposite effect, although technically it is not quite so simple. Mach (1886) stuffed putty into the orbit around one eye so that it could not move. When he then attempted to move the eye voluntarily, he observed that the stationary scene in front of him swung in the same direction as the intended eye-movement. Here we have an efference copy in the absence of an expected reafference. The sign of the matching error will be opposite to that described above for the passive movement case; as a result the illusory perception is in the opposite direction.

So far, we have considered the reafference principle in relation to largely perceptual phenomena; but it applies equally well to the control of motor performance. As indicated above, the differences between the reafference and the efference copy will produce predictable effects depending upon the sign of the mismatch between them. When the reafference is greater than expected on the basis of the efference copy, the movement will end prematurely; if the reafference is too weak, the movement will persist for longer than intended. Liu (1968) carried out an experiment which directly tests these predictions. He instructed subjects to press a key a distance of 3·5 cm with a single quick movement in response to a light signal. In one group, this response was executed against a light counterweight of 500 gm, and in another group a counterweight of 1,000 gm was used. After a training period, the weight was increased to 1,000 gm for the first group, and decreased to 500 gm for the second group. On the subsequent test trials, the light-to-heavy group decreased the extent of the key press distance, and the heavy-to-light group increased by about the same amount. These results are exactly those predicted by the reafference principle.

In Chapter 8, it was pointed out that active movements are superior to passive movements in acquiring adaptation to various forms of sensory arrangement. To account for these findings, Held (1961) extended the reafference principle by introducing a memory component that would allow it to deal with changes over time. This component he termed the *correlation storage*, and described its role as follows:

The Correlation Storage acts as a kind of memory which retains traces of previous combinations of concurrent efferent and reafferent signals. The currently monitored efferent signal is presumed to select the trace combinations containing the identical efferent part and to reactivate the reafferent trace combined with it (p. 30).

A comparator device then compares the current reafferent signal with a revived reafference (i.e. one previously associated with the current command signal) which is selected from the correlation storage. Future performance is dependent on the results of this comparison. As discussed in Chapter 8, adaptation proceeds faster in the case of active movements because the efferent signal 'addresses' the appropriate reafferent traces within the correlation storage and allows them to be accessed more rapidly than in passive movement when the efference copy is absent.

Necessary features of a theory of volition

On the basis of the previous discussion, it is possible to identify at least four hypotheses that are central to an adequate theory of volition. Each of these hypotheses, as we have seen above, is reasonably well supported by empirical data. They are summarized below:

1. *The voluntary act begins with some mental representation of the movements to be performed.* This has been labelled variously by different writers: William James and von Holst called it an 'image'; Miller *et al.* used the term 'plan'; for Luria (1966) it was a 'motor plan'. When the voluntary act is comparatively novel, it is likely that this mental representation is of the sensory consequences of the components involved in the action; but as the movement sequence becomes more practised, it is probable that some more limited representation of the effects of the sequence is sufficient to set it in motion. As stated in Chapter 14, increasing levels of skill make diminishing demands upon the limited capacity of conscious, 'closed-loop' control.

2. *Voluntary behaviour is always learned.* As Kimble and Perlmuter (1970) put it: '... unless we wish to believe in some pretty exotic innate ideas, it is always necessary for a response to have occurred on some other basis for the individual to have the image or plan necessary for a voluntary act' (p. 368).

3. *Voluntary behaviour requires the presence of some kind of comparator or test mechanism.* This is necessary in order that we may monitor our actions from moment to moment to gauge their present status in relation to the ends they seek to achieve. This mechanism not only guides the action but also provides the stop-rule, as indicated both by Miller *et al.* in their TOTE unit and by von Holst in the reafference principle.

4. To account for the advantages conferred by active movements in acquiring adaptation to conditions of sensory rearrangement, *it is necessary to postulate the existence of some storage system.* The function of this system, as in the case of Held's correlation storage, would be to retain traces of efferent signals *together with* their reafferent consequences. For a further discussion of such a mechanism, see Reason (1978).

The voluntary–involuntary distinction

As with other words taken from everyday language to serve in a scientific context, the terms 'involuntary' and 'voluntary' lack precision. We know, for example, that sneezing and blinking are generally taken as involuntary responses; yet in both cases, as in many other forms of apparently involuntary behaviour, we can exercise a degree of voluntary control over them. As Sherrington (1906) wrote: 'the transition from reflex action to volitional is not abrupt and sharp.' Nor, as we have already seen in Chapter 14, is the transition from the voluntary to the comparatively involuntary a clear-cut one either. Typing is generally taken as a voluntary activity, yet the skilled typist, as in the case of other highly practised operators, is executing large segments of the task quite automatically. Even in these relatively obvious examples of involuntary and voluntary behaviour, there is some confusion as to the distinction being drawn.

It seems more appropriate to assume that the terms 'involuntary' and 'voluntary' do not refer to discrete states, but to the extremes of a dimension along which we may exercise varying degrees of conscious control. As stated previously in this chapter, a voluntary response begins as involuntary and acquires its volitional aspect through the gradual development of ideomotor control. But with increasing practice, voluntary acts recede from consciousness, and, in this sense, become more and more involuntary as increasing automaticity is achieved.

We can also suggest that a similarly graded dimension exists between the notions of active and passive movement. An activity like walking is clearly under some form of internal control, even for the sleep walker or the person acting under hypnotic suggestion. At the other extreme, a passenger's movements are externally controlled when he is being transported passively in some vehicle. He can select the vehicle and the destination, but he has little or no control over his immediate state of locomotion. The vehicle operator, however, is in quite a different position. Unlike the passenger, he is an integral part of the vehicle control 'loop', and although the reafference associated with his controlling actions is initially different from that encountered in biologically 'natural' conditions, new efferent–reafferent connections are soon acquired, so that the experienced driver or pilot is essentially an active agent even though he is being moved by means other than his own limbs. This distinction is revealed most dramatically in relation to motion sickness susceptibility. Although both the car driver and his passengers are exposed to the same atypical force environment, only the latter are likely to experience symptoms. It has been argued elsewhere (Reason and Brand, 1975) that this immunity to car sickness enjoyed by the driver is conferred by the high degree of voluntary control he has over the vehicle.

In conclusion, it is worth dwelling briefly on the relationship between the involuntary–voluntary distinction, on the one hand, and the conscious–unconscious (or subconscious) distinction, on the other. As Hilgard (1977) points out, the correspondence between these two continua is an inexact one. When a particular course of action is chosen deliberately and carried out purposefully, we have an experience of conscious action. In this case, voluntary action and conscious control appear almost synonymous. But in highly skilled activity, performance is only intermittently under closed-loop conscious control; for the remainder, actions are run off largely automatically, leaving consciousness free to deal with something quite other than the task in hand. During the course of these routinized or habitual activities, it is not uncommon to find our actions deviating markedly from our current intentions. A frequently occurring 'slip of action' is one in which we fail to apply focal attention to the activity at some critical juncture, so that the guidance of action falls by default under the control of some 'strong' motor program. In other words, we find ourselves performing some frequently or recently executed sequence that is quite inappropriate for the current plan of action. William James (1890) wrote of absent-minded people who go to their bedrooms with the intention of dressing for dinner and end up getting into bed '... merely because that was the habitual issue of the first few movements when performed at a later hour'. A more detailed discussion of how these everyday slips and lapses can provide important clues about the underlying control mechanisms for action is given in Reason (1977b, 1979). Readers wishing to pursue the question of how controls over action can be modified by such conditions as hysteria, or by the use of hypnosis, are recommended to consult the excellent account given by Hilgard (1977).

Chapter 16
Remembering

Introduction

The effects of experience, and indeed the facts of learning, obviously imply that the objects, people and events we encounter are received and registered in some more or less enduring form and may be later utilized in behaviour. On the other hand, much of everyday experience leads us to suppose that retention of past events is far from perfect (we learn only slowly, and we forget) and varies in amount and quality, both from person to person and within the same person at different times. The obvious questions, then, with which the layman and the psychologist are both concerned are: how do we remember, in the sense both of retaining material and of using it later? How, and why, do we forget what we have seen or heard or otherwise learned? Why are there inter-individual and intra-individual differences in the efficiency of remembering? Although this chapter will to some extent deal separately with these questions, they are in fact closely related: for example, what we know of the phenomena of forgetting will obviously influence our view of the nature of remembering, as will our observation of individual differences.

Historically, psychological interest in memory has come from many traditions, including both the Gestalt and the associationist school, which have sought to extend to memory the principles of organization and association derived from the study of perception and learning. Its progress has been inspired, perhaps above all, by the work of two men, Ebbinghaus (1885) and Bartlett (1932). Ebbinghaus in effect founded the experimental investigation of memory, studying the learning and retention of simple material under rigidly controlled conditions. In an effort to render memory phenomena amenable to precise scientific investigation, he employed himself as a highly trained and highly motivated subject, and devised as his material the now famous 'nonsense syllables', consonant–vowel–consonant trigrams such as VUZ or MEP, which it was hoped excluded the effects of prior learning or familiarity. In reaction to this strongly disciplined but obviously limited approach, Bartlett set out to show that memory for meaningful material could also be studied usefully in the laboratory, but in a way bridging the gap between the laboratory and 'real life', and that its study revealed processes which the Ebbinghaus approach could not reveal – notably, the prevalence of 'effort after meaning' in a subject's attempts to retain and recall. Where Ebbinghaus had used nonsense-syllable lists as his basic materials, Bartlett used a variety of materials, pictures and prose passages, often with marked idiosyncrasies both of content and of style; his data were based chiefly on *successive reproduction* of the learned material by the same subject over a period of time, and on *serial reproduction*, in which one subject's reproduction of an original would be passed to a second for memorizing, the reproduction of the second subject on to a third, and so on.

There are in fact very many different situations which have been studied by psychologists under the general title 'memory'. These range through situations involving immediate recall of single stimuli (little different from tachistoscopic perception, discussed in Chapter 10), the recall of lists of items (serial learning) or paired items (paired-associate learning), memory for connected prose or poetry, and the use of previously acquired knowledge in reasoning or problem solving (semantic memory), to the clinically observed phenomena of 'repression', amnesia and fugues. The evidence presented here will be mainly experimental rather than clinical, and it will also be concerned with verbal memory rather than with 'sensory memory' – memory for visual or other sensory events not mediated by language – or with motor memory. Also not considered in this chapter is the important question of the physiological processes of neural *consolidation* which may underlie the formation, maintenance and, perhaps, abolition of 'memory traces'. For discussion of all these areas, and of the Ebbinghaus and Bartlett traditions, see Baddeley (1976).

There are three components of memory which need to be distinguished in principle, although they are not always readily distinguishable in practice. First, if any incoming stimulus is to be remembered it must in the first place be *registered* – learned, or in some sense 'put into storage'. Second, the registered event must be *retained in storage*, rather than lost from it. Third, when the memory item is needed, it must be *retrieved* from storage: in other words, it needs to be not only *available*, in that it has been registered and retained in storage, but also *accessible*, in that it can be 'found' when it is needed. The 'tip-of-the-tongue' phenomenon, or the 'feeling of knowing' experienced in everyday life, bears witness to the reality of this distinction:

it's a common experience to be unable to produce a word or a name although we are aware that we know it and perhaps certain of its characteristics such as number of syllables or initial letter, and although we recognize it with a feeling of certainty if it is produced by someone else or in a dictionary. These common experiences have been discussed and explored by Brown and McNeill (1966) and by Hart (1965). Another basis for the distinction between availability and accessibility is that different methods of measuring retention yield different estimates of memory. One popular method is that of *unaided recall*, in which the subject is required simply to produce previously learned items 'from memory' without any specific cues or hints as to their identity. Another method is that of recognition, in which the subject is shown a number of items and is required to select, from among them, the item or items originally learned. Often a recognition test yields evidence of retention when unaided recall does not; clearly in such a case the material was stored, but required a more sensitive test than that of unaided recall to assist its retrieval.

We shall refer to the distinction between storage and retrieval, at least implicitly and often explicitly, throughout this chapter, particularly in the section concerned with forgetting. However, for a fuller treatment of its special problems, see, for example, Tulving (1968); Baddeley (1976); M. W. Eysenck (1977).

Short-term and long-term memory

Memory and learning

We can only speak of remembering, or forgetting, an item when it has once been registered. It can be said to have been remembered when, having once been registered, it can be recalled or recognized at a later time. It can be said to have been forgotten when, having been registered, it cannot later be recalled. If we wish to study the phenomena of memory, therefore, we must take care that the material which is to be remembered has been registered in the first place: that is, to distinguish memory from learning or from perception.

There are essentially two ways of effecting this distinction. One is to require a subject to learn some material, so that the learning trials themselves constitute evidence of registration, and then to examine performance at a later time to see whether the learned material has been retained. The other method is to present for retention material which is so simple that it must surely be registered – a single word or a three-digit number or a simple picture: items which can certainly be reproduced immediately after presentation. Such material has been described as *subspan* because it is said to be within the span of apprehension – the amount of a given type of material which can be taken in and immediately reproduced after a single brief presentation (see, for example, Woodworth and Schlosberg, 1954). Some experiments in remembering occupy an intermediate position in that they study characteristics of the retention of *supra*-span material, such as a ten-digit number, presented only once (Hebb, 1961; Melton, 1963). It is not clear to what extent such experiments are studying characteristics of learning as well as, or rather than, characteristics of retention; thus, although they are of undoubted importance, they will not be included for consideration in this treatment of remembering.

Experiments on remembering tend, therefore, to be of two different kinds, one involving short-term recall of simple items and the other involving longer-term recall of more complex material which has been previously learned. In everyday life one can readily encounter situations similar to these extremes. A frequently quoted example of short-term memory concerns the dialling of an unfamiliar telephone number; we can remember the number, after reading or hearing it, for long enough to dial, but cannot remember it if asked a few minutes later. At the opposite extreme, our own address (a reasonably complicated series of numbers and words) is so well learned that we can reproduce it apparently without effort if required to do so. From introspective evidence, then, as well as from rather marked differences in the results obtained in experiments of the two kinds, one might suppose that different processes of remembering are involved in the two situations; and this distinction has indeed been made, both in psychological terms and in terms of the underlying processes which have been said to be involved.

Two-store theories of memory

One of the earliest to distinguish between *short-term* and *long-term* memory was William James (1890). He notes that 'as a rule sensations outlast for some little time the objective stimulus which occasioned them': this corresponds to the physiological after-image, and our consciousness of the after-sensation he terms elementary, or primary, memory. If a stimulus lasts for a sufficient length of time it produces a more durable image, which may pass out of consciousness but which can be recalled to it later; James termed this memory proper, or secondary memory. It is defined as 'the knowledge of an event or fact of which meantime we have not been thinking, with the additional consciousness that we have thought or experienced it before'. Secondary memory is thus the recurrence of an image which we know belongs to the past; primary memory is of events which belong to the psychological present, which have occurred 'just now'. Primary memory fades with time; secondary memory, if it has been established at all, is at any rate much less susceptible to decay (we shall return to the hypothesis of decay over time at later stages).

Later proponents of the two-process account of memory have included Broadbent (1958), Treisman (1964b), Waugh and Norman (1965) and Atkinson and Shiffrin (1971). Although the accounts given by different writers vary in detail, they are alike in comparing memory to a storage system comprising two stores, the relation between which, summarized very simply, is shown in Figure 16.1. Any incoming stimulus, when it is registered, enters a short-term or primary memory store (which we may call STS), and may or may not pass further into a long-term or secondary memory store (LTS). If the item does not enter LTS it will soon be lost, since STS has only a limited retention capacity. A recently presented item may, then, be in STS and LTS at one and the same time, or in STS alone; a less recently presented item may be in LTS alone or may have been forgotten – that is, it may have disappeared from STS without having entered LTS. We shall not consider here whether it is possible for items to be lost from LTS; in general it has been assumed that LTS has virtually unlimited capacity. One item may be more likely than another to enter LTS because it was presented

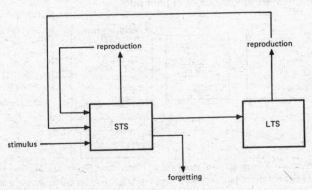

Figure 16.1   A simple model of memory

with greater intensity or for a longer period (James, 1890); because it has been rehearsed while in STS (Waugh and Norman, 1965; Atkinson and Shiffrin, 1971); or because the system is 'set' to select certain items rather than others for storage (Broadbent, 1958). We shall return to the notion of selective retention later in this chapter; it will not be our concern here except to state that two-process theorists generally argue that if selection occurs it does so at a stage between STS and LTS, not before STS, which is catholic in its acceptance.

As a supplement to this very simple statement it may be useful to refer briefly to some additional complexities of the two-process account (generally known as the 'modal model') exemplified by Atkinson and Shiffrin (1971). Their position is represented diagrammatically in Figure 16.2. For a full discussion of the model their article should be consulted; but a few comments can briefly be made here. First, incoming stimuli are shown not as entering STS directly but as passing first through one of a number of 'sensory registers' (depending upon the sensory form of the stimuli). These registers form a *pre-categorical* memory stage, since information in them is hypothesized to be held in a 'raw' or uncategorized state for an extremely brief interval; the registers concerned with visual and auditory stimuli have been termed *iconic* and *echoic* respectively. We shall not deal here with these precategorical stores, but a great deal of work has been devoted to demonstrating their existence and studying their operation, work which is reviewed, for example, by Baddeley (1976) and Neisser (1967). Once material has entered STS it is held to be categorized or *coded*: for example, the capacity of STS for verbal material is a matter of the number of *words* to be held, not the number of syllables or of phonemes.

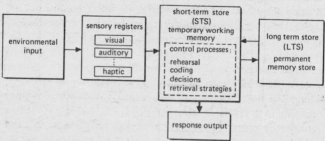

Figure 16.2   A detailed two-store theory of memory. (From Atkinson and Shiffrin, 'The control of short-term memory'. Copyright © 1971 by Scientific American, Inc. All rights reserved)

Second, the role of STS is shown as crucial for the operation of LTS, in two ways. Incoming information cannot gain access to LTS except via STS; and material 'needed' from LTS must re-enter STS in order to be produced as a response. It is in STS that rehearsal occurs, and that coding strategies are implemented, although as we shall see more elaborate coding is reserved for items which enter LTS.

Finally, it should be pointed out that 'STS', as a hypothesized store or stage of processing, and 'short-term memory' are not synonymous. STS is said to be of extremely limited capacity, so that most short-term memory situations will involve both STS and LTS: there are very few experimental situations which can be safely assumed to represent the operation of STS alone.

While the 'modal model' of memory has been a very popular one, it is not universally accepted. Even in its heyday, from the early 1960s to the early 1970s, there have been other theorists who have argued for an essential continuity between short-term and long-term memory (for example, Melton, 1963; Gruneberg, 1970). Not all the evidence regarding short-term memory performance supports the distinctions drawn between STS and LTS. First, STS is said to be of limited capacity, in terms both of the number of items which it can contain and of the length of time for which they can be held, while LTS is of virtually unlimited capacity; but methods of estimating STS capacity are open to question (Watkins, 1974; Baddeley and Hitch, 1976), as is the notion of memory loss from STS 'with time' (Waugh and Norman, 1965). Second, it has been argued that while memory in both STS and LTS is categorical or coded, the type of coding differs for the two stores: coding in STS is said to be on the basis of the *acoustic* properties of the material (put simply, its sound) while coding in LTS is *semantic*, based upon the meaning of the material, its interrelations and its verbal associates. However, although many studies have supported this distinction others have reported evidence of acoustic coding in LTS (Klein, 1972) and semantic coding in STS (Shulman, 1972); it seems at least arguable that the choice of coding strategy is to some extent dependent upon the characteristics of the task (we shall return presently to the discussion of types, or levels, of coding, and their flexibility of use). Finally, rehearsal of items in STS has been said to be crucial for their entry to LTS; but there is some evidence from studies of amnesia that long-term memory performance may be normal even when short-term memory (for example, digit span) is grossly defective (Shallice and Warrington, 1970). Thus, while none of these difficulties neces- sarily involves the discarding of the modal model of memory, the evidence for the existence of distinct stores is less than compelling. Moreover, extension of the modal model to anything other than verbal memory presents further problems of interpretation. Because of problems such as these, many workers have sought other approaches to the conceptualization of memory processes. Notably, there has been an interest in the concepts of *levels of processing* and of *working memory*: concepts which we shall now consider.

Levels of processing and 'working memory'

It is clear that in the perception and storage of events there are several levels at which material may be processed, ranging from the apprehension of such physical characteristics as brightness and loudness, through the recognition of words and of category membership, to the abstraction of meaning via the matching of stimulus items with already stored information – the memorizer's 'knowledge' or his 'semantic memory'.

In an extremely influential paper, Craik and Lockhart (1972) proposed an approach to memory which avoids the assumption of separate stores and instead relates the durability, as well as the characteristics, of memory directly to its level of processing. Rehearsal, they argue, may maintain a memory trace, but cannot strengthen it. Increased durability comes only with 'deeper' processing: processing, that is, which is principally on the basis of cognitive and semantic, rather than structural, properties of the stimulus material. It might be argued that this is an argument not in fact very far removed from that of the modal model, in that the analysis of 'depth' tends in practice to be in terms of two or three levels of processing – for example, acoustic patterning, phonemic coding and semantic coding – which would be predicted also by the modal model. However, there are significant, and useful, differences between the two. For one thing, within a 'levels-of-processing' approach there is scope for considerable refinement in the description of processing levels without the need for postulation of more separate stores to accompany them; indeed, depth of processing can be viewed as essentially a continuum rather than as a succession of stages. For another, Craik and Lockhart suggest that while processing may characteristically involve a passage through successive levels of analysis from 'shallow' to 'deep', levels are to some extent independent: material may be directly processed at a deep level, for example, without the necessity (apart from logical necessity) of being processed first at all shallower levels. The depth at which material is processed depends largely upon task demands, and upon the nature of the task material.

In addition to levels of processing, Craik and Lockhart hypothesize a 'primary memory' system, which is rather different from the primary memory or STS of the modal model, but virtually identical to that proposed by William James. It is said to be a *central processor*, of limited capacity, which has the function of maintaining stimulus information at one level of processing – of *rehearsing* it, of retaining it in *consciousness*, of maintaining *attention* upon it. Primary memory is flexible, in that it can operate at any level of processing; its capacity, and in particular the units or 'chunks' in which it operates, are determined by the depth of processing involved.

The notion of a flexible central processor or 'working memory' has been further explored, notably by Baddeley and Hitch (1974). Because of its association with consciousness and attention deployment, working memory is relevant not only to short-term memory situations but also to long-term memory and to such behaviour as verbal reasoning and prose comprehension. Baddeley and Hitch set out to examine the role of working memory by requiring their subjects to carry out tasks of this kind while at the same time performing an additional task also involving working memory; the memory load of the additional task could be varied and its effect upon performance at the main task observed. For example, subjects might be asked to view a sequence of digits and to write them down either individually, or in sequences of three, or in sequences of six: in the latter cases, obviously, progressively greater loads are placed upon working memory since subjects must wait until a number of digits have been presented, and 'hold' the earlier digits, before writing them down. Baddeley and Hitch found that a heavy load on working memory does affect performance in the main task, although even holding six items in memory does not produce complete breakdown in performance at the main task and holding three items produces little or no impairment. It would appear plausible then to argue that a 'working memory' system is involved in a variety of tasks, and that it is of limited capacity; but its total capacity is clearly greater than the traditional 'memory span' of six or seven items, and far greater than the capacity of two or three items proposed for the STS of a modal model.

From these and other findings Baddeley and Hitch propose a *dual short-term memory system*, comprising a working memory akin to the central processor of Craik and Lockhart, and in addition an *articulatory rehearsal loop* similar to that proposed by Atkinson and Shiffrin. This 'loop' provides extra capacity for two or three items, making no demands upon the central processor; and it is when items are stored in the loop that the phonemic characteristics of the stored material, and also such factors as word length, are likely to be important. To some extent, then, their proposed system brings together the primary memory hypotheses of Craik and Lockhart on the one hand, and Atkinson and Shiffrin on the other; and the notions of working memory and levels of processing have already had some success in accounting for some of the observed phenomena of short-term and long-term memory. Nevertheless, these theoretical positions are still in the early stages of application and testing, and the levels-of-processing approach in particular is at present controversial; its ultimate successfulness, like that of modal models, is still uncertain. One important concomitant of the processing-depth hypothesis, and an essential one for its development, is exploration of the processing or coding strategies which are available, particularly for the organization of long-term memory; this will be the concern of the next section.

Long-term memory organization

Verbal and imaginal coding

It has already been suggested that the type of processing undergone by material in memory is determined largely by the nature of the material and of the task. For example, material of high meaningfulness, such as connected prose, may lend itself to deeper processing than low meaningfulness material, such as lists of arbitrary and unrelated three-letter sequences; and tasks calling for immediate recall of very few items may invite less deep processing than those which involve the recall of lengthy item lists after a delay of hours, days or weeks. In the study of long-term memory the tasks, and the material, used are very diverse, and it follows that general statements about 'the nature of organization in memory' are unwise to the point of folly. Nevertheless, at least one general statement may be made – that in any long-term memory task, from the simplest to the most complex, some tendency to organization is evident on the part of the memorizer.

Largely because of the considerable bias in memory research towards the use of verbal material, there is a strong tendency for organization to be discussed in terms of intraverbal association; but while verbal coding is undoubtedly important in memory organization it is not the only possibility, and recently there has been renewed interest in the role which imagery may play in encoding. This involves the use of sensory representation – for example, visual or auditory images – rather than verbal. As Neisser (1972) has defined it, 'a subject is imaging whenever he employs some of the same cognitive processes that he would use in perceiving, but when the stimulus input that would normally give rise to such perception is absent'.

Clearly, imagery can greatly aid memory. Paivio (1971) has shown, for example, that words which are readily associated with imagery (as evidenced by subjects' ratings) are more easily learned and recalled than other words, and that the association of 'imagery-proneness' with ease of learning and recall is as great as, perhaps greater than, that of meaningfulness or familiarity. Moreover, for certain kinds of material, such as faces, imagery may be virtually the only coding means available.

There has been a tendency to think of sensory memory as a highly specific, essentially 'photographic' record of events or stimuli, and therefore as more superficial than is typical of verbal coding; an example of such sensory memory is the phenomenon of 'eidetic imagery', reported by nineteenth- and early twentieth-century investigators and more recently revisited by, for example, Haber (1969). Eidetic imagery is characterized by a persistent and detailed visual image of a real-life scene or picture immediately after its presentation; it is experienced as occurring 'outside' the imaginer, and, unlike a vivid after-image, it can be scanned by eye movement. It has been suggested that eidetic imagery, which recent investigators have estimated to occur in perhaps 7–10 per cent of children and much more rarely in adults, is a primitive mode of memory which is replaced, with intellectual development, by the more sophisticated, largely verbal, coding methods of normal adult memory. However, if this is so, it is not necessarily the case that all, or even much, of visual memory is of this primitive type. For example, memory for faces may be extremely accurate over long periods of time, a finding which suggests the occurrence of deep, though at least largely imaginal, processing. One current view, therefore, is that imagery may function as a coding system alongside verbal coding, independent of it and with equal status and sophistication of processing (Paivio, 1971); another is that imaginal and verbal coding may coexist as part of the same, unitary semantic memory system, serving a 'common central processor', as M. W. Eysenck (1977) has termed it, which is itself neither verbal nor imaginal but more abstract in nature.

Ordering and categorization

Perhaps the simplest mode of organization is the use of order. Subjects show a marked tendency to recall items in their order of presentation, even when free recall is permitted; and recall is more efficient when material is repeatedly presented for learning in the same order rather than in varying orders on different trials. Consistencies in subjects' order of recall over successive trials have been found to relate positively to performance, and also to be more marked for 'fast learners' than for 'slow learners'. However, it is not altogether clear whether consistency in the order of recall ('subjective organization', as Tulving, 1962, termed it) is necessary for free-recall learning or simply a by-product of it; for a discussion of this point, see Postman (1972).

The use of order is most notable in the recall of comparatively short lists of unrelated items. When lists are somewhat longer and comprise meaningful items such as words, an important characteristic of list recall is that subjects tend to *categorize* items as they learn, and in particular to use category information to aid retrieval at the time of recall. Classic studies, such as those of Bousfield (1953) and Tulving and Pearlstone (1966), explored this tendency in the free recall of lists of words, each of which fell into one of a number of categories: for example, a list might contain equal numbers of proper names, animal names, the names of professions and the names of vegetables. Using a list of this nature, with the words presented in random order, one typically finds *clustering* in recall: that is, subjects tend to produce, first, most or all of the words belonging to one category; then the members of another, and so on. Clustering appears to facilitate recall, in that when one word from a given category is retrieved it 'cues' the rest of the category members in much the same way that an experimenter may cue recall by giving his subjects the *category names* of the words on the list. Tulving and Pearlstone, investigating the cueing technique, found that its effectiveness in enhancing recall lies in the fact that 'uncued' subjects, unlike those who have been supplied with cues, omit whole categories in recall but are equally efficient in recalling the members of those categories which they retrieve at all. The usefulness of categorization is rather dependent upon the number and the size of categories implicit in the material; if list length is constant, recall is generally most efficient when there are a relatively large number of categories each represented by a relatively small number of items. It has been suggested that this is because, when a large number of category members must be retrieved, the search through memory for them is less systematic (Patterson, 1972). This generalization, on the other hand, is limited by the factor of 'category exhaustion': if the members of a category are well known and are *all* represented on the list – for example, the seven days of the week or the twelve months of the year – recall is greatly enhanced and category size becomes an advantage.

The studies so far discussed were concerned with recall of lists into which the experimenters had themselves built a category system; but similar findings have been reported for recall of lists of essentially unrelated words which the subject categorizes for himself (see, for example, Mandler, 1967). Studies of this kind also indicate that *hierarchies* of superordinate and subordinate categories may be used; this bears upon the analysis of 'semantic memory', to be discussed later.

The use of mnemonics

Mnemonics are essentially schemes for making material memorable by coding its 'surface' rather than by deep semantic processing. Hunter (1977) has characterized mnemonic systems as 'rich perceptual chains', rather than the 'rich conceptual maps' of semantic memory. Perhaps because they have tended to be regarded as a matter of tricks or parlour games, their psychological study has not been extensive and has been more often anecdotal than experimental. Nevertheless, they have been of interest to scholars and teachers throughout the ages, and most people at one time or another have found them useful in everyday life.

Most, if not all, mnemonic systems represent one, or a combination of two types of coding: *reduction coding* and *elaboration coding*. Reduction coding serves to reduce the amount of information to be stored and thus its memory load; elaboration coding, on the other hand, adds information in order to make the material more memorable, for example by placing it in a linguistic context, or by the addition of visual imagery. The most extreme form of a reduction code is probably the time-honoured knot in one's handkerchief: it codes material simply as 'something to be remembered', without further detail, and of course has the drawback that such extreme reduction may remind us that we have something to remember without helping us to remember what it was. A more helpful example might be the acronym SOHCAHTOA, which has enabled the writer to remember for some twenty-five years, with no further learning trials, no practical application and very little comprehension, the relation between the lengths of the sides of a right-angled triangle and the sine, cosine and tangent of its acute angles. Mnemonics involving elaboration coding include Every Good Boy Deserves Favour and All Cows Eat Grass, to indicate the musical notes on the lines of the treble clef (E, G, B, D, F) and those in the spaces of the bass clef (A, C, E, G) respectively. Many mnemonics involve both reduction and elaboration coding: for example, 'Richard of York gained battles in vain', a mnemonic for the colours of the visible spectrum in ascending order of wavelength (red, orange, yellow, green, blue, indigo, violet). Reduction coding extracts the initial letters of the colours in order – R, O, Y, G, B, I, V – and elaboration coding then supplies an easily memorable sentence in which successive initial letters correspond to them.

The examples above illustrate the use of *verbal* elaboration coding; imaginal coding is also employed in elaboration mnemonics, and has in fact been rather more often studied. Two methods of imaginal coding, both of them visual, are particularly well known. One, the 'method of loci', has been known since classical times, and involves memorizing first a sequence of locations: for example, the rooms of one's own house, the shelves of a cupboard, a row of framed pictures in a gallery. Each item to be remembered is imagined in one of these locations; at the time of retrieval, the sequence of locations is searched and the associated images can be recalled. In the other, 'pegword' method, a sequence is first learned in which each number is associated with a rhyming word which is capable of giving rise to vivid visual imagery: for example, 'one is a bun, two is a shoe, three is a tree, four is a door' (this method therefore involves not only visual but also perhaps auditory, and certainly verbal, coding.) Each item to be recalled is then associated with the rhyming word corresponding to its number. If we are learning a list of animal names, for example, we may visualize first an elephant (sitting on a bun); second, a tiger (wearing shoes); third, a camel (up a tree); fourth, a donkey (leaning against a door), and so on. These methods can be extremely effective, provided that the initial sequence of loci or pegwords is well learned, both items and cues are clearly visualized and their association is one of interaction, forming a single integrated image. They aid the memorizer, and memory-searcher, by telling him, in effect, 'where to look' to find the desired information.

To some extent mnemonic devices represent features of 'normal' memory – the imaginal and verbal semantic coding which is apparent in long-term and, to some extent and in some circumstances, short-term memory. Generally, however, they seem to be of very limited usefulness in 'everyday' situations or in any situation in which the material to be committed to memory is more complex than a list of unrelated items. This is very clearly argued by Hunter (1977), whose distinction between 'rich perceptual chains' and 'rich conceptual maps' has already been quoted. The distinction is well illustrated by his comparison of the respective techniques adopted by two men, both possessing exceptional powers of memory: first, S. V. Shereshevskii, a professional mnemonist studied by Luria (1969), and second, A. C.

Aitken, an eminent academic mathematician studied by Hunter himself. Of their methods of memory he says:

The chief similarity between Aitken and Shereshevskii is that each comprehends materials in terms of a multiplicity of unconventional properties, knits these properties into fairly unconventional patterns, and durably retains these patterns so as to be able to reconstruct the original materials. The chief difference is the *kind* of property involved and the *kind* of pattern woven. Characteristically, Shereshevskii's kind of property is perception-like, i.e. particular sensory qualities and particular imagined objects: his kind of pattern is the chain, i.e. short-run links between successively encountered items. Characteristically, Aitken's kind of property is conceptual: his kind of pattern is the panorama or map, i.e. long-run groupings of items into overlapping multilayered configurations (1977, p. 162).

It may be that Hunter's distinction between 'perceptual' and 'conceptual' properties, though not that between 'chains' and 'maps', should be viewed with some caution in view of the growing body of opinion, referred to earlier, that imaginal coding should not be seen as inferior to, less 'semantic' or more superficial than, verbal coding. Nevertheless it seems fair to conclude that mnemonic devices have not only their uses but also their limitations and drawbacks; as Hunter put it, 'they involve us in focusing upon the kind of property, and kind of pattern, that has severely limited utility for productive thinking'.

Memory for connected language

Connected language differs from unrelated verbal material in that its components are interrelated in grammatical structure and in meaning: both syntactically and semantically, the identity and placement of items within connected language are not random but *probabilistic*. Language is *redundant* (to use the statistical term) and *predictable* (to use the psychological term, with its inclusion of subjective expectation as well as statistical relation), in that its units do not all occur with equal frequency and in that their order of occurrence is not random but is constrained by context. In English, for example, E is a more common letter than X, and 'dig' more common than 'axolotl'; Q is almost invariably followed by U, 'the' is more often followed by a noun than by an adverb, the missing word in 'Happy —— Year' is more likely to be 'new' than 'old'.

The roles of syntax and semantics in aiding memory for prose have to some extent been studied separately, and their independent roles compared, most notably by *psycholinguists* who derive their psychological hypotheses from modern linguistic theories such as that of Chomsky (1965). We shall consider some of these studies, and their implications for the psychology of language, in Chapter 17. Here it can simply be stated that syntactic structure does aid learning and recall, but that its importance is probably considerably less than that of semantic structure – the meaningful relation of words in sentences.

At least since Bartlett's (1932) treatment of memory it has been clear that memory for connected language (and indeed memory for complex pictorial stimuli) is characterized by what he termed 'effort after meaning'. In learning a prose passage, for example, we try to understand its central ideas, and attempts at recall generally show evidence of *abstraction*: the recall is a precis of the original, in which the more important or striking features are retained and the less important ones lost. Bartlett argued that the process of abstraction, or summarizing, took place during retention of the material over time, and showed that the tendency to abstraction increased with successive attempts to reproduce the original, over what were often considerable lengths of time. More recent investigators (e.g. Gomulicki, 1956) have argued rather that abstraction occurs at input to memory rather than during the retention interval. Johnson (1970), for example, asked his subjects to precis a prose passage by eliminating its less important features; he then required them to learn the complete passage and to recall it after an interval which ranged, for different subjects, from fifteen minutes to sixty-three days. He found that less important items (those which had been omitted in precis) were less well recalled than more important items, but that they were not more rapidly forgotten over time. It is likely that Bartlett's finding of *progressive* abstraction during storage is due to his use of repeated reproduction attempts from the same subject, who may well be recalling his previous recall attempt rather than the original passage.

It has also been shown that the 'effort after meaning' involves not only abstraction 'with reduction' but also construction. For example, Barclay (1973) required his subjects to learn, and afterwards recognize, sentences which described the location of animals in a row: for example, 'the bear is to the left of the moose' and 'the cow is to the right of the bear'. In the recognition tests there was a high incidence of *false* recognition of sentences which had not been presented for learning but which were consistent with those which had been learned; for example, 'the cow is to the right of the moose'. Such evidence (for other studies see Barclay, 1973, and Baddeley, 1976) suggests strongly that subjects use the information which is presented to form a coherent semantic structure, from which other information may then be derived. In this case it would appear that the construction involved the use of visual imagery; however, visual imagery is not *necessarily* involved in construction, since similar false recognition effects have been shown for abstract material.

Whatever may be the medium of coding, it seems clear that in long-term memory items are stored semantically rather than merely as words, and this may well be true not only for connected language but also for relatively 'unrelated' verbal material. This has been demonstrated in experiments using polysemous words – that is, words which have more than one meaning, such as 'jam' – or words whose 'semantic emphasis' is varied by context. For example, the word 'piano' may be embedded in the sentence 'The man tuned the piano', to emphasize the musical function of the instrument, or in the sentence 'The man lifted the piano', to emphasize its weight; a cue to later recall of the word 'piano' might be 'something musical' or 'something heavy'. Words learned in a context stressing one meaning or emphasis are more readily recalled or recognized when a cue, or context, is supplied which stresses the same meaning, but much less readily when cue or context stresses a different meaning (e.g. Barclay *et al.*, 1974). The capacity of words to comprise a range of possible semantic emphases was termed by Barclay *et al.* 'semantic flexibility'; they argued that we learn a semantic emphasis rather than a word. As Baddeley (1976) suggests, 'the subject encodes the information to be remembered in terms of an area of *semantic space*, not in some specific location representing the dictionary definitions of the words in the sequence. Subjects do not learn words; they learn semantic interpretations based on the words presented' (pp. 298–9). Attempts to describe the possible organization of such 'semantic interpretations' in memory will be the concern of the following section.

Semantic memory

Semantic memory has been defined in a classic paper by Tulving (1972), who contrasted it with *episodic memory*, or memory of a specific event – a personal experience, or perhaps memory that an (already familiar) word is 'on the learning list' in a laboratory experiment. Semantic memory is defined as 'a mental thesaurus, organized knowledge a person possesses about words and other verbal symbols, their meanings and referents, about relations among them, and about rules, formulas, and algorhythms for the manipulation of these symbols, concepts, and relations' (p. 386). Clearly semantic memory is very highly organized and efficient, since information can be very rapidly retrieved from what must be a storage system of gigantic proportions: such questions as 'a dog is an animal – true or false?'; 'is "rolt" an English word?'; 'name a fruit beginning with P'; can be answered in a second or less. Much of the work on semantic memory, indeed, takes precisely this form – the experimenter asks 'general knowledge' questions and records the subject's response time.

Some investigations of what we now term semantic memory have been concerned with the analysis of meaning (see, for example, Osgood, Suci and Tannenbaum, 1957), or with its definition in terms of intraverbal associations, semantic relatedness of words being defined in terms of their *associative overlap* – the extent to which they evoked the same range and pattern of words in free association (Deese, 1965, 1970; Slobin, 1971). More recent studies have tended to attempt a description of semantic structure – that is, the possible form of the storage system, either in terms of verbal networks and categories or in terms of 'feature analysis'; such descriptions are often linked to computer simulation.

Models of semantic memory which stress the importance of networks and categories have in common the hypothesis that words which belong to the same category are in some sense 'stored together', and may be linked to subordinate and superordinate categories. One model of this type is the 'category search' model (Landauer and Freedman, 1968); this hypothesizes that words are stored in categories. When the subject is asked 'Is a dog an animal?' he scans the words stored in the 'animal' category to see if 'dog' is among them. Clearly, according to this model category size should influence response time, since the greater the number of words to be scanned, the longer it will take to determine whether the critical word is among them. Whether the correct response is 'yes' or 'no' would also be expected to influence response time; if the sought item is present, 50 per cent of the category members, on average, have to be scanned before it is discovered, while all members have to be scanned to determine that the item is absent. Thus one should find that response times are greater when categories are large and when the correct response is 'no'; this is supported by the data, but one difficulty is that an *interaction* has been reported between the two factors, category size having much more effect in the case of 'no' responses than in the case of 'yes' responses, a finding which is not readily explained in category-search terms.

An alternative, *'network'*, model has been proposed by Collins and Quillian (1969). They propose a hierarchical structure to semantic memory: words are stored in locations which indicate their superordinate and sub-

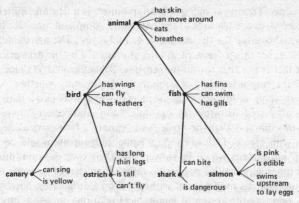

Figure 16.3 Portion of a hypothetical network in semantic memory. (From Collins and Quillian, 1969)

ordinate category relations. An example of a semantic network is shown in Figure 16.3.

The important factor in accessibility (and hence response time), according to this model, is not category size but *nesting*: retrieval of information requires a 'journey' from one node of the network to another. To answer the question 'Is a dog an animal?' the subject must determine that following the network up from 'dog' leads him to 'animal'; the further the journey – that is, the more nodes crossed – the longer the response time. Category size only appears to be important because small categories are often nested inside larger ones. Thus 'Is a collie a dog?' is more quickly answered than 'Is a collie an animal?'; according to the category-search model this is because the category 'animal' is larger than the category 'dog', but according to the network model it is because 'animal' is further away up the network. The closer words are to one another, therefore, the briefer should be response time; however, quite often the reverse is true in practice. This presents a considerable difficulty for the network model, but is predictable from the other main type of model, that which utilizes the notion of *feature analysis*.

According to the feature-analysis approach to semantic structure, storage of information is analogous to a dictionary or filing system. All words are stored separately (not in category-groups), each word with semantic 'features' attached to it. Along with the word 'canary', for example, might be stored entries such as: living; has skin; breathes; eats; moves; can fly; can sing; is yellow. To answer our specimen question 'Is a dog an animal?', the subject compares the features of the two words 'dog' and 'animal'; if there is substantial overlap the subject is able to reply 'yes'. The more similar the words, the easier this judgement will be, as predicted by the network model also; but this is not true for all judgements. Schaeffer and Wallace (1970) observed the response times of subjects in determining whether pairs of words were 'same' or 'different'. Some pairs of words were closer than others in terms of shared features: for example, 'dog' and 'canary' have more features in common than do 'oak' and 'canary'. It was predicted that although with greater feature overlap 'same' judgements would be faster, 'different' judgements would be slower, and their own data on 'different' response times support this prediction rather than that of network theory. The feature-analysis model is not without its own difficulties, however; for example, rejecting the notion of hierarchical relations, and thus any *directionality* of the relation between two words, means that if a canary is a bird, on the basis of overlap, a bird is also a canary!

The study of semantic memory is in its infancy, and it is not unfair to describe its achievements so far as modest (although Baddeley, 1976, and M. W. Eysenck, 1977, should be consulted for a fuller account). No one model so far devised can account for all the evidence available, and different models tend to be very much tied to the specific research paradigms adopted by their proposers. The data on which these models are based are also extremely limited, comprising almost exclusively decision times for two-word comparisons, with virtually no consideration of words other than nouns, let alone items other than words. Further, different models seem to be concerned with rather different aspects of decision and memory: category models are concerned with the structure of storage, feature-analysis models with the processing of information once it has been retrieved. Clearly, more analysis is needed of the separate processes of entry to storage, organization within it, and retrieval from it, with reference to a greater variety of material, before we can speak with any confidence about the storage of knowledge in semantic memory.

Forgetting

Decay

In our consideration of memory processes we have already mentioned certain ideas about forgetting. One such idea is that as time passes the traces left by outside events in the nervous system grow fainter until they can no longer be reactivated (except, of course, by a recurrence of the events which originally produced them); in other words, we forget with the passage of time. In a descriptive sense this is obviously true: memory performance does deteriorate as a (negatively accelerated) function of time since learning, a phenomenon classically demonstrated by Ebbinghaus and shown here in Figure 16.4. However, it should be noted that time is not in itself a variable which could explain changes in performance; the hypothesis is that the passage of time provides the opportunity for *trace decay*. E. L. Thorndike (1932) was the most notable of the supporters of this theory of forgetting. He suggested that one of the laws by which learning and remembering could be understood was, as he termed it, the Law of Exercise; when actions are repeatedly produced or events repeatedly experienced, they become stronger – better learned, more readily produced. When actions or events fall into disuse, and are no longer practised, they become weaker and finally 'lost' from memory.

Two points implied by this account merit explicit consideration. The first is that rehearsal – or repetition to oneself – of an item appears to function

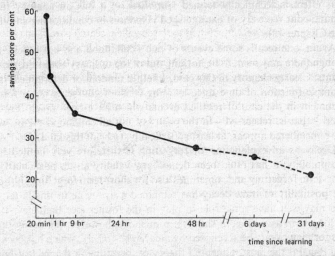

Figure 16.4   The rate of forgetting over time (data from Ebbinghaus, 1885). The 'savings score' represents the reduction in time needed for relearning, as opposed to original learning, of lists of nonsense syllables, expressed as a percentage of the original learning time

in much the same way as actual repeated presentations of the stimulus itself; to a certain extent rehearsal furnishes additional learning trials and so increases the probability that the material will be (relatively) permanently learned. The second point is that remembrance of an item is here equated with action – the active response of recalling. It is this second implication which has created severe problems for decay theory. As we have seen earlier in this chapter, it is necessary to distinguish between the *availability* and the *accessibility* of items in memory; this distinction is not readily handled by a simple explanation of forgetting in terms of 'fading through disuse'. Apart from the evidence already quoted (for example, the varying estimates of retention yielded by different methods of measurement), the most obvious difficulty for decay theory is perhaps, quite simply, that the same item may be recalled at one time, in one situation, and not in another. For example, one may be unable to remember a fact which suddenly and apparently spontaneously emerges into consciousness later on. Clearly the memory was for some reason inaccessible at first but had not 'faded away'. In experiments on learning, it is often noted that a subject is able to recall more items from a learning task after a brief rest interval than immediately after learning. This effect is technically termed *reminiscence*; it has an analogy in the spontaneous recovery of extinguished responses in conditioning situations (see Chapter 13).

Again, one recalls some events of one's childhood and not others, even though there may seem to be nothing out of the ordinary about the recalled events. Clearly memory in this case, whether random or determined, is not a simple function of time since learning (this, of course, is not a forceful argument in the case of recalled events which have been much 'brooded over' – that is, rehearsed – in the past; but not all childhood events which are remembered appear, at least superficially, to be of this kind).

Decay as an explanation of forgetting is therefore very limited in its acceptability; it has often been denied any validity at all, particularly for long-term forgetting and sometimes also for short-term forgetting, although the possibility of trace decay has remained a live issue in this latter area and may well have some role to play in the former (see Baddeley, 1976). In long-term as well as in short-term memory, however, the decay theory has for many years been eclipsed by *interference theory*, which has been and still remains the most influential theory of forgetting in the field of human learning: it is to this theory we now turn.

Interference theory

Although proponents of interference theory have often claimed great
generality for it, most of its development has been based upon very limited
experimental evidence, chiefly relating to the phenomena of *transfer*,
proaction and *retroaction*. It is useful to begin by defining these experimental
situations.

Transfer, as we saw in Chapter 13, may be defined as the effect (positive
or negative) of learning one task upon the learning of a second.

Proaction may be defined as the effect of learning one task upon the
retention of a second, subsequently learned. Thus, having learned French
may influence the ease with which we later learn Italian; this would be
evidence of transfer. Also, having learned French may influence our retention of the Italian which we learn later, quite apart from its possible effect
upon the actual learning. Proaction is therefore similar to but distinct from
transfer, the practical distinction lying chiefly in the measures taken of our
knowledge of the later task. A measure of transfer might be the number of
learning trials required for a particular task – a vocabulary list or a declen-
sion – to be learned to a suitable criterion; a measure of proaction might
be the percentage of the material, once learned to an agreed criterion, which
is recalled after an interval. Of course, there may be a difference between
performance at the last learning trial and performance at recall which is
irrespective of any effects of previous learning: for example, reminiscence
or its opposite, forgetting over time. Consequently, a control group of
subjects learns and recalls the second task without having learned the first,
and the difference between experimental and control subjects provides a
measure of proaction. It is worth noting that the term 'task' is here used quite
generally to refer to any material given to a subject to learn; it might be a
language vocabulary, a list of numbers, a poem, a motor skill such as
dart-throwing or car-driving. Laboratory studies, however, have generally
employed verbal-learning tasks.

Retroaction is defined as the effect of interpolated learning upon the
retention of a task previously learned: if we learn French and then Italian,
retroaction would refer to the effect which learning Italian might have upon
our retention of French. The measures used to assess retroaction are therefore measures of retention – recall, recognition, savings and so on – as in the
case of proaction. Negative retroaction and negative proaction (or retro-
active and proactive inhibition, as they are sometimes called) are therefore
examples of forgetting and have been much used in the explanation of

forgetting in terms of interference. Typical designs of experiments on transfer, proaction and retroaction are shown in Table 16.1.

Table 16.1
Experimental designs used to study (i) transfer, (ii) proaction and (iii) retroaction

(i) *Transfer*			
E group:	Learn task 1		Learn task 2
C group:	—		Learn task 2
(ii) *Proaction*			
E group:	Learn task 1	Learn task 2	Recall task 2
C group:	—	Learn task 2	Recall task 2
(iii) *Retroaction*			
E group:	Learn task 1	Learn task 2	Recall task 1
C group:	Learn task 1	—	Recall task 1

Evidence of *transfer* or of *proaction* is sought by comparing the performance of E and C groups in learning, or recalling, task 2. Evidence of *retroaction* is sought by comparing their final recall of task 1.

Naturally, the experimenter must attempt to ensure that subjects in both groups have *learned* task 1 (or task 2, in the case of proaction) to the same level, or at any rate must make allowances for any differences in original learning when analysing retention scores; this control is more straightforward in principle than in practice.

The amount of proaction or retroaction, and whether it is positive or negative, varies greatly from situation to situation and depends on several factors. One of these is the *amount or degree of learning* of the two tasks. In general, as far as retroaction is concerned, the better task 1 is learned the more resistant it is to negative retroaction, while the better task 2 is learned the more likely it is to cause negative retroaction (although this is true only up to a point; when task 2 is very well learned it becomes if anything rather less likely to interfere with recall of task 1). Somewhat similar findings have been reported for the case of negative proaction, although less unequivocally, perhaps because there are more difficulties in achieving adequate experimental control – for example, of degree of initial learning in experimental and control groups. The *time intervals* employed – between task 1 and task 2 learning, and between task 2 learning and the final recall of task 1 (retroaction) or task 2 (proaction) – may also be important, although investigations have often yielded conflicting results. The most consistent findings have concerned the interval between task 2 and final recall: in the case of negative proaction, a longer interval produces more forgetting, while in the case of retroaction there is no such relation.

Probably the most important factor is the *similarity* between tasks 1 and 2. Clearly, if the two tasks are identical, 'retroaction' and 'proaction' must be positive; yet it has long been held that when tasks are not identical proaction and retroaction are usually negative, and that their extent is greater when the tasks are similar than when they are dissimilar. This apparent contradiction (called, in the literature, the *similarity paradox*) is chiefly due to the fact that two types of similarity, at least, may be distinguished: *stimulus similarity* and *response similarity*. This distinction has already been made, in Chapter 13, in our discussion of transfer phenomena. Often – for example, in the serial learning of a list of items, or in learning a skill – stimulus and response aspects of performance are not easily separated since the same item in a series may act both as a response (to the preceding item) and as a stimulus (to the following item). The different effects of stimulus and response similarity can most easily be seen in *paired-associate* (P-A) learning, in which the subject is presented with items in pairs, his task being to learn the second item of the pair as a response to the first. On subsequent tests the subject is presented with the first stimulus item and is asked to produce the response item. The items used in this type of learning may be verbal, such as words or nonsense syllables; they may be numbers, or nonsense or meaningful diagrams. The pairs of items may be alike or different in nature: a list for learning may, for instance, be composed of paired nonsense syllables, or of verbal stimulus terms paired with numerical responses.

When material of this kind is employed in retroaction experiments it is possible to vary the stimulus and response similarity of tasks 1 and 2 independently. In an A–B, A–C design, as it is termed, the stimuli used in the two tasks are identical and the responses different; in an A–B, C–B design the responses are identical while the stimuli differ, while both are different in an A–B, C–D design. Retroaction and proaction experiments using these designs have produced findings similar to those obtained in transfer experiments and already described in Chapter 13. When stimuli are identical but responses differ, negative effects occur; response identity or very close similarity, with or without stimulus similarity, tends to produce positive effects. Psychologists interested in forgetting have generally used the A–B, A–C design: in this situation negative retroaction or negative proaction occurs, although it grows less as response similarity increases and becomes positive in direction as the responses of the two tasks approach identity.

From data such as these the 'interference' theorists (for example, McGeogh, 1932) argued that forgetting occurs because of *competition* among responses. In retroaction, for example, responses from task 2 compete for production with responses from task 1: when the subject tries to remember B as a response to A, he instead remembers C, the response learned to the same stimulus in the 'interfering task'. This response B is not 'lost' – it has simply been blocked by a stronger rival. Some later proponents of interference theory suggested that competition might be better described as a difficulty in *differentiating* responses from one task from those of the other. If the two tasks have been imperfectly learned, the 'task membership' of responses cannot be readily identified and responses from the wrong task may be produced at recall. With thorough learning of the two tasks, inappropriate responses at recall will be recognized and withheld; this is why, as we have seen, very thorough learning, or over-learning, of task 2 (in the retroaction paradigm) does not produce ever greater decrement in recall of task 1 and may even reduce the decrement shown. Thus, this version of the interference theory relates not to response competition in a molecular sense but to a global difficulty of task differentiation: as Ceraso (1967) termed it, 'crowding'. There is some evidence for either interpretation of interference, and some investigators have suggested that both types occur; for a discussion, see Baddeley (1976).

However, whether competition is viewed as specific or general there is a good deal of evidence that it is not by itself a sufficient explanation of the data. We shall mention only one important difficulty, which was pointed out by Barnes and Underwood (1959). These investigators evolved an experimental technique which they termed M M F R (or 'modified modified free recall', since it was itself a modification of a 'modified free recall' technique devised earlier by Briggs, 1954). After learning two tasks constructed according to the A–B, A–C design, their subjects were asked, when shown each stimulus term, to produce both the responses they had learned to that stimulus, in either order. They found, as interference theory would predict, that when subjects produced both responses task 2 responses were produced first; this clearly indicates that task 2 responses were stronger. However, they also found that even when given plenty of time to produce responses subjects recalled fewer from task 1 than from task 2. Since competition between responses was no longer applicable, it seemed as though some 'unlearning' of task 1 responses must have occurred; not only are rival responses stronger, but the original response itself has weakened.

How might such unlearning occur? Underwood (1964) suggested that the process is essentially one of extinction. When the subject is learning task 2 he often thinks of responses from task 1; if he produces these responses they are treated as incorrect, that is, non-reinforced, and so become less likely to occur. They may be non-reinforced and therefore extinguished even if they are not produced overtly but are simply thought of and then rejected (for a fuller discussion of 'implicit responses', see Barnes and Underwood, 1959).

The interference theory of forgetting has thus become a two-factor theory. First, there may be *competition* or *crowding* between the two tasks which results in recall of inappropriate items or, more commonly perhaps, failure to recall. Second, in the case of retroaction (but not in that of proaction, since there is no additional learning task between the learning and the recall of task 2), responses may prove inaccessible at the time of recall because they have been *unlearned* during the learning of an intervening task. These two factors between them account quite successfully for the empirical data on retroaction and proaction: for example, the difference between proaction and retroaction with respect to the effect of lengthening the interval between task 2 learning and final recall. It is hypothesized that crowding will become worse, and tasks less well differentiated, with a longer gap between learning and recall; so in the case of proaction, where crowding only is involved, a longer interval produces more interference. Unlearning, however, by analogy with extinction, is hypothesized to be *less* severe with a longer interval because of *spontaneous recovery* of the 'unlearned' responses; so in retro-action, where both factors are important, they work in opposition to each other, resulting in little or no consistent time effect. For further evidence in support of this interpretation, see Ceraso (1967).

Two-factor interference theory has been the dominant theory of forgetting for twenty years or more; however, in the last few years it has come increasingly under attack (see, for example, Postman and Underwood, 1973; Baddeley, 1976). On the one hand there have been doubts as to the adequacy of the concepts of competition or crowding and unlearning; as we have seen, it is not clear whether response competition is general, or specific, or both, and the interpretation of MMFR as providing a pure measure of unlearning, uncontaminated by competition, has also been challenged. On the other hand, while interference theory has been extended with some plausibility to other experimental tasks, such as serial learning and conditioning, it has proved disappointing as a predictor of *extra-experimental* interference effects – that is, in experiments where the source of inter- ference is experience outside the laboratory rather than a specific learning task within it. Where verbal material is being learned, it is reasonable to assume that the subject is learning it against a background of previously learned language habits, and retaining it perhaps against a background of language encountered during the retention interval: in other words, learning of a single list constitutes 'everyday proaction' and 'everyday retroaction'. Yet attempts to predict degree and direction of interference in single-list learning, based on the similarity of the material to natural language charac- teristics such as letter sequences and word frequency, have been very largely unsuccessful. Interference appears to be highly *context-dependent*: retro- action and proaction are much diminished when the two tasks learned are learned in very different physical contexts (for example, in different rooms; or, in a number of experiments by Baddeley, respectively on dry land and under water). This limitation means that the status of interference theory as a general theory of everyday forgetting is increasingly hard to defend.

It is possible that classical interference theory will be replaced by, or at any rate modified by contact with, other theories of forgetting. Possible alternative approaches have been reviewed by Baddeley (1976), including use of the concepts of 'encoding variability', trace decay, and some emphasis on cognitive models of memory in terms of semantic networks rather than the basically associationist approach on which interference theory has been based. Such approaches are in their infancy, so that it is difficult to know what success they might achieve in the explanation of 'experimental' and 'everyday' forgetting. It is also possible that interference theory, which has survived many crises and reformulations, may still prove useful as a frame- work for the explanation of forgetting.

'Spontaneous change'

A theory of forgetting which in its day provoked considerable controversy and much experimental work was that of the Gestalt psychologists. We have discussed in earlier chapters the principles of *Prägnanz* and 'belonging' which were assumed by them to govern perceptual organization; and they argued that the same principles could be applied to the organization of memory traces. Where a trace is 'unstable' it may undergo modification in the direc- tion of stability; and it may by the same process be assimilated to other traces and its individual characteristics lost (Koffka, 1935).

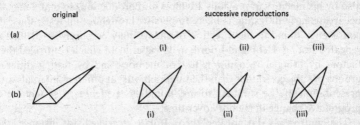

Figure 16.5   Successive changes in reproduction of figures from memory. (From Wulf, 1922, trans. 1938). Figure (a) shows a *sharpening* tendency: special characteristics and irregularities of the presented figures are emphasized in reproduction. Figure (b) shows a *levelling* effect: special characteristics and irregularities are smoothed out in reproduction and the figure tends towards symmetry.

In both cases reproductions were obtained thirty seconds (i), twenty-four hours (ii) and one week (iii) after presentation of the original

Many experiments have sought to show that memory for a given form may undergo spontaneous change in the direction suggested by Gestalt theory. A classic early experiment was carried out by Wulf (1922), who showed his subjects diagrams such as those shown in Figure 16.5. Subjects were asked to reproduce the diagrams from memory, after varying intervals of time. Wulf found that changes occurred in memory, as judged from his subjects' attempts at reproduction, that the change was usually consistent in direction over several tests and that it might be either in the direction of perfect symmetry and loss of any detail implying irregularity, or in the direction of extreme complexity in which any minor irregularity of the original figure became progressively exaggerated. These 'goals' he termed *minimal simplicity* and *maximal simplicity*, respectively, and the processes whereby the goals were approached were respectively described as *levelling* and *sharpening*. Whether in a given case levelling or sharpening occurred would depend principally upon the characteristics of the original figure.

More procedurally sophisticated investigations have thrown considerable doubt on this finding. Hebb and Foord (1945), for example, pointed out that when a subject is asked to reproduce a drawing, changes may occur through inaccurate perception or imperfect drawing skills; such changes have been shown to occur even when the subject is copying a form displayed before him and therefore cannot be taken as evidence of a change in memory. Further, when the subject is tested repeatedly over a period of time, he may be influenced not only by his memory of the original stimulus but also by his memory of previous attempts at reproduction, so that a mistake occurring early in testing is likely to persist throughout all tests; thus, the consistency found in the direction of change may be purely an artifact of repeated testing. Hebb and Foord, in an experiment which controlled these factors by using a recognition test of memory and by testing different groups of subjects, rather than the same subjects, at different intervals after presentation of the stimulus forms, found no evidence of systematic or progressive change in memory over time.

The controversy did not end there. It can be argued, for instance, that the recognition method itself is not an entirely suitable measure of change in memory for form and many experiments have since been aimed at devising methods which are free from criticism. A detailed review of the methodological issues, and of the research findings, in this area has been provided by Riley (1962), and relatively little work has been able to add substantially to our knowledge since his review was published. In summary we can say that very little evidence has been produced to support the Gestalt view, but that the task of providing evidence whose interpretation is unambiguous has so far proved virtually impossible. It should also be pointed out that it is often extremely difficult to predict the change expected in memory, especially when memory other than for form is concerned.

Repression or 'motivated forgetting'

The last theory of forgetting to be considered here is based upon the Freudian theory of repression. Very briefly, Freud (1925) hypothesized that certain ideas and events may be forgotten because they are threatening in content: wishes, feelings or actions which in the past, maybe in childhood, have been met with punishment or the threat of punishment, are 'repressed' – expelled from consciousness – and can be expressed only in distorted form or in very special circumstances, for example, during therapy. Such memories are not 'erased' but become inaccessible; this is a position similar to that of interference theory. It differs from the Gestalt view in that memories are held to be retained in their original form as well as in distorted form, and in that distortion occurs as a result of associated anxiety and threat rather than because of the formal instability of the memory trace. (It should, however, be pointed out in passing that other accounts of mnemonic change have considered both structural and motivational factors to be of importance; see, for example, Bartlett, 1932.)

Numerous experiments have been devised to test the notion of 'motivated forgetting' in the laboratory; a review of such work has been given by McKinnon and Dukes (1962) and more recently by Kline (1972). Such studies would certainly indicate, on the whole, that the affective tone of material may be reflected in its ease of reproduction at a later date; for example, memory for 'pleasant' events is better than that for 'unpleasant' events, and tasks in the laboratory which have been associated with failure and which have therefore gained unpleasant significance are less likely to be recalled than tasks which have no such connotation. There are, however, methodological difficulties with many studies and it is unclear whether the differential recall of pleasant and unpleasant material reflects differences in learning, or in rehearsal, rather than in 'purer' characteristics of retention. It is also worth noting that the orthodox Freudian bases his support for the notion of repression upon clinical evidence rather than experimental; much of the experimental evidence is essentially trivial with respect to the nature of the 'unpleasantness', 'failure' or 'anxiety' which is induced, and Freud himself (quoted by McKinnon and Dukes) held such evidence to be harmless but irrelevant! It seems quite clear that the 'motivated forgetting' hypothesis is only appropriate in rather circumscribed situations, and, like the Gestalt theory of spontaneous change in the memory trace, cannot lay any claim to acceptance as a general theory of forgetting.

Variations in the efficiency of memory

In this final section we shall discuss very briefly some of the principal factors which seem to be related to the efficiency of remembering. One such factor is the age, or maturity, of the rememberer; other factors, and arguably the most significant, relate to the nature of the memory task and the conditions under which it is carried out. Finally, we shall consider some individual differences among rememberers, relating to intelligence, 'cognitive style' and personality.

Memory development

It is well known both that some memory capacity is present even in very young infants (for example, they respond differentially to familiar and to novel stimuli) and that memory capacity, or at any rate memory performance, increases with age. This is true for a wide variety of tasks, ranging through digit span, recall of visual arrays ('Kim's game'), recall of prose, comprehension performance, and the accuracy of testimony. Development continues over perhaps the first twelve years or more of life, and some aspects of memory performance, such as vocabulary growth and semantic memory organization, can be seen to continue development throughout adult life at least until old age.

Studies of memory in young children chiefly employ recognition measures: it is generally assumed that recall develops rather later, although it has been little studied. After this point it appears that the main developmental changes are in the use of *strategies* of encoding and decoding (storage and retrieval), and in the development of semantic memory. Good reviews of memory development in children are provided by Kail and Hagen (1977), Flavell (1977), and Chi (1976) in the case of short-term memory.

In the study of memory strategies in children, the main emphasis has been on the development of verbal encoding (clearly very valuable for many memory tasks), the development of visual encoding, or the use of imagery (equally important, but comparatively neglected) and the relation between the two. Obviously, very young children do not possess a verbal code or can use it only very imperfectly; they rely upon visual coding more than do older children, and this preference can be seen in the sorts of errors made by children of different ages in recognition tasks (see, for example, Perlmutter and Myers, 1975; Cramer, 1976). On the other hand, at any rate after the age of four or five it seems that the deficiency in verbal coding shown by younger children is one of *production* rather than capacity: younger children are capable of verbal rehearsal, for example, when instructed to use it, but do not do so spontaneously. The production deficiency may occur because the verbal rehearsal strategy has not been thoroughly learned; because other strategies, such as visual coding, supplant it; or because the child only imperfectly understands the demands of the memory task or the benefits of verbal rehearsal. The last point relates to the development of what Flavell has termed *metamemory*: the individual's knowledge about memory, both its general laws and his own capacity. Adults generally are fairly competent in this respect; they can usually predict with some accuracy their likely level of performance at a memory task, and it is sometimes a source of gloom for memory researchers that the facts about memory which years of patient investigation have established are precisely those which 'everyone knows' in any case. Young children, on the other hand, have to learn 'what every-one knows', and they cannot accurately estimate their own performance; typically a young child, if asked, will confidently assert that his recall of, say, a ten- or twelve-item visual array will be more or less perfect, and is surprised when it is not. It is likely, then, that a child who is capable of verbal rehearsal does not use it simply because he does not appreciate that rehearsal is needed or that verbal rehearsal, as opposed to (or in addition to) visual encoding, may be profitable.

A rather similar picture emerges from other studies of memory development. Chi (1976) has concluded that the poorer short-term memory performance of young children is attributable to strategy unavailability and production deficiency rather than to limited capacity. It has also been reported that *clustering* in long-term memory increases with age, and that younger children (six-year-olds, say, as opposed to eleven-year-olds) are less likely to use *cueing* when it is available as an optional strategy although they are able to benefit from cueing when it is imposed by the experimenter. Again, this suggests not an incapacity to use categorization but a failure to use it spontaneously.

The study of memory processes in children is still at quite an early, though very active, stage; at the other extreme of development, there is great research interest in memory development in late adulthood and old age. It is a cultural stereotype that old people 'live in the past', that they remember the events and acquaintances of their youth more readily than 'new' events and acquaintances. When reasonable experimental controls are adopted there is no supporting evidence for this view (see, for example, Franklin and Holding, 1977), although naturally enough if there is frequent rehearsal of events which occurred long ago there should also be ready recall of them. Nevertheless, deficits, or at any rate different patterns, of memory do appear when older adults are compared with younger ones (Craik, 1977; M. W. Eysenck, 1977), although the methodological problems involved in studying age differences are particularly acute in the case of old age (see Chapter 22).

Generally, there is little evidence for decrement in short-term memory unless the task carries some extra load – for example, dichotic listening or divided attention (see Chapter 9) – in which case older subjects perform less well. In long-term memory, age deficits have been shown in a variety of tasks: free recall, paired-associate recall, memory for past events and to some extent semantic memory (although it appears to be less affected than episodic memory). It is not entirely clear what the nature of the age deficit may be, but there is some evidence to support several different hypotheses. Older subjects have sometimes (though not always) been found to *encode* material less efficiently – for example, to be less likely to show clustering and categorization, and to employ shallow rather than deep processing. Where this occurs, it may well be a production deficiency: deep processing is possible but older subjects are less likely to use it spontaneously. In paired-associate learning and recall, older subjects seem (comparatively) more likely to use verbal encoding rather than visual, quite an important difference since visual imagery has been found to be very valuable in mediating such performance, and again this seems to be a production deficiency in that visual encoding can be used under instructions to do so (Nebes, 1976).

Other evidence suggests that rather than, or in addition to, an encoding deficiency there are *retrieval* difficulties associated with age: for example, in several tasks age differences are found in recall but not in recognition or when *cued* recall is substituted for uncued. Further, M. W. Eysenck (1975) has demonstrated that apparent retrieval difficulties, with age, in semantic memory may reflect not inefficient retrieval but a slower *decision process*: older subjects are able to retrieve a member of a given category, for example, with no more difficulty than younger subjects, but take more time to confirm the accuracy of the retrieval before reporting the item. It seems probable that deficits of all types may occur in old age, with some tasks being more susceptible to particular deficits than others; more research is needed to establish the relative importance, and more detailed nature, of the various deficits and the extent to which they may be remedied by instruction or other task manipulation.

Task conditions

We have already mentioned, implicitly or explicitly, many characteristics of memory tasks which influence their ease or difficulty. For example, meaningful material is more readily learned and recalled than meaningless (or at any rate less meaningful) material; and connected material, such as continuous prose, more readily than disconnected material such as isolated words. In some memory tasks phonetic similarity among items is important, in other tasks (sometimes in the same task) semantic similarity is influential. In serial learning, the position of an item within a list also usually determines its ease of recall, early items (the so-called *primacy* effect) and later items (the *recency* effect) being favoured. Again, whether material is presented auditorily or visually often greatly influences the results obtained; for a review of such *modality-specific* effects, see Penney (1975). It is well known, too, that the *retention interval* is strongly related to memory efficiency; however the effect is interpreted, it is virtually beyond dispute that memory performance becomes poorer as the time since initial storage increases, and that the subject's activity during the retention interval – whether or not he is able, or chooses, to rehearse the learned material, what strategy he adopts in doing so, whether he is engaged in 'interfering' activity – is of considerable importance. We can predict such effects with some reliability, and authors feel safe in listing them in textbooks, although their theoretical interpretation, as can be seen from the earlier sections of this chapter, is often a matter for debate.

There are other characteristics which can also often be shown to affect memory performance. One concerns the degree to which the conditions of initial learning and of subsequent retention test are alike. Generally speaking, performance is better when the testing situation is similar to that of original learning: for example, when learning and testing are carried out in the same room, with the same experimenter. The most spectacular demonstration of this effect is that of Godden and Baddeley (1975), whose subjects were deep-sea divers who carried out their learning and memory tasks either on the shore or below 20 ft of water. Similarly, retroactive interference has been found to be greatly reduced if task 1 is learned and recalled in the same room while the interfering task 2 is learned in a different room (Greenspoon and Ranyard, 1957). In this sense, then, memory is *context-dependent*; and it has also been shown to be *state-dependent*, in that subjects performing either in a 'normal' state or under the influence of a drug (such as alcohol) yield better memory scores when their states at learning and at testing are alike rather than different (Kumar, Stolerman and Steinberg, 1970).

There are some qualifications to these findings. In some cases (though not in all) the effects of context-dependence disappear when the distracting effect of moving into a different situation between learning and testing is controlled for; the evidence for state-dependent memory has been found to hold for recall but not for recognition, suggesting that these are retrieval effects rather than effects related to encoding (in spite of the fact that such phenomena are usually described under the heading of state-dependent *learning*); and some factors which influence memory do not seem to show state-dependent effects although they are usually interpreted in terms of the internal state of the rememberer. Amongst these factors are time of day, noise and others all of which tend to be grouped together as *arousal* variables.

Time of day, for example, has been shown to affect performance at a number of different occupations (Blake, 1967). On the whole, performance tends to be better in the afternoon or early evening than in the morning on many perceptual-motor tasks; and this seems to be true also of long-term memory, although there is little evidence of any effect upon semantic, as opposed to episodic, memory. It has often been found, however, that immediate memory shows the reverse effect, with performance reaching a peak at mid-morning (rather poorer in the early morning) and declining thereafter through the day. The crucial factor appears to be the time of day at which material is learned, rather than that at which it is recalled (although obviously this can only be tested in the case of long-term memory); neither is there any evidence for the state-dependent hypothesis that material learned at one time of day would be better recalled at that time of day than at another (Folkard *et al.*, 1977; Folkard, 1979).

The usual interpretation of time-of-day effects is in terms of *arousal*: people are held to be less aroused in the morning than in the afternoon/ evening, a hypothesis which is supported by diurnal variation in certain physiological measures, notably body temperature, which are often taken to index arousal (see Chapter 5). The suggestion, then, is that a state of relatively low arousal is more beneficial for immediate memory performance, while high arousal is more beneficial for long-term memory. This interpretation has some support from studies employing other 'arousal' variables: for example, comparing recall for items associated with, respectively, relatively low or relatively high GSR at presentation, or for items learned in noise or in quiet. However, particularly in the case of immediate memory, there have been some inconsistent results (Craik and Blankstein, 1975), and there is no consensus of opinion on the effects of arousal which might mediate its influence on memory performance: for discussion of various views, see M. W. Eysenck (1977). The only clear agreement amongst workers in this field seems to be that 'arousal' effects will depend very greatly upon the demands of the particular memory task employed. Moreover, since (as we saw in Chapter 5) the concept of 'arousal' as a unitary state of the organism is a doubtful one, it is not perhaps too surprising that different 'arousal' variables may yield different effects upon memory performance.

Individual differences

An obvious characteristic of individuals which might be expected to relate to memory performance is *intelligence*: there have been a number of studies seeking to relate the two, a useful survey being given by M. W. Eysenck (1977). Although some studies have found differences in memory between 'superior I.Q.' and 'normal I.Q.' subjects or between normals and retardates, it is on the whole unrealistic to expect any simple relation between 'intelligence' and 'memory', since neither is a unitary concept. Nevertheless, there is evidence that some kinds of memory performance are related to certain aspects of measured intelligence. Subjects high in verbal ability, for example, tend to be superior in some aspects of short-term memory, but only when verbal materials are employed; subjects high in spatial ability have been found to be superior in recall or recognition of geometric forms or pictures. It is likely that such differences reflect the amount, and the nature, of the encoding and rehearsal strategies employed, and it has been suggested that intelligence is related to secondary, rather than primary, memory: but there is rather little evidence available to support or disprove these hypotheses.

Probably the significant differences among memorizers are qualitative, rather than quantitative: rather than seeking 'good' and 'bad' performers, we should perhaps be considering individual differences in the handling of information. One approach of this kind has been the postulation of differences in cognitive style by such investigators as Gardner and Witkin (Gardner *et al.*, 1959; Witkin *et al.*, 1962). For example, the dimensions of *levelling–sharpening* (Gardner *et al.*) and *field-dependence* (Witkin *et al.*; and see also Chapter 21) have been studied with regard to memory, as well as in the contexts of perception and thinking. However, these dimensions present problems of measurement, with rather poor correlations among the tests which are supposed to define them; and field-dependence appears to be related to intelligence and perhaps also to arousal, so that its independent status as a correlate of memory seems doubtful. A further limitation is that investigations of the relation between cognitive style and memory have not on the whole incorporated clear and distinct examination of the different memory processes which, at least in the current theoretical climate, are held to be important and independent: attention, short-term storage capacity, rehearsal strategy, retrieval strategy, and so on. We are in no position to state with any certainty which of these processes, if any, are related to the dimension being studied. The same limitation applies to a large extent to studies of the relation between *personality* or *psychopathology* and memory. For a general review, see Johnson (1974); for more detailed treatment of certain topics, see M. W. Eysenck (1977).

One of the most studied personality dimensions has been that of extraversion/introversion (discussed in Chapter 20); there seems certainly to be some relation between this dimension and performance at a number of learning and memory tasks. Extraverts learn more quickly than introverts, at least when the task is difficult; their recall is better at short retention intervals, but less good at longer intervals; and they appear to retrieve information

more quickly, both from episodic and from semantic memory. These conclusions should be tempered, at least, by the observation that in many cases
it is *neurotic* introverts, rather than non-neurotic introverts, who perform
less well than extraverts; and *anxiety*, a characteristic related to neuroticism,
also appears to be related, negatively, to efficiency in memory, both in
encoding and at retrieval. The effects of anxiety and of extraversion/intro-
version are typically explained in terms of *arousal*, although as we have
already noted the status of arousal as a unitary dimension, which might
show reliable individual differences, is doubtful.

In the case of psychopathology, it has been found that subjects suffering
from *schizophrenia* show consistent and reliable deficiencies of attention (in
short-term memory) and of long-term memory organization (at least in
episodic memory). Studies of memory in schizophrenics have on the whole
assumed a reasonably sophisticated analysis of memory processes, as a
starting point; studies of other dimensions of personality and psychopathology often have not, and it is likely that this lack is at least partly
responsible for the rather poor evidence which they produce for individual differences in memory.

It may well be that personality characteristics, and other individual differences, contribute to memory performance, and that their contribution will
be shown to be substantial when studies are based upon a sensitive
information-processing analysis of memory. It is clear, however, that not
only individual differences but also (and, as far as one can now see, more
importantly) the *task situation* – the memory task itself and its context –
determine the efficiency of memory. There is now increasing interest in
memory (and in particular forgetting) in everyday situations rather than
in the laboratory: studies of 'absent-mindedness', of failures to remember
the names of recent acquaintances or familiar TV actors, of failures to
carry out intended actions such as pill-taking, shopping and other errands.
Such evidence, often derived from questionnaire data (for example, Herrman
and Neisser, 1979), suggests that it is naïve to talk of memory as a unitary
faculty exhibiting reliable individual differences. There *may* be a general
factor of 'good' or 'bad' memory, but it seems also true that people who
are 'good at' remembering faces or names are not necessarily 'good at'
remembering to take their medicine at the appropriate times, or 'good at'
remembering appointments, or 'good at' digit span or the free recall of verbal
lists in the laboratory. The results of memory research are still very heavily
dependent upon the particular experimental paradigms which researchers
have used, and the particular theoretical approaches, such as the S–R

approach, from which these paradigms have derived. It is likely that we need, if not to replace, at least to supplement the traditional laboratory investigations with other, naturalistic methods of research if we are to gain anything approaching a complete understanding of the diverse phenomena of remembering and forgetting.

Chapter 17
Language

'Language' in humans and animals

The possession of a language system, both spoken and written, is generally considered to be an exclusively human attribute, one which demarcates human beings from animals quite unequivocally. However, not all human languages have a written form; and for spoken language, too, the line of demarcation is not at first sight firmly drawn. Animals of domesticated species are able to respond appropriately to verbal commands; certain birds, for example parrots and Indian mynah birds, are able to reproduce strings of words or phrases to which they have been exposed, and anthropoid apes possess communication systems of different sounds which may appear to differ from human language only in degree. There are several 'design features' which language and vocal signalling systems of animals possess in common (see Hockett, 1960), and several of the functions of human language appear to be shared by animal communication systems. For example, sounds emitted by animals may serve to warn intruders encroaching on alien territory, to attract mates, to threaten enemies and to preserve the social structure of large groups.

However, at least four important differences have been claimed between human language systems and the naturally occurring communication systems of animals. First, human beings can talk about objects or events which are remote from the speaker in time or place or both. This feature of language, known as *displacement*, appears to be absent from animal communication, although bee 'dancing', a communication which serves to inform other bees of the location of nectar, has sometimes been said to possess it. The second major difference is that of *productivity*: human beings are capable of producing, and of understanding, utterances which have never been produced or heard before. Human language is thus an 'open' system, capable of infinite expansion; the vocalizations of animals, on the other hand, tend to form a 'closed' system, the repertoire being fixed and finite, with no possibility of coining new vocalizations by rearranging old ones.

This is related to the third and perhaps the most important difference, which Hockett calls *duality of patterning*: in human language a limited range of distinguishable sounds can be combined and recombined into an enormous vocabulary. The size of the human language system is thus not limited by the number of different sounds which a human being can discriminate; in contrast, the lack of duality of patterning in non-human communication systems severely restricts their efficiency and flexibility.

Finally, human language is *transmitted across generations*, and consequently also provides a vehicle for the transmission of knowledge through the processes of teaching and learning; animal communication systems lack this feature or possess it only to a very rudimentary degree. As Roger Brown (1965, p. 250) described it:

Information that one person possesses can be delivered to others who do not have it but could use it. This kind of transmission is possible between generations as well as among contemporaries, and so, with the emergence of language, life experiences begin to be cumulative. Some animal species are able to transmit a small amount of lore across generations; chiefly knowledge of waterholes, feeding places and the habits of enemies. But most of what the aged anthropoid knows perishes with him; the young chimpanzee starts life, as he did millennia ago, from scratch.

The possession of language is thus of enormous significance for the human species, since it grants infinite communication possibilities – including to some extent the communication of private experience, thoughts and emotions – and also provides a vehicle for the expression and transmission of knowledge.

If it is true that human language is different from, and in some sense superior to, animal communication systems, do the differences represent a *discontinuity* or can animal communication systems be viewed as rudimentary language systems? Both views have been strongly argued. The *continuity* view maintains that there is no 'special endowment' of language possessed by man alone, but rather that man simply possesses 'more' of the necessary qualifications for language. One suggestion is that man is 'more intelligent', in some general sense, than animal species lower on the phylogenetic scale; another is that many of the various skills required for language are present in non-human species of various kinds, but only man possesses them all: for example, symbolic ability; the vocal apparatus required for a spoken language; the appropriate social structures, stressing sociability and the reinforcement value of communication. In either case human and non-human 'language' is held to be essentially continuous, man's language exhibiting a superiority of degree rather than of kind.

There have been strong objections to the continuity view. For example, it is both logically and practically difficult to compare the 'general intelligence' of different animal species; and there is little evidence that animals closest to man on the phylogenetic scale exhibit more of the skills necessary for language than do more distant species, evidence which would seem to be required by a continuity argument. Such objections were argued cogently by Lenneberg (1964, 1967), who was perhaps the outstanding proponent of the alternative, *discontinuity* theory: that language is a unique system which is species-specific to man. Among the arguments advanced by Lenneberg in support of this position are the observations that language development does not seem closely dependent upon degree of intelligence or training; that there seems to be a fairly fixed developmental schedule for all children, though not in terms of the chronological age at which a given 'language milestone' will be reached; that while it is difficult to suppress language in humans it is virtually impossible to teach it to non-humans; and that while human languages differ markedly from one another they nevertheless share certain basic characteristics or 'linguistic universals'. Stemming from these arguments, the strongest form of the discontinuity view has been that the human infant is born with a special biological capacity for language – a kind of 'universal grammar' against which the speech he hears about him can be checked and which enables him to deduce the linguistic rules of his community: we shall return to this notion of an 'inbuilt' grammar, or *language acquisition device*, in a later section.

In recent years some doubt has been cast on the human exclusiveness of language by studies attempting to teach language to non-human primates, chiefly chimpanzees and gorillas. Such attempts have quite a long history, but until recently they were notably unsuccessful (for a review, see Kellogg, 1968), not least because they employed vocal language. More recently a number of investigators have employed other media, more suited to primates than the vocal system, such as gestural sign language (chiefly Ameslan, the American sign language for the deaf), the manipulation of plastic symbols indicating words or relationships, or typewriting in a specially devised symbolic language. Teaching projects along these lines have yielded impressive evidence of the ability of chimps, in particular, to acquire several of the linguistic features previously thought to be solely 'human' (see, for example, Fleming, 1975; Linden, 1976). Perhaps the most famous 'linguistic ape' has been Washoe, a female chimp reared for some years in a human home (and more recently in a chimp colony) by human caretakers who talked to her in Ameslan, encouraging her response by imitation, reinforcement of 'babbling' and sometimes instrumental conditioning; her early development has been described by Gardner and Gardner (1969) and her later career by Linden (1976). Washoe has shown the ability to transfer signs learned in one context to use in another; she can generate strings of signs which make sense and which have not been imitated from humans – for example, 'gimme tickle'; she can coin names for new objects, such as 'food drink' for a refrigerator or 'water bird' for duck; and she shows originality in certain usages, referring to little things, for example, as 'baby', and to annoying things as 'dirty'.

Another celebrated chimp pupil, Sarah, has apparently exhibited considerable conceptual skills, relevant to language use, in her comprehension of a 'language' achieved by the ordering of arbitrary plastic symbols to stand for objects or relations (Premack and Premack, 1972). Sarah shows understanding of labels and verbs, interrogatives, the concepts of same/different and if/then, and, to some extent, the hierarchical structure of complex sentences (see pp. 450ff.): for example, she responded correctly to the linguistically complex instruction 'Sarah insert apple pail banana dish', placing the apple in the pail and the banana in the dish rather than, say, the apple in the pail only, or indeed the banana in the pail (although the two symbols are adjacent).

Other chimps, too, in both types of study, have demonstrated similar achievements; however, there is still considerable debate as to their real extent and interpretation. McNeill (1970) and Limber (1977), for example, have argued that Washoe's 'language strings' are not conclusive evidence for the possession of hierarchical structure, and that her productivity does not compare favourably with that of the average three-year-old human. It remains to be seen whether her performance will be bettered by later animals reared in conditions more nearly optimal for language acquisition, in particular those reared virtually from birth by 'foster parents' who are highly fluent Ameslan speakers. While Sarah's achievements seem more impressive conceptually, her exposure to language was very far from naturalistic: she was trained in the laboratory, by standard conditioning and discrimination learning procedures, and without access to her plastic-symbol 'language' other than during training sessions, and her capacity was tested virtually exclusively by comprehension rather than performance. Limber (1977) has argued that her 'creativity' and her possession of displacement are debatable, and that her apparent comprehension may be overestimated by the probabilistic criteria of successful response adopted and by the conditions of testing. In fact, in this debate a great deal hinges upon the precise definition of language, about which there is some lack of consensus.

Moreover, so far there is rather little evidence (although some is accumulating) concerning the use of language by adult, rather than infant, chimps, the incidence and characteristics of Ameslan exchanges among chimps (rather than between chimp and man) or the occurrence of language transmission from 'linguistic' mother to child. It may be that the emergence of clear evidence of linguistic capacity is simply a matter of time; but until such evidence is substantial, the possession of *language*, other than the capacity to acquire alien, conceptually sophisticated 'tricks', in a non-human species must remain a hypothesis to be treated with some caution.

Approaches to the psychology of language

Langue *and* parole

In considering the psychological study of language, it is useful to begin with the distinction between *langue* and *parole*. The Swiss linguist, Ferdinand de Saussure, was the first to make explicit this important distinction, effectively a distinction between language and speech (de Saussure, 1916). Consider, for example, the two statements: 'He is speaking English' and 'He speaks English'. It would be quite fair to say that a mynah bird, under the appropriate circumstances, 'is speaking English' – that is, uttering sound sequences which are acceptable as English – but it would not be appropriate to say that it 'speaks English'. Following de Saussure, it could be said that all those individuals who 'speak English' share a particular *langue* and that the utterances which they produce when they are 'speaking English' are instances of *parole*. All those who 'speak English' produce utterances when they are speaking it which, in spite of the variations between them, can be described in terms of a particular system of rules and relations: that is, in some sense, all these different utterances share the same *structural* characteristics. The utterances, which are instances of *parole*, are taken by the linguist as evidence for the construction of the underlying common structure, namely the *langue*.

The linguist is concerned with describing the *langue*, the language system. The psychologist's interest, on the other hand, is principally in *parole*, language behaviour. He may be guided either by his knowledge of findings, methods and theories in other areas of psychology – notably in the area of learning – or by a knowledge of findings, methods and theories in the area of linguistics. The first approach depends upon the assumption that language behaviour is not essentially different from other kinds of behaviour, and that all kinds are ultimately to be described in the same sorts of terms; the second approach depends upon the assumption that while linguistic concepts are not themselves appropriate as psychological descriptions they may nevertheless suggest parallel psychological concepts which will prove fruitful in the description of language behaviour. For example, the distinction between *langue* and *parole* as linguistic concepts has been paralleled by a psychological distinction between *competence* (defined by McNeill, 1966, as representing 'the knowledge a native speaker of a language must have in order to understand any of the infinitely many grammatical sentences of his language ... a native speaker's linguistic intuition') and *performance* (in McNeill's words, 'the expression of competence in talking or listening to speech'). This is a distinction which will be considered in more detail later.

Until comparatively recently in the long history of psychological studies of language it was possible for various approaches, in particular those drawing upon learning-theory and linguistics, to co-exist and indeed to supplement one another; a good example of such a multidisciplinary approach is that of Miller (1951). This co-existence ended, in effect, in the late 1950s, when it was made explicit, most notably by Chomsky (1959), that many of the assumptions of learning theory were incompatible with those of linguistics. In this section we shall consider, very briefly, some characteristics of these two types of approach, their strength and their weaknesses.

Learning-theory approaches

Learning-theory approaches to the psychology of language represent an extension to language behaviour of principles which were devised to account for the acquisition and modification of non-verbal (and often non-human) behaviour. In a sense the term 'learning-theory approach' is a misnomer, since theories of learning are very diverse with respect to the principles they employ; the 'learning-theory approach' to language has been almost entirely in terms of associative learning and, more narrowly, in terms of conditioning principles. It has been applied not only to verbal responses in simple learning situations but also to integrated verbal behaviour: Skinner (1957), for example, has produced a theory of language acquisition in terms of operant conditioning, and writers such as Bousfield (1961), Mowrer (1960), C. E.

Noble (1963), and Osgood (Osgood, Suci and Tannenbaum, 1957) have offered accounts of meaning and meaningfulness which, while they differ considerably in detail, share a common foundation in associationist (S–R) or mediational (S–O–R) learning theory.

What sort of theoretical account can 'learning theory' give of language behaviour? We shall briefly consider two examples: first, the use of conditioning principles to describe language learning; secondly, the use of serial learning principles to describe the production and comprehension of sentences.

It has often been argued that language learning proceeds in situations analogous to classical and instrumental conditioning. For example, a mother may bring her child a cup of milk and say the word 'milk' at the same time. The sight of the drink produces various responses such as smiling, reaching out, grasping the cup, drinking. The word which accompanies it may then become a *conditioned stimulus* eliciting a conditioned response derived from the response to the drink itself (see Chapter 13). True, the mother may vary what she says to the child when bringing milk. She may only rarely, if ever, speak the single word alone; more often, she will say 'Here's your milk' or 'Drink up your milk' or, on other occasions, 'Do you want some milk?' The child is held to be capable of generalizing from one potential CS to another on the basis of their common word 'milk'; and it is probable that the mother aids such stimulus generalization by placing selective emphasis on the crucial word when speaking. (We shall not consider here the vexed question of what sort of reinforcement, if any, might be held necessary for learning to occur.)

At other times, a child may utter a word-like sound, such as 'do-do'. His mother observes: 'He wants his dolly', and gives the doll to the child. In other words, certain spontaneous vocalizations are selectively and specifically reinforced; later, when the child wants his doll, he may say 'do-do' again, and will receive the doll, and the *instrumental* conditioning of the response 'do-do' is strengthened. Again, if the child says 'do-do' when he is given the doll, he may gain further rewards in the form of praise, attention, perhaps a sweet. Skinner (1957) described the possible principles of such *operant conditioning* in some detail; he argued further that the child's correct pronunciation of the word may be affected by increasingly selective reinforcement, or *shaping*, a process which has been employed in the instrumental conditioning of animals. At first the mother will reward any utterance which bears some similarity to the appropriate word; later on, one might hypothesize, she becomes more selective (perhaps as a result of her acceptance of cultural norms for children's speech, perhaps because it is growing increasingly apparent that the child is improving his control over his own vocalization), and gives the doll to the child only when he produces the word 'dolly' or something close to it.

Of these two situations, the first appears to describe the skill of understanding speech and the second the skill of uttering it. One can hypothesize further that there is transfer from one skill to the other. For example, in the 'classical conditioning' situation one might suppose that the child not only hears his mother say 'milk' but also imitates her; if he repeats 'milk' or some approximation to it, he is further rewarded. Again, if a mother repeats her child's utterance while also rewarding it, the stimulus word will be conditioned to the reward given. Thus the same situation can furnish the opportunity both for classical and for instrumental conditioning.

At first sight this account of language learning possesses elegance and simplicity. However, there are a number of difficulties in the way of its acceptance. In the first place, the theory is less simple than it sounds; it is not clear, for example, what is the nature of the reinforcement needed for language conditioning, or whether the learning of labels is more simply a function of the repeated co-occurrence of word with referent in the child's experience, contiguity alone being needed for the association to be formed.

In the second place, it must be pointed out that the mother's teaching of her child is likely to be irregular and unsystematic. If the child is left by himself he may call for milk or for 'dolly' without being rewarded by the desired object; when he utters 'do-do' he may be given a doll when in fact he wants milk. The conditioning schedule which the mother presents is therefore likely to be one which would prove ineffective in the laboratory.

Finally, the learning techniques outlined above may account in part for the learning of words, or of sounds; but they cannot account for all aspects of language use. It has often been pointed out that humans can produce sentences which they have never learned before, and indeed it would be impossible to maintain that a child learns his repertoire of sentences in the way that he learns a vocabulary, since the range of possible sentences is far too great to render the position tenable. To explain the acquisition and use of connected speech, rather than isolated vocalizations, learning-theory approaches have sometimes had recourse to principles derived from the study of serial learning: for example, maze learning, or the rote learning of lists of verbal material.

Broadly speaking, these approaches suggest that sentences are generated on a left-to-right, non-anticipatory system, each word in the sentence being selected on the basis of preceding words. Thus sentences are thought of as *stimulus–response chains*, with each word serving as a response to the preceding word and as a stimulus for the next. Many learning theorists are aware that an analysis of sentence production in terms of learned stimulus–response chains is inadequate. They have accordingly complicated their accounts in a variety of ways. One such development is to take account of the frequency with which letters and words occur in speech. The twenty-six letters of the alphabet do not all have the same probability of occurrence (in printed English, for instance, E is the most frequent letter and J, Q and Z are the least frequent). Further, the letters are not independent of one another; for instance, U is much more likely to occur following Q than following T. What goes for letters also goes for words. Thus the speaker's knowledge of the relative frequency and interdependence of linguistic units can be presumed to play a part in sentence production: the words comprising a sentence may be 'hooked-up' into chains on the basis of the transitional probabilities between them.

This approach has some plausibility. Listeners have to interpret sentences on a probabilistic basis and it would be biologically economical if they were to produce them in the same way. Furthermore, the mathematics of such systems have been extensively studied under the general topic of *Markov processes*. Thus if human beings could be shown to operate in this way, a great deal would be known about the level of complexity of the grammatical system underlying their linguistic performance. In fact, some aspects of language behaviour do seem to conform quite well with this account. For example, Miller and Selfridge (1950) constructed verbal sequences corresponding in varying degrees to the transitional probabilities of continuous English (see their original report for details of construction methods, and Table 17.1 for examples).

At one extreme, a *zero-order* approximation to English consists simply of a string of words, with no account taken either of the relative frequencies of individual words in the English language, or of the relative frequencies of sequences of words; a *first-order* approximation takes account of the relative frequencies of individual words, in that the string contains, for the most part, fairly common words, with some very common ones – such as *the* and *a* – perhaps occurring more than once; a *second-order* approximation takes some account of the frequencies with which ordered *pairs* of words occur, a *third-order* approximation reflects the frequencies of occurrence of triplets of words, and so on; at high levels of approximation – for example, fifth-, sixth- or seventh-order – the sequences correspond very closely to

Table 17.1
Some word sequences of varying approximations to continuous English.
(Based upon Miller and Selfridge, 1950)

Zero-order approximation:	Byway consequence handsomely financier bent flux cavalry swiftness weatherbeaten extent betwixt trumpeter
First-order approximation:	Her blue the is country hope with the covered camping the hedges
Third-order approximation:	Happened to see Europe again is that trip to the end is
Fifth-order approximation:	Old London was a wonderful place wasn't it even pleasant to talk

those of 'normal' continuous English. With an increased order of approximation it has been found that sequences are easier to learn and recall. The
same effects of prior context are also seen in more 'natural' material: in
speech perception, as Treisman (1966, p. 111) has pointed out, 'unlikely
words like *giraffe* coming after "I sang a ..." need to be much louder than
song and a little louder than *carol* or *ditty*, to be heard correctly'.

Such context effects of course include semantic constraints as well as syntactic; experiments have indicated that both types of constraint are important
in determining ease of perception, comprehension and production. Marks
and Miller (1964), for example, used 'semantic sentences' (in effect, real
sentences in scrambled order, so that semantic interrelations were present
but syntactic constraints virtually absent) and 'syntactic sentences' (in which
syntactic constraints were observed but the words used were not semantically related), and found that both types of anomalous sentence were harder
than normal sentences, but easier than unrelated word strings, to recall (a
similar effect in perception of speech was reported by Miller and Izard,
1963). Further, different types of error were associated with the two-sentence
types. Order and inflectional errors were more common in 'semantic sentences', intrusion errors more common in 'syntactic sentences'; in both cases
the effect was to distort the sentences in the direction of 'normality'. For
further discussion of these and other experiments, see Herriot (1970) and
Greene (1975); examples of sentence types are shown in Table 17.2.

However, two lines of argument suggest that a Markovian model of

Table 17.2
Examples of 'sentences' used by Marks and Miller (1964), see text

Normal sentences:	Furry wildcats fight furious battles
	Respectable jewellers give accurate appraisals
	Lighted cigarettes create smoky fumes
	Gallant gentlemen save distressed damsels
	Soapy detergents dissolve greasy stains
'Semantic sentences':	Furry fight furious wildcat battles
	Jewellers respectable appraisals accurate give
	Create fumes cigarettes lighted smoky
	Distressed gallant save damsels gentlemen
	Stains greasy soapy dissolve detergents
'Syntactic sentences':	Furry jewellers create distressed stains
	Respectable cigarettes save greasy battles
	Lighted gentlemen dissolve furious appraisals
	Gallant detergents fight accurate fumes
	Soapy wildcats give smoky damsels
Word lists:	Furry create distressed jewellers stains
	Cigarettes respectable battles greasy save
	Dissolve appraisals gentlemen lighted furious
	Accurate gallant fight fumes detergents
	Damsels smoke soapy give wildcats

sentence generation, in terms of transitional probability and prior context, is inadequate. First, it is very difficult to account in this way for the generation of certain complex sentence types, such as those characterized by 'nested dependencies', in which one or more sentence structures are embedded within another: for example, 'I must write the address the man who sold us the lamp gave us down'. To explain such sentences it is necessary to conceive of language as being *hierarchically*, rather than simply sequentially, structured (see pp. 450ff.). It is not in fact impossible for a sophisticated associationist learning theory to accommodate these structures, and to describe hierarchical as well as left-to-right (and indeed right-to-left) constraints; see, for example, Kintsch (1970). It is, however, impossible in principle for a Markov grammar to account for infinite degrees of embedding, which a model of grammatical competence would require; for elaboration of this criticism see McNeill (1970). On the other hand, it is arguable that a theory of *perform-*

ance might be adequately based upon learning-theory principles, since performance is finite, time-dependent and largely governed by left-to-right constraints.

The second major difficulty of learning-theory accounts of language is that it is very hard to conceive of a child learning his native language 'from scratch' according to these principles, in the relatively few years which it actually takes him to acquire proficiency in that language; the amount of learning required, particularly from an immature organism given imperfect exposure to language and incomplete training in it, seems too great. Moreover, the learning principles of contiguity and reinforcement applied to language learning are both theoretically problematic (see, for example, Chomsky's attack (1959) upon the Skinnerian position, but also Mac-Corquodale's reply (1970)) and notably difficult to observe precisely in practice.

We shall consider the child's acquisition of its native language, and the extent to which 'language-learning devices' can be observed in it, in a later section of this chapter; first we shall examine the characteristics of 'psycholinguistics' as an approach to the study of language behaviour.

Psycholinguistics

At the beginning of this section a distinction was made between linguistic competence and linguistic performance – the expression of competence, almost inevitably imperfect because of the limitations imposed by sensory and motor efficiency, attention, memory and other performance factors. The chief interest of linguists is in constructing models of competence, based upon structural descriptions of the phenomena of language: the sound system upon which it is based (phonemics and phonology), the rules for the formation of words and sentences (morphology and syntax) and the rules for inferring the meaning of sound sequences (semantics). Psychologists, if they are interested in language, are interested in the expression of competence in actual situations and in the psychological and physiological mechanisms underlying linguistic performance. However, psycholinguists argue that in order to understand language behaviour one must understand the linguistic rules which may underlie it. Thus, the psycholinguist draws upon linguistic concepts in describing competence, and then proceeds to see whether such concepts are useful in the prediction of performance; in other words, whether linguistic rules have psychological reality.

One difficulty for this procedure is that linguistics, like psychology, is a rapidly growing discipline whose models are constantly changing; it is thus dangerous to assume that a given current linguistic concept has universal or lasting validity in its own field and is therefore 'safe' to borrow. The grammatical model which has been most influential in psycholinguistics is that of Chomsky (1957, 1965). Chomsky's is a *generative* grammar, in that (like some, but not all, other grammatical models) it seeks to outline a system of rules which are capable of generating all the grammatical utterances of a language and no ungrammatical ones. Since modern linguistics claims to be empirical and descriptive rather than prescriptive (laying down 'good' or 'correct' usage), the definition of grammaticality is ultimately, in principle, in terms of what a native speaker would accept as a grammatical utterance and what he would reject as ungrammatical (in fact this definition poses some logical and practical problems, though we shall not deal with them here). Chomsky's is also a *transformational* grammar, in a sense, and for reasons which we shall discuss presently.

Central to generative and descriptive grammars is the notion of *phrase structure*: the notion that sentences are hierarchically organized. Thus 'phrase-structure' rules describe the sentence in terms of subdividing or 'rewriting'. A sentence is defined first in terms of general constituents; then those constituents may be further defined in more and more specific terms via further rewriting rules. For example, one might start by specifying that a sentence must consist of a noun phrase followed by a verb phrase: in a conventional, simple terminology,

$$S \longrightarrow NP + VP.$$

The structure of the noun phrase (NP) would then be specified further: for example, it *must* contain a noun (or a pronoun, in which case the following options are excluded); it *may* start with an article, and it *may* include an adjective governing the noun, in which case that adjective must immediately precede the noun. Such a rule can be represented in the following way, the bracketed elements being optional:

$$NP \longrightarrow (Art) + (Adj) + N.$$

Similarly, a third phrase-structure rule will specify the structure of the verb phrase or VP. There may be several possibilities. The verb may simply be an intransitive verb; it may be a transitive verb, followed by a noun phrase as its object; it may be a *copular* verb such as 'be', 'seem' or 'appear', which is followed by an adjective. Thus, a rule for the formation of a verb phrase might be

$$VP \longrightarrow \begin{cases} V\ tr + NP \\ V\ intr \\ V\ cop + Adj. \end{cases}$$

Again, if a noun phrase is contained, our second rule, above, will further specify its structure: so that one simple analysis of a sentence might be represented as in Figure 17.1.

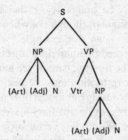

Figure 17.1   Simple diagrammatic representation of the structure of a sentence

From such a simple scheme (sometimes termed a *phrase marker* or a *tree diagram*) a number of quite varied sentences can be generated. In addition to phrase-structure rules, we can hypothesize vocabulary (or lexical) rules which state which words may be substituted for the constituents defined above. For example:

Art $\longrightarrow$ a, the,
Adj $\longrightarrow$ tall, hungry,
N $\longrightarrow$ man, dog, house,
V tr $\longrightarrow$ saw, chased.

Choosing words according to these vocabulary rules to fill in the bottom row of our phrase marker, we can obtain a sizeable number of different sentences even though the hypothesized vocabulary is very small – only three nouns, two verbs, two adjectives. For example:

The tall man saw the dog,
A hungry dog chased a man,
The dog saw a house,
A tall dog saw the house,
Dog chased man,

The hungry house chased the dog,
A house saw the man.

Clearly, from these examples, even our simple model has considerable
generative power, but needs further elaboration. The first three sentences
seem reasonable, but the others all present some difficulty of acceptance.
Can dogs be tall? Perhaps. 'Dog chased man' does not seem acceptable
(except in newspaper headlines), so perhaps a further partial rule is needed to
specify that an article may be obligatory, rather than optional, in noun
phrases when the noun is singular, though not when it is plural (dogs chased
men) or when it is a *mass noun* (for example, 'water', which cannot be
preceded by 'a', or be governed by numerical adjectives such as 'one', 'two'
or 'ten'). A house cannot be hungry, cannot see and cannot chase because
it is *inanimate*: this further restriction must be dealt with by elaboration of
vocabulary rules. Again, obviously our model does not sufficiently define the
structure of the verb in terms of its auxiliary system: the marking of tense
(present or past), the use of 'modal' verbs such as 'may', 'will', 'can',
'must' or 'shall', the expression of perfect or of continuous form (I have
taken, I am going) and so on. Nevertheless, it furnishes an example of
the hierarchical analysis of sentence structure.

There are certain difficulties, however, which are very hard to overcome
by an elaboration of phrase-structure and lexical rules. Some sentences may
have more than one meaning: for example, 'They are eating apples', and 'The
police were ordered to stop drinking at midnight'. The former of these
sentences can easily be marked in two ways to indicate its two senses; the
second is more difficult to deal with. Again, there are some sentences which
are clearly different in logical structure but which have very similar phrase
markers: for example,

The Apache are eager to kill,
The Apache are easy to kill.

John was run over by a car,
John was run over by Peter,
John was run over by the cinema,
John was run over by accident.

Such differences are difficult, if not impossible, to deal with in terms of
superficial structure, even if hierarchically analysed. To deal with such
problems Chomsky proposed that sentences possess not only a surface structure but also a *deep structure*, which specifies the logical relations of their

constituents, and their relation to other sentences (such as 'a car ran over John'), much more directly than does their surface structure (although in very simple sentences the relation between deep and surface structure may be very close). Chomsky argued, therefore, that in order to give a complete account of sentence structure one must outline first the *base rules* which define the deep structure of sentences, and second the *transformational rules* which mediate the translation of deep structure into surface structure.

Some base rules are categorical, or rewriting, rules somewhat similar to the phrase-structure rules already discussed. They define syntactically the constituents of a sentence – its subject and its predicate and the components of each; they specify the derivation of the sentence from other related sentences, and whether it shall be active or passive, affirmative or negative, declaratory, interrogative or imperative, and so on. Other base rules are lexical, governing the choice of words in a given context, taking into account not only the part of speech required but also more specific characteristics. For example, the word John is not only a noun but also animate, human, and male. Thus it can occupy the head of a noun phrase; it must be replaced by *who* or *whom* in a question, rather than by *what*; it is associated with the possessive *his* rather than *her*; it can be the subject of certain verbs, such as *sleep*, or governed by certain adjectives, such as *hungry*.

The base rules, categorical and lexical, between them determine completely the content of a sentence, but not the form in which it is produced by a speaker; for this, deep structure has to be expressed in surface structure by the means of transformational rules, which reorder and modify the deep-structure elements into the conventional expression of a particular language. For example, the deep structure of a verb phrase may specify that it is in the present tense, that the verb is 'sing' and that the sentence is negative. The 'base string' generated by deep structure is therefore

[The boy] + present + sing + neg.
          (-s)   (not)

To express this as an English sentence, three separate transformations have to be carried out. First, the word 'sing' has to be expressed as 'do sing' (a transformational step which is not necessary for more complex verbs). Second, the negative element has to be placed between the auxiliary 'do' and the verb 'sing'. Third, the affix -s which denotes the present tense must be attached to the verb which immediately follows it. Thus 'The boy -s sing not' becomes 'The boy does not sing'.

For fuller accounts of transformational grammar and the role played in it by phonological and semantic components, which have not been discussed here, see, for example, Lyons (1970); Crystal (1971); Palmer (1971); Greene (1972).

There has been a great deal of research aimed at testing the 'psychological reality' of generative grammar in general, and Chomsky's transformational grammar in particular; such work, particularly that based upon Chomsky's theory, is most fully reviewed by Greene (1972, 1975). In general, it appears that there is some psychological reality in the hierarchical structures provided by phrase-structure grammar. For example, Johnson (1965) found that subjects required to learn and recall sentences produced *transitional errors* (in which a correctly recalled word is followed by an incorrect one) more frequently at phrase boundaries than within phrases. In addition, when errors did occur within phrases, they were more likely to occur near the stem of the phrase marker than at the periphery: that is, the larger the constituent unit between which transitions occurred, the greater the probability of making a transitional error. Thus, in the sentence: 'The black cat chased the white mouse', most errors would be expected to occur between the subject and the predicate – that is, between 'cat' and 'chased'; but within the phrase 'chased the white mouse', transitional errors would be more likely to occur between 'chased' and 'the' than between 'the' and 'white', and more likely between 'the' and 'white' than between 'white' and 'mouse'.

Further evidence for the psychological reality of linguistic units, employing a different technique, was reported by Garrett, Bever and Fodor (1966), who asked their subjects to listen to a sentence over which, at one point, a brief click was superimposed, and afterwards to report the point at which the click had occurred; they found that subjects tended to report the click as having occurred at a major phrase boundary.

There is also some support for the distinction between deep and surface structure and, in particular, for the psychological reality of transformational rules: sentences of relatively high transformational complexity, for example, have been found to be more slowly processed, and to impose a higher load on memory, than simpler sentences, in a variety of learning, sentence-matching and evaluation tasks (Miller and McKean, 1964; Savin and Perchonock, 1965; Slobin, 1966b). However, psychological hypotheses based upon strict accounts of transformational theory do not always receive support. One assumption so derived, for example, is that in order to comprehend a sentence the listener (or reader) must *detransform* it, that is, translate its surface structure into deep structure; the 'semantic component', as

Chomsky termed it, then operates upon deep structure to produce comprehension. The more complex the transformation, the longer it will take for the sentence to be 'detransformed' and understood. Thus, negative sentences will be 'processed' more slowly than affirmative ones, passives more slowly than actives, and so on.

Generally, as we have already mentioned, this hypothesis is supported for a number of tasks in which comprehension is measured in terms of perception; matching with sentences of identical or related meaning; evaluation of truth or falsity; and ease of learning or recall. But these tend to be rather unnatural situations, not typical of 'normal' language behaviour, so that it is not entirely clear how far these findings can be generalized; further, alternative explanations of the findings have sometimes been advanced, for example in terms of the *perceptual* complexity of transformed sentences (Fodor and Garrett, 1967); and, finally, some experiments have shown that transformational complexity is not a good predictor of performance when *semantic* factors are involved. Herriot (1969), for example, found that passive sentences take no longer to evaluate than active sentences when it is semantically obvious, or at least semantically probable, which is the *logical subject*, and which the logical object, of the sentence, as in 'The flower was watered by the girl', or 'The patient was treated by the doctor'. Again, Slobin (1966b) and Greene (1970a) have found, with slightly different techniques, that 'false negatives' – that is, negative statements which are in fact false (or in Greene's case to which the reply 'different', rather than 'same', must be given in matching) are *easier* to evaluate than are 'true negatives': thus, the statement 'thirteen does not follow seven' is more quickly evaluated than the statement 'seven does not follow thirteen', and may be evaluated as quickly as 'thirteen follows seven'. They suggested that this is because the natural function of negatives is to contradict, or to signal a change of meaning, and that users therefore find a negative sentence easier to process when it performs that function. In these cases, then, it would seem that semantic factors in effect bypass syntactic analysis and the notions of transformation and detransformation cease to have any predictive power.

Semantic factors have in fact proved a considerable problem, in that Chomsky's argument was that the *syntactic* component of grammar is the generator of sentences, the semantic component being conceived as the processor of sentences already produced. If this is translated into a hypothesized psychological reality, as MacCorquodale (1970) and others have pointed out, it may offer an account of sentence production but leaves the speaker with nothing to say; why should a person speak at all if he does not start from a meaning to be communicated? There have been attempts to make psychological sense of the syntactic generation of sentences (see, for example, Katz and Postal, 1964), but generally it appears likely that psychological models of language use require more possibility of semantic generation than is provided by Chomsky's model. In fact, some later grammars do view the deep structure of sentences as being largely semantic, rather than purely syntactic, in nature (e.g. Fillmore, 1968), but their psychological application is at present in its infancy.

Psycholinguistics has made a clear, positive contribution to the psychology of language in its emphasis upon the creativity, productivity and complex hierarchical structure of language. With respect to language acquisition, the contribution of Chomsky and those influenced by his views has been, as we have already mentioned earlier in this chapter, to stress the likelihood of some biologically based predisposition to language, or Language Acquisition Device, corresponding at least in part to the existence of linguistic universals – that is, to the universal features within the deep structure of all languages. The implication is that certain, specifically linguistic, processing features may be inbuilt, predisposing the child towards the adoption of certain grammatical hypotheses and categories when he receives and processes the linguistic sample provided by his environment. Language acquisition would then basically be a matter of matching the surface structures of the linguistic sample to the deep structures which are inbuilt, resulting in the production of a transformational grammar (with successive modifications) which ultimately corresponds to that of the language of the child's environment. If this hypothesis is accepted, it has the useful effect of reducing the apparent magnitude of the language-learning task with which every young child is faced, and therefore making his mastery of it more comprehensible than in the case of learning-theory approaches. These contributions, and the considerable stimulus which the psycholinguistic approach has given to research, are very much to its credit.

On the debit side, however, even if some linguistic structures are claimed to be innate (and there is really no direct evidence for this claim), there is obviously still a great deal of language to be learned; and while psycholinguists have been eager to reject learning-theory principles as a basis for language learning they have offered no real alternatives. Again, psycholinguistics, by its very dependence upon linguistic theory as the source of hypotheses, has neglected the importance of meaning, and in general the non-linguistic context in which language occurs. Further, as we stated earlier, linguistic models are constantly changing so that they do not necessarily provide a firm basis for psychological hypotheses. Finally, there is some doubt as to the logical status of linguistic models as a source of ideas about language behaviour; is a grammar (as we argued at the beginning of this discussion) a formal description of language, based upon observations of language use but bearing no necessary relation to the actual principles by which we produce and understand speech, or is generative grammar at any rate, as Chomsky has sometimes argued, a branch of cognitive psychology – that is, a psychological theory of language behaviour? Clearly the answer to this question is likely to influence our interpretation of empirical evidence, our formulation of research questions, and indeed the likely usefulness of grammatical models. Is the distinction between competence and performance, seen as crucial for the linguist, really useful for the psychologist, or should some features of performance limitation, as Greene (1972) has suggested, form part of the psychological theory of language? Psycholinguistics has some advantages over earlier approaches to the psychology of language, but is no more likely to provide 'easy answers' to our questions about language behaviour.

In the course of this section, and earlier, we have discussed certain characteristics of the language behaviour of adults, but have said virtually nothing of the nature of language development in the young child; this will be our next concern.

Language development

Some preliminaries

It is useful at the outset to make two general points about language development. First, the emergence and development of language depends upon a variety of different factors. It may depend upon possession of an innate pre-disposition for language (although, as we have seen in earlier sections of this chapter, some at least of the strong circumstantial evidence for this hypothesis has been eroded in recent years). Certainly it depends upon maturational factors: upon changes in the size and weight of the brain, and in its electrical activity patterns, and also upon certain anatomical changes – for example, in the shape of the oral cavity, associated with the absorption of sucking pads at weaning, and with the irruption of teeth – which are necessary for phonological development. Further, language development is clearly dependent upon learning, since it will not emerge in the absence of linguistic input, since every child learns the language of his own community and since the amount of linguistic input, and reinforcement of the child's own speech, does influence the frequency, and sometimes the complexity, of the child's language (we shall return to this point in later sections). Finally, language development is closely associated with other aspects of cognitive development, although the possible *causal* relations between language and thought have been much disputed (again, we shall discuss this in a later section).

The other general point which should be made is that at virtually all stages of language development, phonological, verbal or syntactic, the child's understanding precedes and exceeds his production. A child can understand certain words and constructions, and respond appropriately to them, before he is using them in speech. McCarthy (1954), for example, surveyed a number of studies of language development in children and concluded that the child first shows signs of paying attention to the sound of the human voice, for example, by altering his activity or by stopping altogether or perhaps turning round to face the speaker, at about two months of age. By the time he is six months old he seems able to discriminate between tones of voice, for instance to distinguish between a friendly and a scolding tone, although he is presumably still unable to understand the meanings of the individual words. By the age of nine months children are generally able to respond appropriately to one or two phrases when accompanied by gestures, and to show pleasure at hearing certain words rather than others. The attachment of appropriate responses to particular words increases in the tenth month and before the child is a year old he can stop when told 'no' and can follow some rudimentary commands. Between the ages of thirteen and seventeen months he understands 'Give me that' when it is accompanied by a gesture, and by the age of eighteen months he can point to his nose, eyes or hair when requested. These 'milestones' in the development of comprehension are obviously earlier than those of language production, the first word being typically produced at about one year of age and the first two-word utterance at perhaps eighteen months (albeit with enormous variations around these times even for 'normal' children). In phonological development, too, there is evidence that children may appreciate distinctions between sounds before these distinctions are put into practice: a child who calls his toy fish a 'fiss', for example, may well not accept 'fiss' as its name when spoken by adults but may insist on 'fish' instead.

The superiority of comprehension over production can be overstated, and there are instances of the opposite effect. Clark (1974), for example, quotes a sentence 'Let's go see baby Ivan have a bath', produced by a child less than three years old. At first sight this is a complex sentence, but examination of other utterances in the child's contemporary repertoire makes it clear that the sentence is in fact considerably simpler; 'Baby Ivan have a bath', for example, is *not* a modification of 'Baby Ivan has a bath', as one would suppose from the standpoint of adult grammar, but simply the form the sentence takes when used on its own. Again, there are many instances in which children may quote quite elaborate phrases from nursery rhymes or jingles apparently without comprehension of the structures involved; the writer's son, at thirty-four months, would cheerfully sing of 'a bicycle made for two', but spoil the effect by referring to bicycles seen in the street sometimes as 'bicycle' but often as 'bicycle-made'. However, such instances are more the exception than the rule; generally the child's production gives an underestimate of his capacity, and this of course has implications for research methodology.

There are perhaps four main methods by which a young child's language may be studied. First, and most obvious, is the study of the child's spontaneous speech, preferably in his own home and in the company of his usual caretaker (usually the mother), or in school and play settings in the case of older children. The parents may keep a 'speech diary' in which virtually all the child's utterances are recorded, or an 'outside' observer may enter the home to sample, usually to tape-record, speech on a number of occasions perhaps over a period of months. Both procedures have advantages and disadvantages, and in particular they share the disadvantages that the children studied are often a rather highly-selected sample (the children of highly educated parents, notably of psychologists and linguists!) and that, as we have seen, a child's production may not accurately represent his competence, particularly if observation of his speech is selective. A second method of research is therefore to *elicit* speech from the child rather than simply to record his spontaneous utterances. One simple way of eliciting speech is to ask the child to name objects; another is to require him to *imitate* or repeat the adult's utterance, since it has often been argued that if a child is able to imitate an utterance he is also capable of producing it spontaneously (we shall return to the characteristics of imitation later). Other ways of eliciting speech include the technique of Berko (1958), who asked young children of about four to eight years old to complete sentences which involved the grammatical modification of nonsense words; her findings will be mentioned later. A third method is to test *comprehension*, rather than spontaneous or elicited production. The vocabulary test is a conventional example, in which vocabulary size is estimated by requiring verbal definitions of given words.

Younger children can be asked to point to a picture of the object named, as a test of vocabulary, and it is also possible to test grammatical comprehension by, for example, showing a child two pictures – one of a girl pushing a boy, the other of a boy pushing a girl – and asking him to point to the picture in which 'the boy is pushed by the girl'; this of course provides a test of the child's comprehension of the passive construction. A fourth general research method involves *intervention*: an experimental group of children is given 'extra' linguistic stimulation in a series of informal individual sessions with an 'outsider' adult, perhaps over a period of weeks, and linguistic performance before and after the intervention is compared with that of a control group receiving no 'extra' stimulation. The intervention may consist fairly generally of recasting or commenting upon the child's utterances, or more specifically of exposing him to particular linguistic structures which do not yet appear in his spontaneous speech, such as complex question or verb forms. We shall return to such experiments in our discussion of 'language learning'.

The development of sounds and words

Crudely put, a child develops first sounds, then words, then grammar, although it is obvious that these three aspects of language, initiated in that order, overlap considerably in development; phonological development continues long after the first word and the first sentence have been produced, and an individual's vocabulary continues to grow until very old age.

Typically, a baby's first sound is crying; after a month or two, its vocalization becomes more varied, consisting at first of vowel sounds, particularly 'i' or 'u', which have led to the term 'cooing' to describe this stage. At perhaps four to six months of age there is a considerable increase in the variety and frequency of vocalization with the onset of *babbling*. Consonants emerge, first the 'back consonants' such as 'k' and 'g', then 'labials' such as 'b' and 'p' and 'nasals' such as 'm' and 'n'. Also the baby begins to combine sounds, chiefly consonant-plus-vowel (CV) at first, such as 'ga', 'ka', 'ma', then VCV ('aga') and VC ('uk'), then reduplication of sounds such as 'gaga', 'momo'. Also at this stage there is a development of stress, intonation and rhythm. At about twelve months (but with very wide normal variations, from perhaps seven to twenty-four months), the child produces his first recognizable word, and speech can be said to have begun; often at this stage there is a marked decrease in the frequency of vocalization and sometimes in its variety.

It has sometimes been argued that the babbling stage is an important preparation for speech, in which all the sounds relevant to the child's language are practised, and in some way reinforced, while sounds which are irrelevant become less frequent. In fact the relation between babbling and speech is not quite as straightforward as this would imply; sounds used early, and frequently, in babbling, for example, may not be used appropriately in early speech. The early consonants 'k' and 'g' are typically replaced in childish speech by 'front consonants' such as 't' and 'd': thus, a child may say 'tum' for 'come', 'det' for 'get'. This type of substitution is only one-way, in that children do not typically replace 't' by 'g'; thus, it is regular and not the result of poor discrimination. The substitutions are similar for several languages (though not for all), and are mirrored by the 'baby talk' of adults. On the other hand, there may be a certain continuity between babbling and speech in that on the whole substitution sounds in speech are popular in babbling, while the sounds replaced are less so. Thus it has been suggested that children have 'natural phonological preferences' which are reflected in substitutions: for a discussion, see Dale (1976). Nevertheless, the relation between prelinguistic and linguistic development is still rather unclear, as is the meaning, if any, which is to be attributed to different pre-linguistic vocalizations.

Once the first word has been produced, the growth of vocabulary is very rapid, although exact estimates of vocabulary size at different ages vary enormously, because of both individual differences among children and different estimation methods. The earliest words tend to be nouns, with adjectives also occurring early, and verbs usually rather later. A simple view of this early speech has been that it consists essentially of labelling, or naming; but consideration of the context and also the intonation of one-word utterances has led some investigators to argue that their function is not only referential but also *expressive* of emotion, and *conative* – that is, linked with action, either imperative or self-imperative: the child, for example, may say 'away' and push an undesired object away from him, or say 'doggie' and head purposively for the dog. Indeed, it has been argued that one-word utterances may in fact be sentences, with an implied grammar, and in particular that they often represent the *predicate* of an implied sentence, with the subject unstated. This *holophrastic speech* hypothesis (see, for example, McNeill, 1970) suggests that the child has the competence, even at the one-word stage, for longer, grammatical utterances but that his performance is limited to one word because of such factors as small vocabulary, brief memory and attention span, and perhaps a failure to appreciate the distinction between linguistic and non-linguistic expression of sentence elements. However, this interesting hypothesis is difficult to test, and is opposed, for example, by Bloom (1973), who has argued that the child's limited performance at the one-word stage mirrors a limited competence, dependent in turn upon his more general cognitive development. Certainly it is difficult to demonstrate a child's possession of grammar until the stage at which he produces single utterances of more than one word in length, the words showing evidence of *patterning* in the order in which they are produced.

The development of grammar

The first sentences children produce are typically of two, sometimes three and occasionally four words; thus they are very short compared to adult sentences. The words used are usually *content* words (such as nouns, adjectives, verbs) rather than *function* words (such as articles and prepositions), and typically they lack *inflections* such as the present participle ending -ing, third person singular or past tense endings such as -s and -d. Typical examples of children's early sentences (from Brown) are 'two boot', 'hear tractor', 'Adam make tower'. Similarly, when children imitate adult utterances they abbreviate them, retaining content words but omitting function words and inflections: thus, 'The doggie is eating' becomes 'Doggie eat', and 'Daddy's going to the office' becomes 'Daddy go office' or 'Daddy office'. This has been described by Brown and Fraser (1963) as *telegraphic speech* because of its resemblance to the very efficient condensation of messages, retaining their essential meaning, used in telegraphic communication. This, of course, is not to say that the child consciously devises an efficient reduction process; indeed, the abbreviation process is less serviceable, but still followed, in more heavily inflected languages than English, such as Russian, where the omission of inflections leads to considerable loss of meaning. It is most likely that certain content words are more readily imitated than function words because they are more familiar, and certainly because they are more heavily accented (as are word stems rather than inflectional endings), in adult speech.

Virtually from the start of two-word utterances it is clear that children show evidence of patterning, or of *rules*: words are not joined at random, but systematically, so that, for example, a child watching the dog eat supper will say 'doggie eat' but not 'eat doggie'. Clearly, too, at this stage the child is best seen as possessing a simple grammar or system of generative rules, which is his own, rather than an inferior adult grammar; thus the researcher's task is to discover the child's grammar. The method most often employed in the past has been *distributional analysis*: an examination of the frequency of occurrence of different words and of the positions (for example, initial or terminal) in an utterance that a given word typically occupies, and an allocation of words into grammatical classes on the basis of 'shared distributions' (or 'shared contexts'). Two words in the child's repertoire are considered to belong to the same grammatical category if they appear grammatically interchangeable: if they occur in the same position in an utterance, followed or preceded by the same words and so on. The percentage of overlap

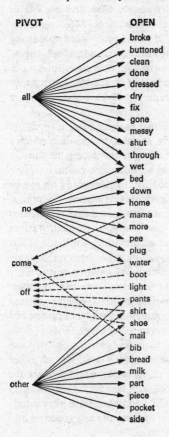

Figure 17.2 Some two-word pivotal constructions (pivot + open and open + pivot) observed in one child, by Braine (1963). Arrows indicate order of utterance: e.g. 'all broke', 'other shirt', 'mama come', 'shirt off'. Note that (a) there are many more open than pivot words, (b) some open words may occur either as the first or as the second word of the utterance, but no pivot words show this flexibility, (c) many open words may occur in association with a given pivot word, but different pivot words rarely 'share' an associated open word. No three (or more) word utterances are shown here, although a few were produced by this child, a boy aged nineteen to twenty-four months

in context between the words which can be accepted as evidence of their grammatical equivalence has to be arbitrarily determined, and this presents some difficulty, particularly since the percentages obtained are likely to be unstable from one set of utterances to another. Brown and Fraser (1963) have suggested that this difficulty may well be one shared by the learning child as well as by the observing adult.

Using the method of distributional analysis, Braine (1963) and others suggested that early speech consists basically of two classes of words, *pivot* and *open*. Pivot words were said to occupy a fixed position in an utterance, to be relatively few in number and to be very frequently used. Open words were said to be greater in number, less frequently used and capable of appearing in different positions in different utterances. Most sentences consisted of a pivot word plus an open word (some pivot words occurring always first in an utterance, others appearing always last); some 'open-open' utterances might also occur, but not 'pivot-pivot' utterances, and open words, but not pivot words, might also stand alone as one-word utterances. Examples of pivotal constructions (from Braine's study) are given in Figure 17.2.

Braine suggested that the pivot-open distinction was an at least partly fortuitous result of *position learning* – that is, learning the position which a word typically occupies in a sentence, and subsequently placing the word in that position in new sentences via a process of *contextual generalization*; pivot words, according to him, were differentiated from open words simply by being words for which a fixed sentence position had been learned. For others, however, such as McNeill (1966, 1970), the pivot and open classes represented a fundamental grammatical distinction upon which, through further differentiation of pivot and open classes, later grammatical development was based. In recent years, the notion of 'pivot grammar' has been increasingly criticized. It does not characterize the utterances of all children, particularly in languages other than English; it does not adequately describe early utterances, in that, for example, words which on other grounds would be classed as 'pivots' do sometimes occur alone or in conjunction with other pivots; and it neglects the *structural meaning* of utterances in many cases. Bloom (1970) quoted the example of Kathryn, a child who used the construction 'Mummy sock' twice in one day: first, on picking up her mother's sock; second, as her mother put her (Kathryn's) sock on her. Pivot grammar would describe the two instances of the utterance identically; clearly, however, their meaning is different. Thus, Bloom (1970), Brown (1973) and others have increasingly suggested that a more appropriate method of analysis of early speech is into its *semantic structures* – in terms of its expression of agent, action, object, location, instrument and so on. This of course parallels a recent trend in transformational grammar (referred to on p. 456).

Nevertheless, much of early speech, at least in English, does have a 'pivot look' about it, and the pivot grammars had at least the virtue of illustrating the great regularity and lawfulness even of very early stages of continuous speech. Obviously, however, the child's grammar will be considerably enlarged and elaborated before it approximates to the adult grammar of his community. One feature of adult speech often lacking in that of young children is that a sentence must contain both a subject and a predicate (or a noun phrase plus a verb phrase); the apparent lack of such a rule in early speech has sometimes been an embarrassment to proponents of an innate LAD, since the subject-predicate rule is one obvious candidate as a universal feature of deep structure. However, Brown and others have pointed out that in early speech children seem to possess a basic order rule, that a sentence consists of agent + action + object + location; if the child produces only two word utterances he will produce any two of these elements, observing the word order of the basic rule; when he progresses to predominantly three-word utterances he will again observe the basic rule in his ordering of elements, and the rule will be fully expressed when four-word utterances are achieved. Thus the later emergence of subject–predicate expressions as a reliable sentence characteristic may represent increasing production capacity rather than the acquisition of a new rule.

Inflections, as we have seen, are typically absent from early speech and there is some suggestion that their order of acquisition is determined in part by frequency of adult use: the present participle ending -ing and the plural ending -s, for example, are very frequent in adult speech and are acquired relatively early, while the possessive -s (as in 'Adam's car') and the third person -s (as in 'doggie eats') are acquired relatively late and are less frequent (although still far from rare) in adult speech. However, other factors are also likely to be important, such as the *surface* complexity of the inflection and its *semantic* complexity. For further discussion of these factors, see Slobin (1966a, 1971).

It is particularly clear in the case cf inflections (and in the case of trans-formations, to be mentioned presently) that children develop not by learning piecemeal but by learning *rules*. Paradoxically, some of the best evidence for rule learning comes from cases in which children make grammatical errors. Often a child will produce a sentence such as 'I digged in the garden' or 'The sheeps runned away' – sentences which they are very unlikely to have learned from parents or other adults, and which show not an absence of grammar but rather an over-generalization of grammatical rules. The point has been further demonstrated experimentally, notably by Berko (1958), whose research method was mentioned earlier. For example, a child would be shown two pictures of an imaginary animal or bird and told: 'This is a wug'. 'This is another wug'. 'Now there are two   '. Even the youngest children were able to produce the regular plural form 'wugs' in completing this sentence; they were similarly able to form regular past tenses of nonsense verbs. They showed, in fact, a strong reluctance to learn *irregular* forms; for example, when given the sequence: 'Here is a goose and there are two geese. Now there are three   ,' most children, especially the younger ones, would complete it with the word 'gooses'. Clearly, these young children possessed a 'productive grammar', highly regular and intolerant of exceptions. The development of plural and past tense rules has also been studied, in more detail, by Ervin (1964), who has charted the way in which such irregular forms as 'feet' are at first produced correctly, then replaced and 'regularized' (foots) when a simple rule is acquired, then further transformed as more complex rules are learned: for example, when a child learns that a word ending in a sibilant (such as 'box') is turned into the plural by the addition of a neutral vowel sound as well as a terminal -s ('boxes') the plural of foot may well become 'footses' or even 'feetses'. The difficult learning task appears to be not the acquisition and generalization of rules but their limitation and partial application.

The importance and ubiquity of rule learning is equally evident in the development of transformations – that is, the emergence of utterances which are not simple, active, affirmative, declarative utterances but which are negative, passive, interrogative or imperative. To take negative sentences as an example, in the formation of 'adult' negative sentences at least two things are needed: there must be a negative element such as 'no' or 'not', and it must be correctly placed in the sentence, after the first auxiliary of the verb (so that 'I have written' in negative form is 'I have not written': the negative form of 'I have been writing' is 'I have not been writing' and so on). Further, if the verb has no auxiliary (as in 'I write') one must be created by a rule known as 'do-support', whereby 'I write' becomes 'I do write' and can then be expressed in the negative as 'I do not write'. Children appear to acquire these rules one by one, and in the above order: thus, a child's earliest negative sentences may be 'no wipe finger' and 'not Teddy', replaced later by such constructions as 'he no bite you' and 'there no squirrels', and later still by 'correct' adult forms. Similarly, in the formation of so-called wh- questions (in which an element such as 'who', 'what' or 'which' is required) a child may successively produce such forms as 'you want what?', 'what you want?' and 'what do you want?'. It would also appear that even when several transformational rules have been acquired performance limitations may prevent more than a few from being applied to the same sentence: thus, a child may, at the same stage of development, produce both 'why can he go out?' and 'why he can't go out?'. For further discussion of the development of transformations, see, e.g., McNeill (1970); Dale (1976).

Finally, the child acquires *complex* sentences – those having characteristics of embedding, of co-ordinate or subordinate classes, and of various kinds of deletions and substitutions. These first occur at perhaps two-and-a-half to three years of age, often taking the form of a sentence as object – as in 'I think it's the wrong way' or 'I don't want you read that book' (for other examples and fuller discussion, see, e.g., Dale (1976)). Such structures may take a considerable time in acquisition, and they also sometimes present problems of interpretation when they first occur (take, for example, the sentence 'Let's go see baby Ivan have a bath' quoted on p. 458).

To summarize, it is clear that at all stages language development is charac-terized by the learning not simply of piecemeal elements but of rules. The tendency is for a few simple, general rules to be learned early, and for more complex and more partial or limited rules to be learned later; and when partial rules are learned they tend to be over-applied as though they were general. In many ways, then, the chief problem for the child learning language, at least after the very early stages, is not acquiring rules but learning to limit their application and to tolerate exceptions and irregul-arities.

Language learning

Although we now know a great deal about the characteristics of young children's language, our knowledge of the means by which language develop-ment proceeds is still rather slight. Given the enormity of his task, the relatively short time taken for its accomplishment and the irregularity of his training, the child's mastering of his native language is certainly impressive. Indeed, it has sometimes been argued (chiefly in the context of the psycho-linguists' attack upon learning-theory principles as a basis for the under-standing of language acquisition) that the process of development is a mystery: that the child somehow induces the structure of his language by an unobservable process (aided no doubt by highly specific inbuilt grammatical hypotheses) and that anything which might look to the naïve observer like a potential learning or teaching situation is irrelevant. It has become increasingly clear in recent years that this is an overstatement of the (admittedly real) difficulty of accounting for language acquisition. In the first place, children do take a considerable time to acquire the chief structures of their language, certainly continuing through, say, the first twelve years or so of life. Second, children typically receive an 'easy introduction' to language, in that the speech of adults, particularly caretakers, to children is simpler, slower, shorter, better-formed grammatically, more repetitive and more limited in vocabulary than is speech among adults; moreover, mothers appear to modify their speech appropriately with the increasing age and skill of their children (Snow, 1972; Fraser and Roberts, 1975; Moerk, 1974). Third, there are in fact certain patterns of 'natural' caretaker–child interaction which may well have importance as language-learning devices. The child imitates adult utterances; he appears to practise grammatical forms once they have been acquired; and adults do set up 'training situations' in which they 'correct' the child's utterances and present model utterances for him to copy. We shall very briefly consider the possible importance of imitation and of 'training situations'; we shall not consider the role of overt practice on the part of the child, since its importance in acquiring new structures is probably very limited (although Moerk, 1974, has argued that certain kinds of practice – so-called 'replacement sequences' – may well be important for expanding and generalizing already acquired constructions).

There has been considerable debate concerning the 'progressiveness' of children's imitations; as we mentioned earlier, it has often been argued that a child will only imitate what he is capable of producing spontaneously, and thus that imitation cannot be a means of acquiring new constructions. However, recent studies suggest that imitation can be progressive, in that children may well be able to imitate utterances more complex than their typical productions when required to do so, although their spontaneous imitations are not more complex, and that even spontaneous imitations may be progressive if the criteria for an imitation (usually an exact, complete and immediate reproduction of the adult utterance) are relaxed somewhat to allow for partial imitation and some measure of delay. It is still not clear that imitation mediates the acquisition of new structures, and perhaps more likely that its (important) role in language development is that it mediates the *production* of structures which are already understood but not yet produced in spontaneous speech (Moerk, 1977; Whitehurst and Vasta, 1975).

As far as parental training is concerned, there is some evidence that specific correction, by an adult, of a young child's utterance is not a particularly successful way to 'improve' his speech. Nelson (1973) has reported that children whose speech is often corrected at the one-word stage may develop more slowly than uncorrected children, and books on language development abound in anecdotes illustrating the resistance of children to correction of their utterances. But parents and other caretakers, in their natural interactions with the child and often without any clear didactic intent, provide a variety of training situations. They provide grammatical models for a child simply by talking to him; by imitating, in expanded form, his utterances; by commenting on what he says; by prompting further elaborations on his part; by setting up question and answer games of various kinds; by telling nursery rhymes and stories which provide vocabulary and syntax more advanced than the child's production. Clearly, all these patterns of interaction are potential learning devices; moreover, many interactions are very rich in that they provide more than one opportunity for learning. A mother's expansion of her child's utterance, for example, provides a 'corrected' model of his own speech, a model of a more complex grammatical structure for him to comprehend and an opportunity for him to translate comprehension into production by imitating her expansion. It is in this context that 'intervention' experiments (mentioned on p. 460) have proved very useful in supplementing observational data: although some studies have shown only a general improvement in linguistic performance to result from systematic language exposure, and some have been inconclusive, several recent reports have shown clear and specific effects of intervention, in that children given exposure to certain linguistic structures show more complex use of such structures, rather than simply a general developmental spurt, as a result (for example, Nelson, Carskaddan and Bonvillian, 1973; Nelson, 1977).

It seems, then, that language learning may prove less of a mystery than has sometimes been claimed, although exactly what learning principles are involved, and, for example, what the *long-term* effects of 'intervention' may be, are still not well understood. Perhaps the most promising aspect of recent research is its implicit or explicit view of language development as an *interactive* process between the child and a sensitive adult, a process which is not purely linguistic but more generally communicative and cognitive, and to be placed firmly within the context of cognitive and social development.

Language and cognition

In the first section of this chapter we remarked on the importance of language as a communication system, as a vehicle for the expression of private experience and the transmission of knowledge. Language, in the sense of verbal report, has traditionally been used very widely, not only in everyday life but also in scientific investigation, as an indicator of non-verbal behaviour and experience: for example, perception, memory and thinking. As we have already seen in our discussion of perception (Chapter 10) and will discuss further in the context of thinking (Chapter 18), verbal report has drawbacks as an indicator: it may not be sufficiently sensitive to mirror experience, and the requirement of verbal report may itself be distorting. In the field of memory too there is abundant evidence of the importance of verbal labelling, both in increasing the accuracy of memory and in introducing a tendency for distortion. Several investigators have shown that the ease with which colour stimuli can be described verbally (that is, their *codeability*) is positively related to the accuracy with which they can be recognized, after delay, in an array of closely similar colours (Brown and Lenneberg, 1954; Lantz and Stefflre, 1964). Similar results have been obtained in cross-cultural studies, comparing memory for colours in cultures whose language differentiates them relatively well or relatively poorly (Lenneberg and Roberts, 1956; Stefflre, Vales and Morely, 1966); however, more recent studies have cast some doubt upon these findings or their inter-

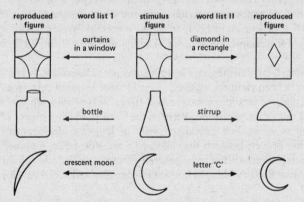

Figure 17.3   The influence of a verbal label upon reproduction of visual forms. (From Carmichael, Hogan and Walter, 1932, p. 80)

pretation (see Rosch, 1977b). Carmichael, Hogan and Walter (1932) showed that naming nonsense shapes can influence their reproduction from memory; examples of their findings are shown in Figure 17.3. In these cases, the ascription of a verbal label results in less accurate, rather than more accurate, memory for a non-verbal stimulus; thus in memory, as in perception, language is a double-edged weapon.

It has sometimes been argued further that language may not only distort the *report* of experienced reality but may itself to some extent determine that experience. This *linguistic relativity* hypothesis was classically stated by Whorf (1956), who argued that the linguistic system is 'not merely a repro- ducing instrument for viewing ideas but rather is itself the shaper of ideas, the program and guide for the individual's mental activity, for his analysis of impressions, for his synthesis of his original stock in trade. Formulation of ideas is not an independent process ... but is part of a particular grammar and differs, from slightly to greatly, as between different grammars. We dissect nature along lines laid down by our native languages' (pp. 212–13).

Whorf illustrated his argument by drawing attention to grammatical dif- ferences between English and the American Indian languages, particularly Hopi, and arguing that these differences must be reflected in the cognitive structures of the respective cultures. Similar work has been carried out by others, and there have also been attempts to investigate more precisely whether differences in vocabulary or grammar among different languages are accompanied by differences in perception or in cognition (for reviews see, e.g., Lloyd, 1972; Rosch, 1977b). The results of these attempts have been essentially negative: although language differences may in some cases serve to direct attention, interpretation and rehearsal, there is no evidence to suggest that they have any effect upon perception in any basic sense or that they restrict cognition to any significant extent. As Greene (1975) has pointed out, it would be naïve to assume from a study of English usage that the Englishman believes that ships are feminine, that mountains have heads and feet, or that identical actions are involved in driving a car, driving on the golf course and driving a hard bargain. This is not to say that language differences, both among and within cultures, are unimportant. It is not insignificant that a scientist should speak of 'sacrificing', rather than killing, an experimental animal; that trade union leaders talk of 'industrial action' when others talk of strikes; that a twenty-five-year-old human male should be called a man while a twenty-five-year-old human female is called a girl (or increasingly, in current usage, a lady). Such differences in terminology afford an interesting insight into the attitudes and prejudices of our society; but they are less pervasive and influential, and more easily overcome, than the linguistic relativity hypothesis would allow. Indeed it is most likely that language differences reflect, rather than shape, cultural attitudes and ideas.

Of some relevance to the linguistic relativity hypothesis is the study of social class differences in language, notably by Bernstein (1973). He argued that patterns of speech, or *codes*, are initially determined by the social relationships, and modes of social control, which characterize the child's family group; once learned, the habitual code may then have repercussions, notably for communication and schooling. The classification of social control systems is not in principle completely identified with social class differences, but tends to be so identified in practice, the distinction being chiefly drawn between 'lower working class' and 'middle class' family structures.

Corresponding to this distinction, Bernstein proposed two distinct language codes – the *restricted code* and the *elaborated code*. The restricted code is characterized by an emphasis on concrete, descriptive, affective levels of response, with little generalization or abstraction, and it tends to be context-dependent, in that comprehension is often difficult in the absence of a non-linguistic 'confirming' context. The elaborated code, in contrast, shows greater syntactic and lexical variety with more subordinate clauses,

Table 17.3
'Typical' restricted-code and elaborated-code descriptions of a series of pictures. (Bernstein, 1973, p. 203)

Restricted code:	They're playing football and he kicks it and it goes through there it breaks the window and they're looking at it and he comes out and shouts at them because they've broken it so they run away and then she looks out and she tells them off.
Elaborated code:	Three boys are playing football and one boy kicks the ball and it goes through the window the ball breaks the window and the boys are looking at it and a man comes out and shouts at them because they've broken the window so they run away and then that lady looks out of her window and she tells the boys off.

Picture series on which the descriptions are based:

1. Some boys are playing football.
2. The ball goes through the window of a house.
3. A woman is looking out of the window and a man is 'making an ominous gesture'.
4. The children are moving away.

complex structures, uncommon adjectives and verbs; it is likely to contain more generalities, abstractions and qualifications; and it is relatively context-free. A comparison of the two codes in the description of a series of pictures is given in Table 17.3.

Other differentiating characteristics are that restricted-code users are more likely to employ 'sociocentric' verbal sequences, such as 'couldn't it?' and 'isn't it?' and more 'total' personal pronouns such as 'you' and 'they'; elaborated-code users are more likely to use 'egocentric' sequences such as 'I think' and, in general, the first person singular pronoun 'I'. These differences have been related to class differences in the source and definition of status, which for lower working class members may be more in terms of group reinforcement and for middle class members more in terms of individual identity.

It has sometimes been suggested that while elaborated-code users have access to a restricted code, restricted-code users do not possess an elaborated code and therefore are at a *cognitive* disadvantage, being barred access to a powerful intellectual vehicle. However, the *cognitive deficit* hypothesis has not been supported by Bernstein himself, who has argued that class differences are differences in habitual performance, not in competence or 'tacit understanding of the linguistic rule system'. It has also been forcibly attacked, for example, by Labov in the context of his studies of Nonstandard Negro English (NNE) in the U.S.A.; he has argued, with cogent illustrations, that NNE is not an inferior language, but a language different from standard English but of equivalent conceptual status. Cazden and others have also pointed out that in comparing subcultural language differences the *context* of use is an all-important determinant of whether an individual employs predominantly an elaborated or a restricted code (for examples of these arguments see the papers by Olim, Labov and Cazden in Williams, 1970; Robinson, 1972).

If there is little or no evidence for the linguistic relativity hypothesis, what is the relation between language and cognition? It has sometimes been proposed, in effect, that thought determines language, at least in the sense that language can only mirror the complexity which cognitive structure has achieved; this has been termed the *cognitive hypothesis* (see, for example, Cromer, 1974), and it clearly resembles the position of, for example, Bloom (1970, 1973) quoted in our discussion of language development. Yet again it has been argued that although language and cognition may be closely related and at times interdependent, they have their separate roots; as Cromer (1974, p. 246) suggests, 'cognitive ability makes meanings available for expression, but we also need linguistic capabilities in order to express those meanings in language. Though language development depends on cognition, language has its own specific sources'. We shall return to these suggestions, and more generally to possible accounts of cognitive development, in Chapter 18.

Chapter 18
Thinking

The definition of thinking

The term 'thinking', as many writers have pointed out (e.g. Thomson, 1957), is not well defined in everyday, or indeed in technical, language; it may refer to many rather different types of activity and to a wide range of situations. Many of the questions which the layman asks about thinking are basically concerned with the legitimacy of applying the term to a particular situation or type of activity. He may ask, for example: Do animals think? Can a machine think? Are we 'thinking' when we dream? Is thinking always rational or can it be irrational? Is 'inspiration' a kind of thinking or some quite different process? Clearly, the answer to these and similar questions must depend upon our definition of the term 'thinking'.

Let us as an example take the question: can animals think? Thinking has sometimes been defined simply as the internal representation of events: thinking is said to have occurred in any situation when behaviour is produced for which 'the relevant cues are not available in the external environment at the time the correct response is required, but must be supplied by the organism itself' (Osgood, 1953, p. 656). While this definition clearly can be applied to many human tasks, from mental arithmetic to poetry writing, it will also cover many learning situations in which animals are tested: for example, those involving *delayed response* and thus some 'internal representation' of prior events, and *alternation learning* problems based upon mazes such as that shown in Figure 18.1 (for amplification, see Osgood, 1953).

In alternation learning tasks, cues to the appropriate response in the sequence are not supplied by the environment, or by the position or orientation of the animal, but must be provided by internal, representational stimuli. If we accept such rather simple situations as appropriate to demonstrate thinking, then it is clear that animals can think. Not only apes and monkeys but also cats, dogs, rats and racoons can solve problems involving delayed response, and several of these species can also learn alternation sequences, although these, and in particular double alternation sequences, present a much more difficult task; the ability to learn such tasks varies

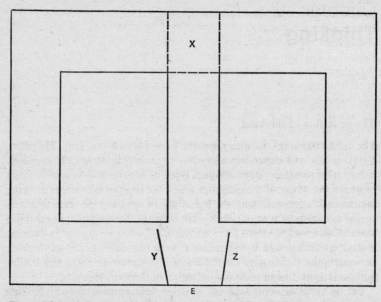

Figure 18.1 A figure-of-eight maze used in alternation learning. The animal enters the maze at E. If it correctly turns right at X, it is rewarded at Z and readmitted to the central alley; if it correctly turns left at X it is rewarded at Y. If an incorrect turn is made the animal is unrewarded at Y or Z, or is stopped before reaching Y or Z and forced to retrace its path, or is punished by administration of electric shock at some point beyond X. 'Correct' response sequences may be in the form of *alternation* (RLRL...) or *double alternation* (RRLL RRLL ...), and in *delayed alternation* the animal may be halted temporarily at some point or points in the sequence

with the character of a species and, in particular, the nature of its adaptation to the environment.

The objection might be made to this evidence that if thinking is defined in these terms it is no different from retention; to be regarded as anything more than synonymous with memory, thinking must be demonstrated in, and defined in terms of, more complicated situations. The construction of such situations has followed from a second definition of thinking in terms of problem-solving behaviour. Humphrey (1951) defined thinking as 'what happens in experience when an organism, human or animal, meets, recognizes and solves a problem' (p. 311). A problem may be said to arise whenever a desired goal is not immediately accessible. Thus, the solution of a problem may be taken as evidence of thinking if it appears that the solution involves internal manipulation of elements of the situation, or the supplying 'from within' of cues which are not perceptually present. It would not be evidence of thinking if an animal solved a problem by trial and error or by repeating a well-learned response which had been rewarded in the past.

Much of the work on problem solving in animals began as an attempt to answer the question: do animals think? More precisely, the question posed was whether animals could exhibit insightful behaviour in a problem situation, as opposed to blind, mechanical trial and error. Such investigators as E. L. Thorndike (1898, 1911) argued that animals typically solve problems by a more or less random trial and elimination of possible responses until the correct response is hit upon, with a gradual and irregular reduction in errors on successive attempts at solution; others, notably Köhler (1925), claimed that an animal might show a grasp of the problem situation as a whole, form hypotheses as to its solution and produce responses which were meaningful in the total context of the problem. Köhler described the process of insightful solution in this way: there is, often, a pause in activity during which the animal, literally, surveys the situation, followed by sudden and swift performance of the responses involved in the solution.

The discrepancy between these accounts may be explained in various ways, not least in terms of the species of animal on which the accounts were based; Köhler's studies involved, principally, the use of apes as subjects, while Thorndike used animals lower in the phylogenetic scale (for example, cats). Generally speaking, however, it is likely that the distinction between 'insightful' and 'blind' solutions is misconceived. Thorndike's animals were tested in 'puzzle boxes', their goal being to open the door of the box and escape to food placed outside it. To open the door they had to perform one or more of a number of responses – lever pushing, pulling at strings, lifting latches – whose connection with the door was not evident from the inside of the cage. Köhler, on the other hand, set problems for his animals in which all the cues to solution were normally present and often within the same field of vision as the 'goal object' (see Figure 18.2). It is likely that an animal faced with a problem will utilize any cues that are available towards solution and that its performance will vary with the number and availability of such cues. If Köhler's animals react on the basis of visual cues they are likely to show 'insight'; if Thorndike's animals react to visual cues they will fail to reach a solution, since the response which produces a solution is basically arbitrary. They must learn to produce an improbable response rather than the responses suggested by the (misleading) cues available.

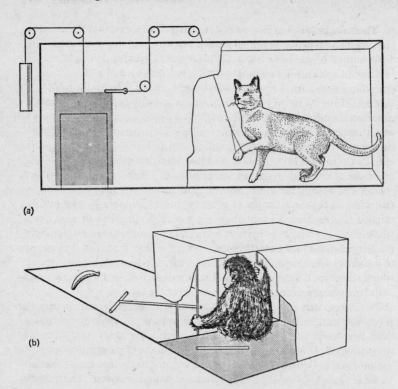

Figure 18.2   Problem-solving situations used by Thorndike and Köhler. (a) A 'puzzle box' of the type used by E. L. Thorndike (1911). To open the door of its box the cat must claw at a loop of string which, outside the box, releases the catch of the door via a pulley system. A separate weight-and-pulley system raises and holds open the door when released. (b) A problem situation of the type used by Köhler (1925). The chimpanzee cannot reach its food with the short stick inside its cage; but it can use the short stick to rake the long stick into reach, and then use the long stick to draw in the fruit

The work carried out in this field has, however, proved extremely useful in providing a good deal of empirical evidence as to the conditions which improve or impair performance at problem solving (see, for example, Riopelle, 1968); and clearly, if we define thinking in terms of the capacity to solve problems, animals, at any rate of some species, must be held to think.

These definitions are not, of course, those likely to be produced by the introspecting layman. When he asks whether animals think, he is probably referring to some such notion as 'inner life': whether animals have self-awareness and abstract ideas. The notion that animals possess awareness, in this sense, appears to be generally rejected, if it is considered at all, although a strong case for its reconsideration has been made by Thorpe (1966). It is in fact extraordinarily difficult to decide what would constitute evidence of such 'inner life', in the absence of its communication by speech. The problem was traditionally solved by recourse to 'Lloyd Morgan's canon' – the principle that animal behaviour is to be explained in the simplest terms possible, and that therefore accounts of animal behaviour involving such notions as 'insight' and 'expectancy' were to be avoided. It is of course debatable whether such accounts are necessarily less 'simple' than the sometimes very complex mechanistic explanations which have instead been offered.

The conclusion to be drawn from such considerations might well be that by a skilful use of definition well-nigh any question about thinking may receive any answer. Partly because of these uncertainties, for many years experimental psychologists tended to avoid the study of cognition – notably behaviourists who sought to account for behaviour without recourse to the notion of 'internal events', which were held to be not directly observable and therefore to lead only to untestable hypotheses. If 'internal events' were incorporated into theories of behaviour, they were incorporated in the form of 'intervening variables' whose independent existence was not considered.

Nevertheless, in recent years there has been a return of interest in the analysis of what has been termed 'the central process', largely but not entirely stimulated by the growth of computer science which has focused attention on the methods by which information can be processed in machines, and perhaps also, in some sense, in man. A classic statement of the nature of thinking (and one which seems currently to be approved by many researchers) was that of Craik (1943), who paved the way for the information-processing approach (see later) by arguing that 'thought models, or parallels, reality'. In some sense, he proposed, 'the organism carries a "small-scale model" of external reality and of its own possible actions within its head.' The thinking process is one of translating external objects and events into *symbols*, operating upon these symbols by inference, hypothesizing, calculation, the utilization of knowledge to produce further symbols, and then translating the symbols thus produced 'back' into external objects or events so that the present 'real' situation can be dealt with successfully.

Thinking, then, might be provisionally defined as 'the internal manipulation of symbols': but it is an inadequate definition. 'Manipulation' suggests
that thinking involves *active* organization rather than, for example, the
automatic association of ideas, although not *necessarily* awareness of such
organization: this seems a reasonable stipulation if thinking is to be differentiated, however weakly, from 'unthinking' activities. However, the
nature of the manipulation, of the rules by which symbols might be analysed
and synthesized, is unstated, and many different types of process might
require discrimination and description (see Neisser, 1963b). Again, the
nature of 'symbols' is not specified: these might be words, numbers, sensory
images or other types of representation (as we shall see later, there have been
numerous attempts to specify the nature of the elements or 'raw stuff' of
thinking). The greatest difficulty of definition, and indeed of research, is
summed up by the use of the word 'internal', since it underlines the basic
problem that thinking is private and unobservable activity. How then can
it be studied?

There are effectively two approaches to unobservable behaviour. One is
via introspection. Thinking is not necessarily 'unobservable' to the thinker;
he may be able to make his private awareness public by reporting on it.
The technique of introspection – that is, of 'observing oneself think' during
the performance of mental tasks and of reporting on the process to an
observer – was extensively used by early investigators although with the
advent of behaviourism it fell into some disrepute.

The difficulties of dealing with introspective data are considerable. Introspective data are by their nature unverifiable; they can represent only those
aspects of thinking of which the thinker is readily aware and therefore can
offer no clue to the existence or nature of 'unconscious' thinking; they are
conveyed only by the verbal report of the thinker and this may not be
sensitive enough to portray all the subtleties of experience. Further, the
process of introspection involves an atypical attitude on the part of the
thinker who is required not only to think but also to 'observe his thinking',
and this may well lead to modification of the thinking process itself. Nevertheless, introspection has been, and is still, a valuable tool in psychological
research (for a fuller discussion of the use of introspection in the study of
thinking, see Humphrey, 1951; McKellar, 1962; Radford and Burton, 1974).

The other source of evidence about 'unobserved behaviour' is, simply,
that there are situations which can only be explained by postulating it. We
have already referred to some of these situations – delayed-response and
alternation problems in the case of animals, problem situations for both

animals and humans – in which activity 'must have occurred' between stimulus and response, since the final behaviour of the subject cannot be held to derive directly from the immediate stimulus situation. In the following section of this chapter we shall consider certain types of 'thinking situations' – problem solving and reasoning, concept formation, creative thinking – with special reference to the (observable) factors which contribute to relative success or failure. On pp. 491–7 we shall look at attempts to examine thinking more closely, in terms of its 'raw material' and in terms of analysing its processes and stages. Finally, on pp. 497–501 we shall mention some aspects of cognitive development. For fuller discussions of these and other areas, see, for example, Reeves (1965); Voss (1969); Bourne, Ekstrand and Dominowski (1971); Bolton (1972); Radford and Burton (1974); Cohen (1977); Johnson-Laird and Wason (1977).

Studies of 'thinking situations'

Problem-solving and reasoning

A general requirement of any behaviour which is to be regarded as problem solving is that it should involve some response which is novel for the individual, which requires the reorganization rather than the simple recall of previously learned responses and which is not simply a specific solution but one which can apply in principle to any of a number of problems. Beyond that generalization, the problem situations which have been employed are very diverse. We have already mentioned some problems employed by psychologists using animals; when humans are studied, problems have ranged from practical construction tasks, via anagrams and 'brain-teasers', to abstract mathematical and logical reasoning. It is not surprising, then, that general conclusions about problem-solving activity are not altogether easy to achieve. Findings tend to depend upon the type of problem used: to a large extent, subjects give the kind of performance which the task requires, and are influenced by the variables which the experimenter has put there to influence them.

Many early experiments in problem solving were carried out under the influence of Gestalt psychology (see Chapter 10), with emphasis upon the perceptual characteristics of the problem situation and the achievement of insight, or else within the framework of S–R learning theory; we have already considered some such experiments with animals as subjects. From these, and other, types of experiment two groups of factors emerge as of great importance for success or failure: certain characteristics of the task, and the prior experience of the problem solver (as well as other factors such as the species of animal tested, its age – which is of course confounded with, but not identical with, prior experience – and its motivational state).

With respect to task characteristics, it has been found that in the case of animals (such as those used by Köhler and Thorndike) problems are much more likely to be solved if all the components of the solution are readily visible: if, for example, the sticks needed for solution of a food-raking problem are left lying at the front of an ape's cage and within the same field of vision as the food. Where humans are concerned, the perceptual presence of cues to solution might be considered less important, since the human subject has greater capacity for representing to himself cues which are not present, for example by words. Nevertheless, there are studies which suggest that perceptual factors are not unimportant in problem solving by humans. A classic series of experiments by Duncker (1945) showed that the spatial arrangement of components given to subjects substantially affected the ease with which they solved construction problems. When subjects were asked to fix three lighted candles against a wall, given only hammer, nails, a box and the candles, the problem was solved more readily when the box and candles were laid out separately than when the candles were presented *in* the box; the solution to this problem is to use the box not in its usual role as a container but as a shelf, which can be nailed to the wall and on which the candles can stand. The implication would seem to be that perceptual characteristics may influence a subject's grasp of the possible functions of elements of the solution; where the presentation of elements favours one functional interpretation, other functions are rendered harder to grasp.

Other task variables which are clearly important in determining ease of solution include complexity, (often) degree of abstractness, and the degree of definition of the initial problem and of the desired goal. For example, Cohen (1977) compares three problems: 'find the square root of 169'; 'mend the car'; 'design a fine town centre'. In the first, both starting point and goal are well defined; in the second the goal is well defined but the initial state ill defined, while the goal is ill defined in the third. It is, incidentally, a limitation of much problem-solving research that it has tended to use problems which are far more well defined, in these terms, than are those of 'everyday life'.

The type of information presented in the initial problem, and the kind of evidence which needs to be utilized in order to solve it, may also be important. An example of this concerns the use of *negative information*, particularly in reasoning tasks (see, for example, Wason and Johnson-Laird, 1972; Johnson-Laird and Wason, 1977). We saw in Chapter 17 that the evaluation of negative sentences has often been found to be more difficult (usually, slower) than that of positive sentences. Rather similarly, subjects who are set *rule evaluation* or *rule discovery* problems tend to choose confirming instances, rather than falsifying ones, to test their hypotheses, although in many cases information of the latter kind would be more illuminating. For example, Wason (1968) presented subjects with four cards, each of which the subject knew bore a letter on one side and a number on the other. The upper surfaces of the cards bore, respectively, 'A', 'D', '4' and '7'. Subjects were given a rule: 'If a card has a vowel on one side, then it has an even number on the other side', and were asked to turn over only those cards which would enable them to test the truth of the rule. Most subjects (who were university students) turned the cards bearing 'A' and '4', or else only the card bearing 'A'; but the two cards which should in fact be chosen are those bearing 'A' and '7', since to find an odd number on the reverse of the former, or a vowel on the reverse of the latter, would disprove the rule. Again, Wason gave other subjects the digit series 2, 4, 6 . . . and asked them to suggest continuations of the series in order to discover the rule governing its generation; the rule in fact was simply 'digits in ascending order'. Many subjects first chose the hypothesis 'digits in ascending order, each exceeding the last by 2': they therefore suggested the additional digits 8, 10, 12 and were told that this was acceptable, but did not go on to suggest, say, 13, 14, 15 . . ., although this would have shown their hypothesis to be invalid since these digits also would have been acceptable.

Why is negative information less readily utilized than affirmative? The explanation considered in Chapter 17 invoked the necessity for syntactic recoding (more specifically, detransformation) before comprehension is possible; it was argued that the evidence for such an explanation is doubtful. Others have argued that semantic, rather than syntactic, recoding is needed, and analyses of the recoding process involved have been suggested by Trabasso, Rollins and Shaughnessy (1971) and by Clark and Chase (1972). As Cohen (1977) has pointed out, a snag with such analyses is that they tend to restate the bias for affirmative rather than negative information, and for affirmative rather than negative response, rather than explaining it. Other explanations have also been suggested; one is in terms of the *emotional* connotations of negative statements, which have been said to be associated with prohibition and frustration and therefore to be likely to evoke anxiety and inhibit response (Eifermann, 1961; Wason and Jones,

1963). This explanation seems considerably less plausible in some contexts than in others. A further explanation is in terms of *ambiguity*: often the information conveyed by negative statements is incomplete. 'The policeman didn't stop the truck' may refer to one of several events: the policeman waved the truck on, the policeman stopped a car, somebody else stopped the truck, and so on. If such sentences are accompanied, in an evaluation task, by pictures which make their meaning unambiguous, they may be no harder to process than affirmatives (Engelkampf and Hörmann, 1974).

The study of deductive and inductive reasoning has been of interest to psychologists throughout the discipline's history, and is currently the focus of much interest. On the whole, errors of reasoning (for example, deviations from the deductive principles of formal logic) are frequently reported, although occasionally investigators have found quite impressive evidence of logical reasoning even in subjects without formal training. People also frequently perform poorly when required to make predictions of uncertain events based upon prior probabilities (Tversky and Kahneman, 1977). Why should such errors occur? One possibility is that personal attitudes, beliefs and emotions may influence readiness to accept logical conclusions. Another is the 'atmosphere effect' first proposed by Woodworth and Sells (1935), who argued that subjects may draw conclusions on the basis of the global impression produced by the premises; this view has often been challenged, notably by Chapman and Chapman (1959), who found rather that subjects made errors principally because their inferences are *inductive* rather than deductive, based upon 'everyday' knowledge and plausibility rather than upon strict logical necessity (and rather similar conclusions are reached by Tversky and Kahneman, 1977, in their study of predictive behaviour). In line with this argument, it has often been reported that *concretization* aids the solution of reasoning problems (and indeed problems of other kinds). Subjects given the premise 'All As are Bs' will often conclude, erroneously, that therefore all Bs are As; but they will not conclude from the statement 'all hedgehogs are animals' that all animals are hedgehogs. On the other hand, Henle (1962) for example has argued that subjects may reason 'correctly', in accordance with logical rules, but reach the wrong conclusion because they have misinterpreted the original premise; thus it may well be premature to claim that formal logic bears no relation to everyday thinking, or that 'people are bad at reasoning', on the basis of the limited evidence so far available.

It does seem clear, however, that prior knowledge, experience and expectation may play an important role in determining success at reasoning tasks;

the same has been repeatedly observed in other types of problems. Generally speaking, experience benefits performance in that it permits the transfer of learned principles and skills to a 'new' problem situation: and many studies could be quoted in support of this, in both animal and human problem solving. However, experience can in certain circumstances lead to impaired performance when learned 'labels' and skills are transferred to inappropriate situations. This has often been termed 'functional fixation'. For example, if an object must be used in a novel way to solve a practical problem, as in the example quoted earlier (Duncker, 1945), it is less likely to be so used if the subject has already seen it used, or used it, for a different purpose; a 'neutral' block of wood is more likely to be seen as serving the purpose of a pendulum weight than is a hammer, which normally has a quite different function. Again, if a given method of problem solving has proved successful in the past, it may be applied again in situations where it is inappropriate and thus hinder solution. A classic example of this is the 'water jar' problem of Luchins (1942) who required his subjects to devise the steps whereby a given volume of water could be obtained, given empty jars of specified capacity: Luchins induced a 'set' for arriving at the desired volume by a specific procedure, and found that this procedure tended to be followed even in the case of problems capable of much simpler solutions. A major task for the problem solver, therefore, is to utilize his experience without being bound by it.

Concept formation

Concept formation denotes the process by which stimuli come to be responded to not merely as individual and unique events but as members of a class of stimuli. When we identify a strange animal as a dog we are indicating that a concept – of 'dogs' – has been formed; and we may run away from a bull encountered in a field, not because we have previously experienced its ferocity but because we respond to its membership of a class of animals from which it is appropriate to run. The classifying, or categorizing, of stimuli can be said to be 'one of the most elementary and general forms of cognition by which man adjusts to his environment' (Bruner, Goodnow and Austin, 1956, p. 2); the function of a concept is basically to relate present to previous experience, so that new situations and events may be appropriately dealt with without further learning. Concept formation has traditionally been studied experimentally by means of *sorting problems*, often involving cards as stimuli. A subject is given a deck of cards, each card bearing certain markings; each card is an exemplar of a certain category and the subject's task is to sort the cards into the appropriate categories – that is, to learn the concepts according to which they should be sorted. Beyond this basic condition experimental conditions and instructions have varied widely; some subjects, for example, have been specifically told that theirs is a concept-formation task, while at the opposite extreme subjects have learnt concepts only incidentally while ostensibly performing an associative-learning task (Hull, 1920). The characteristics which determine the category to which a stimulus belongs also vary in complexity and in degree of abstractness. Further, in some experiments (for example, Goldstein and Scheerer, 1941) concept formation may be 'open ended' rather than 'closed', in the sense that there is no necessarily correct way of classifying the stimuli given; the subject's task is to devise one or more bases of classification. Performance in such tasks has been used to measure cognitive deficit in organic or functional illness.

Clearly, concept formation tasks have much in common with many problem solving tasks, and the factors already quoted as relevant for problem solution are also relevant to success in concept formation. The initial task definition is important: success is more likely when subjects are specifically told to search for 'conceptual' characteristics when sorting stimuli than when they are simply instructed to learn 'the label' which belongs to each stimulus, given that some stimuli share the same label (Reed, 1946). The complexity of the task material, particularly as defined by the number of relevant and irrelevant dimensions and the number of values of each dimension, also affects ease of concept learning, as does the *salience* of the relevant cue (for a review of these and other relevant factors, see Bourne, Ekstrand and Dominowski, 1971). Degree of abstractness of the task materials can also influence success, as was shown in a classic experiment by Heidbreder (1946a,b). She employed a card-sorting task in which the concepts to be learned were either 'concrete', 'spatial' or 'abstract' (a sample of the material used is shown in Figure 18.3), and found that concrete concepts were most easily, and abstract concepts least easily, mastered.

Another important variable is the type of concept which must be formed. For example, Bruner, Goodnow and Austin (1956) have reported that conjunctive concepts are much more readily learnt than disjunctive concepts, even by highly intelligent and sophisticated subjects. A conjunctive concept is one for which all members of the class have one or more characteristics in common; a disjunctive concept represents a class of stimuli which qualify for membership by possession of one of several characteristics. All stimulus cards bearing a green border and a triangle would be an example of a

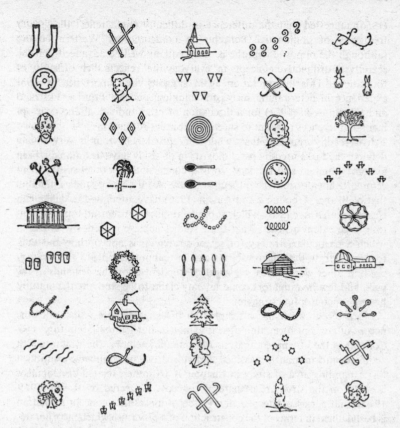

Figure 18.3 Materials used in Heidbreder's study of concept formation. (From Heidbreder, 1946a, p. 182). Note the exemplars of different types of concept: concrete (e.g. faces), spatial (e.g. circular stimuli), and abstract (e.g. five-element stimuli)

conjunctive concept; all cards with either a green border or a triangle, or both, an example of a disjunctive concept. Thus two members of the same distinctive category might be utterly dissimilar, and negative rather than positive instances of the concept are needed for its identification; as in the case of reasoning problems, subjects appear reluctant to seek, and inefficient in utilizing, such negative information (see also Hovland, 1952; and Huttenlocher, 1962, on the use of negative instances). Bruner, Goodnow and Austin

(1956) suggested that the difference in difficulty might reflect the greater frequency of conjunctive concepts in contemporary Western culture (although the opposite hypothesis could equally well be advanced that the scarcity of disjunctive concepts in 'everyday life' reflects their difficulty of formation). This interpretation again suggests the importance of prior experience in determining successful thinking; and see Bourne, Ekstrand and Dominowski (1971) for a discussion of other individual and developmental differences relevant to success in concept formation.

It is readily apparent that, while conceptual behaviour is very widely defined, the tasks used by psychologists in its study have traditionally been extremely limited and artificial, so that conclusions about 'everyday' conceptual behaviour may be difficult to draw. A number of studies, notably that of Bruner, Goodnow and Austin (1956) have attempted to define and classify the *strategies* by which subjects attempt concept attainment; but, to a large extent at least, what these studies achieve is to devise a task in which a particular strategy (or set of strategies) is appropriate and then to demonstrate that their subjects can, or cannot, adopt it. The strategy used, in other words, must be largely dependent upon the demands of the task, and few investigators could lay any claim to be studying the 'natural history' of conceptual behaviour.

More recent work has attempted to investigate more realistically the nature of concept formation as it is exhibited outside the laboratory. One example is the attempted analysis of semantic memory, the way in which acquired information is classified and stored; we have already mentioned this expanding area of study in Chapter 16. Another, related development is work on the structure of natural concepts pioneered by Rosch (1975, 1977a) and her associates. Briefly, Rosch proposes that concept formation is best defined in terms of the construction of a *prototype* which incorporates the features shared, in different degrees, by most instances of the concept: the prototype is, as it were, an 'ideal instance' with which new, potential instances may be compared and to which other instances bear a varying degree of resemblance. Rosch has investigated this hypothesis by means of *rating* experiments, in which subjects rate the extent to which an instance 'fits' their idea of the concept; *priming* experiments, which investigate the facilitating effect of presenting a prototype name (usually a colour) before the picture of an instance is presented for naming; *evaluation-time* experiments of the type used in the study of semantic memory (see Chapter 16); *developmental* studies, and so on. For fuller discussion, see Cohen (1977) and Rosch (1977a). Approaches of this kind are broadening and changing the study of concept formation, and seem likely to provide data and hypotheses which will have quite wide relevance for the study not only of thinking but also of memory and perception.

Creativity

Creativity can be defined as a special case of problem solving. What makes it special may be the 'open-mindedness' of the problem, the originality (and, in some sense, value) of the solution, or the nature of the process by which solution is achieved; creativity is also often taken to indicate a personality characteristic. These four aspects of the definition of creativity are not always well distinguished. We shall very briefly discuss each in turn; for fuller discussion, see, for example, Barron (1969), P. E. Vernon (1970), Bolton (1972), and Radford and Burton (1974).

Problems relevant to creativity include instances of scientific innovation and artistic or literary production, and also so-called 'tests of creativity', such as the 'unusual uses test' (think of as many uses as possible for, say, a brick), fable completion and picture construction tasks, and many more. Such tests have in common that they have no 'right answer' and that they are scored essentially in terms of fluency, productivity, diversity and originality of response: for additional discussion of tests of creativity and their relation to intelligence, see Chapters 20 and 21. With respect to *originality*, it is generally agreed that a creative response is not only novel but also effective and appropriate: Maltzman (1960) in fact defined creativity as 'originality evaluated'. The evaluation of a creative product, whether a scientific discovery, a poem, a painting or a response on the 'unusual uses test', is not always a simple matter; scoring protocols have been devised for tests of creativity, while in other fields recourse has to be made to teachers' ratings of their pupils' achievement, or to the judgement of history, or of fellow-workers in the same discipline, in assessing the creative achievement of artists, scientists, and so on.

It has often been argued that the *creative process* has special characteristics which distinguish it from 'everyday' thinking. Several classic studies have been concerned with the nature of the creative process in artists, poets, writers and scientists, ascertained from introspective reports (Ghiselin, 1952) and occasionally from observation of, and discussion with, the 'creators' at work (Patrick, 1935, 1937). A fairly common theme emerging from these often fascinating reports is that after a certain amount of preparatory work there is characteristically a period of *incubation*, in which conscious work does not occur, and that this period may end in *illumination* – a sudden realization of the solution, which can then be tested and verified – or *inspiration*, in the case of artistic and literary work, which can then be developed and perfected. This led to considerable interest in the nature of the 'insight experience' and of the 'unconscious work', not available to intro-spection and not under voluntary control, which was held to lead to it. McKellar (1957), for example, suggested a distinction between reality-adjusted, or R-thinking, and autistic, or A-thinking. R-thinking is logical, rational and checked against external information; A-thinking is non-rational, proceeding by the association of ideas on a non-logical basis, and independent of external correction, and has affinities with dreams, fantasy and some forms of psychotic thinking. McKellar further suggested that R-thinking and A-thinking may co-exist in many situations, notably in problem solving; when R-thinking has not produced a solution, A-thinking in the absence of conscious work may prove effective. In support of this notion are the many instances, quoted by McKellar, of solutions which occur in fantasy or in dreams and which prove viable on realistic verification. In such situations A-thinking can be regarded as the author, and R-thinking as the editor, of the final production. This account of A-thinking can be compared with psychoanalytic views of autistic thinking and dreaming as wish fulfilment which is unconsciously directed and not subject to realistic assessment. For further discussion of these and related ideas, see Neisser (1963b).

A closely related dichotomy which has been of interest in recent years is that between *convergent* and *divergent* thinking, included in Guilford's analysis of intelligence (see Chapter 20) and extensively studied by, for example, Getzels and Jackson (1962) and Hudson (1966, 1968). Convergent thinking, like McKellar's 'R-thinking', is said to be logical, consciously controlled, reality-oriented and largely dependent upon adherence to pre-viously learned knowledge and skills; divergent thinking is said to be produc-tive rather than reproductive and to proceed by intuitively formed, 'illogical' and unconventional associations and analogies to arrive at novel conclusions rather than the 'right answer'. Interest in convergent and divergent thinking has been strongly associated with the notion of *personality differences* in creativity and with the postulation of (less creative) 'convergers' and (more creative) 'divergers'. The personality characteristics which have been said to be related to these types are described in Chapter 21, and also by Hudson, Barron, Vernon and others in the works already quoted. A summary might be that creative people (or divergers) tend to be verbally fluent, flexible in thinking and (at any rate among actual achievers) dedicated to work, in the sense that they devote a very great deal of time and effort to it. They emerge as independent and individual in judgement and as generally unconventional, sometimes flamboyant, in manner. They have been described as self-centred and difficult to handle and as showing more evidence of psychopathology on clinical tests; on the other hand, it is worth noting that psychoanalysts (for example, Kubie, 1958) have specifically denied that creativity is allied to neurosis or 'genius akin to madness', arguing rather that neurotic or psychotic disorder is more likely to disrupt than to facilitate productive thinking.

However, the distinction between convergers and divergers, or between creative people and the rest of us, should be treated with caution. Whether an individual exhibits convergent or divergent behaviour is quite considerably dependent upon the demands of the task with which he is faced, and when instructions are manipulated 'convergers' can become 'divergers' and *vice versa* (Hudson, 1968). The thinking strategies adopted by an individual are not rigidly determined by his personality, but are largely a function of his situation and of his training; and the large body of work concerned with the *training* of creativity attests to this belief. Methods of creativity training are very varied, ranging from techniques aimed at increasing response originality in word association (Maltzman, 1960), via 'brainstorming' and allied techniques concerned with problem-solving effectiveness, often in a business context (Osborn, 1957; De Bono, 1967), to more or less long-term attempts to 'reform' educational systems in order to encourage creativity rather than conformity (see the review by Radford and Burton, 1974). Many of these techniques can claim success, given the often rather limited criteria which they set for improved performance; what still remains to be demonstrated is the generality and persistence of such improvements.

Analyses of thinking processes

The 'raw stuff' of thinking

What, essentially, are thoughts made of? Early investigators sought the answer to this question by analysing the introspections of trained subjects during 'mental work' such as mental arithmetic, word association or complex problem solving. They were concerned in particular with the relation between thinking and sensory imagery. Many of the ancient and the empiricist philosophers had argued that thinking consists essentially of sensory imagery; and it certainly appears from introspective data that sensory images figure very largely in mental activity. Galton (1883), for example, found that even eminent mathematicians and scientists, whose thinking might be imagined to occupy an 'abstract plane', made use of concrete imagery to aid calculation as well as invention. Might there, however, be 'pure' thought unaccompanied by sensory ideas? Different investigators produced sharply opposing results (see Humphrey, 1951) and no unequivocal answer could be produced. Nevertheless, the role of visual imagery, in particular, in thought remains an interesting subject for study and is currently the focus of much research; see the discussion of imaginal coding in Chapter 16 and also, for example, Richardson (1969); Radford and Burton (1974); Cohen (1977).

Another early suggestion was that *motor* imagery, or subliminal muscular involvement, was also important for thinking: that, essentially, thinking is implicit behaviour. When we think about a specific action, the 'thinking' takes the form of small changes in the peripheral musculature appropriate to the action; when we attempt the solution of a practical problem we do so by 'trying out' possible responses at an amplitude below that required for overt action, until an appropriate response is detected and carried out overtly. For discussion of this 'peripheral' theory of thought, its associated experimentation and some of its problems, see Osgood (1953). The most celebrated statement of a peripheralist view was probably that of Watson (1914) who proposed that thinking consisted essentially of implicit *vocalization* or 'internal speech'. While this was certainly an overstatement, the role of language in thinking is undoubtedly of great importance, and it is common for recent textbooks concerned with thinking to contain substantial chapters on language. We saw in Chapter 17, however, that a wholesale acceptance of language as the vehicle for thought is not justified by the available evidence.

If thought is not necessarily a matter of sensory or motor imagery or of words, where are we to look for its 'raw material'? There are two fairly obvious possibilities (and, no doubt, others). First, we may seek an answer in terms of neurophysiology; Thompson (1969), for example, has argued that 'thinking is nothing more than brain activity, together with associated receptor and effector events. Brain activity, in turn, is nothing more than interactions among individual nerve cells in the brain.' However, although there have been attempts (reviewed by Thompson) to construct neural models of thinking, many investigators would be likely to agree with Fisher's comment (1969) that 'scientists studying brain function from the inside out simply haven't even approached a stage in which the investigation of complex thought processes is either reasonable or possible'. This is not to say that such an investigation will not prove reasonable, or fruitful, in the future as our knowledge advances.

The other obvious argument which can be adopted is that the raw material of thinking may well be anything – images, words, 'neural events' or whatever – which we care to envisage. Thinking is not a unitary activity, and its 'vehicles' are likely to be diverse; it is more profitable to analyse the functions involved in thinking, and their sequence, without any necessary reference to the neural or other organismic processes which might underlie them.

'Models' of thought

In considering analyses of the thinking process we shall be chiefly concerned with what might be termed 'purposive thinking': cases, such as problem solving, in which the goal of thinking is clear. We shall not consider further the nature of what might be termed 'autistic' or divergent thinking as a process distinct from reality-adjusted thinking; this has already been discussed to some extent under the heading of creativity. Moreover, the distinction between purposive and non-purposive thinking, and in particular (as we have seen) the logical nature of purposive thinking, can easily be exaggerated and is sometimes more confusing than enlightening.

Perhaps the earliest systematic approach to the analysis of thinking was that of the empiricist tradition, mentioned in Chapter 1, which sought to explain thinking in terms of the *association of ideas* according to the principles of contiguity, similarity and contrast. The chief criticisms against this approach were that it gave an account of thinking which was reproductive rather than productive, mechanistic rather than purposive and atomistic rather than synthetic and configurational; thus it gave an inadequate description of cognitive phenomena. Nevertheless, the influence of associationism in psychology has been all-pervasive; it is clearly seen, for example, in the study of perceptual organization and development, memory and language, reviewed in earlier chapters, and it largely laid the foundation for S–R theories with the advent of behaviourism. For a review of the classical associationist doctrine, its rise and fall, and its similarities to and differences from S–R behaviourism, see Humphrey (1951).

At first sight S–R behaviourism appears, to say the least, an unpromising starting-point for the study of thinking. Indeed, one of the basic tenets of behaviourism was that it excluded such 'unobservables' as legitimate objects of study, and certainly the kinds of criticism advanced against classical associationism can also be levelled at S–R theory. However, S–R theory is capable of certain sophistications and complexities which make the task of extending it to certain aspects of thinking a more reasonable one (see, e.g., Kintsch, 1970). Maltzman (1955), for example, suggested the elements of a behaviourist theory of thinking which derives from the system proposed by Hull (see Chapter 13). In conditioning, the UCS is at first capable of evoking many responses, of which some are more dominant than others – that is, more likely to be evoked; Hull termed such a group of responses, all related to the same stimulus but with differential strength, a *habit-family hierarchy*. In conditioning what occurs is a 'reshuffling' of the dominance of responses in the hierarchy so that the correct response becomes dominant; and the same model might be applied to the solving of simple problems (see, for example, the behaviourist interpretation of 'insight', as shown by Köhler's apes or by Maier's rats, reported in Osgood, 1953). More complex problem solving Maltzman explains in terms of *compound* habit-family hierarchies; a number of hierarchies may be associated, again with differential strengths, with the stimulus situation which represents the problem, and the solver's task is to select not only the correct response from a hierarchy but also, first, the correct hierarchy of responses.

Another, more notable elaboration of S–R theory which has implications for the analysis of thinking is *mediation theory*, as stated by Osgood (1953). The notion of mediation has been discussed in Chapter 13; in Osgood's view, thinking consists of mediating responses which are fragmentary reduced portions of the overt behaviour which they represent. Mediation theory, as opposed to 'single-stage' S–R theory, appears better able to account for certain aspects of conceptual behaviour: for example, the effects of transfer in concept formation when the basis of classification is changed, studied by Kendler and Kendler (1969) under the heading of 'reversal' and 'non-reversal' shifts. However, it has many difficulties; see, for example, the criticism of the notion of 'representativeness' of the mediating response by Fodor (1965).

Although S–R and mediation theories are still of some influence in psychology, they are strongly rivalled (as we saw in Chapter 13) and currently outweighed by *cognitive* approaches, which stress the purposive, goal-directed and consciously controlled nature of behaviour. The Gestalt school can lay some claim to being regarded as a precursor, at least, of the cognitive approach, with its emphasis upon the organization and structural 'wholeness' of experience. It is a debatable claim, since it could be argued that to the Gestalt psychologist man is a passive recipient, rather than an active shaper, of stimulus information even though that information is viewed as being inherently structured rather than fragmentary. However, particularly in its treatment of thinking (and notably problem solving) Gestalt theory did offer certain notions of organized and goal-directed behaviour which can be interpreted in terms of an active, purposive thinker. We have already noted Köhler's account (1925) of problem solving in animals, which comprises three distinct stages: initial helplessness, a pause in activity and a sudden and smooth performance of the solution. In human problem solving Duncker (1945) provided a careful analysis of stages in problem solving which stressed the rational, purposive nature of the activity involved. Duncker hypothesized that, again, three stages are involved in solution. A subject at first produces a *general range* of possible means of solution, which have been described as reformulating the problem rather than offering solutions to it. When a general line of attack has been chosen, the subject begins to produce *functional solutions*, more detailed but still not entirely specific; the proposal of a functional solution – a notion as to what sort of method might be employed to achieve the goal – leads in turn to *specific solutions* which detail the exact means to be employed. If such solutions are not acceptable, another functional solution will be explored; if all functional solutions arising from a given general line of attack prove unprofitable, the subject rejects that general line and turns to another, which is then pursued in the same way. The process is thus seen to be an enlightened series of trials at solution each of which results in reorganization of the problem until the solution is achieved. An example of behaviour thus analysed is shown in Figure 18.4 (see, incidentally, Maltzman's reanalysis (1955) of Duncker's protocols in terms of response-hierarchy dominance). It is worth adding that, just as many different kinds of learning have been postulated (see Chapter 13), so it is possible to propose different kinds of thinking which would be appropriate to different types of problem situation; thus S–R analysis might provide the 'best' account of one type of activity, a 'cognitive' analysis the 'best' account of another.

Clearly included under the heading of 'cognitive approaches' to thinking is the work of Bruner, Goodnow and Austin (1956), and others, which sets out to explore the *strategies* which subjects adopt in concept attainment tasks and in reasoning and prediction. Here the emphasis is unambiguously on the thinker as an active seeker of solutions, and it is markedly similar in this respect to the 'information-processing' approach, exemplified in the TOTE theory of Miller, Galanter and Pribram (1960) discussed in Chapter 14. A frequent concomitant of the information processing approach is the

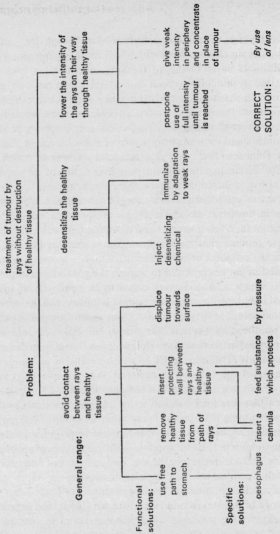

Figure 18.4   Duncker's analysis of problem solving. (From Duncker, 1945, p. 5).
Duncker's problem was as follows: given a human being with an inoperable stomach
tumour and rays that destroy organic tissue at sufficient intensity, by what condition
can one free him of the tumour by these rays and at the same time avoid destroying the
healthy tissue which surrounds it?

use of computers to simulate problem solving. The general method adopted in computer simulation of thinking is as follows: the investigator first makes a provisional analysis on the basis of observations and introspections. When an analysis of thinking has been devised, the investigator writes a *program*, or set of instructions, for the computer, to enable it to carry out the hypothesized process. This program, it has been claimed, is essentially a theory of thinking, couched in computer terms; naturally, it involves more detailed description than is provided by the analyses quoted above. The program, or theory, is then *verified*.

In the verification of a given program there are two questions to be asked. First, is the appropriate goal behaviour produced – for example, is the problem solved? It has been shown often that computers can in fact successfully solve practical and abstract problems and play 'intellectual' games such as chess. Second, is the 'thinking' process carried out by the machine similar to that of a human subject, in general and in detail? Basically, there are two ways of examining the similarity between the protocols produced by human and machine solvers. One of these is to lay the protocols side by side and to count up the differences between them at various stages towards solution; the other is to employ judges who are given a number of protocols and asked to sort them into those produced by machines and those produced by humans. The results of verification are on the whole encouraging (for further detail and discussion, see Reitman, 1965; Newell and Simon, 1972; Cohen, 1977).

Although there have been objections both in principle and in practice to the use of computer models in the analysis of thinking, computer simulation is at the very least a valuable exercise in theoretical precision, in that it necessitates *explicit* formulation of all assumptions made during analysis; in verbal expression it is easy unwittingly to omit, or leave implicit, quite basic assumptions, but an incompletely specified computer program will simply not run. Naturally, many studies of computer simulation are activated by an interest in 'artificial intelligence' in its own right, rather than in relation to human intelligence; whether a general theory of human and machine thinking would ever prove feasible is still very much an open question.

Cognitive development

We have already discussed several aspects of cognitive development: for example, perceptual development in Chapter 11, memory development in

Chapter 16 and language development in Chapter 17. In all these cases it was argued that development in any one area should be viewed as part and parcel of the general development of conceptual behaviour, and thus the points made in earlier chapters are also relevant to the development of thinking. There have of course also been many studies concerned with development of more narrowly defined 'thinking' activities such as problem solving, concept formation and logical reasoning. Vygotsky (1934), for example, has charted the development of object-sorting performance with age from essentially random grouping, through the use of 'concrete and factual' bases of classification with poor response to correction, to 'adequate' conceptualization at perhaps the age of puberty; Bruner, Olver and Green-field (1966) and others have examined the types of conceptual strategy adopted by children of different ages, and much attention has also been paid to the emergence of the 'object concept' (already mentioned in Chapter 11), the concept of number (Piaget 1952b; Bryant 1974) and various aspects of logical thinking (Inhelder and Piaget, 1958, 1964).

It is possible that in some cases at least the cognitive development of the child may have been exaggerated, in that his early abilities may have been underestimated or misconceived. For example, one aspect of logical thinking studied by Piaget is *transitivity*. If we are told that A is greater than B, and B greater than C, we can immediately make the inference that A is greater than C; but children younger than about eight appear not to be able to recognize this. Another example which has been extensively studied concerns *conservation*. If a young child is shown two glasses of identical size and shape, each half full of liquid, he will probably report correctly that the amount of liquid in each is the same; but if, in plain view, the liquid from one glass is poured into a thinner, taller glass the child is likely to say that there is more liquid in the tall glass than in the other, since its level is higher. Only when they are, again, about eight years old do children show appreciation of the 'invariance of quantity': that a given volume of liquid remains the same even when it occupies a container of a different shape. In both cases, then, there would appear to be a deficiency of logical thinking; but Bryant (1974) and others have argued that the 'failure' in these cases may be not logical, but the result of other inadequacies. In the case of transitivity young children may fail because they do not remember the original premises, and Bryant has shown that they can in fact infer the appropriate relations when the initial relations have been well learned; in the case of conservation it might be that young children do understand the principle of invariance of quantity, but that when the situation is one of *conflict* between a judgement based upon invariance and one based upon perceptual cues the child cannot weigh the alternatives appropriately. Again, there is some evidence to support this interpretation of failures of conservation. It is also worth pointing out that as in other aspects of behaviour the stimulus attributes which the experimenter considers important are not always those which are salient for the young child, and that in general the problems of accurately assessing a young child's capacity are considerable (see Flavell, 1977). Nevertheless, the fact of cognitive development, of a remarkable order, over the childhood years is undeniable.

How are we to conceptualize, and explain, the course of cognitive development? S–R and mediation analyses have sometimes been offered; a notable example is that of Kendler and Kendler (1962, 1969) who applied a mediation model to conceptual behaviour in their study of reversal and non-reversal shifts. Subjects were given a number of stimuli which might be, say, large or small and black or white, and were required to learn a concept: perhaps its definition would be 'all large objects'. The basis of classification was then shifted. In a 'reversal shift' – for example, to a definition of 'all small objects' – the relevant dimension could be retained, but reversed in value; in a 'non-reversal shift' – for example, 'all black objects', the relevant dimension would be changed. In the latter case, some, but not all, previously correct responses become incorrect and require relearning: thus if a simple S–R model of learning were adopted relearning should be easier than in the case of reversal shifts, where all previously correct responses become incorrect. However, if a mediational model were assumed, in which the mediating response 'size' has been learned, a reversal shift would not necessitate unlearning and relearning of the mediating response and thus should be easier than non-reversal shift. Kendler and Kendler found that reversal shifts were *easier* than non-reversal shifts for adults and for children over about six years of age, but *harder* for younger children and also for rats. They argued therefore that cognitive development is at least partly a matter of the development of mediational systems, and in particular of *verbal* mediation. Unfortunately for this argument, some studies have shown a superiority of reversal over non-reversal shifts in rats (Shepp and Eimas, 1964) and difficulties of interpretation in the case of young children (Bryant, 1971), so that verbal mediation as an explanatory notion must be regarded with caution.

Some theorists have sought to explain cognitive development essentially along the same lines as perceptual development. We have already mentioned (in Chapter 11) Gibson's (1969) theory of perceptual development as being principally a matter of learning the significance of distinctive features of the perceptual array, and the notion of increasing differentiation which this involves has been postulated as a general feature of development notably by Werner (1948, 1957). In Werner's words (1957, p. 126): 'whenever development occurs it proceeds from a state of relative globality and lack of differentiation to a state of increasing differentiation, articulation and hierarchic integration'. The concept of differentiation has already been discussed in Chapter 3, and the related concept of field-dependence receives mention in Chapters 11, 16 and, notably, 21; thus the relevance of this approach can be seen in a number of different areas of psychology.

On the other hand, it is possible to view the process of cognitive development as largely an escape from dependence upon perceptual input: as Turner (1975) encapsulates it, 'over time the perceptually dominated world of the infant becomes the conceptual world of the adult'. Obviously it would be absurd to argue that as thinking develops the thinker becomes less in contact with reality; but he can be said to become less dominated by present percepts and more capable of independent symbolic activity. In that sense, a child is capable of logical thinking to the extent that he is free from the influence of immediate sensory impression (as in the case of conservation, mentioned earlier). Such a view is contained in the developmental theory of Piaget, who has been unquestionably the greatest single contributor to our knowledge of cognitive development, both in terms of empirical observation and in terms of theory. We shall not attempt to consider his work in any detail here; the omission is an acknowledgement, rather than a denial, of his stature in psychology, which can be compared to that of Freud. Helpful introductions to Piaget's work are provided by, e.g., Turner (1975) and, with more detail, Flavell (1963, 1977).

To Piaget, thinking is operational intelligence, and its essence is adaptation to, and in particular interaction with, the environment. Interaction, and therefore cognitive growth, is achieved by *assimilation* and by *accommodation*. For example, when a young child grasps a ball, he is said to be assimilating the ball to the grasping action (more properly, as Piaget terms it, the grasping *schema*; see the references suggested for more precise definition of this and other terms): he is, as it were, turning the ball into 'something to be grasped'. At the same time he has to accommodate to it, in the sense that the grasping schema has to adjust to the size, weight, texture and position of the ball. At a more complex representational level, the student who is engaged in the action of listening to a lecture is, at one and the same time, assimilating the incoming information to existing schemata and accommodating these schemata to what is new in that information. Thus cognitive development proceeds as the biological drive to adapt to his environment leads the child to assimilate the objects in that environment to his existing schemata, while at the same time the nature of the environmental objects forces upon the child an accommodatory adjustment of these schemata. The *stages* through which intelligence is said to develop have been briefly described in Chapter 3; they describe a path from the earliest, sensory-motor stage in which thinking is inseparable from overt action, through the beginnings of representational and reflective thought, to the stage of 'concrete operations' in which the child is able to deal simultaneously with various relationships or dimensions of objects and finally to the stage of 'formal operations', in which he is capable of general, propositional thinking independent of particular experience. Obviously the references already given should be consulted for a fuller discussion, as should Piaget's own writings (for example, Piaget, 1970; Inhelder and Piaget, 1958, 1964).

Piaget's work has often been criticized on various grounds. It has been said that in his insistence on the importance of 'natural' interaction between organism and environment he has neglected the importance of specific training and formal education for cognitive growth; see, for example, Bruner's (1973) analysis of the influence of schooling, and Flavell's (1977) discussion of the contributions of genetic predisposition and experience in prompting and shaping development. Piaget's hypothesized 'stages' of development have also been criticized: the borderlines between stages are often blurred, a child may attain a given stage in one aspect of his thinking but not in others, and older children may sometimes regress in their thinking. Finally, Piaget's conclusions have often been based upon observation of small and biased samples of children, and more large-scale studies with additional controls have not always confirmed his findings: see, for example, the earlier discussion of transitivity and conservation, and also Bryant (1974) and Flavell (1977). Nevertheless, his work remains the most comprehensive, the most valuable and certainly the most influential attempt to describe and explain the nature of cognitive development.

Chapter 19
Assessment of Individuals

Introduction

Individual differences in task performance are regularly found in all experimental and observational studies in psychology, and these differences are often considerable in extent. In most of the studies discussed so far in this book, individual differences have been regarded as sources of error, and the purpose of experimental designs has been to control or randomize their influence upon the dependent variable. However, individual differences are of interest in their own right, and this chapter, as well as Chapters 20–21, will be concerned directly with their measurement and conceptualization. Additionally, Chapter 22 will consider group differences (in age, sex and race) in psychological functioning. Group differences are one of the concerns of social psychology. Other aspects of the latter constitute the subject matter of Chapter 23.

The number of specific ways in which people can differ is incalculable. Fortunately the human system is such that these specific differences among people tend to be interrelated, or correlated with one another, in a manner which makes possible the specification of more general dimensions of difference. If our aim is to describe the ways in which people vary, it is obviously more economical to do this in terms of general dimensions which subsume a number of systematically related specific forms of behaviour. At the highest level of generality people are said to differ in (1) general cognitive ability, or intelligence, and (2) personality, which includes attitudes, beliefs and characteristic styles of behaving: quantitative definitions of these dimensions are considered in Chapter 20, and qualitative aspects of personality are discussed in Chapter 21.

The formal assessment of individual differences (as distinct from informal assessments, made both by psychologists and by laymen) is dependent upon the existence of adequate measuring devices, or *tests*, constructed and administered in accordance with rather stringent rules. The purpose behind these rules is to ensure that the measuring process is 'objective', in the sense that it is not biased by the personal judgement of the tester. In this chapter our concern is with psychological tests of ability and personality, but the rules apply also to any kind of behavioural measurement.

If the subject's performance on a test is to be free from the influence of the tester, it is important that testers should follow a standard procedure when using the test. To this end, manuals are provided which indicate precisely how the test should be administered and scored. It is of the greatest importance that testers should follow exactly the instructions given, for even small deviations can affect the subject's scores. In addition, manuals usually contain normative data, by which is meant details of the results of administering the test to large samples of subjects. The value of such data is that they enable the tester to interpret a particular individual's score in relation to specified populations of subjects.

However, the effect of the tester's personality can never be completely eliminated. This is because a testing situation is a social one, and the tester has to establish 'rapport' with his subjects: that is, he must secure the co-operation of the subjects and put them sufficiently at ease for them to produce something like their best performance. Individual testers clearly vary in the skill with which they can do this.

Assessments consist of acquiring information about an individual's behaviour in a particular test situation and using the information obtained as the basis for a decision about the testee's ability, or personality, or about his future career. For example, information may be required about an individual's 'mental ability' for the selection of candidates for university training, or, in industrial rehabilitation, for determining the amount and kind of retraining an individual should receive. It is unlikely that in the two examples mentioned the same test of mental ability would be given. Different tests have different advantages; a test which helps materially in making one kind of decision may be of little value in making another. Therefore, no one test of mental ability, for example, can be said to be the best; the choice of a test depends very much on the purpose for which it is required and on the kind of decision to be made.

This does not mean that there are not certain general qualities which distinguish good tests from bad. Among these are the clarity of the directions for use and how easily the test can be administered and scored. A good test has the following characteristics. First, it must be a sensitive measuring instrument which discriminates well between subjects. Second, it must have been standardized on a representative and sizeable sample of the population for which it is intended, so that any individual's score can be interpreted in relation to that of others. Third, it must be valid, in the sense of measuring what it purports to measure, and, fourth, it must be stable or reliable.

There are three main purposes for which tests might be used: selection, diagnosis and description. We shall not be concerned here with diagnostic tests – for example, tests used in locating disorders such as reading disability or mental illness – and will only incidentally consider the use of tests in selection for jobs or training. Our discussion of testing centres round the use of tests for descriptive purposes, that is to say, their use as measures of individual differences in a research context. In the sections that follow we shall first examine certain basic aspects of any kind of psychological measurement, and then describe some of the different kinds of test that have been constructed.

Basic principles of testing

Psychological measurement

The essence of psychological measurement is the assigning of numerical values to behavioural events such that differences in behaviour are represented by differences in score. It involves the application to subjects of a standard procedure which allows the quantification of the responses made. The systematic representation of behavioural events by numbers implies an underlying logic, or set of rules, which governs the relationship between numbers and events. The kinds of statistical transformations of the scores which are permissible depend upon the nature of this logic.

Essentially, there are four different ways of quantifying a variable, or four different kinds of scale that can be employed (Stevens, 1951; Nunnally, 1970). The most primitive is the categorization of subjects or responses into classes: for example, shots at a target can be grouped into hits and misses, or subjects given a test can be grouped into those who pass and those who fail. This kind of quantification is known as *nominal* measurement, and the data it yields are not in the form of scores but in the form of frequencies in different classes. Subjects are placed in groups, but within each group no differentiation is made. An example of nominal measurement might be the classification of subjects as neurotic and normal, or as extraverted and introverted.

The simplest form of measurement which represents each subject or response with a number is *ordinal* measurement. In this, the subjects or responses are placed in rank order with respect to the variable concerned:

thus, shots at a target can be ranked according to their distance from it, or subjects could be ranked according to the number of items in a test they answer correctly.

The information conveyed by ordinal measurement, though greater than in nominal measurement, is still limited, for, since the numbers assigned to subjects or responses only represent their position in a rank order, it is impossible to tell from the numbers themselves whether or not the difference between, for example, the first and second is greater or smaller than the difference between the second and third. The form of measurement which does represent these varying differences numerically is *interval* measurement. The distinctive feature of interval measurement is that the quantifying procedure is such that any one unit difference in score represents the same amount of difference in the variable being quantified as any other unit difference in score. If the measuring procedure yields an interval scale, it means that, for example, if subject A scores 60, subject B 50 and subject C 45, then the difference between subjects A and B on the variable being measured is twice as great as the difference between subjects B and C.

If the measuring procedure, in addition to having the features of interval measurement, also has the property that a score of zero corresponds to the absence of the characteristic being measured, then it is said to yield *ratio* measurement. To use again the example of target shooting, we could measure the distance in inches of each shot from the target, so that a zero score represented a hit. An example of ratio measurement in psychology might be the time taken for a subject to respond to a stimulus, for although it is impossible for a subject to respond in no time at all, the scale used to measure his response has a zero point.

In psychological testing of ability or personality, ratio measurement is in fact never attained and it is doubtful whether tests ever yield a genuine interval scale. Let us again suppose that the scores for subjects A, B and C on an intelligence test are 60, 50 and 45 respectively. We can be reasonably sure that we have ordinal measurement, that the scores tell us that A is more able than B, and B than C (at least for the type of ability measured by the test). But it is very questionable whether we can go on to say that the difference in ability between A and B is twice as great as the difference between B and C. However, if the test is well constructed, we may feel that we have a form of measurement somewhat stronger than ordinal. Thus, though we cannot assert that the difference between A and B is twice the difference between B and C, we may nevertheless feel fairly confident that it is a greater difference, that $A-B > B-C$.

Let us consider further the assumptions which can be made about scores which represent interval measurement. Suppose that a group of subjects takes a test of ability for which interval measurement can be achieved; scores obtained over the group can be described in various ways, most commonly by quoting the *mean* and the *standard deviation* of the scores. The *mean* score of the group is its average score, obtained by summing all scores and dividing the sum by the number of subjects in the group. Strictly speaking the mean can only be calculated when an equal interval scale is employed. However, as a matter of expediency, an equal interval scale is often assumed for the purposes of calculating the mean. The *standard deviation* is a statistic which expresses the degree of variation in a set of scores; it can be defined as the square root of the average of the squared deviations of each score from the mean of the scores. The significance of the standard deviation can be brought out by considering the concept of *frequency distribution*.

When a large number of individuals take a test, their scores can be represented by a *frequency distribution*. The possible scores on the test are plotted along the baseline, or *abscissa*, and the number of individuals obtaining a particular score is shown along a line placed at right angles to the abscissa, the *ordinate*. Suppose that the majority of individuals taking the test obtain a score falling roughly in the middle of the abscissa, while only a few individuals obtain either very high or very low scores. The resulting frequency distribution might look like that shown in Figure 19.1. Such a frequency distribution approximates to what is termed a *normal distribution*.

The normal distribution curve is a purely mathematical concept which has certain special properties:

1. By definition it describes the distribution of an *infinite* number of cases, therefore the two tails of the curve never touch the baseline.
2. It is symmetrical and there are thus an equal number of cases on either side of the mean, the central axis.
3. The mean and two other *measures of central tendency*, the *median* (that is the point on a scale of measurement both above and below which lie exactly half the total number of cases being described) and the *mode* (that value or score which occurs with the highest frequency in the group of cases considered) are all equal to one another.

A further characteristic of the normal curve is its mathematical construction. There are two points on the normal curve where it changes direction from convex to concave. These are known as points of inflexion. The distance from the mean to each point of inflexion represents one standard deviation.

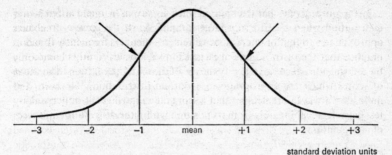

standard deviation units

Figure 19.1   The hypothetical 'normal curve' (see text). Arrows represent points
of inflexion

Using this distance on the abscissa as a standard, points two and three
deviations from the mean in either direction can be found. The distance
between the mean and one, two or three standard deviations away from
it in either direction accounts for a progressively greater percentage of the
total area under the curve, as Figure 19.1 shows; the two tails of the normal
curve approach the abscissa so closely that the distance between plus and
minus three standard deviations accounts for over 99 per cent of the total
area. In principle, however, since the normal curve describes an infinite
number of cases, the abscissa could be divided into an infinite number of
parts, each equal to one standard deviation, and the two tails of the distribution would never reach the abscissa.

Statistical tests of significance based upon interval measurement (so-called
parametric tests) usually assume that the scores on the measure being taken
are normally distributed. Where the distribution of obtained scores grossly
violates this assumption such tests cannot be applied; one usual procedure,
then, is to use *non-parametric* tests which require only ordinal, or in some
cases only nominal, data. For a further discussion of scaling, of statistical
treatments appropriate to various levels of measurement and of the relative
merits of parametric and non-parametric tests, see Siegel (1956) and Robson
(1973).

We may sum up the main points that have been made in this section as
follows. Measures used in most psychological tests of ability and personality
do not fulfil the conditions necessary for ratio scale measurement, and therefore are in no sense 'absolute' measures of these traits. A psychological test
of this kind can be defined as a device for scaling the *differences* between

subjects on a given characteristic in such a way as to yield a frequency distribution when applied to a large sample. When the scaling procedure approximates to that of interval measurement, then it is frequently found in practice that the distributions of large samples are sufficiently close to the theoretical normal curve to justify the use of those statistical transformations of scores which are appropriate to a normal distribution. However, it is important always to remember that a score on an intelligence or personality test gains its meaning only from its position within the distribution of scores of a population.

Estimation of reliability

Given that the purpose of a psychological test is to discriminate between subjects with respect to a certain characteristic, then two of the most important questions we must ask about it are whether it is *reliable* in the sense of always discriminating in the same way, and whether it is *valid* in the sense of discriminating in the way in which it is intended to do. The issues raised by the problems of reliability and validity are central to the theory of testing, and are discussed at length in numerous textbooks (see, for example, Guilford, 1954; E. L. Kelly, 1967; Schofield, 1972). For the present, we shall discuss only the meanings of these terms and the ways in which evidence relevant to their assessment is collected. In choosing a test, for whatever purpose, the psychologist needs to be confident that it is both reliable and valid, and for this reason it is the usual practice to include the relevant evidence in the test manual.

A test is reliable if, whatever it measures, it always measures the same characteristic. If we wish to replicate someone else's experiment using his tests, we need to be assured that they will measure the same thing for us as they did for him. This may seem an obvious statement, but it is in fact of great importance.

When a group of subjects takes a test, the resulting distribution of scores will be a function of both stable differences between them on the variable measured by the test (the subjects' 'true' scores on the test) and also temporary differences between them in mood, motivation, health and so on. These latter factors may be called sources of *error in measurement*, since they may be expected to fluctuate from one testing to another in a random fashion. The more the subjects' scores reflect this error, the more the test is sensitive to differences between subjects which obtain only at the time of testing, then the less reliable and stable the test is as a measure of lasting differences between subjects. To put the point another way, the more the error of measurement, the less will a subject's obtained score reflect his 'true' score on the variable the test measures.

It would follow from this that the most sensible way of checking the reliability of a test is to give it to the same subjects twice and to correlate the two sets of scores. A reliable test would be one which preserved the same relative differences between subjects on the two occasions, as shown by a high, positive correlation coefficient. Of course the actual scores of the subjects may not remain the same. For example, it would be expected that subjects would do better on the second attempt at an intelligence test than on the first. What is important for reliability is that the position of subjects relative to each other stays the same. Any factor, such as practice, which affects all subjects taking a test *in the same way*, raises questions about the validity of the test, not its reliability.

In fact, the test–retest method of estimating reliability is only one of three methods commonly used. In principle each of these methods is applicable to any test. In practice difficulties arise in using one or other method with some tests. For example, reliability based upon the test–retest method may be unduly inflated if the test is such that the subjects can remember clearly on the second testing the responses they made on the first. What is important, however, is that each of the three methods deals with a distinctive source of error. We shall briefly consider each method in turn.

Test–retest reliability. The test–retest reliability coefficient, also known as the *coefficient of stability*, is the correlation between the obtained scores of the same group of subjects taking the same test on two different occasions; the closeness of the coefficient to $+1\cdot00$ indicates the reliability of the test.

One difficulty with test–retest reliability is that the whole of the change in relative scores from one administration to another is regarded as unreliability, and this may not be an appropriate assumption. If the time interval between the two administrations of the test is very short, individuals may remember their previous responses and this may produce an unduly high reliability coefficient. If the interval is unduly long, it affords the opportunity for differential forgetting, and for different amounts and kinds of new learning, among the testees, which would be likely to affect their relative performances at retest; in consequence the reliability coefficient might underestimate the reliability of the test. Test–retest reliability coefficients, when quoted, therefore usually specify the intertest time interval used. In general, the value of the test–retest reliability coefficient falls as the interval increases, indicating the greater likelihood that 'error' variation is contributing to the differences in score.

Equivalent-form reliability. An alternative method of assessing reliability which avoids the problems of retesting is to administer equivalent forms of the same test to the same individuals at more or less the same time. Thus, the Stanford–Binet intelligence test has two forms, L and M, and the correlation between them is about 0·91 (Terman and Merrill, 1937).

This procedure involves the construction of two tests which are in fact equivalent. Strictly, two tests are equivalent or parallel only if, when administered to the same group of individuals, the means, variances (standard deviations squared) and inter-item co-variances are equal. These requirements demand considerable care in the selection of items for the two forms, although in practice the test constructor may not adopt such stringent criteria.

What is meant by 'error' when the equivalent-forms method is used differs from 'error' as defined by the test–retest reliability procedure. The latter treats random *time-to-time* fluctuations in scores as error. The former includes these fluctuations, since necessarily the two forms of a test are administered at different times; but since different items are used in the two forms, fluctuations from *form to form* may also be influential. Thus the equivalent-form procedure provides a compound measure of equivalence and stability.

The types of variation that can contribute to changes in scores from one administration to another are quite diverse, but can be placed in four overlapping categories: temporary, lasting, general, specific. Following Cronbach (1964) these four sources of variation can be depicted as shown in Table 19.1. Random variation (that is, variation which is not uniform in its effect upon all subjects) from any of these sources will decrease the size of a correlation between administrations and thus decrease the apparent reliability of a test.

From what has been said so far, it is apparent that different measures of reliability are concerned with different sources of error. The test–retest procedure measures temporal reliability: the reliability coefficient is increased by any *lasting* determinant of scores, whether general or specific, and is decreased by temporary determinants. In other words, the test–retest procedure regards both general and specific factors as 'true' variance only if they are *lasting*. The equivalent-forms procedure, on the other hand, regards both temporary and lasting factors as 'true' variance only if they are *general*, since the specific items on the two forms are different.

Table 19.1
Possible sources of variation in a test score. (Cronbach, 1964, p. 128; after R. L. Thorndike, 1949, p. 73)

I. Lasting and general characteristics of the individual
  1. General skills (e.g. reading)
  2. General ability to comprehend instructions, testwiseness, techniques of taking tests
  3. Ability to solve problems of the general type presented in this test
  4. Attitudes, emotional reactions or habits generally operating in situations like the test situation (e.g. self-confidence).
II. Lasting and specific characteristics of the individual
  1. Knowledge and skills required by particular problems in the test
  2. Attitudes, emotional reactions or habits related to particular test stimuli (e.g. fear of high places brought to mind by an inquiry about such fears on a personality test).
III. Temporary and general characteristics of the individual (systematically affecting performance on various tests at a particular time)
  1. Health, fatigue and emotional strain
  2. Motivation, rapport with examiner
  3. Effects of heat, light, ventilation, etc.
  4. Level of practice on skills required by tests of this type
  5. Present attitudes, emotional reactions, or strength of habits (in so far as these are departures from the person's average or lasting characteristics – e.g. political attitudes during an election)
IV. Temporary and specific characteristics of the individual
  1. Changes in fatigue or motivation developed by this particular test (e.g. discouragement resulting from failure on a particular item)
  2. Fluctuations in attention, co-ordination or standards of judgement
  3. Fluctuations in memory for particular facts
  4. Level of practice on skills or knowledge required by this particular test (e.g. effects of special coaching)
  5. Temporary emotional states, strength of habits, etc., related to particular test stimuli (e.g. a question calls to mind a recent bad dream)
  6. Luck in the selection of answers by 'guessing'.

A third procedure, less frequently used than the two so far described, is to interpose a similar delay to that involved in retesting between the administration of equivalent forms. In this, the *delayed-equivalence* procedure, both changes in the individual and changes in the items comprising the two forms are likely to lower the correlation and hence are included as error. Thus, in this procedure only *lasting general* factors are regarded as 'true' variance.

Different measurement procedures will therefore yield rather different estimates of the reliability of a test. If all three procedures are used in a given case, it is possible by comparing these estimates to arrive at a statement of the relative contributions of each of the sources of variation quoted – lasting general, lasting specific, temporary general, temporary specific – to the *total variance* of the scores obtained.

Split-half reliability. As we have seen, equivalent forms of a test cannot be administered to the same individuals at the same time, so that the equivalent-forms procedure does not entirely eliminate the possibility of including variation in the true score from occasion to occasion as part of the error score. The split-half method attempts to eliminate this possibility by correlating the scores of the same individuals on one half of the test with their scores on the other half, thus providing as closely as possible a measure of form-to-form fluctuation only.

Such a correlation is sometimes known as a *coefficient of equivalence*. In practice, the items comprising the two split halves are usually selected on an odd–even basis. Thus the scores obtained on the odd items are correlated with the scores obtained by the same subjects on the even items. However, since the reliability of a test is also a function of its length, for reasons which will not be considered here, a correction is needed to determine the reliability of the whole test (see Cronbach, 1964, pp. 129–33).

Split-half reliability differs from other reliability measures in that it is concerned with the homogeneity, or internal consistency, of a test rather than with its reliability from one administration to another. Thus it is more clearly a part of test *construction*, aiding the selection and comparison of test items, than are the other procedures, and is more often used for that purpose.

Estimation of validity

A test which is highly reliable, by any or all of the criteria described above, may still not be *valid*, in the sense that it might give highly reliable scores which are not in fact measures of the characteristic which the test is intended to measure. On the other hand, an entirely unreliable test logically cannot be valid; the reliability of a test must limit its validity.

Like reliability, validity is a concept capable of various definitions, based upon various methods of measurement. Three main types of validity will concern us here. The first is *content validity*, which might be said to employ criteria internal to the tests being examined; the second is *empirical validity*, which is assessed by correlation between test scores and other, 'external' criteria of the characteristic under consideration. Finally, we shall consider the notion of *construct validity*.

Content validity. This subdivides into two further types, *face validity* and *factorial validity.* Face validity refers to how appropriate a test appears to be, either to a potential user or to someone actually taking the test. For example, if a test which purports to measure mechanical aptitude consists solely of items concerned with electrical knowledge, its face validity is low. Factorial validity is a more sophisticated type of content validity which, as its name implies, involves the application of techniques of factor analysis to derive factors which different tests sample in differing degrees and to which psychological values may or may not be assigned (see Chapter 20). The factor loadings of one test can then be compared with those of another.

Empirical validity. The establishment of empirical validity involves relating performance on the test to performance on another, independent measure of the same characteristic; that is, we correlate the test with a criterion. If the criterion measure is taken some time after the test is administered, we speak of *predictive validity*; if scores on the criterion are already available at the time of testing, we speak of *concurrent validity*.

In principle, this method of validating a test is the most direct and obvious. In practice it has one major drawback which severely limits its value, at least for certain kinds of test. Before it can be used, there must be good ground for thinking that the criterion measure itself is valid.

It is only when a test is constructed solely for the purpose of predicting performance in some other, clearly defined situation, and this is usually when the test is required for selection purposes, that the problem does not arise. For example, if a test is constructed for selecting students for a degree course in French, and if the purpose is to choose those who will get good degrees, then performance in the degree examination is a completely valid criterion. Moreover, if the purpose of the test is to predict degree success, then its correlation with degree results is the only possible way of validating the test. In this context, concurrent validity would mean that the test is given to students after they have taken their degree.

A hypothetical correlation between a test and a criterion is shown in Figure

19.2. Let us suppose that individuals who obtain a criterion score above X are satisfactory – that is, they are the individuals the selector wants to select. The problem then becomes one of finding a suitable *cutting score* on the test which will discriminate between those individuals who should be selected on the basis of their probable criterion score and those who should be rejected on the same grounds. Let us further suppose that a cutting score Y has been adopted. The two shaded areas in Figure 19.2 then represent incorrect selection decisions, since the cutting score has failed to select those in group A who would have obtained a satisfactory criterion score and has selected those in group B who failed to obtain a satisfactory criterion score. Those in group A are known as *misses* and those in group B as *false positives*. It can be seen that placing the cutting score at different points on the abscissa results in different proportions of misses, false positives and correct selections. The cutting score is usually determined in accordance with the risks the selector is prepared to undergo. If a large number of misses is unimportant but false positives must be avoided, the cutting score will be placed

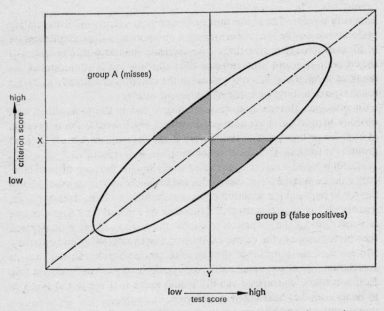

Figure 19.2   Hypothetical relation between a test and a criterion (see text)

somewhere to the right of Y. If, on the other hand, misses must be avoided, even if this means that a large number of false positives will be made, the cutting score will be placed to the left of Y.

To evaluate the usefulness of a test in reaching selection decisions it is also necessary to know the *base rate*, that is, the proportion of individuals who were selected without the test being used as a selection device and who reached a satisfactory criterion score. The proportion of correct decisions made using the test for selection purposes, the *validity rate*, can then be compared with the base rate.

Of course, the construction of tests for selection faces other practical difficulties. To continue the example above, the test of ability at French can only be validated on students who have already been selected for a university course on other criteria. But for this kind of test, the logic of the validating procedure is straightforward enough.

The problems arise when we wish to use criterion validity for a test of some more general individual-difference dimension. The classic example is intelligence. The first 'intelligence' tests to be constructed were often validated against the independent criterion of teachers' ratings for intelligence or success in school subjects. In the light of everyday usage of the term, intelligence, it is reasonable to assume that these criteria have some validity, at least if the sample used is large and representative. But it is also certain that responsiveness to educational influence is determined by other factors than the children's intelligence, such as interest in school subjects and parental encouragement. It follows that, in a large enough sample, we should expect some positive association between performance on a test purporting to measure intelligence and success in school; a zero correlation would certainly cast doubt on the validity of the test. But at the same time, a very high positive correlation would also make us doubt that the test was measuring general intelligence alone.

The difficulty is due to the fact that intelligence is a high level construct, intended to refer to some general feature of the human system which reveals itself in so many different ways that there can be no single independent criterion. For tests designed to measure such general characteristics, correlation with a criterion can only supply modest support of their validity, and greater reliance has to be placed on other methods such as factor analysis. The most appropriate method is probably that of construct validity, discussed below; unfortunately this method requires that the characteristic to be measured be embedded in an explanatory theory, and an adequate theory of this kind does not yet exist for intelligence.

It is always essential that as much care should be taken in the construction of a criterion as in the construction of the test itself. If, for example, the test is capable of making very subtle discriminations among individuals and the criterion is capable only of very gross discriminations, the validity of the test is lowered, not necessarily because the test is poor but because the test and the criterion are not sufficiently well matched for a high validity coefficient to be possible. Finally, it should be added that in practice the tendency is to validate new tests, particularly intelligence tests, by correlating them with well-established existing tests. This is not as circular as it might seem. When a test has been used a great deal in research and selection, and has consistently functioned as we should expect a good test of intelligence to do, we may justly feel more confident in its validity.

Construct validity. As noted above, construct validity is appropriate when the characteristic to be measured is a general dimension of individual difference, such as anxiety, authoritarianism, intelligence or extraversion. The establishment of construct validity is contingent upon the fact that the psychologist has an explanatory theory within which the trait to be measured features as an intervening variable or hypothetical construct, and from which it derives its definition. The validity of the test as an operational measure of a construct within the theory is then bound up with the extent to which predictions derived from the theory are confirmed by experiments using the test as one of the measures (see Cronbach and Meehl, 1955).

As a convenient example of construct validity, we can consider the personality inventory devised by Eysenck, the Maudsley Personality Inventory or MPI (Eysenck, 1959), which is designed to measure extraversion–introversion. Eysenck has developed an elaborate theory of personality, which is outlined briefly in Chapter 20. Within this theory, the personality dimension of extraversion–introversion is associated with differences in physiological functioning and in various measures of performance. Eysenck's theory of cortical inhibition suggests that individuals may differ in the rates at which they build up and dissipate reactive inhibition. Some individuals (introverts) are thought to build up inhibition slowly and to dissipate it rapidly while others (extraverts) build up inhibition rapidly and dissipate it slowly. This in turn suggests that introverts and extraverts will behave differently when tested under conditions of massed and distributed practice or that the performance of extraverts in vigilance situations will decline at a more rapid rate than will that of introverts. Now if predictions regarding the physiological and behavioural correlates of extraversion are sustained by experiments in which extraversion is defined by scores on a personality inventory, then the validity of the test as a measure of a construct within the theory is supported.

However, one of the problems attendant upon the construct validation of a test is knowing when to stop. The theory may generate many predictions, not all of which are sustained. A single negative result implies that the theory needs modification; but it is uncertain how many confirmatory results are required before the theory can be regarded as confirmed, and the test, as a measure of one of its constructs, validated.

Types of test

Tests of achievement

Achievement can be defined as an individual's degree of accomplishment or success in acquiring knowledge or skill in a particular sphere of activity. This can be measured by examination or test performance. For example, different kinds of school achievement can readily be assessed by means of specially devised tests, and test scores then provide *direct* measures of the level of scholastic achievement. In contrast, aptitudes, intelligence, personality and the like are assessed in an *indirect* manner in that such qualities are inferred from psychological test scores. However, in common with all other tests, tests of achievement must be so designed as to give consistent results; that is, they must be reliable. Furthermore, whenever such tests are used for predictive purposes, and they often are, they must be not only reliable but also valid.

Although achievement tests are perhaps not, in a strict sense, psychological tests, their construction, administration and use are subject to the rules which apply to all tests. Not only should they be objective, reliable and valid, but each test must also be standardized on a large sample of the population for which it is to be used. Only in this way can the achievement of a given individual be assessed in relation to the group of which he/she is a member. Standardization consists of evaluating the mean score on the given test (and other measures of central tendency) as well as the standard deviation of scores (or some other measure of scatter) obtained by the individuals in the standardization sample.

There are many different scholastic achievement tests, such as reading tests, language tests, mathematics tests, science tests and so on. There are also proficiency tests for carpenters, for lathe operators, for shorthand typists, etc., as well as driving tests, musical proficiency tests and the like. All such tests of achievement, or performance, investigate what a person can actually do here and now rather than what the person's potential might be. But what a person can do today is often indicative of what he or she may be able to do in the future. Therefore many tests were devised specifically to be predictors of future performance, and were given labels corresponding to what was thought to be essential for such successful performance, for example, musical aptitude, or mechanical aptitude, or verbal fluency, or – quite often – simply, general intelligence. Such tests of general ability or specific aptitude will receive special consideration in following sections.

General ability tests

Compared to many other areas of psychology, the construction of intelligence tests has a long history. A major impetus to its growth came from the need, in the early years of this century, to create a method of classifying children in terms of their educational requirements. The pioneer in the measurement of individual differences was Francis Galton. But probably the most important event, historically, was the decision of the French Ministry of Public Instruction, in 1904, to appoint a committee to inquire into the education of mentally retarded children. As a consequence, Alfred Binet was asked to devise a test which would identify feeble-minded children early in their lives so that they could be given special educational treatment.

Binet's interest in mental testing had begun about twenty years earlier, and in 1905 – in collaboration with Simon – he produced the first test of intelligence. He had earlier criticized the tests of Galton on the grounds that they contained too many measures of sensory ability, and that, in any case, they were too simple to provide adequate measures of intelligence. Binet and Simon's test, therefore, consisted of a number of subtests, each with items ranging widely in difficulty, which attempted to measure such complex psychological processes as memory, imagination, comprehension and aesthetic appreciation. In a monograph translated into English after Binet's death in 1911, Binet and Simon (1916) stated 'to judge well, to comprehend well, to reason well, these are the essential activities of the intelligence' (p. 42).

This first intelligence test was standardized on a very small sample of children, but it was shortly followed by two revisions, both standardized on larger samples. The second of these, in 1911, contained five tests at each age level from three to fifteen years. Moreover, the correlations between scores on the test and external criteria such as teachers' assessments and school examinations were much improved. For a number of years this test served as a model for the construction of other intelligence tests.

Two refinements were introduced shortly after the publication of the 1911 Binet–Simon test. Burt introduced the method of writing answers in a test booklet, as opposed to the oral question-and-answer procedure used by Binet, and Stern suggested the expression of test scores in the form of intelligence quotients, or I.Q.s. Stern (1912) argued that 'this quotient would show what fractional part of the intelligence normal to his age a feeble-minded child obtains' (p. 80).

In 1910 Terman, working at Stanford University, began modifying the Binet tests for administration to American children, and his Stanford Revision of the Binet scales was produced in 1916. This revision made it possible to estimate normal and superior intelligence as well as subnormal. The 1916 Stanford–Binet test was itself revised in 1937 by Terman and Merrill, who published two equivalent forms of the test, forms L and M. The 1960 revision combined the most useful tests from the 1937 version into a single form, L–M, and has an improved scoring system.

All versions of the Binet test are scales; in other words, the test items are grouped together in terms of their difficulty and as the test proceeds the items become more and more difficult. The score a child obtains depends on how many items he can answer correctly rather than how fast he works. However, the level of difficulty of items is also related to age, and a great deal of research has been carried out to find items of suitable difficulty for each age level. For example, an item suitable for the age level of eight years should be answered correctly by some eight-year-olds, by virtually all nine-year-olds and by hardly any seven-year-olds. But assigning values to the terms 'some', 'virtually all' and 'hardly any' has aroused controversy. For instance, does 'some' mean 50, 66 or 75 per cent? Heim (1970a) has argued that the least objectionable figure is 50 per cent. The scoring system of the Binet test is expressed in terms of years and months, and the score a child obtains is his *mental age* (MA). The obtained mental age is equivalent to the chronological age (CA) at which the average child does as well as the testee does. For example, a six-year-old child who correctly answers as many items as the average eight-year-old, earns a mental age of eight years. If 'average' is also taken to mean 50 per cent, then the median mental age of a random sample of six-year-olds will be six years. This does not necessarily imply that the mean mental age will also be six years unless the mental age distribution is completely normal, when the mean will equal the median.

In practice it very rarely happens that a child answers correctly all the items as far as a particular age level and then fails to answer any more; in other words, incorrectly answered items occur at irregular points as the test proceeds. The mental age is therefore calculated by adding age credits (usually two months per test, since most forms of the Binet scale now have six tests at each age level) for each test successfully completed. Testing is normally terminated if three successive tests are failed at a particular age level.

Intelligence quotients which simply express the ratio of mental age to chronological age are known as *ratio I.Q.s*. It is a necessary feature of the ratio I.Q. that as CA increases, the *same* differences in I.Q. correspond to *increasing* differences in MA. If three children have a CA of eight years, and I.Q.s of 70, 110 and 130, then their MAs will be 5·6, 8·8 and 10·4 respectively. At age fifteen, children with the same I.Q.s will have MAs of 10·5, 16·5 and 19·5. The gap in MA between I.Q.s of 70 and 130 has widened from 4·8 years at age eight to nine years at age fifteen. As a consequence, some psychologists have interpreted MA as signifying *amount* of intelligence and I.Q. as indicating *rate of development* of intelligence.

There are, however, several considerations which must qualify these interpretations.

1. Intelligence tests are not absolute measures and hence it is very doubtful if a test score can be taken as indicating 'amount' of intelligence.

2. There is no guarantee that a test attains interval measurement, and therefore that any one-year increase in MA is equivalent to every other.

3. As noted in the section on validity, 'intelligence' is a construct whose relationship to any single test is very much more complicated than, for instance, the relationship between a tape-measure and height. The inference from increased test score to 'development of intelligence' must remain problematic.

4. There is much evidence that improved performance with age on any test tends to reach a ceiling. On some tests, this ceiling is reached by most people by the age of fourteen or fifteen years; on other tests by the age of twenty-five years or more. This implies that *in certain of its aspects*, the growth of intelligence ceases for most people with the attainment of adulthood, and that the calculation of I.Q.s after such growth has stopped is largely meaningless.

5. I.Q.s are not, as was once thought, constant throughout development. It is true that there is fairly high stability of individual differences over a large sample through much of childhood and adolescence (B. S. Bloom, 1964); but the scores of particular individuals may fluctuate quite widely, by as much as twenty I.Q. points or more.

These considerations, together with a number of other technical problems which cannot be discussed here, have led a growing number of psychologists to abandon the concepts of MA and ratio I.Q. Instead, greater reliance is being placed on a *deviation I.Q.* A deviation I.Q. expresses the test result as a standard score; it informs the tester how many standard deviations above or below the average of his age group the testee's score lies. This avoids the notion of mental age, and makes comparisons between different tests easier.

The conversion of test scores into standard scores implies the assumption that intelligence itself is normally distributed. This assumption is impossible to verify directly but the considerable amount of indirect evidence which has been accumulated suggests that it is not untenable and, in addition, it confers considerable practical advantages.

However, the difficulty of intelligence test items affects the normality of the distribution, and the distributions of scores tend to be skewed on tests in which the difficulty of items is not graded in approximately equal steps. In such cases the test is not sensitive enough to spread the scores sufficiently; hence too many scores cluster at one end or the other of the distribution. The relation of test-item difficulty to the distribution of test scores is clearly important in the construction of intelligence tests, although even in carefully constructed tests the distributions of scores at different ages, while normal, may differ in range.

Thus, on the 1937 Stanford–Binet, the standard deviation of ratio I.Q.s is twelve points at six years of age and about twenty points at eleven years of age. This means that a child with the same I.Q. would be placed at two different points in relation to his peers at the two different ages, which leads to confusion, although it is possible to make the standard deviations equivalent by applying appropriate computational procedures. In the 1960 revision of the Stanford–Binet, the test constructors computed the standard of mental ages for each group and whatever mental age fell one standard deviation above the mean was converted into a deviation I.Q. of 116, while the mental age falling one standard deviation below the mean was converted to a deviation I.Q. of 84. The standard score in this case is thus based upon a mean of 100 and a standard deviation of 16. It should be emphasized that these are essentially arbitrary choices.

Psychologists have therefore tended to accept the assumption that intelligence is normally distributed on the grounds that there is no compelling evidence against it and because it is convenient from the point of view of test construction and the analysis and interpretation of test scores. This does not mean that all mental abilities are normally distributed; the distributions of special talents and attainments, such as musical aptitude or scientific creativity, are much more likely to be skewed.

The Stanford–Binet test is heavily weighted on verbal abilities and the scores obtained at different ages reflect differences in these abilities. The various intelligence scales developed by Wechsler, which permit separate estimates to be made of both verbal and non-verbal abilities, provide a useful supplement to the Binet in testing children, as well as providing what is probably the best all-round test of adult intelligence. Wechsler's first test, the Wechsler–Bellevue, developed in 1939, is now no longer in use. However, it has been replaced by three separate scales, the Wechsler Primary and Pre-School Intelligence Scale which was published in 1967, the Wechsler Intelligence Scale for Children (W.I.S.C.) published in 1949, and the Wechsler Adult Intelligence Scale (W.A.I.S.) for testees aged sixteen years and over, which first appeared in 1955. In addition to the introduction of a well-standardized performance scale, Wechsler made use of a deviation I.Q which compares an individual's test score with the expected mean score of his age group. The same raw score will thus be converted to different I.Q.s at different ages, in line with Wechsler's view of the growth and decline of mental abilities throughout the life-span (for further details of age changes in intelligence, see Bayley, 1949, 1955; Botwinick, 1977; Wechsler, 1958). Cronbach (1964) gives an excellent summary of the tests which make up the Wechsler scales and of some representative research concerned with its evaluation (see also Guertin et al., 1966). The Stanford–Binet and Wechsler tests were standardized in America, and this limits somewhat their applicability in this country. To remedy this situation, a new individual general ability test has been developed, and it is known as the British Ability Scales (Elliott, Murray and Pearson, 1978). This test includes traditional items concerned with reasoning, spatial imagery, short-term memory and so on, as well as new-type items, deriving from the investigations of Piaget, and involving 'conservation' by children of length, number, area, volume and weight.

Finally, it should be mentioned that there are also many group tests of intelligence, both verbal and non-verbal. A number of these, for example, the

AH4 and AH5, are concerned with the measurement of superior adult intelligence. For further details of such tests the reader is referred to Cronbach (1964) and P. E. Vernon (1960).

Aptitude tests

Special aptitude tests, achievement tests, and for that matter intelligence tests, rest on a similar conceptual framework and the distinction between them is largely a matter of convenience. One reason why aptitude and achievement tests are frequently considered under separate headings is a historical one; aptitudes were once thought to be innate while achievement was considered to be largely a function of learning and experience. Another is that aptitude tests are frequently used to *predict* future performance while achievement tests, as we have already seen, are used to measure the effectiveness of training procedures already administered. The training procedure may be an industrial one or it may be a school or college course. However, in some instances, achievement tests may be just as effective predictors as aptitude tests and the degree of achievement may correlate highly with aptitude test scores.

Aptitude testing can be considered from two points of view: selection and vocational guidance. When aptitude tests are used to select individuals for a particular occupation, the purpose of the test is to discover the potential which an individual possesses to perform at a certain level of competence in the occupation in question. This potential, which is a combination of innate abilities and of experience, sets a limit on the rate of acquisition of a particular skill and also on the maximum level of performance that the individual is capable of achieving. Thus in selection situations aptitude tests are used as predictors of occupational success. In vocational guidance situations, on the other hand, aptitude tests are used in an attempt to identify an individual's special talents in order to advise him on a range of occupations for which his abilities indicate that he is suitable.

Vocational guidance procedures nearly always include already established batteries of special abilities, about which a great deal of information is available. Two examples are the Differential Aptitudes Test (Bennett, Seashore and Wesman, 1959) and the General Aptitude Test Battery, both of which were developed in the U.S.A. The Differential Aptitudes Test (D.A.T.), which was developed in the 1940s, consists of subtests measuring verbal reasoning, spatial reasoning, clerical speed and accuracy, spelling and the ability to detect faults in grammar, punctuation and spelling in sentences.

The General Aptitude Test Battery (G.A.T.B.) was produced by the United States Employment Service and its subtests include measures of general reasoning ability, verbal aptitude, numerical aptitude, spatial aptitude, form perception, clerical perception, motor co-ordination, finger dexterity and manual dexterity.

There seems little doubt that different occupations are associated, to some extent at least, with different patterns of ability (Thorndike and Hagen, 1959) and in both tests minimum scores in the critical aptitudes for a wide range of occupations have been laid down. It is thus possible to gain a good idea of the occupations for which the testee's ability pattern is best suited. However, possession of the appropriate ability profile does not guarantee occupational success; vocational guidance includes more than aptitude testing and information about interests, attitudes, values and attainment is highly desirable. Furthermore, vocational guidance depends for its success upon extremely close consultation with the client at each stage in the guidance process.

Selection procedures are generally used to screen applicants for a particular job and, unless the screening process is an extremely leisurely one, it is unlikely that already-established aptitude test batteries, involving a broad spectrum of abilities, will be employed. Instead, it is likely that the qualities required for the job in question will already be known, that is, a *job analysis* will have been carried out (European Productivity Agency, 1956), a test based on this analysis will have been given to employees already working at the job and the results compared with a criterion, usually supervisors' ratings. If the match between test and criterion is satisfactory, in other words, if the correlation between them is sufficiently high, the test can then be given to applicants for the job, and to further validate the test, a *follow-up study* of the job performance of the applicants selected by the test will usually be carried out. Such a test will focus on the abilities specific to the job for which it acts as a selection device (for an example of the development of an aptitude test, see Viteles, 1962).

The development of a suitable criterion against which to match test results is clearly very important in the development of an aptitude test. First of all, the notion that there is a criterion for each and every job, as classified for instance in the Department of Employment and Productivity index of job classifications, may be questioned. Second, if there is such a criterion, in most jobs it is unlikely to be a single measure (Ghiselli, 1956). This suggests that the multiple criteria available should be combined into a single over-all criterion. Since, however, these various criteria are unlikely to be equally important in the determination of occupational success, they must be weighted in accordance with their relative importance. There are a number of different ways of doing this but each one is associated with certain methodological problems (Ghiselli and Brown, 1955). Furthermore, the different criteria are quite likely to be unrelated. Speed of work, for instance, is likely to correlate poorly with accuracy, yet both may be important in a particular job. This raises the question as to whether several unrelated criteria can be meaningfully combined into one multiple criterion. Third, the criterion may correlate poorly with itself at different times, that is, its reliability may be low. If this happens, then the correlation between test and criterion is also likely to be low (Ebel, 1961). Thus the low validity of a selection device may sometimes be due to the unreliability of the criterion, although it may also arise from a variety of other factors, among which should be included the quality of management (Ferguson, 1951).

Ghiselli (1966), in an extremely interesting review of occupational aptitude tests and their validity, suggests that in practice two broad types of criteria should be distinguished: first, *training criteria*, that is, criteria which are relevant to the capacity of trainees to learn a job and, second, *proficiency criteria*, criteria relevant to the job proficiency of workers who have already been trained. For further discussion of the usefulness of aptitude tests the reader is referred to Ghiselli's review.

Attitude and personality tests

Ability tests have been described as 'intellective'; by contrast tests of personality are said to be 'non-intellective'. This distinction is much the same as that between cognitive and affective aspects of mental functioning. Personality assessment of the individual thus focuses on his/her non-cognitive characteristics such as temperament, social attitudes, habitual ways of coping with stress, and so on. Numerical assessment, or measurement, of such qualities is not easy; and we shall indicate very briefly how this has been attempted. Much more information on the study of personality and social psychology will be found in Chapters 20–23. As with other types of test already discussed, personality tests, if they are to be useful, must be objective, standardized, reliable and valid to some acceptable degree.

A feature of personality which is perhaps most readily gauged concerns the interests of the individual. There are many ways of obtaining information about a person's interests, but the most convenient is the *interest inventory* method, based upon the use of questionnaires. Some much used inventories have been developed in America. One is the so-called Strong Vocational Interest Blank, another the Kuder General Interest Survey (see review in Aiken, 1971). Tests such as these are mostly used in vocational guidance and personnel selection. They are intended to be predictive of occupational success. In other words, interest tests, apart from being reliable, must also be valid. A novel framework for the study of interests from the standpoint of occupational choices has been developed more recently by Holland (1973).

The *attitudes* an individual adopts towards the various aspects of his environment form an important part of his personality. Newcomb (1964, p. 40) has defined an attitude as

an individual's organization of psychological processes, as inferred from his behaviour, with respect to some aspect of the world which he distinguishes from other aspects. It represents the residue of his experience with which he approaches any subsequent situation including that aspect and, together with the contemporary influences in such a situation, determines his behaviour in it. Attitudes are enduring in the sense that such residues are carried over to new situations, but they change in so far as new residues are acquired through experience in new situations.

There are several ways in which attitudes, and their effect on behaviour, may be measured. If, for example, we are interested in establishing an individual's attitude towards West Indian immigrants, we might (at least in principle) follow him about his everyday occupation and observe his behaviour towards the West Indians he meets. As well as being difficult to implement in practice, this procedure encounters the objection that attitudes are not necessarily, consistently or directly reflected in overt behaviour; a man may have an essentially negative attitude to women but behave towards them with unvarying politeness. Another, and the most common, method of estimating attitude is, essentially, to ask the subject himself, usually by means of an *attitude scale*.

Attitude scales generally consist of a series of statements with which the testee is invited to express his degree of agreement or, sometimes, merely whether he agrees with the statement or not. In some cases a hypothetical situation is described, the respondent is given a range of choices and asked about his probable course of action, which he must often indicate by a simple 'yes' or 'no'. There are three main types of attitude scale, *summated rating scales* (also known as Likert-type scales), *equal appearing interval scales* and *cumulative* or *Guttman scales*.

Summated rating scales consist of items of 'equal attitude value', which means that the scores for all items in the scale can be summed and averaged to give the individual's over-all attitude score. Such scales also allow the intensity with which an attitude is held to be expressed. This increases response variation, and enables finer discriminations to be made between individuals. A disadvantage is that this variation, on summated rating scales at least, often appears to consist mainly of variations attributable to response sets (see below). In equal-appearing interval scales, the items are scaled and are assigned values at equal intervals along an attitude continuum, a procedure which confers considerable statistical advantage. Cumulative scales are concerned with the measurement of one variable, which is supposed to be unidimensional. The first type of scale, using summated ratings, is probably the most widely used, since it is the easiest to work with. For further details of attitude scale construction, see A. L. Edwards (1957b). The concept of attitude, and the possible relation between attitudes and behaviour, are further discussed by Jaspars (1978).

Personality tests vary a great deal, not least because the definition of personality may be very different for different researchers (see Chapters 20 and 21). However, they share a basic problem of validity: it is difficult to conceive of a meaningful criterion against which the test results can be checked. One way in which this problem has been solved is to use criterion groups already selected by society. For instance, if individuals already classified as mentally ill, or as criminals, produce test protocols indicating a high level of maladjustment, then this is considered to be evidence of the validity of the test.

This method of solving the criterion problem has been a popular one and its use has generated a large number of tests which emphasize negative aspects of personality. Indeed, the first personality inventory to be developed was constructed in the First World War for the purpose of identifying soldiers who were unsuited for combat on emotional grounds (Woodworth, 1920). One of the consequences of this preoccupation with maladjustment has been that it is now much easier to detect signs of instability in an apparently normal individual than it is to detect traits that both society in general and the individual himself would regard as desirable.

However, this balance has been to some extent redressed both by the use of *empirical* or *criterion keying* in tests which have sought to distinguish different occupational groups in terms of their interests and attitudes (Strong, 1955) and by the use of construct validation in the study of individual differences (Eysenck, 1957, p. 261). In addition, projective techniques have been used as part of experimental research programmes aimed at identifying the structure of needs and motives in different individuals and exploring the relation between motivation and action (see, for example, Atkinson, 1958).

The most obvious method of personality assessment might appear to be the interview. A great deal has been written on it (see Matarazzo, 1965; Richardson, Dohrenwend and Klein, 1965) and it raises too many issues to be dealt with here. Fortunately some of the main methodological problems encountered in interviewing also occur with other methods. For our present purposes, therefore, we shall consider briefly only three general approaches to the measurement of personality, namely: self-report procedures, inventories and questionnaires; rating procedures; and projective techniques.

Self-report procedures, inventories and questionnaires. Self-report procedures present the testee with a series of questions which he is required to answer, for convenience in scoring, by using fixed response categories such as 'yes', 'no' or 'cannot say'. The questions are usually chosen, initially at least, on the basis of their content validity, so that the resulting questionnaire looks as if it is concerned with the measurement of personality. If the responses to a personality questionnaire are taken at face value, then certain problems of interpretation arise. For instance, several factors limit the degree of trust that can be placed in the responses: subjects can easily fake their responses; they may lack insight and be unable to answer the question usefully; they may approach the test with different response sets or response styles; and finally, because of their ambiguity, test items may be interpreted in ways which the test constructor did not intend.

Test constructors have attempted to counter faking in several different ways. First, they have attempted to conceal the purpose of a test and have disguised personality tests as measures of ability (Campbell, 1957). Second, some test constructors have incorporated verification and correction keys, or lie scales, into the test, for example, by repeating the same item in two different forms. The Kuder Preference Record (Kuder, 1953) and the Minnesota Multiphasic Personality Inventory or M.M.P.I. (Hathaway and McKinley, 1942, 1943) are examples of tests which have one or other of these built-in checks against distortion.

However, one of the most important ways of meeting most of the difficulties that personality inventories face is the method of *criterion keying*. This method makes use of what has been described as actuarial validity and uses the responses gained from a questionnaire administered to already well-defined criterion groups as 'signs' which distinguish one criterion group from another. Because this method makes few or no theoretical assumptions about what the content of personality questionnaires should be, it has given rise to argument concerning the importance of test-item content (Berg, 1959; Norman, 1963). Although items may be selected initially on the basis of content validity, they are retained only if they discriminate between different criterion groups. The M.M.P.I., while not immune to criticism, is an outstanding example of a personality inventory based on the principle of criterion keying and is composed of ten scales which cover most of the various neurotic and psychotic disorders (for further details, see Dahlstrom and Welsh, 1960).

The use of criterion keying also appears to eliminate the problem of lack of insight, in that if a questionnaire can successfully discriminate between criterion groups, it matters little whether items are being answered truthfully from a full knowledge of the respondent's own personality dynamics, or whether the testee is lying or simply 'doesn't know'. However, in order to learn more about the individual personality than the criterion groups to which it belongs, other techniques, such as projective tests, are necessary.

Beginning with two papers by Cronbach (1946, 1950) the effects of *response sets* and *response styles* have been examined in considerable detail in the past thirty years, although complete agreement on the ways in which these two terms should be defined has not been reached. Response set appears to be the more general term while response style refers to the way in which a response set is expressed in a particular situation, for example, when answering a personality questionnaire. An example of a response set is *acquiescence*, which has been regarded as a basic personality trait, while an example of a response style stemming from acquiescence is the disproportionate tendency to select 'yes' as a response to items in a personality inventory. The effects of acquiescent sets and their associated response styles are reviewed by Jackson (1967) and Messick (1967).

Another important response set is the *social desirability variable* (A. L. Edwards, 1957a; 1967a, b); this response set is the tendency to agree with or endorse statements favourable to the respondent. The work of Edwards and his collaborators has demonstrated beyond much doubt that a tendency to present oneself in a favourable light when answering a self-report inventory does exist, that its effects are distinguishable from deliberate lying and that its existence has important implications for personality assessment. This tendency has been related to other personality characteristics, in particular, conformity (Crowne and Marlowe, 1964). One way of minimizing the effects of the social desirability variable is to construct personality questionnaires in accordance with the method of *forced choice keying*, in which items are matched for social desirability, or undesirability, and the respondent is required to choose between pairs of items. This approach to the construction of personality questionnaires is exemplified by the Edwards Personal Preference Schedule (A. L. Edwards, 1959).

The third major response set that has been identified is *deviance* (Adams and Butler, 1967; Berg, 1967), although the consequences of deviance – expressed in the deviation hypothesis (Berg, 1967) – extend far beyond the personality assessment situation. Deviance is expressed in personality inventories as a tendency to respond to items in an uncommon way and the deviation hypothesis is thus much more concerned with non-conformists than with conformists. Berg and his associates have shown that deviance in the personality assessment situation appears to be associated with atypical behaviour in a variety of other situations and hence that deviance can also be considered as a basic personality trait.

Response sets and response styles are considered by some investigators to be sources of error which must be minimized by more careful construction of tests and by others as important dimensions of personality in their own right (see Block, 1965). Although this controversy is far from settled, some of its effects are already apparent in the form of better-constructed self-report procedures.

Rating procedures. In addition to self-report procedures, a number of self-rating procedures have been used to assess personality characteristics, principally in personality research rather than in the clinical situation. These procedures require subjects to rate themselves in relation to various statements as part of a more complex task situation than that involved in self-report procedures. Among the more prominent of such techniques are the *Q sort* (Block, 1961; Stephenson, 1953), which has been used, *inter alia*, to evaluate the effectiveness of psychotherapy (Rogers and Dymond, 1954); the *semantic differential* (Osgood, Suci and Tannenbaum, 1957) and the *Construct Repertory Test* (Bannister and Mair, 1968; G. A. Kelly, 1955). The importance of all three tests for the assessment of personality depends, at present, perhaps more on their potential than on their performance.

Projective techniques. It has been said that the rationale underlying projective techniques is something like 'your unconscious is you, your fantasy is the key to your unconscious, your protocol is the key to your fantasy, therefore your protocol is you'. Lindzey (1961, p. 45) has defined a projective technique as 'an instrument that is considered especially sensitive to covert or unconscious aspects of behavior. It permits or encourages a wide variety of subject responses, is highly multidimensional and it evokes unusually rich or profuse response data with a minimum of subject awareness concerning the purpose of the test.'

Thus projective techniques are essentially unstructured, that is, subjects are presented with ambiguous stimuli such as pictures or incomplete sentences or stories and asked in the first case to describe what they see and in the two latter cases to complete the material with which they have been presented. The number of possible responses open to the subject is, in consequence, virtually unlimited and he is specifically told there are no right or wrong answers.

Two of the most widely used projective techniques are the Rorschach technique (see Klopfer and Kelley, 1942) and the Thematic Apperception Test, or T.A.T. (Murray, 1943; Tomkins, 1949). The Rorschach technique presents the respondent with a series of ink-blots, five in various shades of grey, two grey and red and three in several colours, and the subject is encouraged to describe what he sees in each blot. His descriptions are recorded and, together with the inquiry carried out when all ten blots have been presented, make up his test protocol. One of the principal assumptions underlying the Rorschach is that the way in which the subject structures the series of ambiguous stimuli is linked to his personality structure.

The administration, scoring and interpretation of the Rorschach is a complex matter, discussed in detail by Klopfer and Davidson (1962). The Rorschach can be considered as a psychometric test, since respondents can be assigned scores on various criteria, particularly if certain modifications are made involving an increase in the number of stimuli and the use of criterion keying (Holtzmann *et al.*, 1961), but it seems fair to say that the Rorschach, in its original form, has not coped altogether successfully with its special problems of reliability and validity.

The T.A.T. makes use of stimuli which are more highly structured than in the Rorschach. The subject is presented with a set of black and white pictures depicting various scenes and is asked to say what is happening in the picture, what led up to the events in the picture and what the outcome will be. Because Murray's original scoring system was not very specific, others have been put forward, such as those of McClelland and Eron and their respective colleagues, which emphasize quantitative methods (see Murstein, 1963). The interpretation of the T.A.T. was originally made in terms of psychoanalytic concepts (Murray, 1938), but over the years other interpretative systems have been advanced (e.g., Atkinson, 1958). The

T.A.T., like the Rorschach, faces difficult problems of reliability and validity and the evidence for its general usefulness in the assessment of personality is conflicting (Harrison, 1965). Nevertheless, the experienced examiner can gain a great deal of information about the dynamics of an individual personality both from the Rorschach and from the T.A.T., information which would not be available to him from other sources.

Our concern in this chapter has been with the types of measurement used in the assessment of individual differences in abilities and personality. In the following chapters we turn to the theoretical bases underlying test content, and to the accounts of intelligence and personality structure which have been yielded by assessment procedures.

Chapter 20
Abilities and Personality: Quantitative Approaches

The statistical approach to intelligence

We saw in Chapter 19 how various individual psychological differences may be expressed in quantitative terms. We can now go further and consider how empirical findings based on mental testing could help to advance our knowledge of the character of human abilities and personality. This we may call the statistical approach to intelligence and personality. Starting with the former, we need not attempt to provide a precise and agreed definition; the literature is replete with inconclusive definitions of intelligence (Heim, 1970a); furthermore, the very notion of definition in this context is questionable (Miles, 1957). This is not to say that we can completely disregard the problem of the meaning of intelligence. However, in focusing attention on the empirical study of intellectual activities, we can keep our conception of intelligence elastic and imprecise and at the same time as close to everyday usage as possible (Heim, 1970a).

We customarily separate people into more or less intelligent, depending upon the effectiveness of their responses to certain situations; and we distinguish some tasks as requiring more intelligence for their successful execution than others. These are, of course, relative discriminations; there seems little point in debating whether there are tasks which do not involve intelligence at all. The statistical approach capitalizes upon individual differences in tasks which, by general consensus, are held to call for intelligent action. The basic question asked concerns the dimensionality of intelligence. Is intelligence best conceived of as a single dimension along which individuals differ, or is it a multidimensional ability, such that we can only describe an individual as more intelligent than another with respect to a particular aspect of intelligence?

The statistical approach has a long and controversial history. A major impetus to its development has come from the demands of education, industry and the armed services for tests which will improve selection procedures. The claim that particular tests 'measure intelligence' has provoked the challenge that intelligence is not a single dimension, like height or weight, that can be measured by a single test. To investigate this, researchers have had recourse to the mathematical technique of *factor analysis*, and it is impossible to understand the subsequent controversies, and the difficulty of resolving them, without a minimal awareness of what factor analysis is. A very simple and brief introduction is given below. One general criticism of this approach, however, is that, because it involves the testing of large numbers of individuals and the elaborate mathematical analysis of their scores, the resulting conception of intelligence is too abstract and remote from what actually goes on when people solve problems.

The empirical basis of the statistical approach is the test score. A test (or subtest) is a collection of items which samples a type of behaviour thought to involve intelligence. The items are made to vary in difficulty so that individuals differ in the number they successfully complete, and to discriminate in the same direction so that a total score has meaning. The number of possible tests is in principle unlimited, since they can vary both in the type of task sampled and in the actual items chosen to illustrate a task.

The next step in the argument is this. If two tests are given to a population sample, and are found to correlate positively, it is plausible to infer that this correlation is due to the fact that the two tests measure the same ability or abilities, at least to some extent. To put the point more cautiously, the correlation between two tests (or behavioural items) offers the best, indeed the only, operational definition for the concept of ability. Obviously the two tests must differ if this conclusion is to be informative; the closer the two tests approximate to each other, the more the argument approaches a tautology (this test measures the ability measured by this test).

Finally, if we administer to a population sample a battery of tests, all of which sample operations involving intelligence, and find that the intercorrelations between them are all positive (as in fact tends to be the case), then we can infer that all the tests measure, in varying degree, some common ability which is not unreasonably labelled as intelligence. Moreover, since these intercorrelations will vary in size, the pattern they exhibit should afford a clue to the nature and structure of intelligence. It is at this point that researchers have turned to factor analysis in order to make sense of the pattern of co-variance.

It is of the greatest importance to be clear that factor analysis is a mathematical technique designed to summarize a matrix of values (in this case, intercorrelations between tests) in a small number of 'factors' such that from the factors alone the original matrix can be reproduced. Mathematically, a factor is a value which, when multiplied by another value, yields a product. Every product can be conceived in terms of multiplication of two or more factors, and the number of possible factors for any given product is, of course, infinite. What the factor analysis of a matrix of correlation coefficients does, then, is to reduce the matrix to a smaller set of factor values, the products of which yield the original matrix. It follows that there is an unlimited number of possible sets of factor values from which the original correlations can be calculated.

There are a number of different methods for factor analysing a matrix of correlation coefficients. Any discussion of them, and of the mathematical reasoning that underlies them, is well beyond the scope of this chapter. The reader must consult one of the many textbooks devoted to it (for example, Fruchter, 1954; Horst, 1965). However, in order to understand the controversies which have arisen in the study of intelligence, some conception of what is meant by a factor is necessary. One of the simplest ways of introducing the reader to the notion is to take up the spatial metaphor implicit in the idea of a *dimension* of intellectual difference and to represent the process of factor analysis geometrically. Again, the mathematical justification for doing this must be sought elsewhere; we are using geometrical representation here as a convenient expository device.

If two tests, A and B, are represented by lines, or vectors, of unit length on a plane surface, such that they have a common point of origin, then we can represent the correlation between the two tests by the angle between the two vectors. More accurately, the angle between the vectors must be such that its cosine equals the correlation coefficient (see Figure 20.1).

To represent a correlation coefficient between two tests, then, we need a two-dimensional space. We can now draw in these two dimensions as two

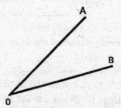

Figure 20.1   Geometric representation of a correlation coefficient between two tests A and B, where r_{AB} = cosine A O B

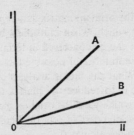

Figure 20.2 Geometric representation of a correlation coefficient with two factors added

lines, again of unit length, and label them factor I and factor II (see Figure 20.2). Note that the dimensions are independent, and therefore drawn at right angles to each other. Moreover, their positions relative to $\angle AOB$ are arbitrary.

The next step is to draw in the projections of both tests upon the two dimensions, or factors (see Figure 20.3). Since the factors are of unit length, these projections will be some value between zero and one. The projection of a test vector upon a factor is called its loading on that factor.

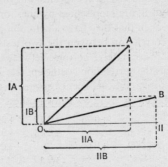

Figure 20.3 Geometric representation of the loadings of two tests, A and B, on factors I and II

Finally, it is now possible to calculate the correlation between tests A and B from a knowledge of their loadings on the two factors. This is done by multiplying the loadings of the two tests on factor I, doing the same for factor II and then summing the products. Thus:

$(IA \times IB) + (IIA \times IIB) = \text{cosine} \angle AOB = r_{AB}$.

It is possible, then, to account for the correlation between two tests in terms of their respective loadings on two factors. When only one correlation is involved there is obviously no point in doing this, for no economy in information would be achieved. But if we imagine six or seven tests, the intercorrelations between which are positive, and such that they can be represented on a single plane surface, then it would effect an economy if we could reduce the information given in the correlations to two sets of factor loadings. In practice, however, with such a number of tests, it is almost certain that more than two dimensions would be needed. But in general the usefulness of factor analysis depends upon the fact that fewer factors are needed than tests.

To return now to Figure 20.3, above, it is obvious that the position of factors I and II is arbitrary. Provided we retain the orthogonal relationship between them, we could rotate the factors generating an unlimited number of possible factor solutions, each of which would permit the recalculation of the original coefficient. Moreover, the factors do not necessarily have to remain orthogonal. It is possible to calculate an oblique factor solution to a matrix of correlation coefficients, though the computation is more complex and it is more difficult to assign psychological meaning to the resulting factor structure.

Table 20.1

Correlation coefficients between six psychological tests. (From P. E. Vernon, 1961, p. 5)

Tests	1	2	3	4	5	6
1. Vocabulary		+0·76	+0·79	+0·45	+0·41	+0·34
2. Analogies	+0·76		+0·68	+0·44	+0·35	+0·26
3. Classifications	+0·79	+0·68		+0·49	+0·39	+0·32
4. Block design	+0·45	+0·44	+0·49		+0·58	+0·44
5. Spatial	+0·41	+0·35	+0·39	+0·58		+0·55
6. Formboard	+0·34	+0·26	+0·32	+0·44	+0·55	

In order to illustrate what has been said so far, a hypothetical example of a correlation matrix is given. It is taken from the excellent introduction to the subject by P. E. Vernon (1961). Table 20.1 gives the correlations which might result if a battery of six tests were given to a large and varied sample of the population. Table 20.2 gives the results of a factor analysis of this matrix.

As can be seen, three factors are necessary to account for the correlations. All the tests have loadings on the first factor, reflecting the fact that all the correlations are positive. The remaining two factors each have positive loadings on three tests and zero loadings on three tests. From the table of factor loadings, it is possible to reconstruct the table of correlations. For example:

$$r_{34} = (0{\cdot}8 \times 0{\cdot}6) + (0{\cdot}3 \times 0) + (0 \times 0{\cdot}4) = 0{\cdot}48.$$

It is true that the correlation is not precisely the same as the original; but it is near enough for the difference to be attributable to error due to the rounding of decimals.

Table 20.2
Completed factor analysis of six psychological tests. (From P. E. Vernon, 1961, p. 7). See below for definitions of g, v and k

Tests	Loadings			Tests	Loadings		
	g	v	k		g	v	k
1. Vocabulary	0·8	0·5		4. Block design	0·6		0·4
2. Analogies	0·7	0·4		5. Spatial	0·5		0·7
3. Classifications	0·8	0·3		6. Formboard	0·4		0·5

So far we have considered only the mathematical concept of a factor. What factor analysis does is to show how many dimensions are needed to accommodate a set of intercorrelations and how the total amount of information given by them may be summarized in terms of loadings on these dimensions. Generally speaking, psychologists who have used factor analysis have not been primarily concerned with achieving economy as such. Rather they have been animated by the conviction that in discovering the dimensional structure of a correlation matrix, they were also discovering something about the structure of intelligence (Thurstone, 1940). For them, 'factor' was a psychological concept as well as a mathematical one. It is with regard to the psychological meaning of factors that all the controversy has arisen. And after years of research, it is now plain that the value of factor analysis as a technique for investigating *psychological* structure is severely limited. Some of these limitations are brought out in the following considerations:

1. Factor analysis can establish that to account for a given set of inter-correlations between tests, a certain minimal number of orthogonal factors is required. But it is possible to rotate these dimensions so that, though the number of dimensions is relatively stable, the loadings of particular tests on these factors is infinitely variable. The normal procedure for assigning psychological meaning to a factor is to name it after what appear to be the relevant characteristics of those tests which have a high loading on it. It follows that the technique does not permit any definitive psychological description of structure. It is true, criteria have been put forward for pre-ferring one factor solution to another. They include 'factor invariance', by which is meant that the same psychological structure can be reproduced using different subjects and tests; but mostly investigators have relied upon their own subjective judgement as to what makes the most psychologically meaningful solution. And such judgements depend upon the theories held by the investigator. A further, related problem is to know when to stop factor analysing. A complex matrix of correlations may require for its complete analysis a number of factors which have very small loadings indeed on any of the tests. Since these factors have little if any psychological value, it is customary to stop the analysis when the main factors have been extracted. This means that an element of approximation enters into the analysis.

2. The factor solutions obtained (in both the mathematical and psycho-logical senses) depend upon the nature and number of tests used, and the sampling procedures adopted. If the tests chosen are relatively homogeneous and the subjects vary widely over the whole range of intellectual difference, then the analysis is likely to yield few factors and to give prominence to one general factor. If on the other hand the tests are very varied and the subjects relatively homogeneous, the analysis is likely to yield a large number of factors and to minimize the likelihood of there being one general factor with loadings on all tests. Plainly, the psychological meaning of the factors obtained under such differing conditions is not comparable.

3. More fundamentally we can ask what it really means to assign psycho-logical meaning to a factor. Early factor analysis tended to assume without question that factors corresponded to abilities. The nature of an ability was determined by inspection of the tests. In the hypothetical example given above, the first factor, common to all tests, is labelled 'general cognitive ability', or g. The second is common to the only three tests which make extensive use of words and hence is called 'verbal ability'. The third is named 'spatial ability', because the tests it has loadings on all involve the perception

of spatial relationships. Obviously the labelling of factors is convenient. The problem lies in interpreting just what is meant when a factor is said to correspond to an ability.

There are two extreme views. On the one hand, some writers have claimed that abilities are actual entities, or circumscribable psychological functions. If a psychological function is unitary, in some sense, then this is presumably because of an underlying physiological unity of structure. Such a view appears to be assumed by Burt (1944) who argued that there were functionally unitary abilities and that these would always show up as factors in a test battery, but that not all factors found in analysis corresponded to abilities. How it is possible to distinguish factors which correspond to abilities from those that do not, other than by intuition, is not clear. Spearman (1927) thought that the general factor, which he found to have loadings on all tests, corresponded to 'mental energy' which existed in varying quantities and which was measured most directly by those tests with a high loading on the general factor. This mental energy found its expression in self-consciousness, the perception of relations and the eduction of correlates.

At the other extreme is G. N. Thomson (1939), who argued that it is naïve to suppose that there are unitary abilities which could correspond to factors. It is worth quoting him at some length.

In brief, then, the author's attitude is that he does not believe in factors if any real existence is attributed to them; but that, of course, he recognizes that any set of correlated human abilities can always be described mathematically by a number of variables or 'factors', *and that in many ways*, among which no doubt some will be more useful or more elegant or more sparing of unnecessary hypotheses. But the mind is very much more complex, and also very much more an integrated whole, than any naïve interpretation of any one mathematical analysis might lead a reader to suppose. Far from being divided into 'unitary factors', the mind is a rich, comparatively undifferentiated complex of innumerable influences – on the physiological side an intricate network of possibilities of intercommunication. Factors are fluid descriptive mathematical coefficients, changing both with the tests used and with the sample of persons, unless we take refuge in sheer definition based upon psychological judgement, which definition would have to specify the particular battery of tests, and the sample of persons, as well as the method of analysis, in order to fix any factor (p. 267).

The conclusions to be drawn from these considerations are unambiguous. As an investigatory technique, factor analysis is meaningless unless it is related to a theory. Moreover, the technique cannot be used to *test* a theory, for to do this, it would not only have to show that a theory fitted the facts but also that alternative, logically incompatible theories are false. Since factors are 'fluid mathematical coefficients', they cannot be used to rule out alternative theories. At best, then, factor analysis will show that a given theory is tenable, and sometimes indicate that some theories are harder to maintain than others. Its main value is as an exploratory technique for shaping hypotheses rather than as a method for finding out whether the hypotheses are true.

It is hoped that by now it will be clear to the reader just why the statistical approach has led to so much unresolvable controversy. There is not space here to review the different theories that have been held, and the research which has gone into their support. This task was done, lucidly and comprehensively, by P. E. Vernon (1961). However, a very brief sketch of four different theories will be given to introduce the reader to the field.

1. The simplest theory is that advocated by Spearman (1927), and is usually called the *two-factor theory*. Spearman argued that individual differences in performance on any test could be accounted for by one factor which was general, and common to all tests, and one which was quite specific to that test. The former he labelled *g*, or general intelligence. Although Spearman defended this theory persuasively, the persistent finding of more than one factor common to several tests in a battery makes it the least easy to maintain.

2. The second view has been dubbed the *hierarchical theory of mental abilities*, and has been popular among British psychologists. This view maintains that individual differences can best be accounted for in terms of one general factor, common to all tests, and a series of group factors each of which has positive loadings on some tests and zero, or near zero, loadings on others. Table 20.2 above is an example of a group factor solution. The number of group factors depends upon the number and variety of tests used. Among the group factors which have been found most consistently are those which have been labelled 'verbal', 'arithmetical', 'spatial' and 'mechanical'. This theory is supported by methods of factor analysis which maximize the total amount of variance due to the common factor, and is an extension of the two-factor theory. It has been defended by Burt (1955) on the grounds that it produces solutions which are closest to the way the term 'intelligence' is generally used.

3. The third theory derives from Thurstone, and is called the *multiple factor theory*. The distinctive feature of Thurstone's use of factor analysis

is the criterion he adopts for selecting a factor solution. This criterion he calls 'simple structure'. By this he means a factor solution which maximizes the number of zero loadings. Ideally, each factor has high loadings on some tests and zero loadings on others. Thurstone maintains that such a solution makes the most satisfying psychological sense. Necessarily, however, it minimizes the likelihood of finding a general factor. Since tests tend in fact to correlate positively with each other, it is not easy to achieve simple structure and Thurstone has been forced to have recourse to oblique factors. This has in turn led to the generation of a 'second order' general factor to account for the correlation between the primary factors. But a theory which conceives of intelligence as a loosely related group of 'primary abilities' is tenable in terms of factor analysis. These primary abilities have been labelled: V (verbal), P (perceptual speed), I (inductive reasoning), N (number) and so on. Advocates of the group factor approach, though they accept that multiple factor analysis is logically possible, would claim that it fails to do justice to the evidence for a general factor.

4. The last theory is of a different kind. The objection which may be brought against the previous theories is that they offer a simplified concept of intelligence and fail to do justice to its richness and variety. In a series of papers and a book, Guilford has sought to give a comprehensive description of intellectual functioning on the basis of test measurement (see Guilford, 1967; Kerlinger 1979). He starts with a logical analysis of intellectual activities. First he distinguishes five types of mental operation: thinking, remembering, divergent production (problem solving which leads to unexpected and original solutions), convergent production (problem solving which leads to the one, correct solution) and evaluating; then six types of product of these operations: units, classes, relations, systems, transformations and implications; and finally, four types of content upon which the operations are performed: figural, symbolic, semantic and behavioural. These classifications generate 120 distinguishable 'abilities', such as, for example, the ability to remember relations between symbols. Guilford then proceeds to construct test batteries designed to yield factors corresponding to these abilities. The project is still incomplete, but most of the abilities have been defined factorially. It would seem that Guilford is trying to do justice to the complex and integrated whole that Thomson described. He has not so far examined the correlations between these abilities. But it is significant that he has used a very select population of subjects in his investigations, namely men chosen to become officers in the United States Army.

There is likely to be little variability in 'general intelligence' in such a population, and therefore the more qualitative aspects of intellectual functioning are more likely to be discernible.

A further development which should be mentioned is due to Cattell (1963b), who has argued that the general factor found in test batteries is really a function of two conceptually distinct but correlated factors. He labels these factors fluid and crystallized intelligence. Crystallized intelligence reveals itself in those cognitive tests which require learned habits of thinking; fluid intelligence operates in new situations where successful adaptation cannot be achieved by the individual's existing repertoire of cognitive skills. Cattell develops a number of predictions about these two components of general intelligence. For example, fluid intelligence is expected to have a greater association with genotypic difference than crystallized, and to have a different growth curve reaching its maximum level earlier. A comparable theoretical distinction had been made by others, for example, Hebb (1949). The distinctive feature of Cattell's approach is his use of factor analysis to support his theory. He claims that factor studies have failed to isolate definitively the nature of general intelligence because they have only used cognitive tests. To isolate intelligence, it is necessary to include personality measures in the battery. This Cattell does in his own study, and is able to extract the two correlated factors demanded by his theory.

Conventional tests of intelligence are usually composed of items which admit of only one correct solution. They are highly structured, in the sense that sufficient information is given for the answer to be reached deductively. For some time there has been a growing suspicion that such tests do not do justice to those people who have the capacity for imaginative and original thinking. Moreover, many, if not most, of the problems which occur in real life have no single correct solution. In the attempt to do justice to this neglected aspect of intelligence, attempts have been made to measure creativity. The tests devised have usually consisted of items in which the subject has to think of as many different but appropriate responses as possible in a given time.

Armed with tests of this kind, some investigators have attempted to show that creativity is a feature of cognitive activity which is largely independent of intelligence as conventionally measured. Getzels and Jackson (1962) compared two groups of adolescent boys, one which was very high on intelligence but relatively low on creativity measures, the other high on creativity but relatively low on intelligence. The authors found that the high creatives were equally good in academic attainment, but were less popular with teachers and tended to differ on a variety of personality measures. Though they found creativity and intelligence to be positively correlated, they claimed that this 'signifies rather that a certain amount of intelligence is required for creativity but that intelligence and creativity are by no means the same' (p. 125).

The study has come in for a good deal of criticism (see De Mille and Merrifield, 1962; Marsh, 1964). In general, it appears that tests of creativity do not correlate highly with each other and tend to be more correlated with intelligence than some investigators claim (see P. E. Vernon, 1964; Hasan and Butcher, 1966). Moreover, it is probably misleading to call these test measures of creativity. Hudson (1966) argued that the term should be dropped and that we should use the term 'divergent thinking' instead. It is obvious that this is an important and growing field in differential psychology.

Quantitative approaches to personality

When we assess people we know, or when we reflect on ourselves as persons, many characteristics are mentioned which are not classifiable as abilities. We think of people as timid or conscientious, or friendly, or dependable, or as the opposite of these descriptive adjectives. It is with this large group of characteristics that the psychology of personality is concerned. This part of psychology deals with the individual as a person rather than as an organism or a member of a biological species. It is an unsatisfactory and confusing branch of the discipline. There are, as R. B. Cattell remarked, 'as many variables claimed to be of outstanding significance' for the description of personality 'as there are psychologists'. There does not appear to be much hope of resolving theoretical differences in the psychology of personality – and there is a large number of different theories. Since definitions of 'personality' are theory-loaded there is not much point in arguing over rival definitions. It is sufficient to suggest that 'personality' refers to that, within the individual, which contributes to the organization of his behaviour (Cattell, 1954, 1965).

The trait approach

One way to conceptualize and investigate the personality was taken over from the study of abilities already discussed in this chapter. It was hoped that factor analysis of test scores, and other measures, of personality characteristics would yield factors of some generality across *different* kinds of specific response, and of some degree of stability over time. Interpretation of these factors might suggest the elements of which our personality is made, and the relationship between the elements would suggest the overall 'structure' or 'system' which constitutes personality as a whole. This approach, featured in several statistically-based theories, depends on the fundamental concept of the *trait*. Trait adjectives are common in everyday assessments. We describe people as 'shy', 'timid', 'anxious', 'conscientious', 'conceited', 'careless', 'punctual', etc. These are general dispositions. When we ascribe timidity to a person we imply that he is consistently liable to react in ways in which he fails to do what he wants, or is required, to do. He fails to put himself forward for promotion at work when entitled to do so; he fails to approach girls to whom he is attracted at social gatherings; he fails to ask questions at a public meeting when curious. If on occasion he acts in a non-timid way – diving into a pond to save a child from drowning – this does not invalidate the general tendency to behave in a timid way. A trait is a situation-response regularity; however, it is not an invariable regularity. Traits are S–R frequency-dispositions. Observing a large set of S-type situations, X *frequently* responds in these in a specific kind of way. If a number of traits regularly go together they are sometimes used to define a psychological *type*. Types are derivatives from the more basic characteristic of traits. A psychological type is defined in terms of traits which co-vary. To illustrate the approach further, we shall consider two trait-type theories – those of Cattell and Eysenck.

Cattell's trait-type theory

Cattell's research assumes that there are basic 'structures', presumably unknown physiological processes, which determine observable consistencies in attitude and action. These traits function at different levels or strata. First-stratum traits, or *surface* traits, are observable in behaviour. They can be detected in psychological tests and experiments. People who answer questionnaire items such as 'I like going to parties'; 'I have a fairly large circle of friends'; 'I dislike being alone' by ticking the 'yes' answer, reveal a consistency of behaving which forms a surface trait of some kind (viz. 'sociability'). Such traits tend to be correlated with each other – they co-vary in a large number of people. If X has one of these to a marked degree he is likely to have certain others. If Y lacks the same trait, he is likely to lack the others as well – although Y will have another cluster of traits which tend to go with each other, e.g. a person who is sociable may be even-

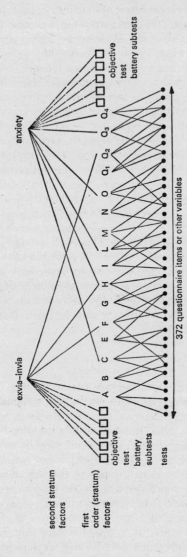

Figure 20.4 Diagram showing hierarchical arrangement of Cattell's first- and second-order factors (After Cattell, 1965, p. 118)

tempered and tolerant while one who is solitary may be quick-tempered and intolerant. At the root of this positive correlation is an underlying second-stratum trait or *source* trait. Source traits are not immediately noticeable in a person's behaviour. They can only be deduced as the result of research using factor analysis.

Cattell began his investigation by taking many adjectives descriptive of common traits and reducing these to two hundred, after synonyms had been eliminated. A hundred adults were rated by acquaintances on these traits, and a factor analysis was performed on the scores. Cattell concluded that forty-two bi-polar traits accounted for the results. These were such common distinctions as: rigid–adaptable; calm–emotional; assertive–submissive; quitting–determined; conscientious–unconscientious and so on, up to forty-two such pairs.

Five hundred adults were now rated by acquaintances on the forty-two bi-polar traits (surface) and the resulting scores were factorized. Twelve factors were extracted. Cattell proceeded to investigate the extent to which these twelve factors were present in three types of data derived from a large sample of subjects: Life-Data; Questionnaire Data; and Objective Test Data. L-data consisted of information from educational, medical and work records, assessed for the twelve traits by psychologists. Q-data were from questionnaires and interviews in which direct questions were put to people concerning their behaviour. OT-data were measures of behaviour from psychological tests and experiments covering a wide range of responses: for example, the speed at which problems in arithmetic can be solved; the accuracy and speed with which a person learns to trace a maze with a finger when blindfold; the speed of completion of broken figure-drawings under time constraint; the choice of book titles as between 'horrific' and 'nice' topics; galvanic skin reaction to neutral and emotionally exciting stimuli, and so on.

Cattell's purpose was to see if he could identify the same twelve factors in all three types of source. Source traits could only be verified if there were matching factors based on positive correlation coefficients across all three domains. Cattell's long and patient research, much of which has been questioned by critics, was claimed to yield sixteen primary factors each representing a bi-polar trait dimension. These are summarized in Table 20.3.

Cattell devised a test to measure individual differences along these sixteen traits, the 16 Personality Factor Inventory. Various revisions since 1954 have been made. There are at least two forms of the test, A and B, for reason-

Table 20.3
Cattell's sixteen primary factors (Cattell, 1963a)

High-score description	Factor	Low-score description
Outgoing, warmhearted, easy-going, participating (Cyclothymia)	A	*Reserved*, detached, critical, cool (Schizothymia)
More intelligent, abstract thinking, bright (Higher scholastic mental capacity)	B	*Less intelligent*, concrete thinking (Lower scholastic mental capacity)
Emotionally stable, faces reality, calm (Higher ego strength)	C	*Affected by feelings*, emotionally less stable, easily upset (Lower ego strength)
Assertive, independent, aggressive, stubborn (Dominance)	E	*Humble*, mild, obedient, conforming (Submissiveness)
Happy-go-lucky, heedless, gay, enthusiastic (Surgency)	F	*Sober*, prudent, serious, taciturn (Desurgency)
Conscientious, persevering, staid, rule-bound (Stronger superego strength)	G	*Expedient*, a law to himself, by-passes obligations (Weaker superego strength)
Venturesome, socially bold, uninhibited, spontaneous (Parmia)	H	*Shy*, restrained, diffident, timid (Threctia)
Tender-minded, dependent, over-protected, sensitive (Premsia)	I	*Tough-minded*, self-reliant, realistic, no-nonsense (Harria)
Suspicious, self-opinionated, hard to fool (Protension)	L	*Trusting*, adaptable, free of jealousy, easy to get on with (Alaxia)
Imaginative, wrapped up in inner urgencies, careless of practical matters, bohemian (Autia)	M	*Practical*, careful, conventional, regulated by external realities, proper (Praxernia)
Shrewd, calculating, worldly, penetrating (Shrewdness)	N	*Forthright*, natural, artless, sentimental (Artlessness)

Table 20.3–*Continued*

High-score description	Factor	Low-score description
Apprehensive, worrying, depressive, troubled (Guilt proneness)	O	*Placid*, self-assured, confident, serene (Untroubled adequacy)
Experimenting, critical, liberal, analytical, free-thinking (Radicalism)	Q_1	*Conservative*, respecting established ideas, tolerant of traditional difficulties (Conservatism)
Self-sufficient, prefers own decisions, resourceful (Self-sufficiency)	Q_2	*Group-dependent*, a 'joiner' and sound follower (Group adherence)
Controlled, socially precise, self-disciplined, compulsive (High self-concept control)	Q_3	*Casual*, careless of protocol, untidy, follows own urges (Low integration)
Tense, driven, overwrought, fretful (High ergic tension)	Q_4	*Relaxed*, tranquil, torpid, unfrustrated (Low ergic tension)

ably literate adults, two others for those with poorer vocabulary and a simple version E for low-literacy adults. There are also versions for children. The test has been used both for clinical diagnosis in psychiatric units and for occupational assessments. It has also been given to occupational groups such as airline pilots to find out whether or not they have a similar personality rating. The pilots were found to be free from anxiety proneness and to be above average in alertness, being tough-minded and determined, persevering, conscientious and responsible – a reassuring result.

Cattell investigated correlations amongst these second-stratum source traits and discovered some second-order factors (Figure 20.4). Among these were Extraversion and Anxiety. Since traits A, F, H and Q2 correlate to indicate 'Extraversion' and C, L, O, Q4 inter-correlate to a basic underlying 'Anxiety' factor, Cattell is now dealing with psychological types. Extraversion is associated with the 'going together' of adaptability, warm-heartedness, enthusiasm, cheerfulness, impulsiveness, conventionality and gregariousness. Anxiety is associated with suspiciousness, guilt-proneness, tension due to frustration, worry, lack of determination and lack of persistence.

There are different sorts of trait within Cattell's system. *Ability* traits, assessed in cognitive tests, account for individual differences in adapting means to ends. *Temperamental* traits determine the speed and energy and emotive quality of actions. *Dynamic* traits direct behaviour towards specific goals in terms of our wants and needs.

Cattell's earlier research tended to concentrate on temperament. More recently he has been concerned with motivation, learning and intelligence. He is interested in what he calls structural learning. This involves not only the acquisition of new habits and skills but the restructuring of emotional attachments. Different motivational factors get linked and converge upon a single goal. Thus a skilled mathematician may get curious and become emotive about the uses to which mathematical knowledge can be put. He may find himself forming the ambition to train as an engineer. Cattell is thus interested in the different ways in which traits become manifest in specific behaviours – how moods, social role shifts and other states affect traits. This work is still under way and is not yet completed. His recent publications (1971, 1973) give some account of these developments.

Cattell's work on temperament is paralleled by that of J. P. Guilford (1959). Guilford, using factorial methods, has identified fifteen factors involved in temperament. He believes that there are five basic dimensions which indicate the *style* or *manner* in which people exhibit a wide variety of responses.

1. Positive as contrasted with negative attitudes towards objects and events.
2. Variation in responsiveness or discriminative acuity to stimuli.
3. Actively initiating reaction as contrasting with passive, unadventurous reaction.
4. Controlled organized reaction as contrasted with unorganized, imprecise, vacillating reaction.
5. Objective, detached, dispassionate attitude as contrasted with emotional, egocentric attitude.

Those who are positive (1) tend to be self-confident, cheerful and optimistic in outlook, and socially ascendant and assertive. These traits tend to go together in individuals indicating a temperamental dimension. Those who are active (3) tend to take the initiative in social encounters and accept the role of leader in a group. They can be impulsive and of nervous disposition – being readily anxious.

Sells and his associates (1971) carried out research applying Guilford's personality test to 2,011 U.S. airmen. Items from Cattell's 16 PF Inventory were also applied. The results were factorized. This reduced the data to the level of correlations between highly specific action-tendencies in the experimental data. There was considerable agreement between the two systems. Guilford's separate traits for depression, immaturity, nervousness, were all seen as variations along an 'emotional stability' dimension. His trait of 'ascendance' was split into two – friendliness and sociability – in the Sells study. Whatever criticisms may be made of Cattell or Guilford, this study suggests that the conception of primary traits of temperament, which are widely distributed among human beings, has some plausibility.

Cattell's work in particular has been subjected to criticisms. It has been argued by Becker (1960) that his basic researches have failed to produce correlations sufficiently high to warrant the extraction of the factors on which source traits are postulated. Speculative assumptions are needed to create the trait system and there is inadequate cross-matching across L-data, Q-data, and OT-data – the source of Cattell's factorizing. Moreover, Overall (1964) has questioned the basic strategy in terms of which Cattell has proceeded to investigate personality. Overall used the physical dimension of books as his datum. He devised twelve equations, each of which gave a measure as a linear function of height, width and thickness of a book. He then devised three pure 'marker' variables to represent the primary physical dimensions of any book. One hundred books were measured in terms of these criteria. A factorial analysis of the correlations between all the measures was performed and this produced three factors. These factors failed to correspond with what are unquestionably the primary dimensions of books (e.g., one could only be interpreted as a book's 'obesity', a strange way to describe a book).

Does factor analysis detect underlying natural structures in areas where these are uncertain? Factor analysis is a legitimate tool for reducing complex data to simpler form and for suggesting possible hypotheses for testing by further empirical research. Is Cattell putting it to a use for which it is not suitable? Cattell does hope to detect hitherto unknown source traits and type dimensions on the basis of extracted factors – using the technique to identify the unknown bases of surface traits. Psychologists (Passini and Norman, 1966; D'Andrade, 1965; Mulaik, 1964) have produced experiments to suggest that Cattell's research reveals, not basic traits, but merely conventional *verbal* classifications – those which people use to describe each other. It is not the underlying structure of the experimental subject's behaviour but rather the conceptual–verbal habits of the raters, in questionnaire studies, which come out in the factors.

Even if Cattell's traits do have some objective basis it is argued by others that they are too abstract, general and bloodless to give much information about a person. If X is rated on the 16 PF Inventory as abnormally high in anxiety this is a statistical observation. We cannot deduce why X is anxious, what he tends to be anxious about, how he construes his own anxiety-states and with what consequences for his actions, or how he came to be anxious. Only clinical investigations can answer such questions in detail – and this, according to some clinical psychologists, is beyond the scope of Cattell's system.

Eysenck's trait-type system

Eysenck has worked chiefly in the area of clinical psychology. He began by being dissatisfied with orthodox psychiatric theories and classifications. He decided to construct a theory of normal and abnormal personality on a strictly scientific basis. The structure of personality could be tackled by psychometrics, especially by factor analysis, showing how highly correlated *traits* determine psychological *types*. Each type could be delineated in terms of a few typological dimensions. Experimental psychology could account for the dynamic functioning of personality by postulating underlying psycho-neurological processes at the root of traits and types. Eysenck employed a distinctive method. Research is aimed at plotting individual differences along a specific dimension and obtaining test scores for, e.g., intelligence or extraversion–introversion. Highly inter-correlated trait measures define these grosser scores. It is then hypothesized that individuals who differ along the dimension (e.g. those with consistently high or low scores) will be correspondingly differentiated on some measure of behaviour derived from a theory in experimental psychology (viz. learning theory). If the prediction about relationships between inferences from the personality dimension, and from the experimental theory, are confirmed, this strengthens the assumptions about the personality variables (see also Chapter 19).

Eysenck also used the technique of criterion analysis. A group of people are selected who share a common, socially defined characteristic, e.g., they have all been diagnosed as schizophrenic or neurotic by psychiatrists. A second group of 'normal' people are also organized as subjects. Both groups are subjected to a large number of experimental and test measures. The question now is which measures serve to clearly differentiate between the groups? Neurotics may obtain high scores on measures of 'anxiety' while normals have low scores. Can the items measured be related to any hypotheses generated by the personality 'model' under construction? Do assumptions about the personality dimensions account for the scores in such research? Eysenck in 1947 published the result of investigations with 700 neurotic soldiers. A factor analysis of many inter-correlated measures suggested that two dimensions (second-order factors) might account for these results. Eysenck suggested that extraversion–introversion and neuroticism–stability were the psychological characteristics of these two dimensions. Further researches (1952) with normal subjects as well as psychiatric patients supported the original findings. In addition to the two dimensions mentioned Eysenck also postulated the dimension of psychoticism–normality and included that of intelligence. These four dimensions are used to study variations in personality.

Eysenck postulated a hierarchy of psychological functions. People display highly specific behaviours – volunteering for committee work in social club and church; enjoying parties by participating in many games; going to as many social gatherings each week as possible; joining new societies. Such habits are the basis of traits such as 'highly sociable' and 'warm, outgoing, friendly'. Several such traits inter-correlate to form a second-order dimension such as extraversion/introversion. It is such higher order dimen-

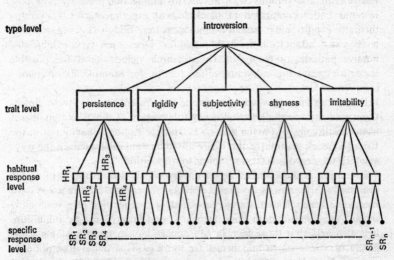

Figure 20.5   Eysenck's hierarchical model of personality structure as it relates to the introversion dimension. (From Eysenck, 1953, p. 13)

sions which Eysenck selects as basic terms for describing personality. Extraverts display such traits as being sociable, impulsive, uninhibited. They tend to crave excitement, they dislike solitude, enjoy change, are carefree, optimistic. They can be quick-tempered and aggressive. Introverts are quiet and retiring; tend to be introspective and reserved, except with intimate friends. They tend to plan carefully and distrust impulsive decisions. They keep their feelings under control, are highly ethical and tend to be pessimistic.

On the second dimension those people who are strong in neuroticism are not necessarily neurotic in a clinical sense. They may avoid breakdown all their lives and be adequately adjusted in work, sexual life, family and social settings. They are subject to wide swings of mood and are easily upset emotionally. They tend to over-react in situations in which a stable person remains calm and detached. They complain of many psychosomatic symptoms – headaches, digestive disorders, insomnia. They suffer from anxiety and under severe stress they may become neurotic more readily than those with high measures at the 'stability' end of this dimension. These are the dimensions as defined in the early work. Eysenck's research was aimed at investigating individuals with high scores in extraversion, introversion, neuroticism and stability with a view to finding out precisely how they respond under conditions of psychological experimentation, subjecting them to conditioning, reaction-time measures, body-sway suggestibility tests, visual adaptation to dark measures. Does each type exhibit distinctive patterns of response? This research yielded items for possible scales for measuring individual differences in, for example, extraversion–introversion.

Eysenck extended his work to provide a biological basis for these dimensions, and the specific traits associated with them. Taking his hypotheses from the theories of Pavlov and C. L. Hull, a leading behaviourist in the 1950s, Eysenck postulated that there are individual differences in the ways in which the nervous system responds to stimulation.

Excitation is the building up of energy which then erupts into motor response. Inhibition is a fatigue-like process for cutting off a reaction once energy has been released. It was postulated by Eysenck that extraverts show slower, weaker excitation than introverts, and faster, stronger inhibition. It is also held that those high in neuroticism have a more unstable autonomic nervous system and hence are more easily aroused to emotional reaction. Since Pavlov held that cortical excitation facilitates the forming of *conditioned* reflexes Eysenck predicted that extraverts will *condition* less readily than introverts. From this hypothesis considerable experimental research has resulted. In spite of its bulk it is inconclusive and this particular hypothesis has not been firmly established.

From 1967 onwards Eysenck has modified the theory. The human brain has a Reticular Activating System (RAS) which controls its degree of arousal or alertness (see Chapter 4). Eysenck postulated that introverts have lower thresholds for reticular arousal than extraverts. He also held that reticular arousal can be produced by emotion. Since emotional arousal is connected with the limbic system (or visceral brain), differences in threshold for visceral arousal are thought to be the basis for differences along the neuroticism–stability dimension. Individuals with low thresholds for emotional arousal (high in neuroticism) are also likely, in Eysenck's view, to be introverts; since high levels of arousal in the visceral system lead to the arousal of the reticular system, this is synonymous with the capacity to react quickly to stimuli – a sign of introversion. A great deal of experimental research has gone into the testing of implications of this development of Eysenckian theory. Reviews of this work (Brody, 1972) seem to agree that many empirical findings go against the theory and that hypotheses derived from the theory sometimes depend on purely *ad hoc* assumptions. Nevertheless the theory has been applied to various practical problems. Eysenck's test, the Eysenck Personality Inventory (1964), differentiates two groups of neurotics: dysthymia (depression, anxiety, obsessions) and hysteria and psychopathy. Dysthymics have high scores in neuroticism and introversion. Hysterics and psychopaths have high scores in neuroticism and extraversion. Eysenck explains dysthymic disorders as due to emotional responses (fear and anxiety) becoming conditioned readily to neutral stimuli. Hysterics do not condition so easily, on his theory, unless the stimulation is excessive and traumatic, e.g., accidents or battle stress.

Eysenck also applied his theory to criminality. His thesis is that extraverts and introverts react to conditioning very differently. This has implications for social learning. Extraverts are 'under-socialized' in the sense that they do not learn social rules quickly. If high extraversion is combined with high neuroticism, a person may become so under-socialized as to acquire criminal habits. The theory has not received much support. Cochrane (1974) questions its validity after a close review of the evidence. One generally accepted finding is that criminals are not markedly higher in extraversion than normal people. The empirical support for Eysenck's theory is weak. There are also logical objections. It has been argued that the hypotheses of Eysenck's system are not genuinely scientific but merely *ad hoc* hypotheses. That is, the only evidence for the basic assumptions are facts which it is the point of the hypotheses to explain. The existence of an extraversion–introversion dimension is taken as a discovery of the theory – a natural phenomenon (resting on somewhat speculative neurological processes). This does not seem to be the case. The distinction between extraversion–introversion is a descriptive-classificatory one which remains to be justified, and even to be explained. Nevertheless Eysenck's theory has generated hypotheses capable of empirical testing under experimental conditions – a rare feature of personality research. Much of interest has emerged from this extensive work.

Scepticism concerning traits

More recently there has been some disillusionment with the trait concept. Walter Mischel (1968, 1973) cast doubts on the usefulness of traits. He produced an impressive array of empirical evidence, and a critical analysis of statistical techniques as used by trait-psychologists. This seemed to show that there is little consistency in behaviour across different situations. Variations in the environmental situation affect alleged traits markedly.

It is evident that the behaviours which are often construed as stable personality trait indicators actually are highly specific and depend on the details of the evoking situations and the response mode employed to measure them (Mischel, 1968).

William P. Alston (1976) finds Mischel's case ambiguous. However, he provides an analysis of traits as stimulus–response frequency dispositions. Given a range of Sx-type situations X will exhibit response R in a large number of instances when Sx is presented. Alston accepts the utility of this concept but maintains that there are several response-categories, relevant to the description of personality, which do not fit the trait model. These include abilities, motives and needs. In any particular situation a range of different personality variables become active and interact, not only with each other but with properties of the situation. Traits alone cannot account for behaviour and an 'interactionist' account relating personality with situation is essential.

Argyle (1976) argues that provided psychologists sample persons and situations equally widely, overt behaviour constitutes the data, and appropriate statistical measures are employed, it is possible to demonstrate that behaviour is a function of person, situation, and person–situation interaction. Moreover, person–situation variance ($P \times S$) accounts for the greater amount of variability. Only an interactionist model is valid. Behaviour is always a function of P, S, and P × S – not simply a function of P alone. 'Traits' are exclusively P-variables, properties carried about within the person.

There are difficulties about using an interactionist model. Argyle points out (1976) that people can choose the situation, rejecting some situations and seeking others. Also in some situations a person can do things intelligently to change the situation. Cognitive functioning complicates the formula for 'interaction'. Again, the exact proportions of variance between P, S, and P × S cannot be determined since it is not possible, in practice, to sample P and S variables in a strictly comparable manner. Finally a situation does not always exist *per se*. It is perceived and defined as a particular sort of situation in terms of a person's interpretations and these are often strongly influenced by the behaviours of another person with whom the percipient is interacting. Argyle has a remedy, a complicated model derived from linguistics (Rule-Games model). This may not be acceptable to all critics as a workable remedy. However, the general upshot of this review is that the psychology of personality based on factor analysis relies too exclusively on the trait and this constitutes a weakness.

Psychologists have plenty of alternatives to select in place of the trait. Only a large and comprehensive text could cover even the more influential ones. In the next chapter we will take a highly selective look at other approaches to the study of personality.

Chapter 21
Models of Personality

The study of personality has involved the proliferation of an apparently unending series of theories, or models, each concentrating on *different* personal characteristics, or situational variables, as crucial to the description of persons and the delineation of individual differences of personality between persons. Each developed its own distinctive methodology for research and assessment. The earliest views on human personality were put forward by philosophers and men of letters. These often contain valuable observations and insights, many of which may be true and accurate but which are not subjected to systematic empirical investigation within such humanistic contexts.

The second phase, preceding that undertaken by psychologists, was conducted by medical practitioners interested in treating psychiatric cases. From the 1880s neurosis was being identified and investigated systematically for the first time and several psychiatrists devised general psychological systems within which to view deviant behaviours. Sigmund Freud was one of these pioneers who developed a theory of personality. It was not until near the end of his life that psychologists such as G. W. Allport (1937) and H. A. Murray (1938) began to construct alternative theories.

Psycho-dynamic theories

Freud

It is not easy to deal with Freud's contribution to the theory of personality. He changed his views several times during his lifetime but never attained any final synthesis or revision. Moreover, Freud's followers did not agree among themselves regarding the interpretation of his ideas and several seceded to found rival theories. Ruth L. Munroe (1955) gives a comprehensive account of Freud's theories and of those divergences from his original system developed by Jung, Adler, Horney, Reik and Sullivan. It is often useful to take a historical approach to Freud describing how his views developed and changed. Martha Robert (1966) and Richard Wollheim (1971) have written excellent historically-oriented reviews of Freud's thought. Here, we can only deal with some of his main ideas and note the major differences between his view before and after the period 1914–18. However, throughout his shifting conceptualizations certain basic ideas seem to have remained constant.

Freud regarded man as an energy system. The nervous system has a limited quantity of energy for discharge in the form of motor activity or mental activity. Neurons can only contain a limited amount of energy (or, to put it differently, endure a limited degree of stimulation); once a maximal quantity is stored any excess beyond this produces stress, tension, and the need to discharge the energy in action. If energy cannot be released along one pathway it can take an alternative. Thus energy associated with sexual impulse may be 'sublimated' or discharged in activity which has nothing to do with sexual gratification. This idea led Freud to accept a form of hedonism as a fundamental law of psychology. Build-up of energy in the neurons produces tension: release of the energy produces 'pleasure'.

In its most basic form energy appears as instinctive response. Freud always regarded instinct as important in man as in animals. His views on instinct changed but he came to think of two main groups of instincts. On the one hand were sexual, reproductive, life-preserving instincts and, on the other, aggressive–destructive impulses which could either be directed outwards or turned inwards against the self. To gratify instinctive impulses was pleasurable – a release from painful tension and stress. To have them blocked was frustrating and distressful. Even with a complex brain and the ability to learn and reason, human beings are subject to the powerful drives which come directly from our basic energies.

Unfortunately man's intelligence and his gregarious nature have resulted in complicated social organizations which often inhibit the direct and satisfying expression of instinctual need in behaviour. Many of the rules, conventions and customs on which social co-operation, with its great benefits, depends run counter to instinct. There is often a conflict between the needs of instinctual gratification and the need to conform to social requirements. One of the consequences of this is that man, although subject to pressure from powerful instincts, has developed tricks for managing them and handling the conflicts they engender – although these tricks tend to work imperfectly and produce maladaptive behaviours.

It is another axiom of Freud's that consciousness and rationality, our explicit awareness of our condition, is less significant than we commonly take it to be. It is a somewhat ineffectual monitor of our ongoing interaction with the environment. The causes of our behaviour and the processes which control it are located below the threshold of consciousness.

Freud regarded man as being organized by a set of interrelated processes called the unconscious mind. It is the functioning of these hidden processes which accounts for our actions and our personality. The laws governing the processes of the unconscious are different from those applying to conscious thought and feeling. Freud regarded himself as a scientist who had discovered the existence of the unconscious and its ways of working. Of course this claim has been challenged on both logical and empirical grounds. Thus for those psychologists who question the validity of Freud's postulation of 'The Unconscious' the problem remains of saying what, if anything, is the significance of his observations.

It is plausible to single out two distinct phases in Freudian theory as being of primary importance. The first is from 1900 to 1914 and the second from about 1920 until Freud's death in 1939. In the first phase Freud was attempting to account for the ways in which overt behaviour and conscious experience were the products of unconscious processes energized by instinct. Two central parts of his theory were his view on infantile sexuality and his postulation of the Oedipus complex. In his theory of infantile sexuality Freud argued that the eruption of instinct involves physical tensions which at different stages of infant development are centred on specific parts of the body – the erogenous zones. The first of these is the mouth. During this oral stage of individual development, which lasts from birth until the age of two years, instinctual gratification is manifested in sucking, feeding, and other oral sensations. When the teeth appear aggressive instincts are expressed in biting. The second stage, from two to three years, is the anal stage. Instinct is centred on anal sensations. During this phase toilet and cleanliness training by parents begins. Infants get satisfaction not only from retention-release of faeces but in the influence they exercise over their parents' behaviour through bowel function (e.g. in getting rewards for learning a routine). The third stage is the phallic stage in which instinctual life centres on the genital organs. This lasts until five or even six years of age. After this instinctual development remains 'latent' until puberty.

Towards the end of the phallic phase children undergo a developmental crisis, beginning to experience sexually biased feelings directed towards the parent of the opposite sex. In males tenderness towards the mother is associated with feelings of jealousy, dislike and fear directed towards the father who is a rival for the mother's love and attention. At the same time the boy identifies with the father as a 'model' and loves and admires him. There ensues a confused, intense and painful conflict which Freud named the Oedipus complex. The emotions and confused thoughts tend to be repressed but the effects of the conflict remain. For girls the experience of feeling attracted by the father and rejective of the mother occurs but it is less intense and less complex than for males. If the male child can keep his love for his mother but so strongly identify with his father that he can drop the 'rivalry' and hold both parents in positive relationships, with reducing conflict, then he can grow towards being a mature adult. If not he is in danger of becoming a neurotic personality unable to adopt a properly male role. Identifying with the parent of the same sex is the critical factor – it can take many different forms and it can go 'wrong' in a variety of ways. The Oedipal crisis is an important watershed in the growth of personality.

Freud also held that during the three stages of instinctual development in infancy a child might fail to move on smoothly from one phase to the next. It may remain 'fixated' at, for example, the oral stage for too long. Either too little or too much gratification at this stage could produce such fixation. This could have lasting effects. Under stress of any kind later in life there is a tendency to regress to an earlier, more simple, infantile mode of adaptation. In the case of a person strongly fixated at the oral stage stress in adult life may lead to heavy drinking of alcohol, over-eating and perhaps smoking – signs of a withdrawal within to a soporific state of opting out.

Tendencies to regress towards infantile modes of instinctual gratification – albeit repressed and unconscious – may determine general personality characteristics. Freud believed that regression to oral modes is associated with certain dominant traits in adult personality – self-centredness, being neurotically over-demanding of help and attention, being envious, greedy, impatient. Since the oral type is over-dependent on others and does not always receive the somewhat excessive help demanded, such a person is often insecure and anxious and easily depressed. The anal type is obstinate, orderly and parsimonious, 'holding on' and being rigid in adherence to rules. These traits are supposed to be derivative of a fixation with infantile interests during toilet training. The phallic type has over-reacted to stresses during the Oedipal conflict. Male or female status is over-emphasized and there is an over-concern with achievement in work and in marriage. Such types are still competing with the model set by their mother or father at the time of the Oedipal phase.

Freud was concerned with the primacy of instincts – the vicissitudes of their development, and with the enduring traces in the unconscious of the crises in which such drives were gratified, or thwarted, and the idiosyncratic ways in which the individual learned to cope with conflicts engendered during the course of instinctual development.

However, this emphasis was changed in his writings from 1920 onwards. In the last two decades of his life Freud introduced some completely new concepts into his system. Important among these was the distinction between three different types of behaviour, designated by the terms id, ego and super-ego. The id is the product of heredity and is the instinctual level of response. It is the main source of mental energy and is concerned with self-preserva-tion, reproduction and aggression against threats. The primitive tensions and needs of the id demand discharge in some kind of activity – if only fantasies. The ego is those activities of the brain which express themselves in intelligent actions. Whatever the primitive wishes of the id, reality must prevail. We learn to know and accept the facts of existence and to inhibit any impulses which would fail to be adaptive. Freud made a big concession to human rationality and conscious experience – played down in his earlier version of the theory – when he introduced the concept of ego. The ego-functions adjust or inhibit more primitive impulses to the complicated requirements of the social environment. There are thus two systems for organizing behaviour: the id with its instinctual needs and the ego which makes use of the skills of intellect. However, the capacities of the ego-function to control the person are precarious and limited. The id and the ego often conflict. The ego cannot always rule and compromises between conflicting tendencies can produce vacillating or ineffective adaptations.

The ego is often threatened by impulses from the id as well as by external dangers in the environment and when this happens anxiety occurs. Freud regarded anxiety as a regular and powerful source of pain which played a basic role in the organization of the person. Anxiety became a topic of central importance during this later period for Freud. He became interested in the ways in which the ego is protected against acute anxiety resulting from con-flict between rival impulses and postulated a number of defence strategies. In this later theory 'repression' simply is one such strategy. It is a sort of amnesia for avoiding the conscious experience of threatening impulses, wishes, memories, associations, motives. Another defence is 'projection' in which an anxiety-provoking impulse or emotion is attributed to another person. If one has a spite against X one comes to see X as being spiteful towards oneself and others – one feels uncomfortable but it is less disturbing to attribute the unpleasant attributes to somebody other than oneself. Freud considered many such 'defences' and argued that the sort of defence a person adopts for coping with anxiety produced by conflict is an important clue to personality.

The super-ego is a refinement of the ego-function. It defines the values accepted by a person as a result of identifying with parents in childhood – and later modifying these on a basis of social experience. At the root of our values are very primitive emotions of fear and guilt acquired in childhood during the Oedipus crisis. Hence the super-ego can be as irrational and impulsive as the id in prompting responses which threaten the ego and so provoke anxiety. The ego-functions must control and refine the promptings of the super-ego and so produce sophisticated and rational 'moral' values out of cruder material. Conflicts can be engendered in this process which are as stressful as those from the functioning of the id-system. Thus in Freud's later thinking ego-functioning and its ways of coping with anxiety are important and constitute a change in the theory. The unconscious and repressed impulses from the id are still important factors but they are no longer the only determinants of behaviour. Man is rational and the strengthening of his ego-functions is a move towards maturity. However, the ego is regularly in conflict with other parts of his nature and has only a precarious hold on the person as a whole. Freud saw man as an over-complex, ill-balanced, conflicted being who is not especially well adapted to the requirements of survival and control of his environment. His superior powers of intellect and socialization within civilized communities have evolved at some cost to his stability as an organism.

The difference between the earlier and later versions of Freud's theory can be illustrated by the change in his use of the concepts of 'repression' and 'anxiety'. In his early theory anxiety is caused by the repression of socially unacceptable sexual impulses. The impulse continues to exist and operate in the unconscious. In his later theory anxiety is a quasi-intelligent reaction to threat. If the anxiety is too intense and we cannot get rid of it in action then we 'repress' by switching the anxiety away from its original object to a less threatening object. This 'trick' reduces the anxiety to tolerable limits and enables us to cope after a fashion. Thus anxiety and repression are conceived in a new way in the later version.

Previously repression refers to a hidden process in the unconscious which, like a toxic substance in the bloodstream, disturbs normal functioning. Later, repression is a way of responding to threat and anxiety, a defensive reaction. The former tries to explain behaviour; the latter merely describes or classifies behaviour as performing a specific function. In the earlier theory repression names a hidden and active force, occurring in an inaccessible region of the

564 Models of Personality

person. Later, repression describes a sort of inhibition of emotion or attitude to an event in consciousness. The weakness in Freud's later thinking is that he lacked a theory of emotion, despite the importance of this idea of emotion and its inhibition in redefining 'repression'.

Freud seemed unhappy with two ways of looking at mental life – id-functioning (unconscious control) and ego-functioning (rational, conscious motivation). He constructed a theory of motivation bringing both under the control of the 'pleasure principle', thereby invoking hedonism. This hedonism is of a strangely negative sort since pleasure is release from tension, frustration, suffering of some kind. The rational choices of the ego and its devious defensive strategies against anxiety and conflict are merely a refinement of the same principle which governs instinct.

Thus Freud does not present a consistent theory. Controversy regarding the interpretation of his views continues. However, he initiated the attempt to work out a psychology of the individual person. Even if his theory is logically incoherent and difficult to test empirically he indicated significant aspects of behaviour for future investigation. What was his achievement? Peter Lomas (1973) thinks that Freud put forward certain broad generalizations which remain of value.

1. He re-discovered that childhood, especially early childhood, leaves its mark on adult personality to a greater extent than most eighteenth- and nineteenth-century thinkers had understood. Many of our traits have their origins early in our personal history, and child-like modes of response persist.

2. People have primitive biological appetites and needs. We tend to fail to recognize these for what they are, e.g., failure to accept sexual gratifications of a highly idiosyncratic and irrational kind can have negatively disturbing effects on a person.

3. Love and hate are powerful sentiments which are capable of dominating wide stretches of experience and behaviour. It is easy to try to ignore this fact. At the same time they are difficult to dissipate into less harmful channels. The power and commonality of these passions makes living in closely-knit groups, and especially the family, a hazardous business. Painful conflicts and unworkable defences are often generated within the family and leave traces in adult personality.

4. People adapt to the complex demands of society only with loss to the satisfaction of basic human needs. Sexual relations have become problematic for humans in a way in which they are not for other animals.

5. People often protect themselves against stress by indulging in wish-

fulfilling fantasies. In extreme cases fantasies come to dominate and the person regresses towards child-like modes of behaviour and thought. A powerful barrier is erected between the person and the 'real' world.

6. People in a state of psychological conflict express themselves in a language which is very different from the language of conscious, rational thought. The imagery and symbols of dreams and fantasies are closer to this language of 'the unconscious' and psychologists must learn to decipher the meanings of this language.

Thus our self-appraisals can easily become distorted and misleading. The term 'unconscious' is less controversial when used as an adjective (unconscious hatred of a brother) instead of the name of a hidden set of processes ('the unconscious'). An unconscious hate is not hate which you have but do not feel. You both have and feel hate and have impulses of an aggressive kind. It is simply that you fail to perceive, recognize, acknowledge your state as hate: a sort of amnesia, blockage or confusion of awareness operates and inhibits understanding of your own condition. This assumes a paradigm or conventional case in which you have and feel hate and are able to recognize and acknowledge it for what it is. That such blockage or confusion occurs, under certain special circumstances, seems to be the case. Freud's use of the term 'unconscious', applied as an adjective, to impulses, wishes, motives, does seem to describe this sort of occurrence. His theory of 'the unconscious' as an inaccessible region or inaccessible forces is much more dubious.

Derivations and deviations

Freud's theories were challenged and questioned by many of his original followers from 1911 onwards. Although starting from some Freudian position several theorists constructed alternatives to the Freudian model. They form a diverse group of 'psycho-dynamic type' theories, owing something to Freud but diverging strongly from the original. One of Freud's earliest disciples was Alfred Adler (1870–1937). Adler quickly disagreed with Freud over the theory of infantile sexuality. Indeed, he had little time for either instinct or the unconscious. Instead Adler believed that social influences are of greater significance in shaping personality. Aggression is more potent than sex. Men strive to master the environment and to win socially rewarded 'success'. However, the weakness and dependence of childhood bring a sense of inferiority. This can be double-edged. It can drive a person to over-compensate by becoming over-competitive. Or it can help towards the realization that the individual can only achieve a limited amount by his own effort. A mature person develops 'social interest' – the understanding that co-operation with others for commonly-shared benefits within society is the best strategy. Self-interest and social co-operation must be reconciled. Only those who achieve this style of life are mature persons. This process of development can go wrong in many ways. Adler's studies of neurotics were based on an attempt to identify failures to achieve 'social interest'. He believed that training given to children in both pre-school and primary school years was often mistaken and that aggression and strivings failed to become socialized and sublimated to useful ends. Adler had an experimental school and a child guidance clinic where children could be studied and his ideas on child rearing tested.

Perhaps closer to Freud was Karen Horney (1883–1952). Horney began as an orthodox Freudian but came to modify her position. Horney believed in the primacy of anxiety in human experience. The helplessness and confusion of every child in a complex social environment, which takes many years to master, ensures this 'basic anxiety'; relationships within the family make this anxiety more difficult to appease. Dominating parents, indifferent parents, over-protective parents, quarrelsome parents – each presents a child with stresses which aggravate the basic anxiety which arises in any case. Children react in different ways. Some go on the attack and become highly aggressive. Others are over-submissive and timid. Others withdraw from contact with other people as far as they can; others make excessive demands for attention and support. Horney lists many alternative strategies for coping with anxiety which structure the developing personality. These strategies, when exaggerated, produce a neurotic type. Even if mildly followed they tend to be less than effective in coping. Horney attempts in her therapy to devise means of training people to cope with anxiety and do so realistically and effectively.

She accepts 'repression' and confused, blocked aims and wishes. However, she rejects Freud's theory of instincts, and the sexual factor in personality development. She regards 'unconscious' factors as relevant only in more extreme neuroses and regards social and interpersonal relationships as a more widespread source of stress and anxiety. There is thus some debt to Freud but also wide divergence from his teaching in Horney's approach.

There are many writers on personality, mostly psychotherapists and clinical psychologists, within this broad psycho-dynamic tradition initiated by Freud, and also by C. G. Jung whose more esoteric views on the unconscious are well described by such writers as Fordham (1953) and C. S. Hall (Hall and Nordby, 1974). The data for much of this tradition are taken from the case-histories of patients 'treated' by psychoanalysts and other practitioners. It is often regarded as 'unscientific' and speculative by many psychologists. Attempts have been made to test psychoanalytic hypotheses empirically (Lee and Herbert, 1970; Fisher and Greenberg, 1977), but the results have been diverse. This approach remains problematic. Yet it constitutes a chapter in the theory of personality which cannot be ignored. Many hypotheses generated within this area remain to be tested empirically.

Behaviouristic approaches

Another group of theories derives from 'behaviourism' in a broad sense of that term. Of course, strict behaviourists such as N. E. Miller, B. F. Skinner and O. H. Mowrer have derived theories of personality on the lines of their theories of learning and motivation. Many, however, hold that it would take more than a lifetime for a human being to learn common social skills and roles if he were restricted to operant conditioning, reinforcement schedules or trial-and-error learning as required by a strictly behaviourist theory.

More flexible versions of behaviourism are most popular in the psychology of personality. These emphasize that the sources of behaviour lie in the environment rather than within the person. Traits, cognitive organization, physiological programmes within the head, are not favoured as the key to personality. Learning, the effects of environmental variations, is the source: situational variables must be sought and intensively studied. Let us consider two theories which follow this line.

Observational learning

This theory is associated with Albert Bandura and Richard Walters (1963) and begins from an emphasis on imitation. Individuals learn through rewards and punishments, as in traditional behaviourist models. But they also learn by observing the effects of reward and punishment on other people whom they watch attentively. Vicarious reinforcement of this kind is as important as direct reinforcement.

In a celebrated experiment nursery school children were shown a film of adult models behaving aggressively towards a large doll. When these children were introduced into a room containing games, toys and a replica of the doll they not only behaved aggressively to the doll, but closely matched many of the behaviours they had been shown on the film. Children who had not been shown the film did not attack the doll but preferred to play with the toys and games. Vicarious reinforcement can influence the acquisition of new responses and many social behaviours may be acquired in this way from models in the social environment.

Vicarious reinforcement can also lead to inhibitions and to the removal of inhibition of suppressed responses. Children who were shown a film of an adult being punished for displaying aggressive behaviour refrained from such behaviour when given the opportunity to imitate. In the original experiment some of the aggressive responses to the doll had not been demonstrated by the model – presumably the exposure must have had an effect of removing inhibition from these children.

Bandura and Walters make a distinction between acquiring knowledge how to act in a situation (through observational learning) and the actual performance of the actions. They have investigated the situational variables which control the actual use of what is learned and the factors which modify performance. How vicarious reinforcement influences the development of self-control was studied by Bandura and Mischel (1965) in an experiment on the ability of young children to delay gratification by choosing a larger reward at a later time rather than a smaller reward immediately. Children learned to achieve this measure of self-control through observations of adult models.

Studies of aggression in adolescents, with controlled situational variables, have been characteristic of Bandura's work with emphasis on the conditions under which reinforcements and punishments for aggressive responses are acquired. The learning of social roles is also a phenomenon which has been investigated and as a result of these and other studies the theory enjoyed a certain prestige as being more rigorously empirical than rival theories.

However, it is regarded as too restricted in its insistence that personality must be reduced to the direct or vicarious learning of an individual. Moreover, Brody (1972) suggests that a series of experiments by Epstein and Fenz, on the reactions of parachutists to the approach–avoidance conflicts, engendered by early jumps from an airplane, goes against the Bandura–Walters theory:

This research provides evidence of a lawful and orderly development of displacement as a function of experience such that fear is expressed to more and more remote cues. The processes by which this displacement occur are apparently intrapsychic in nature and develop in a manner which appears relatively autonomous, viz. independent of the influence of extrapsychic or vicarious reinforcement.

Again, the observational learning approach relies on reducing personality development to each specific situation eliciting a particular response (rewarded or punished directly or vicariously) for the individual. No genotypal influences (which exist prior to and distinct from social learning) are allowed. It can be argued that there is some evidence for genotypal factors: e.g. if extraversion–introversion refers to a basic temperamental difference, or if Guilford and Cattell's evidence for some behaviours having a genetic influence is reasonably sound, we have reason to question such a strongly situational emphasis.

Social learning

Another behavioural emphasis is to be found in the social learning theory of J. B. Rotter (1954). This theory, however, stresses environment only as it is meaningful to the person. Any situation, by virtue of previous learning, contains cues which arouse in a person the expectation that certain behaviour will bring a specific form of reward or punishment. Personal learning and the acquisition of common information enable a person to know the meaning of most situations which occur. Human behaviour is a function of the environmental situation. This situation is intelligible through the person's expectancies and his own reinforcement values (what is most strongly rewarding in specific circumstances and hence a goal).

Rotter uses three main concepts. Behaviour-potential is the probability that a person will display behaviour B in situation S for some specific reinforcement R. B thus depends not only on the occurrence of S as stimulus, but on the person's expectancy that B will yield R, and the acceptance that R has positive value for the person. Thus what the person *thinks* B will bring about and how he *evaluates* its consequences is important. Human behaviour is adaptive – aimed at obtaining rewards and avoiding punishments – but it is intelligently adaptive. Rotter held that several behaviours, B_1, B_2, B_3, may be linked by the fact that their reinforcements are very similar (or even identical). When behaviours have this inter-relationship Rotter refers to their common 'need potential': 'not only do they share a common goal but their success and failure generalize to each other due to their functional similarity.' The reinforcements cumulate into a more overriding 'need'. Expectancy also can generalize widely. When a set of linked behaviours has a common reinforcement value there are different behavioural routes to a common goal. This constitutes 'freedom of movement' for a particular class of reinforcements. Thus a person may aim at public recognition and prestige from his group through performing a variety of different actions. He has a certain choice of action in order to get his reward.

An example of a generalized expectancy is Rotter's dimension of the internal–external control of reinforcement. Rotter postulates a continuum (for which he has a scale for measuring individual differences): at one extreme (internal control) are people who believe that their behaviour can control the outcome of most reinforcing events. What happens to them they expect to be generally under their own control. At the other extreme (external control) are those who expect that what happens to them is not in their control but is due to fate, chance or those in positions of social power. People tend to acquire general expectancies about the locus of control over events in the personal environment; they feel in command, or otherwise, over a wide range of situations. This distinction has generated a considerable amount of research. What sort of learning leads to 'internal' or 'external' control expectations? What other personality characteristics are associated with these two opposed attitudes? Are internals more achieving and socially dominant while externals are anxious and depressed? Do these attitudes have an influence on the effects of reinforcement or can strong reinforcements cut across these attitudes? Results tend not to be clear or consistent and it is not certain whether the considerable interest shown in this aspect of Rotter's theory has been fruitful or not.

Rotter has another generalized expectancy for which a scale has been provided – inter-personal trust. People vary in the extent to which they expect others to keep their promises and adhere to other moral rules. Rotter's test suggests that people who have a strong religious faith are much more trusting of others than agnostics or atheists, and that the higher a person is on the socio-economic ladder the more trusting he tends to be.

It is a fairly obvious criticism of Rotter's theory that it does not remain consistently 'situational'. Concepts like 'need potential' and 'freedom of movement' imply that a person can change his own reinforcement rules by thinking and imagining different possibilities of behaviour and outcome. Cognitive functioning comes into the model through the back door. Organization and control within the organism produce behaviour to change the situation. The main source is not exclusively situational variables. Just as observational learning and social learning theory corrected the overemphasis of trait-state approaches, so cognitive theory is required to correct theories emphasizing situational influences on personality.

Cognitive approaches

Personal constructs

The most comprehensive theory to study personality in terms of the contents of thought is that of George A. Kelly (1955). Kelly's starting-point was that the psychologist regards himself as a scientist with the intelligent purpose of experimenting in order to test hypotheses and to apply the results to the explanations of human behaviour. However, the psychologist often treats his subjects as creatures of impulse or as controlled by reflexes conditioned to stimuli in the environment – a complex set of mechanisms. The subjects whom the psychologist investigates, according to Kelly's point of view, are interested no less than the psychologist in trying to understand and control behaviour. The ordinary human being needs to be able to anticipate events, to predict what is likely to happen next.

Each individual is constantly engaged in interpreting information coming to the brain through his perceptual apparatus in terms of a set of 'constructs'. Events are represented meaningfully in consciousness. An object is distant or near, heavy or light; another person is friendly or hostile; a situation is supportive or threatening. What is happening is represented by a 'construct' or 'thought'. Each person builds up his own *system* of personal constructs in terms of which his experiences are interpreted, and in line with which his behaviour is directed.

This system is the personality. To study an individual's personal construct system is to study his personality. Kelly stated his theory in a formal manner. From a fundamental postulate follow eleven corollaries.

The postulate which structures the whole theory states: 'a person's processes are psychologically channelled by the way he anticipates events.' Constructs originate, according to Kelly, through people noticing repetitions or replications within their experiences. Yet each person differs from every other in the way he construes events. There are similarities and overlaps, but the system which each person operates is highly idiosyncratic. However, constructs always take a bipolar form. If A and B are construed as 'heavy' they contrast with C who is 'light'. Events occur so that A is 'before' B and B is 'after' A. What goes 'up' must come 'down'. Each particular construct has two contrasting 'poles'. Any event to which a construct is applied is placed at one or other of its two poles.

Constructs cannot be applied to events indiscriminately. Each has its appropriate 'range of convenience' of events to which it can be applied and a 'focus' of convenience which renders its application more precise in a specific context. If a construct is not applied to events within its range of convenience any actions carried out under its guidance will fail to be adaptive.

The point of the system is its efficiency in accurately predicting events and so rendering behaviour adaptive rather than maladaptive. A person learns to 'select' that alternative in any bipolar construct which enables him to do this. As Kelly, somewhat obscurely, puts it: 'he chooses that construct through which he anticipates the greater possibility for the elaboration of his system.' Constructs must become sufficiently precise and the range of their convenience sufficiently extensive if the system is to work properly: to be accurate in predicting events for most of the time. The construct system is likely to remain stable for a person who lives a routine existence in a relatively unchanging environment. If experience is of a changing environment then the personal construct system must adapt in order to deal with new patterns of events and their consequences.

Kelly takes an unconventional line on emotion and motivation. He holds that an emotion such as 'anxiety' is a sort of ignorance and confusion, the inability to understand a situation and hence to cope with it. One's construct system fails to operate, one does not know what to do with the demands of the situation and is thrown into confusion. Kelly dislikes the image of man being pushed or pulled into action by impulses, drives or being lured by aspirations for future reward. Man is continually active, ongoing, interactive with events. It is simply the direction of behaviour that has to be explained. The construing of events is sufficient to account for this direction.

Kelly devised a technique for generating tests which would elicit and assess the personal construct system – what specific constructs a person relies upon and how they are inter-related – the Role Construct Repertory Grid (Rep. Test). Individuals do not have an indefinite number of constructs or an infinite variety of ways of linking them together; the system can be delineated without difficulty.

In the original form of the test each subject is given a list of role titles: father, mother, boss, best friend, teacher liked, teacher disliked, etc. until twenty to thirty such roles are available. The name of a person filling each role in his experience is written on a card. The experimenter then takes three role figures and asks the subject to say which two (say A and B) are alike in some respect and different from the third figure (C) who is the opposite. The subject is using a construct and applying one pole to A and B and the contrasting pole to C. The result is recorded on a 'grid' chart. As the procedure is repeated over and over again with different sets of three role figures, certain constructs are used. Father, best friend and boss may be 'warm, friendly' while teacher disliked and brother are 'cold and distant'. After the completion of the test we find patterns amongst the constructs used. We may note that a number of constructs with similar meanings have been used to describe and compare people. Hence all people are seen in a rigid manner as either friendly or hostile; easy-going and relaxed or over-sensitive and anxious. A person who sees people in terms of such sharp contrasts has a distinctive attitude towards other people and their relationship with him.

Not only roles but types of situation can be presented on cards to elicit constructs, e.g., disturbing events (illness, quarrels with parents and friends, being reprimanded at work for an error). How does the person construe and compare these significant happenings or crises? The Repertory Test is flexible and has been adapted by clinical psychologists and by research psychologists interested in cognitive functioning.

Kelly's system has been criticized as ambiguous and abstract. How is a specific construct selected in order to interpret an ongoing event? Is it like a choice or decision? Or is it determined by an independent process? What exactly is happening when a person construes his experiences as this or that? Kelly does not make this clear. Again, how do actions follow from the selection of a given construct? Kelly seems to have no theory of action. His constructs simply occur within a person's consciousness but it is not easy to see how action is initiated and guided.

Kelly holds that the system is confirmed if constructs, in guiding activity, help us to predict accurately and consistently what is going to happen. But if a construct is invalidated, as sometimes is the case, how exactly does this affect future construings? How does the construct become modified, or even rejected? Kelly says this does happen but not how it happens.

The situation and its changing pattern of events must impinge upon the construer – his information must come through perception. But how environment and cognitive activity are related is left obscure.

It is probable that drastic revision, and additions, to Kelly's system might remedy these and other serious weaknesses. However, Kelly has at least corrected a bias in the psychology of personality. Man is partially a rational animal. Intelligent adaptation has often been neglected in favour of the dominance of instincts, emotions, drives, reinforcing stimuli, etc. Cognitive functioning must be an important aspect of a person, and individual differences in the personal construct system are part of the total picture. Kelly's use of his Repertory Test does suggest that such differences in the content of cognitive response are important factors.

Cognitive styles

It is one thing to study the specific content of thinking. It is another to study how a person thinks – his strategies and styles for organizing contents into effective behaviours. A new approach to personality in the 1960s came with the topic of 'styles'.

H. A. Witkin (1962) maintained that people exhibit consistent cognitive styles, common to perceptual and problem-solving activities. He began by studying a familiar distinction derived from the Gestalt experimentalists of the 1930s – field dependency–independency. In his well-known Rod and Frame Test, Witkin places the subject in a darkened room and sets the task of adjusting the position of a luminous rod to its true vertical within a luminous square frame. The experimenter can tilt the rod and the frame and the subject has to make corrections on his controls when rod and frame tilt in opposite directions. The chair in which the subject sits is also tilted. Scores are calculated on the absolute deviations of the settings from the true vertical under conditions of body tilt, frame tilt and rod tilt. People differ consistently in their performance from each other. What is crucial is an ability to ignore the misleading features of the frame and the body so that the rod can be isolated and fixated in relation to its true vertical. Some have this ability to a marked degree. Others lack it. Witkin describes those who consistently succeed as 'highly differentiated'.

In another study the subject is placed in a small room that can be tilted. The chair in which he sits can also be tilted independently of the room. The task is to keep the chair at its true vertical when the room is tilted. Again the subject must avoid getting 'embedded' in the context. He must discount cues from the tilting room. Witkin argues that these experiments demonstrate that some people interpret the information in an undifferentiated style. They cannot isolate parts and their inter-relationships from the total or 'global' presentation. Others who are differentiated in style can discriminate parts within the whole field. These differences are called by different names – articulated as compared with global style or field-independent as compared with field-dependent.

In addition to the two 'tilting' setting studies, Witkin has a picture test in which figures are embedded in highly complicated designs – the task being to promptly extract the figures. The three test scores are combined into a measure called 'perceptual index' which purports to give a score for one's place on the differentiation dimension. The tests are highly stable: individuals on being retested at intervals tend to get a similar rating on the measures. Subjects tested over a period of fourteen years had a retest correlation of 0·66. However, the three tests do not correlate well with each other and there are problems regarding what exactly they assess.

Some investigators have found a high correlation between perceptual index scores and measures of general intelligence. It is thought that Witkin's tests measure non-verbal intelligence factors rather than an independent personality function.

One study by Minard and Mooney (1969) investigated the relationship between differentiation measures and response to emotive words. It was argued that the effect of emotion on perceptual recognition was totally unrelated to measures of intelligence included in the experiment. This suggested that differentiation as a style is something other than a manifestation of non-verbal intelligence. In another study Vernon (1972) found that, with effects of intelligence controlled and eliminated, differentiation measures had little relationship to a number of personality variables. Thus the issue regarding the meaning of 'differentiation' is open and unresolved. Yet intelligence, organized strategically for certain difficult tasks, does seem to display interesting individual differences in the style and effectiveness of the subjects' performance. Witkin's work has highlighted the importance of differences in the way we *use* our intelligence in problem-solving situations.

Another difference in cognitive style derives from the work of Getzels and Jackson (1962) mentioned in Chapters 18 and 20. Their distinction between convergent and divergent styles of thinking is well known. A series of experiments was carried out with high school children whose average I.Q. was over 132. Several standard intelligence tests were administered but so were tests alleged to assess 'creativity'. The creativity tests included word tests in which as many differences in definition of abstract words as possible had to be found under pressure of time. Again, given an object, as many different actual uses of the object as possible had to be identified in a brief period. It was found that the correlation between these 'creativity' tests and the intelligence tests was low − ·27. Indeed the scholars were divided by their scores into two groups:

(a) Those high in 'creativity' but lower than average for the groups in I.Q. (divergent);

(b) Those high in I.Q. but lower than average for the groups in 'creativity' test scores (convergent).

The personality characteristics of these two groups seemed to be different. The divergent group were unconventional and sometimes rebellious against conventions. They displayed humour and violence much more in their fantasies (making up stories or interpreting pictures). They were more impulsive and unpredictable and less popular with teachers. The convergers were more orthodox, staid, unadventurous, restrained and obedient – accepting rules and authority without demur.

It has been suggested by subsequent researchers that with a large and heterogeneous population convergent and divergent scores tend to be highly intercorrelated (Ripple and May, 1962) – the Getzels and Jackson study was made with a highly selected group of bright, middle-class children. It has also been suggested that the minority groups who exhibit the highly convergent versus highly divergent results are each groups with distinctive personality profiles. Highly divergent, less highly intelligent people tend to lack ego-control. Their needs demand immediate gratification and they tend to be excessively impulsive and aggressive. The highly intelligent, less divergent group tend to be gregarious, easy-going, lacking in dominance and drive. It is probable that the two 'styles' represent 'extreme' personality types which manifest themselves in cognitive functioning as well as in other more obvious ways. The studies do suggest that cognitive efficiency is affected by strategies for processing information and solving problems which are due to dominant personality organization. It is clear that however inadequate the theories and research, cognitive functioning must be taken into account in investigations of personality. How we think and understand the situations of life reflects differences of personality.

An interactionist compromise

More recently there have been attempts to combine cognitive with social learning approaches to the study of personality. Walter Mischel (1973) has put forward a proposal. He repeats the case against exclusive reliance on traits. There is evidence for extensive person–situation interaction. Indeed 'behaviour is idiosyncratically organized for each individual' in virtue of variability within the situation, and the person, and the discriminative sensitivity of persons to these.

The key is how the individual construes his particular situation as it affects him. Specific situational variables evoke and sustain cognitive reactions and behaviour but only as 'processed' by the intelligence of the agent. Sometimes the situation is 'strong' and imposes its impress. At other times it is 'weak' and has little effect. Social learning methodology can investigate situational variables but cognitive functioning must also be brought into any account of personality.

People differ, according to Mischel, in their 'construction competencies'. Even if people have similar information and beliefs about what is the most appropriate action to take in a specific situation, and are similarly motivated to act, they differ as to whether they can perform the action, or perform it efficiently. Differences in behaviour also depend on the individual ways in which people categorize a situation. There are different ways of encoding, grouping, labelling, discriminating the same events. Differences in perform- ance depend, again, on differences in the agent's expected outcome of actions, and with the agent's predictions regarding how the situation is likely to develop independently of his action. To these outcomes different subjective values are applied – some being perceived as desirable, preferable, useful, others seen as the opposite. Finally, plans and 'self regulatory systems' differ from person to person.

Thus all these cognitive orientations interact with changing features of the environmental situation to structure behaviour precisely. Cognitive as well as situational variables are essential. There are three perspectives in relation to personality which Mischel regards as equally important:

1. From the point of view of the psychologist interested in the control of behaviour it is useful to concentrate on the environmental conditions related to changes in behaviour. People can be made to perform, or influenced to perform, quite specific actions through control of the stimulus situation.

2. From the point of view of the theorist trying to explain how such operations on the environment produce changes in performance it is useful to focus on alterations in information processes and upon such factors as con- structs, expectations, subjective values, rules and other cognitive variables. These mediate the effects of the stimulus situation upon behaviour.

3. From the point of view of the experiencing agent it is useful to think of these same events in terms of their phenomenological impact – as thoughts, feelings and other subjective or internal states.

'The same events may be alternatively construed from each of these perspectives.' The influence of Kelly's approach is apparent – although Mischel's starting point in social learning theory helps him to include the environmental situation as interacting with information processing. There is no one model for construing personality – a flexible approach is needed. This constitutes a departure from behavioural psychology of the orthodox behaviourists although it incorporates some of their achievements in studying the control of behaviour through the manipulation of situational variables.

Motivation and personality

William P. Alston (1976) writes '. . . the question of how to conceptualize personality is the question of how to conceptualize what contribution the person makes to the determination of behaviour. And how we answer that question will depend on our general theory of motivation.' As we saw in Chapter 6 motivation has proved a difficult topic for psychologists. One traditional approach has been to draw up lists of typical motives commonly found in human nature. Jeremy Bentham's *A Table of the Springs of Action* (1815) is an example from the past which retains a very modern look. It is similar in many respects to the theory of Henry A. Murray (1938).

Murray began by conducting longitudinal studies over many years with a small group of people who were intensively investigated from a number of different angles. This study, supported later by his work with the United States Army during the Second World War on the psychological assessment of personnel, gave him empirical data from which to construct a system. In Murray's system 'needs' within the person and 'presses' from the environment are the basic concepts, although by no means the only technical terms.

However, at the centre of Murray's theory is a set of twenty dominant types of 'need' which many humans strive to satisfy. These are long-term motives, highly generalized goals which can be realized only by setting and attaining a succession of more specific exemplars of the goal-type. The 'need for achievement' is one such motive-type. This takes many possible forms: to overcome obstacles; to rival and surpass other people in competitive social situations; to accomplish difficult tasks successfully; to organize – people, ideas or even physical things – to some purpose of one's own; etc. etc.

A considerable range of specific goal-directed behaviours, capable of being observed, are covered by the 'achievement motive' – but they have a *common* type of aim and fulfilment. A given individual may be seen, over a period of time, as a 'high achiever', constantly setting goals for socially recognized 'success' – at school, at college, at work, in leisure and sporting pursuits, in 'social' activities. Others do not seem to be concerned with the business of being 'successful' in these recognized ways.

The other 'needs' in Murray are: affiliation, aggression, autonomy, counteraction (overcoming fear and other weaknesses), defence, deference, dominance, exhibition, harm-avoidance, infavoidance (avoiding failure, humiliation), nurturance, order, play, rejection, sentience, sex, succorance, understanding.

It is the need for achievement which has been investigated most rigorously, by D. C. McClelland, J. W. Atkinson, and their associates. This research has been adventurous and comprehensive and has shown that long-term motives to achieve do have a considerable role in the behaviour of many individuals. The research is not without its problems. For example, the most widely used method of obtaining measures of a person's need for achievement is the Thematic Apperception Test (T.A.T.). This consists of a set of pictures showing people in an ambiguous situation. Subjects respond to the pictures by writing a short story about how they see the scene represented – what is happening, what the people are thinking and feeling, what is the likely inter-personal outcome. It is argued that people project something of their own personalities into the story and reveal such basic motives as 'aggression', 'exhibition', 'achievement', through dominant interpretations and themes. Obviously inferences and scores in such an open-ended projective test are subject to dispute. Test-retest reliability tends to be low.

Attempts to provide alternative measures to those of the T.A.T. have not proved much more successful. Moreover, attempts to quantify relationships between 'variables' involved in the achievement motive such as degree of motivation, fear of failure, and the incentive value of a specific goal, are also open to criticism. In spite of technical difficulties a great deal of informa-tion about high and low achievers has been amassed, and this is a beginning into the investigation of typical long-term patterns of motivation as clues to personality.

However, individuals often strive for goals which seem highly idiosyn-cratic and personal – only loosely linked to typical, broad patterns of motivation. It is with regard to these that the psychodynamic psychologists from Freud and Jung onwards come into the picture. The theories of such psychologists are, as we have seen, open to doubt. They picture all thoughts, feelings and actions as being determined by complex interacting processes operating in 'the unconscious'. There are logical (McIntyre, 1958) and empirical grounds (Kline, 1972; Fisher and Greenberg, 1977) for questioning the validity of 'the unconscious'. However, if one looks at the many case-histories reported by 'analysts' and the events during therapy, material emerges which is not implicated in the theory. Much of this throws light on how the individual comes to act from specific motives. The patients treated by 'analysts' do not seem to manifest obscure instincts but to be confused, anxious or guilt-ridden about their strivings towards specific objectives in their personal relationships.

As R. S. Peters (1958) has pointed out, Freud was much concerned with motive. When he talked of ego-functioning, guided by the reality principle, he was referring to our everyday way of explaining intelligent, goal-directed actions. A person wants G and believes that certain actions will prove, both practically and in terms of social convention, an efficient means to G. However, when Freud speaks of id-functioning, under the guidance of the pleasure principle, he is referring to more devious motives. People can seek specific gratifications or avoid certain frustrations without being able to discriminate or identify their own behaviour for what it is. As we have already noted a person can have feelings associated with hatred and behave in a hostile and harmful manner towards another person without being able to recognize that he does hate that person and is behaving maliciously. He perhaps rationalizes and justifies his actions as 'righteous indignation' directed against the unacceptable in the other person's character. At the same time the faults attributed to this other person might justly be referred to the agent himself – 'unconsciously' he 'projects' these guilt-productive activities on to an innocent victim.

How such inabilities to know and acknowledge one's own motives come about is not easy to explain. The explanations of psychoanalytic, and similar type, psychologies may not be capable of much solid support. Whether 'conflict' or 'confusion' or 'amnesia' are apt analogies it is not easy to decide. Nevertheless when it comes to *describing* the behaviour involved in such cases, its onset in specific circumstances, its relation to previous developmental history of the persons involved, then the literature of psychodynamic psychology has much to offer. It does throw some light on the idiosyncratic character of motivation, and how there is common ground between the abnormal motives of the neurotic and psychotic and the minor psychopathologies of everyday life. This descriptive psychology – taken out of the complicated theoretical structure within which it is usually presented – has something to offer the student of personality. R. S. Peters' *The Concept of Motivation* (1958) shows how a philosophical critique of Freud can separate the misleading from the illuminating metaphors, and how Freud has something of interest to show about human motivation. Even if it is descriptive rather than explanatory it is one of the few sources of information on the subject of concrete manifestations of motive as a clue to personality. The goals we select and the means we adopt to reach them provide us with important variables for the description of personality.

Values and self-identity

Several psychologists, especially Gordon Allport and Carl Rogers, have emphasized the importance of the beliefs and attitudes a person has about himself. Self-concepts may imply self-satisfaction or self-confidence or self-disgust. They may be incongruent with the pictures which other people have of the person and so create anxiety. They may be remarkably inaccurate on any reasonable criterion of assessment or they may appear to observers as quite accurate. Our self-concepts and self-evaluations are regarded as an important aspect of our personality and there is now a considerable literature of empirical studies (Wylie, 1961).

Self-evaluation has been stressed by A. H. Maslow (1968, 1973), a clinical psychologist who was originally interested in defining what constitutes robust, positive mental health – the far end of a dimension well beyond the risk of neurotic maladjustments. Maslow maintained that there are two distinct types of motivation and that these are related to a hierarchy of basic human needs. Once simpler needs are met adequately, a higher type of need arises to motivate a person. At first we strive towards goals which are necessary in order to satisfy various *deficiencies*.

At the lowest level are needs for food, drink, shelter, warmth. Next come safety needs for protection against dangers. If these are well satisfied there are then psychological needs for affection, belonging with others, acceptance by others. If these are not satisfied people become maladjusted. There are also needs for esteem – self-respect, and respect from other people. We require status and a sense of worth as members of a society. All these are 'deficiency needs'. Without satisfaction they produce frustration and unrest, and striving to satisfy such needs is what Maslow calls 'deficiency motivation'.

However, once most deficiency needs are satisfied, we are subject to a different kind of motivation – growth motivation. There is a need to develop our powers and capabilities and our basic character in order to be able to enjoy higher forms of satisfaction which Maslow classifies as 'self-actualization'.

He has studied what he believes to be self-actualized individuals with a view to discovering their personality characteristics. These he takes to be synonymous with positive, robust mental health. Self-actualized people who are satisfying the needs of growth motivation tend to have certain personality characteristics. They are more objective in their perception of what is happening in their inter-personal environment; they are tolerant and accepting of self and others; they are more interested in problems outside of themselves rather than in egocentric problems; they are calm and detached in emotionally arousing situations; they are spontaneous in thought and action; they are liberal and democratic in outlook; they are 'creative' in various ways; they experience occasionally a sort of 'mystical' euphoria.

There is much that is obscure in Maslow's writings. He appears to treat the need for self-actualization as a natural growth process which is inbuilt, rather than a socio-cultural acquisition of privileged persons in a complex society. If we look carefully at the criteria used to specify states of self-actualization these seem to be definable in terms of normative or value-judgements. The goals of self-actualization indicate activities or states of mind which are, in some sense, intrinsically commendable or worthwhile. These states and activities are worth having or worth doing for their own sake. They are not a means to any ends *extrinsic* to themselves. Deficiency motivation involves reaching goals in order to be safe from danger, or in order to avoid stress leading to neurosis. But the goals of self-actualization are simply achieved for their own sake – they are prescribed in terms of criteria of value (ethical, prudential, aesthetic).

Maslow is pointing out that people do develop ways of appraising events, states of mind, actions and their consequences in terms of value-judgements. They employ moral and aesthetic concepts to interpret experience as well as empirical concepts to explain what happens and to predict the future. Such normative concepts are applied to people – we regularly pass judgements on other people's behaviour and on their characters. We also apply such moral appraisals to ourselves. Actions are seen as 'immoral', 'vulgar', 'disgusting', or as 'duties', or 'delightful', or 'admirable'. Many activities are governed by the intrinsic satisfaction of doing or having something which we regard positively in terms of some criterion of value – going to concerts and listening to music; collecting (and playing) gramophone records or collecting paintings or decorative ornaments. Our 'interests' show how we choose to spend our time and energy when we are not having to make necessary adjustments to the environment – doing all kinds of gratuitous things such as riding horses (for fun, not as basic transport), collecting postage stamps or coins, etc.

People also have aspirations directed towards the future. We want to be different in some ways – having skills, accomplishments, enjoyments, understanding, which at present we lack. This involves self-appraisal, a setting up of a future or ideal self. Such thinking is largely in terms of what we value, as much as a matter of planning efficient means to ends. Our self-concepts, the sort of person we conceive ourselves to be, and the sort of person we want to become, give us a locus for self-identity, our claim to be a particular person, different from all others. Maslow is moving into the area where the acquisition of personal values and the application of value-judgements in relation to self-concepts is a central concern. This is part of our 'personality' and some psychologists regard it as the most significant part.

Summary comments

The psychology of personality is an area of controversy. There is no agreement regarding what are the essential variables to investigate or the most appropriate methods for research and assessment. Albert Mehrabian (1968) has argued that each theory is rooted in a metaphor or analogy, arbitrarily and intuitively chosen by the author. This determines the categories, assumptions and hypotheses of the theory and the sort of observations favoured. He makes a fair case for the a priori and arbitrary nature of personality theories. There is no need to take sides. All one can do is to classify the main areas within which significant variables for the description of individuals as persons may be sought. R. R. Holt (1969) gives us a lead here, even if some of the classifications involve a degree of overlapping.

Abilities

There is some evidence in favour of the idea that we can assess individual differences along a dimension of general intelligence. Also that specific 'factors' within this dimension can be detected. Individuals do not merely operate at a characteristic level of performance in relation to an average for their group. They develop special aptitudes for certain skills – for mathematics, music, athletics. One's intellectual capacity and one's aptitude to perform well in specific endeavours are part of one's personality. So, too, are the strategies which organize our cognitive reactions – 'cognitive styles'. Cognitive factors are a basic key to personality.

Temperament

It has been a longstanding belief, to which the work of Cattell and Guilford lends some support, that people exhibit individual differences in the level of energy and emotion with which they respond to a considerable range of stimuli. Some are more active, persistent, vigorous than others in everything they do. Some people are noticeably more apathetic, lethargic, dilatory. Again, some persons display more emotion and express it more explicitly and spontaneously than others who are more inhibited or calmly detached. We vary in our emotional lability. Moreover, the frequency and intensity of some specific emotion, such as anger or fear, occur variedly between persons. There are anxious types and irascible types and cheerful types. Such highly generalized reaction-tendencies are believed to be the result of genetic endowment and early experiences. Temperamental traits appear early in life and tend to persist.

Character traits

Learning and developmental history leave traces which enable us, in every-day situations, to describe people as 'generous', 'miserly', 'conscientious', 'punctual', 'timid', 'brave', 'humourless'. Whether, as Cattell and Eysenck believe, such surface traits are determined by more basic dispositions, we certainly find dictionaries full of such adjectives for classifying stimulus–response frequency dispositions as defined by Alston (1976).

Motives

Behaviour is sometimes seen as intelligently and intentionally directed towards a specific goal. Certain actions are thus a means to an end. The agent knows what he wants and how he intends to achieve it. However, observations of an individual over time may suggest that specific goal-directed actions have something in common; follow a pattern. They are instances of a more general long-term motive – to achieve success in social activities (work, leisure) to dominate and lead other people in various group activities; to think, research, understand. Long-term motives are clues to personality: how a person is likely to behave in different situations. The sort of goals an individual prefers and the ways he strives for them are important aspects of a person.

Values, interests, attitudes and ideals

We react to situations, not only by identifying objects, events, relationships, and anticipating probable outcomes, but by evaluating them. Normative criteria prescribe our likes and dislikes, what is fair or unjust, good or evil in human conduct. We develop ethical and aesthetic values. A person's interests and hobbies, what he chooses to do with 'spare' time, tell us something about what he values positively. Again, many fundamental beliefs and attitudes may be the products of normative rather than empirical reasoning. People develop political or religious ideologies and some of their activities are closely related to the 'constructions' derived from the principles involved in the ideology. Our self-concepts are closely related to our values. Self-satisfaction, self-criticism and self-distrust are the products of appraisal in terms of ethical norms. Thus we have to consider individual differences in value-systems, accounting for personality. The self is thus the system of beliefs and attitudes we have at any particular time about ourselves and the way in which we apply our concepts of value to ourselves. It is not synonymous with 'personality' but it constitutes an aspect of the whole which may be of some importance.

Identity

Self-concepts and attitudes would seem to be relevant to the organization of behaviour. How a person thinks and feels about himself at work, how he regards the social groups of which he is a member, how he sees himself as a person in comparison with other persons and what he sees as his most prominent characteristics all help to define identity as a particular person. Are a person's dominant attitudes towards himself positive or negative? Has he a clearly defined conception of himself or are his ideas obscure and incomplete so that his sense of identity is imperfect? Does the person's description of himself correspond closely to that of observers? Or is there a marked discrepancy between self-description and the assessments of other people who know him well? Do differences in self-concepts relate to differences in behaviour? Some psychologists regard the approach to personality through the study of self-concepts as important for the understanding of the person.

Developmental history

The clinical approach encourages us to account for dominant trends in terms of past history and development. The family situation in childhood and adolescence may have initiated and structured developments which have left an imprint. What aspects of present personality result from ethnic background, religious upbringing, socio-economic status during formative years? Is a person rooted in early training and 'models' or has he deviated strongly away from them, and, if so, why? What events and people have influenced the person strongly and helped to form basic traits? What accidents of personal history have turned the individual in a specific direction? Has he succumbed to trauma or handicaps or struggled to overcome them? What gratifications and fulfilments have become important, and do any derive from the experiences of early life? Are there any basic patterns in relationships with other people which have been acquired in the past and strengthened by subsequent experiences? How does the person construe certain types of inter-personal encounter? Each case-history presents a unique developmental account which suggests certain developmental trends leading to the present and having persisting effects.

Stability, adjustment and mental health

Psychiatry and clinical psychology make familiar the conception of individual differences in the extent to which people adjust effectively to their social environment and deal with its stresses and strains. Without being neurotic or psychotic normal people vary in stability and mental health and occasionally exhibit minor maladjustments. One does not have to be diagnosed as an acute case to experience disturbing anxiety or a tendency to depressive moods – disruptions which do not get out of hand but which affect the whole quality of everyday life. There are variations in stability which seem to be a matter of degree rather than a qualitative difference between the healthy and the sick. The Eysenck discussion of neuroticism–stability is one approach for assessing this aspect of behavioural organization – how adequately an individual is coping, or tending to cope, with the problems of adjustment.

It is unlikely that assessments within these categories can be systematized into a coherent whole. Adler, the Viennese psychiatrist who was one of Freud's early associates, believed that all our various personality characteristics summate into a distinctive and discernible 'style of life'. However, this has never proved a widely accepted conception. Just as artists can create effective caricatures with a few deft strokes, so a psychologist who is verbally fluent may give a sketch of the main convergences from various assessment procedures. However, a caricature is not the same as a portrait and a portrait does not include an analysis in anatomical or physiological terms of a body. The best we can manage is probably a sketchy summary of the main impressions. There is no one way of conceptualizing personality or one proven method of investigation. The search for more adequate conceptualizations remains a task. For the student who can tolerate ambiguity, uncertainty and open-ended problems, this branch of psychology does at least provide some fascination, and a challenge to make his own interpretation of its data.

Chapter 22
Group Differences

Introduction

People, like all stimuli, are responded to not solely in terms of their unique characteristics (even in so far as these can be readily perceived) but in terms of their group membership. Assessment of individuals may well be influenced by the apparent group membership of the individual appraised, and by the group membership of the appraiser, and membership of a group may in turn impose a strain upon the objectivity of one's evaluation of certain issues and evidence.

There are many 'groups' membership of which renders an individual liable to stereotyped judgement: for example, social class or religious affiliation; but sex, age and race are perhaps the most obvious (and most studied) group differences of interest to the psychologist, if only for the reason that an individual's sex, racial origin and approximate age can usually be readily determined at a first, and at a superficial, meeting, and it is these dimensions which will be considered in this chapter. All are characterized by the prevalence of *stereotypes* and of prejudice. Such prejudgements are important in that they may be used as the basis not only of individual interpersonal relations but also of political action and legal and occupational discrimination. It is not surprising that people may feel themselves threatened by the hypothesis that there are stable and substantial psychological differences associated with sex, age and racial origin; hence the pejorative terms sexism, racism and ageism, and the forcefulness of campaigns for 'women's liberation', racial equality and (more in the U.S.A. than in Britain) a fair deal for the aged – for example, an end to inflexible age criteria for compulsory retirement.

Another issue common to all three fields is that of assessing the relative contributions of biological and environmental or social determinants to any psychological group differences which may be established. This is most evident in the case of sex and race differences, but it is also of some importance to discover to what extent age differences – and in particular performance decrements with increased age – are an inevitable concomitant of 'normal ageing' and to what extent they are socially or culturally determined. Again understandably, there has been a strong tendency for opponents of 'sexism', 'racism' and 'ageism' to deny any biological foundation for such group differences as might be reliably observed. Ultimately, the only hope for an end to 'unfair' discrimination on the basis of group membership must lie in objective, and non-polemic, assessment of the nature and extent of sex, race and age differences and, as far as can logically be determined, their causation. We are still very far from arriving at such an assessment: this chapter can only give a brief indication of the principal directions which psychological research is currently taking.

Sex differences

Sex differences in behaviour

It is clear that in many, if not all, societies men and women differ in their behaviour, and there is considerable (though not complete) concordance in the nature of such differences (see, for example, D'Andrade, 1966). Women tend to be occupied in domestic duties and in the rearing of children; men tend to be active outside the home, rather than within it, and to be the hunters, the warriors or the breadwinners, according to the basic economy of the society in which they live. Sex differences are obvious in the behaviour, and training, of children as well as in adults: Barry, Bacon and Child (1957), for example, found that in most societies examined by them girls are trained to be nurturant, responsible and obedient, and boys to be self-reliant and achieving. Many sex differences are linked, historically at least, to physical differences. It is women who bear children and who are able to breast-feed them; men are physically stronger, at least in certain respects, and these differences are more or less sufficient in a primitive society to dictate that women will be tied to the home and men will be the providers. In more developed societies, in which physical strength is less relevant to the business of making a living and in which there are adequate substitutes for breast-feeding, such differences are far less important; there are no obvious sex qualifications for many occupations, and, as Schaffer (1977) has expressed it, mother need not be a woman. The crucial questions then are, firstly, whether differences in role between the sexes are only historical residues or whether they represent enduringly important differences in temperament, personality, interests, attitudes and other cognitive abilities and styles; secondly, whether if such differences exist they represent principally innate, genetically (or hormonally) determined gender differentiation or principally learned sexual identity. As in any instance of a nature-nurture controversy, it is unlikely that a simple 'either/or' question is appropriate (see, for example, Archer and Lloyd, 1975); but the dichotomy between innate and learned determinants remains more alive in the study of sex differences (and also, for example, in the study of racial differences) because, as we have already said, the problem of defining sexual identity is not only physiological and psychological but also ideological and political (see, for example, Millett, 1970; Hartnett, Boden and Fuller, 1979).

There are a considerable number of beliefs about sex differences in temperament and personality, as well as in cognitive style; for reviews, see, e.g., Garai and Scheinfeld (1968); Hutt (1972); Maccoby and Jacklin (1974); Lloyd and Archer (1976). Boys, and men, are often said to be more active, more aggressive, dominant, competitive and achievement-oriented; girls, and women, are more anxious, timid and compliant, have lower self-esteem, and are more 'social' in orientation, more concerned with nurturance, co-operation and affiliation. As far as cognitive performance is concerned, it has been argued, for example, that girls excel in verbal ability and boys in visual–spatial, and also in mathematical, ability; that girls are superior in simple, repetitive clerical tasks (for example, digit-symbol substitution, a subtest of Wechsler intelligence tests – see Chapter 19) while boys are superior in more complex cognitive tasks and, above all, in creative achievement in 'real life', both in science and in the arts. While there are not sex differences in 'average intelligence' (not surprisingly, since intelligence tests are generally so standardized as to eliminate sex differences), sex differences in subtests which are related to the above characteristics have been reported. Further, Heim (1970b) has pointed out that although men and women do not differ in mean I.Q. the *spread* of scores differs, men showing more extremes both of high and of low I.Q.; and similarly, when women go to university they are more likely to gain second-class degrees, and less likely to gain firsts and thirds, than are men.

There is some evidence for all of these assertions, and also for differences in interests (for example, preferred play) in even quite young children; see, for example, Fling and Manosevitz (1972). However, the evidence in many cases is conflicting, and based on ill-controlled or otherwise unreliable studies. Maccoby and Jacklin (1974) concluded from an extensive review that relatively few sex differences are reliably documented – among those few, differences in verbal, visual–spatial and mathematical ability and in aggression; and later reviews have suggested even further qualifications upon their conclusions when methodological problems are taken into account (Block, 1976; Fairweather, 1976). Sex differences can be overestimated for various reasons: for example, there is a certain bias, on the part both of investigators and of publishers, against the publication of negative findings, so that positive sex-difference findings are likely to be over-represented in the published literature and failures to find, or to replicate, such differences neglected. They may also be underestimated by poor design of experiments, inadequate sample sizes and the assumption that a failure to show sex differences means that no such difference exists. Other complications include the importance of the experimenter's sex (girls, for example, have sometimes been found to show superiority in performance when the experimenter is a woman, while boys excel when the experimenter is a man), and, above all, the age of the subjects. On the whole, observed sex differences are minimal in the case of infants and very young children and increasingly evident with older children and with adults; it is not easy to say to what extent this is attributable to social learning and to what extent it reflects the enormous difficulties of gaining reliable test scores from very young subjects. Further, a sex difference at one age may be reversed at another, as appears to be the case with certain aspects of motor skill, in which girls tend to be superior to boys at younger ages, inferior to them at older ages; and a number of sex differences in motor and spatial skills have been shown to disappear rapidly with practice when, as happens quite rarely, practice trials are included in the experimental design. Thus, while there has in the past been considerable agreement as to the existence, and direction, of sex differences, the problems of experimental investigation and interpretation should lead us to treat these postulated differences with extreme caution.

One way of examining sex differences has been the construction of masculinity–femininity (or M–F) scales, based upon responses to questionnaire items on which men and women have been found to differ. The argument is that an individual's score on an M–F scale will measure sex-role orientation with more sensitivity than simply labelling him or her as biologically 'male' or 'female'; and such scales have been found to discriminate, for example, between passive and active male homosexuals (defined by their preference for the 'feminine' or the 'masculine' role, respectively, in sexual behaviour). Further, Bem (1974, 1977) has devised an *androgyny* scale, based upon separate subscales of masculinity and femininity, which measures the extent to which an individual possesses both 'masculine' and 'feminine' psychological characteristics; she has argued, as have Bakan (1966) and

Block (1973), that androgyny contributes positively to mental health. However, as Constantinople (1973) has pointed out, the assumptions generally made by M–F tests, either that masculinity and femininity represent opposite ends of a single dimension or that masculinity and femininity are *unitary* dimensions independent of each other, are almost certainly unwarranted. Much recent work has been directed at further analysis of the concepts of masculinity, femininity and androgyny and their behavioural correlates (see, e.g., Bem, Martyna and Watson, 1976), and at more precise definition of sex-role orientation, preference and adoption (see, e.g., Biller, Singer and Fullerton, 1969).

The origin of sex differences

It has been argued that from an evolutionary point of view some sex differences at least might be genetically linked, because they have led in the past to more successful reproduction: 'non-achieving' men and 'non-domestic' women would in past generations have been less likely to reproduce than those whose genetic endowment predisposed them to 'appropriate' sexual and parental behaviour. On the other hand, there are societies in which the 'traditional' modal sex roles are absent or reversed (see, e.g., Mead, 1949, 1961; Rosenberg and Sutton-Smith, 1972), so that biological differences cannot be held completely to determine differences in social role. Further, as Willerman (1979) has pointed out, 'one should not expect too much of the genetic differences between males and females. The two sexes have forty-five/forty-six of their chromosomes in common, and the one that differs (the Y) contains the smallest proportion of genetic material' (pp. 366–367).

It must also be borne in mind that the biology of sex differences is not simply a matter of genetic sex; the crucial factor is less chromosomal sex *per se* than its associated differences in hormonal activity. The essential contribution of the sex chromosomes is to determine the development of the gonads or sex glands, either ovaries or testes, at an early stage of prenatal development. The *gonads*, in turn, secrete the sex hormones, predominantly *androgens* (and in particular *testosterone*) in the case of a male, predominantly *estrogens* and *progesterone* in the case of a female; and hormonal secretion influences the development of internal and external sexual organs. The role of testosterone is particularly crucial, since it appears that the 'natural' form is the female; in the absence of testosterone a female will develop, even if the ovaries are removed at a very early stage of development. There are, rarely, individuals for whom genetic sex is not accurately expressed in prenatal (and, indeed, postnatal) hormonal activity, due to the presence of some other genetic defect; in extreme cases, because of the incongruous development of external sexual organs, an infant may be wrongly assigned, from the point of view of his or her genetic make-up, as a girl or as a boy (see, e.g., Hutt, 1972; Money and Ehrhardt, 1972). In the so-called *adreno-genital syndrome* (AGS), for example, excessive secretion of androgen results in the masculine development of external organs, though not of internal organs, in females; similar effects have occurred in the case of girls whose mothers were given synthetic androgens during pregnancy to prevent abortion. Studies of girls affected by AGS have indicated that they tend to be 'tomboyish' in their behaviour, preferring rough-and-tumble play with boys, and play with 'boys' toys', rather than play with dolls or centred around baby care and domestic activities; however, this finding has not always been supported (McGuire, Ryan and Omenn, 1975), and the girls studied, who had all been recognized, and reared, as female, appeared to regard themselves as female and to accept 'feminine' social roles. In another disorder, the *androgen insensitivity syndrome* (AIS), genetic males may be unresponsive to testosterone, with the resultant development of female external genitalia and incomplete development of female internal organs. Such infants are generally reared as girls, and it has been reported that in childhood and adulthood they appear conventionally 'feminine' in behaviour, interests and attitudes.

Cases such as this, in which sex has been assigned and the child therefore reared in accordance with external appearance and in contradiction of genetic sex, have supported the belief of many investigators that sexual identity is largely, though not completely, a matter of learning on the basis of differential rearing and socialization, and that the individual is psychologically neuter at birth (see, however, the argument for genetically and hormonally determined sexual bias at birth strongly advanced, for example, by Hutt, 1972). According to this belief, children learn *gender identity* – the 'private' experience of being male or female – and *gender role* – the public expression of sexually appropriate behaviour – through observational learning and social reinforcement from parents, other adults and peers. There is considerable evidence to encourage this view. As has already been mentioned, there is a general tendency for sex differences to become greater with increased age; this seems likely to be, at least largely, a reflection of socialization, with the reinforcement of appropriate behaviour and discouragement of the inappropriate. Certain aspects of family structure, and hence the opportunity for observational learning, also appear to influence the strength of sex-appropriate behaviour: for example, the presence or absence of a father, whether or not the mother works outside the home, and the sex and comparative age of siblings (see, for example, Lips and Colwill, 1978). Further, it is at least suggestive that sex-appropriate behaviour tends to emerge comparatively early in children of above-average intelligence, and comparatively late in mentally retarded children (Kohlberg and Zigler, 1967; Clark, 1963).

Certainly the material of sexual indoctrination is evident in our society. The formal education of girls in Western culture has traditionally been different from, and in crucial respects inferior to, that of boys (see, for example, Kamm's review (1965) of the history of girls' education in England): it is unwise to assume too readily that the distinction is now a thing of the past. Children's books, plays and films often enshrine sexual stereotypes, and toys, too, reinforce cultural expectations of sex-typed interests. At Christmas 1979, for example, the 'Lego' toy company was advertising train sets 'for boys six and over', and technical sets 'for Lego experts of nine and over' with the comment that 'older boys are fascinated by the way things work'. 'Girls six and over' were offered Lego dolls' houses, with which 'a girl can be a nurse in her own hospital, a hairdresser in her own salon or a mother in her own home'. While indoctrination by parents is unlikely to be so uncompromising, they tend to buy conventionally 'sex-appropriate' toys for their children and to reinforce, and model by their own behaviour, sex-appropriate occupations and attitudes while discouraging those seen as inappropriate. Some examples of such discrimination in child-rearing and socialization are discussed by Block (1973).

A striking example of the extent to which parental shaping can determine gender identity, quoted by Money and Ehrhardt (1972), concerned identical twin boys, one of whom suffered accidental ablation of the penis at a few months of age and was subsequently 'reassigned' as a girl, with appropriate surgical reconstruction and hormonal therapy. The parents, with professional guidance, implemented a programme of sex-appropriate rearing. Their new daughter was clothed in pretty dresses, frills, ribbons and bracelets: neatness and cleanness were encouraged more than with her brother, as was helping with the housework, while tomboyish activities were discouraged in favour of polite, 'ladylike' behaviour; and the children were taught the facts of sexual reproduction and of male and female societal roles, in such a way as to emphasize the advantages of masculinity to the boy and those of femininity to the girl. Reports of the children's progress (Money and Ehrhardt, 1972; Money, 1975) have so far suggested that the programme was producing its desired effect. The 'girl' was neater and tidier than her brother; she was interested in housework while he was not; she asked for (and received) dolls, a doll's house and a pram for Christmas while his choice was a garage with cars, petrol pumps and tools; she wanted, when she grew up, to be a doctor or perhaps a teacher, while the boy wanted to be a fireman or a policeman.

It is an interesting comment on the prevalence and importance of sexual stereotype that a programme of gender indoctrination was felt, no doubt rightly, to be essential for the child's future happiness; however, the conscious, systematic adoption of such a programme in (mercifully very rare) cases of obligatory sex reassignment is not necessarily indicative of the extent, or the determining role, of sexual bias in normal child rearing. Maccoby and Jacklin (1974) in fact found rather little evidence to support 'social learning' explanations of sex differences in such characteristics as aggression; boys are more physically aggressive, and more active and exploratory, than girls even at very young ages at which there is very little indication that parents are more protective towards girls, or more likely to prohibit overt aggression in them (although such biases are evident in parental attitudes towards school-age children). It seems more likely that early sex differences in aggression and activity are linked to differences in physical strength, and also in hormonal activity: the greater aggressiveness of males occurs in all human societies for which relevant data exist and also in non-human primates, and aggression in animals is related to level of androgen secretion (e.g. Harlow, 1965; Goy, 1968). Studies of the menstrual cycle in women provide further evidence that variation in sex-hormone secretion is associated with variation in mood and in the incidence of mood-related behaviour, such as visiting the doctor, entering hospital, and suicide (see Parlee, 1973).

Hutt (1972) has also pointed out that cases in which assigned sex is inconsistent with genetic sex can be seen as supporting a 'biological' explanation of sex differences, since it is generally when hormonal activity is inconsistent with genetic sex and consistent with assigned sex that such cases occur. Moreover, considerable doubt is cast on the all-dominant influence of rearing upon gender identity by a number of case histories recently reported by Imperato-McGinley et al. (1974). The individuals concerned, all genetic males sharing a common ancestor, have a genetic defect related to the conversion of testosterone which results in ambiguous secondary sexual characteristics at birth. They were reared as girls, until at puberty increased testosterone secretion produced the sexual characteristics of males: the voice

deepened, muscle mass increased, the testes descended and the penis enlarged. The girls became boys, and they appear to have accepted their new sex
roles, taking men's jobs and marrying women. Thus the sex of rearing does
not seem to have produced irreversible gender identity, although it is
arguable that in a community accustomed to the possibility of gender change
and prepared to accept it, sexual indoctrination will be less complete than in
more 'usual' societies.

Nevertheless, it has been argued that such cases provide evidence for
'preprogrammed maleness', brought about by the prenatal action of testosterone. It is apparent that the hypothalamus functions differently in males
and females, at least in its control (in conjunction with the pituitary gland)
of hormonal secretion, which is *tonic*, or relatively constant, in output level
for males and *phasic*, or cyclic, for females. There is also some evidence for a
'sex centre', whose structure is different for males and females, in the brains
of rats, although direct evidence of this kind has not been reported for other
species. Differential development in turn appears to be due to the action of
sex hormones, the critical period being early prenatal in the case of humans,
immediately postnatal in rats and mice (for reviews of the evidence, see Hutt,
1972; Money and Ehrhardt, 1972). Particularly in the case of humans, the
magnitude, and the implications, of sex differences in brain development
remain largely unknown.

It would clearly be unwise to argue that there are no biologically based
sex differences in behaviour other than those directly concerned with
reproduction or inevitably associated with physical strength. It would also be
absurd to ignore the importance of social influences which might readily
counteract, but are more likely to reinforce and exaggerate, any existing
differences and indeed to create others. Moreover, it is likely that biological
and social influences are not merely additive but interactive. The effect of a
given social influence (such as, say, parental protectiveness) may vary with
the sex of the individual concerned, and biological functioning (for example,
hormonal activity) can in turn be influenced by social environment; for
further examples, and discussion of an interactive model of sex differences,
see Archer and Lloyd (1975). The nature and extent of such interactions,
and the magnitude of psychological sex differences when unenhanced by
stereotype, are still very much open questions.

Race differences

The definition of race

The levels of classification with which we are primarily concerned in the discussion of race are first the species and second the subdivision of the species into subspecies or races. A species can be defined genetically as a breeding population whose members are capable through interbreeding of producing fertile offspring; horses and donkeys, for instance, belong to different species since the result of their interbreeding, the mule, is infertile. Members of the same species thus preserve a comparatively high degree of genetic similarity through breeding more or less exclusively with partners drawn from their own numbers. The comparative similarity of genetic background has morphological consequences, so that in terms of structural characteristics members of the same species are much more likely to resemble each other than to resemble members of a different species.

Within any one species there is clearly considerable geographical variation, and in different parts of the world members of the same species exhibit variations of size, colour and of other morphological characteristics, which have been extensively documented by animal taxonomists. One approach that has been taken to the classification of intra-species variation is the development of the concept of 'subspecies', originally considered to be a new species in the process of being born (see Ehrlich and Feldman, 1977). One of the earliest definitions of a subspecies was provided by Mayr (1942), who stated that 'the subspecies, or geographic race, is a geographically localized subdivision of the species, which differs genetically and taxonomically from other subdivisions of the species'. However, as zoologists began to employ the subspecies classification so the number of subspecies proliferated. For example, according to Gould (1980), in a monograph published in 1942 seventy-eight subspecies of the Hawaiian tree snail (*Achatinella apexfulva*) were identified, with an additional sixty 'microgeographic races', a term reserved for units which could not be clearly assigned to a particular subspecies; and according to Ehrlich and Feldman (1977), more than 150 subspecies of the North American pocket gopher (*Thomomys bottae*) have been named.

Since members of different subspecies can successfully interbreed, the result being 'hybrids', a subspecies cannot be a fixed and finite taxonomic category and, although the concept of subspecies has survived, it has not been immune from criticism. Wilson and Brown (1953), for example, argued that intra-species variations in morphological characteristics were highly˙discordant and hence that the number of subspecies identified within a given species was, with few exceptions, a function of the particular characteristic or set of characteristics in which the taxonomist was interested. Inevitably, therefore, there is a certain degree of arbitrariness in the classification of subspecies and Gould (1980) has suggested that the concept is unhelpful and, indeed, liable to be misleading, in the investigation of intra-species variation.

The terms 'subspecies' and 'race' are virtually synonymous, and hence the criticisms levelled at the concept of subspecies can also be applied to the concept of race (see Brace, 1964; Ehrlich and Feldman, 1977; Livingstone, 1962). Taxonomists generally divide the human species into geographical races and subraces, such as local races or populations and microraces (see, for example, Garn, 1971). A geographical race is a collection of breeding populations, which has historically been separated from other collections of breeding populations by major geographical barriers such as oceans, mountain ranges or deserts, and has thus been confined to a particular geographical region. As a result comparatively little interbreeding has taken place with members of other geographical races, and the breeding populations within a particular geographical race have come to resemble one another more closely in morphological characteristics than they resemble breeding populations drawn from other geographical races.

The Australian continent, for example, was the last continent to be settled by man, some time between 25,000 B.C. and 8,000 B.C. The origins of these early settlers are uncertain, but it is probable that they came from South-East Asia. During the various Ice Ages, the last of which ended in about 10,000 B.C., the eastern border of the Asian mainland was formed by what is called the Wallace Divide (after Darwin's contemporary A. R. Wallace), a deep channel in the ocean bed about thirty miles wide, which runs through the Makassar Straits between Borneo and the Celebes and extends southwards between Bali and Lambok in present-day Indonesia. Thus comparatively advanced marine technology would have been required, even during periods of extreme glaciation, when sea-levels were much reduced, for settlements to have been established in Australia. After about 10,000 B.C., when sea-levels had risen again as the climate became warmer, the population of Australia remained largely isolated for some 450 generations until the arrival of European settlers, mostly British convicts and their guards, in 1788. The population of Australia at this time has been estimated to be around 215,000 (see McEvedy and Jones, 1978) and since the economy was predominantly based on hunting, fishing and plant-gathering, it had probably never risen much above this level. Breeding populations of Australian aborigines were thus isolated from other breeding populations for a considerable period of time and, as a result, differ both morphologically and genetically (see Garn, 1971) from other racial groups, such as the Amerindians, the original inhabitants of North and South America. But within geographical races, there are 'natural' breeding populations or local races, such as the South African bushmen, where the barriers to interbreeding with members of other local populations may be as much social or cultural as geographical, and also micro-races, or 'significant pockets of variation' (Gottesman, 1968), as in the remoter parts of Wales or Scotland, where assortative mating may have occurred as a result of low mobility occasioned by local environmental conditions. Breeding populations differ among themselves in several respects, for example in the frequency of different blood groups, in the incidence of taste blindness for certain chemical substances, in fingerprint indices, in the susceptibility to various rare hereditary diseases, in estimated gene frequencies, as well as in skin colour, dental structure, head and nose shape, hair type and average height. A considerable amount of evidence concerning genetic differences among breeding populations has been accumulated in recent years (see Garn, 1971) and when combined with the wealth of data relating to morphological differences (see Baker, 1974) provides the basis for the classification of races. Nevertheless, different authorities provide different accounts of the number of geographical races into which the human species is supposedly divided (see Table 22.1), a state of affairs that is more

Table 22.1
Taxonomy of human geographical races, according to the authorities cited.

from Baker (1974), p. 625	from Osborne et al (1978), p. xvii	from Garn (1971), p. 155
Australid	Australoid	Australian
Europid	Caucasoid	European
Negrid	Negroid	African
Khoisanid	Capoid	Asiatic
Mongolid	Mongoloid	American
Indianid		Indian
		Melanesian
		Polynesian
		Micronesian

or less inevitable, given that racial classifications depend upon a taxonomist's judgement of the number of discrete groupings that can be derived from a very large selection of, for the most part, continuous variables.

Whatever biological foundations the concept of race may possess, and these remain somewhat controversial, the racial classification of human beings, usually on the basis of such visible characteristics as skin colour, invariably has social consequences. In almost all societies, different racial groups have, historically, enjoyed differential access to social rewards, with the result that on virtually any index of socio-economic status there are, on average, large differences between them. In Western industrialized societies such as the United States and Britain these differences are, of course, especially marked between whites and blacks. In the following section we examine race differences in behaviour, with particular emphasis upon black–white differences.

Race differences in behaviour

It is clear from studies of psychological differences between racial groups, in particular between American whites and American blacks, that, with very few exceptions, there has been 'a shocking lack of precision in defining "race"' (Dreger and Miller, 1968). As Dreger and Miller pointed out, in a review of comparative psychological studies of Negroes and Whites in the United States between 1959 and 1965,

Most investigators identify their groups by an implicit acceptance of self-designation and community designation of individuals as 'White' or 'Negro' ... Very few investigators use even simple color tops, color cards, or color wheels for skin colors. Few employ other specified characteristics than skin color. None utilize blood-type gene pools, or genetic patterns underlying certain morphological characteristics.

Dreger and Miller further commented that

We would not go so far as to say that all racial comparisons are vitiated by this grand carelessness in defining an independent variable, for possibly sociological isolation has tended to allow 'averaging out', so that groups designated 'Negro' and 'White' probably tend to be more or less what they purport to be. Nevertheless, investigations presuming to assess the effects of *genetic* differences on performance but failing to take obvious steps to identify genes (and not merely phenotypes) would be laughed out of court in any other field of genetic investigation (p. 25, their italics).

Although Dreger and Miller's strictures were confined to the set of studies mentioned above it seems probable that many of the subsequently conducted investigations of race differences in behaviour have employed similar procedures, involving self or community designation of racial membership, for racial classification. Although these procedural deficiencies should be borne in mind when evaluating possible explanations of race differences in behaviour, it does appear, nevertheless, that there are both genetic and behavioural differences among groups of people classified as belonging to different racial groups, such as Caucasoid, Negroid, Mongoloid and so on (see Table 22.1). However, it is unclear just what part, if any, is played by genetic factors in the determination of behavioural differences, and the behavioural differences themselves are far from being consistent in direction; in some kinds of behavioural tests, for example, Negroids are superior to Caucasoids and Mongoloids, in others Mongoloids are superior to Caucasoids and Negroids and in others still Caucasoids are superior to Negroids and Mongoloids (see Dreger and Miller, 1968; Lynn, 1978; and Noble, 1978, for examples). But undoubtedly the area of investigation which has caused the greatest furore in recent years is that of race differences in intelligence between white and black Americans and it is with this topic that the remainder of this section is concerned.

The population of the United States has long been a melting pot, in which the main ingredients are: 1) the original inhabitants, the North American Indians, whose ancestors probably crossed from Siberia around 10,000 B.C.; 2) a slave population of around 500,000 imported from Africa between 1550 and 1850; and 3) successive waves of European immigrants, totalling altogether about 42,000,000 between 1500 and 1975 (these figures are taken from McEvedy and Jones, 1978). In 1975 the population of the continental United States, excluding Hawaii, was 210,000,000, of whom 20,000,000 were black Americans. As noted earlier, one of the ways in which breeding populations differ is in terms of gene frequencies, and certain genes are found to occur with differential frequency in Caucasian and African black populations (see Cavalli-Sforza and Bodmer, 1971). From information of this kind it is possible to calculate the degree of Caucasian genetic admixture in American black populations and hence to estimate the extent to which interbreeding has taken place between American whites and American blacks. Such calculations yield, on average, an admixture percentage of around 21 per cent, although there are substantial regional differences, ranging from 9 per cent in the Deep South to 27·3 per cent on the West Coast (see Reed, 1969). Since, on average, an individual shares 25 per cent of his or her genes with a single grandparent, the average Caucasian admixture found in American blacks can be viewed, very roughly, as being virtually equivalent to having one white grandparent (see Willerman, 1979), although the same percentage admixture could be achieved in other ways. Although the degree and range of Caucasian admixture in American blacks further complicate the practical problem of racial classification in studies of race differences in behaviour, it does not appear that there is any significant relationship between direct measures of genetic admixture and mental ability in black and white American schoolchildren (Loehlin, Vandenberg and Osborne, 1975).

The measurement and nature of intelligence or general mental ability were outlined in Chapters 19 and 20 and it is clear that measures of intelligence, such as the intelligence quotient or I.Q., derived from a number of different tests, are quite strongly related to measures of academic achievement, as indeed they were originally designed to be, but somewhat less strongly related to occupational status and less strongly related still to income level and measures of job proficiency (see Block and Dworkin, 1977, and Jencks, 1972, for further discussion). I.Q. cannot therefore be regarded as being the sole determinant of access to social rewards and benefits (Loehlin, Lindzey and Spuhler, 1975) although it is certainly of some importance and some psychologists would argue that its determining influence is considerable: see, for example, Jensen (1969). It is just possible, however, that if the current rate of technological change is accelerated, or even maintained, then I.Q. may come to play a more crucial role in 'life success' than it appears to do at present (see Herrnstein, 1971, 1973, for a development of this argument and Chomsky, 1977, for a critique).

I.Q. scores typically vary among socio-economic classes and among racial groups. According to a review by Lynn (1978), international comparisons of intelligence test performance suggest that, in general, Mongoloid populations originating in Japan and China, and Caucasoid populations from Northern Europe, obtain the highest average I.Q. scores. A sizeable literature also exists which indicates that, on average, white Americans achieve higher mean I.Q. scores than do black Americans. These differences become apparent from about three to four years of age. There are, however, noticeable regional variations (perhaps explicable in terms of selective migration), with the difference in mean I.Q. scores being greater in rural areas and in the South and being smaller in urban areas and in the north and west of the United States. Reviews of this evidence can be found in Dreger and Miller (1968), Loehlin, Lindzey and Spuhler (1975), Shuey (1966), and Willerman (1979).

The existence of such differences in the mean I.Q. scores of American blacks and American whites has long been recognized and has been variously interpreted. One set of interpretations, the environmentalist viewpoint, emphasizes the importance of socio-economic and cultural differences in accounting for the mean difference in I.Q. scores between black and white Americans. On average, the socio-economic status (generally defined in terms of the occupation, educational level and income of the head of the household) of black Americans is lower than that of white Americans. Socio-economic status is known to be moderately correlated with I.Q. Thus a difference in mean I.Q. between blacks and whites could be the result of differences in socio-economic status. However, a mean difference in I.Q., though slightly reduced, is still obtained when socio-economic status is controlled for and tends to become greater with increasing socio-economic status, even in pre-school children (Broman, Nichols and Kennedy, 1975). But it has been argued not only that there are, on average, differences between blacks and whites in terms of socio-economic status, but also that blacks are effectively assigned to a different caste, and that caste differences are not removed when the socio-economic status of blacks and whites is equated. The awareness of belonging to a different caste, and the consequent prejudice and discrimination, probably emerge quite early in life, and are almost certainly reflected in the differences between black and white American children on measures of own-race preference and self-esteem (see Shuey, 1978, for a comprehensive review). These factors may exert some influence on I.Q. scores, even in young children, for example by affecting motivation in the test situation or perhaps, less straightforwardly, through an indirect effect on patterns of parent–child interaction, although such conjectures are merely speculative. For further discussion of socio-economic status, culture and subculture in relation to intelligence, see Vernon (1979).

If poorer environments depress I.Q. scores, and it is probable that they exert at least a marginal effect, and if American blacks are more likely to be exposed to conditions of social deprivation, that is, to poorer environments, as they almost certainly are, then it is possible that the effects of such conditions increase with age, resulting in a cumulative deficit which would be reflected in a proportional increase with age in the difference between the I.Q. scores of black and white Americans. The cumulative deficit hypothesis was originally put forward in the 1920s to explain the proportional, and absolute, decline in I.Q. with age in disadvantaged white children, both in Britain and America, but the evidence relevant to the hypothesis from comparative studies of American blacks and whites is equivocal. Jensen (1974a), for example, found no evidence to support the hypothesis of a cumulative deficit in I.Q. scores in American black children in a study carried out in the university

town of Berkeley, California, but did obtain evidence favouring the hypothesis in a study conducted in rural Georgia. However, the interpretation of
both of these studies has been questioned by Kamin (1978) and in general
the cumulative deficit hypothesis, at least with respect to I.Q. scores obtained
by American blacks, does not appear to be particularly well supported.

Environmental interpretations of race differences in I.Q. have also focused
upon the nature of the intelligence tests employed and upon the testing situation itself, and have suggested that because of cultural differences between
blacks and whites it is inappropriate to use tests originally standardized on
white populations in order to obtain measures of intelligence from blacks. In
other words, most standard intelligence tests are culturally biased against
blacks, with the result that the mean I.Q. difference between whites and
blacks will be exaggerated. For example, as noted in Chapter 17 some
linguists have drawn attention to the fact that many American blacks use a
dialect, known as Nonstandard Negro English or NNE, which differs from
standard English in several respects. It is possible, therefore, that the
presentation of an intelligence test in standard English would adversely affect
the performance of blacks. But in a study comparing performance at two
versions of the Stanford–Binet Intelligence Test (see Chapter 19), one presented in standard English and the other in NNE, Quay (1971) reported no
difference in the I.Q. scores obtained on the two versions by black pre-school
children. Furthermore, whites generally perform better than blacks on non-
verbal tests of intelligence, such as the Raven's Matrices Test, where, presumably, linguistic problems do not arise. The mean difference in I.Q. score
obtained from non-verbal tests of intelligence tends to be as great as, or
greater than, the mean difference obtained from verbal intelligence tests
(Jensen, 1974b). Black Americans also tend to perform relatively better on
the verbal scales of standard intelligence tests, such as the Wechsler (see
Chapter 19) than on the non-verbal or performance scales (see Loehlin,
Lindzey and Spuhler, 1975). In general, the evidence for any systematic
cultural bias against American blacks in standard intelligence tests is not as
strong as it might be (see Jensen, 1974b, for a review), although aspects of
the testing situation itself, such as the examiner's race, may affect white and
black examinees differentially (see Dreger and Miller, 1968) and it is possible
that the motivational level of black examinees may, in general, be lower.
However, when tests are used for predictive purposes, for example to select
job applicants, and when there is an average difference in the test scores of
two populations from which the individuals to be selected are drawn, then
other problems of test bias are likely to arise, in that tests which are 'fair'

to the individual, are liable to be 'unfair' to the group, and *vice versa* (see Schmidt and Hunter, 1974). Depending upon which kind of test is chosen, individual members from one or other of the two populations will be 'disadvantaged'.

The environmental approach implies that because of their experience of cultural deprivation, American black children have failed to acquire several of the skills or attitudes which are prerequisites for the attainment of their academic potential during their school years. In the 1960s a number of 'intervention programmes', the best-known probably being 'Project Headstart', were established in the United States, with the aim of rectifying this state of affairs. In 1969, Jensen wrote a paper for the *Harvard Educational Review*, in which the effects of these intervention programmes were evaluated and reasons for their apparent failure examined. Jensen noted that school achievement was related to I.Q. and that mean I.Q. scores were lower for blacks than for whites and, on the basis of a detailed examination of the available evidence, suggested that I.Q. was highly heritable (in his view about 80 per cent of the variation in I.Q. scores being associated with variation in genetic factors). He concluded that the bulk of the difference in mean I.Q. scores between blacks and whites was attributable to genetic sources and that, in consequence, intervention programmes designed to 'boost I.Q. and school achievement' were virtually bound to be unsuccessful. Jensen's thesis was immediately attacked, often in virulently abusive terms (see the preface to Jensen, 1972) and the 'I.Q. controversy' (see Block and Dworkin, 1977) began to rage. Some of the major themes of this controversy are now briefly summarized.

One of the fundamental questions about I.Q. scores is the extent to which they can be said to be inherited, that is, the value of the heritability component of the I.Q. in a particular population of individuals. Population geneticists use the term 'heritability' to refer to the extent to which the variation in a particular measurable characteristic or trait in a particular population at a particular time can be associated with variations in genotype (see Chapter 3) among the individuals comprising that population. The simplest way of expressing a heritability value for a particular population is in terms of the ratio of the total genotypic variance in the trait under investigation to the total phenotype variance and the resulting coefficient can vary between 0 (zero heritability) and 1 (maximum heritability). Discussions of the procedures for calculating heritability coefficients and of the assumptions underlying these procedures can be found in Fuller and Thompson (1960) and in Loehlin, Lindzey and Spuhler (1975).

Heritability is thus the property of a particular population at a particular time, and not that of a particular characteristic or trait. The heritability coefficient for a particular trait may well be different for different populations at a particular time, and for the same population at different times. As far as the heritability of I.Q. is concerned, the major source of data has been the relationships between the I.Q. scores of different members of the same family and, in particular, the comparatively few studies of identical twins reared in the same or in different environments (see Chapter 3). Reviews of these studies propose heritability coefficients ranging very widely from around 0·8 (Jensen, 1969) to around zero (Kamin, 1974), with most estimates falling somewhere in between these extremes. Most of these studies have been conducted with white populations and the results of the few studies of the heritability of I.Q. in blacks are inconclusive. Jensen's argument has been heavily criticized (see, for example, Block and Dworkin, 1977) and while Kamin's painstaking analysis has exposed the weaknesses of much of the research taken to support the hereditarian point of view, his arguments, too, have been criticized, in detail, as being too one-sided (see, for example, Mackintosh, 1975). One can only conclude that the heritability coefficient for I.Q., in both white and black populations, probably lies somewhere between zero and 0·8, a range so wide as to render speculation useless; further, the values for whites and blacks may well be different. The point has been made on several occasions, perhaps most forcibly by Kempthorne (1978), that the data presently available do not permit any satisfactory estimate to be made of the relative contributions of genetic and environmental variation to the variation of I.Q. scores. In the case of plants and animals, selective breeding experiments can be conducted which allow a reasonable conclusion to be drawn concerning the relative contribution of genetic and environmental variations to phenotypic variation. Such experiments have not yet been conducted with human beings and are not likely to be. Thus genetic factors, and for that matter many environmental factors, cannot be manipulated to enable a chain of causal inference to be established concerning the relative contributions of heredity and environment to I.Q. scores. The only experiments which can be conducted with respect to human intelligence, and they are far from being ideal, are intervention programmes, which, at least in some cases, have produced initially promising results (see, for example, Cowen, 1973; Heber *et al.*, 1972; Stanley, 1972). Even if it were the case that I.Q. possessed a large heritability component, this would not preclude either increasing the mean level of I.Q. or reducing the mean difference in I.Q. score between two populations through the manipulation of environmental influences.

Age differences

The nature of ageing

The study of age differences is obviously concerned, in principle, with hypotheses of change and of continuity over the life span. Psychologists have paid great attention to child development, and this attention is reflected in several of the chapters of this book; interest in adult development and ageing, and more generally in life-span developmental psychology, has been much less marked, although in recent years it has increased considerably. The relative neglect of post-maturity development is perhaps, at least in part, because ageing has traditionally, and popularly, been regarded not as the gradual realization of potential but rather as a depressing matter of declining cognitive ability, ossification of attitudes and disintegration of personality leading to senility, disease and death. We shall see that this view is over-pessimistic; there are many ways of conceptualizing adult age differences, only one of which is in terms of general decline. Many psychological functions remain stable (and indeed may improve) throughout adulthood, at least until very old age, and others can be described as developing in the direction of 'decrement-with-compensation'.

A frequent observation in the psychological study of ageing is that very high intersubject variability in performance is a feature of older age groups, much more so than for younger subjects; clearly, chronological age, measured in terms of years since birth, is an extremely crude measure of ageing since different speeds and patterns of adult development characterize different individuals. Some investigators have suggested that what is needed is a measure not of chronological age but rather of *functional* age, or the position occupied by an individual on his own 'life-trajectory', with perhaps different estimates of functional age for different psychological characteristics (e.g. Nuttall, 1972; see also Wohlwill, 1970). It has also been suggested more specifically that the important measure of age is not distance from birth but rather distance from death, the most explicit statement in this view being the *terminal drop* hypothesis advanced, for example, by Kleemeier (1962) and by Riegel and Riegel (1972). This hypothesis states that decline in cognitive functioning is principally associated with the approach of death – that is, with declining health and 'organic disintegration' which may occur over the last few years of life – rather than with gradual ageing; when gradual changes in performance are observed with increasing age this simply reflects the gradually increasing number of subjects at older ages who are experiencing terminal drop and who therefore exhibit comparatively sudden decline. In support of this hypothesis it has been shown that 'non-survivors' – subjects who die within five years of testing – typically have lower scores than 'survivors' (e.g. Riegel and Riegel, 1972) and that distance from death is at least sometimes a powerful predictor of performance, although the evidence, and its interpretation, are not altogether clearcut; see, e.g., Siegler (1975). The greatest practical problem of adopting distance from death as the independent variable in age research is obviously that it necessitates a delay of years, until a substantial number of subjects have died, before data can be analysed and the result published; thus as a matter of expediency, if not of logic, distance from birth is almost universally adopted as the criterion of ageing.

Even if distance from birth were perfectly (inversely) correlated, across the population, with distance from death, its ambiguities as a measure would remain. What precisely is meant by 'normal' ageing? Which changes with advancing age are 'normal' and which are pathological? There are various biological theories of ageing, although none is entirely convincing, and a good deal is known about neurological and sensory changes which characterize old age; see, for example, the relevant chapters in Birren and Schaie (1977). Nevertheless, it also appears that performance decrements in old age may be largely the result of environmental and social factors, life experiences and illness or other physical changes (for example, sensory deprivation resulting from impairment of vision, hearing and other senses) which are in principle reversible or at any rate remediable. As Siegler (1976) has put it:

Many of the problems of aging are problems of poverty, chronic disease, unemployment, widowhood, etc. These problems are not the exclusive property of the elderly, and remedies proven effective for younger populations may also prove effective for older persons. Often, what is unique about the elderly is not *the* problem; rather, there are multiple problems, and many of the resources available for younger persons (through jobs, family members) are not available to older persons (pp. 103–4).

It is a tragic consequence of 'ageism' that changes, in particular impairments, in functioning which would provoke immediate investigation, treatment and perhaps cure if they occurred in young people may be dismissed as the inevitable concomitants of old age and therefore left untreated in the elderly.

In this brief account of the psychology of ageing we shall concentrate upon some findings relating chiefly to cognitive, and in particular intellectual, ability and to attitudes and personality; for more complete coverage see, e.g., Bromley (1974); Siegler (1976); Birren and Schaie (1977). However, it is an essential preliminary to point out that the study of age changes is beset by methodological problems. This is true to some extent of all developmental studies, including those concerned solely with behavioural changes through infancy and childhood; but certain problems are particularly great in the study of adulthood and old age because of the very considerable time span which requires investigation. We have already indicated, for example, that the definition of 'normal ageing' can be problematic; other difficulties, more specifically concerned with the design of investigations, will be the concern of the following section.

Methodological problems

Most studies of adult age differences have involved the *cross-sectional* method of investigation, in which groups of adults differing in age are compared, with respect to some aspect of performance, at the same point in time. This method clearly may provide information concerning *age differences*, but it is less clear to what extent it can provide information concerning *age changes*, or the modifications which advancing age brings about in the individual (Schaie, 1977). In particular the cross-sectional method confounds *age* with so-called *cohort* differences: the age groups differ not only in chronological age *per se* but also, obviously, in the era in which their members were born and the historical, social and cultural experiences through which they have lived. More often than not, such cohort differences are likely to depress the comparative performance of older age groups. For example, the nutritional, social and educational early environment of a cohort born in 1900 may be generally inferior to that of a cohort born in 1960, with a resultant advantage for twenty-year-olds over eighty-year-olds in, say, intelligence test performance in 1980.

To some extent specific cohort differences can be eliminated – for example, by selecting subject samples equivalent in educational level; and where such controls are applied, age differences tend to be smaller than are otherwise observed (e.g. Green, 1969). However, one problem with matching procedures is that the selected sample of older subjects may be less representative of its population than that of younger subjects. Other aspects of differential experience, and reaction to that experience, which might be thought to be part of the definition of a cohort (e.g. Rosow, 1978), are difficult or impossible to control, and indeed it has sometimes been suggested that to do so would be to some extent an artificial exercise.

Nevertheless, it is generally acknowledged that the interpretation of age differences obtained by cross-sectional studies is problematic, and in particular that the cross-sectional method is likely to exaggerate age-related changes (although it may also underestimate them, since particularly in older age groups it tends to be more able, more healthy and more motivated individuals who make themselves available for testing; see Riegel and Riegel, 1972). The obvious alternative is a *longitudinal* method, in which the same subjects are retested throughout at least a considerable part of the adult life span. The practical difficulties of such research are apparent: the study must continue for years and perhaps involve different generations (and cohorts) of testers, an adequate number of subjects must remain available for retesting, and the findings are susceptible to so-called 'secular' or time-of-testing effects: that is, historical, social and cultural changes which might affect performance at different times of testing and thus become confounded with age. Perhaps the most serious problem is that of selective dropout or 'subject attrition'. Not all subjects tested at one point in time will be available for retesting, say twenty years later; in many cases those who drop out are likely to do so because of ill health or 'terminal drop' (and indeed death) and low motivation or low interest in being tested, with the result that a sampling bias favourable to the older testing age is introduced. Further, subjects who remain available for testing tend to be those who initially obtained high scores, at least in studies of intellectual performance (e.g. Siegler and Botwinick, 1979), and there is some evidence that these more able individuals show less age change, at least into very old age, than the less able, although contrary data have sometimes been reported (e.g. Owens, 1959); for a review, see Botwinick (1977). Thus longitudinal studies may well underestimate age changes while cross-sectional studies tend to overestimate them; and in fact the decline in performance found in cross-sectional studies is generally greater than that shown in longitudinal studies, which have sometimes found no decline or even an improvement in performance with increasing age.

Schaie (e.g. 1965, 1977) has suggested a type of research design which goes some way towards avoiding the major problems of cross-sectional and longitudinal approaches; this type is often referred to generally as the *cross-sequential* method (although Schaie in fact distinguishes among cross-sequential, cohort-sequential and time-sequential designs). The essence of this method is that subjects from different cohorts are tested at successive times, so that the effects of age and cohort – and, with some additional design features, time of testing – can be disentangled. For example, a group of twenty-year-olds may be tested in 1950; in 1970 they are retested (now at age forty), and so are a group of contemporary twenty-year-olds; in 1990 both groups will again be tested (at the respective ages of sixty and forty) as will yet another group of contemporary twenty-year-olds. For a diagrammatic representation of this design (a cohort-sequential design) and the types of comparisons it makes possible, see Table 22.2; for further discussion of cross-sequential and related designs, see Schaie (1977) and Palmore (1978).

This type of procedure, like others, has its problems, many of which are shared with the longitudinal approach. For example, repeated testing of subjects produces practice effects which need to be controlled by additional design features; studies still stretch over impracticable lengths of years, unless the age intervals tapped are so small that they may yield very little evidence of age changes; selective subject attrition remains a serious difficulty. Nevertheless, the comparatively few studies which do employ cross-sequential designs contribute very significantly to our understanding of data derived from cross-sectional and longitudinal studies.

Finally, there remain other problems of methodology, such as the comparability of motivation for subjects of different ages and the 'age-fairness' of the tests used (similar to the problem of culture-fairness when race differences

Table 22.2
Example of a cohort-sequential research design. (After Troll, 1975, p.10)

Time 1	Time 2	Time 3
		Group 1c, Survivors of 1a, who are now 60-year-olds
	Group 1b Survivors of 1a, who are now 40-year-olds	Group 2b Survivors of 2a, who are now 40-year-olds
Group 1a 20-year-olds	Group 2a 20-year-olds	Group 3 20-year-olds

Cross-sectional comparisons:	Groups 2a and 1b
	Groups 3, 2b, and 1c
Longitudinal comparisons:	Groups 1a, 1b, and 1c
	Groups 2a and 2b
Cultural-change comparisons:	Groups 1a, 2a, and 3
	Groups 1b and 2b

are investigated: see pp. 604–5). In the assessment of intelligence, for example, certain types of test such as picture arrangement and digit-symbol substitution may be more remote from everyday experience, and much less recently practised, for older than for younger subjects, and specific items in vocabulary and general information tests may be more appropriate for one age group than for another. There is of course the logical difficulty that in attempting to ensure 'age-fairness' by eliminating certain types of test from his assessment battery, an investigator may in fact be eliminating the aspects of performance in which real age differences lie. Such problems cannot ultimately be solved purely by the redesign of investigations; they can be solved only, if at all, by a consensus of definition as to those aspects of performance change which are to be 'taken seriously', or considered conceptually significant, and those which are not.

Cognitive abilities

Our discussion of age-related changes in cognitive ability will be chiefly concerned with intellectual ability, as measured by such intelligence tests as the Primary Mental Abilities (P.M.A.) test (Thurstone and Thurstone, 1949) and the Wechsler Adult Intelligence Scale or W.A.I.S., discussed in Chapter 19. Decline in intelligence-test performance has traditionally been associated with age; indeed, early studies seemed to show a decline from the late 'teens or early twenties onward (Wechsler, 1958). However, later studies, both cross-sectional and longitudinal, tend to show *increasing* I.Q. scores throughout early adulthood, with decline appearing only after the mid forties and reaching significant proportions only after sixty or even seventy years of age (Schaie, 1958; Doppelt and Wallace, 1955). Moreover, when decline occurs it is by no means general. There is, rather, a 'classic ageing pattern': verbal sub-tests (for example, vocabulary or similarities tests) decline much less sharply than performance sub-tests (such as picture arrangement and digit-symbol substitution). This pattern appears even if older and younger subjects are matched on total W.A.I.S. score; in that case older subjects have been found superior to younger ones on verbal items and inferior on performance items (Harwood and Naylor, 1971).

It has been argued that the classic ageing pattern principally reflects not a decline in intellectual abilities but rather a decline in speed of performance; there is considerable evidence that response speed generally declines with age (Welford, 1965), and performance sub-tests are very heavily timed. However, this is unlikely to be the whole explanation of the pattern, since some investigators have removed time limits from various sub-tests, and have reported that age differences are not reduced to zero, may not be reduced at all (Doppelt and Wallace, 1955) and may for some sub-tests even be increased (Schaie, Rosenthal and Perlman, 1953). A more likely explanation may lie in the distinction between *fluid* and *crystallized* intelligence (see Chapter 20). Factor analytic studies have shown that older subjects may be equivalent, or superior, to young ones in tests which tap accumulated knowledge and acculturation, and in which, in Birren's (1952) words, 'their performance is determined by what they already know rather than by what new information they can elicit from the test situation' (p. 404); they are likely to be inferior in tests heavily loaded on fluid intelligence, reflecting learning capacity not dependent upon previous learning but more directly upon the neural and other physiological structures which support intellectual functioning and which may be held to deteriorate with age (e.g. Horn and Cattell, 1967). However, the relations among crystallized intelligence, fluid intelligence and age require further elucidation.

There is considerable evidence that learning may be impaired in the elderly (Arenberg and Robertson-Tchabo, 1977), as may memory (see Chapter 16), although the precise nature of the deficit, or deficits, involved is not always clear. Various factors may operate to depress performance: for example, response slowness; response reluctance; a failure to use efficient learning strategies, which can, however, be adopted when appropriate instructions are given; and increased susceptibility to interference. Such factors, many of which are important also for memory functioning, suggest that decreased ability may reflect difficulties in *performance* rather than reduced learning capacity *per se*; this distinction between capacity and performance may also be very important in assessing age changes (or, more often, age differences) in intelligence-test scores.

Finally, it must be reiterated that the methodological problems mentioned in earlier sections are of crucial relevance to the interpretation of age-related intelligence differences. For example, a number of studies have found that age differences contribute less to score variance than do educational differences (e.g. Birren and Morrison, 1961; Green, 1969), and cross-sequential analyses (e.g. Schaie and Labouvie-Vief, 1974; Schaie and Parham, 1977) have indicated that generational (or cohort) effects are greater than age effects, at least until the late sixties, while age changes are more influential, but still not always substantial, thereafter. Such considerations as selective drop-out, the 'age-fairness' of test items and experimental tasks, and the health and motivation of subjects clearly require to be taken into account.

The existence and extent of adult age changes in intellectual functioning remain a matter of considerable debate (see, for example, Horn and Donaldson, 1976; Baltes and Schaie, 1976), and it is unwise at present to accept too readily any precise estimate of the magnitude of cognitive decline with age. Probably it is most reasonable to conclude that intellectual decline does occur in most people of advanced age, but that the decline is typically smaller, more partial, and later in onset than has often been assumed.

Moreover, while decline in intellectual abilities may be found in closely controlled tests and laboratory settings it is less likely to be in evidence in 'everyday life' where it is often possible to compensate for lessened ability and to preserve performance. Rabbitt (1977) concluded from a review of age changes in problem solving and creative ability that:

... in considering the real-life performance of older people, it is naïve to regard them as passive victims of a cognitive degeneration of which they are helplessly unaware. On the contrary, older people may be said to both conserve and to exploit their intellectual resources more fully than do the young, to have a more subtle perception of points at which the complexity of decisions exceeds their capacities, and to thereby avoid unnecessary blunders ... the study of performance with age is not merely the study of *decrements in performance*. Unless we recognize that it is also the study of *adaptation* to decrements of performance, we shall completely miss the point (p. 623).

Rabbitt's conclusion was based chiefly upon the study of gifted older individuals in professional employment, and as we have already seen there is some evidence that age is kinder to the initially more able. Nevertheless, it is unlikely that recognition of one's limitations and of the necessity, and the means, of compensating for them is the sole prerogative of the intellectually gifted and professionally trained.

Personality and attitudes

Studies of personality changes with age are hampered by the problems, already discussed, of defining and investigating age changes and also by the problems, discussed in Chapters 19, 20 and 21, of defining and measuring 'personality'; moreover, it is not altogether clear that a given personality trait has the same significance, or that constellations of traits have the same inter-relations, at different ages. The relation between personality and age has been studied from a variety of conceptual positions, using many different tools of measurement and with reference to many different personality dimensions.

We can mention only a few findings here; for reviews, see, for example, Troll (1975); Kalish (1975); and Neugarten (1977).

One set of somewhat related findings which has emerged with some consistency from a number of studies is that older individuals are characterized by increased passivity, 'interiority' or inner-directedness, and introversion (see Chapter 20). Such findings helped to give rise to the *disengagement* theory first proposed by Cumming and Henry (1961), who argued that later life is characterized by mutual withdrawal of the individual from social interaction (though not from societal values) and of society from the individual. Cumming and Henry further stated that degree of disengagement is positively related to high morale and life satisfaction; others have reported that the opposite is generally the case, but that there is considerable diversity among individuals and that the relation between disengagement and life satisfaction depends upon personality type (see, e.g., Neugarten, 1968).

Sex differences in personality change have also been reported: in particular, increasing age has been found to be associated with greater affiliation and nurturance, and reduced aggression and achievement motivation, in men, but with reduced affiliation and greater aggression in women (e.g. Neugarten *et al.*, 1964; and for discussion of the personality dimensions quoted, see Chapter 21). The nature of these differences has led to the hypothesis that older people are more *androgynous* (see pp. 591–2), although the evidence for the hypothesis is scanty and far from conclusive (e.g. Hyde and Phillis, 1979). It seems likely that age–sex interactions of this kind would be associated with changes in familial and social role and in social expectation.

It has often been argued that older people are more rigid in their opinions, attitudes and methods of work, more cautious, conservative and resistant to change. There is considerable evidence for this view, not only from studies of personality and attitude change but also from studies of cognitive performance such as problem solving (e.g. Rabbitt, 1977). However, as a generalization it should be accepted only with caution. Chown (1961) has pointed out that 'rigidity' is not a unitary dimension, and that many age differences in 'rigidities' can also be attributed to differences in non-verbal intelligence. Botwinick (1966, 1969) found that older subjects were more 'cautious' in response on a questionnaire involving choices among alternative courses of action differing in riskiness though also in reward (see Chapter 23), but that the age difference disappeared when the questionnaire was so modified that some degree of risk was present in all alternatives offered; he argued that older subjects avoid situations, or discussions, involving risk when possible (and this avoidance can of course be adaptive rather than maladaptive), but are not more cautious than younger subjects when some degree of risk is unavoidable. Further, Herzog (1979), for example, has reported that older subjects were rather *more* susceptible than younger ones to persuasive communication, although this may be counteracted by decreased capacity to receive and retain information; and it is possible that age differences in conservatism of attitude are largely to be attributed to generational differences rather than to age changes (e.g. Pressey and Jones, 1955; Cutler *et al.*, 1980).

Most studies of personality change are cross-sectional, while such longitudinal studies as exist have been limited in the age range investigated. Cross-sequential studies such as that of Schaie and Parham (1976), in which cohort effects can be separated from age effects, have tended to show stability, rather than change, in personality with age. Indeed, it is hardly surprising that cohort effects may be important contributors to age–personality differences. Personality changes could well be related to biological, and indeed sensory, changes with senescence; they are almost certainly related to 'life experiences', which differ for different cohorts.

Some life experiences, however, are common to many or most people: for example, puberty, marriage, parenthood; pregnancy, menopause and the 'empty nest' (departure of grown-up children from the home) in women; retirement, bereavement, and so on. Many psychologists, and sociologists, have therefore concentrated upon studying the impact of such life experiences and patterns of adaptation to them. Such consistencies as have been observed point to very complex relationships. Many potential crises may in fact be less stressful, and lead to more successful adaptation, than is sometimes assumed (e.g. Palmore *et al.*, 1979). Pre-existing personality characteristics are likely to determine the nature and success of adaptation to life experiences, and modes of adaptation successful at one age may not be so at another: for example, Lieberman (1975) has found that 'grouchiness', pugnaciousness and paranoia may be conducive to survival in old age although they are not traditionally associated with good psychological health. Again, Neugarten (1970) has pointed out that the impact of life experiences is much greater when they occur 'off-time' – when, for example, bereavement or major illness occur much earlier than expected. This illustrates the existence of *age–role expectations*: norms of age-appropriate behaviour, and of 'suitable ages' for events such as leaving home, marriage, the first child, retirement and so on, set both by individuals for themselves and by a society for its members. To some extent such personality changes as may be observed in older people (notably, perhaps, increased 'passivity', interiority and dis-engagement) may reflect changes in the role which is imposed upon them by society; this may be a more powerful influence in the case of old (for example, post-retirement) people than in, say, the case of the middle aged, for whom social expectations may be less narrow or less compelling.

Although modern industrial societies have programmes of care for old age, attitudes to the aged are often unfavourable, more so in fact than in pre-literate societies, in which the aged have often been viewed as repositories of wisdom and therefore objects of reverence (although sometimes also of fear). It has been forcefully stated that 'ageism' is a social evil, and a source of real discrimination, comparable with racism and sexism (e.g. Bennett and Eck-man, 1973; Butler, 1975; Palmore and Manton, 1973). It may be, as Schaie (1973) and others have argued, that we should strive through re-education of the young and the middle aged towards an 'ageless' society, in which age changes are recognized as more or less irrelevant to social policy, and in which behaviour is not required to be 'age-appropriate' (for example, in which educational and vocational opportunity is not restricted to younger age groups and retirement is not compulsory on the basis of age). In such a society age differences, like sex and race differences, would be regarded as less important, at any rate, than individual differences; nevertheless, it is an essential part of any advance towards that Utopia that we should ack-nowledge the existence of such differences as appear stable, assess accurately their nature, extent and practical significance, and devise and make available the support systems and remedial measures needed to mitigate any dis-advantages they may entail.

Chapter 23
Social Behaviour

Introduction

Social psychology is concerned with describing and explaining psychological phenomena which arise from the direct and indirect influence of people on one another's thoughts, feelings and behaviour. To a degree, of course, nearly everything an individual does is influenced by social factors, and for this reason the demarcation between social psychology and other branches of the discipline is often unclear. There are, however, a number of psychological phenomena that are irreducibly social in character since they have no independent existence apart from the social context in which they occur. Included in this category are audience and coaction effects, group polarization, and some of the phenomena associated with non-verbal communication. These matters are discussed in some depth in this chapter.

It is impossible in a single chapter to do justice to all the topics commonly dealt with in more extended treatments of social psychology. The discussion that follows centres on a small but varied selection from the core of social psychological theorizing and research, but omits a number of important topics altogether and mentions others only in passing. These include attitudes and attitude change, aggression, attribution theory, prejudice and inter-group relations, conformity and obedience, group structure and leadership, interpersonal attraction, cognitive dissonance, altruism, and mob behaviour. A more expansive account of social psychology is given by Tajfel and Fraser (1978).

Audience and coaction effects

It was not until the end of the nineteenth century that the first serious attempt was made to perform a controlled experiment in order to solve a problem in the field of social psychology. In 1897 Norman Triplett carried out an experiment to answer the question: does an individual's task performance improve when other people are present? Not only was this the first recorded experiment in social psychology, but it centred on what, at least on the face of it, was the simplest and most fundamental of all social psychological questions. Triplett did not succeed in solving the problem once and for all, partly because his question turned out to have been too crudely formulated. In fact, variants of the same basic question continued to dominate social psychology for the next thirty years (Allport, 1968). Research activity began to dwindle in the late 1930s, probably on account of the wealth of seemingly contradictory results which had by then accumulated, but a revival of interest occurred in recent years following a theoretical contribution by Zajonc (1965, 1966) which suggested a possible resolution of the apparent conflict of evidence.

Triplett's interest was originally aroused by a perusal of the official records of bicycle races. He noticed that, compared with attempts by a solitary rider to beat an established time, a cyclist's maximum speed was on average approximately 20 per cent higher when he was not alone on the track. In order to investigate under controlled conditions whether a quite different kind of task performance would be enhanced by the presence of coactors (people working together at the same task), he recruited forty ten- to twelve-year-old children and presented them with the task of executing 150 winds on a fishing-reel as quickly as possible. All the children performed the task six times: thrice working entirely alone and thrice competing against each other in pairs. Triplett was shrewd enough to control for order effects such as fatigue, practice, etc., by alternating the solitary and coaction conditions. His experimental design did, however, suffer from the flaw that coaction was confounded with competition in such a way that his results could be attributed to either or both of these two factors. The outcome of the experiment was nevertheless quite striking: exactly half the children performed better in the coaction than in the solitary condition, one quarter performed better in the solitary condition, and one quarter performed at essentially the same level in both conditions. Triplett therefore concluded that on average the effect of the presence of another individual is an improvement in task performance. He explained his results in terms of the then fashionable doctrine of *dynamogenesis*, which held that an idea of a bodily movement, once it enters a person's mind, always evokes the actual movement to some degree. Triplett thought that the sight of the other competitors in the coaction condition evoked ideas of movement and speed and that these ideas produced dynamogenic effects.

Triplett's results can, of course, quite easily be interpreted in terms of the effects of competition, without invoking dynamogenesis, but his historic finding should not be dismissed as trivial or obvious on that account: similar effects were soon shown to occur under conditions in which there was no question of either competition or dynamogenesis being the cause. This is true, for example, in the case of pure audience effects, i.e. the effects of passive spectators rather than coactors. Since audience effects seem to arise from the *mere presence* of other people, they are in a sense even more basic than co-action effects.

The first experimental evidence for audience effects was reported by Meumann (1904). While working on muscular fatigue using an ergograph (an instrument for recording the amount of effort expended in repetitive muscular contractions), Meumann made the accidental discovery that, although a subject may be striving to work at the upper limit of his capacity, a significant increase in muscular output is typically recorded when passive observers are present.

A similar positive audience effect was found by Travis (1925) in the performance of subjects on a well-learned perceptual-motor skill. The subjects in this experiment were first of all trained for several consecutive days until they had mastered the task of using an articulated stylus to track a small metal target near the edge of a disc revolving at 60 r.p.m. This apparatus, which is called a *pursuit rotor*, records time and errors automatically. One day after the conclusion of his training each subject was given several trials alone and then in the presence of a handful of spectators who had been instructed to watch quietly but attentively. A small though very consistent positive audience effect was found.

Dashiell (1930, 1935) conducted a series of rather more sophisticated experiments in this area. Mindful of the complexity of the problem, he examined the performance of subjects while working (a) alone, (b) under observation by an audience of quiet spectators, (c) in the presence of coacting non-competitors, and (d) in the presence of competitors. The tasks presented to the subjects were simple multiplication problems, analogies ('rain is to summer as snow is to ——'), and a word-association test to see how quickly the subject could produce a chain of meaningfully associated responses to a stimulus word. The design was properly counterbalanced for order effects. The results showed that subjects worked *faster* when under observation from passive spectators than in the other conditions, but the *accuracy* of their performance was somewhat *lower* with an audience. The subjects were also found to be slightly faster at solving analogies and multiplication problems in the presence of competitors than when working alone or with coacting non-competitors. Finally, it was established that speed was generally greater in the presence of coacting non-competitors than in the genuinely 'alone' condition. Dashiell concluded that the crucial social factors which enhance the speed (though not the accuracy) of an individual's performance are 'the presence of some of the competitive attitude or else some of the being-observed attitude' (1930, p. 196).

Bergum and Lehr (1963) found a very marked positive audience effect on vigilance performance in a group of National Guard trainees. The subjects' task entailed pressing a button whenever a light failed to go on in a pre-determined sequence on a panel in front of them. After a twenty-minute training session, subjects in one condition performed the task alone, while others were told that from time to time an officer would visit them to observe their performance. The performance of both groups declined over time as a result of fatigue, but the detection accuracy of the supervised subjects remained on average 34 per cent higher than that of the subjects working alone, and towards the end of the session it was more than twice as high.

The experiments outlined above have all pointed to positive audience effects, but matters are not in fact quite so straightforward. As early as 1931, Husband reported that an audience interferes with the learning of a finger maze. This finding of a negative audience effect was replicated by Pessin and Husband (1933). Pessin (1933) reported an experiment in which subjects had to learn lists of nonsense syllables; the results showed that the subjects required more trials to learn a seven-item list in front of an audience, and that the average number of errors was considerably lower when they worked alone. Once learned, however, recall of the nonsense syllables was better under audience than solitary conditions.

The findings on audience effects seem to contradict one another: sometimes the effect is positive and sometimes negative. This confusing state of affairs appears to have had a demoralizing effect on research workers until the mid 1960s when Robert Zajonc (1965, 1966) drew attention to a 'subtle consistency' in the findings which had hitherto been overlooked. He pointed out that positive audience effects had usually been found on the performance of well-learned or over-learned tasks (such as repetitive muscular contractions, well-practised pursuit-rotor skills, easy multiplication sums, simple analogies, word-associations and routine vigilance tasks) while negative audience effects had been reported on the learning of novel tasks (such as finger mazes and lists of nonsense syllables). He suggested therefore that the effect of an audience is to facilitate performance but to impair learning. A close examination of the findings reveals that this generalization fits less than perfectly; but it does offer some clarification although it is more in the nature of a description than an explanation of the phenomenon. Zajonc therefore developed his hypothesis further with some bold theoretical speculations.

During the early stages of learning, wrong responses tend to predominate. Once a task has been mastered, however, correct responses gain dominance in an individual's task-relevant behavioural repertoire. The conflicting evidence can therefore be comprehended if it is assumed that the effect of an audience is to enhance the emission of dominant responses; if the above speculations are correct, this could account for the facilitation of performance and the impairment of learning. Zajonc (1965, 1966) hypothesized further that the reasons for this enhancement of dominant responses are the motivational or arousal properties of the audience. The primary effect of an audience may be to increase motivation or arousal, and this in turn may enhance the emission of dominant responses, thus facilitating performance but impairing the learning of novel tasks.

How effective is Zajonc's hypothesis in accounting for the results of experiments on coaction rather than audience effects? Triplett's (1897) results clearly fall into the expected pattern since the subjects in that experiment were performing fairly well-practised movements (winding fishing-reels) and a positive coaction effect was indeed observed. Further examples of positive effects have been reported in investigations of eating behaviour in animals (e.g. Bayer, 1929; Harlow, 1932; James, 1953, 1960; James and Cannon, 1955; Tolman and Wilson, 1965) and even in nest-building activity in ants (Chen, 1937). In all these cases positive coaction effects are expected on the basis of the hypothesis since the dominant responses are instinctive. Learning experiments with animals have on the other hand usually produced the expected negative coaction effects (e.g., Gates and Allee, 1933; Allee and Masure, 1936; Rasmussen, 1939; Klopfer, 1958).

The best known experiments in this area are undoubtedly those of Floyd Allport (1920) using human subjects. In these experiments subjects worked either separately in cubicles or together seated round a table. In an attempt to minimize competitive tendencies, subjects in the coaction conditions were forbidden to compare their responses and were told that the experimenters would not make such comparisons either. Several types of task were presented to the subjects, including producing a chain of meaningful word-associations, cancelling all the vowels in a set of newspaper articles, performing simple multiplications, and refuting false syllogisms. On all these tasks except the last, the performance of the subjects was enhanced by coaction. On the logic test, however, subjects performed better in the solitary condition. Commenting on his results, Allport suggested that the presence of coactors increases the quantity and strength of responses though it may sometimes impair their intellectual quality. He later coined the term *social facilitation* to denote the effects of audiences and coactors (Allport, 1924), but since the effects subsequently turned out to be as often negative as positive, this term, although still widely used, seems something of a misnomer. Zajonc (1965, 1966) has argued that Allport's results strongly support his hypothesis, since in all these tasks, with the exception of the logic test, it seems reasonable to assume that the dominant responses are correct ones. The logic test, for its part, involved refuting false syllogisms; in this case incorrect response tendencies are quite strong since there are many wrong responses and only one correct one.

Recent contributions in this area have, in general, been directed either towards testing Zajonc's hypothesis or towards shedding light on the apparently drive-increasing effects of audiences and coactors. Kelley and Thibaut (1969) and Weiss and Miller (1971) have drawn together various strands of evidence which support the claim that an individual's motivational level is normally increased under social conditions. Zajonc and Sales (1966) and Zajonc, Heingartner and Herman (1969) provided direct experimental support for the assertion that both audiences and coactors lead to an enhancement of performance when correct responses are dominant but impair performance when incorrect responses predominate. Cottrell, Rittle and Wack (1967) showed that, in a paired-associate learning task, when correct responses are salient (e.g. when a subject has to learn to produce the response word *skilful* to the stimulus word *adept*), audiences have a facilitating effect, but when they are not (e.g. *dessert-leading*), negative audience effects occur. All these experiments provide support for Zajonc's hypothesis.

Several researchers, starting with Cottrell (1968), have argued that the 'mere presence' of others is not in itself crucial to the enhancement of dominant responses. The physical presence of others has been found to be neither a sufficient condition – Cottrell found no effects from a blindfolded audience – nor a necessary one: Criddle (1971) demonstrated an enhancement of dominant responses when subjects know they are being observed through a one-way screen. On the basis of evidence from an experiment on the social facilitation of laughter in children (Chapman, 1973) and an electromyographic study of audience effects, Chapman (1974) suggested that what is important in increasing drive level is the 'psychological presence' rather than the 'mere (physical) presence' of other people.

It may be the case, however, that even 'psychological presence' is not in itself the decisive drive-increasing factor. Cottrell (1968) originally put forward the hypothesis that what is crucial is *evaluation apprehension*, i.e.

anxiety arising from the feeling that one's performance is being judged by others. When this ingredient is missing from an audience or coaction situation, according to Cottrell and his followers, no effects should occur. Experimental support for this refinement of Zajonc's hypothesis has been provided by Cottrell *et al.* (1968), Henchy and Glass (1968), Klinger (1969) and Paulus and Murdoch (1971). Unfortunately, some evidence contradicting this hypothesis has also been reported (e.g. Burwitz and Newell, 1972).

An alternative suggestion has therefore been put forward and has gained a number of supporters. This hypothesis centres on the *distracting* quality of audiences and coactors (Baron, Moore and Saunders, 1978; Freedman, Sears and Carlsmith, 1978). According to this hypothesis, distraction that arises in certain social situations takes the form of attentional conflict which has drive-increasing properties. Audience and coaction effects are expected to occur only when people are in a state of conflict between concentrating on the task in hand and attending to the task-irrelevant distraction. Some evidence supporting this hypothesis has been reported (e.g. Baron, Moore and Saunders, 1978).

The original problem posed by Triplett in 1897 has not been finally solved, but it is fair to say that we have come some way towards an understanding of the effects of audiences and coactors on an individual's performance. The potential relevance of this line of research to everyday problems in industry, education and the performing arts should not be overlooked. Should students study in isolation and should examinations take place in groups? How should offices and factories be laid out? Why do music students often go to pieces in front of an audience while professional musicians give their best performances under such conditions? What are the precise mechanisms of 'stage fright'? The literature on audience and coaction effects offers some illumination to such questions as these.

The group polarization phenomenon

An important and paradoxical phenomenon was discovered by Ziller in 1957 and independently re-discovered in a Masters thesis by Stoner a few years later (Stoner, 1961). The discovery was that group decisions are usually riskier than individual decisions. This came as a surprise because it had always been assumed that committees and similar decision-making groups stifle individual boldness and daring and tend to produce cautious and unenterprising decisions. Although a number of plausible explanations were put forward for what somewhat misleadingly became known as the *risky shift* phenomenon, experimental evidence soon cast doubt on most of them and forced social psychologists to search further afield for a satisfactory explanation. After a decade of intensive experimental research, Moscovici and Zavalloni (1969) suggested that the risky shift was merely a special case of a more general group polarization phenomenon, and by the end of 1974 this interpretation had become more or less universally accepted.

The instrument used by Stoner (1961) and many subsequent researchers in this area was the *Choice Dilemmas Questionnaire* (Kogan and Wallach, 1964). The CDQ comprises twelve hypothetical situations, outlined in some detail, in each of which a protagonist has to choose between a safe course of action and a more attractive but riskier one. The dilemmas include choosing between a moderately satisfactory job and a more attractive one in a firm which might collapse, playing for a safe draw in a chess match or playing for a win and thereby risking defeat, and choosing a safe career as a physician or a potentially more rewarding but riskier one as a concert pianist. In responding to the CDQ, a subject is asked to specify the lowest probability or odds (one in ten, three in ten, etc.) of the risky alternative proving successful which would lead him to recommend that course of action to the hypothetical protagonist.

Stoner (1961) found that when a number of people respond to the CDQ on an individual basis and then come together to discuss the dilemmas and arrive at a series of unanimous group decisions, the group decisions tend to be riskier (i.e. lower probabilities are chosen) than the average of the individual decisions. This finding generated a wave of research on group risk taking, and Stoner's results were replicated in a dozen different Western industrialized countries and among a wide range of subject populations, including males and females, undergraduate and postgraduate students, senior executives, professional people, soldiers, and elementary school children. The phenomenon was also shown to generalize beyond the CDQ to more lifelike situations in which real rewards and punishments result from the subjects' decisions, for example choices between expensive but safe person-to-person long-distance telephone calls and cheaper but riskier station-to-station calls. The literature on group risk taking has been reviewed by Clark (1971) and Pruitt (1971) among others, and more general reviews of the group polarization phenomenon have been provided by Myers and Lamm (1976) and Lamm and Myers (1978).

One of the most superficially plausible hypotheses which were put forward to account for the risky shift was the *familiarization* hypothesis (Bateson, 1966). Animals and humans, it was argued, typically behave in a hesitant and

cautious manner in unfamiliar surroundings, and after a period of exploration and 'feeling out' they usually exhibit greater boldness and daring. An
analogous effect could account for the risky shift if it could be assumed that
it is familiarization with the dilemmas in the group context which emboldens
the subjects and causes them to make riskier decisions. There are two reasons,
however, why this hypothesis was soon rejected by researchers in this area.

The first problem with this hypothesis arises from the results of experiments designed to test it directly. An implication of Bateson's suggestion is
that the risky shift is a pseudo-group effect; although it occurs in groups it
is not actually the result of any group process, and it should be possible to
demonstrate the effect in subjects who are familiarized with the CDQ
dilemmas on an individual basis. Bateson reported such a risky shift in
individuals, but almost every attempt to replicate his findings, using a wide
range of individually-based familiarization techniques, has failed dismally
(e.g. Teger *et al.*, 1970).

The second difficulty with the familiarization hypothesis arose from the
discovery that reliable cautious shifts occur in certain situations. Two of
the items on the original CDQ, one involving a choice between a safe
domestic investment and a risky investment abroad, and the other a choice
between a safe decision not to marry and a risky one to marry, turned out to
produce consistent and easily replicable cautious shifts. A large number of
hypothetical and naturalistic decision-making situations have since been
found which generate reliable cautious shifts. While it is true that animals
and humans sometimes become even more hesitant and cautious as a result of
familiarization with their environments, it was widely felt that this hypothesis
could not convincingly account for all the specific cautious shifts which were
discovered.

A completely different approach to the problem was suggested by
Marquis's (1962) *leadership* hypothesis. The central idea is that the kind of
person who is most outspoken and persuasive in a group discussion is likely
also to possess the personality attributes of a high risk taker; the risky shift
may therefore be due to the influence of risky leaders persuading the other
group members to their points of view.

Several rather serious objections to this hypothesis have been raised.
Firstly, evidence is lacking that leadership ability is a strong personality trait;
a great deal of evidence has accumulated that an individual who is a leader in
one situation is not necessarily a leader in another. It is not possible therefore
to devise a meaningful test of the assumption that leaders tend to be high
risk takers. Secondly, experiments in which subjects have been asked to rate

the influence of the various group members following the discussions have not always confirmed the predictions of the leadership hypothesis (e.g. Rabow *et al.*, 1966). Thirdly, the hypothesis seems quite incapable of accounting for the cautious shifts mentioned earlier. Finally and most seriously, Vidmar (1970) demonstrated that in groups which are homogeneous with respect to the initial risk level of the individual members, a risky shift nevertheless occurs; and particularly in the case of groups composed entirely of low risk takers, this finding decisively refutes the leadership hypothesis.

A third hypothesis, in terms of *diffusion of responsibility*, was put forward by Wallach, Kogan and Bem (1962). The phenomenon of responsibility diffusion has proved useful in accounting for a number of other group effects, such as the tendency for lynch mobs in the United States in the 1920s and 1930s (and other mobs) to perform acts which none of their constituent members would risk as individuals (e.g. Jones and Gerard, 1967, pp. 622–4), and the reduced likelihood of bystanders to display altruism in going to the help of a person in distress when others are present (e.g. Darley and Latané, 1968). As an explanation for the risky shift, this hypothesis assumes that people can afford to take greater risks when they are part of a group than when they are alone, because responsibility for the decision is shared among the group members rather than weighing on any individual's conscience.

The force of the responsibility diffusion hypothesis is seriously weakened by several considerations. Firstly, it has been found that unanimous group decisions are not a necessary prerequisite for the occurrence of the risky shift: the effect has been found to occur in a slightly diminished form following group discussions without the requirement of unanimity (e.g. Wallach and Kogan, 1965). Under these conditions, an explanation in terms of diffusion of responsibility loses a great deal of its cogency since there is no question of the group members sharing responsibility for a single joint decision. Secondly, even active group participation has turned out to be unnecessary: small risky shifts have been found in individuals who have passively listened in on the deliberations of groups of which they are not a part (e.g. Lamm, 1967). This finding is also somewhat damaging to the hypothesis, although it is possible to imagine some sort of vicarious diffusion of responsibility occurring under conditions like these. Most seriously, however, the responsibility diffusion hypothesis seems as impotent as any of the theories discussed above in the face of cautious shifts, which remain entirely unaccounted for.

The most successful explanation for the risky shift, and the only one which seems adequately to account for cautious shifts and other group polarization effects, is Brown's (1965) *value* hypothesis. Brown suggested two different mechanisms, as will be explained later, but the most powerful variant of this theory, which is often referred to as the *interpersonal comparison* hypothesis, argues ingeniously as follows. Risk is a value in Western culture in the sense that we tend generally to admire risk takers rather than people who are timid and cautious. In order to maintain favourable images of ourselves, we therefore like to consider ourselves at least as willing to take risks as our peers. When responding to the CDQ on an individual basis, subjects assume, in the absence of any opportunity for social comparison, that they are making riskier decisions relative to their peers than they really are. In the group situation however, most of them discover that there are others whose risk level is higher than their own, so in order to restore their self-images as people who are at least as risky as their peers, they modify their decisions in the direction of greater risk taking.

A minor elaboration of the interpersonal comparison hypothesis allows it to provide a theoretically adequate explanation for cautious shifts. An assumption has to be made that while risk is valued in a wide range of decision-making contexts, there are some situations in which caution is valued. We consider a person foolhardy if he takes risks on questions like investment (CDQ item 5) and marriage (CDQ item 12) which have been found to produce cautious group shifts.

This hypothesis dangles on the end of a chain of assumptions, but the links in this chain have stood up remarkably well to experimental tests. The assumptions that people admire risk taking in the areas which are known to produce risky shifts, and that they tend to overestimate their own risk levels relative to their peers, were confirmed in a simple but elegant experiment by Levinger and Schneider (1969) whose results have been replicated many times (Myers, 1973, has listed more than twenty-four studies). In Levinger and Schneider's experiment, subjects responded to the CDQ on an individual basis three times: first of all giving their own responses in the usual way, secondly giving their estimates of the responses of the majority of their peers, and thirdly indicating the responses they would most admire. As predicted by the theory, on most of the items the subjects tended to consider their own decisions as more risky than those of their peers but as less risky than those they would most admire. On the items that generate cautious group shifts (items 5 and 12), Levinger and Schneider and subsequent researchers have usually found self-ideal discrepancies in the opposite direction, precisely as predicted by the theory. The interpersonal comparison hypothesis also generates the prediction that no risky shifts will be observed in cultures in which risk taking is not generally valued, and this has been confirmed by Carlson and Davis (1971) with a sample of Ugandan Africans.

As the interpersonal comparison hypothesis gained ascendancy in the late 1960s, it gradually became apparent that a phenomenon of wider generality was at the root of risky and cautious shifts. An influential French study was largely responsible for the theoretical and empirical reorientation which occurred. The results of this study demonstrated that the favourable attitudes of a group of French school children towards de Gaulle became even more positive, and that their unfavourable attitudes towards Americans became even more negative, as a result of a group discussion (Moscovici and Zavalloni, 1969). Since risk and caution are clearly irrelevant here, Moscovici and Zavalloni explained their findings in terms of the more general concept of *group polarization*. What is implied by this term is an amplification of the dominant attitudinal tendency within a group rather than a spreading apart of individual attitudes. An assumption of this theory is that a risky shift should be found on CDQ items only when the subjects' individual judgements tend initially towards the risky pole, and that cautious shifts should occur when, as is usually the case on CDQ items 5 and 12, the initial dominant tendency is towards caution. This assumption has been amply confirmed (e.g. Clark and Willems, 1969) and it is now possible to invent risky or cautious shift items to order.

The group polarization phenomenon has been observed in a wide range of experimental and naturalistic studies (reviewed by Myers and Lamm, 1976; and Lamm and Myers, 1978). Discussion groups were found to enhance the negative attitudes of French architectural students towards their college. Simulated juries were found, following group deliberation, to become even more definite in their judgements of innocence when the accused was made to appear innocent, and even more emphatic in their judgements of guilt when he was made to appear guilty. Bargaining teams, whose individual tendencies were to set high aspiration levels when their bargaining position was strong and *vice versa*, were found to adjust their aspirations upward and downward following group discussion in accordance with predictions. The initial cautious inclinations of most race track punters were reported, in a field study, to be strengthened when the bets were placed by groups rather than by individuals. The preferences of students for continuous assessment rather than examinations were shown to polarize towards greater extremity following group discussion. Peer counsellors acting in groups were found to give more extreme advice in the direction of their individual inclinations.

Numerous other examples of group polarization have been reported in the literature and there are no doubt more to come.

How is the group polarization phenomenon to be accounted for? Since the risky shift can now be seen to be nothing more than a special case of this more general effect, it follows logically that any putative explanation which fails to account for the risky shift can be dismissed as an inadequate general theory of group polarization. Interest therefore centres naturally on the inter-personal comparison hypothesis which proved uniquely successful as an explanation of the risky shift. But can this hypothesis account adequately for the findings on group polarization?

In order to cope with the group polarization findings, three assumptions have to be incorporated into an elaborated version of the interpersonal comparison hypothesis. Firstly, it must be assumed that people admire attitudes which deviate from neutrality in the same direction as their own. The second assumption is that people like to consider themselves at least as polarized as their peers on all issues, or at least on all issues which generate polarization effects (exceptions may come to light). Finally, people must be assumed generally to overestimate their own degree of polarization relative to their peers on a wide range of issues (most of the French school children, for example, must have thought they were more pro-de Gaulle and more anti-American than their classmates). The first of these assumptions is indirectly supported by a great deal of research on interpersonal attraction (see, e.g., Duck, 1977). The second seems intuitively likely as a natural consequence of the first. The third has not received much attention from investigators, but like the other two assumptions, is well supported by research in the specific area of risk taking.

The group polarization phenomenon therefore appears to be reasonably well explained by an elaborated version of Brown's (1965) interpersonal comparison hypothesis. There is reason to believe, however, that another related group process, also originally suggested by Brown, may be necessary to account fully for the observed effects. A second version of the value theory suggested a tendency of people in discussions to express arguments which favour the dominant group opinion, out of a desire, perhaps, to present themselves favourably. The hypothesized *biased flow of information* in group discussions may lead to mutual reinforcing of pre-existing attitudinal tendencies and thereby enhance the polarization effect. This process cannot account on its own for the group polarization effect because small risky shifts have been observed in groups whose members simply exchange information about their individual decisions without any discussion of arguments (Teger and Pruitt, 1967). There is, however, evidence that it is a contributing factor (Lamm and Myers, 1978).

It is worth noting that the theories and findings discussed above have important implications for a wide range of everyday social events, from the emergence of extremist movements in certain social contexts to the decisions of trade union mass meetings, which are usually more militant than the results of individual ballots. The literature on the group polarization phenomenon, and its progenitor, the risky shift, have contributed to our understanding of these and many other important social issues.

Non-verbal communication

In 1839 Charles Darwin's first child was born, and as he later described in his autobiography, he immediately began to make extensive notes on the first dawn of the infant's emotional expressions, 'for I felt convinced, even at this early period, that the most complex and fine shades of expression must all have had a gradual and natural origin' (Darwin, 1887, pp. 131–2). These early observations were eventually incorporated into a book, *Expression of the Emotions in Man and Animals*, published in 1872, which is an early landmark in the scientific study of non-verbal communication. During the early decades of the present century, a smattering of scholarly studies of facial expressions and gestures appeared, but it was not until the 1960s and 1970s that research on all facets of non-verbal communication began to take place on a truly extravagant scale. The explosion of research activity and publications in this area is no doubt due in part to the increasing availability of sophisticated audio-visual recording apparatus, though more subtle cultural factors are probably also involved. Numerous detailed reviews of the literature on non-verbal communication have recently appeared, among the best of which are those by Harper, Wiens and Matarazzo (1978) and Knapp (1978). The discussion that follows will centre on five principal areas of investigation: (a) paralanguage, (b) facial expression, (c) kinesics, (d) proxemics, and (e) inconsistency between channels.

Paralanguage

There is a strong temptation to think of human communication solely in terms of language, because the verbal component absorbs most of our attention when we communicate. Nevertheless, quite apart from information conveyed by the face and body, a great deal of the information that is transmitted by the vocal apparatus is non-verbal in character. In addition to the verbal content of what the speaker says, variations in loudness, pitch, timbre, rate, inflection, rhythm and enunciation inevitably convey additional information. These non-verbal properties of speech are usually referred to as *paralanguage*. Research in this area is concerned not with *what* is said, but with *how* it is said, though paralinguistic factors can of course influence the meaning of a verbal message. Consider the qualitatively different meanings conveyed by the following: '*Will* you marry me?'; 'Will *you* marry me?'; 'Will you *marry* me?'; 'Will you marry *me*?'. It is possible to say 'I like that' in a manner which conveys displeasure, and as lawyers who defend rapists frequently point out, it is even possible to say 'no' in a way which indicates 'yes'.

Certain aspects of a spoken message, particularly emotions and attitudes, are communicated less by the words a person uses than by non-verbal factors including paralanguage. On the basis of experimental findings, Mehrabian (1972) has proposed the following formula to indicate the relative weight of three factors in determining the emotion or attitude conveyed by a spoken message: *Total Impact = 0·07 Verbal + 0·38 Paralinguistic + 0·55 Facial*. This formula suggests that paralinguistic factors are more than five times as influential as the verbal content and that facial expressions (see below) are even more important. Mehrabian's formula was based in part on some ingenious experiments in which tape recordings of speech fragments were passed through an electronic filter to eliminate frequencies above 200 cycles per second (in the case of women speakers) or 100 cycles per second (for men). This had the effect of making the words unintelligible while leaving most of the paralinguistic qualities intact. Subjects were able rather easily, and with a high degree of agreement, to perform the task of judging the amount of liking expressed in the filtered speech. One group judged a transcript of what was said (the verbal content) for the amount of liking conveyed, a second group judged the filtered speech (the paralinguistic content), and a third group judged the complete recorded message. The paralinguistic component turned out to be much more influential than the verbal component in determining the total impact of the message.

Weitz (1972) found that paralinguistic cues were more accurate indicators of inter-racial attitudes than the verbal content of speech in eighty white 'liberal' students who were expecting to interact with black people. Tape recordings of the subjects' speech were rated on such dimensions as *warm–cold*, *pleasant–unpleasant*, etc. and their attitudes towards blacks were assessed by conventional paper-and-pencil scales and also by observing

certain aspects of their behaviour such as chair placement, whether they preferred to wait together with or apart from the black person and the like. The
findings revealed a general pattern of overt friendliness and covert rejection;
the more friendly the subjects' verbal communication, the less friendly were
their assessed attitudes towards blacks. The paralinguistic cues on the other
hand showed a strong positive relationship with attitudes.

A number of factors influence the judgement of emotion from paralinguistic cues. There are large individual differences in the ability of speakers to
convey emotion and in the ability of listeners to perceive it. Snyder (1974)
found that some people are more conscious of their expressive behaviour
and have more control over it than others, and there seems to be a tendency
for high 'self-monitors' to be the best judges of emotion in other people.

It is difficult to make generalizations about the specific paralinguistic cues
associated with various emotions because they vary from speaker to speaker
and from situation to situation. Davitz (1964) has however presented a rough
guide to the typical features associated with several emotions. Affection, for
example, is normally conveyed by soft, low, resonant, slow, regular and
slurred speech with a slightly upward inflection, while sadness is communicated by the same paralinguistic cues except that the rhythm is irregular and
the inflection is downward.

Numerous investigators have studied the paralinguistic cues associated in
particular with stress and anxiety (see the review by Murray, 1971). Experiments have shown that under stress, accents and dialects become stronger
and that 'non-ah' speech errors tend to increase. 'Non-ah' speech errors are
repetitions, stutters, and all dysfluencies apart from the most common ones
which are pauses filled with 'ah', 'um' and 'er'. Speech rate tends to rise under
mild stress but to fall under severe stress. There is also some evidence
indicating that stress produces muscle tension in the larynx and suppresses
the microtremors which show up as rapid oscillations, undetectable by the
unaided ear, in the pitch of relaxed speech. This is the idea behind the
Psychological Stress Evaluator (P.S.E.) which its inventors rather im-
plausibly claim can identify truth-tellers with 94·7 per cent accuracy. The
P.S.E. has been used as a lie-detector in several recent court cases in the
United States. The use of any stress indicator as a lie-detector is of course
open to the objection that liars may sometimes be relaxed and truth-tellers
are often tense. Nevertheless, a person who displays a strong stress reaction
when questioned about (let us say) neckties but is relaxed when discussing
a variety of other similar objects might reasonably be assumed to have
some inside knowledge of a crime which happened to involve neckties,

even if he denies any knowledge of the crime (Podlesny and Raskin, 1977).

A final area of paralinguistic research has centred on the effects of accents on the perception of speakers and of the messages which they communicate (see the review by Giles and Powesland, 1975). In England, for example, it has been found that speakers using Received Pronunciation (the 'standard B.B.C.' accent) are generally perceived as more *competent* (high in social status, intelligent, self-confident etc.) but lower in *personal integrity* and *social attractiveness* (i.e. less good-natured, kind-hearted, humorous, sincere, etc.) than speakers using Cockney, Yorkshire accented speech and other regional accents. The quality of arguments delivered in R.P. is more favourably perceived, though the messages are not always found to be more persuasive. In spite of 'accent loyalty', these findings hold good for listeners whatever their own speech styles.

Facial expression

On the basis of some detailed observations of expressive behaviour, including a cross-cultural survey and a handful of rudimentary experiments, Darwin (1872) concluded that 'only a few expressive movements' such as turning the eyes upward in devotion, nodding and shaking the head, and kissing, are acquired by learning. 'The far greater number of movements of expression, and all the more important ones, are, as we have seen, innate or inherited' (p. 373). This hereditarian hypothesis implies that non-verbal communication constitutes a sort of universal code, transcending the barriers of language and culture, which has been biologically programmed into us through natural selection.

A vast number of important non-verbal signs are now known to differ arbitrarily from one culture to another (see the discussion of kinesics below). But with regard to facial expression, which was Darwin's main focus of attention, convincing evidence has continued to accumulate in favour of the hereditarian hypothesis. Numerous cross-cultural investigations (reviewed by Ekman, 1972) have somewhat surprisingly confirmed Darwin's findings in so far as they have shown that the same distinctive movements of the facial muscles accompany the primary expressions of happiness, sadness, surprise, fear, anger and disgust, even among culturally isolated primitive tribesmen. The kinds of events which are *elicitors* of various emotions differ from one culture to another, and there are different *display rules* governing the degree to which facial expressions of emotion are intensified or masked in different cultures, but the quality of the primary facial expressions appears to be invariant.

In one study concerned with display rules, American and Japanese students were shown either a disagreeable film of a surgical operation or a neutral film, and their facial expressions were surreptitiously observed. Under these conditions a high correlation was found between the expressions of the Americans and Japanese. In subsequent personal interviews, however, display rules came into play and the Japanese subjects engaged in culturally prescribed masking behaviour while the Americans continued to show negative facial affect when discussing the disagreeable film (Ekman, Friesen and Ellsworth, 1972, p. 165).

The most decisive evidence in support of the hereditarian hypothesis has been provided by studies of the facial expressions of very young infants, and especially of those born blind and deaf (Eibl-Eibesfeldt, 1973). In such cases it is virtually impossible to imagine facial expressions being acquired through learning. The fact that these infants typically display the expected facial expressions in response to various elicitors therefore provides overwhelming evidence in favour of the hereditarian hypothesis.

Ekman and Friesen (1975), who are the major investigators in this area, have in addition found evidence for differences in display styles among individuals within a single culture group: revealers, withholders, unwitting expressors, frozen-affect expressors and so on. They have developed a scoring technique, based upon the separate coding of the upper, middle and lower parts of the face, known as the Facial Affect Scoring Technique (FAST). Transcending individual display styles, it turns out that the primary expressions are revealed to different degrees in each of these three facial areas. Sadness, for example, is most reliably revealed in the upper area (the inner corners of the eyebrows are drawn up) while disgust shows most clearly in the middle and lower areas (the nose is wrinkled and the upper lip is raised).

Analysis of facial expressions using the FAST system has revealed that the appearance of vertical 'frown' lines between the brows is most closely associated with feelings of anger or perplexity. In the light of this, a study by Trujillo and Warthin (1968), which pre-dates Ekman and Friesen's work, is particularly intriguing. These investigators asked 126 chronic duodenal ulcer patients and 274 control patients to frown, and counted the number of visible frown lines. The results revealed that 85 per cent of the ulcer patients had three or more furrows compared with only 6 per cent of the control patients. In fact more than half the ulcer patients had four or more furrows.

Research on the *decoding* or recognition of facial expressions rather than their *encoding* or portrayal has had a rather unhappy history. Several studies in the 1920s appeared to demonstrate that subjects could not identify emotions through the face any better than chance, and these findings had the effect of discouraging research in this area for several decades. The early experiments were, however, marred by poor design and used *static* photographs of *artificially posed* emotions. More recent research has refuted the early findings and has also revealed that there are large individual differences in the ability to interpret facial expressions. Specific training greatly enhances this ability (Ekman and Friesen, 1975) and there is some evidence that females are in general better interpreters and portrayers of facial expressions than males (e.g. Zuckerman *et al.*, 1977).

Interpretation of facial expressions is an extremely complex skill which requires attention to subtle detail. Although we have only a few words to describe facial expressions – smile, frown, grimace, etc. – our facial musculature is sufficiently complex to allow us to display more than a thousand distinguishable expressions (Ekman, Friesen and Ellsworth, 1972, p. 1). The facial movements may moreover be so slight or so rapid that they sometimes cannot be seen at all. Schwartz (1974), for example, found that electrodes attached to only four facial muscles generated electromyogram recordings which enabled joyful, angry and sad thoughts to be reliably distinguished even in the absence of any visible changes in facial expression. Using a completely different procedure, Haggard and Isaacs (1966) found evidence for facial expressions which were also invisible, in this case because of their rapidity. Filmed interactions between psychotherapists and patients, when slowed down, revealed changes in the patients' faces – e.g. from a smile to a grimace to a smile – which lasted for between one eighth and one fifth of a second. During periods of apparent emotional conflict, these *micromomentary facial expressions* often gave the lie to what the patient was expressing verbally.

A great deal of research, reviewed by Argyle and Cook (1976), has been devoted to a specific aspect of facial activity, namely eye movements. People tend to *gaze* (into another person's eyes) more when interacting with someone they like than they do with a disliked partner. Increased gazing, however, may also indicate social dominance. Mutual gaze, or *eye contact*, signals intimacy, and it tends to diminish if other cues to intimacy, such as physical closeness, are artificially increased. This decrease in gazing is a compensating mechanism motivated by a desire to re-establish an equilibrium level, according to an hypothesis put forward by Argyle and Dean. Eye contact is satisfying and rewarding but it becomes uncomfortable if it exceeds an appropriate level for the degree of intimacy of the interaction. People gaze less when being interviewed about intimate topics than when discussing neutral issues. Furthermore, people who have been induced to tell lies, with the exception of 'Machiavellian' or manipulative personalities, have been found to indulge in less gazing than control subjects, and people who are trying to be persuasive portray greater credibility by gazing more while they are speaking.

Kendon (1967) has provided clear evidence for the importance of gaze and eye contact in regulating the flow of speech in social interactions. The whites of the eyes help us to perceive gaze direction in others with considerable accuracy, and this may be why humans, unlike our non-talking fellow primates, have evolved this unusual facial feature. Gaze and eye contact were shown by Kendon to follow a pattern during verbal interactions. The first generalization is that people gaze more and produce longer glances when listening than when speaking. The normal pattern is as follows. The speaker gazes at the beginning and end of each utterance and at the natural pauses, during which the listener nods or gives other *back-channel signals* to indicate that he is attending. During hesitations (e.g. when searching for the right word) on the other hand, the speaker nearly always looks away. As he approaches the end of his utterance, the speaker gazes at his partner and eye contact occurs, but eye contact episodes seldom last more than one and a half seconds. The partner starts to speak and usually looks away to indicate that he has taken the floor, and the cycle begins again.

Departures from the normal pattern of gaze and eye contact are usually associated with a disruption of the smooth flow of conversation. The importance of the regulatory function of gaze has been confirmed in an experiment in which conversations between people wearing dark glasses were found to contain abnormally long pauses and hesitations (Argyle, Lalljee and Cook, 1968). Autistic children display extreme gaze aversion (Hutt and Ounstead, 1966) and among adult mental patients, schizophrenics and depressives may possibly manifest abnormal gaze patterns, though the evidence is somewhat confusing on this point (Rutter, 1973).

Some research has been directed at trying to discover the possible expressive and communicative functions of pupil dilation and constriction. This line of research arose from a claim first made by Hess and Polt in 1960 that pupil dilation signals interest or liking and constriction signals aversion. The advertising industry invested huge sums of money in pupillometry on account of its commercial potential, and a great deal of research took place in this field. Unfortunately, numerous negative findings have now been reported and it seems clear that no simple generalizations can be made about attitude and pupil size (see, e.g., Harper, Wiens and Matarazzo, 1978, pp. 228–33).

Kinesics

A vivid illustration of the importance and subtlety of non-verbal communication through kinesics (expressive body movements) was provided by the scandal surrounding the famous horse, Clever Hans, which was owned by Herr von Osten of Berlin in the first decade of this century. By tapping his front hoof according to a pre-arranged code, Clever Hans demonstrated what appeared to be a remarkable intelligence: he had a complete comprehension of spoken and written German and he could perform difficult tasks in mental arithmetic, tell the time and recall musical pitches whether or not Herr von Osten was present. An investigating committee of learned professors attested to the genuineness of these and sundry other abilities, but the psychologist Pfungst (1911) later demonstrated that the apparent equine intelligence was an illusion. Pfungst's crucial experiment involved having one investigator whisper a number into the horse's left ear while another investigator whispered a different number into his right ear. When Clever Hans was asked to add the two numbers, he was stumped. The reason, as further experiments showed, was that the horse could only give correct answers when there was someone in his visual field who knew the answer: he could not perform when blindfolded. What Clever Hans had evidently learned to do was simply to start tapping his hoof when onlookers adopted an expectant posture, and to stop as soon as they made slight anticipatory head and eye movements. Credit should, however, be given to Clever Hans for having developed a remarkable skill at kinesic decoding.

Ekman and Friesen (1969) have distinguished between four types of kinesic behaviour according to function: (a) *emblems*, which are simply gestural substitutes for words; (b) *illustrators*, used to accent and elucidate speech; (c) *regulators*, which control the verbal flow in social interactions; and (d) *adaptors*, which are related to emotion and attitude. *Expressors*, confined largely to facial expressions, have already been discussed.

The most systematic study of American emblems was undertaken by Johnson, Ekman and Friesen in 1975. Subjects were given a list of verbal statements and phrases and asked to produce appropriate gestural translations. Those that were coded similarly by at least 70 per cent of the subjects were, together with some additions, performed in front of a fresh group of subjects who were asked to translate them back into words. More than sixty emblems were uncovered which were similarly interpreted by 70 per cent or more of the second group of subjects. These include waving ('goodbye'), putting a finger to the lips ('be silent') and making a ring with thumb and forefinger ('O.K.').

There are, however, almost unlimited cultural variations in gestural emblems (see the 'gesture maps' provided by Morris et al., 1979). The forefinger and thumb ring, for example, signifies 'O.K.' in the United States, but it means 'money' in Japan and, if accompanied by a downturned mouth, it means 'zero' or 'worthless' in France. The Chin Flick emblem in which the underside of the chin is tapped with the backs of the fingers is unknown in England, but in France, Northern Italy and Tunisia it means 'get lost', while between Rome and Naples it simply means 'no'. Similarly, beckoning someone to 'come here' is done with the palm up in some countries and with the palm down in others; the palm-down version is not found in England, Holland and France but is much more common than the palm-up version in Spain and Italy.

Illustrators, which serve the functions of accenting and elucidating speech, have been studied with the aid of slow-motion films of human interactions by Condon and Ogston (1966). These researchers have described the remarkable *interaction synchrony* whereby points of change in the flow of speech are mirrored by changes in body postures, altnough the universality of this phenomenon has recently been questioned by McDowall (1978). The movements of the speaker and listener tend to coincide as if they were puppets on a single set of strings, especially for small speech fragments up to the word level but less so for larger segments, so that the fine detail of the synchrony is difficult or impossible to see with the unaided eye. The most obvious and visible illustrators are hand gestures such as stabbing the air for emphasis or making a slow sweeping movement to illustrate 'a long time', and gross postural changes which tend to occur in both listeners and speakers when a new topic of conversation is broached.

Regulators play a prominent role in initiating and terminating conversations and also in monitoring turn-taking in speech during continuing conversations. Some of these regulatory movements have already been described in connection with gaze and eye contact. With regard to greetings, vast cultural differences have been observed. Europeans often shake hands as a form of greeting, but Polynesians stroke their own faces with each other's hands, the Lapps rub noses, the Dahomeans snap their fingers, and the Loangoese clap hands (Argyle, 1975, p. 78).

Adaptors have been investigated primarily in connection with their relationship to emotions. Krout (1954) reported an experiment in which subjects were interviewed in a manner calculated to arouse various emotions, and twenty-four gestures were found which appeared to be associated with particular emotions when speech was blocked. Most striking were self-touching gestures, like nose-touching (fear), fist-clenching (anger) and lip-touching (shame). More recent research has tended to indicate that shame or embarrassment is most often accompanied by eye-covering gestures, and that picking or scratching the face is associated with self-blame, that fingernail-picking and other restless movements usually denote either anxiety or boredom, and that rubbing or smoothing gestures indicate self-assurance.

Scheflen (1965) has identified a number of kinesic cues associated with courtship behaviour. *Courtship readiness* is normally accompanied by high muscle tone, reduced bagginess beneath the eyes, less jowl and stomach sag and reduced slouch. *Positioning cues* are body postures which are calculated to exclude other people from the interaction. *Preening behaviours* involve hair smoothing, tie straightening, etc. Finally, *appeal and invitation actions* include flirtatious gaze behaviours and, particularly among women, showing a palm, which according to Scheflen is rarely observed in non-courtship interactions involving Anglo-Saxon women. Observation of therapeutic encounters, business meetings and conferences, however, revealed a high frequency of quasi-courtship behaviours which do not have specifically sexual implications.

Ekman and Friesen (1972, 1974) have reported some interesting research on non-verbal 'leakage' of information in people who are engaging in deception. Their hypothesis was that since people are most aware of their faces as sources of non-verbal information regarding emotion, they are therefore most adept at monitoring facial cues and least skilful in controlling bodily kinesic cues when lying or concealing emotion according to display rules. Subjects who were shown videotapes of only the body movements of a group of nurses who had been induced to lie were found to be more accurate at identifying the deception than were those who viewed the face only. This was true, however, only when the subjects had first become acquainted with the nurses' normal kinesic behaviour. When lying, in contrast to their behaviour when telling the truth, the nurses manifested significantly more face-touching adaptors, and the Hand Shrug emblem (turning the palms of both hands up in a manner which is normally used to communicate helplessness) occurred significantly more often, although the nurses were unaware of this leakage.

Proxemics

People attach a great deal of significance to the way they position themselves relative to one another. The study of the spatial features of social interaction is commonly referred to as *proxemics*. An important aspect of proxemics research is the investigation of *personal space*, i.e. the area surrounding a person's body which others may not enter without evoking some kind of negative reaction. Research on these topics has been reviewed by Evans and Howard (1973) and by Harper, Wiens and Matarazzo (1978).

Interpersonal distances vary according to the nature of the interactions taking place, but they are nevertheless governed by strict, though largely unrecognized, social conventions. In our culture the optimal nose-to-nose distance in ordinary conversations is 30–48 in. (76–122 cm) and even quite small deviations outside these limits in either direction tend to cause discomfort and are usually followed by attempts to re-establish an 'appropriate' distance.

In crowded situations, of course, closer interpersonal distances are tolerated. In dense crowds the average interpersonal distance has been found to be about 15 in. (38 cm) from which we can calculate that each person occupies about 6 sq. ft. (0·56 sq. m.). In loose crowds the average interpersonal distance is about 20 in. (51 cm) with each person occupying 10 sq. ft. (0·93 sq. m.). The size of a crowd can therefore be estimated by dividing the area occupied in square feet (or square metres), by an appropriate figure between 6 (or 0·56) and 10 (or 0·93) and such estimates have been found to correspond quite closely with head counts made from aerial photographs (Sommer, 1969, pp. 27–8).

Other cultures have different, though evidently equally strict, norms governing interpersonal distances in non-crowded situations. Arab cultures, and to some extent Latin American and Mediterranean cultures, prescribe closer interpersonal distances for ordinary conversations. When a Northern European or an American talks to an Arab, therefore, the former may keep retreating as the latter keeps advancing, and both may feel uncomfortable (Watson and Graves, 1966). In general, those cultures which prescribe close interpersonal distances, the so-called *contact cultures*, also allow more touching than is permitted in *non-contact cultures*. Jourard (1966) counted the number of times couples in cafés in various cities touched each other, and the results per hour were: San Juan 180, Paris 110, Gainesville, Fla 2, and London 0.

The narrowing of interpersonal distance normally communicates an

attempt to create a higher level of intimacy. The optimal distance for intimate conversations in Anglo-American cultures is about 6–18 in (15–46 cm)
and, if both parties to an interaction agree that the relationship is intimate,
they may not feel at all uncomfortable at this distance and may even attempt
to diminish it further. If one of the parties does not accept this implied
definition of the situation, however, he or she may try to increase the interpersonal distance, or failing that, reduce the level of intimacy conveyed by
other verbal and non-verbal signals to compensate for the close physical
proximity (Patterson, 1973). Intimacy-reducing behaviours such as gaze
aversion and inhibition of facial expression have also been observed in situations of enforced closeness such as lifts and underground trains.

In non-intimate situations, close interpersonal distances generate high
levels of arousal and tension in most people. In an unusual but well-designed
field experiment in a public lavatory, for example, Middlemist, Knowles and
Matter (1976) found that tension induced by the close proximity of another
man using a urinal (about 17 in or 43 cm) led to a measurable delay in the
onset of urination and to a shorter duration of urination than was observed
in men whose interpersonal distance from another user was greater (about
53 in or 135 cm).

There is reliable evidence from a number of studies that women require
less personal space than men (see Evans and Howard, 1973). Status
factors are also important determiners of interpersonal distances: people of
equal status tend to approach each other closer than people of unequal status
(e.g. Lott and Sommer, 1967) and higher status individuals occupy more
personal space than those of lower status. The relationship between personal
space and status depends, however, on who is approaching whom. In one
experiment, for example, student subjects allowed white-coated experimenters to approach them much more closely than they would themselves
approach the experimenters (Hartnett, Bailey and Gibson, 1970). Kinzel
(1970) has provided evidence that violent prisoners, in contrast to non-
violent prisoners, have larger personal space areas particularly in the region
behind their backs.

Inconsistency between channels

In many social interactions, the messages transmitted through the verbal
and non-verbal channels reinforce each other in a manner which simply
increases their impact. In other cases, however, a conflict arises between the verbal and the non-verbal components of the aggregate message.

This may occur, as has been shown, when a person is speaking untruthfully. Consider a person who declares 'Of course I love you!' in a loud voice, frowning deeply and clenching his fists. The verbal component of the message implies affection, but the paralinguistic, facial and kinesic cues all indicate anger.

Verbal communication is most powerful and efficient at conveying information about facts or events external to the speaker and the speaker-listener relationship, and in these circumstances inconsistency between channels is unlikely to arise. Non-verbal communication, on the other hand, is more or less restricted to conveying information about internal feelings or about the quality of the speaker–listener relationship. (Exceptions to this rule are found in certain gestural emblems.) It is when speaking about attitudes, emotions, or matters related to the relationship with the listener, therefore, that inconsistency between channels may arise.

An interesting experiment concerning inconsistent messages about the speaker–listener relationship was reported by Argyle *et al.* (1970). The subjects were exposed to videotapes of a woman requesting volunteers for an experiment, using either superior, neutral or deferential language combined with either superior, neutral or deferential non-verbal signals. Each subject gave his or her impression of the messages on a set of semantic differential scales, and the design allowed the relative impact of the verbal and non-verbal components to be quantified precisely by Analysis of Variance. The results showed that non-verbal cues had 21·7 times the effect of verbal cues in influencing the variance in the subjects' ratings; in the case of female subjects the relative impact of the non-verbal cues was even greater and for male subjects it was slightly less.

The above experiment was concerned with messages which communicated information about the quality of interpersonal relationships. As has already been mentioned, Mehrabian (1972) proposed the following formula for the relative weight of verbal and non-verbal factors in determining the attitude or emotion conveyed by a message: *Total Impact: 0·07 Verbal + 0·38 Paralinguistic + 0·55 Facial.* From this formula we can calculate the non-verbal/verbal ratio to be 13·1 : 1. Mehrabian does not always make it clear that his findings apply to the communication of internal feelings only, and not to information of all kinds. Taken together, however, the results of the studies discussed above show that messages concerned with both internal feelings (attitudes, emotions, etc.) and the quality of relationships are conveyed largely through the non-verbal channel, and that when inconsistencies exist between channels, the recipients of the messages are overwhelmingly influenced by the non-verbal component. These findings relate to adults; there is evidence that children respond primarily to verbal cues once they have learned to comprehend language. Bugental *et al.* (1970) showed that inconsistent messages such as a criticism spoken with a smile, are interpreted more negatively by children than by adults, especially when the speaker is a woman.

There are many people who habitually emit messages whose verbal and non-verbal components are inconsistent, even when they are not lying or deceiving in any conscious sense. There are others whose paralinguistic behaviour in particular is abnormal: usually they speak too softly, indistinctly and slowly in a flat, monotonous tone. Some people habitually display a blank, unsmiling facial expression and show continuous gaze aversion, and still others manifest a sort of kinesic 'freezing' and seem never to have acquired appropriate proxemic habits. A person who manifests one of these non-verbal peculiarities very often displays most or all of the others to some degree. People in all these categories are often described as suffering from *social skills deficits*. Work has begun in England, and to a lesser extent elsewhere, in an attempt to remedy these deficits by means of *social skills training* (Trower, Bryant and Argyle, 1978) and the early results look very encouraging. This work is an example of applied social psychology, and it is a field in which considerable expansion is likely to take place in the future.

Chapter 24
Psychology's Applications

Introduction

Knowledge in any field, including psychology, may or may not be of direct practical use. On occasion, however, 'useless' knowledge of yesterday has proved useful today; and today's basic knowledge could find valuable applicability tomorrow. Thus, a sharp distinction between 'pure' and applied knowledge is never possible. Likewise, basic and applied research are not necessarily distinct, though the former focuses on gaining knowledge, as such, while the latter is a response to, and seeks to meet, a practical need.

The bulk of the present book is concerned with psychological knowledge and research that might be described as non-applied, but certainly not as non-applicable. Some fields of study, such as the assessment of individuals dealt with in Chapter 19, have obvious applications in educational, clinical and occupational psychology. Other topics introduced in earlier chapters, e.g., attention, perceptual organization, skilled performance, or remembering, could have relevance to practical problems, although the extent of their applicability is a matter of debate. Some kinds of work that applied psychologists have to undertake are not directly based on any one branch of academic psychology, but such work may nevertheless make use of techniques and experimental procedures developed within the discipline of psychology, making it possible for real-life psychological problems to be tackled in a professional rather than an amateurish manner.

It is clearly impossible in this short chapter to survey comprehensively the many applications of psychology. However, the reader may find it useful at the close of the book to be told something about the activities of applied psychology. This we propose to do by giving what may be regarded as a quick bird's-eye view of the fields in which applied psychologists of diverse kinds are working.

Educational psychology

Very broadly conceived, educational psychology would be concerned with every aspect of learning (and remembering), with cognitive and social development from birth to maturity, with the assessment of ability and personality, as well as with a host of specific problems, such as teacher–pupil relationships, methods of examining pupils and students, educational retardation and so on (Stones, 1966). In practice, educational psychology refers to a range of activities of educational psychologists who in the United Kingdom are chiefly employed by local authorities in school psychological services, often associated with child guidance clinics. Some educational psychologists work in other settings, such as paediatric assessment units which may be attached to university departments, hospitals or other centres.

Educational psychologists' work is normally carried out in collaboration with other professional people, viz. social workers, psychiatrists, speech therapists, community physicians and various specialist remedial teachers. It involves (a) investigating children's and adolescents' learning and/or behaviour and/or emotional problems, and (b) advising upon and/or undertaking remedial treatments. It should be noted that educational psychologists have certain statutory responsibilities connected with the ascertainment of special needs of school-age children handicapped by impairments of sight, hearing or language and suffering from other disabilities, e.g. epilepsy; they also have the duty to assess the needs of children considered to be disturbed or maladjusted; and they are required to make appropriate arrangements for the education of all such children.

A distinction is sometimes drawn between educational psychology and the psychology of education. The former, defined by the educational psychologists' range of activities, might be extended to embrace also what educational psychologists could or should do beyond what they actually do. The latter, the psychology of education, refers less to practice than to the body of knowledge concerning the applicability of psychology to problems of education. The ambit of possible applicability is a wide one; it includes motivation, attention and perception, learning principles, retention and recall, language development and concept formation, as well as individual differences in intelligence and personality (Child, 1977). A specific example would be the question as to how the existing knowledge of perceptual and cognitive development of children could be used in constructing school curricula for different age groups. Likewise one would wish to know how the established general knowledge of conditions conducive to effective learning might specifically be applied to the teaching of different school subjects (Riding. 1977).

It may, of course, be cogently argued that many areas of study do not fit the distinction mentioned above. One of the many possible examples would be educational assessment, which includes conventional examinations as well as the so-called continuous assessment of academic progress. This is certainly a field which is of interest to both psychology and education. While presenting many thorny theoretical problems, assessment in some form is clearly necessary to provide feedback to teachers and essential information to parents and potential employers of school leavers. There is, too, the important area of research concerning educational handicaps (Shakespeare, 1975). These include physical disabilities and cognitive deficits, as well as personality and behaviour disturbances. The latter are, of course, also of particular interest and concern to clinical psychologists; and it is the field of clinical psychology to which we must now turn.

Clinical psychology

The roots of clinical psychology lie in the study of abnormal psychological states and psychopathology. Traditionally, clinical psychologists, together with psychiatrists, have been involved in the diagnosis of mental illness; more latterly, they have also been using their special skills by giving to patients certain kinds of therapeutic treatment. References to mental illness imply a medical-model approach by clinical psychology, that is a view that, just as a person can be either physically well or physically ill, so also he/she may be well or ill mentally. In more recent years this medical model has been criticized. Many problems with which clinical psychologists have to deal in practice may be described as problems of living rather than of mental illness (Mackay, 1975). Such are not only problems of marital discord, loneliness, bereavement, etc., but also perhaps anxiety, phobias and the like. It has been argued that the medical model is inappropriate in such cases, although it makes good sense in relation to conditions of severe disturbance – perhaps those described as psychotic, such as schizophrenia or acute clinical depression.

In Britain, clinical psychologists generally, but not invariably, function within the National Health Service. They investigate individuals by means of clinical interviews and psychological tests designed to assess abilities, personality and any possible brain damage. Of all the treatments available, the one entirely pioneered by psychologists is behaviour therapy/modification. It derives from the application of learning principles, more especially classical and operant conditioning, to practical situations. These range from the management of patients in hospitals for the mentally handicapped, to the imparting of social skills to individuals who experience difficulties in coping with everyday problems.

In giving an account, no matter how brief, of the work of clinical psychologists it is necessary to start with the process of clinical assessment which is set in train by the referral of the client or patient. Here the psychologist has an armoury of tools at his/her disposal. First of all, there is, of course, the interview, both with the referred individual and with persons who are familiar with him/her. Interviews range from highly structured ones, virtually verbal questionnaires, to wholly unstructured 'free-wheeling' open types of interview. When members of the family are seen, this is often done by another member of the team, the social worker. To aid the assessment of the problem, the client's life history records may be consulted. Then there are psychological tests; various kinds have been extensively used since the early days of the century. Tests are used to obtain information about the client's abilities and personality; the latter subsumes attitudes, emotional needs, expectancies, interests, cognitive style and so on. Equally important, if not more so, are situational observations of the client. Such observations, during the interview and testing sessions, as well as in other situations if possible, can confirm, or shed doubt on, the assessment arrived at by the more formal means. Standard textbooks of clinical psychology deal at great length with methods and problems of assessment and diagnosis (see, for example, Phares, 1979).

The other phase of the clinical psychologist's work is psychological treatment, intervention or therapy. Here, too, there are many methods available; and there are deep divisions of opinion about the efficacy of the different approaches. Medication and such forms of physical treatment as electro-convulsive therapy apart, which are the psychiatrists' prerogatives, the clinical psychologist, broadly speaking, may try to modify the client's functioning either by psychotherapy or by behaviour therapy. In the former case, what essentially happens is that the therapist listens and talks to the client; but there are very many ways of doing this, in accordance with different underlying notions about the nature of the therapeutic process. Perhaps most forms, though by no means all, of psychotherapy derive from the psychoanalytic or psychodynamic tradition. The therapist attempts to interpret the client's problems, quite often in terms of his/her childhood experiences. Being at the receiving end of such treatment is an emotional experience of some intensity; the client may, however, gain a measure of insight into his/her problems which should help him/her to cope better with them. Other forms of psychotherapy have their roots mainly in the phenomenological and humanistic traditions. Quite widely practised are the so-called personal-construct therapy, client-centred therapy, Gestalt therapy, rational-emotive therapy, as well as experiential group methods.

Psychotherapy of any kind is expected to bring about in its wake some changes of behaviour; but such changes are regarded as secondary effects. In contrast, behaviour therapy is a treatment which aims directly at modifying the individual's behaviour; the expectation is that this would essentially provide the solution to the problem with which the clinical psychologist has been called upon to deal. In general, the behavioural approach uses techniques which derive straight from learning principles established by research in the field of conditioning, both classical and operant. These techniques include systematic desensitization, relaxation, aversive training and so on. Such treatments nowadays often go hand in hand with a form of psychotherapy known as cognitive restructuring, which may be conducive to behaviour changes. Conditions most frequently treated by behaviour therapy include anxiety, phobias, alcohol and drug dependence, and other addictions such as smoking and compulsive eating. Learning principles are also relied upon in devising programmes of rehabilitation and the training of mentally-handicapped patients.

Interprofessional issues loom large in all areas of applied psychology, but, perhaps nowhere more so than in clinical psychology. Psychological methods of treatment form, of course, part of the work of all helping professions. In addition to psychologists, professionals such as psychiatrists, psychiatric nurses and social workers engage in psychotherapy and/or behaviour therapy of some description. The striking growth and transformation of clinical psychology in Britain since the late 1950s has contributed to the demarcation problems and disputes. Up to the late 1950s there were relatively few practising clinical psychologists, and their role was mainly confined to psychological testing. Nowadays psychological assessment involves much more than routine testing; above all, psychologists have in recent years been developing new forms of treatment. All this has entailed much more interaction, and sometimes some friction, with others working in psychiatric and subnormality hospitals, such as psychiatrists, social workers and nurses. There is also some uncertainty as to where the boundary lies between clinical psychology and educational psychology when, for instance, conduct disorders in children are concerned. However, clinical psychologists themselves are searching for improvements in the guidelines for their day-to-day work and relationships with neighbouring professional groups. This is important in view of the new directions evident in present-day clinical psychology. One which is increasingly promising is the collaboration with neurosurgeons. This, among other things, involves the assessment of memory disorders with a view to pin-pointing brain lesions and, later, evaluating the outcomes of neurosurgical procedures. Quite a different direction in which clinical psychology is developing concerns welfare arrangements in hospital wards and institutions. Yet another development is the help provided by clinical psychologists to general practitioners and health visitors; generally, such techniques as behaviour modification have a role to play in public-health education.

Criminological psychology

It is to be hoped that it will become more and more feasible to apply psychology to the understanding and treatment of criminal behaviour. Forensic psychology, as this branch of applied psychology is sometimes called, is still in its infancy, but interest in it is markedly on the increase. In Britain psychologists are employed in the prison service, helping with the design, development and evaluation of prison régimes and the training of prison officers. There is a wealth of statistics on crime in relation to age, intelligence, race and other such variables. The most psychologically interesting are perhaps the possible relationships of crime and psychopathy to personality characteristics, such as impulsivity. Unfortunately, however, it continues to be true that 'there is little substantial evidence to differentiate the criminal from the non-criminal, particularly in a predictive manner' (J. M. Brown *et al.*, 1966, p. 524).

Crime is well known to be associated with various environmental factors. It tends to be more frequent among those of low socio-economic status, although it is an open question as to whether poor living conditions contribute towards criminal behaviour, or whether such conditions and crime both result from a common cause. Modes of upbringing had long been suspected to influence the individual's later behaviour with regard to delinquency. Glueck and Glueck (1959) found among other things that children exposed to inconsistent discipline and deprived of affection have a greater proneness to crime in later life. Gibson (1969) investigated the family circumstances of over 400 boys, aged eight years, who had records of delinquency; he found an association between homes broken by parental desertion, rather than by death, and delinquent acts; the age, however, at which a child suffered emotional deprivation was not predictive of the child's degree or type of delinquency.

Empirical findings, such as those mentioned above, shed light on criminal behaviour, but do not provide a proper understanding of it. What is needed is an explanatory theory of crime. There have been interesting attempts to provide such a psychological theory in terms of learning principles (e.g. Trasler, 1962). However, our general knowledge of the lasting effects of early experience is somewhat uncertain, and learning theory itself is in a state of turmoil (see Chapters 12 and 13). Therefore, it does not look as if a psychology of criminality could be built upon firm foundations. Nevertheless, criminological and legal psychology does constitute a body of empirical knowledge and practice. Some of this relates to problems of detection of deception and of court-room procedures.

Individuals who are suspected of having committed a crime will more often than not attempt to conceal any delinquency of which they may be guilty. It is often said that the untruths told by a person under interrogation can be revealed by means of the so-called lie detector. There is no such thing, however, as a genuine lie detector; there is only apparatus which can indicate certain physiological changes occurring while the individual being questioned gives his/her answers. The physiological measures usually monitored in such circumstances include blood pressure, pulse rate, breathing rate and the electrical conductivity of the subject's skin (known as the psychogalvanic reflex). Telling a lie is commonly associated with emotional arousal which is reflected in the various physiological responses just mentioned. However, it is recognized that changes associated with emotional states may occur not only, or even not primarily, as a result of lying. Therefore the messages provided by 'lie detectors' must be interpreted with great caution.

A different concern of forensic psychology is the role of the psychologist in the court of law. It is thought that the psychologist's contribution to evidence is, or should be, different from that of the psychiatrist. The latter attempts a psychiatric diagnosis of the individual on trial. The psychologist, however, perhaps like the pathologist, can offer factual evidence within his competence and state the logical implications of his findings. Thus, the results of psychological tests may well have a bearing on the suitability of the offender for different types of training. A longer-term prospect might be the contribution that psychology could make to the training of magistrates and judges. So far as research is concerned, psychological follow-up studies of convicted offenders may be able to shed more light on criminal behaviour and the best remedial measures available to those who administer the law.

Occupational psychology

Occupational psychology is concerned with people at work; by definition, then, its potential importance for human well-being can scarcely be exaggerated, since work is a central feature of life in modern industrial society. Occupational psychology tends to be concerned with industrial work, but other occupations such as commerce, the civil service and the armed forces are also within its province. Thus occupational psychologists may be employed by government organizations, such as the Department of Employment and the Manpower Services Commission, or by such organizations as the Civil Service, the Post Office and the Greater London Council; they may be employed by private companies, either singly or as part of a research unit. Occupational psychologists may also be involved as teachers, for example, in management training.

The business of occupational psychology has been traditionally defined as 'fitting the man to the job' and 'fitting the job to the man'. The first heading refers to such activities as vocational guidance and the selection and training of personnel. Vocational guidance is concerned with assisting an individual's choice of career, while selection is concerned with choosing an individual for a job from among a number of applicants, or perhaps with the allocation of successful applicants to one area or another of the work of a company. Although obviously the occupational psychologist's primary interest is rather differently placed in the two cases, they have features in common: both involve the use of interviews and tests of aptitude, interests and perhaps personality, and the analysis of occupations, for example in terms of 'job descriptions' specifying the conditions and details of work and the qualities required for adequate job performance. Once selection is made, by the individual and by the employer, the chosen applicant usually requires more or less formal job training, even in occupations where the traditional training method has been 'sitting by Nellie', or learning by observation 'on the job'. The occupational psychologist has an important, and increasing, part to play in the design and evaluation of training courses and learning systems, including the development of managerial skills (see Stammers and Patrick, 1975).

Vocational guidance and training have typically been experiences supplied to the individual once in his lifetime, at the end of the school (or university) career and the beginning of employment; but they are becoming increasingly relevant at later stages in life. Individuals may make an initial error in their choice of career; their needs (for example, domestic responsibilities) may change; they may suffer physical or psychological disablement; with technological change their job may cease to exist. The 'growth areas' in fitting the man for the job may well be life-long vocational counselling and the development of selection and training procedures suitable for older people embarking on a 'second career' (Belbin and Belbin, 1972); the development of 'retirement planning programmes' to enable people to make the transition from work to retirement more easily is also likely to become increasingly important.

One important aspect of 'fitting the job to the man' is *ergonomics* (e.g. Murrell, 1965), also sometimes called human engineering or human factors research. The aim of ergonomics is to improve work efficiency by tailoring the conditions and requirements of the job to the anatomical, physiological and psychological characteristics of the worker. The psychologist working in ergonomics, for example, may be concerned with the design of visual displays, such as warning lights, scales and representational displays of processing systems. He may also be concerned with the design and positioning of controls, such as levers, cranks, handwheels, knobs and footpedals, as well as with improving the efficiency of monitoring or inspection and with the effects of more general characteristics of the work place, such as ambient noise and temperature levels. Increasingly, too, the ergonomist is concerned with the design and evaluation of 'man–machine systems' (see Singleton, 1974).

The aim of ergonomics research is explicitly to increase efficiency and productivity; some research in occupational psychology is less directly concerned with performance levels and more with job satisfaction. Although, according to Tilgher (1962), 'to the Greeks work was a curse and nothing else', for many people work is a major activity in which personal achievement and 'self-actualization' may be sought, and a number of methods have been explored for increasing satisfaction: for example, job rotation, enlargement or enrichment, aimed at increasing the variety and interest of work and, in the latter cases at least, the sense of personal responsibility of the individual worker for the final product. Differences in organizational structure, the 'working group' and managerial style have also been explored (in what is sometimes termed 'organizational psychology') in relation to satisfaction. Most studies of job satisfaction are not simply philanthropic but are initiated on the assumption that increased satisfaction, high morale and 'intrinsic motivation' will in fact be reflected in greater working efficiency and lower rates of absenteeism and turnover. This assumption is more clearly justified with respect to absenteeism and turnover than with respect to productivity, and it is also worth noting that the role of job satisfaction, and more generally attitudes to work, appear to differ substantially among individuals and among occupations.

The term 'occupational psychology' clearly covers a very wide range of applications of psychology to problems of work, drawing not only upon explicitly 'applied' research findings but also upon 'basic' research data in the fields of individual differences (in vocational guidance and selection), perception, learning, memory and skill (in training and in ergonomics), social psychology and group differences (in organization and work design and in considering the special characteristics of women at work and of older workers). For further discussion of occupational psychology, see, for example, Davies and Shackleton (1975) and Warr and Wall (1975).

Consumer psychology

Very broadly conceived, occupational psychology would include those aspects of market research which are concerned with people's attitudes to diverse products, ranging from margarine and detergents to television programmes and road discipline. However, the study of such attitudes – and especially attitude changes resulting from exposure, advertising and propaganda – has long been regarded as a separate branch of applied psychology known as consumer psychology (Bass and Barrett, 1972; Tuck, 1976). Continual monitoring of changes in consumer attitudes is of vital importance to manufacturers, advertisers, broadcasters and government departments (e.g. D.H.S.S. in its concern with health education). Consumer psychology involves the application of traditional social-psychological methods of attitude measurement. A typical consumer research is a 'before-and-after' study which compares the views of people before and after exposure to a campaign of persuasion, e.g. that it is best to smoke a certain brand of cigarettes, or that smoking is bad for health. Sometimes, however, before-and-after studies assess attitude changes which are not deliberately fostered but which occur quite spontaneously.

In conducting attitude studies, qualitative judgements are sometimes required, for example, of the texture of wool, the taste of cheese, the attractiveness of colours and so on. Work of this kind relies on well-established psycho-physical laboratory methods. When objective information is needed on time spent looking at advertisements, eye-movement cameras developed by students of visual perception have been used. In questionnaire construction, series of well-worded questions have to be put together, and established social-psychological procedures have been used for this purpose. Survey research techniques, including opinion polls, involving the gathering of information from representative samples of consumers, have been developing all the time. Representative samples are commonly samples of individuals drawn at random; often, however, samples are suitably stratified so as to ensure that the various sections of the total population are represented in correct proportions. Thus, observational, experimental and statistical methods of academic psychology have been found to be applicable to consumer research in a variety of ways.

The so-called motivation research attempts to go further than the traditional consumer research; it asks additionally *why* are the attitudes found such as they are. Direct questions will often not reveal the motives for particular attitudes. Indirect questions, however, might disclose the consumers' secret fears, urges and hopes (Henry, 1958; Packard, 1960). The so-called depth interviews are used to obtain such information. Data could be gathered this way on the unconscious reasons for preferring, for example, a particular brand of soap or tooth-paste. Then, information of this kind would be utilized for introducing the most effective mode of appeal in advertising any given product. However, the interpretations of depth interviews are very uncertain. Above all, the ethics of basing advertising on this type of depth interview research is questionable. For these reasons there has been some disenchantment with motivation research, and it is much less popular today than a decade or two ago. The more traditional consumer research, however, including product testing, advertising-effectiveness testing, radio and television audience research, and the like, is flourishing.

Environmental psychology

To some extent environmental psychology represents an extension of occupational psychology, in that it is concerned with the effect of man's physical environment on behaviour in occupational and more especially residential settings. In a sense, of course, the term 'environmental psychology' could be taken to subsume most of the subject matter of this book; in practice it has been used to denote an interest in the effects of particular aspects of the built environment – in particular, the design of homes, schools, hospitals and cities. Like ergonomics, environmental psychology is essentially multidisciplinary, and its practitioners work (at least ideally) alongside architects, planners, geographers, biologists, engineers, sociologists and politicians. In fact environmental psychology tends to be a subsidiary research interest of psychologists basically employed otherwise, for example as university teachers, although a few psychologists are employed by building research units, others may teach in schools of architecture, and there is a growing number of graduate courses in environmental psychology particularly in the U.S.A.

Methods used in research are quite varied, ranging from laboratory studies of population density in rats, via ecological observations of people in their own homes or neighbourhoods, to correlational studies of housing area (and therefore housing type) and the incidence of schizophrenia and other pathology. Studies of noise and other environmental stresses (Chapter 9), and of the characteristics of 'personal space' (Chapter 23) and the desire for privacy, are relevant, as is population research; there has been much interest in the effect upon 'inmate activity' of school size and location and the layout of hospital wards, and above all in aspects of the urban environment – housing density, the possession of gardens, house size, 'high-rise' living and so on – and their effect upon adult behaviour and well-being and upon child development.

Man is the manipulator *par excellence* of his own physical environment: it is clearly important to discover to what extent, and in what ways, people are in turn influenced by the environment which they (or others of their species) have created. However, such relations, and in particular their causal nature, are very difficult to determine. Consider the concept of *crowding* (Freedman, 1975). Some people live crowded together in blocks of flats, and in low-income areas the density of population sometimes reaches a high value. It is well known that animals kept in crowded conditions fail to thrive and appear to suffer from prolonged stress; thus it seemed natural to hypothesize that high-density living might have detrimental psychological effects upon humans. Early findings, indeed, showed positive correlations between population density on the one hand and the incidence of mental illness and juvenile delinquency on the other. Closer investigations, however, showed that such effects were associated with low socio-economic status and that therefore crowding *per se* could not be said to be the cause of high rates of abnormal psychological conditions. It also appears that 'crowding' is not determined solely by population density, as measured by the number of people per unit space, but also by such factors as competition for resources, the amount of social contact among inhabitants of the same space, and the homogeneity, in terms of shared value systems, of those inhabitants. Further, some individuals, and some cultures, may for various reasons be better able to tolerate high population density than others.

Clearly, much more research and conceptual analysis is needed before the findings of environmental psychology can safely be used, as ideally they should be used, as a basis for planning decisions. Indeed, Mercer (1975, p. 219) has concluded that 'the scientific inquiry of environmental psychology cannot answer the questions of what is the best environment for man and the best man for the environment; all it can do is to make the inevitably value-loaded answers to these questions slightly less than complete shots in the dark'. Even with this cautious view of their potential, future developments could be exciting and worth while. For further discussion of environmental psychology, see Ittelson *et al.* (1974); Mercer (1975, 1978); Lee (1976).

Careers in psychology and related fields

Earlier sections of this chapter will have shown that the activities of applied psychologists range far and wide. Perhaps a distinction ought to be made between careers in the recognized areas of applied psychology and careers in fields where the background of psychological knowledge is not a *sine qua non* but where it is nevertheless highly relevant.

In Britain the professions of educational and clinical psychology are well established. Occupational psychology has not quite the same uniform structure with regard to the nature of work and pay. Nevertheless, in Government service psychologists, as such, are employed in various fields, e.g. in the prison service, in the Armed Forces, in industrial rehabilitation centres, in research centres (such as, for instance, the Road Research Laboratory) and so on. To all these may be added employment in the teaching of psychology as well as in research funded by official bodies, such as the Science and Engineering Research Council, the Social Science Research Council or the Medical Research Council.

In addition to those areas where a recognized psychology qualification is essential there are the ones in which it can be useful. Thus, psychology graduates often pursue careers in market research and advertising, in personnel management, in social work, in school teaching, and so on, as well as in work in the mass media – the press, radio and television.

The *British Psychological Society*, which has been in existence since the beginning of the century, has as its aim the promotion of the study of psychology and its applications. One of its main concerns is the maintenance of standards of professional qualifications and conduct. Among other things, the Society publishes information booklets on the various careers in psychology. There are similar associations of psychologists in many other countries. The fields in which knowledge of psychology is of relevance are many and varied. It will be exciting to see what impact the ever-widening range of applications of psychology will have on the society of tomorrow.

References

ADAMS, H. E., and BUTLER, J. R. (1967), 'The deviation hypothesis: a review of the evidence', in I. A. Berg (ed.), *Response Set in Personality Assessment*, Aldine.

ADAMS, J. A. (1969), 'Acquisition of motor responses', in M. H. Marx (ed.), *Learning Processes*, Macmillan.

ADAMS, J. A. (1971), 'A closed-loop theory of motor learning', *J. Motor Behav.*, vol. 3, pp. 111–49.

ADES, H. W. (1959), 'Central auditory mechanisms', in J. Field, H. W. Magoun and V. E. Hall (eds.), *Handbook of Physiology*, vol. 1, Williams & Wilkins.

ADLER, A. (1939), *Social Interest*, Putnam.

AGNEW, H. W., WEBB, W. B., and WILLIAMS, R. L. (1967), 'Comparison of stage four and 1 – REM sleep deprivation', *Percept. Motor Skills*, vol. 24, pp. 851–8.

AIKEN, L. R. (1971), *Psychological and Educational Testing*, Allyn & Bacon.

AINSWORTH, M. D. *et al.* (1962), *Deprivation of Maternal Care: A Reassessment of its Results*, World Health Organization.

ALLEE, W. C. and MASURE, R. H. (1936), 'A comparison of maze behavior in paired and isolated shell parakeets (*Melopsittacus undulatus*, Shaw)', *Physiol. Zool.*, vol. 22, pp. 131–56.

ALLISON, T., and CICCHETTI, D. V. (1976), 'Sleep in mammals: ecological and constitutional correlates', *Science*, vol. 194, pp. 732–4.

ALLPORT, A., ANTONIS, B., and REYNOLDS, P. (1972), 'On the division of attention: a disproof of the single channel hypothesis', *Quart. J. exp. Psychol.*, vol. 24, pp. 225–35.

ALLPORT, D. A. (1980), 'Attention and performance', in G. Claxton (ed.), *Cognitive Psychology: New Directions*, Routledge & Kegan Paul.

ALLPORT, F. H. (1920), 'The influence of the group upon association and thought', *J. exp. Psychol.*, vol. 3, pp. 159–82.

ALLPORT, F. H. (1924), *Social Psychology*, Houghton Mifflin.

ALLPORT, F. H. (1955), *Theories of Perception and the Concept of Structure*, Wiley.

ALLPORT, G. W. (1937), *Personality: A Psychological Interpretation*, Holt, Rinehart & Winston.

ALLPORT, G. W. (1961), *Pattern and Growth in Personality*, Holt, Rinehart & Winston.

ALLPORT, G. W. (1968), 'The historical background of modern social psychology', in G. Lindzey, and E. Aronson (eds.), *The Handbook of Social Psychology*, vol. 1, pp. 1–80, Addison-Wesley.

ALSTON, W. P. (1976), 'Traits, consistency and conceptual alternatives in personality theory', in R. Harré (ed.), *Personality*, pp. 63–97, Blackwell.

ALTMAN, J., and DAS, G. D. (1964), 'Autoradiographic examination of the effects of enriched environment on the rate of glial multiplication in the adult rat brain', *Nature*, vol. 204, pp. 1161–3.

ANAND, B. D., and BROBECK, J. R. (1951), 'Hypothalamic control of food intake', *Yale J. biol. Med.*, vol. 24, pp. 123–40.

ANASTASI, A. (1958), *Differential Psychology*, Macmillan.

ANGELL, J. R. (1916), 'A reconsideration of James's theory of emotion in the light of recent criticisms', *Psychol. Rev.*, vol. 23, pp. 251–61.

ANNETT, J. (1969), *Feedback and Human Behaviour*, Penguin Books.

ANNETT, J., and KAY, H. (1956), 'Skilled performance', *Occup. Psychol.*, vol. 30, pp. 112–17.

ANNETT, J., *et al.* (1974), *Human Information Processing*, vol. 1, Open University Press.

ANNETT, M. (1972), 'The distribution of manual preference', *Brit. J. Psychol.*, vol. 63, pp. 343–58.

ANTROBUS, J., ANTROBUS, J. S., and FISHER, C. (1965), 'Discrimination of dreaming and non-dreaming sleep', *Arch. gen. Psychiat.*, vol. 12, pp. 395–401.

APTER, M. J. (1970), *The Computer Simulation of Behaviour*, Hutchinson.

ARCHER, J. (1973), 'Tests of emotionality in the rat', *Animal Behav.*, vol. 21, pp. 205–35.

ARCHER, J., and LLOYD, B. (1975), 'Sex differences: biological and social interaction', in R. Lewis (ed.), *Child Alive: New Insights into the Development of Young Children*, Temple Smith.

ARENBERG, D., and ROBERTSON-TCHABO, E. (1977), 'Learning and aging', in J. E. Birren and K. W. Schaie (eds.), *Handbook of the Psychology of Aging*, Van Nostrand.

ARGYLE, M. (1975), *Bodily Communication*, Methuen.

ARGYLE, M. (1976), 'Personality and social behaviour', in R. Harré (ed.), *Personality*, Blackwell.

ARGYLE, M., and COOK, M. (1976), *Gaze and Mutual Gaze*, Cambridge University Press.

ARGYLE, M., LALLJEE, M., and COOK, M. (1968), 'The effects of visibility on interaction in a dyad', *Hum. Rel.*, vol. 21, pp. 3–17.

ARGYLE, M., *et al.* (1970), 'The communication of inferior and superior attitudes by verbal and non-verbal signals', *Brit. J. soc. clin. Psychol.*, vol. 9, pp. 222–31.

ARONSON, E., and ROSENBLOOM, S. (1971), 'Space perception in early infancy: perception within a common auditory–visual space', *Science*, vol. 172, pp. 1161–3.

ARONSON, L. R., *et al.* (eds.) (1970), *Development and Evolution of Behavior*, Freeman.

ASERINSKY, E., and KLEITMAN, N. (1953), 'Regularly occurring periods of eye motility and concomitant phenomena during sleep', *Science*, vol. 118, pp. 273–4.

ASHBY, W. R. (1952), *Design for a Brain*, Chapman & Hall.

ATKINSON, J. W. (ed.) (1958), *Motives in Fantasy, Action and Society*, Van Nostrand.

ATKINSON, J. W., and FEATHER, N. T. (eds.) (1966), *A Theory of Achievement Motivation*, Wiley.

ATKINSON, R. C., and SHIFFRIN, R. M. (1971), 'The control of short-term memory', *Scient. Amer.*, vol. 225, pp. 82–90.

ATKINSON, R. M., and RINGUETTE, E. L. (1967), 'A survey of biographical and psychological features in extraordinary fatness', *Psychosom. Med.*, vol. 29, pp. 121–33.

AUSUBEL, D. P. (1958), *Theory and Problems of Child Development*, Grune & Stratton.

AVERILL, J. R. (1969), 'Autonomic response patterns during sadness and mirth', *Psychophysiology*, vol. 5, pp. 399–414.

AVERILL, J. R. (1976), 'Emotion and anxiety: sociocultural, biological and psychological determinants', in M. Zuckerman and C. D. Spielberger (eds.), *Emotions and Anxiety: New Concepts, Methods and Applications*, Lawrence Erlbaum.

AVERILL, J. R., OPTON, E. M. Jr., and LAZARUS, R. S. (1969), 'Cross-cultural studies of psychophysiological responses during stress and emotion', *Int. J. Psychol.*, vol. 4, pp. 33–102.

AX, A. F. (1953), 'The physiological differentiation between fear and anger in humans', *Psychosom. Med.*, vol. 15, pp. 433–42.

BADDELEY, A. D. (1976), *The Psychology of Memory*, Harper & Row.

BADDELEY, A. D., et al. (1970), 'Memory and time of day', *Quart. J. exp. Psychol.* vol. 22, pp. 606–9.

BADDELEY, A. D., and HITCH, G. (1974), 'Working memory', in G. H. Bower (ed.), *The Psychology of Learning and Motivation: Advances in Research & Theory*, vol. 8, Academic Press.

BADDELEY, A. D., and HITCH, G. (1976), 'Recency reexamined', in S. Dornic (ed.) *Attention and Performance, VI*, Academic Press.

BAEKELAND, F., and LASKY, R. (1966), 'Exercise and sleep patterns in college athletes', *Percept. Motor Skills*, vol. 23, pp. 1203–7.

BAIR, J. H. (1901), 'Development of voluntary control', *Psychol. Rev.*, vol. 8, pp. 474–510.

BAKAN, D. (1966), *The Duality of Human Existence*, Rand McNally.

BAKER, C. H. (1963), 'Further toward a theory of vigilance', in D. N. Buckner and J. J. McGrath (eds.), *Vigilance: A Symposium*, McGraw-Hill.

BAKER J. R. (1974), *Race*, Oxford University Press.

BALTES, P. B., and SCHAIE, K. W. (1976), 'On the plasticity of intelligence in adulthood and old age: where Horn and Donaldson fail', *Amer. Psychologist*, vol. 31, pp. 720–25.

BANDURA, A. (1962), 'Social learning through imitation', in M. R. Jones (ed.), *Nebraska Symposium on Motivation*, University of Nebraska Press.

BANDURA, A., and MISCHEL, W. (1965), 'Modification of self-imposed delay of reward', *J. Pers. soc. Psychol.*, vol. 2, pp. 698–705.

BANDURA, A., and WALTERS, R. H. (1963), *Social Learning and Personality Development*, Holt, Rinehart & Winston.

BANNISTER, D., and MAIR, J. M. M. (1968), *The Evaluation of Personal Constructs*, Academic Press.

BARASH, D. P. (1979), *Sociobiology and Behavior*, Heinemann.

BARCLAY, J. R. (1973), 'The role of comprehension in the remembering of sentences', *Cognit. Psychol.*, vol. 4, pp. 229–54.

BARCLAY, J. R., *et al.* (1974), 'Comprehension and semantic flexibility', *J. verb. Learn. verb. Behav.*, vol. 13, pp. 471–81.

BARD, P. (1928), 'A diencephalic mechanism for the expression of rage with special reference to the sympathetic nervous system', *Amer. J. Physiol.*, vol. 84, pp. 490–515.

BARLOW, H. B., and HILL, R. M. (1963), 'Evidence for a physiological explanation of the waterfall phenomenon and figural after-effects', *Nature*, vol. 200, pp. 1345–7.

BARNES, J. M., and UNDERWOOD, B. J. (1959), '"Fate" of first-list associations in transfer theory', *J. exp. Psychol.*, vol. 58, pp. 95–105.

BARON, R. S., MOORE, O., and SAUNDERS, G. S. (1978), 'Distraction as a source of drive in social facilitation research', *J. Pers. soc. Psychol.*, vol. 36, pp. 816–24.

BARRON, F. (1969), *Creative Person and Creative Process*, Holt, Rinehart & Winston.

BARRY, H., BACON, M., and CHILD, I. L. (1957), 'A cross-cultural survey of some sex differences in socialization', *J. abnorm. soc. Psychol.*, vol. 55, pp. 327–32.

BARTLETT, F. C. (1932), *Remembering: A Study in Experimental and Social Psychology*, Cambridge University Press.

BARTLETT, F. C. (1943), 'Fatigue following highly skilled work', *Proc. Roy. Soc. (Series B)*, vol. 131, pp. 247–57.

BARTLETT, F. C. (1948), 'The measurement of human skill', *Occup. Psychol.*, vol. 22, pp. 31–8.

BARTLETT, F. C. (1958), *Thinking: An Experimental and Social Study*, Allen & Unwin.

BARTOSHUK, A. K. (1972), 'Motivation', in J. W. Kling and L. A. Riggs (eds.), *Woodworth and Sholosberg's Experimental Psychology*, Methuen, revised edn.

BASS, B. M., and BARRETT, G. U. (1972), *Man, Work and Organization: An Introduction to Industrial and Organizational Psychology*, Allyn & Bacon.

BASSER, L. (1962), 'Hemiplegia of early onset and the faculty of speech with special reference to the effects of hemispherectomy', *Brain*, vol. 85, pp. 427–60.

BATESON, N. (1966), 'Familiarization, group discussion, and risk taking', *J. exp. soc. Psychol.*, vol. 2, pp. 119–29.

BATESON, P. P. G. (1966), 'The characteristics and context of imprinting', *Biol. Rev.*, vol. 41, pp. 177–200.

BATESON, P. P. G., and CHANTREY, D. F. (1972), 'Retardation of discrimination learning in monkeys and chicks previously exposed to both stimuli', *Nature*, vol. 237, pp. 173–4.

BATESON, P. P. G., and HINDE, R. A. (1976), *Growing Points in Ethology*, Cambridge University Press.

BATINI, C. *et al.* (1958), 'Persistent patterns of wakefulness in the pretrigeminal midpontine preparation', *Science*, vol. 128, pp. 30–32.

BATSEL, H. L. (1960), 'Electroencephalographic synchronization and desynchronization in the chronic "cerveau isolé" of the dog', *EEG clin. Neurophysiol.*, vol. 12, pp. 421–30.

BAUER, H. G. (1954), 'Endocrine and other clinical manifestations of hypothalamic disease', *J. clin. Endoc. Metabolism*, vol. 14, pp. 13–31.

BAYER, E. (1929), 'Beitrage zur Zweikomponenttheorie des Hungers', *Zeitschrift für Psychologie*, vol. 112, pp. 1–54.

BAYLEY, N. (1949), 'Consistency and variability in the growth of intelligence from birth to eighteen', *J. Gen. Psychol.*, vol. 75, pp. 165–96.

BAYLEY, N. (1955), 'On the growth of intelligence', *Amer. Psychologist*, vol. 10, pp. 805–18.

BEACH, F. A. (1955), 'The descent of instinct', *Psychol. Rev.*, vol. 62, pp. 401–10.

BEACH, F. A., and JAYNES, J. (1955), 'Effects of early experience upon the behavior of animals', *Psychol. Bull.*, vol. 51, pp. 239–63.

BEATTY, J., and KAHNEMAN, D. (1966), 'Pupillary changes in two memory tasks', *Psychon. Sci.*, vol. 5, pp. 371–2.

BEATTY, J., and WAGONER, B. L. (1978), 'Pupillometric signs of brain activation vary with level of cognitive processing', *Science*, vol. 199, pp. 1216–18.

BEAUMONT, J. G. (1974), 'Handedness and hemisphere function', in S. J. Dimond and J. G. Beaumont (eds.), *Hemisphere Function in the Human Brain*, Elek.

BECKER, W. C. (1960), 'The matching of behavior rating and questionnaire personality factors', *Psychol. Bull.*, vol. 57, pp. 202–12.

BELBIN, E., and BELBIN, R. M. (1972), *Problems in Adult Retraining*, Heinemann.

BELOFF, J. (1973), *Psychological Sciences: A Review of Modern Psychology*, Crosby Lockwood Staples.

BEM, S. L. (1974), 'The measurement of psychological androgyny', *J. consult. clin. Psychol.*, vol. 42, 155–62.

BEM, S. L. (1977), 'On the utility of alternative procedures for assessing psychological androgyny', *J. consult. clin. Psychol.*, vol. 45, pp. 196–205.

BEM, S. L., MARTYNA, W., and WATSON, C. (1976), 'Sex typing and androgyny: further explorations of the expressive domain', *J. Pers. soc. Psychol.*, vol. 34, pp. 1016–23.

BENN, S. I., and PETERS, R. (1965), *Principles of Political Thought*, Free Press of Glencoe.

BENNETT, E. L. *et al.* (1964), 'Chemical and anatomical plasticity of the brain', *Science*, vol. 146, pp. 610–19.

664 References

BENNETT, G. K., SEASHORE, H. G., and WESMAN, A. G. (1959), *Manual for the Differential Aptitude Tests*, Psychological Corporation, 3rd edn.

BENNETT, R., and ECKMAN, J. (1973), 'Attitudes towards aging: a critical examination of recent literature and implications for future research', in C. Eisdorfer and M. P. Lawton (eds.), *The Psychology of Adult Development and Aging*, American Psychological Association.

BENSON, D. F. *et al.* (1973), 'Conduction aphasia', *Arch. Neurol.*, vol. 28, pp. 339–46.

BENTHAM, J. (1815), 'A table of the springs of action', in P. McReynolds (ed.), *Four Early Works on Motivation*, Scholars' Facsimile & Reprints (1969).

BENTON, A. L. (1968), 'Disorders of spatial orientation', in P. J. Vinken and G. W. Bruyn (eds.), *Handbook of Clinical Neurology*, vol. 3, North-Holland.

BERG, I. A. (1959), 'The unimportance of test item content', in B. M. Bass and I. A. Berg (eds.), *Objective Approaches to Personality Assessment*, Van Nostrand.

BERG, I. A. (1967), 'The deviation hypothesis: a broad statement of its assumptions and postulates', in I. A. Berg (ed.), *Response Set in Personality Assessment*, Aldine.

BERGER, R. J. (1961), 'Tonus of extrinsic laryngeal muscles during sleep and dreaming', *Science*, vol. 134, p. 840.

BERGER, R. J. (1969), 'Oculomotor control: a possible function for REM sleep', *Psychol. Rev.*, vol. 76, pp. 144–64.

BERGER, R. J., and OSWALD, I. (1962), 'Effects of sleep deprivation on behaviour, subsequent sleep and dreaming', *J. mental Sci.*, vol. 108, pp. 457–65.

BERGUM, B. O., and LEHR, D. J. (1963), 'Effects of authoritarianism on vigilance performance', *J. appl. Psychol.*, vol. 47, pp. 75–7.

BERKELEY, G. (1910), *An Essay Toward a New Theory of Vision*, Dutton.

BERKO, J. (1958), 'The child's learning of English morphology', *Word*, vol. 14, pp. 150–77.

BERLYNE, D. E. (1960), *Conflict, Arousal and Curiosity*, McGraw-Hill.

BERNARD, L. L. (1924), *Instinct: A Study of Social Psychology*, Holt, Rinehart & Winston.

BERNSTEIN, B. (1973), *Class, Codes and Control*, Paladin.

BHASKAR, R. (1979), *The Possibility of Naturalism*, Harvester Press.

BILLER, H. B., SINGER, D. L., and FULLERTON, M. (1969), 'Sex-role development and creative potential in kindergarten-age boys', *Devel. Psychol.*, vol. 1, pp. 291–6.

BINET, A., and SIMON, T. (1916), *The Development of Intelligence in Children*, translated by E. S. Kite, Williams & Wilkins.

BIRREN, J. E. (1952), 'A factorial analysis of the Wechsler–Bellevue scale given to an elderly population', *J. consult. Psychol.*, vol. 16, pp. 399–405.

BIRREN, J. E., and MORRISON, D. F. (1961), 'Analysis of the WAIS subtests in relation to age and education', *J. Gerontol.*, vol. 16, pp. 363–9.

BIRREN, J. E., and SCHAIE, K. W. (eds.) (1977), *Handbook of the Psychology of Aging*, Van Nostrand.

BITTERMAN, M. E. (1960), 'Toward a comparative psychology of learning', *Amer. Psychol.*, vol. 15, pp. 704–12.

BITTERMAN, M. E. (1965), 'The evolution of intelligence', *Scient. Amer.*, vol. 212, pp. 92–101.

BITTERMAN, M. E. (1968), 'Phyletic differences in learning', in N. S. Endler, L. R. Boulter, and H. Osser (eds.), *Contemporary Issues in Developmental Psychology*, Holt, Rinehart & Winston.

BLACKMAN, D. (1974), *Operant Conditioning*, Methuen.

BLAKE, M. J. F. (1967), 'Time of day effects on performance in a range of tasks', *Psychon. Sci.*, vol. 9, pp. 349–50.

BLAKEMORE, C. (1975), 'Central visual processing', in M. S. Gazzaniga and C. Blakemore (eds.), *Handbook of Psychobiology*, Academic Press.

BLINKOV, S. M., and GLASER, I. I. (1968), *The Human Brain: A Quantitative Handbook*, Basic Books & Plenum Press.

BLOCK, J. A. (1961), *The Q-Sort Method in Personality Assessment and Psychiatric Research*, Charles C. Thomas.

BLOCK J. A. (1965), *The Challenge of Response Sets: Unconfounding Meaning, Acquiescence and Social Desirability in the M.M.P.I.*, Appleton-Century-Crofts.

BLOCK, J. H. (1973), 'Conceptions of sex role', *Amer. Psychol.*, vol. 28, pp. 512–26.

BLOCK, J. H. (1976), 'Issues, problems and pitfalls in assessing sex differences: a critical review of *The Psychology of Sex Differences*', *Merrill-Palmer Q.*, vol. 22, no. 4.

BLOCK, N., and DWORKIN, G. (1977), *The I.Q. Controversy*, Quartet Books.

BLODGETT, H. C. (1929), 'The effect of the introduction of reward upon the maze performance of rats', *Univ. Calif. Publ. Psychol.*, vol. 4, pp. 113–34.

BLOOM, B. S. (1964), *Stability and Change in Human Characteristics*, Wiley.

BLOOM, L. (1970), *Language Development: Form and Function in Developing Grammars*, M.I.T. Press.

BLOOM, L. (1973), *One Word at a Time*, Mouton.

BLURTON JONES, N. (ed.). (1972), *Ethological Studies of Child Behaviour*, Cambridge University Press.

BODEN, M. A. (1972), *Purposive Explanation in Psychology*, Harvester Press.

BOGEN, J. E., and BOGEN, G. M. (1976), 'Wernicke's region – Where is it?' *Ann. N. Y Acad. Sci.*, vol. 280, pp. 834–43.

BOLLES, R. C. (1975), *Theory of Motivation*, Harper & Row, 2nd edn.

BOLLES, R. C. (1979), *Learning Theory*, Holt, Rinehart & Winston.

BOLTON, N. (1972), *The Psychology of Thinking*, Methuen.

BOOTH, D. A. (1977), 'Satiety and appetite are conditioned reactions', *Psychosom. Med.*, vol. 39, pp. 76–81.

BORING, E. G. (1930), 'A new ambiguous figure', *Amer. J. Psychol.*, vol. 42, pp. 444–5.

BORING, E. G. (1942), *Sensation and Perception in the History of Experimental Psychology*, Appleton-Century-Crofts.

BORING, E. G. (1943), 'The moon illusion', *Amer. J. Phys.*, vol. 11, pp. 55–60.

BORING, E. G. (1957), *A History of Experimental Psychology*, Appleton-Century-Crofts, 2nd edn.

BOTWINICK, J. (1966), 'Cautiousness in advanced age', *J. Gerontol.*, vol. 21, pp. 347–53.

BOTWINICK, J. (1969), 'Disinclination to venture response vs cautiousness in responding: age differences', *J. genet. Psychol.*, vol. 115, pp. 55–62.

BOTWINICK, J. (1977), 'Intellectual abilities', in J. E. Birren and K. W. Schaie (eds.), *Handbook of the Psychology of Aging*, Van Nostrand.

BOURNE, L. E., EKSTRAND, B. R., and DOMINOWSKI, R. L. (1971), *The Psychology of Thinking*, Prentice-Hall.

BOUSFIELD, W. A. (1953), 'The occurrence of clustering in recall of randomly arranged associates', *J. gen. Psychol.*, vol. 49, pp. 229–40.

BOUSFIELD, W. A. (1961), 'The problem of meaning in verbal learning', in Cofer, C. N. (ed.), *Verbal Learning and Verbal Behavior*, McGraw-Hill.

BOWER, T. G. R. (1966), 'The visual world of infants', *Scient. Amer.*, vol. 215, pp. 80–92.

BOWER, T. G. R. (1974), *Development in Infancy*, Freeman.

BOWER, T. G. R. (1977), *The Perceptual World of the Child*, Fontana/Open Books.

BOWER, T. G. R., BROUGHTON, J. M., and MOORE, M. K. (1970), 'Infant responses to approaching objects: an indicator of response to distal variables', *Percept. Psychophys.*, vol. 9, pp. 193–6.

BOWLBY, J. (1944), 'Forty-four juvenile thieves: their characters and home life', *Int. J. Psychoanal.*, vol. 25, pp. 19–52, 107–27.

BOWLBY, J. (1951), *Maternal Care and Mental Health*, World Health Organization.

BOWLBY, J., *et al.* (1956), 'The effects of mother–child separation: a follow-up study', *Brit. J. med. Psychol.*, vol. 29, pp. 211–47.

BRACE, C. L. (1964), 'A non racial approach towards the understanding of human diversity', in A. Montagu (ed.), *The Concept of Race*, Free Press of Glencoe.

BRAINE, M. D. S. (1963), 'The ontogeny of English phrase structure: the first phase', *Language*, vol. 39, pp. 1–13.

BRANDT, T. H., DICHGANS, J., and BÜCHELE, W. (1974), 'Motion habituation: inverted self-motion, perception and optokinetic after-nystagmus', *Exp. Brain Res.*, vol. 21, pp. 337–52.

BRELAND K., and BRELAND, M. (1961), 'The misbehavior of organisms', *Amer. Psychologist*, vol. 61, pp. 681–4.

BREMER, F. (1954), 'The neurophysiological problem of sleep', in E. D. Adrian *et al.* (eds.), *Brain Mechanisms and Consciousness*, Blackwell.

BRENER, J. (1967), 'Heart rate', in P. H. Venables and I. Martin (eds.), *A Manual of Psychophysiological Methods*, North-Holland.

BRENER, J. (1974), 'A general model of voluntary control applied to the phenomena of learned cardiovascular change', in P. A. Oberst *et al.* (eds.), *Cardiovascular Physiology*, Academic Press.

BRENER, J. (1977), 'Visceral perception', in J. Beatty and H. Legewie (eds.), *Biofeedback and Behavior*, Plenum Press.

BRIDGES, K. M. B. (1932), 'Emotional development in early infancy', *Child Devel.*, vol. 3, pp. 324–41.

BRIGGS, G. E. (1954), 'Acquisition, extinction and recovery functions in retro-active inhibition', *J. exp. Psychol.*, vol. 47, pp. 285–93.

BROADBENT, D. E. (1954), 'The role of auditory localization in attention and memory span', *J. exp. Psychol.*, vol. 47, pp. 191–6.

BROADBENT, D. E. (1958), *Perception and Communication*, Pergamon.

BROADBENT, D. E. (1963), 'Differences and interactions between stresses', *Quart. J. exp. Psychol.*, vol. 15, pp. 205–11.

BROADBENT, D. E. (1963), 'Possibilities and difficulties in the concept of arousal', in D. N. Buckner and J. J. McGrath (eds.), *Vigilance: A Symposium*, McGraw-Hill.

BROADBENT, D. E. (1970), 'Stimulus set and response set: two kinds of selective attention', in D. I. Mostofsky (ed.), *Attention: Contemporary Theories and Analysis*, Appleton-Century-Crofts.

BROADBENT, D. E. (1971), *Decision and Stress*, Academic Press.

BROADBENT, D. E. (1973), *In Defence of Empirical Psychology*, Methuen.

BROADBENT, D. E. (1977), 'The hidden pre-attentive processes', *Amer. Psychologist*, vol. 32, pp. 109–18.

BROADBENT, D. E. (1979), 'Human performance in noise', in C. M. Harris (ed.), *Handbook of Noise Control*, McGraw-Hill, 2nd edn.

BROADBENT, D. E., and GREGORY, M. (1967), 'Perception of emotionally toned words', *Nature*, vol. 215, pp. 581–4.

BROADHURST, P. L. (1960), 'Experiments in psychogenetics', in H. J. Eysenck (ed.), *Experiments in Personality*, vol. 1, Routledge & Kegan Paul.

BROADHURST, P. L. (1963), *The Science of Animal Behaviour*, Penguin Books.

BROCA, P. (1965), 'Sur le siège de la faculté du langage articulé', *Bull. Soc. d'Anthropol.*, vol. 6, pp. 337–93.

BRODY, N. (1972), *Personality: Research and Theory*, Academic Press.

BROMAN, S. H., NICHOLS, P. L., and KENNEDY, W. A. (1975) *Preschool I.Q. Prenatal and Early Developmental Correlates*, Lawrence Erlbaum.

BROMLEY, D. B. (1974), *The Psychology of Human Ageing*, Penguin Books.

BROOKS, V. B., and STONEY, S. D. (1971), 'Motor mechanisms: the role of the pyramidal system in motor control', *Annual Rev. Physiol.*, vol. 33, pp. 337–92.

BROWN, C. C. (1967), *Methods of Psychophysiology*, Williams & Wilkins.

BROWN, C. C. (1972), 'Instruments in psychophysiology', in N. S. Greenfield and R. A. Sternbach (eds.), *Handbook of Psychophysiology*, Holt, Rinehart & Winston.

BROWN, I. D. (1966), 'Measuring the difficulty of perceptual-motor tasks: some limitations to dual-task techniques'. Paper presented to the Ergonomics Research Society Annual Conference.

BROWN, J. A. C. (1961), *Freud and the Post-Freudians*, Penguin Books.

BROWN, J. M., BERRIEN, F. K., and RUSSELL, D. L. (1966), *Applied Psychology*, Macmillan.

BROWN, R. (1965), *Social Psychology*, Free Press.

BROWN, R. (1973), *A First Language: The Early Stages*, Allen & Unwin.

BROWN, R., and FRASER, C. (1963), 'The acquisition of syntax', in C. N. Cofer and B. S. Musgrave (eds.), *Verbal Behavior and Learning*, McGraw-Hill.

BROWN, R., and LENNEBERG, E. H. (1954), 'A study in language and cognition', *J. abnorm. soc. Psychol.*, vol. 49, pp. 454–62.

BROWN, R., and MCNEILL, D. (1966), 'The "tip of the tongue" phenomenon', *J. verb. Learn. verb. Behav.*, vol. 5, pp. 325–37.

BROWN, S., and SCHAEFER, E. A. (1888), 'An investigation into the functions of the occipital and temporal lobes of the monkey's brain', *Phil. Trans. Roy. Soc.*, vol. 179, pp. 303–27.

BROWN, W. P. (1961), 'Conceptions of perceptual defence', *Brit. J. Psychol., Monogr. Supp.*, no. 35, Cambridge University Press.

BRUNER, J. S. (1973), *Beyond the Information Given*, Norton.

BRUNER, J. S., GOODNOW, J. S., and AUSTIN, G. A. (1956), *A Study of Thinking*, Wiley.

BRUNER, J. S., OLVER, R. R., and GREENFIELD, P. M. (1966), *Studies in Cognitive Growth*, Wiley.

BRUNER, J. S., and POSTMAN, L. (1949), 'On the perception of incongruity: a paradigm', *J. Personal.*, vol. 18, pp. 206–23.

BRYAN, W. L., and HARTER, N. (1897), 'Studies in the physiology and psychology of the telegraphic language', *Psychol. Rev.*, vol. 4, pp. 27–53.

BRYAN, W. L., and HARTER, N. (1899), 'Studies on the telegraphic language: the acquisition of a hierarchy of habits', *Psychol. Rev.*, vol. 6, pp. 345–75.

BRYANT, P. E. (1971), 'Discrimination learning and the study of transfer in young children', *Brit. J. Psychol.*, vol. 62, pp. 1–11.

BRYANT, P. E. (1974), *Perception and Understanding in Young Children*, Methuen.

BUCHANAN, J. (1812), *The Philosophy of Human Nature*, Grimes.

BUGENTAL, D., *et al.* (1970), 'Child vs adult perception of evaluative messages in verbal, vocal, and visual channels', *Devel. Psychol.*, vol. 2, pp. 367–75.

BULLOCK, T. H. (1977), *Introduction to Nervous Systems*, Freeman.

BURNETT, C. T. (1906), 'An experimental test of the classical theory of volition', in J. H. Tufts *et al.* (eds.), *Studies in Philosophy and Psychology*, Houghton Mifflin.

BURT, C. (1944), 'Mental abilities and mental factors', *Brit. J. educ. Psychol.*, vol. 14, pp. 85–94.

BURT, C. (1955), 'The evidence for the concept of intelligence', *Brit. J. educ. Psychol.*, vol. 25, pp. 158–77.

BURT, C. (1966), 'The genetic determination of differences in intelligence: a study of monozygotic twins reared together and apart', *Brit. J. Psychol.*, vol. 57, pp. 137–53.

BURWITZ, L., and NEWELL, K. M. (1972), 'The effects of the mere presence of coactors on learning a motor skill', *J. Motor Behav.*, vol. 4, pp. 71–126.

BUSS, A. H., and BUSS, E. H. (1956), 'The effect of verbal reinforcement combinations on conceptual learning', *J. exp. Psychol.*, vol. 52, pp. 283–7.

BUTLER, R. A. (1954), 'Incentive conditions which influence visual exploration', *J. exp. Psychol.*, vol. 48, pp. 19–23.

BUTLER, R. N. (1975), *Why Survive? Being Old in America*, Harper & Row.

CAMPBELL, D. T. (1957), 'A typology of tests, projective and otherwise', *J. consult. Psychol.*, vol. 21, pp. 207–10.

CANNON, W. B. (1927), 'The James–Lange theory of emotions: a critical examination and an alternative theory', *Amer. J. Psychol.*, vol. 39, pp. 106–24.

CANNON, W. B. (1931), 'Again the James–Lange and the thalamic theories of emotions', *Psychol. Rev.*, vol. 38, pp. 281–95.

CANNON, W. B. (1932), *The Wisdom of the Body*, Norton.

CARLSON, J. A., and DAVIS, C. M. (1971), 'Cultural values and the risky shift: a cross-cultural test in Uganda and the United States', *J. Pers. soc. Psychol.*, vol. 20, pp. 392–9.

CARMICHAEL, L. (1926), 'The development of behavior in vertebrates experimentally removed from the influence of external stimulation', *Psychol. Rev.*, vol. 33, pp. 51–8.

CARMICHAEL, L. (1927), 'A further study of the development of behavior in verte-brates experimentally removed from the influence of external stimulation', *Psychol. Rev.*, vol. 34, pp. 34–47.

CARMICHAEL, L. (1954), 'The onset and early development of behavior', in L. Carmichael (ed.), *Manual of Child Psychology*, Wiley, 2nd edn.

CARMICHAEL, L., HOGAN, H. P., and WALTER, A. A. (1932), 'An experimental study of the effect of language on the reproduction of visually perceived forms' *J. exp. Psychol.*, vol. 15, pp. 73–86.

CARTWRIGHT, R., MONROE, L., and PALMER, C. (1967), 'Individual differences in response to REM deprivation', *Arch. gen. Psychiat.*, vol. 16, pp. 297–303.

CATTELL, R. B. (1954), *The Sixteen Personality Factor Questionnaire*, Institute for Personality and Ability Testing.

CATTELL, R. B. (1963a), *The Sixteen Personality Factor Questionnaire* (The 16 PF), Institute for Personality and Ability Testing.

CATTELL, R. B. (1963b), 'Theory of fluid and crystallized intelligence: a critical experiment', *J. educ. Psychol.*, vol. 54, pp. 1–22.

CATTELL, R. B. (1965), *The Scientific Analysis of Personality*, Penguin Books.

CATTELL, R. B. (1971), *Abilities: Their Structure, Growth and Action*, Houghton Mifflin.

CATTELL, R. B. (1973), 'Key issues in motivation theory in relation to learning and dynamic calculus', in J. R. Royce (ed.), *Multivariate Analysis and Psychological Theory*, Academic Press.

CAVALLI-SFORZA, L. L., and BODMER, W. F. (1971), *The Genetics of Human Population*, Freeman.

CERASO, J. (1967), 'The interference theory of forgetting', *Scient. Amer.*, vol. 217, pp. 117–24.

CHAPMAN, A. J. (1973), 'Social facilitation of laughter in children', *J. exp. soc. Psychol.*, vol. 9, pp. 528–41.

CHAPMAN, A. J. (1974), 'An electromyographic study of social facilitation: A test of the "mere presence" hypothesis', *Brit. J. Psychol.*, vol. 65, pp. 123–8.

CHAPMAN, L. J., and CHAPMAN, J. D. (1959), 'Atmosphere effect re-examined', *J. exp. Psychol.*, vol. 58, pp. 220–26.

CHEN, S. C. (1937), 'Social modification of the activity of ants in nest-building', *Physiol. Zool.*, vol. 10, pp. 420–36.

CHERRY, E. C. (1953), 'Some experiments on the recognition of speech, with one and two ears', *J. acoust. Soc. Amer.*, vol. 25, pp. 975–9.

CHERRY, E. C., and TAYLOR, W. K. (1954), 'Some further experiments upon the recognition of speech with one and two ears', *J. acoust. Soc. Amer.*, vol. 26, pp. 554–9.

CHI, M. T. H. (1976), 'Short-term memory limitations in children: capacity or processing deficits?', *Memory & Cognition*, vol. 4, pp. 559–72.

CHILD, D. (1977), *Psychology and the Teacher*, Holt, Rinehart & Winston.

CHOMSKY, N. (1957), *Syntactic Structures*, Mouton.

CHOMSKY, N. (1959), 'Review of Skinner's *Verbal Behavior*', *Language*, vol. 35, pp. 26–58.

CHOMSKY, N. (1965), *Aspects of the Theory of Syntax*, M.I.T. Press.

CHOMSKY, N. (1977), 'The fallacy of Richard Herrnstein's I.Q.', in N. Block and G. Dworkin (eds.), *The I.Q. Controversy*, Quartet Books.

CHOWN, S. L. (1961), 'Age and the rigidities', *J. Gerontol.*, vol. 16, pp. 353–62.

CHURCH, R. M. (1963), 'The varied effects of punishment on behavior', *Psychol. Rev.*, vol. 70, pp. 369–402.

CLARK, E. (1963), 'Sex-role preference in mentally retarded children', *Amer. J. ment. Deficiency*, vol. 67, pp. 606–10.

CLARK, H. H., and CHASE, W. G. (1972), 'On the process of comparing sentences against pictures', *Cognit. Psychol.*, vol. 3, pp. 472–517.

CLARK, R. (1974), 'Performing without competence', *J. Child Lang.*, vol. 1, pp. 1–10.

CLARK, R. D., III (1971), 'Group-induced shift toward risk: a critical appraisal', *Psychol. Bull.*, vol. 76, pp. 251–70.

CLARK, R. D., and WILLEMS, E. P. (1969), 'Risk preferences as related to judged consequences of failure', *Psychol. Rep.*, vol. 25, 827–30.

CLARKE, A. M., and CLARKE, A. D. B. (1976), *Early Experience: Myth and Evidence*, Open Books.

CLAUSEN, J., SERSEN, E., and LIDSKY, A. (1974), 'Variability of sleep measures in normal subjects', *Psychophysiol.*, vol. 11, pp. 509–16.

CLEMES, S., and DEMENT, W. C. (1967), 'The effect of REM-sleep deprivation on psychological functioning', *J. nerv. ment. Dis.*, vol. 144, pp. 485–90.

CLIFT, A. D. (ed.) (1975), *Sleep Disturbance and Hypnotic Drug Dependence*, Excerpta Medica.

COCHRANE, R. (1974), 'Crime and personality: theory and evidence', *Bull. Brit. Psychol. Soc.*, vol. 12, pp. 175–87.

COGHILL, G. E. (1929), *Anatomy and the Problem of Behaviour*, Cambridge University Press.

COHEN, D. (1979), *J. B. Watson: A Biography*, Routledge & Kegan Paul.

COHEN, D. B. (1970), 'Current research on the frequency of dream recall', *Psychol. Bull.*, vol. 73, pp. 433–40.

COHEN, D. B. (1974), 'Toward a theory of dream recall', *Psychol. Bull.*, vol. 81, pp. 138–54.

COHEN, G. (1977), *The Psychology of Cognition*, Academic Press.

COHEN, J. (1969), *Operant Behavior and Operant Conditioning*, Rand McNally.

COHEN, S. (1980), 'After-effects of stress on human performance and social behavior: a review of research and theory', *Psychol. Bull.*, vol. 88, pp. 82–108.

COHEN, S., and SPACAPAN, S. (1978), 'The after-effects of stress: an attentional interpretation', *Envir. Psychol. nonverb. Behav.*, vol. 3, pp. 43–57.

COLLINS, A. M., and QUILLIAN, M. R. (1969), 'Retrieval time from semantic memory', *J. verb. Learn. verb. Behav.*, vol. 8, pp. 240–7.

COLLINS, T. B. (1965), 'Strength of the following response in the chick in relation to degree of "parent" contact', *J. comp. physiol. Psychol.*, vol. 60, pp. 192–5.

COLQUHOUN, W. P. (1971), 'Circadian variations in mental efficiency', in W. P. Colquhoun (ed.), *Biological Rhythms & Human Performance*, Academic Press.

CONDON, W. S., and OGSTON, W. D. (1966), 'Sound film analysis of normal and pathological behavior patterns', *J. nerv. ment. Dis.*, vol. 143, pp. 338–47.

CONNOLLY, K. J. (ed.) (1971), *Mechanisms of Motor Skill Development*, Academic Press.

CONNOLLY, K. J., and BRUNER, J. S. (eds.) (1974), *The Growth of Competence*, Academic Press.

CONRAD, K. (1954), 'New problems of aphasia', *Brain*, vol. 77, pp. 491–509.

CONRAD, R. (1951), 'Speed and load stress in a sensori-motor skill', *Brit. J. indust. Med.*, vol. 8, pp. 1–7.

CONRAD, R. (1953), 'Timing', *MRC Appl. Res. Unit Rep.*, no. 188.

CONSTANTINOPLE, A. (1973), 'Masculinity–femininity: an exception to a famous dictum?', *Psychol. Bull.*, vol. 80, pp. 389–407.

COOPER, R., OSSELTON, J. W., and SHAW, J. C. (1974), *EEG Technology*, Butterworth, 2nd edn.

COOPER, R. M., and ZUBEK, J. P. (1958), 'Effects of enriched and restricted early environment on the learning ability of "bright" and "dull" rats', *Canad. J. Psychol.*, vol. 12, pp. 159–64.

CORDEAU, J. P., and MANCIA, A. (1959), 'Evidence for the existence of an EEG synchronization mechanism originating in the lower brainstem', *EEG clin. Neurophysiol.*, vol. 11, pp. 551–64.

CORTEEN, R. S., and DUNN, D. (1974), 'Shock-associated words in a non-attended message: a test for momentary awareness', *J. exp. Psychol.*, vol. 102, 1143–4.

CORTEEN, R. S., and WOOD, B. (1972), 'Autonomic responses to shock-associated words in an unattended channel', *J. exp. Psychol.*, vol. 94, pp. 308–13.

COTTRELL, N. B. (1968), 'Performance in the presence of other human beings: mere presence, audience and affiliation effects', in E. C. Simmel, R. A. Hoppe and G. A. Milton (eds.), *Social Facilitation and Imitative Behavior*, Allyn & Bacon.

COTTRELL, N. B., RITTLE, R. H., and WACK, D. L. (1967), 'Presence of an audience and list type (competitional or non-competitional) as joint determinants of performance in paired-associate learning', *J. Person.*, vol. 35, pp. 425–34.

COTTRELL, N. B., *et al.* (1968), 'Social facilitation of dominant responses by the presence of an audience and the mere presence of others', *J. Person. soc. Psychol.*, vol. 9, pp. 245–50.

COWEN, E. L. (1973), 'Social and community interventions: introduction – scope of field', *Annual Rev. Psychol.*, vol. 24, pp. 423–72.

CRAIK, F. I. M. (1977), 'Age differences in human memory', in J. E. Birren and K. W. Schaie (eds.), *Handbook of the Psychology of Aging*, Van Nostrand.

CRAIK, F. I. M., and BLANKSTEIN, K. R. (1975), 'Psychophysiology and human memory', in P. H. Venables and M. J. Christie (eds.), *Research in Psychophysiology*, Wiley.

CRAIK, F. I. M., and LOCKHART, R. S. (1972), 'Levels of processing: a framework for memory research', *J. verb. Learn. verb. Behav.*, vol. 11, pp. 671–84.

CRAIK, K. (1948), 'Theory of the human operator in control systems', *Brit. J. Psychol.*, vol. 38, pp. 56–61, 142–8.

CRAIK, K. J. W. (1943), *The Nature of Explanation*, Cambridge University Press.

CRAIK, K. J. W., and MACKWORTH, N. H. (1943), Cited in MACKWORTH, N. H. (1950), *Researches on the Measurement of Human Performance* (MRC Special Rep. 268), H.M.S.O., MRC.

CRAMER, P. (1976), 'Changes from visual to verbal memory organization as a function of age', *J. exp. Child Psychol.*, vol. 22, pp. 50–57.

CRIDDLE, W. D. (1971), 'The physical presence of other individuals as a factor in social facilitation', *Psychon. Sci.*, vol. 22, pp. 229–30.

CRIDER, A., and LUNN, R. (1971), 'Electrodermal lability as a personality dimension', *J. exp. Res. Personality*, vol. 5, pp. 145–50.

CROMER, R. F. (1974), 'The development of language and cognition: the cognitive hypothesis', in B. M. Foss (ed.), *New Perspectives in Child Development*, Penguin Books.

CRONBACH, L. J. (1946). 'Response sets and test validity', *Educ. psychol. Meas.*, vol. 6, 475–94.

CRONBACH, L. J. (1950), 'Further evidence on response sets and test design', *Educ. psychol. Meas.*, vol. 10, pp. 3–31.

CRONBACH, L. J. (1964), *Essentials of Psychological Testing*, Harper & Row, 2nd edn.

CRONBACH, L. J., and MEEHL, P. E. (1955), 'Construct validity in psychological tests', *Psychol. Bull.*, vol. 52, pp. 281–302.

CROSSMAN, E. R. F. W. (1959), 'A theory of the acquisition of speed-skill', *Ergonomics*, vol. 2, pp. 153–66.

CROW, T. J. (1975), 'The physiological basis of sleep', in A. D. Clift (ed.), *Sleep Disturbance and Hypnotic Drug Dependence*, Excerpta Medica.

CROWNE, D. P., and MARLOWE, D. (1964), *The Approval Motive: Studies in Evaluative Dependence*, Wiley.

CRUIKSHANK, R. M. (1941), 'The development of visual size constancy in early infancy', *J. genet. Psychol.*, vol. 58, pp. 327–51.

CRYSTAL, D. (1971), *Linguistics*, Penguin Books.

CUMMING, E., and HENRY, W. E. (1961), *Growing Old*, Basic Books

CUTLER, S. J., et .al. (1980), 'Aging and conservatism: cohort changes in attitudes about legalized abortion', *J. Gerontol.*, vol. 35, pp. 115–23.

DAHLSTROM, W. G., and WELSH, G. S. (1960), *An M.M.P.I. Handbook: A Guide to Use in Clinical Practice and Research*, University of Minnesota Press.

DALE, P. S. (1976), *Language Development*, Holt, Rinehart & Winston, 2nd edn.

DALY, M. (1973), 'Early stimulation in rodents', *Brit. J. Psychol.*, vol. 64, pp. 435–60.

DANA, C. I. (1921), 'The anatomic seat of the emotions: a discussion of the James–Lange theory', *Arch. Neurol. Psychiat.*, vol. 6, pp. 634–9.

D'ANDRADE, R. G. (1965), 'Trait psychology and trait-componential analysis', *Amer. Psychol.*, vol. 67, pp. 215–28.

D'ANDRADE, R. G. (1966), 'Sex differences and cultural institutions', in E. E. Maccoby (ed.), *The Development of Sex Differences*, Stanford University Press.

DARLEY, J. M., and LATANÉ, B. (1968), 'Bystander intervention in emergencies: Diffusion of responsibility', *J. Personal. soc. Psychol.*, vol. 8, pp. 377–83.

DARROW, C. W. (1943), 'Physiological and clinical tests of autonomic function and autonomic balance', *Physiol. Rev.*, vol. 23, pp. 1–36.

DARWIN, C. (1872). *Expression of the Emotions in Man and Animals*, Murray, revised edn. 1890 (ed. F. Darwin).

DARWIN, C. (1887), *The Autobiography of Charles Darwin*, Collins, revised edn. 1958 (ed. N. Barlow).

DASHIELL, J. F. (1930), 'An experimental analysis of some group effects', *J. abnorm. soc. Psychol.*, vol. 25, pp. 190–99.

DASHIELL, J. F. (1935), 'Experimental studies of the influence of social situations on the behavior of individual human adults', in C. Murchison (ed.), *A Handbook of Social Psychology*, Clark University Press.

DAVIES, D. R., and JONES, D. M. (1975), 'The effects of noise and incentives upon attention in short-term memory', *Brit. J. Psychol.*, vol. 66, pp. 61–8.

DAVIES, D. R. and JONES, D. M. (1982), 'Hearing and noise', in W. T. Singleton (ed.), *The Body at Work*, Cambridge University Press.

DAVIES, D. R., and KRKOVIC, A. (1965), 'Skin conductance, alpha-activity and vigilance', *Amer. J. Psychol.*, vol. 78, pp. 304–6.

DAVIES, D. R., and PARASURAMAN, R. (1977), 'Cortical evoked potentials and vigilance: A decision theory analysis', in R. R. Mackie (ed.), *Vigilance: Theory, Operational Performance and Physiological Correlates*, Plenum Press.

DAVIES, D. R., and PARASURAMAN, R. (1981), *The Psychology of Vigilance*, Academic Press.

DAVIES, D. R., and SHACKLETON, V. J. (1975), *Psychology and Work*, Methuen.

DAVIES, D. R., SHACKLETON, V. J., and PARASURAMAN, R. (in press), 'Monotony and boredom', in G. R. J. Hockey (ed.), *Stress and Fatigue*, Wiley.

DAVIES, D. R., and TUNE, G. S. (1970), *Human Vigilance Performance*, Staples.

DAVIS, L. H. (1979), *Theory of Action*, Prentice-Hall.

DAVITZ, J. R. (ed.) (1964), *The Communication of Emotional Meaning*, McGraw-Hill.

DE BONO, E. (1967), *The Use of Lateral Thinking*, Cape.

DECI, E. L. (1975), *Intrinsic Motivation*, Plenum Press.

DEEKE, L., SCHEID, P., and KORNHUBER, H. H. (1969), 'Distribution of readiness potential, pre-motion positivity, and motor potential of the human cerebral cortex preceding voluntary finger movements', *Exp. Brain Res.*, vol. 7, pp. 158–68.

DEESE, J. (1965), *Structure of Association in Language and Thought*, Johns Hopkins Press.

DEESE, J. (1970), *Psycholinguistics*, Allyn & Bacon.

DELGADO, J. M. R., and ANAND, B. K. (1953), 'Increased food intake induced by electrical stimulation of the lateral hypothalamus', *Amer. J. Physiol.*, vol. 172, pp. 162–8.

DELGADO, J. M. R., ROBERTS, W. W., and MILLER, N. E. (1954), 'Learning motivated by electrical stimulation of the brain', *Amer. J. Physiol.*, vol. 179, pp. 587–93.

DEMBER, W. N., and WARM, J. S. (1979), *Psychology of Perception*, Holt, Rinehart & Winston, 2nd edn.

DEMENT, W. C. (1960), 'The effect of dream deprivation', *Science*, vol. 131, pp. 1705–1707.

DEMENT, W. C. (1965), 'An essay on dreams', in T. M. Newcomb (ed.), *New Directions in Psychology II*, Holt, Rinehart & Winston.

DEMENT, W. C. (1969), 'The biological role of REM sleep (circa 1968)', in A. Kales (ed.), *Sleep: Physiology and Pathology*, Lippincott.

DEMENT, W. C. (1973), 'Commentary', in W. B. Webb (ed.), *Sleep: An Active Process*, Scott, Foresman.

DEMENT, W. C., and FISHER, C. (1963), 'Experimental interference with the sleep cycle', *Canad. psychiat. Assoc. J.*, vol. 8, pp. 400–405.

DEMENT, W. C., and GREENBERG, S. (1966), 'Changes in total amount of stage four sleep as a function of partial sleep deprivation', *EEG clin. Neurophysiol.*, vol. 20, pp. 523–6.

DEMENT, W. C., and KLEITMAN, N. (1957a), 'Cyclic variations in EEG during sleep and their relation to eye movements, body motility and dreaming', *EEG clin. Neurophysiol.*, vol. 9, pp. 673–90.

DEMENT, W. C., and KLEITMAN, N. (1957b), 'Relation of eye movements during sleep to dream activity: an objective method for the study of dreaming', *J. exp. Psychol.*, vol. 53, pp. 339–46.

DE MILLE, R., and MERRIFIELD, P. R. (1962), 'Review of *Creativity and Intelligence* by Getzels and Jackson', *Educ. psychol. Meas.*, vol. 22, pp. 803–808.

DENENBERG, V. (1959), 'The interactive effects of infantile and adult shock levels upon learning', *Psychol. Rep.*, vol. 5, pp. 357–64.

DENENBERG, V. (1963), 'Early experience and emotional development', *Scient. Amer.*, vol. 208, pp. 138–46.

DENNIS, W. (1948), *Readings in the History of Psychology*, Appleton-Century-Crofts.

DENNIS, W. (1960), 'Causes of retardation among institutional children: Iran', *J. genet. Psychol.*, vol. 96, pp. 47–59.

DENNIS, W., and DENNIS, M. G. (1940), 'The effect of cradling practices upon the onset of walking in Hopi children', *J. genet. Psychol.*, vol. 56, pp. 77–86.

DE SAUSSURE, F. (1916). *Cours de linguistique générale*. Paris: Payot. English translation by Wade Baskin, (1959) *Course in General Linguistics*, Philosophical Library.

DEUTSCH, J. A. (1960), *The Structural Basis of Behaviour*, Cambridge University Press.

DEUTSCH, J. A., and DEUTSCH, D. (1963), 'Attention: some theoretical considerations', *Psychol. Rev.*, vol. 70, pp. 80–90.

DEWAN, E. M. (1969), 'The programing (P) hypothesis for REM sleep', in E. Hartmann (ed.), *Sleep and Dreaming*, Little, Brown.

DEWEY, J. (1898). *Psychology*, Harper, 3rd edn.

DICHGANS, J., and BRANDT, T. (1978), 'Visual–vestibular interaction', in R. Held, H. W. Leibowitz and H.-L. Tauber (eds.), *Handbook of Sensory Physiology, VIII: Perception*, Springer-Verlag.

DIMOND, S. J. (1970), *The Social Behaviour of Animals*, Batsford.

DIMOND, S. J. (1972), *The Double Brain*, Churchill Livingstone.

DIXON, N. (1972), *Subliminal Perception: the Nature of a Controversy*, McGraw-Hill.

DONCHIN, E. (1975), 'Brain electrical correlates of pattern recognition', in G. F. Inbar (ed.), *Signal Analysis and Pattern Recognition in Biomedical Engineering*, Wiley.

DONCHIN, E., RITTER, W., and MCCALLUM, W. C. (1978), 'Cognitive psychophysiology: the endogenous components of the ERP', in E. Calloway and S. H. Koslow (eds.), *Event-related Brain Potentials in Man*, Academic Press.

DOPPELT, J. E., and WALLACE, W. L. (1955), 'Standardization of the Wechsler Adult Intelligence Scale for older persons', *J. abnorm. soc. Psychol.*, vol. 51, 312–30.

DREGER. R. M., and MILLER, K. S. (1968), 'Comparative psychological studies of negroes and whites in the United States: 1959–1965', *Psychol. Bull. Monogr. Suppl.*, vol. 70, (3, pt. 2).

DREVER, J. (1961), 'Perceptions and action', *Bull. Brit. psychol. Soc.*, vol. 45, pp. 1–9.

DREWE, E. A., *et al.* (1970), 'A comparative review of the results of neurophysiological research on man and monkey', *Cortex*, vol. 6, pp. 129–63.

DUCK, S. (ed.) (1977), *Theory and Practice in Interpersonal Attraction*, Academic Press.

DUFFY, E. (1932), 'The relationship between muscular tension and quality of performance', *Amer. J. Psychol.*, vol. 44, pp. 535–46.

DUFFY, E. (1962), *Activation and Behavior*, Wiley.

DUFFY, E. (1972), 'Activation', in N. S. Greenfield and R. A. Sternbach (eds.), *Handbook of Psychophysiology*, Holt, Rinehart & Winston.

DUNCAN, J. (1980), 'The locus of interference in the perception of simultaneous stimuli', *Psychol. Rev.*, vol. 87, pp. 272–300.

DUNCKER, K. (1945), 'On problem solving', *Psychol. Monogr.*, vol. 58(5), no. 270.

DUSSER DE BARENNE, J. G. (1920). 'Recherches expérimentales sur les fonctions du système nerveux central, faites en particulier sur deux chats donc le néopallium a été enlevé', *Arch. Neurol. Physiol.*, vol. 4, pp. 31–123.

DYER, F. N. (1973), 'The Stroop phenomenon and its use in the study of perceptual, cognitive, and response processes', *Memory & Cognition*, vol. 1, pp. 106–20.

EASTERBROOK, J. A. (1959), 'The effect of emotion on cue utilization and the organization of behavior', *Psychol. Rev.*, vol. 66, pp. 183–201.

EASTON, R. D., and SHOR, R. E. (1975), 'Information processing analysis of the Chevreal pendulum illusion', *J. exp. Psychol.: Human Perception & Performance*, vol. 1, pp. 231–6.

EBBINGHAUS, H. (1885), *Ueber das Gedächtnis*, Dunker (translated 1913 by H. A. Ruger and C. E. Bussenius as *Memory: A Contribution to Experimental Psychology*, Teachers College, Columbia University Press).

EBEL, R. L. (1961), 'Must all tests be valid?', *Amer. Psychol.*, vol. 16, pp. 640–47.

EDELBERG, R. (1972), 'Electrical activity of the skin: its measurement and uses in psychophysiology', in N. S. Greenfield and R. A. Sternbach (eds.), *Handbook of Psychophysiology*, Holt, Rinehart & Winston.

EDWARDS, A. L. (1957a), *The Social Desirability Variable in Personality Assessment and Research*, Holt, Rinehart & Winston.

EDWARDS, A. L. (1957b), *Techniques of Attitude Scale Construction*, Appleton-Century-Crofts.

EDWARDS, A. L. (1959), *Edwards Personal Preference Schedule*, Psychological Corporation.

EDWARDS, A. L. (1967a), 'The social desirability variable: a broad statement', in I. A. Berg (ed.), *Response Set in Personality Assessment*, Aldine.

EDWARDS, A. L. (1967b), 'The social desirability variable: a review of the evidence', in I. A. Berg (ed.), *Response Set in Personality Assessment*, Aldine.

EDWARDS, A. L. (1967c), *Statistical Methods*, Holt, Rinehart & Winston, 2nd edn.

EGETH, H. E., and SAGER, L. C. (1977), 'On the locus of visual dominance', *Percept. Psychophys.*, vol. 22, pp. 77–86.

EHRLICH, P. R., and FELDMAN, S. S. (1977), *The Race Bomb: Skin Color, Prejudice and Intelligence*, Quadrangle/New York Times Book Co.

EIBL-EIBESFELDT, I. (1970), *Ethology*, Holt, Rinehart & Winston.

EIBL-EIBESFELDT, I. (1973), 'The expressive behaviour of the deaf- and- blind-born', in M. V. Cranach and I. Vine (eds.), *Social Communication and Movement*, Academic Press.

EIFERMANN, R. R. (1961), 'Negation: a linguistic variable', *Acta Psychol.*, vol. 18, pp. 258–73.

EIJKMAN, E., and VENDRIK, A. J. H. (1965), 'Can a sensory system be specified by its internal noise?', *J. acoust. Soc. Amer.*, vol. 37, pp. 1102–1109.

EKMAN, P. (1972), 'Universal and cultural differences in facial expressions of emotion', in J. K. Cole (ed.), *Nebraska Symposium on Motivation*, vol. 19. University of Nebraska Press.

EKMAN, P., and FRIESEN, W. V. (1969), 'The repertoire of nonverbal behavior: categories, origins, usage, and coding', *Semiotica*, vol. 1, pp. 49–98.

EKMAN, P., and FRIESEN, W. V. (1972), 'Hand movements', *J. Comm.*, vol. 22, pp. 353–74.

EKMAN, P., and FRIESEN, W. V. (1974), 'Detecting deception from the body or face', *J. Pers. soc. Psychol.*, vol. 29, pp. 288–98.

EKMAN, P., and FRIESEN, W. V. (1975), *Unmasking the Face: a Guide to Recognizing Emotions from Facial Expressions*, Prentice-Hall.

EKMAN, P., FRIESEN, W. V., and ELLSWORTH, P. (1972), *Emotion in the Human Face: Guidelines for Research and an Integration of the Findings*, Pergamon.

ELLIOTT, C. D., MURRAY, D. J., and PEARSON, L. S. (1978), *British Ability Scales*, N.F.E.R. Publ. Co.

ELLISON, G. D., and FLYNN, J. P. (1968), 'Organized aggressive behavior in cats after surgical isolation of the hypothalamus', *Arch. Italiennes de Biologie*, vol. 106, pp. 1–20.

ELMADJIAN, F., HOPE, J. M., and LAMSON, E. T. (1957), 'Excretion of epinephrine and norepinephrine in various emotional states', *J. clin. Endocrin. & Metab.*, vol. 17, pp. 608–20.

ENGEL, B. T. (1972), 'Response specificity', in N. S. Greenfield and R. A. Sternbach (eds.), *Handbook of Psychophysiology*, Holt, Rinehart & Winston.

ENGELKAMPF, J., and HÖRMANN, H. (1974), 'The effect of non-verbal information on the recall of negation', *Quart. J. exp. Psychol.*, vol. 26, pp. 98–105.

EPHRON, H. S., and CARRINGTON, P. C. (1966), 'Rapid eye movement sleep and cortical homeostasis', *Psychol. Rev.*, vol. 73, pp. 500–526.

EPSTEIN, S., and FENZ, W. D. (1962), 'Theory and experiment on the measurement of approach–avoidance conflict', *J. abnorm. soc. Psychol.*, vol. 64, pp. 97–112.

EPSTEIN, W. (1967), *Varieties of Perceptual Learning*, McGraw-Hill.

ERDMAN, G., and JANKE, W. (1978), 'Interaction between physiological and cognitive determinants of emotions: experimental studies on Schachter's theory of emotions', *Biol. Psychol.*, vol. 6, pp. 61–74.

ERIKSEN, C. W. (1960), 'Discrimination and learning without awareness: a methodological survey and evaluation', *Psychol. Rev.*, vol. 67, pp. 279–300.

ERLENMEYER-KIMLING, L., and JARVIK, L. F. (1963), 'Genetics and intelligence: a review', *Science*, vol. 142, pp. 1477–9.

ERVIN, S. M. (1964), 'Imitation and structural change in children's language', in E. H. Lenneberg (ed.), *New Directions in the Study of Language*, M. I. T. Press.

ESTES, W. K. (1944), 'An experimental study of punishment', *Psychol. Monogr.: Gen & Appl.* vol. 54, no. 263.

ESTES, W. K. (1950), 'Toward a statistical theory of learning', *Psychol. Rev.*, vol. 57, pp. 94–107.

ETKIN, W. (ed.) (1964), *Social Behavior and Organization among Vertebrates*, University of Chicago Press.

EUROPEAN PRODUCTIVITY AGENCY (1956), *Job Analysis: A Tool of Productivity*. Organization for Economic Co-operation and Development.

EVANS, G., and HOWARD, R. B. (1973), 'Personal space', *Psychol. Bull.*, vol. 80, pp. 334–44.

EVARTS, E. V. (1974), 'Sensorimotor cortex activity associated with movements triggered by visual as compared to somesthenic inputs', in F. O. Schmitt and F. G. Warden (eds.), *The Neurosciences: Third Study Program*, M. I. T. Press.

EXNER, S. (1888), 'Einige Beobachtungen über Bewegungsnachbilder (Some observations of movement after images)', *Centralblatt f. Physiologie*, vol. 1, pp. 135–40.

EYSENCK, H. J. (1947), *Dimensions of Personality*, Routledge & Kegan Paul.

EYSENCK, H. J. (1952), *The Scientific Study of Personality*, Routledge & Kegan Paul.

EYSENCK, H. J. (1953), *The Structure of Human Personality*, Methuen.

EYSENCK, H. J. (1956), 'The inheritance of extraversion–introversion', *Acta Psychol.*, vol. 12, pp. 95–110.

EYSENCK, H. J. (1957), *The Dynamics of Anxiety and Hysteria*, Routledge & Kegan Paul.

EYSENCK, H. J. (1959), *The Maudsley Personality Inventory*, University of London Press.

EYSENCK, H. J. (ed.) (1964), *Experiments in Motivation*, Pergamon.

EYSENCK, H. J. (1977), *Crime and Personality*, Routledge & Kegan Paul.

EYSENCK, H. J., and PRELL, D. B. (1951), 'The inheritance of neuroticism: an experimental study', *J. ment. Sci.*, vol. 97, pp. 441–65.

EYSENCK, H. J., and RACHMAN, S. (1965), *The Causes and Cures of Neurosis*, Routledge & Kegan Paul.

EYSENCK, M. W. (1975), 'Retrieval from semantic memory as a function of age', *J. Gerontol.*, vol. 30, pp. 174–80.

EYSENCK, M. W. (1977), *Human Memory: Theory, Research and Individual Differences*, Pergamon.

EYSENCK, M. W., and FOLKARD, S. (1980), 'Personality, time of day and caffeine: some theoretical and conceptual problems in Revelle *et al.*', *J. exp. Psychol.: General*, vol. 109, pp. 32–41.

FAIRWEATHER, H. (1976), 'Sex differences in cognition', *Cognition*, vol. 4, pp. 231–80.

FANTZ, R. L. (1961), 'The origin of form perception', *Scient. Amer.*, vol. 204(5), 66–72.

FAVREAU, O. (1976), 'Interference in colour-contingent motion after-effect', *Quart. J. exp. Psychol.*, vol. 28, pp. 553–60.

FAVREAU, O., and CORBALLIS, M. C. (1976), 'Negative after-effects in visual perception', *Scient. Amer.*, vol. 235(6), pp. 42–8.

FEHR, F. S., and STERN, J. A. (1970), 'Peripheral physiological variables and emotion: the James–Lange theory revisited', *Psychol. Bull.*, vol. 74, pp. 411–24.

FEINBERG, I., and CARLSON, V. R. (1968), 'Sleep variables as a function of age in man', *Arch. gen. Psychiat.*, vol. 18, pp. 239–50.

FERGUSON, L. W. (1951), 'Management quality and its effects on selection test validity', *Pers. Psychol.*, vol. 4, pp. 141–50.

FERSTER, B. C., and SKINNER, B. F. (1957), *Schedules of Reinforcement*, Appleton-Century-Crofts.

FESTINGER, L. (1957), *Theory of Cognitive Dissonance*, Row, Peterson & Co.

FILLMORE, C. J. (1968), 'The case for case', in E. Bach and R. T. Harms (eds.), *Universals in Linguistic Theory*, Holt, Rinehart & Winston.

FISHER, A. E. (1969), 'Problems in the analysis of complex neural function: discussion of Professor Thompson's paper', in J. F. Voss (ed.), *Approaches to Thought*, Merrill.

FISHER, S., and GREENBERG, R. F. (1977), *Scientific Credibility of Freud's Theories and Therapy*, Harvester Press.

FITTS, P. M. (1964), 'Perceptual motor skill learning', in A. W. Melton (ed.), *Categories of Human Learning*, Academic Press.

FITTS, P. M. (1965), 'Factors in complex skill training', in R. Glasser (ed.), *Training Research and Education*, Wiley.

FITTS, P. M., and POSNER, M. R. (1967), *Human Performance*, Brooks/Cole.

FLAVELL, J. H. (1963), *The Developmental Psychology of Jean Piaget*, Van Nostrand.

FLAVELL, J. H. (1977), *Cognitive Development*, Prentice-Hall.

FLEMING, J. (1975), 'The state of the apes', *Psychology Today* (English edition) no. 1.

FLING, S., and MANOSEVITZ, M. (1972), 'Sex typing in nursery school children's play interests', *Devel. Psychol.*, vol. 7, pp. 146–52.

FODOR, J. (1965), 'Could meaning be an r_m?', *J. verb. Learn. verb. Behav.*, vol. 4, pp. 73–81.

FODOR, J. A., and GARRETT, M. (1967), 'Some syntactic determinants of sentential complexity', *Percept. Psychophys.*, vol. 2, pp. 289–96.

FOLKARD, S. (1975), 'Diurnal variation in logical reasoning', *Brit. J. Psychol.*, vol. 66, pp. 1–8.

FOLKARD, S. (1979), 'Time of day effects in immediate and delayed memory', in M. M. Gruneberg, P. E. Morris and R. N. Sykes (eds.), *Proc. Int. Conference on Practical Aspects of Memory*, Academic Press.

FOLKARD, S., et al. (1977), 'Time of day effects in school children's immediate and delayed recall of meaningful material', *Brit. J. Psychol.*, vol. 68, pp. 45–50.

FORDHAM, F. (1953), *An Introduction to Jung's Psychology*, Penguin Books.

FORSTER, P. M., and GOVIER, E. (1978), 'Discrimination without awareness?', *Quart. J. exp. Psychol.*, vol. 30, pp. 289–95.

FOULKES, D. (1962), 'Dream reports from different stages of sleep', *J. abnorm. soc. Psychol.*, vol. 65, pp. 14–25.

FOULKES, D. (1966), *The Psychology of Sleep*, Scribners.

FOULKES, D., and FLEISHER, S. (1975), 'Mental activity in relaxed wakefulness', *J. abnorm. Psychol.*, vol. 84, pp. 66–75.

FOULKES, D., SPEAR, P. S., and SIMMONDS, J. D. (1966), 'Individual differences in mental activity at sleep onset', *J. abnorm. Psychol.*, vol. 71, pp. 280–87.

FOULKES, D., and VOGEL, G. W. (1965), 'Mental activity at sleep onset', *J. abnorm. Psychol.*, vol. 70, pp. 231–43.

FOWLER, C. J. H., and WILDING, J. (1979), 'Differential effects of noise and incentives on learning', *Brit. J. Psychol.*, vol. 70, pp. 149–53.

FRANCOLINI, C. M., and EGETH, H. E. (1979), 'Perceptual selectivity is task-dependent: The pop-out effect poops out', *Percept. Psychophys.*, vol. 25, pp. 99–110.

FRANCOLINI, C. M., and EGETH, H. E. (1980), 'On the nonautomaticity of "automatic" activation: evidence of selective seeing', *Percept. Psychophys.*, vol. 27, pp. 331–42.

FRANKENHAEUSER, M. (1975), 'Experimental approaches to the study of catecholamines and emotion', in L. Levi (ed.), *Emotions: Their Parameters and Measurement*, Raven Press.

FRANKLIN, H. C., and HOLDING, D. H. (1977), 'Personal memories at different ages', *Quart. J. exp. Psychol.*, vol. 29, pp. 527–32.

FRASER, C., and ROBERTS, N. (1975), 'Mothers' speech to children of four different ages', *J. psycholing. Res.*, vol. 4, pp. 9–16.

FREEDMAN, D. G., and KELLER, B. (1963), 'Inheritance of behaviour in infants', *Science*, vol. 140, pp. 196–8.

FREEDMAN, J. L. (1975), *Crowding and Behavior*, Freeman.

FREEDMAN, J. L., SEARS, D. O., and CARLSMITH, J. M. (1978), *Social Psychology*, Prentice-Hall, 3rd edn.

FREEMAN, G. L. (1940), 'The relationship between performance level and bodily activity level', *J. exp. Psychol.*, vol. 26, pp. 602–608.

FREUD, S. (1915), 'Instincts and their vicissitudes', translated in *Collected Papers of Sigmund Freud*, vol. IV, Hogarth Press.

FREUD, S. (1925), 'Repression', in *Collected Papers*, vol. IV, Hogarth Press.

FREUD, S. (1938), 'Psychopathology of everyday life', in A. Brill (ed.), *The Basic Writings of Sigmund Freud*, Modern Library.

FREUD, S. (1949), *Three Essays on the Theory of Sexuality*, translated by J. Strachey, Imago Publishers.

FREUD, S. (1954), *The Interpretation of Dreams*, translated by J. Strachey, Allen & Unwin.

FRIEDMAN, H., and MARSHALL, D. A. (1965), 'Position reversal training in the Virginia opossum: evidence for the acquisition of a learning set', *Quart. J. exp. Psychol.*, vol. 17, pp. 250–54.

FRIEDMAN, M. I., and STRICKER, E. M. (1976), 'The physiological psychology of hunger: a physiological perspective', *Psychol. Rev.*, vol. 83, pp. 409–31.

FRISBY, J. (1979), *Seeing*, Oxford University Press.

FROMME, A. (1941), 'An experimental study of the factors of maturation and practice in the behavioral development of the embryo of the frog, *Rana pipiens*', *Genet. Psychol. Monogr.*, vol. 24, pp. 219–56.

FRUCHTER, B. (1954), *Introduction to Factor Analysis*, Van Nostrand.

FULLER, J. L., and CLARKE, L. D. (1966), 'Genetic and treatment factors modifying the post-isolation syndrome in dogs', *J. comp. physiol. Psychol..* vol. 61, pp. 251–7.

FULLER, J. L., and THOMPSON, W. R. (1960), *Behavior Genetics*, Wiley.

FUNKENSTEIN, D. H., KING, S. H., and DROLETTE, M. E. (1957), *Mastery of Stress*, Harvard University Press.

GAGNÉ, R. M. (1967), *The Conditions of Learning*, Holt, Rinehart & Winston.

GALABURDA, A. M., *et al.* (1978), 'Right-left asymmetries in the brain'. *Science*, vol. 199, pp. 852–6.

GALE, A. (1977), 'Some EEG correlates of sustained attention', in R. R. Mackie (ed.), *Vigilance: Theory, Operational Performance and Physiological Correlates*, Plenum Press.

GALIN, D., and ORNSTEIN, R. (1972), 'Lateral organization of cognitive mode: an EEG study', *Psychophysiology*, vol. 9, pp. 412–18.

GALLISTEL, C. R. (1964), 'Electrical self-stimulation and its theoretical implications', *Psychol. Bull.*, vol. 61, pp. 23–4.

GALTON, F. (1869), *Hereditary Genius*, Macmillan.

GALTON, F. (1883), *Inquiry into Human Faculty and its Development*, Macmillan.

GARAI, J. E., and SCHEINFELD, A. (1968), 'Sex differences in mental and behavioral tasks', *Genet. Psychol. Monogr.*, vol. 77, pp. 169–299.

GARCIA, J., HANKINS, W. G., and RUSINIAK, K. W. (1974), 'Behavioral regulation of the milieu interne in man and rat', *Science*, vol. 185, pp. 824–31.

GARCIA, J., *et al.* (1968), 'Cues: their effectiveness as a function of the reinforcer', *Science*, vol. 160, pp. 794–5.

GARDNER, R. A., and GARDNER, B. T. (1969), 'Teaching sign language to a chimpanzee', *Science*, vol. 165, pp. 664–72.

GARDNER, R. W., *et al.* (1959), 'Cognitive controls: a study of individual consistencies in cognitive behavior', *Psychol. Issues*, vol. 1, no. 4.

GARN, S. M. (1971), *Human Races*, Thomas.

GARRETT, M., BEVER, T. G., and FODOR, J. A. (1966), 'The active use of grammar in speech perception', *Percept. Psychophys.*, vol. 1, pp. 30–32.

GATES, M. G., and ALLEE, W. C. (1933), 'Conditioned behavior of isolated and grouped cockroaches on a simple maze', *J. comp. Psychol.*, vol. 13, pp. 331–58.

GAULD, A., and SHOTTER, J. (1977), *Human Action and its Psychological Investigation*, Methuen.

GAUPP, L. A., STERN, R. M., and GALBRAITH, G. G. (1972), 'False heart-rate feedback and reciprocal inhibition by aversion relief in the treatment of snake avoidance behaviour', *Behav. Ther.*, vol. 3, pp. 7–20.

GAZZANIGA, M. (ed.) (1979), *Handbook of Neurobiology*, vol. 2,: *Neuropsychology*, Plenum Press.

GAZZANIGA, M. S., and HILLYARD, S. A. (1973), 'Attention mechanisms following brain bisection', in S. Kornblum (ed.), *Attention and Performance IV*, Academic Press.

GELDARD, F. A. (1972), *The Human Senses*, Wiley.

GESCHWIND, N. (1970), 'The organization of language and the brain', *Science*, vol. 170, pp. 940–44.

GESCHWIND, N. (1975), 'The apraxias: neural mechanisms of disorders of learned movement', *Amer. Scient.*, vol. 63, pp. 188–95.

GESELL, A. (1929), 'Maturation and infant behavior patterns', *Psychol. Rev.*, vol. 36, pp. 307–19.

GESELL, A. (1954), 'The ontogenesis of infant behavior', in L. Carmichael (ed.), *Handbook of Child Psychology*, Wiley, 2nd edn.

GESELL, A., and ILG, F. L. (1949), *Child Development*, Harper & Row.

GESELL, A., and THOMPSON, H. (1929), 'Learning and growth in identical twins', *Genet. Psychol. Monogr.*, vol. 6, pp. 1–124.

GESELL, A., and THOMPSON, H. (1941), 'Twins T and C from infancy to adolescence: a biogenetic study of individual differences by the method of co-twin control', *Genet. Psychol. Monogr.*, vol. 24, pp. 3–121.

GETZELS, J. W., and JACKSON, P. W. (1962), *Creativity and Intelligence: Explorations with Gifted Students*, Wiley.

GHENT, L. (1960), 'Recognition by children of realistic figures presented in various orientations', *Canad. J. Psychol.*, vol. 14, pp. 249–56.

GHISELIN, B. (1952), *The Creative Process*, University of California Press.

GHISELLI, E. E. (1956), 'Dimensional problems of criteria', *J. appl. Psychol.*, vol. 40, pp. 1–4.

GHISELLI, E. E. (1966), *The Validity of Occupational Aptitude Tests*, Wiley.

GHISELLI, E. E., and BROWN, C. W. (1955), *Personnel and Industrial Psychology*, McGraw-Hill.

GIBSON, E. J. (1969), *Principles of Perceptual Learning and Development*, Appleton-Century-Crofts.

GIBSON, E. J., *et al.* (1962), 'A developmental study of the discrimination of letter-like forms', *J. comp. physiol. Psychol.*, vol. 55, pp. 897–906.

GIBSON, H. B. (1969), 'Early delinquency in relation to broken homes', *J. Child Psychol. Psychiat.*, vol. 10, pp. 195–204.

GIBSON, J. J. (1933), 'Adaptation, after-effect and contrast in the perception of curved lines', *J. exp. Psychol.*, vol. 16, pp. 1–31.

GIBSON, J. J. (1937), 'Adaptation with negative after-effect', *Psychol. Rev.*, vol. 44, pp. 222–44.

GIBSON, J. J. (1950), *The Perception of the Visual World*, Houghton Mifflin.

GIBSON, J. J. (1968), *The Senses Considered as Perceptual Systems*, Allen & Unwin.

GIBSON, J. J., and GIBSON, E. J. (1955), 'Perceptual learning: differentiation or enrichment?', *Psychol. Rev.*, vol. 62, pp. 32–41.

GILES, H., and POWESLAND, P. F. (1975), *Speech Style and Social Evaluation*, Academic Press.

GLASS, D. C., and SINGER, J. L. (1972), *Urban Stress*, Academic Press.

GLAUBMAN, H., *et al.* (1978), 'REM deprivation and divergent thinking', *Psychophysiology*, vol. 15, pp. 75–9.

GLENCROSS, D. J. (1977), 'Control of skilled movements', *Psychol. Bull.*, vol. 84, pp. 14–29.

GLUECK, S., and GLUECK, E. T. (1959), *Predicting Delinquency and Crime*, Harvard University Press.

GODDARD, G. V. (1964), 'Functions of the amygdala', *Psychol. Bull.*, vol. 62, pp. 89–109.

GODDEN, D. R., and BADDELEY, A. D. (1975), 'Context-dependent memory in two natural environments: on land and under water', *Brit. J. Psychol.*, vol. 66, pp. 325–32.

GOLD, R. M. (1973), 'Hypothalamic obesity: the myth of the ventromedial nucleus', *Science*, vol. 182, pp. 488–90.

GOLDFARB, W. (1943), 'Effects of institutional care on adolescent personality', *J. exp. Educ.*, vol. 12, pp. 106–29.

GOLDIAMOND, I. (1958), 'Indicators of perception: I. Subliminal perception, subception, unconscious perception: an analysis in terms of psychophysical indicator methodology', *Psychol. Bull*, vol. 55, pp. 373–412.

GOLDSTEIN, D., FINK, D., and METTEE, D. R. (1972), 'Cognition of arousal and actual arousal as determinants of emotion', *J. Pers. soc. Psychol.*, vol. 21, pp. 41–51.

GOLDSTEIN, K., and SCHEERER, M. (1941), 'Abstract and concrete behavior: an experimental study with special tests', *Psychol. Monogr.*, vol. 53, no. 2.

GOMULICKI, B. R. (1956), 'Recall as an abstractive process', *Acta Psychol.*, vol. 12, pp. 77–94.

GOODENOUGH, D. R., *et al.* (1959), 'A comparison of "dreamers" and "non-dreamers": eye movements, electroencephalograms and the recall of dreams', *J. abnorm. soc. Psychol.*, vol. 59, pp. 295–302.

GOODENOUGH, D. R., *et al.* (1965), 'Dream reporting following abrupt and gradual awakenings from different types of sleep', *J. Pers. soc. Psychol.*, vol. 2, pp. 170–79.

GOTTESMAN, I. I. (1963), 'Heritability and personality', *Psychol. Monogr.*, vol. 77, no. 9.

GOTTESMAN, I. I. (1968), 'Biogenetics of race and class', in M. Deutsch, I. Katz and A. R. Jensen (eds.), *Social Class, Race, and Psychological Development*, Holt, Rinehart & Winston.

GOULD, S. J. (1980), *Ever since Darwin: Reflections in Natural History*, Penguin Books.

GOY, R. W. (1968), 'Organising effects of androgen on the behavior of rhesus monkeys', in R. P. Michael (ed.), *Endocrinology and Human Behaviour*, Oxford University Press.

GRAY, J. A., and WEDDERBURN, A. A. I. (1960), 'Grouping strategies with simultaneous stimuli', *Quart. J. exp. Psychol.*, vol. 12, pp. 180–84.

GREEN, R. F. (1969), 'Age-intelligence relationship between ages sixteen and sixty-four: a rising trend', *Devel. Psychol.*, vol. 1, pp. 618–27.

GREENBERG, R., and PEARLMAN, C. (1974), 'Cutting the REM nerve: an approach to the adaptive role of REM sleep', *Perspect. Biol. & Med.*, vol. 17, pp. 513–21.

GREENE, J. M. (1970a), 'The semantic function of negatives and passives', *Brit. J Psychol.*, vol. 61, pp. 17–22.

GREENE, J. M. (1970b), 'Syntactic form and semantic function', *Quart. J. exp. Psychol.*, vol. 22, pp. 14–27.

GREENE, J. M. (1972), *Psycholinguistics: Chomsky and Psychology*, Penguin Books.

GREENE, J. M. (1975), *Thinking and Language*, Methuen.

GREENFIELD, N. S., and STERNBACH, R. A. (1972), *Handbook of Psychophysiology*, Holt, Rinehart & Winston.

GREENSPOON, J., and RANYARD, R. (1957), 'Stimulus conditions and retroactive inhibition', *J. exp. Psychol.*, vol. 53, pp. 55–9.

GREENWALD, A. G. (1970), 'Sensory feedback mechanisms in performance control', *Psychol. Rev.*, vol. 77, pp. 73–99.

GREENWALD, A. G. (1972), 'On doing two things at once: time sharing as a function of ideomotor compatibility', *J. exp. Psychol.*, vol. 94, pp. 52–7.

GREENWALD, A. G., and SHULMAN, H. G. (1973), 'On doing two things at once: II. Elimination of the psychological refractory period effect', *J. exp. Psychol.*, vol. 101, pp. 70–76.

GREGOR, A. J., and MCPHERSON, D. A. (1965), 'A study of susceptibility to geometrical illusion among cultural subgroups of Australian aborigines', *Psychol. Afric.*, vol. 11, pp. 1–13.

GREGORY, R. L. (1961), 'The brain as an engineering problem', in W. H. Thorpe and O. L. Zangwill (eds.), *Current Problems in Animal Behaviour*, Cambridge University Press.

GREGORY, R. L. (1966), *Eye and Brain*, Weidenfeld & Nicolson, 2nd edn (1973).

GREGORY, R. L., and WALLACE, J. G. (1963), 'Recovery from early blindness: a case study', *Exp. Psychol. Soc. Monogr.*, vol. 2.

GROSSMAN, S. P. (1975), 'Role of the hypothalamus in the regulation of food and water intake', *Psychol. Rev.*, vol. 82, pp. 200–224.

GROSSMAN, S. P., and GROSSMAN, L. (1973), 'Persisting deficits in rats "recovered" from transections of fibers which enter or leave hypothalamus laterally', *J. comp. physiol. Psychol.*, vol. 85, pp. 515–27.

GROVES, P. M., and THOMPSON, R. F. (1970), 'Habituation', *Psychol. Rev.*, vol. 77, pp. 419–50.

GRUNEBERG, M. M. (1970), 'A dichotomous theory of memory – unproved and unprovable?', *Acta Psychol.*, vol. 34, pp. 489–96.

GUERTIN, W. H. *et al.* (1966), 'Research with the Wechsler Intelligence Scales for Adults: 1960–1965', *Psychol. Bull.*, vol. 66, pp. 385–409.

GUILFORD, J. P. (1954), *Psychometric Methods*, McGraw-Hill, 2nd edn.

GUILFORD, J. P. (1959), *Personality*, McGraw-Hill.

GUILFORD, J. P. (1967), *The Nature of Human Intelligence*, McGraw-Hill.

GUILFORD, J. P. (1972), 'Executive functions and a model of behaviour', *J. gen. Psychol.*, vol. 86, pp. 279–87.

GUITON, P. (1959), 'Socialisation and imprinting in Brown Leghorn chicks', *Anim. Behav.*, vol. 7, pp. 26–34.

GULEVICH, G., DEMENT, W. C., and JOHNSON, L. C. (1966), 'Psychiatric and EEG observations on a case of prolonged (264 hr) wakefulness', *Arch. gen. Psychiat.*, vol. 15, pp. 29–35.

GUNN, C. G. *et al.* (1972), 'Psychophysiology of the cardiovascular system', in N. S. Greenfield and R. A. Sternbach (eds.), *Handbook of Psychophysiology*, Holt, Rinehart & Winston.

GUTHRIE, G., and WIENER, M. (1966), 'Subliminal perception or perception of partial cue with pictorial stimuli', *J. Pers. soc. Psychol.*, vol. 3, pp. 619–28.

HABER, R. N. (1966), 'Nature of the effect of set on perception', *Psychol. Rev.*, vol. 73, pp. 335–51.

HABER, R. N. (1969), 'Eidetic images', *Scient. Amer.*, vol. 220, pp. 36–44.

HABER, R. N., and HERSCHENSON, M. (1973), *The Psychology of Visual Perception*, Holt, Rinehart & Winston.

HAGGARD, E. A., and ISAACS, K. S. (1966), 'Micromomentary facial expressions as indicators of ego mechanisms in psychotherapy', in L. A. Gottschalk and A. H. Auerbach (eds.), *Methods of Research in Psychotherapy*, Appleton-Century-Crofts.

HALL, C. S. (1951), 'The genetics of behavior', in S. S. Stevens (ed.), *Handbook of Experimental Psychology*, Wiley.

HALL, C. S. (1954), *A Primer of Freudian Psychology*, World Publ. Co.

HALL, C. S., and NORDBY, V. J. (1974), *A Primer of Jungian Psychology*, Croom Helm.

HALL, K. R. L. (1963), 'Observational learning in monkeys and apes', *Brit. J. Psychol.*, vol. 54, pp. 201–26.

HAMILTON, P., HOCKEY, G. R. J., and REJMAN, A. (1977), 'The place of the concept of activation in human information processing theory: an integrative approach', in S. Dornic (ed.), *Attention and Performance*, VI, Lawrence Erlbaum.

HARDYCK, C., and PETRINOVICH, L. F. (1977), 'Left-handedness', *Psychol. Bull.*, vol. 84, pp. 385–404.

HARLOW, H. (1965), 'Sexual behavior of the rhesus monkey', in F. A. Beach (ed.), *Sex and Behavior*, Wiley.

HARLOW, H. F. (1932), 'Social facilitation of feeding in the albino rat', *J. genet. Psychol.*, vol. 41, pp. 211–21.

HARLOW, H. F. (1949), 'The formation of learning sets', *Psychol. Rev.*, vol. 56, pp. 51–65.

HARLOW, H. F. (1959), 'Love in infant monkeys', *Scient. Amer.*, vol. 200, pp. 68–74.

HARLOW, H. F. *et al.* (1952), 'Analysis of frontal and posterior association syndromes in brain-damaged monkeys', *J. comp. physiol. Psychol.*, vol. 45, pp. 419–29.

HARLOW, H. F., AKERT, K., and SCHILTZ, K. A. (1964), 'The effects of bilateral prefrontal lesions on learned behavior of neonatal infant and pre-adolescent monkeys', in J. M. Warren and K. Akert (eds.), *The Frontal Granular Cortex and Behavior*, McGraw-Hill.

HARLOW, H. F., and HARLOW, M. K. (1962), 'Social deprivation in monkeys', *Scient. Amer.*, vol. 207, pp. 137–46.

HARLOW, H. F., and ZIMMERMANN, R. R. (1959), 'Affectional responses in the infant monkey', *Science,* vol. 130, pp. 421–32.

HARPER, R. G., WIENS, A. N., and MATARAZZO, J. D. (1978), *Nonverbal Communication: The State of the Art*, Wiley.

HARRIS, C. S. (1965), 'Perceptual adaptation to inverted, reversed and displaced vision, *Psychol. Rev.*, vol. 72, pp. 419–44.

HARRISON, R. (1965), 'Thematic apperceptive methods', in B. B. Wolman (ed.), *Handbook of Clinical Psychology*, McGraw-Hill.

HART, H. L. A. (1968), *Punishment and Responsibility: Essays in the Philosophy of Law*. Clarendon Press.

HART, J. T. (1965), 'Memory and the feeling of knowing experience', *J. educ. Psychol.*, vol. 56, pp. 208–16.

HARTMANN, E. (1973), *The Functions of Sleep*, York University Press.

HARTNETT, J. J., BAILEY, K. G., and GIBSON, F. W., JR. (1970), 'Personal space as influenced by sex and type of movement', *J. Psychol.*, vol. 76, pp. 139–44.

HARTNETT, O., BODEN, G., and FULLER, M. (eds.) (1979), *Sex-role Stereotyping*, Tavistock.

HARWAY, N. I. (1963), 'The judgment of distance in children and adults', *J. exp. Psychol.*, vol. 65, pp. 385–90.

HARWOOD, E., and NAYLOR, G. F. K. (1971), 'Changes in the constitution of the WAIS intelligence pattern with advancing age', *Austral. J. Psychol.*, vol. 23, pp. 297–303.

HASAN, P., and BUTCHER, H. J. (1966), 'Creativity and intelligence: a partial replication with Scottish children of Getzels and Jackson's study', *Brit. J. Psychol.*, vol. 57, pp. 129–35.

HASSETT, J. (1978), *A Primer of Psychophysiology*, Freeman.

HASTRUP, J. L., and KATKIN, E. S. (1976), 'Electrodermal lability: an attempt to measure its physiological correlates', *Psychophysiology*, vol. 13, pp. 296–301.

HATHAWAY, S. R., and McKINLEY, J. C. (1942), *Minnesota Multiphasic Personality Inventory*, University of Minnesota Press.

HATHAWAY, S. R., and McKINLEY, J. C. (1943), *Manual for the Minnesota Multiphasic Personality Inventory*, Psychological Corporation.

HAURI, P. (1970), 'What is good sleep?', in E. Hartmann (ed.), *Sleep and Dreaming*, Little, Brown.

HEAD, H. (1923), 'The conception of nervous and mental energy, II.: Vigilance: a physiological state of the nervous system', *Brit. J. Psychol.*, vol. 14, pp. 126–47.

HEARNSHAW, L. S. (1964), *A Short History of British Psychology*, Methuen.

HEATH, R. G. (1955), 'Correlations between levels of psychological awareness and physiological activity in the central nervous system', *Psychosom. Med.*, vol. 17, pp. 383–95.

HEBB, D. O. (1946), 'Emotion in man and animal: an analysis of the intuitive processes of recognition', *Psychol. Rev.*, vol. 53, pp. 88–106.

HEBB, D. O. (1949), *The Organization of Behavior*, Wiley.

HEBB, D. O. (1955), 'Drives and the C.N.S. (conceptual nervous system)', *Psychol. Rev.*, vol. 62, pp. 243–53.

HEBB, D. O. (1958), *A Textbook of Psychology*, Saunders.

HEBB, D. O. (1961), 'Distinctive features of learning in the higher animals', in J. Delafresnaye (ed.), *Brain Mechanisms in Learning*, Oxford University Press.

HEBB, D. O. (1966), *A Textbook of Psychology*, Saunders, 2nd edn.

HEBB, D. O., and FOORD, E. N. (1945), 'Errors of visual recognition and the nature of the trace', *J. exp. Psychol.*, vol. 35, pp. 335–48.

HEBER, R., *et al.* (1972), *Rehabilitation of families at risk for mental retardation*, University of Wisconsin.

HECAEN, H. (1979), 'Aphasias', in M. Gazzaniga (ed.), *Handbook of Behavioral Neurobiology*, vol. 2.: *Neuropsychology*, Plenum Press.

HEIDBREDER, E. (1946a), 'The attainment of concepts: I. Terminology and methodology', *J. genet. Psychol.*, vol. 35, pp. 173–89.

HEIDBREDER, E. (1946b), 'The attainment of concepts: II. The problem', *J. genet. Psychol.*, vol. 35, pp. 191–223.

HEIM, A. W. (1970a), *Intelligence and Personality*, Penguin Books.

HEIM, A. W. (1970b), *The Appraisal of Intelligence*, National Foundation for Educational Research.

HELD, R. (1961), 'Exposure history as a factor in maintaining stability of perception and co-ordination', *J. nerv. ment. Dis.*, vol. 132, pp. 26–32.

HELD, R. (1965), 'Plasticity in sensory-motor systems', *Scient. Amer.*, vol. 213, pp. 84–94.

HELD, R., and FREEMAN, S. J. (1963), 'Plasticity in human sensory-motor control', *Science*, vol. 142, pp. 455–62.

HELD, R., and HEIN, A. (1963), 'Movement-produced stimulation in the development of visually guided behavior', *J. comp. physiol. Psychol.*, vol. 56, pp. 607–13.

HELD, R., and RICHARDS, W. (1972), *Perception: Mechanisms and Models*, W. H. Freeman.

HENCHY, T., and GLASS, C. D. (1968), 'Evaluation apprehension and the social facilitation of dominant and subordinate responses', *J. Pers. soc. Psychol.*, vol. 10, pp. 446–54.

HENLE, M. (1962), 'On the relation between logic and thinking', *Psychol. Rev.*, vol. 69, pp. 366–78.

HENRY, H. (1958), *Motivation Research*, Frederick Unger.

HEPLER, N. (1968), 'Color: a motion-contingent after-effect', *Science*, vol. 162, pp. 376–7.

HERRIOT, P. (1969), 'The comprehension of active and passive sentences as a function of pragmatic expectations', *J. verb. Learn. verb. Behav.*, vol. 8, pp. 166–9.

HERRIOT, P. (1970), *An Introduction to the Psychology of Language*, Methuen.

HERRMAN, D. J., and NEISSER, U. (1979), 'An inventory of everyday memory experiences', in M. M. Gruneberg, P. E. Morris and R. N. Sykes (eds.), *Proc. Int. Conference on Practical Aspects of Memory*, Academic Press.

HERRNSTEIN, R. (1971), 'I.Q.', *The Atlantic*, vol. 228(3), pp. 43–64.

HERRNSTEIN, R. (1973), *I.Q. in the Meritocracy*, Little, Brown.

HERZOG, A. R. (1979), 'Attitude change in older age: an experimental study', *J. Gerontol.*, vol. 34, pp. 697–703.

HESS, E. H. (1959), 'Imprinting', *Science*, vol. 130, pp. 133–41.

HESS, E. H., and POLT, J. M. (1960), 'Pupil size as related to interest value of visual stimuli', *Science*, vol. 132, pp. 349–50.

HESS, E. H., and POLT, J. M. (1964), 'Pupil size in relation to mental activity during simple problem-solving', *Science*, vol. 143, pp. 1190–92.

HESS, W. R. (1954), *Diencephalon: Autonomic and Extrapyramidal Functions*, Grune & Stratton.

HETHERINGTON, A. W., and RANSON, S. W. (1942), 'The spontaneous activity and food intake of rats with hypothalamic lesions', *Amer. J. Physiol.*, vol. 136, pp. 609–17.

HICK, W. E., and BATES, J. A. V. (1950), 'The human operator of control mechanisms', *Permanent Records of Research & Development*, no. 17, p. 204, Ministry of Supply, H.M.S.O.

HILGARD, E. R. (1977), *Divided Consciousness: Multiple Controls in Human Thought and Action*, Wiley.

HILGARD, E. R., and BOWER, G. H. (1966), *Theories of Learning*, Appleton-Century-Crofts.

HILGARD, E. R., and MARQUIS, D. G. (1961), *Conditioning and Learning*, Methuen.

HILL, W. F. (1972), *Learning: A Survey of Psychological Interpretations*, Methuen.

HILLYARD, S., and PICTON, T. W. (1978), 'Event-related brain potentials and selective information processing in man', in J. E. Desmedt (ed.), *Progress in Clinical Neurophysiology*, vol. 6: *Cognitive Components in Event-related Cerebral Potentials*, Karger.

HILLYARD, S. A., and WOODS, D. L. (1979), 'Electrophysiological analysis of human brain function', in M. Gazzaniga (ed.), *Handbook of Neurobiology*, vol. 2: *Neuropsychology*, Plenum Press.

HINDE, R. A. (1970), *Animal Behaviour: A Synthesis of Ethology and Comparative Psychology*, McGraw-Hill, 2nd edn.

HINDE, R. A. (1974), *Biological Bases of Human Social Behaviour*, McGraw-Hill.

HINDE, R. A., and STEVENSON-HINDE, J. (eds.) (1973), *Constraints on Learning*, Academic Press.

HINK, R. F., *et al.* (1978), 'Vigilance and human attention under conditions of methylphenidate and secobarbital intoxication: an assessment using brain potentials', *Psychophysiol.*, vol. 15, pp. 116–25.

HIRSCH, J. (1964), 'Breeding analysis of natural units in behavior genetics', *Amer. Zool.*, vol. 4, pp. 139–45.

HIRSCHMANN, R. D. (1975), 'Cross modal effects of anticipatory bogus heart rate feedback in a negative emotional context', *J. Pers. soc. Psychol.*, vol. 31, pp. 13–19.

HOBSON, J. A., and BRAZIER, M. B. (eds.) (1980), *The Reticular Formation Revisited: Specifying Functions for a Nonspecific System*, Raven Press.

HOBSON, J. A., MCCARLEY, R. W., and WYZINSKI, P. W. (1975), 'Sleep cycle oscillation: reciprocal discharge by two brainstem neuronal groups', *Science*, vol. 189, pp. 55–8.

HOCHBERG, J. E. (1962), 'Nativism and empiricism in perception', in L. Postman (ed.), *Psychology in the Making*, Knopf.

HOCHBERG, J. E. (1964), *Perception*, Prentice-Hall.

HOCKETT, C. F. (1960), 'The origin of speech', *Scient. Amer.*, vol. 203, pp. 89–96.

HOCKEY, G. R. J. (1970a), 'Effect of loud noise on attentional selectivity', *Quart. J. exp. Psychol.*, vol. 22, pp. 28–36.

HOCKEY, G. R. J. (1970b), 'Changes in attention allocation in a multicomponent task under loss of sleep', *Brit. J. Psychol.*, vol. 61, pp. 473–80.

HOCKEY, G. R. J., and COLQUHOUN, W. P. (1972), 'Diurnal variation in human performance: a review', in W. P. Colquhoun (ed.), *Aspects of Human Efficiency: Diurnal Rhythm and Loss of Sleep*, English Universities Press.

HOCKEY, G. R. J., DAVIES, S., and GRAY, M. M. (1972), 'Forgetting as a function of sleep at different times of day', *Quart. J. exp. Psychol.*, vol. 24, pp. 386–93.

HOCKEY, G. R. J., and HAMILTON, P. (1970), 'Arousal and information selection in short-term memory', *Nature*, vol. 226, pp. 866–7.

HODES, R., and DEMENT, W. C. (1964), 'Depression of electrically induced reflexes ("H-reflexes") in man during low voltage EEG "sleep"', *EEG clin. Neurophysiol.*, vol. 17, pp. 617–29.

HOEBEL, B. G., and TEITELBAUM, P. (1966), 'Weight regulation in normal and hypothalamic hyperphagic rats', *J. comp. physiol. Psychol.*, vol. 61, pp. 189–93.

HOHMANN, G. W. (1966), 'Some effects of spinal cord lesions on experienced emotional feelings', *Psychophysiol.*, vol. 3, pp. 143–56.

HOLDING, D. H. (1965), *Principles of Training*, Pergamon Press.

HOLLAND, H. C. (1965), *The Spiral After-Effect*, Pergamon Press.

HOLLAND, J. I. (1973), *Making Vocational Choices*, Prentice-Hall.

HOLT, R. R. (1969), *Assessing Personality*, Harcourt, Brace, Jovanovich.

HOLTZMANN, W. H., *et al.* (1961), *Inkblot Perception and Personality: Holtzmann Inkblot Technique*, University of Texas Press.

HORN, J. L., and CATTELL, R. B. (1967), 'Age differences in fluid and crystallized intelligence', *Acta Psychol.*, vol. 26, pp. 107–29.

HORN, J. L., and DONALDSON, G. (1976), 'On the myth of intellectual decline in adulthood', *Amer. Psychol.*, vol. 31, pp. 701–19.

690 References

HORNE, J. A. (1975), 'Binocular convergence in man during total sleep deprivation', *Biol. Psychol.*, vol. 3, pp. 309–19.

HORNE, J. A. (1977), 'Factors relating to energy conservation during sleep in mammals', *Physiol. Psychol.*, vol. 5, pp. 403–8.

HORNE, J. A. (1978), 'A review of the biological effects of total sleep deprivation in man', *Biol. Psychol.*, vol. 7, pp. 55–102.

HORNE, J. A. (1979), 'Restitution and human sleep: a critical review', *Physiol. Psychol.*, vol. 7, pp. 115–25.

HORNE, J. A., and PORTER, J. M. (1976), 'Time of day effects with standardised exercise upon subsequent sleep', *EEG clin. Neurophysiol.*, vol. 40, pp. 178–84.

HORNEY, K. (1937), *Collected Works*, Norton, 2 vols.

HORST, P. (1965), *Factor Analysis of Data Matrices*, Holt, Rinehart & Winston.

HOSKINS, R. G. (1933), *The Tides of Life*, Norton.

HOSPERS, J. (1973), *An Introduction to Philosophical Analysis*, Routledge & Kegan Paul, revised edn.

HOVLAND, C. I. (1937), 'The generalization of conditioned responses', *J. gen. Psychol.*, vol. 17, pp. 125–48.

HOVLAND, C. I. (1952), 'A "communication analysis" of concept learning', *Psychol. Rev.*, vol. 59, pp. 461–72.

HOWARD, I., and TEMPLETON, W. (1966), *Human Spatial Orientation*, Wiley.

HOWARD, I. P. (1970), 'The adaptability of the visual-motor system', in K. J. Connolly (ed.), *Mechanisms of Motor Skill Development*, Academic Press.

HOWES, D. H., and SOLOMON, R. L. (1950), 'A note on McGinnies' "Emotionality and perceptual defense"', *Psychol. Rev.*, vol. 57, pp. 229–34.

HUBEL, D. H. (1963), 'The visual cortex of the brain', *Scient. Amer.*, vol. 209, pp. 54–62.

HUBEL, D. H., and WIESEL, T. N. (1962), 'Receptive fields, binocular interaction and functional architecture in the cat's visual cortex', *J. Physiol.*, vol. 160, pp. 106–54.

HUDSON, L. (1966), *Contrary Imaginations*, Methuen.

HUDSON, L. (1968), *Frames of Mind: Ability, Perception and Self-perception in the Arts and Sciences*, Methuen.

HUDSON, L. (1972), *The Cult of the Fact*, Cape.

HUGHES, K. R., and ZUBEK, J. P. (1956), 'Effect of glutamic acid on the learning ability of "bright" and "dull" rats: I', *Canad. J. Psychol.*, vol. 10, pp. 132–8.

HUGHES, K. R., and ZUBEK, J. P. (1957), 'Effect of glutamic acid on the learning ability of "bright" and "dull" rats: II', *Canad. J. Psychol.*, vol. 11, pp. 182–4.

HULL, C. L. (1920), 'Quantitative aspects of the evolution of concepts', *Psychol. Monogr.*, vol. 28(1), whole no. 123.

HULL, C. L. (1943), *Principles of Behavior*, Appleton-Century-Crofts.

HULL, C. L. (1952), *A Behavior System: An Introduction to Behavior Theory Covering the Individual Organism*, Yale University Press.

HULL, C. L. (1954), 'Autobiography', in E. G. Boring, *et al.* (eds.), *A History of Psychology in Autobiography*, vol. IV, Clark University Press.

HULSE, S. H., FOWLER, H., and HONIG, W. K. (eds.) (1978), *Cognitive Processes in Animal Behavior*, Lawrence Erlbaum.

HUMPHREY, G. (1951), *Thinking: An Introduction to its Experimental Psychology*, Methuen.

HUNT, J. McV., *et al.* (1947), 'Studies of the effects of infantile experience on adult behavior in rats: I. Effects of infantile feeding frustration on adult hoarding', *J. comp. physiol. Psychol.*, vol. 40, pp. 291–304.

HUNTER, I. M. L. (1977), 'An exceptional memory', *Brit. J. Psychol.*, vol. 68, pp. 155–64.

HUSBAND, R. W. (1931), 'Analysis of methods in human maze learning', *J. genet. Psychol.*, vol. 39, pp. 258–77.

HUSEN, T. (1959), *Psychological Twin Research*, Almquist & Wiksell.

HUTT, C. (1972), *Males and Females*, Penguin Books.

HUTT, C., and OUNSTEAD, C. (1966), 'The biological significance of gaze aversion with particular reference to the syndrome of infantile autism', *Behav. Sci.*, vol. 11, pp. 346–56.

HUTTENLOCHER, J. (1962), 'Some effects of negative instances on the formation of simple concepts', *Psychol. Rep.*, vol. 11, pp. 35–42.

HYDE, J. S., and PHILLIS, D. E. (1979), 'Androgyny across the life span', *Devel. Psychol.*, vol. 15, pp. 334–6.

HYMOVITCH, B. (1952), 'The effects of experimental variations on problem solving in rats', *J. comp. physiol. Psychol.*, vol. 45, pp. 313–20.

IMMELMANN, K. (1972), 'Sexual and other long-term aspects of imprinting in birds and other species', in D. S. Lehrman, R. A. Hinde and E. Shaw (eds.), *Advances in the Study of Behavior*, vol. 4, Academic Press.

IMPERATO-MCGINLEY, J., *et al.* (1974), 'Steroid 5 alpha-reductase deficiency in man: an inherited form of male pseudohermaphroditism', *Science*, vol. 186, pp. 1213–15.

INHELDER, B., and PIAGET, J. (1958), *The Growth of Logical Thinking from Childhood to Adolescence*, Basic Books.

INHELDER, B., and PIAGET, J. (1964), *The Early Growth of Logic in the Child*, Routledge & Kegan Paul.

IRWIN, F. W., (1971), *Intentional Behavior and Motivation: A Cognitive Theory*, Lippincott.

ISAACSON, R. L. (1974), *The Limbic System*, Plenum Press.

ITTELSON, W. H. (1952), *The Ames Demonstrations in Perception*, Princeton University Press.

ITTELSON, W. H. et al. (1974), *An Introduction to Environmental Psychology*, Holt, Rinehart & Winston.

IZARD, C. (1971), *The Face of Emotion*, Appleton-Century-Crofts.

IZARD, C. (1977), *Human Emotions*, Plenum Press.

JACKSON, D. N. (1967), 'Acquiescence response styles: problems of identification and control', in I. A. Berg (ed.), *Response Set in Personality Assessment*, Aldine.

JACOBSON, L. E. (1932), 'The electrophysiology of mental activities', *Amer. J. Psychol.*, vol. 44, pp. 677–94.

JAHODA, G. (1966), 'Geometric illusions and environment: a study in Ghana', *Brit. J. Psychol.*, vol. 57, pp. 193–9.

JAHODA, G., and STACEY, B. (1970), 'Susceptibility to geometrical illusions according to culture and professional training', *Percept. Psychophys.*, vol. 7, pp. 179–84.

JAMES, W. (1884), 'What is emotion?', *Mind*, vol. 9, pp. 188–205.

JAMES, W. (1890), *The Principles of Psychology*, Henry Holt, 2 vols. (reprinted, 1950, Dover).

JAMES, W. (1961), *Psychology: The Briefer Course*, Harper & Bros.

JAMES, W. T. (1953), 'Social facilitation of eating behavior in puppies after satiation'. *J. comp. physiol. Psychol.*, vol. 46, pp. 427–8.

JAMES, W. T. (1960), 'The development of social facilitation of eating behavior in puppies', *J. genet. Psychol.*, vol. 96, pp. 123–7.

JAMES, W. T., and CANNON, D. J. (1955), 'Variation in social facilitation of eating behavior in puppies', *J. genet. Psychol.*, vol. 87, pp. 225–8.

JANISSE, M. P. (1977), *Pupillometry*, Hemisphere Publ. Corpn./Wiley.

JASPARS, J. M. F. (1978), 'The nature and measurement of attitudes', in H. Tajfel and C. Fraser (eds.), *Introducing Social Psychology*, Penguin Books.

JASPER, H. H. (1958), 'The ten-twenty system of the International Federation', *EEG clin. Neurophysiol.*, vol. 10, pp. 371–5.

JENCKS, C. (1972), *Inequality*, Penguin Books.

JENKINS, J. J. (1963), 'Mediated associations: paradigms and situations', in C. N. Cofer and B. S. Musgrave (eds), *Verbal Behavior and Learning*, McGraw-Hill.

JENKINS, W. O., McFANN, H., and CLAYTON, F. L. (1950), 'A methodological study of extinction following aperiodic and continuous reinforcement', *J. comp. physiol. Psychol.*, vol. 43, pp. 155–67.

JENKINS, W. O., and RIGBY, M. K. (1950), 'Partial (periodic) versus continuous reinforcement in resistance to extinction', *J. comp. physiol. Psychol.*, vol. 43, pp. 30–40.

JENNINGS, H. S. (1906), *Behavior of the Lower Organisms*, Columbia University Press.

JENSEN, A. R. (1969), 'How much can we boost I.Q. and scholastic achievement?', *Harvard Educ. Rev.*, vol. 39, pp. 1–123.

JENSEN, A. R. (1972), *Genetics and Education*, Methuen.

JENSEN, A. R. (1974a), 'Cumulative deficit: a testable hypothesis?', *Devel. Psychol.*, vol. 10, pp. 996–1019.

JENSEN, A. R. (1974b), 'How biased are culture-loaded tests?', *Genet. Psychol. Monogr.*, vol. 90, pp. 185–244.

JERISON, H. J. (1973), *Evolution of the Brain and Intelligence*, Academic Press.

JOHNSON, H. G., EKMAN, P., and FRIESEN, W. V. (1975), 'Communicative body movements: American emblems', *Semiotica*, vol. 15, pp. 335–53.

JOHNSON, J. H. (1974), 'Memory and personality: an information processing approach', *J. Res. Pers.*, vol. 8, pp. 1–32.

JOHNSON, L. C. (1973), 'Are stages of sleep related to waking behavior?', *Amer. Sci.*, vol. 61, pp. 326–38.

JOHNSON, L. C., SLYE, E. S., and DEMENT, W. (1965), 'Electroencephalographic and autonomic activity during and after prolonged sleep deprivation', *Psychosom. Med.*, vol. 27, pp. 415–22.

JOHNSON, N. F. (1965), 'The psychological reality of phrase-structure rules', *J. verb. Learn. verb. Behav.*, vol. 4, pp. 469–75.

JOHNSON, R. E. (1970), 'Recall of prose as a function of the structural importance of the linguistic units', *J. verb. Learn. verb. Behav.*, vol. 9, pp. 12–20.

JOHNSON, R. N. (1972), *Aggression in Man and Animals*, Saunders.

JOHNSON-LAIRD, P. N., and WASON, P. C. (eds.) (1977), *Thinking: Readings in Cognitive Science*, Cambridge University Press.

JOHNSTON, W. A., and HEINZ, S. P. (1978), 'The flexibility and capacity demands of attention', *J. exp. Psychol.: General*, vol. 107, pp. 420–35.

JONES, E. (1955), *The Life and Work of Sigmund Freud*, vol. 2, Basic Books.

JONES, E. E., and GERARD, H. B. (1967), *Foundations of Social Psychology*, Wiley.

JONES, H. S., and OSWALD, I. (1968), 'Two cases of healthy insomnia', *EEG clin. Neurophysiol.*, vol. 24, pp. 378–80.

JOUANDET, M., and GAZZANIGA, M. S. (1979), 'The frontal lobes', in M. Gazzaniga (ed.), *Handbook of Behavioral Neurobiology*, vol. 2: *Neuropsychology*, Plenum Press.

JOURARD, S. M. (1966), 'An exploratory study of body-accessibility', *Brit. J. soc. clin. Psychol.*, vol. 5, pp. 221–31.

JOUVET, M. (1967), 'The states of sleep', *Scient. Amer.*, vol. 216, pp. 62–72.

JOUVET, M. (1969), 'Biogenic amines and the states of sleep', *Science*, vol. 163, pp. 32–41.

JOUVET, M., MICHEL, F., and MOUNIER, D. (1959), 'Analyse électroencéphalographique comparée du sommeil physiologique chez le chat et chez l'homme', *Rev. Neurol. (Paris)*, vol. 103, pp. 189–204.

JOYNSON, R. B. (1974), *Psychology and Common Sense*, Routledge & Kegan Paul.

KAADA, B. R. (1972), 'Stimulation and regional ablation of the amygdaloid complex with reference to functional representations', in B. E. Eleftheriou (ed.), *The Neurobiology of the Amygdala*, Plenum Press.

KAHN, E., and FISHER, C. (1969), 'The sleep characteristics of the normal aged male', *J. nerv. ment. Dis.*, vol. 148, pp. 477–505.

KAHNEMAN, D. (1973), *Attention and Effort*, Prentice-Hall.

KAHNEMAN, D., and BEATTY, J. (1966), 'Pupil diameter and load on memory', *Science*, vol. 154, pp. 1583–5.

KAIL, R. V., and HAGEN, J. W. (1977), *Perspectives on the Development of Memory and Cognition*, Lawrence Erlbaum.

KALES, A. (1972), 'The evaluation and treatment of sleep disorders: Pharmacological and psychological studies', in M. Chase (ed.), *The Sleeping Brain*, Brain Information Service.

KALISH, R. M. (1975), *Late Adulthood: Perspectives on Human Development*, Brooks/Cole.

KALLMAN, F. J., and SANDER, G. (1949), 'Twin studies on senescence', *Amer. J. Psychiat.*, vol. 106, pp. 29–36.

KAMIN, L. J. (1974), *The Science and Politics of I.Q.*, Lawrence Erlbaum.

KAMIN, L. J. (1978), 'Positive interpretation of apparent cumulative deficit', *Devel. Psychol.*, vol. 14, pp. 195–6.

KAMM, J. (1965), *Hope Deferred: Girls' Education in English History*, Methuen.

KARACAN, I., *et al.* (1970), 'changes in stage 1 – REM and stage 4 sleep during naps', *Biol. Psychiat.*, vol. 2, pp. 261–5.

KATZ, I. (1967), 'The socialization of academic motivation in minority-group children', in D. Levine (ed.), *Nebraska Symposium on Motivation*, vol. 15, University of Nebraska Press.

KATZ, J. J., and POSTAL, P. M. (1964), *An Integrated Theory of Linguistic Descriptions*, M. I. T. Press.

KAUFMAN, L., and ROCK, I. (1962), 'The moon illusion', *Scient. Amer.*, vol. 207(1), pp. 120–32.

KEELE, S. W. (1973), *Attention and Human Performance*, Goodyear Publ. Co.

KEELE, S. W., and NEILL, W. T. (1978), 'Mechanisms of attention, in E. C. Carterette and M. P. Friedman (eds.), *Handbook of Perception*, vol. 9, Academic Press.

KEELE, S. W., and SUMMERS, J. J. (1976), 'The structure of motor programs', in G. E. Stelmach (ed.), *Motor Control: Issues and Trends*, Academic Press.

KEESEY, R. E., and POWLEY, T. L. (1975), 'Hypothalamic regulation of body weight', *Amer. Scient.*, vol. 63, pp. 558–65.

KELLEY, H. H., and THIBAUT, J. W. (1969), 'Group problem solving', in G. Lindzey and E. Aronson (eds.), *The Handbook of Social Psychology*, vol. IV. Addison-Wesley, 2nd edn.

KELLOGG, W. N. (1968), 'Communication and language in the home-raised chimpanzee', *Science*, vol. 162, pp. 423–7.

KELLY, E. L. (1967), *Assessment of Human Characteristics*, Wadsworth.

KELLY, G. A. (1955), *The Psychology of Personal Constructs*, Norton.

KEMPER, T. D. (1978), *A Social Interactional Theory of Emotions*, Wiley.

KEMPTHORNE, O. (1978), 'Logical epistemological and statistical aspects of nature–nurture data interpretation', *Biometrics*, vol. 34, pp. 1–23.

KENDLER, H. H., and KENDLER, T. S. (1962), 'Vertical and horizontal processes in problem-solving', *Psychol. Rev.*, vol. 69, pp. 1–16.

KENDLER, H. H., and KENDLER, T. S. (1969), 'Reversal-shift behavior: some basic issues', *Psychol. Bull.*, vol. 72, pp. 229–32.

KENDON, A. (1967), 'Some functions of gaze-direction in social interaction', *Acta Psychol.*, vol. 26, pp. 22–63.

KENNY, A. (1963), *Action, Emotion and Will*, Routledge & Kegan Paul.

KENT, R. N., WILSON, G. T., and NELSON, R. (1972), 'Effects of false heart-rate feedback on avoidance behavior: an investigation of "cognitive" desensitization', *Behav. Ther.*, vol. 3, pp. 1–6.

KEREN, G. (1976), 'Some considerations of two alleged kinds of selective attention', *J. exp. Psychol.: General*, vol. 105, pp. 349–74.

KERLINGER, F. N. (1979), *Behavioral Research*, Holt, Rinehart & Winston.

KESSEN, W. (1960), 'Research design in the study of developmental problems', in P. H. Mussen (ed.), *Handbook of Research Methods in Child Development*, Wiley.

KIMBLE, G. A., and PERLMUTER, L. C. (1970), 'The problem of volition', *Psychol. Rev.*, vol. 77, pp. 361–84.

KIMURA, D. (1967), 'Functional asymmetry of the brain in dichotic listening', *Cortex*, vol. 3, pp. 163–78.

KING, C. D. (1974), '5-Hydroxytryptamine and sleep in the cat: a brief overview', *Adv. in Biochem. Psychopharmacol.*, vol. 11, pp. 211–16.

KINTSCH, W. (1970), *Learning, Memory and Conceptual Processes*, Wiley.

KINZEL, A. F. (1970), 'Body buffer zone in violent prisoners', *Amer. J. Psychiat.*, vol. 127, pp. 59–64.

KIPLING, R. (1937), *Something of Myself*, Macmillan.

KLEEMEIER, R. W. (1962), 'Intellectual changes in the senium', *Proc. Amer. Stat. Assoc.*, vol. 1, pp. 290–95.

KLEIN, G. A. (1972), 'Temporal changes in acoustic and semantic confusion effects', *J. exp. Psychol.*, vol. 86, pp. 236–40.

KLEITMAN, N. (1939), *Sleep and Wakefulness*, Chicago University Press, 1st edn.

KLEITMAN, N. (1963). *Sleep and Wakefulness*, Chicago University Press, 2nd edn.

KLEITMAN, N. (1970), 'Implications for organization of activities', in E. Hartmann (ed.), *Sleep and Dreaming*, Little, Brown.

KLINE, P. (1972), *Fact and Fantasy in Freudian Theory*, Methuen.

KLING, J. W., and RIGGS, L. A. (eds.) (1972), *Woodworth & Schlosberg's Experimental Psychology*, Methuen.

KLINGER, E. (1969), 'Feedback effects and social facilitation of vigilance performance: mere coaction vs. potential evaluation', *Psychon. Sci.*, vol. 14, pp. 161–2.

KLOPFER, B., and DAVIDSON, H. H. (1962), *The Rorschach Technique: An Introductory Manual*, Harcourt, Brace.

KLOPFER, B., and KELLEY, D. M. (1942), *The Rorschach Technique*, Harcourt, Brace.

KLOPFER, P. H. (1958), 'Influence of social interaction on learning rates in birds', *Science*, vol. 128, pp. 903–4.

KLÜVER, H., and BUCY, P. C. (1937), ' "Psychic blindness" and other symptoms following bilateral temporal lobectomy in rhesus monkeys', *Amer. J. Physiol.*, vol. 119, pp. 352–3.

KLÜVER, H., and BUCY, P. C. (1938), 'An analysis of certain effects of bilateral temporal lobectomy in the rhesus monkey, with special reference to "psychic blindness" ', *J. Psychol.*, vol. 5, pp. 33–54.

KLÜVER, H., and BUCY, P. C. (1939), 'Preliminary analysis of functions of the temporal lobes in monkeys', *Arch. Neurol. Psychiat.*, vol. 42, pp. 979–1000.

KNAPP, M. L. (1978), *Nonverbal Communication in Human Interaction*, 2nd edn., Holt, Rinehart & Winston, 2nd edn.

KOFFKA, K. (1935), *Principles of Gestalt Psychology*, Harcourt, Brace and Routledge & Kegan Paul.

KOGAN, N., and WALLACH, M. A. (1964), *Risk Taking: A Study in Cognition and Personality*, Holt, Rinehart & Winston.

KOHLBERG, L., and ZIGLER, E. (1967), 'The impact of cognitive maturity on the development of sex-role attitudes in the years 4 to 8', *Genet. Psychol. Monogr.*, vol. 75, pp. 84–165.

KOHLER, I. (1964), *The Formation and Transformation of the Perceptual World*, translated by H. Fiss, International Universities Press.

KÖHLER, W. (1925), *The Mentality of Apes*, Harcourt, Brace.

KONORSKI, J. (1967), *Integrative Activity of the Brain*, University of Chicago Press.

KORMAN, A. (1974), *The Psychology of Motivation*, Prentice-Hall.

KORNHUBER, H. H. (1974), 'Cerebral cortex, cerebellum and basal ganglia: An introduction to their motor functions', in F. O. Schmitt and F. G. Warden (eds.), *The Neurosciences: Third Study Program*, M. I. T. Press.

KRAMER, M. *et al.* (1976), 'Do dreams have meaning? An empirical enquiry', *Amer. J. Psychiat.*, vol. 133, pp. 778–81.

KRASHEN, S. (1973), 'Lateralization, language learning, and the critical period: some new evidence', *Lang. Learn.*, vol. 23, pp. 63–74.

KRECH, D., ROSENZWEIG, R., and BENNETT, E. L. (1956), 'Dimensions of discrimination and level of cholinesterase in the cerebral cortex of the rat', *J. comp. physiol. Psychol.*, vol. 49, pp. 261–8.

KRIPKE, D. F. (1974), 'Ultradian rhythms in sleep and wakefulness', in E. D. Weitzmann (ed.), *Advances in Sleep Research*, Spectrum.

KROUT, M. H. (1954), 'An experimental attempt to determine the significance of unconscious manual symbolic movements', *J. gen. Psychol.*, vol. 51, pp. 121–52.

KUBIE, L. S. (1958), *Neurotic Distortion of the Creative Process*, University of Kansas Press.

KUDER, G. F. (1953), *Kuder Preference Record, Form A – Personal*, Science Research Associates.

KUFFLER, S. W. (1953), 'Discharge patterns and functional organisation of mammalian retina', *J. Neurophysiol.*, vol. 16, pp. 37–68.

KUHN, T. S. (1970), *The Structure of Scientific Revolutions*, University of Chicago Press.

KUMAR, R., STOLERMAN, I. P., and STEINBERG, H. (1970), 'Psychopharmacology', *Ann. Rev. Psychol.*, vol. 21, pp. 595–628.

KUO, Z. Y. (1939), 'Total pattern or local reflex', *Psychol. Rev.*, vol. 46, pp. 93–122.

LACEY, J. I., BATEMAN, D. E., and VAN LEHN, R. (1953), 'Autonomic response specificity: an experimental study', *Psychosom. Med.*, vol. 15, pp. 8–21.

LACEY, J. I., and LACEY, B. C. (1958), 'The relationship of resting autonomic activity to motor impulsivity', *Res. Publ. Assoc. nerv. ment. Dis.*, vol. 36, pp. 144–209.

LADER, M. H. (1967), 'Pneumatic plethysmography', in P. H. Venables and I. Martin (eds.), *A Manual of Psychophysiological Methods*, North-Holland.

LAMM, H. (1967), 'Will an observer advise higher risk taking after hearing a discussion of the decision problem?', *J. Pers. soc. Psychol.*, vol. 6, pp. 467–71.

LAMM, H., and MYERS, D. G. (1978), 'Group-induced polarization of attitudes and behavior', *Adv. exp. soc. Psychol.*, vol. 11, pp. 145–95.

LANDAUER, T. K., and FREEDMAN, J. L. (1968), 'Information retrieval from long-term memory', *J. verb. Learn. verb. Behav.*, vol. 7, pp. 291–5.

LANGE, C. (1885), *Om Sindsbevaegelser et psyko-fysiolog. studie*, Krønar. English translation in K. Dunlap (ed.), *The Emotions*, Hafner, 1967.

LANGFORD, G. W., MEDDIS, R., and PEARSON, A. J. D. (1974), 'Awakening latency from sleep for meaningful and non-meaningful stimuli', *Psychophysiology*, vol. 11, pp. 1–5.

LANTZ, D., and STEFFLRE, V. (1964), 'Language and cognition revisited', *J. abnorm. soc. Psychol.*, vol. 69, pp. 472–81.

LASHLEY, K. (1931), 'Mass action in cerebral function', *Science*, vol. 73, pp. 245–54.

LASHLEY, K. S. (1917), 'The accuracy of movement in the absence of excitation from the moving organ', *Amer. J. Physiol.*, vol. 43, pp. 169–94.

LASHLEY, K. S. (1951), 'The problem of serial order in behaviour', in L. A. Jeffress (ed.), *Cerebral Mechanisms in Behaviour: The Hixon Symposium*, Wiley.

LAWLER, E. E. (1971), *Pay and Organizational Effectiveness: A Psychological View*, McGraw-Hill.

LAWRENCE, D. H., and COLES, G. R. (1954), 'Accuracy of recognition with alternatives before and after the stimulus', *J. exp. Psychol.*, vol. 47, pp. 208–14.

LAWRENCE, D. H., and LABERGE, D. L. (1956), 'Relationship between recognition accuracy and order of reporting stimulus dimensions', *J. exp. Psychol.*, vol. 51, pp. 12–18.

LAZARUS, R. S. (1966), *Psychological Stress and the Coping Process*, McGraw-Hill.

LAZARUS, R. S. (1968), 'Emotions and adaptation: conceptual and empirical relations', in W. J. Arnold (ed.), *Nebraska Symposium on Motivation*, University of Nebraska Press.

LAZARUS, R. S. (1968), 'Emotions and adaptation: conceptual and empirical theory of emotion', in M. B. Arnold (ed.), *Feelings and Emotions: The Loyola Symposium*, Academic Press.

LEE, D. N. (1974), 'Visual information during locomotion', in R. B. McLeod and H. L. Pick (eds.), *Perception: Essays in Honor of James J. Gibson*, Cornell University Press.

LEE, D. N., and LISHMAN, J. R. (1975), 'Vision in movement and balance', *New Scient.*, vol. 65, pp. 59–61.

LEE, S. G. M., and HERBERT, M. (1970), *Freud and Psychology*, Penguin Books.

LEE, T. (1976), *Psychology and the Environment*, Methuen.

LEEPER, R. (1935), 'A study of a neglected portion of the field of learning – the development of sensory organization', *J. genet. Psychol.*, vol. 46, pp. 41–75.

LEEPER, R. W. (1965), 'Some needed developments in the motivational theory of emotion', in D. Levine (ed.), *Nebraska Symposium on Motivation*, University of Nebraska Press.

LEFCOURT, H. (1973), 'The function of the illusions of control and freedom', *Amer. Psychol.*, vol. 28, pp. 417–25.

LEHMANN, A. (1914), *Die Hauptgesetze des menschlichen Gefuehlslebens*, Reisland.

LEHRMAN, D. S. (1970), 'Semantic and conceptual issues in the nature–nurture problem', in L. R. Aronson *et al.* (eds.), *Development and Evolution of Behavior*, Freeman.

LE MAGNEN, J. (1971), 'Advances in studies on the physiological control and regulation of food intake', in E. Stellar and J. M. Sprague (eds.), *Progress in Physiological Psychology*, vol. 4, Academic Press.

LENNEBERG, E. H. (ed.) (1964), *New Directions in the Study of Language*, M. I. T. Press.

LENNEBERG, E. H. (1967), *Biological Foundations of Language*, Wiley.

LENNEBERG, E. H., and ROBERTS, J. (1956), 'The language of experience, a study in methodology', *Int. J. Amer. Linguist.*, vol. 22, p. 443.

LEON, G. R., and ROTH, L. (1977), 'Obesity: psychological causes, correlations and speculations', *Psychol. Bull.*, vol. 84, pp. 117–39.

LEVENTHAL, H. (1974), 'Emotions: a basic problem for social psychology', in C. Nemeth (ed.), *Social Psychology: Classic and Contemporary Integrations*, Rand McNally.

LEVI, L. (1965), 'The urinary output of adrenalin and noradrenalin during pleasant and unpleasant emotional states: a preliminary report', *Psychosom. Med.*, vol. 27, pp. 80–85.

LEVI, L. (1966), 'Life stress and urinary excretion of adrenaline and noradrenaline', in W. Raab (ed.), *Prevention of Ischemic Heart Disease: Principles and Practice*, Thomas.

LEVINE, M. (1975), *A Cognitive Theory of Learning*, Wiley.

LEVINE, S. (1956), 'A further study of infantile handling and adult avoidance learning', *J. Pers.*, vol. 25, pp. 70–80.

LEVINE, S. (1960), 'Stimulation in infancy', *Scient. Amer.*, vol. 202, pp. 81–6.

LEVINE, S. (1969), 'Infantile stimulation', in A. Ambrose (ed.), *Stimulation in Early Infancy*, Academic Press.

LEVINE, S., and BROADHURST, P. L. (1963), 'Genetic and ontogenetic determinants of adult behavior in the rat', *J. comp. physiol. Psychol.*, vol. 56, pp. 423–8.

LEVINGER, G., and SCHNEIDER, D. J. (1969), 'Test of the "risk is a value" hypothesis', *J. Pers. soc. Psychol.*, vol. 11, pp. 165–9.

LEWIN, I., and GLAUBMAN, H. (1975), 'The effect of REM deprivation: is it detrimental, beneficial or neutral?', *Psychophysiol.*, vol. 12, pp. 349–53.

LEWIN, K. (1936), *Principles of Topological Psychology*, McGraw-Hill.

LEWIN, K. (1938), *The Conceptual Representation and Measurement of Psychological Forces*, Duke University Press.

LEWINSOHN, P. M. (1956), 'Some individual differences in physiological reactivity to stress', *J. comp. physiol. Psychol.*, vol. 49, pp. 271–7.

LEWIS, J. L. (1970), 'Semantic processing of unattended messages using dichotic listening', *J. exp. Psychol.*, vol. 85, pp. 225–8.

LIEBERMAN, M. A. (1975), 'Adaptive processes in later life', in N. Datan and L. Ginsberg (eds.), *Life-span Developmental Psychology: Normative Life Crises*, Academic Press.

LILLY, J. C. (1956), 'Mental effects of reduction of ordinary levels of physical stimuli on intact, healthy persons', *Psychiat. Res. Rep.*, vol. 5, pp. 1–9.

LIMBER, J. (1977), 'Language in child and chimp?', *Amer. Psychol.*, vol. 32, pp. 280–95.

LINDEN, E. (1976), *Apes, Men and Language*, Penguin Books.

LINDSAY, P. H., and NORMAN, D. A. (1977), *Human Information Processing*, Academic Press, 2nd edn.

LINDSLEY, D. B. (1951), 'Emotion', in S. S. Stevens (ed.), *Handbook of Experimental Psychology*, Wiley.

LINDSLEY, D. B. (1960), 'Attention, consciousness, sleep and wakefulness', in J. Field, H. W. Magoun and V. E. Hall (eds.), *Handbook of Physiology*, sect. 1, vol. 3, American Physiological Society.

LINDSLEY, D. B. (1961), 'Common factors in sensory deprivation, sensory distortion and sensory overload', in P. Solomon *et al.* (eds.), *Sensory Deprivation*, Harvard University Press.

LINDSLEY, D. B., BOWDEN, J. W., and MAGOUN, H. W. (1949), 'Effect upon the EEG of acute injury to the brainstem activating system', *EEG clin. Neurophysiol.*, vol. 1, pp. 475–86.

LINDSLEY, D. B., *et al.* (1950), 'Behavioral and EEG changes following chronic brain stem lesions in the cat', *EEG clin. Neurophysiol.*, vol. 2, pp. 483–98.

LINDZEY, G. (1961), *Projective Techniques and Crosscultural Research*, Appleton-Century-Crofts.

LIPS, H. M., and COLWILL, N. L. (1978), *The Psychology of Sex Differences*, Prentice-Hall.

LIU, I. (1968), 'Effects of repetition of voluntary responses: from voluntary to involuntary', *J. exp. Psychol.*, vol. 76, pp. 398–406.

LIVINGSTONE, F. B. (1962), 'On the non-existence of human races', *Curr. Anthropol.*, vol. 3, p. 279.

LLOYD, B. (1972), *Perception and Cognition*, Penguin Books.

LLOYD, B., and ARCHER, J. (1976), *Exploring Sex Differences*, Academic Press.

LOCKARD, R. B. (1968), 'The albino rat', *Amer. Psychol.*, vol. 23, pp. 734–42.

LOCKARD, R. B. (1971), 'Reflections on the fall of comparative psychology', *Amer. Psychol.*, vol. 26, pp. 168–79.

LOEHLIN, J. C., LINDZEY, G., and SPUHLER, J. N. (1975), *Race Differences in Intelligence*, Freeman.

LOEHLIN, J. C., VANDENBERG, S. G., and OSBORNE, R. T. (1973), 'Blood group genes and Negro–white ability differences', *Behav. Genet.*, vol. 3, pp. 263–70.

LOEVINGER, J. (1943), 'On the proportional contribution of differences in nature and in nurture to differences in intelligence', *Psychol. Bull.*, vol. 40, pp. 725–56.

LOMAS, P. (1973), *True and False Experience*, Allen Lane.

LOOMIS, A. L., HARVEY, E. N., and HOBART, G. (1937), 'Cerebral states during sleep as studied by human brain potentials', *J. exp. Psychol.*, vol. 21, pp. 127–44.

LORENZ, K. (1937), 'The companion in the bird's world', *Auk*, vol. 54, pp. 245–73.

LORENZ, K. (1950), 'The comparative method in studying innate behaviour patterns', *Symp. Soc. exp. Biol.*, vol. 4, pp. 221–68.

LORENZ, K. (1952), *King Solomon's Ring*, Methuen.

LORENZ, K. (1966), *On Aggression*, Methuen.

LOTT, D. F., and SOMMER, R. (1967), 'Seating arrangements and status', *J. Pers. soc. Psychol.*, vol. 7, pp. 90–95.

LOTZE, R. H. (1852), *Medizinische Psychologie*, Weidmann.

LUBOW, R. E. (1973), 'Latent inhibition', *Psychol. Bull.*, vol. 79, pp. 398–407.

LUCHINS, A. S. (1942), 'Mechanization in problem solving: the effect of *Einstellung*', *Psychol. Monogr.*, vol. 54(6), whole no. 248.

LURIA, A. R. (1961), *The Role of Speech in the Regulation of Normal and Abnormal Behavior*, Liveright.

LURIA, A. R. (1966), *Higher Cortical Functions in Man*, Basic Books.

LURIA, A. R. (1969), *The Mind of a Mnemonist*, Cape.

LURIA, A. R. (1973), *The Working Brain: An Introduction to Neuropsychology*, Penguin Books.

LYNN, R. (1978), 'Ethnic and racial differences in intelligence: international comparisons', in R. T. Osborne, C. E. Noble and N. Weyl (eds.), *Human Variation: the Biopsychology of Age, Race and Sex*, Academic Press.

LYONS, J. (1970), *Chomsky*, Fontana/Collins.

LYWOOD, D. W. (1967), 'Blood pressure', in P. H. Venables and I. Martin (eds.), *A Manual of Psychophysiological Methods*, North-Holland.

MACCOBY, E. E., and JACKLIN, C. N. (1974), *The Psychology of Sex Differences*, Stanford University Press.

MACCORQUODALE, K. (1970), 'On Chomsky's review of Skinner's *Verbal Behavior*', *J. exp. Anal. Behav.*, vol. 13, pp. 83–99.

MACCORQUODALE, K., and MEEHL, P. E. (1948), 'On a distinction between hypothetical constructs and intervening variables', *Psychol. Rev.*, vol. 55, pp. 95–107.

MACFARLANE, D. A. (1930), 'The role of kinesthesis in maze learning', *Calif. Univ. Publ. Psychol.*, vol. 4, pp. 277–305.

MACH, E. (1886), *The Analysis of Sensations*, Fischer

MACH, E. (1914), *The Analysis of Sensations*, Open Court Publ. Co.

MACKAY, D. (1975), *Clinical Psychology: Theory and Therapy*, Methuen.

MACKINTOSH, N. J. (1975), 'Critical notice: Kamin, L. J., *The Science and Politics of I.Q.*', *Quart. J. exp. Psychol.*, vol. 27, pp. 672–86.

MACKINTOSH, N. J. (1978), 'Conditioning', in B. M. Foss (ed.), *Psychology Survey No. 1*, Allen & Unwin.

MACKWORTH, N. H. (1950), 'Researches on the measurement of human performance', *MRC Special Report Series*, no. 268, H.M.S.O.

MACKWORTH, N. H. (1957), 'Some factors affecting vigilance', *Adv. Sci.*, vol. 53, pp. 389–93.

MACLEAN, P. D. (1949), 'Psychosomatic disease and the "visceral brain"', *Psychosom. Med.*, vol. 11, pp. 338–53.

MACLEAN, P. D. (1970), 'The limbic brain in relation to the psychoses', in P. D. Black (ed.), *Physiological Correlates of Emotion*, Academic Press.

MAGNES, J., MORUZZI, G., and POMPEIANO, O. (1961), 'Synchronization of the EEG produced by low frequency electrical stimulation of the region of the solitary tract', *Arch. Ital. Biol.*, vol. 103, pp. 596–608.

MAGOUN, H. W. (1958), *The Waking Brain*, Thomas.

MALINOWSKI, B. (1922), *Argonauts of the Western Pacific*, Dutton (reprinted 1953).

MALMO, R. B. (1959), 'Activation: a neuropsychological dimension', *Psychol. Rev.*, vol. 66, pp. 367–86.

MALTZMAN, I. (1955), 'Thinking: from a behavioristic point of view', *Psychol. Rev.*, vol. 62, pp. 275–86.

MALTZMAN, I. (1960), 'On the training of originality', *Psychol. Rev.*, vol. 67, pp. 229–42.

MANDLER, G. (1960), 'Emotion', in T. M. Newcomb (ed.), *New Directions in Psychology*, vol. 1, Holt, Rinehart & Winston.

MANDLER, G. (1967), 'Organization and memory', in K. W. Spence and J. T. Spence (eds.), *The Psychology of Learning and Motivation*, vol. 1, Academic Press.

MANDLER, G. (1975), *Mind and Emotion*, Wiley.

MANDLER, G., and KAHN, M. (1960), 'Discrimination of changes in heart rate: two unsuccessful attempts', *J. exp. Anal. Behav.*, vol. 3, pp. 21–5.

MANDLER, G., and KREMEN, I. (1958), 'Autonomic feedback: a correlational study', *J. Pers.*, vol. 26, pp. 388–99.

MANDLER, G., MANDLER, J. M., and UVILLER, E. T. (1958), 'Autonomic feedback: the perception of autonomic activity', *J. abnorm. soc. Psychol.*, vol. 56, pp. 367–73.

MANNING, A. (1976), *An Introduction to Animal Behaviour*, Arnold.

MARAÑON, G. (1924), 'Contribution à l'étude de l'action émotive de l'adrenalin', *Rev. franç. d'endocrinol.*, vol. 2, pp. 301–25.

MARIN, O. S. M., SCHWARTZ, M. F., and SAFFRAN, E. M. (1979), 'Origins and distribution of language', in M. Gazzaniga (ed.), *Handbook of Behavioral Neurobiology*, vol. 2: *Neuropsychology*, Plenum Press.

MARKS, L., and MILLER, G. A. (1964), 'The role of semantic and syntactic constraints in the memorization of English sentences', *J. verb. Learn. verb. Behav.*, vol. 3, pp. 1–5.

MARLOWE, W. B., MANCALL, E. L., and THOMAS, J. J. (1975), 'Complete Klüver-Bucy syndrome in man', *Cortex*, vol. 11, pp. 53–9.

MARON, L., RECHTSCHAFFEN, A., and WOLPERT, E. A. (1964), 'Sleep cycle during napping', *Arch. gen. Psychiat.*, vol. 11, pp. 503–8.

MARQUIS, D. G. (1935), 'Phylogenetic interpretation of the functions of the visual cortex', *Arch. Neurol. Psychiat.*, vol. 33, pp. 807–15.

MARQUIS, D. G. (1962), 'Individual responsibility and group decisions involving risk', *Indust. Manag. Rev.*, vol. 3, pp. 8–23.

MARSH, R. W. (1964), 'A statistical re-analysis of Getzels' and Jackson's data', *Brit. J. educ. Psychol.*, vol. 34, pp. 91–3.

MARSHALL, G. (1976), 'The affective consequences of "inadequately explained" physiological arousal', unpubl. doctoral dissertation, Stanford University.

MARSHALL, H. H. (1965), 'The effect of punishment on children: a review of the literature and a suggested hypothesis', *J. genet. Psychol.*, vol. 106, pp. 23–33.

MARTIN, B. (1961), 'The assessment of anxiety by physiological behavioral measures', *Psychol. Bull.*, vol. 58, pp. 234–55.

MARTINI, L., MOTTA, M., and FRASCHINI, F. (eds.) (1970), *The Hypothalamus*, Academic Press.

MASLACH, C. (1979), 'The emotional consequences of arousal without reason', in C. E. Izard (ed.), *Emotions in Personality and Psychopathology*, Plenum Press.

MASLAND, R. H. (1969), 'Visual motion perception: experimental modification', *Science*, vol. 165, pp. 819–21.

MASLOW, A. H. (1968), *Toward a Psychology of Being*, Van Nostrand.

MASLOW, A. H. (1973), *The Farther Reaches of Human Nature*, Penguin Books.

MASON, J. W. (1972), 'Organization of psychoendocrine mechanisms: a review and reconsideration of research', in N. S. Greenfield and R. A. Sternbach (eds.), *Handbook of Psychophysiology*, Holt, Rinehart & Winston.

MASSERMAN, J. H. (1943), *Behavior and Neurosis*, University of Chicago Press.

MASTERTON, J. C. (1965), 'Patterns of sleep', in O. G. Edholm and A. L. Bacharach (eds.), *The Physiology of Human Survival*, Academic Press.

MATARAZZO, J. D. (1965), 'The interview', in B. B. Wolman (ed.), *Handbook of Clinical Psychology*, McGraw-Hill.

MAX, L. W. (1935), 'An experimental study of the motor theory of consciousness. III. Action-current responses in deaf mutes during sleep, sensory stimulation and dreams', *J. comp. Psychol.*, vol. 19, pp. 469–86.

MAX, L. W. (1937), 'An experimental study of the motor theory of consciousness: IV. Action-current responses in the deaf during awakening, kinaesthetic imagery, and abstract thinking', *J. comp. Psychol.*, vol. 24, pp. 301–44.

MAYER, J. (1955), 'Regulation of energy intake and the body weight: the glucostatic theory and the lipostatic theory', *Ann. N. Y. Acad. Sci.*, vol. 63, pp. 15–42.

MAYES, A., and BEAUMONT, G. (1977), 'Does visual evoked potential asymmetry index cognitive activity?', *Neuropsychol.*, vol. 15, pp. 249–56.

MAYES, A. R. (1979),'The physiology of fear and anxiety', in W. Sluckin (ed.), *Fear in Animals and Man*, Van Nostrand.

MAYR, E. (1942), *Systematics and the Origin of Species*, Columbia University Press.

McCARLEY, R. W. and HOBSON, J. A. (1975), 'Neuronal excitability modulation over the sleep cycle: a structural and mathematical model', *Science*, 189, 58–60.

McCARTHY, D. (1954), 'Language development in children', in L. Carmichael (ed.), *Manual of Child Psychology*, Wiley, 2nd edn.

McCLEARN, G. E., and DeFRIES, J. C. (1973), *Introduction to Behavioral Genetics*, Freeman.

McCLEARY, R. A., and MOORE, R. Y. (1965), *Subcortical Mechanisms of Behavior*, Basic Books.

McCLELLAND, D. C. (1961), *The Achieving Society*, Van Nostrand.

McCLELLAND, D. C., *et al.* (1953), *The Achievement Motive*, Appleton-Century-Crofts.

McCOLLOUGH, C. (1965), 'Color adaptation of edge-detectors in the human visual system', *Science*, vol. 149, pp. 1115–16.

McDOUGALL, W. (1908), *Introduction to Social Psychology*, Methuen.

McDOUGALL, W. (1912), *Psychology: The Study of Behaviour*, Williams & Norgate.

McDOUGALL, W. (1926), 'Men or robots?', in C. Murchison (ed.), *Psychologies of 1925*, Clark University Press.

McDOWALL, J. J. (1978), 'Interaction synchrony: a reappraisal', *J. Pers. soc. Psychol.*, vol. 36, pp. 963–75.

McEVEDY, C., and JONES, R. (1978), *Atlas of World Population History*, Allen Lane.

McGEOGH, J. A. (1932), 'Forgetting and the law of disuse', *Psychol. Rev.*, vol. 39, pp. 352–70.

McGRATH, M. J., and COHEN, D. B. (1978), 'REM sleep facilitation of adaptive waking behavior: a review of the literature', *Psychol. Bull.*, vol. 85, pp. 24–57.

McGRAW, M. B. (1940), 'Neural maturation as exemplified by the achievement of bladder control', *J. Pediat.*, vol. 16, pp. 580–90.

McGUIRE, L. S., RYAN, K. O., and OMENN, G. S. (1975), 'Congenital adrenal hyperphasia, II.: Cognitive and behavioral studies', *Behav. Genet.*, vol. 5, pp. 175–88.

McGUIRE, T. R., and HIRSCH, J. (1977), 'General intelligence and heritability', in I. C. Uzgiris and F. Weizmann (eds.), *The Structuring of Experience*, Plenum Press.

McGURK, H. (1974), 'Visual perception in young infants', in B. M. Foss (ed.), *New Perspectives in Child Development*, Penguin Books.

McINTYRE, A. (1958), *The Unconscious*, Routledge & Kegan Paul.

McKELLAR, P. (1957), *Imagination and Thinking*, Cohen & West.

McKELLAR, P. (1962), 'The method of introspection', in J. Scher (ed.), *Theories of the Mind*, Free Press of Glencoe.

McKINNON, D. W., and DUKES, W. F. (1962), 'Repression', in L. Postman (ed.), *Psychology in the Making*, Knopf.

McNEILL, D. (1966), 'Developmental psycholinguistics', in F. Smith and G. A. Miller (eds.), *The Genesis of Language*, M. I. T. Press.

McNEILL, D. (1970), *The Acquisition of Language*, Harper & Row.

McNICOL, D. (1972), *A Primer of Signal Detection Theory*, Allen & Unwin.

MEAD, M. (1928), *Coming of Age in Samoa*, Morrow.

MEAD, M. (1949), *Male and Female*, Morrow.

MEAD, M. (1961), 'Cultural determinants of sexual behavior', in W. C. Young (ed.), *Sex and Internal Secretions*, vol. II, Williams & Wilkins.

MEDDIS, R. (1975), 'On the function of sleep', *Anim. Behav.*, vol. 23, pp. 676–91.

MEDDIS, R. (1977), *The Sleep Instinct*, Routledge & Kegan Paul.

MEDDIS, R. (1979), 'The evolution and function of sleep', in D. A. Oakley and H. C. Plotkin (eds.), *Brain, Behaviour and Evolution*, Methuen.

MEDDIS, R., PEARSON, A. J. D., and LANGFORD, G. (1973), 'An extreme case of healthy insomnia', *EEG clin. Neurophysiol.*, vol. 35, pp. 213–24.

MEHRABIAN, A. C. (1968), *An Analysis of Personality Theories*, Prentice-Hall.

MEHRABIAN, A. (1972), *Nonverbal Communication*, Aldine-Atherton.

MELTON, A. W. (1963), 'Implications of short-term memory for a general theory of memory', *J. verb. Learn. verb. Behav.*, vol. 2, pp. 1–21.

MENEGHINI, K. A., and LEIBOWITZ, H. W. (1967), 'The effect of stimulus distance and age on shape constancy', *J. exp. Psychol.*, vol. 74, pp. 241–8.

MERCER, C. (1975), *Living in Cities*, Penguin Books.

MERCER, C. (1978), 'Environmental psychology', in B. M. Foss (ed.), *Psychology Survey No. 1*, Allen & Unwin.

MESSICK, S. J. (1967), 'The psychology of acquiescence: an interpretation of the research evidence', in I. A. Berg (ed.), *Response Set in Personality Assessment*, Aldine.

MEUMANN, E. (1904), 'Haus- und Schularbeit: Experimente an Kindern der Volkschule', *Die Deutsche Schule*, vol. 8, pp. 278–303, 337–59, 416–31.

MICHAEL, C. R. (1969), 'Retinal processing of visual images', *Scient. Amer.*, vol. 220, pp. 104–14.

MIDDLEMIST, R. D., KNOWLES, E. S., and MATTER, C. F. (1976), 'Personal space invasions in the lavatory: suggestive evidence for arousal', *J. Pers. soc. Psychol.*, vol. 33, pp. 541–6.

MILES, T. R. (1957), 'Contributions to intelligence testing and the theory of intelligence: I. On defining intelligence', *Brit. J. educ. Psychol.*, vol. 27, pp. 153–65.

MILLER, G. A. (1951), *Language and Communication*, McGraw-Hill.

MILLER, G. A., GALANTER, E., and PRIBRAM, K. H. (1960), *Plans and the Structure of Behavior*, Holt, Rinehart & Winston.

MILLER, G. A., and IZARD, S. (1963), 'Some perceptual consequences of linguistic rules', *J. verb. Learn. verb. Behav.*, vol. 2, pp. 217–20.

MILLER, G. A., and McKEAN, K. E. (1964), 'A chronometric study of some relations between sentences', *Quart. J. exp. Psychol.*, vol. 16, pp. 297–308.

MILLER, G. A., and SELFRIDGE, J. A. (1950), 'Verbal context and the recall of meaningful material', *Amer. J. Psychol.*, vol. 63, pp. 176–85.

MILLER, N. E. (1957), 'Experiments on motivation', *Science*, vol. 126, pp. 1271–8.

MILLER, N. E., BAILEY, C. J., and STEVENSON, J. A. F. (1950), 'Decreased "hunger" but increased food intake resulting from hypothalamic lesions', *Science*, vol. 112, pp. 256–9.

MILLER, N. E., and DOLLARD, J. (1941), *Social Learning and Imitation*, Yale University Press.

MILLER, R. E., CAUL, W. F., and MIRSKY, I. A. (1967), 'Communication of affects between feral and sonally isolated monkeys', *J. Pers. soc. Psychol.*, vol. 7, pp. 231–9.

MILLETT, K. (1970), *Sexual Politics*, Doubleday.

MILNER, B. (1974), 'Hemispheric specialization: scope and limits', in F. O. Schmitt and F. G. Warden (eds.), *The Neurosciences: Third Study Program*, M. I. T. Press.

MILNER, B., BRANCH, C., and RASMUSSEN, T. (1966), 'Evidence for bilateral speech representation in some non-right handers', *Trans. Amer. neurol. Assoc.*, vol. 91, pp. 306–8.

MINARD, J. G. (1965), 'Response-bias interpretation of "perceptual defense": a selective review and an evaluation of recent research', *Psychol. Rev.*, vol. 72, pp. 74–88.

MINARD, J. G., and MOONEY, W. (1969), 'Psychological differentiation and perceptual defense and studies of the separation of perception from emotion'. *J. abnorm. soc. Psychol.*, vol. 74, pp. 131–9.

MISCHEL, T. (1975), 'Psychological explanations and their vicissitudes', *Nebraska Symposium on Motivation*, vol. 23, pp. 133–204.

MISCHEL, W. (1968), *Personality and Assessment*, Wiley.

MISCHEL, W. (1973), 'Toward a cognitive and social learning reconceptualization of personality', *Psychol. Rev.*, vol. 80, pp. 257–83.

MOERK, E. (1974), 'Changes in verbal child–mother interaction with increasing language skills of the child', *J. Psycholinguist. Res.*, vol. 3, 101–16.

MOERK, E. (1977), 'Processes and products of imitation: additional evidence that imitation is progressive', *J. Psycholinguist. Res.*, vol. 6, pp. 187–202.

MOHR, J. P. (1976), 'Broca's area and Broca's aphasia', in H. Whitaker and H. A. Whitaker (eds.), *Studies in Neurolinguistics*, vol. 1, Academic Press.

MOLLON, J. (1974), 'After-effects and the brain', *New Scient.*, vol. 61, pp. 479–82.

MOLTZ, H. (ed.) (1971), *The Ontogeny of Vertebrate Behavior*, Academic Press.

MONEY, J. (1975), 'Ablatio penis: normal male infant sex-reassigned as a girl', *Arch. sex. Behav.*, vol. 4, pp. 65–72.

MONEY, J., and EHRHARDT, A. A. (1972), *Man and Woman, Boy and Girl*, Johns Hopkins Press.

MONROE, L. J. (1967), 'Psychological and physiological differences between good and poor sleepers', *J. abnorm. Psychol.*, vol. 72, pp. 255–64.

MONROE, L. J., *et al.* (1965), 'Discriminability of REM and NREM reports', *J. Pers. soc. Psychol.*, vol. 2, pp. 246–60.

MONTAGU, J. D., and COLES, R. (1966), 'Mechanism and measurement of the galvanic skin response', *Psychol. Bull.*, vol. 65, pp. 261–79.

MONTGOMERY, K. C. (1954), 'The role of exploratory drive in learning', *J. comp. physiol. Psychol.*, vol. 47, pp. 60–64.

MOORE, J. J., and MASSARO, D. W. (1973), 'Attention and processing capacity in auditory recognition', *J. exp. Psychol.*, vol. 99, pp. 49–54.

MORAY, N. (1958), 'The effect of the relative intensities of dichotic messages in speech shadowing', *Language and Speech*, vol. 1, pp. 110–13.

MORAY, N. (1959), 'Attention in dichotic listening: affective cues and the influence of instructions', *Quart. J. exp. Psychol.*, vol. 11, pp. 56–60.

MORAY, N. (1967), 'Where is capacity limited? A survey and a model', *Acta Psychol.*, vol. 27, pp. 84–92.

MORAY, N. (1969), *Attention: Selective Processes in Vision and Learning*, Hutchinson.

MORAY, N., BATES, A., and BARNETT, T. (1965), 'Experiments on the four-eared man', *J. acoust. Soc. Amer.*, vol. 38, pp. 196–201.

MORAY, N., and FITTER, M. (1973), 'A theory and the measurement of attention: tutorial review', in S. Kornblum (ed.), *Attention and Performance*, IV, Academic Press.

MORGAN, C. T. (1965), *Physiological Psychology*, McGraw-Hill.

MORRIS, D., *et al.* (1979), *Gestures: Their Origins and Distribution*, Cape.

MORUZZI, G., and MAGOUN, H. W. (1949), 'Brain stem reticular formation and activation of the EEG', *EEG clin. Neurophysiol.*, vol. 1, pp. 455–73.

MOSCOVICI, S., and ZAVALLONI, M. (1969), 'The group as a polarizer of attitudes', *J. Pers. soc. Psychol.*, vol. 12, pp. 125–35.

MOSCOVITCH, M. (1979), 'Information processing and the cerebral hemispheres', in M. Gazzaniga (ed.), *Handbook of Behavioral Neurobiology*, vol. 2. *Neuropsychology*, Plenum Press.

MOWRER, O. H. (1960), *Learning Theory and Behavior*, Wiley.

MOYER, K. E. (1968), 'Kinds of aggression and their physiological bases', *Commun. Behav. Biol.*, vol. 2, pp. 65–87.

MULAIK, S. A. (1964), 'Are personality factors raters' conceptual factors?', *J. consult. Psychol.*, vol. 28, pp. 506–11.

MUNROE, R. L. (1955), *Schools of Psycho-analytic Thought*, Dryden.

MURPHY, G. (1947), *Personality: A Biosocial Approach to Origins and Structure*, Harper.

MURRAY, D. C. (1971), 'Talk, silence and anxiety', *Psychol. Bull.*, vol. 75, pp. 244–60.

MURRAY, H. A. (1937), 'Facts which support the concept of need or drive', *J. Psychol.*, vol. 3, pp. 27–42.

MURRAY, H. A. (1938), *Explorations in Personality*, Oxford University Press.

MURRAY, H. A. (1943), *Thematic Apperception Test Manual*, Harvard University Press.

MURRELL, K. F. H. (1965), *Ergonomics*, Chapman & Hall.

MURSTEIN, B. I. (1963), *Theory and Research in Projective Techniques (Emphasizing the TAT)*, Wiley.

MYERS, D. G. (1973), 'Summary and bibliography of experiments on group-induced response shift', *Catalog of Selected Documents in Psychology*, vol. 3, no. 123.

MYERS, D. G., and LAMM, H. (1976), 'The group polarization phenomenon', *Psychol. Bull.*, vol. 83, pp. 602–27.

NAITOH, P. (1975), 'Sleep deprivation in humans', in P. H. Venables and M. J. Christie (eds.), *Research in Psychophysiology*, Wiley.

NATSOULAS, T. (1965), 'Converging operations for perceptual defense', *Psychol. Bull.*, vol. 64, pp. 393–401.

NAUTA, W. J. H. (1946), 'Hypothalamic regulation of sleep in rats. Experimental study', *J. Neurophysiol.*, vol. 9, pp. 285–316.

NEBES, R. (1976), 'Verbal-pictorial recording in the elderly', *J. Gerontol.*, vol. 31, pp. 421–7.

NEBES, R. D. (1974), 'Hemispheric specialization in commissurotomized man', *Psychol. Bull.*, vol. 81, pp. 1–14.

NEFF, W. D. (1960), 'Sensory discrimination', in J. Field, H. W. Magoun and V. E. Hall (eds.), *Handbook of Physiology*, sect. 1, vol. 3, American Physiological Society.

NEISSER, U. (1963a), 'Decision time without reaction time: experiments in visual scanning', *Amer. J. Psychol.*, vol. 76, pp. 376–85.

NEISSER, U. (1963b), 'The multiplicity of thought', *Brit. J. Psychol.*, vol. 54, pp. 1–14.

NEISSER, U. (1964), 'Visual search', *Scient. Amer.*, vol. 210, pp. 94–102.

NEISSER, U. (1967), *Cognitive Psychology*, Appleton-Century-Crofts.

NEISSER, U. (1971), 'Selective reading: a method for the study of visual attention', *Proc. 19th Int. Congress of Psychology, London, 1969*.

NEISSER, U. (1972), 'Changing conceptions of imagery', in P. N. Sheehan (ed.), *The Function and Nature of Imagery*, Academic Press.

NEISSER, U. (1976), *Cognition and Reality*, Freeman.

NEISSER, U., and BECKLEN, R. (1975), 'Selective looking: attending to visually-specified events', *Cognit. Psychol.*, vol. 7, pp. 480–94.

NEISSER, U., NOVICK, R., and LAZAR, R. (1964), 'Searching for ten targets simultaneously', *Percept. Motor Skills*, vol. 17, pp. 955–61.

NELSON, K. (1973), 'Structure and strategy in learning to talk', *Monogr. Soc. Res. Child Devel.*, vol. 38, no. 149.

NELSON, K. E. (1977), 'Facilitating children's syntax acquisition', *Devel. Psychol.*, vol. 13, pp. 101–7.

NELSON, K. E., CARSKADDON, G., and BONVILLIAN, J. D. (1973), 'Syntax acquisition: impact of experimental variation in adult verbal interaction with the child', *Child Devel.*, vol. 44, pp. 497–504.

NEUGARTEN, B. L. (ed.) (1968), *Middle Age and Aging*, University of Chicago Press.

NEUGARTEN, B. L. (1970), 'Adaptation and the life cycle', *J. geriat. Psychol.*, vol. 4, pp. 71–87.

NEUGARTEN, B. L. (1977), 'Personality and aging', in J. E. Birren and K. W. Schaie (eds.), *Handbook of the Psychology of Aging*, Van Nostrand.

NEUGARTEN, B. L. *et al.* (1964), *Personality in Middle and Late Life*, Atherton.

NEWCOMB, T. M. (1964), 'Attitude', in J. Gould and W. L. Kolb (eds.), *A Dictionary of the Social Sciences*, Tavistock.

NEWELL, A., SHAW, J. C., and SIMON, H. A. (1958), 'Elements of a theory of human problem solving', *Psychol. Rev.*, vol. 65, pp. 151–66.

NEWELL, A., and SIMON, H. A. (1972), *Human Problem Solving*, Prentice-Hall.

NEWMAN, E. B., PERKINS, F. T., and WHEELER, R. H. (1930), 'Cannon's theory of emotion: a critique', *Psychol. Rev.*, vol. 37, pp. 305–26.

NOBACK, C. R., and MOSKOWITZ, N. (1962), 'Structural and functional correlates of "encephalization" in the primate brain', *Ann. N. Y. Acad. Sci.*, vol. 102, pp. 210–18.

NOBLE, C. E. (1963), 'Meaningfulness and familiarity', in C. N. Cofer and B. S. Musgrave (eds.), *Verbal Learning and Behavior*, McGraw-Hill.

NOBLE, C. E. (1978), 'Age, race and sex in learning and performance of psychomotor skills', in R. T. Osborne, C. E. Noble and N. Weyl (eds.), *Human Variation: the Biopsychology of Age, Race and Sex*, Academic Press.

NORMAN, D. A. (1968), 'Towards a theory of memory and attention', *Psychol. Rev.*, vol. 75, pp. 522–36.

NORMAN, D. A. (1969), 'Memory while shadowing', *Quart. J. exp. Psychol.*, vol. 21, pp. 85–94.

NORMAN, W. T. (1963), 'Relative importance of test item content', *J. consult. Psychol.*, vol. 27, pp. 166–74.

NOTTEBOHM, F. (1979), 'Origins and mechanisms in the establishment of cerebral dominance', in M. Gazzaniga (ed.), *Handbook of Behavioral Neurobiology*, vol. 2, *Neuropsychology*, Plenum Press.

NOWLIS, V. (1963), 'The concept of mood', in S. M. Farber and R. H. L. Wilson (eds.), *Conflict and Creativity*, McGraw-Hill.

NOWLIS, V. (1970), 'Mood: behavior and experience', in M. B. Arnold (ed.), *Feelings and Emotions: The Loyola Symposium*, Academic Press.

NUNNALLY, J. C. (1970), *Introduction to Psychological Measurement*, McGraw-Hill.

NUTTALL, R. L. (1972), 'The strategy of functional age research', *Aging & Hum. Devel.*, vol. 3, pp. 149–52.

OAKLEY, D. A. (1979), 'Cerebral cortex and adaptive behaviour', in D. A. Oakley and H. C. Plotkin (eds.), *Brain, Behaviour and Evolution*, Methuen.

O'HANLON, J. F., and BEATTY, J. (1977), 'Concurrence of electroencephalographic and performance changes during a simulated radar watch and some implications for the arousal theory of vigilance', in R. R. Mackie (ed.), *Vigilance: Theory, Operational Performance and Physiological Correlates*, Plenum Press.

OLDS, J. (1958), 'Self-stimulation of the brain', *Science*, vol. 127, pp. 315–23.

OLDS, J. (1961), 'Differential effects of drives and drugs on self-stimulation at different brain sites', in D. E. Sheer (ed.), *Electrical Stimulation of the Brain*, University of Texas Press.

OLDS, J., and MILNER, P. (1954), 'Positive reinforcement produced by electrical stimulation of septal area and other regions of rat brain', *J. comp. physiol. Psychol.*, vol. 47, pp. 419–27.

OSBORN, A. F. (1957), *Applied Imagination*, Scribners.

OSBORNE, K., and GALE, A. (1975), 'Bilateral EEG differentiation of stimuli', *Biol. Psychol.*, vol. 4, pp. 185–96.

OSBORNE, R. T., NOBLE, C. E., and WEYL, N. (eds.) (1978), *Human Variation: the Biopsychology of Age, Race and Sex*, Academic Press.

OSGOOD, C. E. (1953), *Method and Theory in Experimental Psychology*, Oxford University Press.

OSGOOD, C. E., SUCI, G. J., and TANNENBAUM, P. H. (1957), *The Measurement of Meaning*, University of Illinois Press.

OSWALD, I. (1973), 'Drug research and human sleep', *Ann. Rev. Pharmacol.*, vol. 13, pp. 243–52.

OSWALD, I. (1976), 'The function of sleep', *Postgrad. Med. J.*, vol. 52, pp. 15–18.

OSWALD, I., TAYLOR, A. M., and TREISMAN, M. (1960), 'Discrimination responses to stimulation during human sleep', *Brain*, vol. 83, pp. 440–53.

OVER, R. (1971), 'Comparison of normalization theory and neural enhancement explanation of negative after-effects', *Psychol. Bull.*, vol. 75, pp. 225–43.

OVERALL, J. E. (1964), 'A note on the scientific status of factors', *Psychol. Bull.*, vol. 61, pp. 270–76:

OWENS, W. A. (1959), 'Is age kinder to the initially more able?', *J. Gerontol.*, vol. 14, pp. 334–7.

PACKARD, V. (1960), *The Hidden Persuaders*, Penguin Books.

PAIVIO, A. (1971), *Imagery and Verbal Processes*, Holt, Rinehart & Winston.

PALMER, F. (1971), *Grammar*, Penguin Books.

PALMORE, E. *et al.* (1979), 'Stress and adaptation in later life', *J. Gerontol.*, vol. 34, pp. 841–51.

PALMORE, E. B. (1978), 'When can age, period and cohort be separated?', *Soc. Forces*, vol. 57, pp. 282–95.

PALMORE, E. B., and MANTON, K. (1973), 'Ageism compared to racism and sexism', *J. Gerontol.*, vol. 28, pp. 363–9.

PAPEZ, J. W. (1937), 'A proposed mechanism of emotion', *Arch. Neurol. Psychiat.*, vol. 38, pp. 725–43.

PARASURAMAN, R. (1979), 'Memory load and event rate control sensitivity decrements in sustained attention', *Science*, vol. 205, pp. 924–7.

PARASURAMAN, R., and DAVIES, D. R. (1976), 'Decision theory analysis of response latencies in vigilance', *J. exp. Psychol.: Human Perception & Performance*, vol. 2, pp. 569–82.

PARASURAMAN, R., and DAVIES, D. R. (1977), 'A taxonomic analysis of vigilance performance', in R. R. Mackie (ed.), *Vigilance: Theory, Operational Performance and Physiological Correlates*, Plenum Press.

PARLEE, M. B. (1973), 'The premenstrual syndrome', *Psychol. Bull.*, vol. 80, pp. 454–65.

PARMELEE, A., SCHULZ, H., and DISBROW, M. (1961), 'Sleep patterns of the newborn', *J. Pediat.*, vol. 58, pp. 241–50.

PARMELEE, A. H. *et al.* (1967), 'Sleep states in premature infants', *Devel. Med. Child Neurol.*, vol. 9, pp. 70–77.

PASSINI, F. T., and NORMAN, W. T. (1966), 'A universal conception of personality structures', *J. Pers. soc. Psychol.*, vol. 4, pp. 4–45.

PASTORE, N. (1971), *Selective History of Theories of Visual Perception 1650–1950*, Oxford University Press.

PATKAI, P. (1971), 'Catecholamine excretion in pleasant and unpleasant situations', *Acta Psycholog.*, vol. 35, pp. 352–63.

PATRICK, C. (1935), 'Creative thought in poets', *Arch. Psychol.*, vol. 26, pp. 1–74.

PATRICK, C. (1937), 'Creative thought in artists', *J. Psychol.*, vol. 4, pp. 35–73.

PATRICK, G. T. W., and GILBERT, J. A. (1896), 'On the effects of loss of sleep', *Psychol. Rev.*, vol. 3, pp. 469–83.

PATTERSON, K. E. (1972), 'Some characteristics of retrieval limitation in long-term memory', *J. verb. Learn. verb. Behav.*, vol. 11, pp. 685–91.

PATTERSON, M. L. (1973), 'Compensation in nonverbal immediacy behaviors: a review', *Sociometry*, vol. 36, pp. 237–52.

PAULUS, P. B., and MURDOCH, P. (1971), 'Anticipated evaluation and audience presence in the enhancement of dominant responses', *J. exp. soc. Psychol.*, vol. 7, pp. 280–91.

PAVLOV, I. P. (1927), *Conditioned Reflexes*, Oxford University Press.

PENFIELD, W., and ROBERTS, L. (1959), *Speech and Brain Mechanisms*, Princeton University Press.

PENNEY, C. G. (1975), 'Modality effects in short-term verbal memory', *Psychol. Bull.*, vol. 82, pp. 68–84.

PERKOFF, G. T. *et al.* (1959), 'Studies of the diurnal variation of plasma 17-hydroxycorticosteroids in man', *J. clin. Endocrin. Metabol.*, vol. 19, pp. 700–10.

PERLMUTTER, M., and MYERS, N. A. (1975), 'Young children's coding and storage of visual and verbal material', *Child Devel.*, vol. 46, pp. 215–19.

PESSIN, J. (1933), 'The comparative effects of social and mechanical stimulation on memorizing', *Amer. J. Psychol.*, vol. 45, pp. 263–70.

PESSIN, J., and HUSBAND, R. W. (1933), 'Effects of social stimulation on human maze learning', *J. abnorm. soc. Psychol.*, vol. 28, pp. 148–54.

PETERS, R. S. (1958), *The Concept of Motivation*, Routledge & Kegan Paul.

PETERS, R. S. (1969), 'Motivation, emotion, and the conceptual schemes of common sense', in T. Mischel (ed.), *Human Action: Conceptual and Empirical Issues*, Academic Press.

PETRINOVICH, L., and McGAUGH, J. L. (1976), *Knowing, Thinking and Believing*, Plenum Press.

PEW, R. W. (1966), 'Acquisition of hierarchical control over the temporal organisation of a skill', *J. exp. Psychol.*, vol. 71, pp. 764–71.

PFUNGST, O. (1911), *Clever Hans, the Horse of Mr. von Osten*, Holt, Rinehart & Winston.

PHARES, E. J. (1979), *Clinical Psychology*, Dorsey Press.

PIAGET, J. (1937), *La construction du réel chez l'enfant*, Delachaux & Niestlé, translated as *The Construction of Reality in the Child*, 1955, Routledge & Kegan Paul.

PIAGET, J. (1952a), *The Origins of Intelligence in Children*, International Universities Press.

PIAGET, J. (1952b), *The Child's Conception of Number*, Routledge & Kegan Paul.

PIAGET, J. (1970), *Genetic Epistemology*, Columbia University Press.

PICK, H. L., HAY, J. C., and PABST, J. (1963), 'Kinaesthetic adaptation to visual distortion'; paper read at Midwestern Psychological Association, Chicago, and cited by C. S. Harris in *Psychol. Rev.* (1965), vol. 72, pp. 419–44.

PLUTCHIK, R. (1956), 'The psychophysiology of skin temperature: a critical review', *J. gen. Psychol.*, vol. 55, pp. 249–68.

PLUTCHIK, R., and AX, A. F. (1967), 'A critique of "Determinants of Emotional State" by Schachter and Singer (1962)', *Psychophysiol.*, vol. 4, pp. 79–82.

PODLESNY, J. A., and RASKIN, D. C. (1977), 'Physiological measures and the detection of deception', *Psychol. Bull.*, vol. 84, pp. 782–99.

POLLACK, R. H., and SILVAR, S. D. (1967), 'Magnitude of the Müller–Lyer illusion in children as a function of pigmentation of the fundus oculi'. *Psychon. Sci.*, vol. 8, pp. 83–4.

POPPER, K. R. (1963), *Conjectures and Refutations: The Growth of Scientific Knowledge*, Routledge & Kegan Paul.

PORTER, L. W., and LAWLER, E. E. (1968), *Managerial Attitudes and Performance*, Irwin.

POSNER, M. I. (1975), 'Psychobiology of attention', in M. S. Gazzaniga and C. Blakemore (eds.), *Handbook of Psychobiology*, Academic Press.

POSNER, M. I., NISSEN, M. J., and KLEIN, R. M. (1976), 'Visual dominance: an information-processing account of its origins and significance', *Psychol. Rev.*, vol. 83, 157–71.

POSNER, M. I., and SNYDER, C. R. (1975), 'Attention and cognitive control', in R. L. Solso (ed.), *Information Processing and Cognition*, Lawrence Erlbaum.

POSTMAN, L. (1962), 'Rewards and punishments in human learning', in L. Postman (ed.), *Psychology in the Making*, Knopf.

POSTMAN, L. (1972), 'A pragmatic view of organization theory', in E. Tulving and W. Donaldson (eds.), *Organization of Memory*, Academic Press.

POSTMAN, L., and LEYTHAM, G. (1951), 'Perceptual selectivity and ambivalence of stimuli', *J. Pers.*, vol. 19, pp. 390–405.

POSTMAN, L. and UNDERWOOD, B. J. (1973), 'Critical issues in interference theory', *Memory and Cognition*, vol. 1, pp. 19–40.

POULTON, C. (1971), 'Skilled performance and stress', in P. B. Warr (ed.), *Psychology at Work*, Penguin Books.

POWLEY, T. L. (1977), 'The ventromedial hypothalamic syndrome, satiety, and a cephalic phase hypothesis', *Psychol. Rev.*, vol. 84, pp. 89–126.

POWLEY, T. L., and OPSAHL, C. A. (1974), 'Ventromedial hypothalamic obesity abolished by subdiaphragmatic vagotomy', *Amer. J. Physiol.*, vol. 226, pp. 25–33.

PREMACK, A. J., and PREMACK, D. (1972), 'Teaching language to an ape', *Scient. Amer.*, vol. 227, pp. 92–9.

PRESSEY, S. L., and JONES, A. W. (1955), '1923–1953 and 20–60 age changes in moral codes, anxieties and interests, as shown by the X-O tests', *J. Psychol.*, vol. 79, pp. 485–502.

PRESSEY, S. L., and KUHLEN, R. G. (1957), *Psychological Development Through the Life Span*, Harper & Row.

PRIBRAM, K. H. (1954), 'Toward a science of neuropsychology', in R. A. Patton (ed.), *Current Trends in Psychology and the Behavioral Sciences*, University of Pittsburgh Press.

PRICE, L. J., and KREMEN, I. (1980), 'Variation in behavioral response threshold within the REM period of human sleep', *Psychophysiology*, vol. 17(2), pp. 133–40.

PRITCHARD, R. M. (1961), 'Stabilised images on the retina', *Scient. Amer.*, vol. 204, pp. 72–8.

PRUITT, D. G. (1971), 'Choice shifts in group discussion: an introductory review', *J. Pers. soc. Psychol.*, vol. 20, pp. 339–60.

QUAY, L. C. (1971), 'Language dialect, reinforcement, and the intelligence-test performance of Negro children', *Child Devel.*, vol. 42, pp. 5–15.

RABBITT, P. M. A. (1977), 'Changes in problem solving ability in old age', in J. E. Birren and K. W. Schaie (eds.), *Handbook of the Psychology of Aging*, Van Nostrand.

RABBITT, P. M. A. (1978), 'Sorting, categorization and visual search', in E. C. Carterette and M. P. Friedman (eds.), *Handbook of Perception*, vol. 9, Academic Press.

RABOW, J. *et al.* (1966), 'The role of social norms and leadership in risk taking', *Sociometry*, vol. 29, pp. 16–27.

RADFORD, J., and BURTON, A. (1974), *Thinking: Its Nature and Development*, Wiley.

RASMUSSEN, E. (1939), 'Social facilitation in albino rats', *Acta Psychol.*, vol. 4, pp. 275–94.

REASON, J. T. (1974), *Man in Motion*, Weidenfeld & Nicolson.

REASON, J. T. (1977a), 'Learning to cope with atypical force environments', in M. Howe (ed.), *Adult Learning*, Wiley.

REASON, J. T. (1977b), 'Skill and error in everyday life', in M. Howe (ed.), *Adult Learning*, Wiley.

REASON, J. T. (1978), 'Motion sickness adaptation: a neural mismatch model', *J. Roy. Soc. Med.*, vol. 71, pp. 819–29.

REASON, J. T. (1979), 'Actions not as planned', in R. Stevens and G. Underwood (eds.), *Aspects of Consciousness*, Academic Press.

REASON, J. T., and BENSON, A. (1978), 'Voluntary movement control and adaptation to cross-coupled stimulation', *Aviation, Space and Envir. Med.*, vol. 49, pp. 1275–80.

REASON, J. T., and BRAND, J. J. (1975), *Motion Sickness*, Academic Press.

RECHTSCHAFFEN, A. (1973), 'The psychophysiology of mental activity during sleep', in F. McGuigan and E. Schoonover (eds.), *The Psychophysiology of Thinking*, Academic Press.

RECHTSCHAFFEN, A., and DEMENT, W. C. (1969), 'Narcolepsy and hypersomnia', in A. Kales (ed.), *Sleep: Physiology and Pathology*, Lippincott.

RECHTSCHAFFEN, A., and KALES, A. (eds.) (1968), *The Manual of Standardized Terminology, Techniques and Scoring System for Sleep Stages of Human Subjects*, N. I. H. Publication no. 204.

RECHTSCHAFFEN, A., VOGEL, G. W., and SHAIKUN, G. (1963), 'Interrelatedness of mental activity during sleep', *Arch. gen. Psychiat.*, vol. 9, pp. 536–47.

REED, G. (1972), *The Psychology of Anomalous Experience*, Hutchinson.

REED, H. B. (1946), 'Factors influencing the learning and retention of concepts: I. The influence of set', *J. exp. Psychol.*, vol. 36, pp. 71–87.

REED, T. E. (1969), 'Caucasian genes in American Negroes', *Science*, vol. 165, pp. 762–8.

REEVES, J. W. (1965), *Thinking about Thinking*, Secker & Warburg.

REITMAN, W. R. (1965), *Cognition and Thought: An Information-processing Approach*, Wiley.

RESCORLA, R. A., and SOLOMON, R. L. (1967), 'Two-process learning theory: relationships between Pavlovian conditioning and instrumental learning', *Psychol. Rev.*, vol. 74, pp. 151–82.

RESTLE, F. (1957), 'Discrimination of cues in mazes: a resolution of the "Place-vs.-Response" question', *Psychol. Rev.*, vol. 64, pp. 217–28.

RESTLE, F. (1970), 'Moon illusion explained on the basis of relative size', *Science*, vol. 167, pp. 1092–6.

REVUSKY, S. H., and BEDARF, E. W. (1967), 'Association of illness with prior ingestion of novel foods', *Science*, vol. 155, pp. 219–20.

RICHARDSON, A. (1969), *Mental Imagery*, Routledge & Kegan Paul.

RICHARDSON, S. A., DOHRENWEND, B. S., and KLEIN, D. (1965), *Interviewing: Its Forms and Functions*, Basic Books.

RIDING, R. J. (1977), *School Learning*, Open Books.

RIEGEL, K. F., and RIEGEL, R. M. (1972), 'Development, drop, and death', *Devel. Psychol.*, vol. 6, pp. 306–19.

RIESEN, A. H. (1947), 'The development of visual perception in man and chimpanzee', *Science*, vol. 106, pp. 107–8.

RILEY, D. (1962), 'Memory for form', in L. Postman (ed.), *Psychology in the Making*, Knopf.

RIOPELLE, A. J. (ed.) (1968), *Animal Problem Solving*, Penguin Books.

RIPPLE, R. E., and MAY, F. B. (1962), 'Caution in comparing creativity and I.Q.', *Psychol. Rep.*, vol. 10, pp. 229–30.

ROBB, M. D. (1972), *The Dynamics of Motor-Skill Acquisition*, Prentice-Hall.

ROBERT, M. (1966), *The Psycho-analytic Revolution*, Allen & Unwin.

ROBERTS, W. W., and ROBINSON, T. C. L. (1969), 'Relaxation and sleep induced by warming of preoptic region and anterior hypothalamus in cats', *Exp. Neurol.*, vol. 25, pp. 282–94.

ROBINSON, J. O. (1972), *The Psychology of Visual Illusion*, Hutchinson.

ROBINSON, W. P. (1972), *Language and Social Behaviour*, Penguin Books.

ROBSON, C. (1973), *Experiment, Design and Statistics in Psychology*, Penguin Books.

ROCK, I. (1957), 'The role of repetition in associative learning', *Amer. J. Psychol.*, vol. 70, pp. 186–93.

ROCK, I. (1966), *The Nature of Perceptual Adaptation*, Basic Books.

ROCK, I. (1975), *An Introduction to Perception*, Macmillan.

ROCK, I., and VICTOR, J. (1964), 'Vision and touch: an experimentally created conflict between the senses', *Science*, vol. 143, pp. 594–6.

ROCKWELL, T. (1972), 'Skills, judgement and information acquisition in driving', in T. W. Forbes (ed.), *Human Factors in Highway Traffic Safety Research*, Wiley.

RODERICK, J. H. (1960), 'Selection for cholinesterase activity in the cerebral cortex of the rat', *Genetics*, vol. 45, pp. 1123–40.

ROFFWARG, H. P., DEMENT, W. C., and FISHER, C. (1964), 'Preliminary observations of the sleep-dream pattern in neonates, infants, children and adults', in E. Harms (ed.), *Problems of Sleep and Dream in Children: International Series of Monographs on Child Psychiatry*, vol. 2, Macmillan.

ROFFWARG, H. P., MUZIO, J. N., and DEMENT, W. C. (1966), 'Ontogenetic development of human sleep-dream cycle', *Science*, vol. 152, pp. 604–18.

ROGERS, C. R., and DYMOND, R. F. (1954), *Psychotherapy and Personality Change*, University of Chicago Press.

ROLFE, J. M. (1971), 'The secondary task as a measure of mental load', in W. T. Singleton, J. G. Fox and D. Whitfield (eds.), *Measurement of Man at Work*, Taylor & Francis.

ROSCH, E. (1975), 'Cognitive reference points', *Cognit. Psychol.*, vol. 7, pp. 532–47.

ROSCH, E. (1977a), 'Classification of real-world objects: origins and representations in cognition', in P. N. Johnson-Laird and P. C. Wason (eds.), *Thinking: Readings in Cognitive Science*, Cambridge University Press.

ROSCH, E. (1977b), 'Linguistic relativity', in P. N. Johnson-Laird and P. C. Wason (eds.), *Thinking: Readings in Cognitive Science*, Cambridge University Press.

ROSENBERG, B. G., and SUTTON-SMITH, B. (1972), *Sex and Identity*, Holt, Rinehart & Winston.

ROSOW, I. (1978), 'What is a cohort and why?', *Human Devel.*, vol. 21, pp. 65–75.

ROTTER, J. B. (1954), *Social Learning and Clinical Psychology*, Prentice-Hall.

ROUTTENBERG, A. (1966), 'Neural mechanisms of sleep: changing view of reticular formation function', *Psychol. Rev.*, vol. 73, pp. 481–99.

ROWLAND, N. E., and ANTELMAN, S. M. (1976), 'Stress-induced hyperphagia and obesity in rats: a possible model for understanding human obesity', *Science*, vol. 191, pp. 310–12.

RUBIN, E. (1921), *Visuell wahrgenommene figuren*, Gyldendalske Boghandel.

RUCH, T. C. (1935), 'Cortical localization of somatic sensibility. The effect of precentral, postcentral and posterior parietal lesions upon the performance of monkeys trained to discriminate weights', *Res. Publ. Assoc. nerv. ment. Dis.*, vol. 15, pp. 289–330.

RUCKMICK, C. A. (1936), *The Psychology of Feeling and Emotion*, McGraw-Hill.

RUSE, M. (1979), *Sociobiology: Sense or Nonsense?*, Reidel.

RUTTER, D. R. (1973), 'Visual interaction in psychiatric patients: a review', *Brit. J. Psychiat.*, vol. 123, pp. 193–202.

RUTTER, M. (1972), *Maternal Deprivation Reassessed*, Penguin Books.

RYAN, T. A. (1970), *Intentional Behavior: An Approach to Human Motivation*, Ronald.

SACKETT, G. P. (1965), 'Effects of rearing conditions upon the behaviour of rhesus monkeys', *Child Devel.*, vol. 36, pp. 855–68.

SACKETT, G. P., PORTER, M., and HOLMES, H. (1965), 'Choice behavior in rhesus monkeys: effect of stimulation during the first month of life', *Science*, vol. 147, pp. 304–6.

SALAMY, J. (1970), 'Instrumental responding to internal cues associated with REM sleep', *Psychon. Sci.*, vol. 18, pp. 342–3.

SAMPSON, H. (1966), 'Psychological effects of deprivation of dreaming sleep', *J. nerv. ment. Dis.*, vol. 143, pp. 305–17.

SASSIN, J. F., *et al.* (1969), 'Human growth hormone release: relation to slow-wave sleep and sleep-waking cycles', *Science*, vol. 165, pp. 513–15.

SATZ, P., *et al.* (1965), 'Order of report, ear asymmetry and handedness in dichotic listening', *Cortex*, vol. 1, pp. 377–96.

SAVIN, H. B., and PERCHONOCK, E. (1965), 'Grammatical structure and the immediate recall of English sentences', *J. verb. Learn. verb. Behav.*, vol. 4, pp. 348–53.

SCHACHTER, J. (1957), 'Pain, fear and anger in hypertensives and normotensives', *Psychosom. Med.*, vol. 19, pp. 17–29.

SCHACHTER, S. (1964), 'The interaction of cognitive and physiological determinants of emotional state', in L. Berkowitz (ed.), *Advances in Experimental Social Psychology*, vol. 1, Academic Press.

SCHACHTER, S. (1970), 'The assumption of identity and peripheralist-centralist controversies in motivation and emotion', in M. Arnold (ed.), *Feelings and Emotion*, Academic Press.

SCHACHTER, S. (1971), 'Some extraordinary facts about obese humans and rats', *Amer. Psychol.*, vol. 26, pp. 129–44.

SCHACHTER, S., GOLDMAN, R., and GORDON, A. (1968), 'Effects of fear, food deprivation and obesity on eating', *J. pers. soc. Psychol.*, vol. 10, pp. 91–7.

SCHACHTER, S., and SINGER, J. E. (1962), 'Cognitive, social and physiological determinants of emotional state', *Psychol. Rev.*, vol. 69, pp. 379–99.

SCHACHTER, S., and WHEELER, L. (1962), 'Epinephrine chlorpromazine and amusement', *J. abnorm. soc. Psychol.*, vol. 65, pp. 121–8.

SCHAEFFER, B., and WALLACE, R. (1970), 'Semantic similarity and the comparison of word meanings', *J. exp. Psychol.*, vol. 82, pp. 343–6.

SCHAFFER, H. R. (1966), 'The onset of fear of strangers and the incongruity hypothesis', *J. Child Psychol. Psychiat.*, vol. 7, pp. 95–106.

SCHAFFER, H. R., and PARRY, M. H. (1969), 'Perceptual-motor behaviour in infancy as a function of age and stimulus familiarity', *Brit. J. Psychol.*, vol. 60, pp. 1–9.

SCHAFFER, R. (1977), *Mothering*, Fontana/Open Books.

SCHAIE, K. W. (1958), 'Rigidity–flexibility and intelligence: a cross-sectional study of the adult life-span from 20 to 70', *Psychol. Monogr.*, vol. 72, (9), whole no. 462.

SCHAIE, K. W. (1965), 'A general model for the study of developmental problems', *Psychol. Bull.*, vol. 64, pp. 92–107.

SCHAIE, K. W. (1967), 'Age changes and age differences', *Gerontologist*, vol. 7, pp. 128–32.

SCHAIE, K. W. (1973), 'Reflections on papers by Looft, Peterson & Sparks: Towards an ageless society?', *Gerontol.*, vol. 13, pp. 31–5.

SCHAIE, K. W. (1977), 'Quasi-experimental designs in the psychology of aging', in J. E. Birren and K. W. Schaie (eds.), *Handbook of the Psychology of Aging*, Van Nostrand Reinhold.

SCHAIE, K. W., and LABOUVIE-VIEF, G. (1974), 'Generational vs. ontogenetic components of change in adult cognitive behavior: a fourteen-year cross-sequential study', *Devel. Psychol.*, vol. 10, pp. 305–20.

SCHAIE, K. W., and PARHAM, I. A. (1976), 'Stability of adult personality: fact or fable?', *J. Pers. soc. Psychol.*, vol. 34, pp. 146–58.

SCHAIE, K. W., and PARHAM, I. A. (1977), 'Cohort-sequential analyses of adult intellectual development', *Devel. Psychol.*, vol. 13, pp. 649–53.

SCHAIE, K. W., ROSENTHAL, F., and PERLMAN, R. M. (1953), 'Differential mental deterioration of factorially "pure" functions in later maturity', *J. Gerontol.*, vol. 8, pp. 191–6.

SCHARLOCK, D. P., TUCKER, T. J., and STROMINGER, N. L. (1963), 'Auditory discrimination by the cat after neonatal ablation of temporal cortex', *Science*, vol. 141, pp. 1197–8.

SCHEFLEN, A. E. (1965), 'Quasi-courtship behavior in psychotherapy', *Psychiatry*, vol. 28, pp. 245–57.

SCHIFFMAN, H. R. (1976), *Sensation and Perception: An Integrated Approach*, Wiley.

SCHILDKRAUT, J. J., and KETY, S. S. (1967), 'Biogenic amines and emotion', *Science*, vol. 156, pp. 21–30.

SCHMIDT, F. L., and HUNTER, J. E. (1974), 'Racial and ethnic bias in psychological tests: Divergent implications of two definitions of test bias', *Amer. Psychol.*, vol. 29, pp. 1–8.

SCHMIDT, R. A. (1968), 'Anticipation and timing in human motor performance', *Psychol. Bull.*, vol. 70, pp. 631–46.

SCHMITT, F. O. (1979), 'Introduction', in F. O. Schmitt and F. G. Warden (eds.), *The Neurosciences: Fourth Study Program*, M. I. T. Press.

SCHNEIRLA, T. G., and ROSENBLATT, J. S. (1963), ' "Critical periods" in the development of behavior', *Science*, vol. 139, pp. 1110–15.

SCHOFIELD, H. (1972), *Assessment and Testing*, Allen & Unwin.

SCHUTZ, F. (1965), 'Sexuelle Prägung bei Anatiden', *Z. Tierpsychol.*, vol. 22, pp. 50–103.

SCHWARTZ, G. E. (1974), 'Facial expression and depression: An electromyographic study', *Psychosom. Med.*, vol. 36, p. 458. (Abstr.)

SCHWARTZ, G. E. (1975), 'Biofeedback, self-regulation, and the patterning of physio-logical processes', *Amer. Sci.*, vol. 63, pp. 314–24.

SCOTT, D. (1976), *Understanding EEG*, Duckworth.

SCOTT, J. P. (1958a), *Animal Behavior*, University of Chicago Press.

SCOTT, J. P. (1958b), 'Critical periods in the development of social behavior in puppies', *Psychosom. Med.*, vol. 20, pp. 42–54.

SCOTT, J. P. (1962), 'Critical periods in behavioral development', *Science*, vol. 138, pp. 949–58.

SCOTT, J. P. (1963), 'The process of primary socialization in canine and human infants', *Monogr. Soc. Res. Child Devel.*, vol. 28, no. 1, pp. 1–47.

SCOTT, J. P. (1968), *Early Experience and the Organization of Behavior*, Wadsworth.

SCOTT, J. P., and FULLER, J. L. (1965), *Genetics and the Social Behavior of the Dog*, University of Chicago Press.

SEARLE, L. V. (1949), 'The organization of hereditary maze-brightness and maze-dullness', *Genet. Psychol. Monogr.*, vol. 39, pp. 279–325.

SEARLEMAN, A. (1977), 'A review of right hemisphere linguistic capabilities', *Psychol. Bull.*, vol. 84, pp. 503–28.

SEARS, R. R., MACCOBY, E. E., and LEVIN, H. (1957), *Patterns of Child Rearing*, Row, Peterson.

SECHENOV, I. M. (1863), *Collected Works*, State Publishing House (1935).

SEGALL, M. H., CAMPBELL, D. T., and HERSKOVITS, M. J. (1963), 'Cultural differences in the perception of geometrical illusions', *Science*, vol. 139, pp. 769–71.

SEKULER, R. (1975), 'Visual motion perception', in E. C. Carterette and M. P. Friedman (eds.), *Handbook of Perception*, vol. V, Academic Press.

SELIGMAN, M. E. P. (1970), 'On the generality of the laws of learning', *Psychol. Rev.*, vol. 77, pp. 406–18.

SELIGMAN, M. E. P., and HAGER, J. L. (eds.) (1972), *Biological Boundaries of Learning*, Appleton-Century-Crofts.

SELLS, S. B., DEMARCE, R. G., and WILL, D. P. (1971), 'Dimensions of personality, II. Separate factor structures in Guilford and Cattell's trait markers', *Multivar. Behav. Res.*, vol. 6, pp. 135–86.

SEM-JACOBSEN, C. W. (1968), *Depth-electrographic Stimulation of the Human Brain and Behavior*, Thomas.

SEVERIN, W. (1973), *Discovering Man in Psychology: A Humanist Approach*, McGraw-Hill.

SHAFFER, L. H. (1975), 'Multiple attention in continuous verbal tasks', in P. M. A. Rabbitt and S. Dornic (eds.), *Attention and Performance*, V, Academic Press.

SHAGASS, C. (1972), 'Electrical activity of the brain', in N. S. Greenfield and R. A. Sternbach (eds.), *Handbook of Psychobiology*, Holt, Rinehart & Winston.

SHAKESPEARE, R. (1975), *The Psychology of Handicap*, Methuen.

SHALLICE, T. (1972), 'Dual functions of consciousness', *Psychol. Rev.*, vol. 79, pp. 383–93.

SHALLICE, T., and WARRINGTON, E. K. (1970), 'Independent functioning of verbal memory stores: a neuropsychological study', *Quart. J. exp. Psychol.*, vol. 22, pp. 261–73.

SHANNON, C. E., and WEAVER, W. (1949), *The Mathematical Theory of Communication*, University of Illinois Press.

SHAPIRO, D., and CRIDER, A. (1969), 'Psychophysiological approaches in social psychology', in G. Lindzey and E. Aronson (eds.), *Handbook of Social Psychology*, vol. 3, Addison-Wesley.

SHAPIRO, D., and SCHWARTZ, G. E. (1970), 'Psychophysiological contributions to social psychology', *Ann. Rev. Psychol.*, vol. 21, pp. 87–112.

SHEEHAN, F. W. (1972), *The Function and Nature of Imagery*, Academic Press.

SHEFFIELD, F. D., and ROBY, T. B. (1950), 'Reward value of a non-nutritive sweet taste', *J. comp. physiol. Psychol.*, vol. 43, pp. 471–81.

SHEFFIELD, F. D., ROBY, T. B., and CAMPBELL, B. A. (1954), 'Drive reduction vs. consummatory behavior as determinants of reinforcement', *J. comp. physiol. Psychol.*, vol. 47, pp. 349–54.

SHEFFIELD, F. D., WULFF, J. J., and BACKER, R. (1951), 'Reward value of copulation without sex drive reduction', *J. comp. physiol. Psychol.*, vol. 44, pp. 3–8.

SHELDON, M. H. (1968), 'Learning', in L. Weiskrantz (ed.), *Analysis of Behavioral Change*, Harper & Row.

SHEPP, B. E., and EIMAS, P. D. (1964), 'Intradimensional and extradimensional shifts in the rat', *J. comp. physiol. Psychol.*, vol. 57, pp. 357–61.

SHERRINGTON, C. S. (1906), *The Integrative Action of the Nervous System*, Yale University Press.

SHETTLEWORTH, S. J. (1972), 'Constraints on learning', in D. S. Lehrman, R. A. Hinde and E. Shaw (eds.), *Advances in the Study of Behavior*, vol. 4, Academic Press.

SHIELDS, J. (1962), *Monozygotic Twins*, Oxford University Press.

SHIELDS, J., and SLATER, E. (1961), 'Heredity and psychological abnormality', in H. J. Eysenck (ed.), *Handbook of Abnormal Psychology*, Basic Books.

SHIFFRIN, R. M., and SCHNEIDER, W. (1977), 'Controlled and automatic human information processing: II. Perceptual learning, automatic attending, and a general theory', *Psychol. Rev.*, vol. 84, pp. 127–90.

SHOCK, N. W. (1951), 'Growth curves', in S. S. Stevens (ed.), *Handbook of Experimental Psychology*, Wiley.

SHUEY, A. M. (1966), *The Testing of Negro Intelligence*, Social Science Press, 2nd edn.

SHUEY, A. M. (1978), 'Own-race preference and self-esteem in young negroid and caucasoid children', in R. T. Osborne, C. E. Noble and N. Weyl (eds.), *Human Variation: The Biopsychology of Age, Race and Sex*, Academic Press.

SHULMAN, H. G. (1972), 'Semantic confusion errors in short-term memory', *J. verb. Learn. verb. Behav.*, vol. 11, pp. 221–7.

SIEGEL, S. (1956), *Non-parametric Statistics*, McGraw-Hill.

SIEGLER, I. C. (1975), 'The terminal drop hypothesis: fact or artifact?', *Exp. Aging Res.*, vol. 1, pp. 169–85.

SIEGLER, I. C. (1976), 'Life span developmental psychology and clinical geropsychology', in W. D. Gentry (ed.), *Geropsychology: A Model of Training and Clinical Service*, Ballinger Press.

SIEGLER, I. C., and BOTWINICK, J. (1979), 'A long-term longitudinal study of intellectual ability of older adults: the matter of selective subject attrition', *J. Gerontol.*, vol. 34, pp. 242–5.

SILVERMAN, A. J., and COHEN, S. I. (1960), 'Affect and vascular correlates to catecholamines', in L. J. West and M. Greenblatt (eds.), *Explorations in the Physiology of Emotions*, Psychiatric Research Reports of the A. P. A., no. 12.

SILVERSTONE, J. T. (1968), 'Obesity', *Proc. Roy. Soc. Med.*, vol. 61, pp. 371–5.

SIMON, H. A., and NEWELL, A. (1971), *Human Problem Solving*, Prentice-Hall.

SINGLETON, W. T. (1974), *Man-Machine Systems*, Penguin Books.

SKINNER, B. F. (1938), *The Behavior of Organisms*, Appleton-Century-Crofts.

SKINNER, B. F. (1950), 'Are theories of learning necessary?', *Psychol. Rev.*, vol. 57, pp. 193–216.,

SKINNER, B. F. (1953), *Science and Human Behavior*, Macmillan.

SKINNER, B. F. (1957), *Verbal Behavior*, Appleton-Century-Crofts.

SKINNER, B. F. (1971), *Beyond Freedom and Dignity*, Cape.

SLOBIN, D. I. (1966a), 'The acquisition of Russian as a native language', in F. Smith and G. A. Miller (eds.), *The Genesis of Language: A Psycholinguistic Approach*, M. I. T. Press.

SLOBIN, D. I. (1966b), 'Grammatical transformations and sentence comprehension in childhood and adulthood', *J. verb. Learn. verb. Behav.*, vol. 5, pp. 219–27.

SLOBIN, D. I. (1971), *Psycholinguistics*, Scott, Foresman.

SLUCKIN, W. (1960), *Minds and Machines*, Penguin Books.

SLUCKIN, W. (1970), *Early Learning in Man and Animal*, Allen & Unwin.

SLUCKIN, W. (1972), *Imprinting and Early Learning*, Methuen.

SLUCKIN, W. (ed.) (1979), *Fear in Animals and Man*, Van Nostrand Reinhold.

SNOW, C. (1972), 'Mothers' speech to children learning language', *Child Devel.*, vol. 43, pp. 439–65.

SNYDER, F. (1966), 'Toward an evolutionary theory of dreaming', *Amer. J. Psychiat.*, vol. 123, pp. 121–36.

SNYDER, F., and SCOTT, J. (1972), 'The psychophysiology of sleep', in N. S. Greenfield and R. A. Sternbach (eds.), *Handbook of Psychophysiology*, Holt, Rinehart & Winston.

SNYDER, M. (1974), 'Self-monitoring of expressive behavior', *J. Pers. soc. Psychol.*, vol. 30, pp. 526–37.

SOLOMON, R. L. (1964), 'Punishment', *Amer. J. Psychol.*, vol. 19, pp. 239–53.

SOLOMON, R. L., KAMIN, L. J., and WYNNE, L. C. (1953), 'Traumatic avoidance learning: the outcome of several extinction procedures with dogs', *J. abnorm. soc. Psychol.*, vol. 48, pp. 291–302.

SOMMER, R. (1969), *Personal Space: The Behavioral Basis of Design*, Prentice-Hall.

SPEARMAN, C. (1927), *The Abilities of Man*, Macmillan.

SPELKE, E., HIRST, W., and NEISSER, U. (1976), 'Skills of divided attention', *Cognition*, vol. 4, pp. 215–30.

SPERRY, R. W. (1964), 'The great cerebral commissure', *Scient. Amer.*, vol. 210, pp. 42–52.

SPERRY, R. W. (1974), 'Lateral specialization in the surgically separated hemispheres', in F. O. Schmitt and F. G. Warden (eds.), *The Neurosciences: Third Study Program*, M. I. T. Press.

SPITZ, R. A. (1945), 'Hospitalism: an inquiry into the genesis of psychiatric conditions in early childhood', *Psychoanal. Stud. Child*, vol. 1, pp. 53–74.

SPITZ, R. A. (1946), 'Anaclitic depression', *Psychoanal. Stud. Child*, vol. 2, pp. 313–42.

STAMMERS, R., and PATRICK, J. (1975), *The Psychology of Training*, Methuen.

STANLEY, J. C. (ed.) (1972), *Preschool Programs for the Disadvantaged*, Johns Hopkins University Press.

STEFFLRE, V., VALES, V. C., and MORELY, L. (1966), 'Language and cognition in Yucatan: a cross cultural replication', *J. Pers. soc. Psychol.*, vol. 4, pp. 112–15.

STELLAR, E. (1954), 'The physiology of motivation', *Psychol. Rev.*, vol. 61, pp. 5–22.

STELLAR, E. (1960), 'Drive and motivation', in J. Field, H. W. Magoun and V. E. Hall (eds.), *Handbook of Physiology*, sect. I, vol. 3, American Physiological Society.

STELMACH, G. E. (1976), *Motor Control: Issues and Trends*, Academic Press.

STEPHENSON, W. (1953), *The Study of Behavior: Q-Technique and its Methodology*, University of Chicago Press.

STERMAN, M. B., and CLEMENTE, C. D. (1962), 'Forebrain inhibitory mechanisms: Cortical synchronization induced by basal forebrain stimulation', *Exp. Neurol.*, vol. 6, pp. 91–102.

STERN, W. (1912), *The Psychological Methods of Testing Intelligence*, translated by G. M. Whipple, Warwick and York, 1914.

STERNBACH, R. A. (1966), *Principles of Psychophysiology*, Academic Press.

STEVENS, S. S. (1951), 'Mathematics, measurement and psychophysics', in S. S. Stevens (ed.), *Handbook of Experimental Psychology*, Wiley.

STONE, C. P., and BARKER, R. C. (1939), 'The attitudes and interests of pre-menarcheal and post-menarcheal girls', *J. genet. Psychol.*, vol. 54, pp. 27–71.

STONEHILL, E. (1976), 'Insomnia in psychiatric illness', *Postgrad. Med. J.*, vol. 52, pp. 19–25.

STONER, J. A. F. (1961), 'A comparison of individual and group decisions involving risk', unpublished Master's thesis. M. I. T. School of Industrial Management, Cambridge, Mass.

STONES, E. (1966), *An Introduction to Educational Psychology*, Methuen.

STRATTON, G. M. (1897), 'Vision without inversion of the retinal image', *Psychol. Rev.*, vol. 4, pp. 341–81; 466–71; 480–81.

STROMEYER, C. F., and MANSFIELD, R. J. W. (1970), 'Colored after-effects produced with moving edges', *Percept. Psychophys.*, vol. 7, pp. 108–14.

STRONG, E. K. (1955), *Vocational Interests Eighteen Years after College*, University of Minnesota Press.

STUNKARD, A. J. (1975), 'Satiety is a conditioned reflex', *Psychosom. Med.*, vol. 37, pp. 383–7.

STUNKARD, A. J., and KOCH, C. (1964), 'The interpretation of gastric motility: I. Apparent bias in the reports of hunger by obese persons', *Arch. ɡ.n. Psychiat.*, vol. 11, pp. 74–81.

SUSHINSKY, L. W., and BOOTZIN, R. R. (1970), 'Cognitive desensitization as a model of systematic desensitization', *Behav. Res. Ther.*, vol. 8, pp. 29–33.

SUTHERLAND, N. S. (1961), 'Figural after-effects and apparent size', *Quart. J. exp. Psychol.*, vol. 13, pp. 222–8.

SWETS, J. A. (1977), 'Signal detection theory applied to vigilance', in R. R. Mackie (ed.), *Vigilance: Theory, Operational Performance and Physiological Correlates*, Plenum Press.

TAJFEL, H., and FRASER, C. (eds.) (1978), *Introducing Social Psychology*, Penguin Books.

TANNER, J. M. (1962), *Growth at Adolescence*, Blackwell, 2nd edn.

TANNER, J. M. (1963), 'The regulation of human growth', *Child Devel.*, vol. 34, pp. 817–47.

TAUB, J. M., and BERGER, R. J. (1969), 'Extended sleep and performance: the Rip van Winkle effect', *Psychon. Sci.*, vol. 16, pp. 204–5.

TAUB, J. H., and BERGER, R. J. (1974), 'Acute shifts in the sleep–wakefulness cycle: effects on performance and mood', *Psychosom. Med.*, vol. 36, pp. 164–73

TAYLOR, J. G. (1962), *The Behavioral Basis of Perception*, Yale University Press.

TEGER, A. I., and PRUITT, D. G. (1967), 'Components of group risk taking', *J. exp soc. Psychol.*, vol. 3, pp. 189–205.

TEGER, A. I., *et al.* (1970), 'A re-examination of the familiarization hypothesis in group risk taking', *J. exp. soc. Psychol.*, vol. 6, pp. 346–50.

TEITELBAUM, P. (1955), 'Sensory control of hypothalamic hyperphagia', *J. comp. physiol. Psychol.*, vol. 48, pp. 156–63.

TEITELBAUM, P. (1971), 'The encephalization of hunger', in E. Stellar and J. M. Sprague (eds.), *Progress in Physiological Psychology*, vol. 4, Academic Press.

TEITELBAUM, P., and EPSTEIN, A. N. (1962), 'The lateral hypothalamic syndrome: recovery of feeding and drinking after lateral hypothalamic lesions', *Psychol. Rev.*, vol. 69, pp. 74–90.

TERMAN, L. M., and MERRILL, M. A. (1937), *Measuring Intelligence*, Houghton Mifflin.

TERZIAN, H., and ORE, G. D. (1955), 'Syndrome of Klüver & Bucy: reproduced in man by bilateral removal of the temporal lobes', *Neurology*, vol. 5, pp. 373–80.

TEUBER, H.-L. (1955), 'Physiological psychology', *Ann. Rev. Psychol.*, vol. 6, pp. 267–96.

TEUBER, H.-L. (1964), 'The riddle of frontal lobe function in man', in J. M. Warren and K. Akert (eds.), *The Frontal Granular Cortex and Behavior*, McGraw-Hill.

THATCHER, R. W. (1978), 'Issues in neurolinguistics: evoked-potential analysis of cognition and language', in D. A. Otto (ed.), *Multidisciplinary Perspectives in Event-related Brain Potential Research*, U. S. Environmental Protection Agency.

THAYER, R. E. (1970), 'Activation states as assessed by verbal report and four psycho-physiological variables', *Psychophysiol.*, vol. 7, pp. 86–94.

722 References

THOMPSON, R. F. (1969), 'Neurophysiology and thought: the neural substrates of thinking', in J. F. Voss (ed.), *Approaches to Thought*, Merrill.

THOMPSON, S. P. (1880), 'Optical illusions of motion', *Brain*, vol. 3, pp. 289–96.

THOMPSON, W. R., and MELZACK, R. (1956), 'Early environment', *Scient. Amer.*, vol. 194, pp. 38–42.

THOMSON, G. N. (1939), *The Factorial Analysis of Human Abilities*, University of London Press.

THOMSON, R. (1957), *The Psychology of Thinking*, Penguin Books.

THOMSON, R. (1968), *The Pelican History of Psychology*, Penguin Books.

THORNDIKE, E. L. (1898), 'Animal intelligence: an experimental study of the associative processes in animals', *Psychol. Rev. Monog. Suppl.*, vol. 2, no. 4.

THORNDIKE, E. L. (1911), *Animal Intelligence*, Macmillan.

THORNDIKE, E. L. (1913), 'Ideo-motor action', *Psychol. Rev.*, vol. 20, pp. 91–106.

THORNDIKE, E. L. (1932), *The Fundamentals of Learning*, Teachers College Bureau of Publications.

THORNDIKE, E. L. (1949), *Personnel Selection*, Wiley.

THORNDIKE, E. L., and HAGEN, E. (1959), *Ten Thousand Careers*, Wiley.

THORPE, W. H. (1963), *Learning and Instinct in Animals*, Methuen, 2nd edn.

THORPE, W. H. (1966), 'Ethology and consciousness', in J. C. Eccles (ed.), *Brain and Conscious Experience*, Springer Verlag.

THOULESS, R. H. (1932), 'Individual differences in phenomenal regression', *Brit. J. Psychol.*, vol. 22, pp. 216–41.

THURSTONE, L. L. (1940), 'Current issues in factor analysis', *Psychol. Bull.*, vol. 37, pp. 189–236.

THURSTONE, L. L., and THURSTONE, T. G. (1949), *SRA Primary Mental Abilities*, Science Research Associates.

TILGHER, A. (1962), 'Work through the ages', reprinted in S. Nosow and W. H. Form (eds.), *Man, Work and Society*, Basic Books.

TILTON, J. W. (1939), 'The effect of "right" and "wrong" upon the learning of nonsense syllables in multiple-choice arrangement', *J. educ. Psychol.*, vol. 30, pp. 95–115.

TINBERGEN, N. (1951), *The Study of Instinct*, Clarendon Press.

TINBERGEN, N. (1953), *Social Behaviour in Animals*, Methuen.

TITCHENER, E. B. (1908), *Lectures on the Elementary Psychology of Feeling and Attention*, Macmillan.

TOBIAS, P. V. (1971), *The Brain in Hominid Evolution*, Columbia University Press.

TOLMAN, C. W., and WILSON, G. F. (1965), 'Social feeding in domestic chicks', *Anim. Behav.*, vol. 13, pp. 134–42.

TOLMAN, E. C. (1932), *Purposive Behavior in Animals and Men*, Appleton-Century-Crofts (reprinted 1967).

TOLMAN, E. C. (1939), 'Prediction of vicarious trial and error by means of the schematic sowbug', *Psychol. Rev.*, vol. 46, pp. 318–36.

TOLMAN, E. C., and HONZIK, C. H. (1930), 'Introduction and removal of reward, and maze performance in rats', *Univ. Calif. Publ. Psychol.*, vol. 4, pp. 257–75.

TOMKINS, S. S. (1949), 'The present status of the Thematic Apperception Test', *Amer. J. Orthopsychiat.*, vol. 19, pp. 358–62.

TOMKINS, S. S. (1962), *Affect, Imagery, and Consciousness: The Positive Affects*, Springer.

TOMKINS, S. S. (1963), *Affect, Imagery, and Consciousness: The Negative Affects*, Springer.

TOWNSEND, J. T. (1974), 'Issues and models concerning the processing of a finite number of inputs', in B. Kantowitz (ed.), *Human Information Processing: Tutorials in Performance and Cognition*, Lawrence Erlbaum.

TOWNSEND, R. E., PRINZ, P. N., and OBRIST, W. D. (1973), 'Human cerebral blood flow during sleep and waking', *J. appl. Physiol.*, vol. 35, pp. 620–25.

TRABASSO, T., ROLLINS, H., and SHAUGHNESSY, E. (1971), 'Storage and verification stages in processing concepts', *Cognit. Psychol.*, vol. 2, pp. 239–89.

TRASLER, G. (1962), *The Explanation of Criminality*, Routledge & Kegan Paul.

TRAVIS, L. E. (1925), 'The effects of a small audience upon eye-hand coordination', *J. abnorm. soc. Psychol.*, vol. 20, pp. 142–6.

TREISMAN, A. M. (1960), 'Contextual cues in selective listening', *Quart. J. exp. Psychol.*, vol. 12, pp. 242–8.

TREISMAN, A. M. (1964a), 'Verbal cues, language and meaning in selective attention', *Amer. J. Psychol.*, vol. 77, pp. 206–19.

TREISMAN, A. M. (1964b), 'Selective attention in man', *Brit. Med. Bull.*, vol. 20, pp. 12–16.

TREISMAN, A. M. (1966), 'Human attention', in B. M. Foss (ed.), *New Horizons in Psychology*, Penguin Books.

TREISMAN, A. M. (1969), 'Strategies and models of selective attention', *Psychol. Rev.*, vol. 76, pp. 282–99.

TREISMAN, A. M., and DAVIES, A. (1973), 'Divided attention to ear and eye', in S. Kornblum (ed.), *Attention and Performance*, IV, Academic Press.

TREISMAN, A. M., SQUIRE, R., and GREEN, J. (1974), 'Semantic processing in dichotic listening? A replication', *Memory & Cognition*, vol. 2, pp. 641–6.

TREISMAN, M. (1977), 'Motion sickness: an evolutionary hypothesis', *Science*, vol. 197, pp. 493–5.

TRIPLETT, N. (1897), 'The dynamogenic factors in pacemaking and competition', *Amer. J. Psychol.*, vol. 9, pp. 507–33.

TROLL, L. E. (1975), *Early and Middle Adulthood: the best is yet to be – maybe*, Brooks/Cole (Wadsworth).

TROWER, P., BRYANT, B., and ARGYLE, M. (1978), *Social Skills and Mental Health*, Methuen.

TRUJILLO, N. P., and WARTHIN, T. A. (1968), 'The frowning sign: multiple forehead furrows in peptic ulcer', *J. Amer. Med. Assoc.*, vol. 205, p. 470.

TRYON, R. C. (1940), 'Genetic differences in maze learning ability in rats', *39th Yearbook Nat. Soc. Stud. Educ.* (Part 1), 111–19.

TUCK, M. (1976), *How Do We Choose?*, Methuen.

TUETING, P. (1978), 'Event-related potentials, cognitive events and information Processing', in D. A. Otto (ed.), *Multidisciplinary Perspectives in Event-Related Potential Research*, U.S. Environmental Protection Agency.

TULVING, E. (1962), 'Subjective organization in free recall of "unrelated" words', *Psychol. Rev.*, vol. 69, pp. 344–54.

TULVING, E. (1968), 'Theoretical issues in free recall', in T. R. Dixon and D. L. Horton (eds.), *Verbal Behavior and General Behavior Theory*, Prentice-Hall.

TULVING, E. (1972), 'Episodic and semantic memory', in E. Tulving and W. Donaldson (eds.), *Organization of Memory*, Academic Press.

TULVING, E., and PEARLSTONE, Z. (1966), 'Availability vs. accessibility of information in memory for words', *J. verb. Learn. verb. Behav.*, vol. 5, pp. 381–91.

TUNE, G. S. (1968), 'The human sleep debt', *Sci. J.*, vol. 4(12), pp. 67–71.

TUNE, G. S. (1969), 'The influence of age and temperament on the adult human sleep–wakefulness pattern', *Brit. J. Psychol.*, vol. 60, pp. 431–41.

TURNER, J. (1975), *Cognitive Development*, Methuen.

TVERSKY, A., and KAHNEMAN, D. (1977), 'Judgment under uncertainty: heuristics and bases', in P. N. Johnson-Laird and P. C. Wason (eds.), *Thinking: Readings in Cognitive Science*, Cambridge University Press.

UNDERWOOD, B. J. (1964), 'Forgetting', *Scient. Amer.*, vol. 210, pp. 91–9.

UNDERWOOD, B. J. (1966), *Experimental Psychology*, Appleton-Century-Crofts.

UNDERWOOD, G. (1976), *Attention and Memory*, Pergamon Press.

VALENSTEIN, E. S., COX, V. C., and KAKOLEWSKI, J. W. (1970), 'Re-examination of the role of the hypothalamus in motivation', *Psychol. Rev.*, vol. 77, pp. 16–31.

VALINS, S. (1970), 'The perception and labeling of bodily changes as determinants of emotional behavior', in P. Black (ed.), *Physiological Correlates of Emotion*, Academic Press.

VALINS, S., and RAY, A. (1967), 'Effects of cognitive desensitization on avoidance behavior', *J. Pers. soc. Psychol.*, vol. 7, pp. 345–50.

VAN EYL, F. P. (1972), 'Induced vestibular stimulation and the moon illusion', *J. exp. Psychol.*, vol. 94, pp. 326–8.

VAN TOLLER, C. (1979), *The Nervous Body: An Introduction to the Autonomic Nervous System and Behaviour*, Wiley.

VENABLES, P. H., and MARTIN, I. (1967), 'Skin resistance and skin potential', in P. H. Venables and I. Martin (eds.), *A Manual of Psychophysiological Methods*, North-Holland.

VENABLES, P. H., and SAYER, E. (1963), 'On the measurement of the level of the skin potential', *Brit. J. Psychol.*, vol. 54, pp. 251–60.

VERNON, M. D. (1970), *Perception Through Experience*, Methuen.

VERNON, P. E. (1960), *Intelligence and Attainment Tests*, University of London Press.

VERNON, P. E. (1961), *The Structure of Human Abilities*, Methuen.

VERNON, P. E. (1964), 'Creativity and intelligence', *Educ. Res.*, vol. 6, pp. 163–9.

VERNON, P. E. (1970), *Creativity*, Penguin Books.

VERNON, P. E. (1972), 'The distinctiveness of field dependence', *J. Pers.*, vol. 40, pp. 366–91.

VERNON, P. E. (1979), *Intelligence: Heredity and Environment*, Freeman.

VIDMAR, N. (1970), 'Group composition and the risky shift', *J. exp. soc. Psychol.*, vol. 6, pp. 153–96.

VITELES, M. S. (1962), *Industrial Psychology*, Cape, 2nd edn.

VOGEL, G., *et al.* (1975), 'REM sleep reduction effects on depression syndromes', *Arch. gen. Psychiat.*, vol. 32, pp. 765–77.

VOGEL, G. W. (1975), 'A review of REM sleep deprivation', *Arch. Gen. Psychiat.*, vol. 32, pp. 749–61.

VOGEL, G. W., and TRAUB, A. C. (1968), 'REM deprivation: 1. The effect on schizophrenic patients', *Arch. gen. Psychiat.*, vol. 18, pp. 287–300.

VON HOLST, E. (1954), 'Relations between the central nervous system and the peripheral organs', *Brit. J. Anim. Behav.*, vol. 2, pp. 89–94.

VON SENDEN, M. (1932), *Space and Sight: The Perception of Space and Shape in the Congenitally Blind Before and After Operation*, Methuen, translated by P. Heath, 1960.

VON WRIGHT, J. M., ANDERSON, K., and STENMAN, U. (1975), 'Generalization of conditioned GSRs in dichotic listening', in P. M. A. Rabbitt and S. Dornic (eds.), *Attention and Performance*, V, Academic Press.

VOSS, J. F. (ed.) (1969), *Approaches to Thought*, Merrill.

VROOM, V. H. (1964), *Work and Motivation*, Wiley.

VURPILLOT, E. (1976), *The Visual World of the Child*, Allen & Unwin.

VYGOTSKY, L. S. (1934), *Thought and Language*, translated by E. Haufman and G. Vakar, 1962, M. I. T. Press.

WADA, J. (1949), 'A new method for the determination of the site of cerebral speech dominance: a preliminary report on the intracarotid injection of sodium amytal', *Igaky to Seibutsugaku* (*Medicine and Biology*), vol. 14, pp. 221–2 (Japanese).

WALK, R. D., and GIBSON, E. J. (1961), 'A comparative and analytical study of visual depth perception', *Psychol. Monogr.*, vol. 75, no. 519.

WALKER, E. L. (1967), *Conditioning and Instrumental Learning*, Brooks/Cole.

WALKER, E. L. (1969), 'Reinforcement: the one ring', in J. T. Tapp (ed.), *Reinforcement and Behavior*, Academic Press.

WALKER, S. F. (1980), 'Lateralization of functions in the vertebrate brain: a review', *Brit. J. Psychol.*, vol. 71, pp. 329–68.

WALLACH, M. A., and KOGAN, N. (1965), 'The roles of information, discussion, and consensus in group risk taking', *J. exp. soc. Psychol.*, vol. 1, pp. 1–19.

WALLACH, M. A., KOGAN, N., and BEM, D. J. (1962), 'Group influence on individual risk taking', *J. abnorm. soc. Psychol.*, vol. 65, pp. 75–86.

WALTERS, R. H., and PARKE, R. D. (1965), 'The role of distance receptors in the development of social responsiveness', in L. P. Lipsitt and C. C. Spiker (eds.), *Advances in Child Development and Behavior*, vol. 2, Academic Press.

WAMPLER, R. S. (1973), 'Increased motivation in rats with ventromedial hypo-thalamic lesions', *J. comp. physiol. Psychol.*, vol. 84, pp. 275–85.

WARDEN, C. J., and JACKSON, T. A. (1935), 'Imitative behavior in the rhesus monkey', *Pedagog. Sem. & J. genet. Psychol.*, vol. 46, pp. 103–25.

WARDLAW, K. A., and KROLL, N. A. E. (1976), 'Autonomic responses to shock-associated words in a nonattended message: a failure to replicate', *J. exp. Psychol.: Human Perception & Performance*, vol. 2, pp. 357–60.

WARM, J. S. (1977), 'Psychological processes in sustained attention', in R. R. Mackie (ed.), *Vigilance: Theory, Operational Performance and Physiological Correlates*, Plenum Press.

WARR, P. B., and WALL, T. (1975), *Work and Well-being*, Penguin Books.

WASON, P. C. (1968), 'Reason about a rule', *Quart. J. exp. Psychol.*, vol. 20, pp. 273–81.

WASON, P. C., and JOHNSON-LAIRD, P. N. (1972), *The Psychology of Reasoning: Structure and Content*, Batsford.

WASON, P. C., and JONES, S. (1963), 'Negatives: denotation and connotation', *Brit. J. Psychol.*, vol. 54, pp. 299–307.

WATKINS, M. J. (1974), 'Concept and measurement of primary memory', *Psychol. Bull.*, vol. 81, pp. 695–711.

WATSON, J. B. (1907), 'Kinaesthetic and organic sensations: their role in the reactions of the white rat to the maze', *Psychol. rev. Monogr. Suppl.*, whole no. 33.

WATSON, J. B. (1914), *Behavior: An Introduction to Comparative Psychology*, Holt.

WATSON, J. B. (1930), *Behaviorism*, University of Chicago Press, 2nd edn.

WATSON, O. M., and GRAVES, T. D. (1966), 'Quantitative research in proxemic behavior', *Amer. Anthropol.*, vol. 68, pp. 971–85.

WAUGH, N. C., and NORMAN, D. A. (1965), 'Primary memory', *Psychol. Rev.*, vol. 72, pp. 89–104.

WEBB, W. B. (1965), 'Sleep characteristics of human subjects', *Bull. Brit. Psychol. Soc.*, vol. 18 (6), pp. 1–10.

WEBB, W. B. (1970), 'Individual differences in sleep length', in E. Hartmann (ed.), *Sleep and Dreaming*, Little, Brown.

WEBB, W. B. (1972), 'Patterns of sleep behavior', in W. P. Colquhoun (ed.), *Aspects of Human Efficiency*, English Universities Press.

WEBB, W. B. (ed.) (1973), *Sleep: An Active Process*, Scott, Foresman.

WEBB, W. B., and AGNEW, H. W. (1965), 'Sleep: Effects of a restricted regime', *Science*, vol. 150, pp. 1745–7.

WEBB, W. B., and AGNEW, H. W., Jr. (1969), 'Measurement and characteristics of nocturnal sleep', in L. E. Abt and B. F. Reiss (eds.), *Progress in Clinical Psychology*, vol. 3, Grune & Stratton.

WEBB, W. B., and AGNEW, H. W. (1974), 'The effects of a chronic limitation of sleep length', *Psychophysiol.*, vol. 11, pp. 265–74.

WEBB, W. B., and CARTWRIGHT, R. D. (1978), 'Sleep and dreams', *Ann. Rev. Psychol.*, vol. 29, pp. 223–52.

WECHSLER, D. (1958), *The Measurement and Appraisal of Adult Intelligence*, Williams & Wilkins, 4th edn.

WEINER, B. (1972), *Theories of Motivation: From Mechanism to Cognition*, Markham.

WEINMAN, J. (1967), 'Photoplethysmography', in P. H. Venables and I. Martin (eds.), *A Manual of Psychophysiological Methods*, North-Holland.

WEISKRANTZ, L. (1961), 'Encephalisation and the scotoma', in W. H. Thorpe and O. L. Zangwill (eds.), *Current Problems in Animal Behaviour*, Cambridge University Press.

WEISKRANTZ, L. (1968a), 'Treatments, inferences and brain function', in L. Weiskrantz (ed.), *Analysis of Behavior Change*, Harper & Row.

WEISKRANTZ, L. (1968b), 'Some traps and pontifications', in L. Weiskrantz (ed.), *Analysis of Behavior Change*, Harper & Row.

WEISKRANTZ, L. (1977), 'Trying to bridge some neuropsychological gaps between monkey and man', *Brit. J. Psychol.*, vol. 68, pp. 431–45.

WEISS, R. F., and MILLER, F. G. (1971), 'The drive theory of social facilitation', *Psychol. Rev.*, vol. 78, pp. 44–57.

WEITZ, S. (1972), 'Attitude, voice, and behavior: a repressed affect model of interracial interaction', *J. Pers. soc. Psychol.*, vol. 24, pp. 14–21.

WELFORD, A. T. (1965), 'Performance, biological mechanisms and age: a theoretical sketch', in A. T. Welford and J. E. Birren (eds.), *Behavior, Aging and the Nervous System*, Thomas.

WELFORD, A. T. (1968), *Fundamentals of Skill*, Methuen.

WELFORD, A. T. (1976), *Skilled Performance: Perceptual and Motor Skills*, Scott, Foresman.

WENGER, M. A. (1950), 'Emotion as visceral action: an extension of Lange's theory', in M. L. Reymert (ed.), *Feelings and Emotions*, McGraw-Hill.

WENGER, M. A. (1966), 'Studies of autonomic balance: a summary', *Psychophysiol.*, vol. 2, pp. 173–86.

WENGER, M. A., *et al.* (1960), 'Autonomic response patterns during intravenous infusion of epinephrine and norepinephrine', *Psychosom. Med.*, vol. 22, pp. 294–307.

WENGER, M. A., and CULLEN, T. D. (1972), 'Studies of autonomic balance in children and adults', in N. S. Greenfield and R. A. Sternbach (eds.), *Handbook of Psychophysiology*, Holt, Rinehart & Winston.

WENGER, M. A., JONES, F. N., and JONES, M. H. (1956), *Physiological Psychology*, Holt.

WERNER, H. (1948), *Comparative Psychology of Mental Development*, Follett.

WERNER, H. (1957), 'The concept of development from a comparative and organismic point of view', in D. Harris (ed.), *The Concept of Development*, University of Minnesota Press.

WERTHEIMER, M. (1923), 'Untersuchungen zur Lehre von der Gestalt. II', *Psychol. Forsch.*, vol. 4, pp. 301–50. Translated by W. D. Ellis, *A Source Book of Gestalt Psychology*, Routledge, 1938.

WERTHEIMER, M. (1961), 'Psychomotor co-ordination of auditory–visual space at birth', *Science*, vol. 134, p. 1692.

728   References

WEST, D. (1969), 'Emotion and the psychologist', *New Scient.*, vol. 44, pp. 354–5.

WESTCOTT, M. R. (1976), 'Free will: An exercise in metaphysical truth or psychological consequences', unpubl. paper.

WHITE, B. L., CASTLE, P., and HELD, R. (1964), 'Observations on the development of visually directed reading', *Child Devel.*, vol. 35, pp. 349–64.

WHITEHURST, G. J., and VASTA, R. (1975), 'Is language acquired through imitation?', *J. psycholinguist. Res.*, vol. 4, pp. 37–59.

WHITING, J. W. M., and CHILD, I. L. (1953), *Child Training and Personality: A Cross Cultural Study*, Yale University Press.

WHORF, B. L. (1956), *Language, Thought and Reality*, Wiley.

WIENER, N. (1948), *Cybernetics*, Wiley.

WILCOXON, H. C. (1969), 'Historical introduction to the problem of reinforcement', in J. T. Tapp (ed.), *Reinforcement and Behavior*, Academic Press.

WILCOXON, H. C., DRAGOIN, W. B., and KRAL, P. A. (1971), 'Illness-induced aversions in rat and quail', *Science*, vol. 171, pp. 826–9.

WILKINSON, R. T. (1965), 'Sleep deprivation', in O. G. Edholm and A. L. Bacharach (eds.), *The Physiology of Human Survival*, Academic Press.

WILKINSON, R. T. (1968), 'Sleep deprivation: performance tests for partial and selective sleep deprivation', in L. E. Abt and B. F. Reiss (eds.), *Progress in clinical Psychology*, vol. 7, Grune & Stratton.

WILKINSON, R. T. (1972), 'Sleep deprivation: Eight questions', in W. P. Colquhoun (ed.), *Aspects of Human Efficiency: Diurnal Rhythm and Loss of Sleep*, English Universities Press.

WILKINSON, R. T., and HAINES, E. (1970), 'Evoked response correlates of expectancy during vigilance', *Acta Psychol.*, vol. 33, pp. 402–13.

WILLERMAN, L. (1979), *The Psychology of Individual and Group Differences*, Freeman.

WILLIAMS, E., and SCOTT, J. P. (1953), 'The development of social behaviour patterns in the mouse, in relation to natural periods', *Behaviour*, vol. 6, pp. 35–64.

WILLIAMS, F. (ed.) (1970), *Language and Poverty*, Rand McNally.

WILLIAMS, H. L., HOLLOWAY, F. A., and GRIFFITHS, W. J. (1973), 'Physiological psychology: sleep', *Ann. Rev. Psychol.*, vol. 24, pp. 279–316.

WILLIAMS, H. L., LUBIN, A., and GOODNOW, J. J. (1959), 'Impaired performance with acute sleep loss', *Psychol. Monogr.: Gen. & Appl.*, vol. 73, pp. 1–26.

WILLIAMS, H. L., MORLOCK, H. C., and MORLOCK, J. V. (1966), 'Instrumental behavior during sleep', *Psychophysiol.*, vol. 2, pp. 208–15.

WILLIAMS, R. L., AGNEW, H. W., and WEBB, W. B. (1964), 'Sleep patterns in young adults: an EEG study', *EEG clin. Neurophysiol.*, vol. 17, pp. 376–81.

WILLIAMS, R. L., KARACAN, I., and HURSCH, C. (1974), *EEG of Human Sleep*, Wiley.

WILLOWS, D. M., and MCKINNON, G. E. (1973), 'Selective reading: attention to the "unattended" lines', *Canad. J. Psychol.*, vol. 27, pp. 292–304.

WILM, E. C. (1925), *The Theories of Instinct: A Study in the History of Psychology*, cited by Cofer, C. N., and Appley, M. H. (1964) in *Motivation: Theory and Research*, Wiley, p. 24.

WILSON, E. O. (1975), *Sociobiology: The New Synthesis*, Harvard University Press.

WILSON, E. O., and BROWN, W. L. (1953), 'The subspecies concept and its taxonomic application', *System. Zool.*, vol. 2, pp. 97–111.

WITELSON, S. F., and PALLIE, W. (1973), 'Left-hemisphere specialization in the human newborn: Neuro-anatomical evidence of asymmetry', *Brain*, vol. 96, pp. 641–6.

WITKIN, H. A., *et al.* (1962), *Psychological Differentiation: Studies of Development*, Wiley.

WOHLGEMUTH, A. (1911), 'On the after-effect of seen movement', *Brit. J. Psychol., Monogr. Suppl.*, vol. 1.

WOHLWILL, J. F. (1960), 'Developmental studies of perception', *Psychol. Bull.*, vol. 57, pp. 249–88.

WOHLWILL, J. F. (1963), 'The development of "overconstancy" in space perception', in L. P. Lipsitt and C. C. Spiker (eds.), *Advances in Child Development and Behavior*, vol. 1, Academic Press.

WOHLWILL, J. F. (1965), 'Texture of the stimulus field and age as variables in the perception of relative distance in photographic slides', *J. exp. Child Psychol.*, vol 2, pp. 163–77.

WOHLWILL, J. F. (1970), 'The age variable in psychological research', *Psychol. Rev.*, vol. 77, pp. 49–64.

WOLF, S., and WOLFF, H. G. (1943), *Human Gastric Function*, Oxford University Press.

WOLLHEIM, R. (1971), *Freud*, Fontana/Collins.

WOODS, D. L., and HILLYARD, S. A. (1978), 'Attention at the cocktail party: brainstem evoked responses reveal no peripheral gating', in D. A. Otto (ed.), *Multidisciplinary Perspectives in Event-related Brain Potential Research*, U.S. Environmental Protection Agency.

WOODWORTH, R. S. (1899), 'The accuracy of voluntary movement', *Psychol. Rev. Monogr. Suppl.*, whole no. 13.

WOODWORTH, R. S. (1906), 'The cause for a voluntary movement', in J. H. Tufts *et al.* (eds.), *Studies in Philosophy and Psychology*, Houghton Mifflin.

WOODWORTH, R. S. (1918), *Dynamic Psychology*, Columbia University Press.

WOODWORTH, R. S. (1920), *Personal Data Sheet*, Stoelting.

WOODWORTH, R. S. (1958), *Dynamics of Behavior*, Holt.

WOODWORTH, R. S. (1963), *Contemporary Schools of Psychology*, Methuen, 8th edn.

WOODWORTH, R. S. and SCHLOSBERG, H. (1954), *Experimental Psychology*, Holt.

WOODWORTH, R. S., and SELLS, S. B. (1935), 'An atmosphere effect in formal syllogistic reasoning', *J. exp. Psychol.*, vol. 18, pp. 451–60.

WOODWORTH, R. S., and SHERRINGTON, C. S. (1904), 'A pseudoaffective reflex and its spinal path', *J. Physiol.*, vol. 31, pp. 234–43.

WULF, F. (1922), 'Über die Veränderung von Vorstellungen (Gedachtnis und

Gestalt)', *Psychol. Forsch.*, vol. 1, pp. 333–73. Translated in W. D. Ellis, *A Source Book of Gestalt Psychology*, Routledge, 1938.

WYATT, R. J. (1972), 'The serotonin-catecholamine-dream bicycle: a clinical study', *Biol. Psychiat.*, vol. 5, pp. 33–64.

WYLIE, R. (1961), *The Self Concept*, University of Nebraska Press.

YOUNG, P. T. (1936). *Motivation of Behavior: The Fundamental Determinants of Human and Animal Activity*, Wiley.

YOUNG, R. M. (1970), *Mind, Brain and Adaptation in the Nineteenth Century: Cerebral Localization and its Biological Context from Gall to Ferrier*, Clarendon Press.

ZAJONC, R. B. (1965), 'Social facilitation', *Science*, vol. 149, pp. 269–74.

ZAJONC, R. B. (1966), *Social Psychology: An Experimental Approach*, Wadsworth.

ZAJONC, R. B., HEINGARTNER, A., and HERMAN, E. M. (1969), 'Social enhancement and impairment of performance in the cockroach', *J. Pers. soc. Psychol.*, vol. 13, pp. 83–92.

ZAJONC, R. B., and SALES, S. M. (1966), 'Social facilitation of dominant and subordinate responses', *J. exp. soc. Psychol.*, vol. 2, pp. 160–68.

ZANGWILL, O. L. (1961), 'Lashley's concept of cerebral mass action', in W. H. Thorpe and O. L. Zangwill (eds.), *Current Problems in Animal Behaviour*, Cambridge University Press.

ZEIGLER, H. P. (1964), 'Displacement activity and motivational theory', *Psychol. Bull.*, vol. 61, pp. 362–76.

ZEPELIN, H., and RECHTSCHAFFEN, A. (1974), 'Mammalian sleep, longevity, and energy metabolism', *Brain, Behav. and Evol.*, vol. 10, pp. 425–70.

ZERNICKI, B. (1968), 'Pretrigeminal cat', *Brain Res.*, vol. 9, pp. 1–14.

ZILLER, R. C. (1957), 'Four techniques of group decision making under uncertainty', *J. appl. Psychol.*, vol. 41, pp. 384–8.

ZIMMERMANN, R. R., and TORREY, C. C. (1965), 'Ontogeny of learning', in A. M. Schrier, H. F. Harlow and F. Stollnitz (eds.), *Behavior of Non-Human Primates*, Academic Press.

ZUBEK, J. P. (ed.) (1969), *Sensory Deprivation: Fifteen Years of Research*, Appleton-Century-Crofts.

ZUCKERMAN, M., *et al.* (1977), 'Encoding and decoding of spontaneous and posed facial expressions', *J. Pers. soc. Psychol.*, vol. 34. pp. 966–77.

ZUNG, W. W. K. (1970), 'Insomnia and disordered sleep', in E. Hartmann (ed.), *Sleep and Dreaming*, Little, Brown.

Acknowledgements

Acknowledgement is due to the following for permission to use figures and tables in this volume.

Figure 3.2, Humanities Press and Routledge & Kegan Paul; Figure 4.1 Addison-Wesley Publishing Co.; Figure 4.2, B.B.C. Publications; Figure 4.7, McGraw-Hill Book Company; Figure 4.8 Basic Books; Figure 4.9, Basic Books; Figure 4.10, Blackwell Scientific Publications; Figure 4.13, W. W. Norton & Co. Inc.; Figure 4.15, Oxford University Press; Figure 5.6, *EEG and Clinical Neurophysiology*; Figure 6.1, American Psychological Association; Figure 7.2, Basic Books; Figure 8.1, first appeared in *New Scientist*, London, the weekly review of science and technology; Figure 8.2, Rockefeller University Press; Figure 8.5, *Scientific American*; Figure 8.6, *Scientific American*; Figure 8.7, Academic Press from *Human Information Processing*, 2nd edn.; Figure 8.8, reprinted by permission from *Nature*, 200, pp. 1345–7. Copyright © 1982 Macmillan Journals Ltd.; Figure 10.1(b), Gyldendalske Boghandel; Figure 10.1(c), University of Illinois Press; Figure 10.2, Humanities Press and Routledge & Kegan Paul; Figure 11.1, Weidenfeld & Nicolson; Figure 11.2, *Scientific American*; Figure 11.5, *Scientific American*; Figure 11.6, American Psychological Association; Figure 13.1, Journal Press; Figure 13.2, American Psychological Association; Figure 14.1, Academic Press; Figure 16.2, *Scientific American*; Figure 16.3, Academic Press; Figure 16.5, Humanities Press and Routledge & Kegan Paul.

Table 9.1, *Psychological Review*; Table 19.1, John Wiley & Sons Inc.; Table 20.1, Methuen and Co. Ltd; Table 20.2, Methuen & Co. Ltd.

Subject Index

Authors Index

Hyde, J. S. 615
Hymovitch, B. 324

Ilg, F. L. 74
Immelmann, K. 327
Imperato-McGinley, J. 595
Inhelder, B. 498, 501
Irwin, F. W. 188
Isaacs, K. S. 636
Isaacson, R. L. 93, 217
Ittelson, W. H. 301, 657
Izard, C. 128, 192–3
Izard, S. 447

Jacklin, C. M. 590, 595
Jackson, D. N. 529
Jackson, P. W. 490, 543, 575–6
Jackson T. A. 346
Jacobson, L. E. 214
Jahoda, G. 292
James, W. 20–21, 165, 194–7, 200–204, 253–4, 276, 296, 365, 370, 381–2, 384–7, 391–2, 398, 402, 404
James, W. T. 622
Janet, P. 22
Janisse, M. P. 106
Janke, W. 209–10
Jarvick, L. F. 56
Jaspars, J. M. F. 527
Jasper, C. 85
Jaynes, J. 305
Jencks, C. 602
Jenkins, J. J. 353
Jenkins, W. O. 341
Jennings, H. S. 337
Jensen, A. R. 602–6
Jerison, H. J. 125–6, 128
Johnson, H. G. 638
Johnson, J. H. 435
Johnson, L. C. 134, 140–41, 144
Johnson, N. F. 454
Johnson, R. E. 414
Johnson, R. N. 190
Johnson-Laird, P. N. 481, 483
Johnston, W. A. 266
Jones, A. W. 616
Jones, D. M. 267, 269
Jones, E. 170

Jones, E. E. 627
Jones, F. N. 195
Jones, H. S. 138
Jones, M. H. 195
Jones, R. 598, 601
Jones, S. 483
Jouandet, M. 127
Jourard, S. M. 641
Jouvet, M. 145, 146, 150, 151
Joynson, R. B. 24
Jung, C. G. 173, 558, 566

Kaada, B. R. 217
Kahn, E. 136
Kahneman, D. 265–7, 275, 484
Kail, R. V. 430
Kakolearski, J. W. 185
Kales, A. 131, 138
Kalish, R. M. 615
Kallman, F. J. 62
Kamin, L. J. 59, 352, 604, 606
Kamm, J. 594
Karacan, I. 135–6
Katkin, E. S. 105, 212
Katz, I. 188
Katz, J. J. 456
Kaufman, L. 290
Kay, H. 370
Keele, S. W. 253, 377–8
Keesey, R. E. 184
Keller, B. 67
Kelley, D. M. 531
Kelley, H. H. 623
Kellogg, W. N. 440
Kelly, E. L. 508
Kelly, G. A. 530, 571–3, 577
Kemper, T. D. 209–10
Kempthorne, O. 606
Kendler, H. H. 494, 499
Kendler, T. S. 494, 499
Kendon, A. 637
Kennedy, J. 198
Kennedy, W. A. 603
Kenny, A. 192
Kent, R. N. 211
Keren, G. 263
Kerlinger, F. N. 542
Kessen, W. 60–61

More About Penguins
and Pelicans

For further information about books available from
Penguins please write to Dept EP, Penguin Books Ltd.
Harmondsworth, Middlesex UB7 0DA.

In the U.S.A.: For a complete list of books available
from Penguins in the United States write to Dept CS,
Penguin Books, 625 Madison Avenue, New York,
New York 10022.

In Canada: For a complete list of books available
from Penguins in Canada write to Penguins Books
Canada Ltd, 2801 John Street, Markham, Ontario
L3R 1B4.

In Australia: For a complete list of books available
from Penguins in Australia write to the Marketing
Department, Penguin Books Australia Ltd, P.O. Box
257, Ringwood, Victoria 3134.

In New Zealand: For a complete list of books
available from Penguins in New Zealand write to the
Marketing Department, Penguin Books (N.Z.) Ltd,
P.O. Box 4019, Auckland 10.

A selection of books on Psychology and Psychiatry

THE FOUR FUNDAMENTAL CONCEPTS OF PSYCHO-ANALYSIS
Jacques Lacan

Jacques Lacan's writings have provoked intense controversy in French psychoanalytic circles, requiring as they do a radical reappraisal of the legacy bequeathed by Freud. In this volume, based on addresses to a larger and less specialized audience than ever before, he wanted to discuss 'the major concepts on which psychoanalysis is based', namely: *the unconscious, repetition, the transference* and *the drive.*

THE MYTH OF THE HYPERACTIVE CHILD
And other Means of Child Control
Peter Schrag and Diane Divoky

A well-researched and thoughtfully argued brief intended to stimulate action against the widespread use of drugs, psychological testing, and behaviour modification used by agents of the state to control children's lives and undermine their rights' – *The New York Times Book Review*

THE LANGUAGE OF MADNESS
David Cooper

The language of madness, maintains David Cooper, expresses both a need, and a challenge to the world which fails to recognize that need. It therefore demonstrates our corporate failure to bring together our sexuality, our lives and our autonomy. Cooper claims that we must accept this indictment and points to ways in which we can rectify the situation.

THE PSYCHOLOGY OF HUMAN AGEING
D. B. Bromley

Infant and adolescent psychology have been very thoroughly explored, but the study of ageing lags behind. This new introduction to human ageing and its mental effects is written by the Scientific Advisor in Gerontology to the Medical Research Council, and is of importance to both the student of psychology and the layman.

THE PSYCHOLOGY OF LEARNING
R. Borger and A. E. M. Seaborne

Only a small part of learning takes place in schools. In this book two psychologists discuss the laws which seem to govern the process of learning in its widest sense. They also provide a thorough survey of programmed learning techniques and the newer developments in the formal teaching of schools and universities.

THE PSYCHOLOGY OF STUDY
C. A. Mace

An explanation of the mental processes by which we all 'read, mark, learn and inwardly digest' information of all kinds. There are chapters on perception, memory, original thinking, concentration and preparation for exams.

THE PSYCHOLOGY OF THINKING
R. Thomson

The achievements and limitations of recent studies into 'thinking' are discussed and evaluated. The direct experimental investigation of adult thought processes, and the intelligent behaviour of animals, are also dealt with.

FREUD AND HIS FOLLOWERS
Paul Roazen

'An extremely rich book . . . It would seem to be essential reading for all who are interested in the history of psychoanalysis or the history of ideas in the twentieth century' – *Guardian*

Paul Roazen interviewed more than seventy people who had known Freud and probed minutely into Freud's home-life, his friends and disciples – Jung, Ernst Jones, Ruth Mack Brunswick, Melanie Klein among others – to reveal the rich, productive world where 'the theories that were to revolutionize what we think of ourselves' took root and ripened.

THE PIGGLE
An Account of the Psychoanalytic Treatment of a Little Girl
D. W. Winnicott

From the age of two until the age of five, the Piggle – seriously disturbed by the birth of a younger sister – visited the late Dr Winnicott on sixteen occasions. A verbatim account of her visits is accompanied by illuminating excerpts from letters written to the analyst by the child's parents and an invaluable commentary by Dr Winnicott.

MUSEUMS OF MADNESS
The Social Organization of Insanity in Nineteenth-century England
Andrew T. Scull

Andrew Scull traces the developments in the treatment of insanity in nineteenth-century England, from the iron cages of Bethlem to the non-restraint policies of the reformers. He follows the progress of the movement for reform, analyses the motives of its opponents, assesses its impact on the 'mad' trade and asks what proof have we that the shift from 'madness' to 'mental illness' has been accompanied by any progress in the treatment of the insane.

THE DIVIDED SELF
R. D. Laing

'It is a study that makes all others I have read on schizophrenia seem fragmentary ... the author brings through his vision and perception, that particular touch of genius which causes one to say "Yes, I have always thought that, why have I never thought of it before?"' – *Journal of Analytical Psychology*

NEW HORIZONS IN PSYCHOLOGY, VOLUME ONE
Ed. Brian M. Foss

Genetics, motivation, drugs, operant conditioning, programmed learning and behaviour therapy are some of the new developments in psychology affecting scientific thinking and influencing our lives today. This expert volume is both a progress report and an indication of future directions.

THE SAVAGE GOD
A Study of Suicide
A. Alvarez

This controversial study of this often taboo area of human behaviour embraces both cultural attitudes and the development of theoretical studies, giving a broad basis for Alvarez's examination of suicide from the perspective of literature. Here, he follows the black thread leading from Dante through Donne and the Romantic Agony, to Dada and the Savage God at the heart of modern literature.

HUMAN AGGRESSION
Anthony Storr

In this monograph the author of *Sexual Deviation* and *The Integrity of the Personality* writes both as a psychotherapist and as a human being living in an age when 'The End is Nigh' could well be the truth. But the coin of aggression, as he shows, bears two faces. As a positive and natural drive he discusses its normal role in the social structure of both animals and men and its function in childhood, adult life, and sexual relations: in its negative aspect he considers hostility in relation to depressive, schizoid, paranoid, and psychopathic personalities.

HOW CHILDREN FAIL
John Holt

'It is possibly the most penetrating, and probably the most eloquent book on education to be published in recent years. To anyone who deals with children and cares about children, it cannot be too highly recommended' – *New York Times*

'John Holt has done a good and necessary job. A very good book indeed' – A. S. Neill

SUCCESS AND FAILURE IN LEARNING TO READ
Ronald Morris

No educational issue has given rise to such a mountain of research and argument as the teaching of reading. The debates, the texts, the hypotheses continue to appear, and unlike many complex educational issues they very largely appear in public. For reading is perhaps the major ground on which the public at large chooses to question and challenge the teaching profession. Is Johnny reading or not? And if not, why not?

SPARE RIB READER

A celebration of ten years of *Spare Rib*.

'I used to be a Tupperware groupie – until I discovered *Spare Rib* ... its sizzling prose blew my hibernating mind ... and whipped up within me a passionate wish to identify with the growing sisterhood of bold, thinking women' – Val Hennessy in the *Evening Standard*, 1979

'*Spare Rib* has earned its hundredth birthday celebrations' – *Guardian*, 1980

THE FEMININE MYSTIQUE
Betty Friedan

First published in the sixties *The Feminine Mystique* still remains a powerful and illuminating analysis of the position of women in Western society.

'Brilliantly researched, passionately argued book – a time-bomb flung into the Mom-and-Apple-Pie image ... Out of the debris of that shattered ideal, the Woman's Liberation Movement was born' – Ann Leslie

THE SCEPTICAL FEMINIST
Janet Radcliffe Richards

In this important and original study, Janet Radcliffe Richards demonstrates with incisive, systematic and often unexpected arguments the precise nature of the injustice women suffer, and exposes the fallacious arguments by which it has been justified. Her analysis leads her to considerable criticism of many commonly held feminist views, but from it emerges the outline of a new and more powerful feminism which sacrifices neither rationality nor radicalism.

'It's a model of how to write a book on *any* topic; on a contentious subject like this *it's a triumph*' – *Sunday Times*

CHILDMINDER
Brian Jackson and Sonia Jackson

'Who minds the child?' is a basic question for working-class communities and for families struggling to establish themselves. But it is also the crunch for middle-class parents, when both of them *choose* to work, and for many more.

Childminder – 'a rare piece of research, a vivid, warm and often harrowing book' (*Social Work Today*) – 'raised questions and faced answers that are hard to ignore' (*Guardian*) in a way that 'reads more like a novel than a research report' (*New Society*).

But Brian and Sonia Jackson go beyond revealing the best and the most horrendous, further even than 'a plethora of suggestions, practical and positive' (*Guardian*) to argue for a change in the whole status of childminding in the community.

And happily, beyond the news stories, the reviews and the TV programmes that publication generated, *Childminder* did indeed, as the *Daily Telegraph* prophesied, 'change official attitudes to children.'

NURSERIES NOW
A Fair Deal for Parents and Children
Hughes, Mayall, Perry, Petrie and Pinkerton

The need for nurseries is greater in Britain now than ever before. *Nurseries Now* combines a consumer's guide to what nurseries are available with a sensible critique of the gaps and anomalies in the present system. The authors emphasize the importance of equal opportunities, of more choice for parents in child-care, and of a greater involvement by men in their children's upbringing. Nurseries alone cannot achieve these aims, and the book also looks at some of the other measures needed, including radical changes in the employment patterns of both sexes.